SAMS Teach Yourself

Digital Video and DVD Authoring

Jeff Sengstack

All in One

SAMS 800 East 96th Street, Indianapolis, Indiana, 46240 USA

Sams Teach Yourself Digital Video and DVD Authoring All in One

International Standard Book Number: 0-672-32689-2

Library of Congress Catalog Card Number: 2004091348

Printed in the United States of America

First Printing: February 2005

08   07   06   05   4   3   2

Trademarks

Warning and Disclaimer

Bulk Sales

Sams Publishing offers excellent discounts on this book when ordered in quantity for bulk purchases or special sales. For more information, please contact

U.S. Corporate and Government Sales

1-800-382-3419

corpsales@pearsontechgroup.com

For sales outside of the U.S., please contact

International Sales

international@pearsoned.com

Acquisitions Editor
Linda A. Harrison

Development Editor
Damon Jordan

Managing Editor
Charlotte Clapp

Project Editor
George E. Nedeff

Copy Editor
Barbara Hacha

Indexer
Erika Millen

Proofreader
Jessica McCarty

Technical Editor
Weymouth Kirkland

Publishing Coordinator
Vanessa Evans

Multimedia Developer
Dan Scherf

Interior Designer
Gary Adair

Cover Designer
Alan Clements

Contents at a Glance

Table of Contents

About the Author

Jeff Sengstack has worn many hats: TV news reporter/anchor, video producer, writer focusing on PC technology, high school math/science teacher, radio station disk jockey, music publisher, marketing director, and (presently) school board trustee. As a news reporter he won a regional Emmy and two Society of Professional Journalists first-place awards. He's an Adobe Certified Expert and Trainer on Premiere and wrote Adobe's Higher Education, *Digital Video Curriculum Guide*. He's written 300 articles and six books, including *Sams Teach Yourself Adobe Premiere Pro in 24 Hours*. Visit his website at www.sengstack.com.

Acknowledgments

My thanks to this book's technical editor—my friend and fellow Occidental Community Choir member—Weymouth Kirkland (www.dejavuvideography.com).

And the staff at Sams applied just the right editorial touch to make this book better. I appreciate that.

We Want to Hear from You!

As the reader of this book, *you* are our most important critic and commentator. We value your opinion and want to know what we're doing right, what we could do better, what areas you'd like to see us publish in, and any other words of wisdom you're willing to pass our way.

You can email or write me directly to let me know what you did or didn't like about this book—as well as what we can do to make our books stronger.

Please note that I cannot help you with technical problems related to the topic of this book, and that due to the high volume of mail I receive, I might not be able to reply to every message.

When you write, please be sure to include this book's title and author as well as your name and phone or email address. I will carefully review your comments and share them with the author and editors who worked on the book.

E-mail: consumer@samspublishing.com

Mail: Mark Taber
           Associate Publisher
           Sams Publishing
           800 East 96th Street
           Indianapolis, IN 46240 USA

Reader Services

For more information about this book or another Sams Publishing title, visit our website at www.samspublishing.com. Type the ISBN (excluding hyphens) or the title of a book in the Search field to find the page you're looking for.

Introduction

Making videos on your PC is fun, creative, and exciting. There's no limit to the cool things you can do with your videos.

I've been making videos for years and continue to be amazed as the quality of digital video camcorders and video-editing software continues to improve.

▶ Digital video (DV) camcorders have dropped in price, yet now offer sharper images, better color reproduction, and more controls.

▶ Video-editing software now has more features—exciting special effects, snazzy transitions, and easy-to-use text tools—to let you create professional-looking videos.

You also have more output options. Not only can you record your videos to VHS or DV tape to play back on your VCR or camcorder, but now you can create

▶ Streaming videos to play on the Internet

▶ Video files that run on any PC

▶ DVDs that can play on your PC and your home, office, or portable DV player

What Will Work Best for You

So how do you tap all that creative potential? Which software and hardware will work best for you? I answer those questions in this book.

During the past few years I've tested more than 20 PC video editors and DVD creation ("authoring") products—from entry level to high end.

I am an Adobe Certified Instructor on Adobe's professional video editor—Premiere Pro—and have written two *Sams Teach Yourself* books on that powerful $700 product. I've conducted a master class and made trade-show presentations on Adobe Encore DVD, Adobe's $550 DVD-authoring tool.

But using Premiere Pro or Encore DVD to take your first steps into video editing or DVD authoring is like taking your first flying lesson in a 747. A tad overwhelming.

Easing into Video Editing and DVD Authoring

The purpose of this book is to *ease* you into video editing and DVD authoring. I've selected what I think are the best (and most reasonably priced) consumer- and intermediate-level video-editing and DVD-authoring products. Then I give you step-by-step instructions on how to use those particular products to create videos and DVDs that you can be proud of.

This is a different approach from most other books in this field. Those other books typically give you generic video-editing instructions using *multiple* video-editing software products as examples. I think those kinds of books waste your time. You shouldn't have to spin your wheels trying out less than the best-of-breed products. I cut to the chase.

Keeping It in Context

There is one other reason *Sams Teach Yourself Digital Video and DVD Authoring All in One* is different from the rest of the DV and DVD how-to books: context. Those other books either are highly detailed or greatly simplified reference manuals using impenetrable vernacular, or they are collections of step-by-step instructions focusing solely on software functions. Both types fail to create lasting impressions and they don't teach you how to make videos.

What's missing is context. I think of those books as sort of like instructing budding artists how to use a paintbrush by telling them to swab the brush in paint and slather it on a canvas. Where's the art?

My goal with *Sams Teach Yourself Digital Video and DVD Authoring All in One* is to help you create high-quality videos and DVDs. Rather than simply presenting a collection of disconnected tutorials, I'll frequently remind you of the big picture and what you're trying to accomplish. However, I haven't skimped on useful nuts-and-bolts instructions. I've tried to present them in a logical, easy-to-follow manner that reflects the way most video producers approach editing.

The timing is right for this book, both on a personal level and in the marketplace. It fits my career path to a T. I have extensive television production credentials— TV anchor, reporter, photographer, and editor—plus I'm a recipient of a regional Emmy award and two Society of Professional Journalists first-place awards. I've written hundreds of articles, written or worked on nine books, and have been a high school science and math teacher.

Book Organization

I start by presenting an overview of digital video. Then it's on to making your raw ingredients: shooting video, creating still images, and acquiring audio.

In a departure from traditional digital video how-to books, I follow those introductory chapters with something of a collaborative project. I contacted several of my friends and former colleagues in the TV news and video-production business, and they provided dozens of expert tips. I've compiled them—along with some of my own—in a chapter intended to help you learn more about the overall art of story creation and video production. For instance, they offer advice about shooting high-quality video, writing effectively, and creating professional voiceovers.

Editing Your First Videos

From there I venture into video editing by first showing you the least-expensive way to edit your initial video—Windows Movie Maker 2. This free product works only with Windows XP (Home or Professional). Movie Maker 2 can ease those on a shoestring budget into video editing. Despite its many limitations, it is very popular.

I cover Movie Maker 2 in Chapters 7 and 8. Because I use those chapters to introduce some video-editing concepts, I recommend that you read both chapters, even if your immediate preference is to start editing video on the higher-level product I cover later.

Two Other Video Editors

The goal of this book is to take you well beyond the limited features of Movie Maker 2. I chose Pinnacle Studio ($100—you can download a free, fully functional trial version that you can use while working with this book) as the principal video-editing software to cover in this book. I've worked with all of Pinnacle Studio's competitors and have reached the conclusion that Studio is the best entry- and intermediate-level video software. It has a logically laid-out workspace, an easy-to-follow workflow, a solid DVD-authoring module, and many special effects and transitions.

However, I don't want to ignore two other Windows PC–based video editors: Adobe Premiere Elements and Adobe Premiere Pro 1.5.

▶ **Adobe Premiere Elements** competes head-to-head with Pinnacle Studio. Adobe released version one of Premiere Elements in October 2004. It has many features found in its professional-level sibling—Premiere Pro—and might be a bit overwhelming for those trying video editing on their PC for the first time. It also has a weak DVD-authoring module. Nevertheless, it was a tough call for me to select one product over the other. So I will introduce you to Premiere Elements in Chapter 14.

▶ **Adobe Premiere Pro 1.5** is the best professional-quality PC video editor. Its capabilities go way beyond the scope of this book. But I want to give you an idea of what else is out there for those who want to take their video editing to a much higher level. I give you a brief overview of its features in Chapter 14.

DVD Authoring—Exciting New Technology

The final step in video editing is to output your finished product. I go over three formats—tape, data files, and streaming Internet files—in the final chapter of the Pinnacle Studio video-editing section of the book. I save the one other output format—DVD—for the final two sections of this book.

This, too, is a departure from most of the books in this genre. They tend to toss DVD authoring in the mix only as an afterthought. Instead, in my view, it should be a significant feature of a book like this because it is the de facto standard output format.

DVD authoring is a relative newcomer to the PC video production process. For years, only Hollywood film companies with deep pockets could afford the hardware and software to create those DVDs you've become accustomed to seeing with their video menus, animated buttons, scene selection options, multiple languages, director comments, and subtitles.

Thanks largely to one company—Sonic Solutions—DVD authoring is now available to anyone with a DVD recorder and some inexpensive software.

You can use DVD-authoring software to create myriad video productions that you can play on your living room or boardroom TV:

▶ Archive your favorite TV programs—you can use Sonic MyDVD 6 to store up to four hours of programming onto one single-layer DVD.

- ▶ Family vacation videos, photo slideshows, family tree histories, and your child's soccer season complete with statistics.

- ▶ Business people can now use DVDs for marketing, employee training, and catalogs.

- ▶ Event videographers can offer clients wedding DVDs with easy menu access to specific moments. No more wading through a long videocassette to get to "I do."

DVD production can be as simple as recording your old VHS videotapes directly to DVDs or as complex as creating DVDs with multiple menus, subtitles, and extra audio tracks.

Using DVD-authoring software, you can create interactive experiences that allow viewers of your DVDs to easily select separate videos, images, and music using menus you design.

DVDs Dominate the Video Market

DVD is the fastest-growing consumer electronics product in history. It has had faster consumer acceptance than TVs and VCRs. There are nearly 500 million DVD players worldwide and more than 60 million DVD-recorder-equipped PCs in the market today.

DVD will soon replace tape as the video publishing format of choice for video professionals and video enthusiasts.

DVDs use high-quality (better than VHS) digital media—images, video, and sound. DVDs are also more compact and more durable than videotapes.

DVDs can store massive amounts of video, images, music, and data; they offer amazing versatility and have near universal compatibility. They are excellent media to archive, publish, and share data and multimedia.

After you make your first DVD, you'll never want to use videocassettes again.

MyDVD 6 and DVDit! 5

In this book's final two sections, I first cover the DVD-authoring module that comes with Pinnacle Studio. Pinnacle presents it as a very limited and consumer-friendly product. I show you that side of this module but also present several undocumented features that let you take even more control over the creation of your DVDs. Studio's DVD module lets you create some very slick-looking DVDs.

However, my goal for this book is to help you go beyond the limited capabilities of Studio's DVD-authoring toolset. So in the final chapters I give you step-by-step instructions on two DVD-authoring titles from Sonic Solutions: MyDVD 6 ($70) and DVDit! 5 ($300). These are easily the two best DVD-authoring products at their price points.

MyDVD 6 is an entry-level product that uses wizards and other streamlined processes to help you easily build DVDs with many of the features you find in Hollywood movie DVDs.

DVDit! 5 takes that authoring process to a higher level, offering more options and giving you greater control over the final product.

Bottom line: If you follow the tasks in this book, I'm sure you will create videos and DVDs you can be proud of—video productions that you will want to show your family, friends, or clients.

Conventions Used in This Book

This book uses the following conventions:

Text that you type and text that you see onscreen appears in bold `monospace` type.

Try It Yourself exercises are the core of this book. They are step-by-step, hands-on instructions that show you how to accomplish tasks. The goal is for you to create high-quality, professional-looking videos and DVDs. This book's many Try It Yourself tasks will help you accomplish that.

By the Way presents interesting information related to the discussion.

Did You Know? offers advice or shows you an easier way to do something.

Watch Out! alerts you to a possible problem and gives you advice on how to avoid it.

PART I

Production Preparation: Videos, Images, Sound, and Story

CHAPTER 1

Digital Video and DVDs— Getting Acquainted

What You'll Learn in This Chapter:

- ▶ Converging technologies
- ▶ Introducing nonlinear video-editing
- ▶ What's DVD authoring?
- ▶ Making sure your PC hardware makes the grade

That you can easily create high-quality videos and DVDs on your PC is a recent and exciting development—the result of converging technologies. I explain what that means in this chapter. To create those videos, you need to use **digital video, nonlinear** editing software. That's a huge shift from older, tape-based, **analog linear** editing machines. I explain those concepts in this chapter.

No longer are you restricted to recording your videos on VHS videotape. Your **output** options include DV tape, PC files, CDs, the Internet, and DVDs. That latter format— DVDs—opens a whole new creative realm. To create Hollywood-style DVDs, with all their menus, buttons, multiple languages, subtitles, and scene selection options, requires using DVD-**authoring** software. I introduce DVD authoring in this chapter. Finally, to exploit these technologies, your PC needs to be up to snuff. I go over some hardware recommendations at the conclusion of this chapter.

Converging Technologies

Harken back to the multimedia days of yore, back when it was a real struggle to create anything on a PC worth presenting in public. Compatibility issues with sound cards and video displays as well as software conflicts fostered uncertainty. Getting your project to run on any PC other than your own was nearly impossible. And if you used video, it ran in postage-stamp-sized windows.

Fast forward to today. Now it's relatively easy to take videos, images, music, narration, and data and build a multimedia project on a PC or DVD. It's not only relatively easy, but also almost guaranteed to play back without a hitch. For instance, you can drop your DVD into any newer-model DVD player, grab the remote, and amaze and astound your viewers.

This dramatic development comes courtesy of several technological advances:

- ▶ Digital video
- ▶ DV camcorders—higher quality and lower prices
- ▶ IEEE 1394—"FireWire"—connectivity
- ▶ High-speed PC processors
- ▶ DVD format
- ▶ MPEG-2 video compression
- ▶ DVD recorders
- ▶ DVD-authoring software

Digital Video Camcorders

Digital video (DV) changes everything.

In the old days (a few years ago) analog video was it. Analog video, when edited on a computer, requires lots of hard drive storage space and leads to quality loss during tape editing and copying.

An analog video signal is a continuous waveform. Small disruptions to that otherwise smooth, continuous signal degrade image and color quality.

Electronically duplicating a waveform is very difficult. Simply dubbing (recording) an analog tape to another tape results in some quality loss. With each additional dub—each added "generation"—images look less defined, colors become increasingly washed out, and the pictures get grainy.

In tape-only editing systems, to make simple scene transitions such as dissolves or to add special effects such as showing videos in moving boxes means doing multiple edits or recording passes. Each pass adds more video "noise" to the tape.

DV Retains Video and Audio Quality

DV makes generation quality loss a thing of the past. DV is a binary signal: a collection of bits—0s and 1s. Unlike an analog signal, which has a wide range of data possibilities and many ways for electronic equipment to misinterpret it, a digital signal rarely loses quality during editing and doesn't suffer from generation loss during copying.

Any copies merely duplicate those bits, meaning a copy looks the same as the original. Electronic equipment looks only for 0s and 1s.

As Figure 1.1 shows, a little noise is not enough to create quality loss, which also means transferring DV from a camcorder to a PC is remarkably easy.

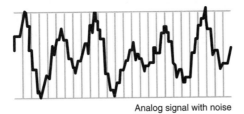

Analog signal with noise

FIGURE 1.1
Signal noise can dramatically affect analog signals but has virtually no impact on binary signals.

Digital (binary) signal with noise

DV is **compressed** video; that is, some data are removed to save storage space. A half-dozen flavors of DV are available with varying degrees of compression and quality. The consumer standard is DV25 (25 mega*bits* per second). To put that in terms we're used to dealing with, that amounts to

3.6 mega*bytes* per second, or 216MB per minute, or 13 gigabytes (GB) per hour.

Why 25 Mega*bits* Equals 3.6 Megabytes

To convert bits to bytes, you divide by 8. Thus, 25 megabits/8=3.125 megabytes. So where does the 3.6 megabytes figure come from? Audio. DV25 refers to 25 megabits of *video* data. The extra *audio* data makes up the balance of the 3.6 megabytes-per-second data rate of DV25.

By the Way

An analog TV signal is about nine times that rate, or about 117GB an hour. Not only would editing straight, uncompressed analog video on a PC require massive hard drive space, but incredible processor power to handle that data rate.

Long-Distance Digital Video

Home satellite systems that use those pizza-sized dishes are digital. To reach your home, those digital TV signals travel from an earth-based transmitter to a satellite in geosynchronous orbit (22,000 miles into space) back to your parabolic pizza pie receiver—44,000 miles and the picture is crystal clear.

Digital Video Looks Better Than Analog

The reason digital video looks better than analog is that it has more lines of resolution.

This can be a bit confusing because TV sets, within each international standard, have the same number of lines of resolution: NTSC (see "TV Standards" sidebar) is 525 lines (although only about 500 are visible), and PAL is 650 lines. Anyone who has visited Europe and viewed TV there has probably noticed the higher-quality image.

But signals sent to those TVs might not have that full resolution, so the signal is interpolated to expand it to fill the screen.

VHS offers 240 lines of information and S-VHS and Hi-8 have 400 lines. Consumer DV tops them all with 500–530 lines. It therefore looks sharper than its predecessors.

TV Standards

NTSC, PAL, and SECAM—what's with all the different (and incompatible) standards?

- ▶ National Television Standard Committee (NTSC) is the TV standard for most of North and South America as well as Japan. It's clearly the worst of these three TV standards. It has only 525 lines of resolution and displays at a nearly incomprehensible 29.97 frames per second (film displays at 24 frames per second).
- ▶ Phase Alternate Line (PAL) at 625 lines has better resolution and displays at 25 frames per second. It's available in Western Europe and Australia.
- ▶ Sequential Couleur A'memorie (SECAM) has the highest resolution—819 lines—as well as a separate channel for color information. Like PAL, it runs at 25FPS. It's used in France and in scattered locations around the Middle East and Africa. Note: SECAM is not an output option for any of the products covered in this book.

Because of NTSC's tendency toward color variability, engineers jokingly refer to it as "Never The Same Color." There is a glimmer of hope: North America is grudgingly elbowing the higher-resolution PAL and SECAM folks aside with High-Definition TV (HDTV), which is set for full adoption in the United States by 2006.

HDTV has a 16:9 screen aspect ratio that matches a typical movie theater screen. Its image is twice as sharp as standard-definition TV. It also features 5.1 theater-style surround sound.

HD is the future. But you won't see HDTV editing options in entry-level video-editing software for a while yet for two reasons:

▶ The massive data throughput to display at a high resolution requires some specialized and expensive hardware.

▶ HD camcorders are still expensive, so few entry-level videographers have them.

DV Camcorders—Higher Quality and Lower Prices

Back in those old days, DV equipment—camcorders and editing machines—was ridiculously expensive and used only by professional or **prosumer** videographers with fat wallets. It was definitely not a budget video production option.

Now you can buy a high-quality DV camcorder for only a few hundred dollars. And you can move up to prosumer quality (a step up from consumer, but still not broadcast quality) with its sharper images, excellent low-light capability, and other high-end features for less than $1,000.

If you don't have a camcorder (analog or DV), buy a DV camcorder. I'll offer some buying tips in Chapter 2, "Shooting Great Videos."

If you have an analog camcorder and are not ready to spend the money for a DV camcorder, you still can edit your videos on your PC. See "Making Sure Your PC Hardware Makes the Grade" later in this chapter for an explanation.

IEEE 1394—"FireWire"—Connectivity

Mac users have long known of FireWire connectivity. Apple Computer invented this data transfer technology in 1986. The IEEE (a standards-setting organization) adopted it as a standard in 1995. IEEE 1394 allows data transfer between devices such as camcorders, printers, scanners, PCs, and hard drives. In addition, it allows direct control—including VCR-style buttons—of connected devices.

Virtually all DV camcorders have IEEE-1394 ports permitting easy connectivity to your PC. I'll explain how you transfer video between your PC and camcorder in Chapter 7, "Capturing and Editing Video with Windows Movie Maker 2," and Chapter 9, " Capturing Video and Cuts-Only Editing with Pinnacle Studio Plus."

High-Speed PC Processors

Video, even compressed DV25, requires a lot of processor power to achieve smooth playback on a PC. Until recently, the only way to view full-screen, full-frame-rate DV on a PC was to run it through an expensive video card. With 3GHz processors now commonplace, software playback of DV is the norm, and viewing DVD movies on your PC is routine.

DVD Format Adoption

DVDs have their roots in audio CDs. That format emerged in 1982 and single-handedly boosted music industry sales.

By the mid-1990s, the movie industry needed a similar jolt. Cable TV and movies via satellite had eroded video sales and rentals. Noting that PC game developers had learned how to put video on CDs, the movie industry sought ways to expand the capacity of those optical discs.

The DVD Logo is a trademark of DVD Format/Logo Licensing Corporation, which is registered in the United States, Japan, and other countries.

The result was DVD-ROM. With a capacity seven times that of a CD-ROM, it launched a consumer technological shift never before seen. DVD players, usually referred to as **set-top boxes**, launched in the U.S. in 1997 and now number about 500 million worldwide. More than half of all U.S. households own a DVD player.

Blue Laser DVDs: Will They Make Your DVD Recordable Drives Obsolete?

Even though most DVDs can hold up to two hours of high-quality video, that's not enough for some movies. And the ongoing DVD-recordable standards disagreements might continue to fragment the DVD market (I'll cover the competing—some might say combating—DVD recordable standards in Chapter 16, "Getting Your Gear in Order—DVD Recorders and Media").

In early 2002, in a move to resolve those issues, a consortium of consumer electronics firms agreed on new DVD recording and playback standards. Those new drives, now shipping in Japan, use blue laser beams instead of red.

Blue beams have a narrower focus and will expand single-sided DVD capacity from their current 4.7GB to 27GB. Double-sided discs will hold an extraordinary 50GB.

Blue laser drives will not be automatically backward-compatible with DVD drives. It'll be up to individual manufacturers to decide whether they want to ship higher-priced drives incorporating both laser technologies.

Does this mean you should wait on the sidelines until these drives ship before buying a DVD recorder or player? The answer is NO.

Those drives are probably a couple years from mass production and availability in the U.S. Also, the new standards come from the same group that brought us the current set of incompatible DVD recordable standards. There's no telling how well the blue-laser standards will withstand competitive interests as time passes.

By its nature, the technology industry is fraught with change and uncertainty. DVDs are not necessarily here to stay. But by the time blue-laser DVDs hit the marketplace, red-laser DVDs will be ubiquitous. It'll take more than a blue light special to change that.

MPEG-2 Video Compression

If movie companies relied on standard analog TV signal data rates, a DVD could hold only three minutes of video. If they used DV (at the consumer standard of 25 megabits per second) DVDs could hold only 21 minutes of video. To reach the magic, Hollywood-mandated two-hour figure (most movies are two hours or less), they needed to digitally compress the video signal.

As the movie industry formulated the DVD specifications, it chose to use two data-compression technologies for DVD video. Created by the Motion Picture Experts Group, an international image standards setting organization, MPEG-1 (finalized in 1988) and MPEG-2 (finalized in 1994) dramatically reduce video signal data rates while retaining image and audio quality. MPEG-1 approximates VHS video quality, and MPEG-2 matches broadcast quality. Both can play back at varying data rates, but at standard DVD-quality rates, an MPEG-2 video is 1/40 the size of its original TV signal.

Edit DV—Output to MPEG

The reason you use DV instead of MPEG-2 video for most video-editing applications is that DV offers more precise—frame-specific—editing than MPEG-2 and does not lose quality during editing. MPEG-2's primary function is for playback. After editing a video (in its original DV format) you then can output it as an MPEG file for distribution on a DVD, CD, as a PC file, or on the Internet.

By the Way

DVD Recorders

In the early days of DVD—from 1997 on—only Hollywood film companies and their DVD development studios could afford DVD recorders. Priced at about $10,000, they fit into a narrow market niche.

Now, thanks to market leader Pioneer Electronics, DVD recorders such as Pioneer's popular DVR-A07 have dropped in price to about $100 while increasing in performance (see Figure 1.2). You probably already have a DVD recorder in your PC. If not, or in case you plan to upgrade, I'll discuss the latest batch of recorders in Chapter 16.

FIGURE 1.2
Pioneer's DVR-A07 DVD-recordable drive retails for about $100.

DVD-Authoring Software

Coinciding with those high-priced DVD recorders, Hollywood studios purchased very expensive DVD-authoring software. Prices for those specialized products frequently exceeded $20,000. That software, along with some skilled technicians, created the slick DVDs—with their motion menus, animated buttons, scene selection options, multiple languages, and subtitles—we've come to expect from Hollywood. But forget about doing that for your home movies.

Then along came Sonic Solutions. In the mid-1990s, the former digital-audio workstation manufacturer chose to shift to DVD-production hardware and software. In 1999 Sonic released DVDit! at the market-busting price of $500. By the fall of 2004, Sonic had shipped more than 10 million DVD creation applications and owned 65% of the DVD creation market. A mind-boggling array of DVD recorders, PCs, and video-editing products from the likes of Pioneer, Microsoft, Sony, Dell, Adobe, and Toshiba come bundled with Sonic Solutions DVD-authoring titles or core technology.

I'll feature two Sonic Solutions products in the DVD-authoring sections of this book. I chose them because they are the best products at each of their price points.

Taken together, these seven converging technologies have created a PC video-editing and DVD-production revolution. You now get to reap the rewards by creating videos and DVDs on your PC.

Introducing Nonlinear Video Editing

You will create videos on your PC using a **nonlinear editor** (NLE). It looks and feels a whole lot different from standard, linear videotape-editing systems. This might be patently obvious to some of you, but bear with me a bit.

On tape systems, you need to lay down edits consecutively and contiguously. Basically, the way it works is that you put your original **raw** footage (a **field tape** in TV news parlance) in a videotape player, cue it up to a clip you like, and then copy that segment to another tape. Then you repeat this process over and over—cuing up both tapes, pressing an edit button, and waiting for the two videotape machines to make the edit. At some point you also might add a narration and music.

If you decide to expand a story already edited on tape by inserting an interview snippet—a sound **bite**—in the middle, you cannot simply slip that bite into the piece and slide everything after it farther along on the edited tape.

You need to edit in that sound bite *on top of* your existing edits (essentially erasing them and recording the sound bite in their place) and re-edit everything after it. Alternatively, you first can make a dub of the story segment after the new edit point and lay that down after adding the sound bite (causing generation quality loss in the process).

Midstory Changes—The Horror

Makes me shudder to think of the news stories I produced, back in the days of videotape-only editing, that screamed for some minor midstory fixes. But I knew those fixes would have taken too much time and caused too much reporter/editor grumbling. Such is life in deadline-driven TV news.

As newsrooms have moved to NLEs, reporter/editor tension (at least over silly little things such as adding a sound bite in the middle of a piece—ah-hem) has dissipated.

By the Way

Pinnacle Studio (the principal NLE covered in this book) and other NLEs like it have come to the rescue. Now you can make changes with a few mouse clicks. If you want to edit the all-important production closing shots before editing anything else, that's fine. It's nonlinear. Feel free to do things nonsequentially.

All your original video clips are stored on your hard drive. Each time you make an edit, all the NLE does is to note the exact start and end points of the edit on both the original video clip and the finished product. No tapes to cue up and no need to worry about sliding a video clip in the middle of an already edited section.

The other overwhelming improvement over videotape-editing systems is immediate access to your video clips. No longer do you need to endlessly fast forward or rewind through miles of tape to find that one moment of natural sound. With Pinnacle Studio and other NLEs, it's all a mouse click away.

Multiple Methods to View Your Videos

Editing your video is only part of the video production experience. You have several choices when it comes to how your audience will view your finished product.

You can stick with DV—retaining all the quality of your original, raw footage. In that case, you'd record it back to a DV tape for viewing from your camcorder to a TV set. Because the NLE you work with will create a separate DV video file, you can view it on your PC or record it to a CD or DVD (if the file does not exceed either medium's capacity).

A more likely scenario is that you will put it in a file format that allows for viewing on the Internet. Depending on the bandwidth—dial-up, DSL, cable, LAN (local area network)—you can create a file with multiple options for your website's visitors.

Finally, you might opt to put it on a DVD, not as a DV file but as an MPEG-2 video that is viewable on a typical DVD player. To do that final option you need to **author** a DVD.

What's DVD Authoring?

DVDs are much more than simply a new type of videocassette or a repository for 4.7GB of data (or more with two-sided, double-layer, or blue laser DVDs). They have the following benefits:

- ▶ They are interactive.
- ▶ They can readily handle all types of media.
- ▶ They are easily customized.
- ▶ The image and audio quality are markedly better than videotape.
- ▶ They allow instant access to video segments or other media.

That's what makes this technology so compelling—its versatility.

By the
Way

DVD Officially Stands for...DVD

That characteristic—versatility—has more or less officially crept into the DVD acronym. The movie industry originally said DVD stood for "digital video disc." But when PC users began using DVDs a few years later, they considered them primarily to be data-only discs.

A mini-political battle ensued between the movie and PC industries. The result? DVD ended up officially standing for nothing. Nevertheless, a news reporter suggested giving it the moniker "digital *versatile* disc," and that has come to be the de facto descriptor. The DVD Forum, the group behind one of the three DVD recordable formats, now includes "versatile" in its literature.

To exploit DVDs' creative potential, you'll need DVD-authoring software. Depending on how many features you want to include on your DVDs, that software can range in price from free (bundled with a DVD recorder or video-editing software), to a few hundred dollars for prosumer-quality products, to $10,000+ for Hollywood-style software.

Most DVD-authoring titles perform the same basic functions. They facilitate

- ▶ Menu creation with buttons and text
- ▶ Adding special features such as video chapters (scene selection menus), extra audio tracks, or subtitles
- ▶ Video conversion to MPEG
- ▶ DVD burning of single DVDs and masters for mass production

Equally as important, they must work within the DVD specification, which is surprisingly configurable, to ensure that your finished DVD meets those specs and runs on *most* DVD set-top boxes.

Watch Out!

DVD Player Compatibility Issues

Some older DVD set-top players do not handle all aspects of the DVD spec—thus, the caveat is that not all DVDs you create with your PC's DVD recorder will work on all DVD players.

Also, three basic types of DVD recordable media exist: DVD-R (dash-R), DVD+R (plus-R) and DVD-RAM. The dash and plus formats also offer rewritable (RW) formats: DVD-RW and DVD+RW. Some players work with some formats and not others.

Finally, with the recent advent of double-layer, recordable DVD recorders and media, there are additional compatibility issues. I explain more about what some call the "format wars" in Chapter 16.

Higher-priced DVD-authoring products have correspondingly higher-level functionality that pushes the DVD spec to its limits—allowing things such as games on DVDs. The first *Harry Potter* movie DVD is a good example—it "remembers" your previous answers despite working in a DVD set-top that has no memory. I will not cover that very high level of DVD authoring in this book.

I will give a more thorough overview of DVD-production ideas and the DVD-authoring process in Chapter 15, "What DVDs and DVD-Authoring Software Can Do for You."

Making Sure Your PC Hardware Makes the Grade

Yes, that technology convergence I referred to earlier means you now can make videos and Hollywood-style DVDs on your PC. But that doesn't mean just any old plain vanilla PC. Here are a few considerations to keep in mind:

▶ Enough processor power

▶ Windows XP—Home or Professional Edition

▶ Sufficient RAM

▶ Large and fast hard drive(s)

▶ FireWire connection

▶ DVD recorder

▶ 3D video card

Enough Processor Power

Video playback and display of special effects takes a lot of processor juice. A Pentium 4 2.0GHz (or the AMD equivalent CPU) is the minimum. You can get by with a bit less, but the stuttering playback will become frustrating.

Windows XP—Home or Professional Edition

This is a must. Microsoft added some excellent video playback enhancements to XP. Coupled with DirectX 9, XP will make your video editing and display much more satisfying. Topping that, if you want to work with Sonic Solutions prosumer DVD-authoring product—DVDit! 5—or Windows Movie Maker 2, you have to have Windows XP.

Sufficient RAM

The bare-bones minimum is 256MB of RAM, but your video and special effects will play more smoothly with 512MB and better still with 1GB (Windows Movie Maker's product manager recommends 1GB).

Large and Fast Hard Drive(s)

One hour of DV consumes 13GB of hard drive space. When you videotape events—weddings, sports, meetings—you might shoot about two hours, or 26GB, of material. This hard drive usage is over and above whatever space your software consumes. Hard drives are relatively inexpensive—pop for one or more that allow you plenty of headroom.

Current drives typically are Serial ATA that operate at 7,200RPM. These have very fast access times and will work fine for DV editing. No need to buy the more expensive 10,000RPM or SCSI drives. Older IDE drives probably will not have fast enough throughput to handle DV.

Finally, consider adding a RAID 0 (Redundant Array of Independent/Inexpensive Drives) controller. RAID 0 splits data into segments and distributes it over two drives, speeding up performance. (RAID 1 duplicates—or mirrors—the data on two drives for improved backup and security, but does not improve performance.) If you're configuring a new system, a RAID 0 controller costs only about $30, but you do need to buy two drives.

FireWire Connection

This is an absolute must. To get DV from your camcorder or videotape machine to your PC, you need to use a FireWire (or IEEE 1394) cable and connectors. True, some camcorders do have USB connectors, but USB does not have the remote control capability of FireWire. Most new PCs selling for more than a few hundred dollars have FireWire connectors. Usually you'll find a FireWire plug on the sound card.

DVD Recorder

If you want to make DVDs, you have to have a DVD recorder (you can make video CDs using a CD recorder but the video quality is poor). There are several flavors of DVD recorders on the market. I cover the full spectrum in Chapter 16. In general, DVD+R/RW (plus) or DVD-R/RW (dash) both work fine. Some newer DVD recorders let you record either plus or dash media. Do not get DVD-RAM.

3D Video Card

Your video card needs to support 3D graphics, DirectX 7.1 or later, have at least 64MB or video RAM, and can display in 1024×768 video resolution. For the best performance, get an ATI Radeon or NVidia GeForce or any of their more recent cards.

If you plan to work only with an analog video camcorder, you need to buy a specialized analog video **capture** device. These run the gamut from low-cost ($60) internal cards to high-end cards ($250 and up) with so-called **break-out boxes**. I will go over the various varieties in Chapter 9.

Summary

These are exciting times. Because of recent technological advances in hardware and software, you now can edit videos and create DVDs on your PC. Consumer digital video camcorders have plummeted in price and have improved in quality to the point where they approach professional camcorders in quality and features.

Nonlinear video-editing software lets you make and change edits in seconds with only a few mouse clicks—a far cry from ancient, linear editing machines.

And you now can play back your videos in multiple ways, from videotape and PC data files to DVDs and the Internet.

CHAPTER 2

Shooting Great Videos

What You'll Learn in This Chapter:

▶ Choosing a digital video camcorder
▶ Sixteen video shooting tips
▶ Expert advice from a TV news chief photographer

To make an excellent video production, you need to start with high-quality raw material—the original footage. Your first step is your camcorder. In this chapter I give you a full complement of camera-buying tips.

With camcorder in hand, your task becomes shooting great scenes. Most books on video editing gloss over camcorder shooting tips, but no amount of clever, whiz-bang editing can turn mediocre raw video or audio into a dazzling final product.

The old computer-programming adage applies: garbage in, garbage out. In the TV world, that adage has a slightly different twist: You *can't* fix it in post. That is, post-production editing techniques will not resurrect reels of video junk.

I have 15 years of experience in broadcast TV and video production. I've done my own shooting and have worked with some of the best photographers in the business. In this hour, I pass along my video-shooting tips along with some from an expert friend of mine to start you on the right track to a finished product you can be proud of.

Choosing a Digital Video Camcorder

If you already have a DV camcorder—great! You're ready to make videos on your PC. Nevertheless, you might want to read this section to compare your camcorder's features to those I recommend. Technology marches forward (as does planned obsolescence). You know that the moment you buy the latest, coolest gadget, a cooler, less-expensive gadget hits the market.

If you don't have a DV camcorder, your first order of business is to buy, borrow, or rent one. A purchase will run you from $300 for a low-end consumer model to $4,000 for a full-featured prosumer camcorder.

Finding a digital camcorder that fits your project needs and budget is no small task. The possibilities can be overwhelming, so your first task is to narrow down the field.

Three things drive camcorder prices and quality:

▶ Number of image-gathering chips—one or three

▶ Lens quality and optical zoom value

▶ Features such as a larger viewfinder, focus ring, image stabilization, and faster shutter speed options

One or Three Chips—CCDs

Camcorders use one or three chips called CCDs—Charged Coupled Devices—to convert light and color to a digital signal. These are the same type of chips used in digital still cameras.

Three-chip camcorders use a prism to divide incoming light into separate red, green, and blue (RGB) hues, thus letting each respective CCD gather more information within its designated segment of the color spectrum.

Single-chip camcorders use special RGB filters to help their one CCD interpret color data.

Three-chip cameras have distinctly better color and low-light capabilities and create sharper images.

Top-of-the-line three-chip camcorders also provide very accurate imaging and many manual options (critically important for advanced video-shooting techniques): focus, iris, shutter speed, and white balance.

Your choice in camcorders comes down to your audience:

▶ If your videos are only for home or web page viewing, a single-chip camcorder will work fine.

▶ If you'll be projecting your videos on large screens for sales presentations or shareholder meetings, you should give strong consideration to a three-chip camcorder.

▶ If you want to move into the prosumer or professional video-production business, a three-CCD camcorder is a must. Showing up at a client's office with a palm-sized, single-chip camcorder is a sure way to jinx a deal.

Features Worth Strong Consideration

As you compare camcorders, there are some features worth considering and others that should have little or no bearing on your buying decision. Here are my deal makers or breakers:

▶ **Substantial optical zoom**—It should be at least 10X, but more is better. Do not confuse this with **digital zoom**, which is useless (see the section "Features Not Worth Considering" later in this chapter).

▶ **Comfortable, accessible, logical controls**—This falls into the try-before-you-buy category. I recommend that you test a camcorder before purchasing it to make sure it feels right to you.

▶ **Easy-to-use viewfinder and easy-to-read LCD display**—These should also have sensible digital setup and controls.

▶ **Optical image stabilizing using prisms or some other means**—Instead of the less-desirable electronic stabilization.

▶ **Input and output capabilities**—IEEE 1394 (the industry-standard technology used to transfer digital video) is a must, as is a means to record from and to an analog VCR or other analog camcorder (S-Video connectors are better than composite ones).

▶ **An external mic plug**—This is a necessity, as is a headphone plug.

▶ **High shutter-speed settings**—These are necessary to capture crisp images of fast-moving subjects.

Two Features of Interest: Progressive Scan and True Widescreen

Your TV set, despite its size, has a lower resolution (dots or pixels per square inch) than photos made with digital cameras (get up really close to a TV set and you'll see how fuzzy the image really is). A typical digital still camera uses a multi-megapixel CCD—that is, a CCD capable of capturing an image with several million pixels. The DV signal standard (which does not vary from camcorder to camcorder) is only 340,000 pixels—a 720×480 resolution. Larger TV sets simply display fatter pixels.

Midrange digital still cameras have resolutions reaching up to 2048×1536. Photo quality is much better than video quality.

For some time now, some DV camcorders have offered megapixel CCDs for still photos—making them sort of dual-function digital camcorder/cameras. For the most part, that has been more a marketing gimmick than something of real value. Those extra capacity CCDs did nothing to improve the quality of the digital video, and the resulting still images were typically lower resolution than most digital still cameras. But that's changing for the better for two reasons: progressive scan and larger-capacity CCDs.

Progressive Scan and Larger-Capacity CCDs

Standard video—both DV and analog—is **interlaced**; that is, each frame is actually two separate images or fields combined into one. Video cameras record at 60 fields per second (FPS) for NTSC and 50FPS for PAL and then combine those fields into **frames** (30FPS for NTSC and 25FPS for PAL).

Video is displayed in horizontal lines. Field "A" is the odd numbered lines and Field "B" is the even-numbered lines. Interlace them together and you have a full frame. The problem is, when there is rapid action, images get blurred because every other line is recorded 1/60 of a second apart.

That means still photos of action taken with a standard DV camcorder look blurry.

Progressive scan fixes that. Progressive—or noninterlaced—display is how computer monitors work. All the horizontal lines for each frame are recorded and displayed sequentially. That's one reason computer monitors look much better than TV sets.

So—if you want to use a DV camcorder as a still camera, make sure it has a Progressive Scan mode. Also check the number of megapixels. Anything less than 2 megapixels means that your still image won't be all that great anyway—progressive scan or not.

True Anamorphic 16:9 Widescreen Mode

This, too, is a result of manufacturers adding higher-capacity CCDs to their DV camcorders. You know that when you watch a Hollywood movie DVD on a standard TV set, you generally have the option of viewing it in a widescreen mode.

The advantage is that you see the entire width of the film that movie theater audiences got to see.

The disadvantage is that it appears in a **letterbox** format—centered vertically on the screen between two horizontal black rectangles. If you have a true widescreen TV set, there is no letterbox; the widescreen mode fills the screen. Nice.

Until recently, consumer and prosumer DV camcorders offered a faux widescreen mode that simply placed black boxes above and below the image, slicing off about a third of the view.

However, some camcorders now offer a true, so-called anamorphic, 16:9 **aspect ratio** widescreen option. The reason: larger CCDs that can accommodate the extra pixels needed for that format. In addition, video-editing software such as Pinnacle Studio and DVD-authoring software such as Sonic Solutions' MyDVD 6, both of which I feature in this book, now let you edit true, anamorphic video. This is an exciting development. Depending on your needs, you might consider buying a camera with a true 16:9 widescreen option.

Features Not Worth Considering

Camcorders have many superfluous, worthless features. Don't make your buying decision based on any of the following:

- ▶ **Digital zoom**—All you get are chunky pixels. Use your video-editing software's zoom feature to handle this.

- ▶ **Titler, fade-in, fade-out, and digital special video effects**—Your video-editing software will take care of these as well.

- ▶ **Presets for special lighting conditions**—These include backlit, low light, portrait, sports, and extremely bright settings (surf and snow). You should use manual controls to more accurately handle these situations.

Camcorders to Avoid Entirely

There are four basic types of consumer DV camcorders. If you're at all serious about your video editing, you will not even consider three of them.

Limit your camcorder search to MiniDV. This uses standard MiniDV cassettes and records in the standard DV format. Don't even bother checking out these three other camcorder types:

- ▶ **Digital8**—Uses the DV format but records on Hi-8 tapes. This was a bridge technology for videographers with Hi-8 analog camcorders making the transition to DV.

▶ **MicroDV**—A proprietary format from Sony that records in MPEG-2. That highly compressed format (lower quality than DV) is fine if you plan only to transfer videos directly to DVD, but it's lousy for editing.

▶ **DVD camcorders**—This is some marketing guy's idea of ease-of-use, but it's a kludge. It, too, records in a couple flavors of MPEG (both lower quality than DV).

Doing Some Homework

Start by using the Internet to get an overview of what's available (later you'll visit a local electronics or camera store for a hands-on trial).

I suggest starting your online research at www.camcorderinfo.com/ or reviews.cnet.com. At CNET in particular, click Camcorders, and then check out the Editors' Top Camcorders. Then take a look at their Camcorder Buying Guide. You will see dozens of camcorders (see Figure 2.1). If you click a specific camcorder, sometimes CNET offers up a brief video review. It's worth checking out.

FIGURE 2.1
CNET.com is a good starting point for your DV camcorder quest.

The Editors' Top Camcorder list is divided into pricing categories such as Home-movie, Enthusiast, and Three-chip Camcorders. You can arrange the listings by rating, alphabetically by manufacturer, or from lowest to highest price.

As you page through the listings, you'll note five main manufacturers. Topping the charts, in my view, are Sony, Canon, and Panasonic. The also-rans are JVC and Sharp.

Although CNET has five pricing categories, I'll limit my overview to three: entry-level, mid-level, and prosumer. Keep in mind that this is a fast-moving business. Camcorder makers regularly release new models and take others off the market.

Entry-Level Camcorders

Entry-level camcorders range in price from $300 to $600. Figure 2.2 shows three popular models near the top of this category's price range.

Canon Elura 60   Panasonic PV-GS15   Sony DCR-HC30

FIGURE 2.2
Three entry-level (but still high quality) digital video camcorders. From left to right: Canon Elura 60, Panasonic PV-GS15, and Sony DCR-HC30.

All three have a traditional look and feel; however, the Sony is an **ultra-compact**; that is, pretty darned small. As I mention later, you really should try out a camcorder at your local retail outlet before buying.

These three reasonably priced camcorders all have many options but are missing some higher-end characteristics, such as improved image quality, longer zoom, microphone plug, and smoother controls.

Mid-Priced Camcorders

Mid-priced camcorders cost from $1,000 to $2,000. Figure 2.3 shows three excellent models in this category.

This price range is rapidly approaching prosumer in quality. The Panasonic PV-GS200 is a 3CCD camcorder that retails for only $700! It does not offer some higher-end features, but the image is sharp and the colors rich. The Canon Optura line features ultracompacts. At the high end of the line—Optura 500—prices are about $1,000, but you get some excellent quality and features. The Sony HC1000 also is a 3CCD camcorder with a price that reflects that: about $1,300.

FIGURE 2.3
These three mid-priced DV camcorders cost between $700 and $1,300. From left to right: Canon Optura 40, Panasonic PV-GS200, and Sony DCR-HC1000.

Canon Optura 40   Panasonic PV-GS200   Sony DCR-HC1000

Prosumer Camcorders

Finally, if you want a top-quality prosumer model, you'll need to spend from $1,800 to $2,500. Figure 2.4 shows the three industry-leading camcorders.

FIGURE 2.4
These are three excellent prosumer DV camcorders. From left to right: Canon GL2, Panasonic PV-GS400, and Sony DCR-VX2100.

Canon GL2   Panasonic PV-GS400   Sony DCR-VX2100

These are not the most expensive camcorders available. There are professional models that have features few budding video enthusiasts would use. To learn more about what's available, visit the three top camcorder manufacturers' websites and view their consumer, industrial, business, or professional camcorder sections: www.usa.canon.com/html/canonindex.html, www.sony.com/, and www.panasonic.com/flash.html.

Take Some Camcorders for a Test Drive

Visit a retail camera or electronics store. Camcorder buying is one of those things that might simply come down to "feel." Try out a few camcorders. Here are some tips:

▶ Does the camcorder fit well in your hands, are the controls logical and accessible, do the menus make sense, and how do the images look?

▶ With the color LCD viewfinder open, aim the camcorder at a window facing outside; then pan to an interior view. How quickly and accurately does the auto-white balance change?

▶ Move the camcorder as close as possible to an object. How close can you get before losing the focus? Closer is better.

▶ Pan the camcorder from a close-up to a distant object and then back to the close-up. Watch how the autofocus handles the move. Is it fast? Did it focus past the new scene and then come back into focus?

▶ Jiggle the camera. How well does the image stabilization system work?

▶ Aim the camera somewhere where there is little ambient light. Does the image remain sharp or get grainy?

No amount of Internet research can trump the value of hands-on testing.

Legacy Analog Camcorders

You might own a legacy analog camcorder—VHS (dread the thought), S-VHS, or Hi-8—and aren't ready to shell out the cash for a DV camcorder. Your old clunker might get the job done, but the results will be several cuts below pure DV video.

Image quality from most legacy camcorders falls below today's DV camcorders (Hi-8 still looks pretty good, and professional analog Beta SP is better than pro-sumer DV). But no matter how good the original video looks, the final edited product will not look that great.

That's largely because when loading the analog video into your PC (video capture), your software converts it to a digital video file (losing some quality in the process). When recording it back to analog tape for viewing, it will lose even more quality (there is no quality lost during editing).

One other minor fly in the ointment: You'll need to buy a video capture card with analog input connectors (see Chapter 9, "Capturing Video with Pinnacle Studio Plus"). A straightforward FireWire connection will not work with an analog camcorder.

Sixteen Tips on Shooting Great Video

With your camcorder of choice in hand, it's time to venture off and shoot videos.

Here are my video-shooting axioms:

▶ Plan your shoot.

▶ Adhere to the "rule of thirds."

- ▶ Use additional still-camera composition techniques.

- ▶ Get a closing shot.

- ▶ Get an establishing shot.

- ▶ Get a good mix of shots—unusual angles, wide and tight, matched action, and sequences.

- ▶ Lean into or away from subjects.

- ▶ Keep your shots steady—use a tripod.

- ▶ Let your camera follow the action.

- ▶ Use trucking shots to move with the action.

- ▶ Avoid fast pans and snap zooms—they're for MTV only.

- ▶ Shoot cutaways to avoid jump cuts.

- ▶ Don't break the "plane."

- ▶ Get plenty of natural sound.

- ▶ Shoot enough continuous audio.

- ▶ Use lights to make your project brilliant.

I've jammed a lot into these 16 items. All will help make your video shine with a professional glow. I discuss each in detail in the following sections.

Video camera work has two fundamental differences from still photography: action and sequential storytelling. With that in mind, here are my video-shooting tips.

Plan Your Shoot

When you consider a video project, plan what you need to shoot to tell the story. Videotaping your kid's soccer championship match, a corporate backgrounder, or a medical procedure—each requires planning to ensure success. Know what you want your final video project to say and think of what you need to videotape to tell that story.

Even the best-laid plans and most carefully scripted projects might need some adjusting after you start rolling and recording in the field. No matter how you envision the finished project, be willing to make changes as the situation warrants.

Adhere to the Rule of Thirds

Composition is the most fundamental element of camerawork, and the rule of thirds is the textbook. When composing your shot, think of your viewfinder as being crisscrossed by two horizontal and two vertical lines. The center of interest should fall on one of the four intersections. See Figure 2.5 for a simple diagram.

The standard amateur-photographer mistake is to put the center of attention at the center of the image. The most common is portraits in which the eyes of the subject are dead center in the photo, leaving all sorts of empty space above the subject's head.

A good rule is to look around the viewfinder as you shoot, not just stare at its center. Check the edges to see whether you're filling the frame with interesting images. Avoid large areas of blank space.

FIGURE 2.5
The rule of thirds: Putting your image's most important element at one of these intersections will make it more pleasing to the eye.

Use Additional Still-Camera Composition Techniques

I cover still-camera shooting tips in Chapter 3, "Creating Compelling Still Images." Briefly stated, here are three admonitions: add foreground elements to your shot, keep your subject(s) off-center, and shoot at oblique angles.

Get a Closing Shot

This might seem like I'm taking things out of order, but the one shot that should be uppermost in your mind is the closing shot of your video production (the opening shot or shots are important but have a much-less lasting viewer impact). Your closing images are what stick in people's minds. They're what your audience takes away from your video production. If you start a shoot without knowing what your closing shot will be, you should be constantly on the lookout for that one shot or sequence that best wraps up your story.

> ### Dotson's Rule
>
> The importance of the closing shot came through loud and clear at a seminar I attended given by NBC-TV's premier feature reporter Bob Dotson (see Chapter 6, "Story-Creation and Video-Production Tips"). He and his photographer never fail to find a closing shot. It could be as simple as someone closing a door, capping a pen, petting a dog, turning out the lights, or releasing a butterfly from their cupped hands. If you happen to see a Dotson feature story, consider its close. It's sure to be memorable.

Get an Establishing Shot

An establishing shot sets a scene. It doesn't have to be the opening shot. One of the greatest establishing shots of all time is in the middle of Robert Redford's *The Natural*. Those who have seen this film know what I'm talking about: the shot from the top row of the baseball stadium during a night game that takes in the entire field with blazing lights ringing the park. Anyone who has been to a major league ballpark gets goose bumps when that image appears onscreen. It tells a dramatic story in one image.

That should be your goal for your project's establishing shot or shots (you might need several if you're covering several topics in one video).

> ### Think Different
>
> Although super-wide works sometimes—aerials make great establishing shots—it pays to think "outside the box." Don't fall back on the old standbys, such as the scoreboard, the corporate sign, or the medium shot of a hospital operating room. Try something different: a tight shot of a soccer ball with natural sound of children's voices, a low-angle image through a glass table of someone using your client's product, or a close-up of a scalpel with light glinting off its surface.
>
> Each grabs the viewer's attention and helps tell your story.

Get a Good Mix of Shots

The following methods will help you get a good mix:

- ▶ **Use unusual angles**—Move your camcorder away from eye level. Shots taken at shoulder height have their place—they represent probably as much as 80% of all video—but getting the camcorder off your shoulder leads to more interesting and enjoyable shots. Ground-level "ferret-cam" shots are great for cavorting puppies or crawling babies. Climb a ladder or use a tall building to get a crane shot. Shoot through other objects or people while keeping the focus on your subject.

▶ **Use wide and tight shots**—Most novice videographers create one medium shot after another. The reason: It fits our experience. Our eyes tend to take in things the same way. Instead, think wide and tight. Grab a wide shot and a tight shot of your subject. It's much more interesting.

Don't Zoom—Move

It's all too easy to rely heavily on your zoom lenses. Wide and tight shots work well, but instead of zooming in for the tight shot, physically move your camera in close. In addition, audio is clearer when you're closer to the subject. When you edit you can use the audio you got in a close-up shot when displaying your wide shot (just turn down its volume a bit). It's much more interesting to change positions rather than simply toggle that zoom button.

Did you Know?

▶ **Match action with multiple shots**—If you're shooting a wood carver, get a wide shot and then move in for a tight shot of his hands in the same position as in the wide shot. If you're shooting repetitive action—assembly-line machinery, a golf swing, or a barber—shoot an entire sequence in one long shot. Then go in tight and shoot the same sequence a couple more times, getting a variety of close-ups. You'll use your nonlinear editor to match the action.

▶ **Shoot sequences mixing tight, wide, and matched action**—Sequences help tell your story, build interest, and frequently can replace a narration. This works well with repetitive action such as a golfer making an approach shot. Shoot the golfer's face as he looks up the fairway, shoot a view from behind as he turns to his golf bag, get a tight shot as he selects a short iron, and so on as he lines up the shot and finally takes a swing. This takes some cooperation from that golfer as you set up each shot. A good finish is to shoot a wide shot from up the fairway and then a tight shot as the ball lands on the green (or in some unexpected, comical location).

Lean Into or Away from Subjects

Too many shooters rely too heavily on the zoom lens. A better way to move in close or away from a subject is simply to lean in or out. Lean way in and start your shot tight on someone's hands as he works on a wood carving; then smoothly lean way back (perhaps widening your zoom lens as well) to reveal that he is working in a sweatshop full of folks hunched over their handiwork. It's much more effective than a standard lens zoom and a lot easier to pull off.

Keep Your Shots Steady—Use a Tripod

We all know that videographers take the images we view on TV and that they use cameras to create them. But as video creators, we don't want to remind viewers of that. We want to give them the sense that they're looking through a window or, better yet, are there on location.

A shaky camera shatters that illusion.

Despite a recent trend away from the use of tripods—MTV started it and shows such as *48 Hours* have run with it—there's plenty to be said for smooth-looking video. If you're doing a sit-down interview or grabbing close-ups, put your camcorder on "sticks." When possible, use a tripod with a fluid head. That'll enable you to make smooth pans or tilts. Good tripods aren't cheap. Reasonably high-quality sticks start at about $150. See Figure 2.6 for a top-of-the-line example.

FIGURE 2.6
The Sachtler DA 75 L aluminum tripod (right) weighs only 2kg. Its DV 2 fluid head works well with lightweight camcorders.

Did you Know?

Makeshift Tripods

If a tripod is too expensive, cumbersome, or inconvenient; if the action is too fast paced; or if you need to move the camera during the shot, try to find some way to stabilize the shot. For still shots, lean against a wall, put your elbows on a table, or place the camcorder on a solid object. For moving shots, get the camcorder off your shoulder, hold it about waist high, and let your arms work as shock absorbers.

Another alternative is to buy or make a Steadicam. A Steadicam Jr—complete with a built-in monitor—that works with prosumer camcorders costs $900. See www.steadicam.com/prohh_jr.htm.

Here's a website for a home-built steady cam: www-2.cs.cmu.edu/~johnny/steadycam/. It's a heck of a lot cheaper.

Stop-Action and Time-Lapse Tips

You'll need a tripod to create stop-action or time-lapse photography. Both methods require that the camera remain steady. The other requirement is that the focal length and aperture cannot change. So, when you set up your camcorder to shoot the same scene for a long time, planning to compress time during editing, make sure that your autofocus, auto-white balance, and auto-iris are turned off.

Did you Know?

Let Your Camera Follow the Action

This might seem obvious, but keep your viewfinder on the ball (or puck, face, conveyor belt, and so on). Your viewers' eyes will want to follow the action, so give them what they want.

One nifty trick is to use directed movement as a pan motivator. That is, follow a leaf's progress as it floats down a stream and then continue your camera motion past the leaf—panning—and widen out to show something unexpected: a waterfall, a huge industrial complex, or a fisherman.

Amateur camcorder users often attempt to *create* action with zooms, pans, and tilts. Minimize those moves, and let the action take place in your viewfinder. If you need to pan or tilt to follow action, do that.

Use Trucking Shots to Move with the Action

This is an excellent way to follow action (so named because using a camera on a moving vehicle is one way to get this shot). Truck right along with some action. If you're shooting a golf ball rolling toward the cup, tag along right behind, in front of, or beside it. When walking through tall grass, dangle your camcorder at knee level and walk right through it, letting the grass blades smack into the lens.

Ever wonder how they get those cool downhill snow-skiing shots? The cameraperson skis backwards with a heavy electronic news-gathering (ENG) camera on his shoulder or dangling from his hand at snow level. I've watched my good friend Karl Petersen (see the upcoming section, "Expert Advice from Karl Petersen") do that amazing maneuver several times.

Become One with the Trucking Shot

Here's a corollary to the trucking shot: Put your camcorder on a moving object—a shopping cart, hospital gurney, bicycle, and so on—to create a different point of view. Here you don't move with the action; you become the action.

Did you Know?

Avoid Fast Pans and Snap Zooms

These moves fall into MTV and amateur-video territory. Few circumstances call for such stomach-churning camerawork. In general, it's best to minimize all pans and zooms. As with a shaky camera, they remind viewers that they're watching TV.

If you do zoom or pan, do it for a purpose: to reveal something, to follow someone's gaze from his or her eyes to the subject of interest, or to continue the flow of action (as in the floating leaf example earlier). A slow zoom in, with only a minimal change to the focal length, can add drama to a sound bite. Again, do it sparingly.

Keep on Rolling Along

Don't let this no-fast-moves admonition force you to stop rolling while you zoom or pan. If you see something that warrants a quick close-up shot or you need to suddenly pan to grab some possibly fleeting footage, keep rolling. Don't press the record/pause button. You can always edit around that sudden movement later.

If you stop recording to make the pan or zoom and adjust the focus, you might lose some or all of whatever it was you were trying so desperately to shoot. If you keep recording, you also won't miss any accompanying natural sound.

Shoot Cutaways to Avoid Jump Cuts

Cutaways literally let you cut away from the action or interview subject. One important use is to avoid **jumpcuts**—two clips that, when edited one after the other, create a disconnect in the viewer's mind.

Consider the standard news or corporate interview. You might want to edit together two 10-second sound bites from the same person. Doing so would mean the interviewee would look like he suddenly moved. To avoid that jump cut—that sudden disconcerting shift—you make a cutaway of the interview. That could be a wide shot, a hand shot, or a reverse-angle shot of the interviewer over the interviewee's shoulder. You then edit in the cutaway over the juncture of the two sound bites to cover the jump cut.

The same holds true for a soccer game. It can be disconcerting simply to cut from one wide shot of players on the field to another. If you shoot some crowd reactions or the scoreboard, you can use those shots to cover up what would have been a jump cut.

Don't Break the Plane

This is another of those viewer disconnects you want to avoid. If you're shooting in one direction, you don't want your next shot to be looking back at your previous camera location.

For instance, if you're shooting an interview with the camera peering over the left shoulder of the interviewer, you want to shoot your reverse cutaways behind the interviewee and over his right shoulder. That keeps the camera on the same side of the plane—an imaginary vertical flat surface running through the interviewer and interviewee. To shoot over your subject's left shoulder would break that plane, meaning the viewer would think the camera that took the previous shot should somehow be in view.

Figure 2.7 shows an interview with correct and incorrect (broken plane) camera placements. This also applies to larger settings, such as shooting from both sides of a basketball court or football field.

In general, you want to keep all your camera positions on one side of that plane. This isn't true for all situations. Consider a TV show of a rock group performance. Camera crew members typically scramble all over the stage, grabbing shots from multiple angles, and frequently appear on camera themselves. That's much different from breaking the plane in a formal sit-down interview.

Did you Know?

Switch Sides

If you conduct formal, sit-down interviews with more than one person for the same piece, consider shooting each subject from a different side of the interviewer. That is, if you shoot one subject with the camera positioned over the left shoulder of the reporter, position the camera over the right shoulder of the reporter for the next interview. That avoids a subtle jump cut that happens when you edit two bites from two individuals who are both facing the same way.

Get Plenty of Natural Sound

This is absolutely critical. We tend to take sound for granted. However, relying on your camcorder's built-in mic as well as taking extra steps to improve the audio quality will dramatically improve the production value of your projects. I'll cover audio issues in depth in Chapter 4, "Acquiring Audio." For now, think in terms of using additional mics: **shotgun** mics to narrow the focus of your sound and avoid extraneous noise, **lavalieres** tucked out of sight for interviews, and **wireless** mics to get sound when your camera can't be close enough to get just what you need.

FIGURE 2.7
The *plane* is an imaginary vertical wall running, in this case, through the reporter and inter-viewee. Breaking the plane—particu-larly when shooting a reverse cut-away—leads to camera shots that cause viewer dis-connects.

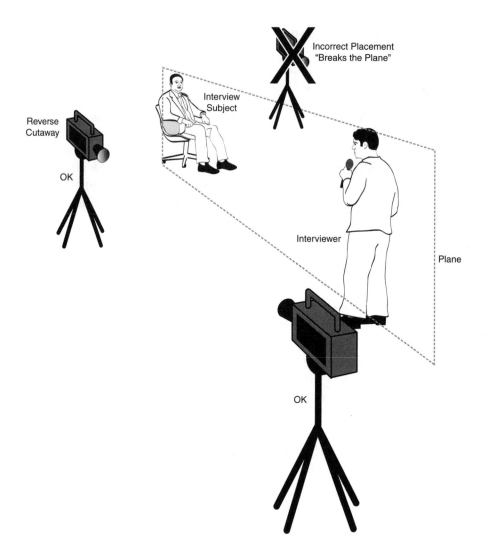

Shoot Enough Continuous Audio

This applies primarily when shooting anything with music—dancing (weddings are the most frequent instance), choir, marching band, or your kid's piano recital. You need to keep the camera rolling for as much of the musical piece as you'll want to include in the final video. The purpose is to get a continuous flow of music. When you make your edited video you'll lay down that tune and then edit in other shots (video-only—no associated natural sound) without breaking up the smooth flow of music. At a wedding, for example, you'll shoot a dance number, wait for another tune with a similar beat, and grab some more shots you can edit over the first dance number.

Did you Know?

Shoot the Same Song Twice

If you have some control over a video shoot that involves music, your best bet is to shoot it twice. For example, I videotaped an elementary school class singing their favorite song. Rolling the entire time (never pressing the Record/Pause button), I generally stayed wide, occasionally changing my position to get some different angles. Then I had them sing it again and I went in close for some face shots. I later edited in the close-ups without breaking the audio. I did something similar for a piano recital, shooting the entire performance as a wide shot. As other pianists played, I grabbed audience shots including applause. Finally, after the show was over and the audience had left, I went on stage and had the original performer play the songs again. I grabbed close-ups of her hands, face, and even inside the grand piano.

Use Lights to Make Your Project Brilliant

Lights add dazzle and depth to otherwise bland and flat scenes. An onboard camcorder fill light is a convenient way to brighten dull shots. And a full (but admittedly cumbersome and expensive) lighting kit with a few colored gels can liven up an otherwise dull research laboratory.

If you don't have the time, money, patience, or personnel to deal with adding lights, do whatever you can to increase the available light. Open curtains, turn on all the lights, or bring a couple desk lamps into the room. One caveat: Low-light situations can be dramatic, and flipping on a few desk lamps can destroy that mood in a moment.

Did you Know?

Watch Your White Balance

No matter what kind of lighting situation you're in, you always need to watch your **white balance**. Different lights operate with different color temperatures. Your eyes automatically compensate for those color differences, but your camcorder is not that proficient. These days, most camcorders have auto-white balance, and many have manual-white balance as well. Auto-white balance works in most situations. As you move from room to room or from inside to outside, the camera "assumes" that everything in its field of view is gray and adjusts its color balance accordingly.

Tricky Lighting Situations

Problems arise when you shoot indoors and have a window in the scene. In that circumstance, whatever you see through the window probably will have a blue tint. The other tricky white balance situation is when you shoot a scene with a predominant color, such as doing product shots using a solid-color background. The auto-white balance will think that solid color is gray, and the image will look horrible. That's when you need to place a gray or white card in the scene, fill the viewfinder with that card under whatever lighting you plan to use for the product shots, and click the manual-white balance button. For a fun practical lesson in the value of a manual-white balance, roll tape throughout this procedure or when you walk from indoors to outdoors to watch the colors change.

Expert Advice from Karl Petersen

Karl Petersen—Chief Photographer, KGW-TV, Portland, Oregon.

Karl Petersen is my favorite TV news photographer. We met in Boise, Idaho, where we worked at competing stations. We later worked together at KSL-TV in Salt Lake City. We formed a video production company in Oregon called Glint Video (we always tried to get a "glint" shot in all our news pieces). Then Karl moved on to KGW-TV in Portland, where he is now chief photographer.

Karl has seen and done it all. Absolutely nothing fazes him. He'll venture into the tensest situation and shoot with aplomb. When we went out on stories, we had an unspoken understanding: I never had to tell Karl what kind of images and sound I needed. I knew he would always get exactly what would make the story work. Karl's regular beat these days is chopper photography. "Sky 8," KGW's Bell 407 helicopter, has two Flir cameras. One is infrared and can operate in *total* darkness. Karl's advice is worth much more than the price of this book. Take it to heart:

▶ My first shooting advice is, don't do it. Pursue a career of doctor, lawyer, teamster, stevedore, bordello piano player, whatever.

▶ Having failed that, my first tip is always to shoot as an editor. Always think about how to get from one shot to the next. Try to get some kind of transition shot with either an entry or exit. Close-ups are especially helpful in editing to get from point A to point B.

- Get a good shot mix—wide, medium, close-up (extreme close-ups work well), and unusual angles. Get lots of shots. Variety is an editor's friend.

- Get an establishing shot that tells viewers where you are.

- Fundamentals: Make sure that you have freshly charged batteries, always monitor audio by wearing an earpiece (if you don't, you're guaranteed to get burned), and watch your color balance.

- For all indoor interviews, I recommend using at least two lights, three if you have time (I usually don't—TV news is hectic). If I'm to the reporter's right, I place a light with an umbrella reflector slightly to his left. That means the interviewee is looking toward the light. I place a Lowel Omni with "barn doors" (to keep it from shining into the lens) behind and over the left shoulder of the interview subject (that is, to my right). This adds nice highlights. If I have time, I place a third umbrella well behind the camera to add fill (see Figure 2.8).

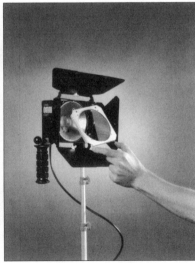

FIGURE 2.8
A Lowel Tota with an umbrella (left) and a Lowel Omni with barn doors. Images courtesy of Lowel-Light.

- If I'm shooting in a room with sunlight coming in a window, I use blue gels—especially balanced for daylight—and then color balance for sunlight.

- For underwater photography, I recommend using an Ewa-Marine plastic bag video camcorder housing (see www.ewa-marine.de/English/e-start.htm). They're good to a depth of about 30 feet, easy to use, and relatively inexpensive (about $350).

When shooting from "Sky 8," I sit in the warmth and comfort of the back seat and operate the cameras with a laptop and a joystick. Not many video producers have this luxury. For those who must shoot from a side window, here are some tips:

▶ Think safety first. Make sure that nothing can fall off the camera—such as a lens shade—or out of the back seat and possibly hit the rotor. That makes the chopper spin like crazy, so you get real dizzy before you die.

▶ Shooting with the door off is ideal (remove it *before* you take off).

▶ Try to keep the camera slightly inside the door frame to keep it out of the wind.

▶ Have the pilot "crab" (fly sort of sideways) so that you can shoot straight ahead. That's much more dramatic. It's a great way to fly along a river for instance.

▶ Have the pilot fly low. This allows cool reveal shots, such as flying over a ridge to reveal an expansive vista.

Finally, don't forget to grab that "glint" shot.

Summary

A high-quality video production must start with excellent video. Your camcorder is paramount.

Digital video has become the de facto consumer/prosumer camcorder standard. It has many advantages over analog—VHS, 8mm, and Hi-8. If you're in the market for your first camcorder, choose a DV camcorder. If you have an analog camcorder and your budget is tight, that can work for you, but it has drawbacks such as video quality loss during capture and the need for a specialized video capture card.

When selecting a DV camcorder, consider the number of CCDs, the lens quality, and important features such as manual control of focus, shutter speed, and aperture. Ultimately, your DV-buying decision might simply come down to "feel," so be sure you try before you buy. Look for easily accessible controls as well as menus that make sense.

With your camcorder in hand, use my video shooting tips to give your productions some professional polish. When shooting your raw video, think outside the box. Don't settle for standard, boring shoulder shots. Get in close, get down low, look for that unusual angle. Natural sound is essential, and lighting adds sizzle.

CHAPTER 3

Creating Compelling Still Images

What You'll Learn in This Chapter:

▶ Digital or film cameras—what will work best for you

▶ Digital camera buying tips

▶ Making high-quality photos—tips and tricks

▶ Importing and scanning images

▶ Formatting images for videos and DVDs

▶ Editing images with Adobe Photoshop Elements

Photos and other still images can play a major role in your video production. Consider the Ken Burns documentaries that consist almost entirely of old black-and-white photos.

But simply taking a bunch of poorly exposed or composed snapshots and dropping them into a video or slapping them on a DVD will not transform them into works of art.

In this chapter, I offer tips on digital camera selection. I also present some picture-taking dos and don'ts and cover three new digital image technological developments.

Even if you are a digital camera devotee, you still probably have scrapbooks loaded with photos shot on film. To get them into your video productions and DVDs, you'll need to use a scanner. In this chapter I give you scanner buying and usage tips. Finally I introduce Photoshop Elements, the younger sibling of the most popular image-editing software.

Digital or Film Cameras—What Will Work Best for You

My quick answer is film for sure. Digital? Maybe.

I am not a big fan of digital still cameras. They cannot yet replace film cameras because they have too many drawbacks, including the following:

- ▶ **Shutter lag time**—You must press the button and wait for up to two seconds to actually take the photo (see the sidebar titled "Consumer Digital Cameras Don't Do Action," later in this chapter).

- ▶ **Delay between shots**—This ranges from two to five seconds.

- ▶ **Battery consumption**—They devour batteries.

- ▶ **Slow autofocus.**

- ▶ **Poor flash metering**—They use "pre-flashes" instead of responding to light during the actual exposure.

- ▶ **Frequent color or white balance miscues.**

- ▶ **Digital focal multiplier**—Your 35mm SLR (single lens reflex) camera wide-angle lens won't work properly on a digital SLR (see the sidebar titled "Three Rapidly Changing Digital Image Technologies," later in this chapter).

- ▶ **Rapid obsolescence**—You can buy a digital camera one day and see a better, less-expensive model advertised the next day.

- ▶ **Learning curve**—Yet another technology to learn with frequently complicated, arcane, and incomprehensible controls.

- ▶ **Poor low-light capabilities.**

- ▶ **Expensive printers and paper.**

Despite these drawbacks, millions of digital camera users can't all be wrong. Digital cameras have the following advantages:

- ▶ Immediate feedback—if you don't like how the photo turned out, you can erase it and try again.

- ▶ You never have to buy film again.

- ▶ You don't have to pay to process your film.

- ▶ You can print only the photos you need when you need them.

- ▶ You can quickly and easily upload pictures to your PC.

▶ You don't need to use a scanner.

▶ Prices are dropping, and quality is increasing.

▶ You can give a digital camera to your kids without worrying about them wasting film.

Digital still cameras are not completely ready for prime time, but they can be tremendously useful for certain applications:

▶ Real estate agents emailing photos of homes to out-of-town clients

▶ Insurance adjusters photographing property damage

▶ Employee security badges, credit card photos, or driver's license photos

▶ Posting images to websites

Consumer Digital Cameras Don't Do Action

The first time you try a digital camera, I guarantee you'll wonder what's going wrong.

You'll look through the viewfinder and see nothing. You'll think, "Oops, I need to turn the darned thing on." You'll press the On button or open the sliding lens cover, you'll wait, and the camera will finally finish its startup process and be ready to shoot.

You'll then compose a shot and press the shutter button, but nothing will happen. You'll probably press the shutter again, a bit harder, and still nothing will happen. So, you'll hold it down longer—a second or two—and finally you'll hear a click and whir and an image will appear. But it won't be the image you thought you were going to get—it won't be that moment, frozen in time, that you visualized when you pressed the shutter.

That moment passed your digital camera by. Why? Electronics, surprisingly, can be slow.

Here's what occurs as you press the shutter: As with a film camera, a digital camera emits an infrared signal to set the focus, then adjusts the autoexposure by changing the aperture (f-stop) and the shutter speed, and (if it's dark) sends out a small burst of light to determine how much flash to use. At this point, a film camera snaps the picture. But a digital camera has much more work to do.

The digital camera flushes the photosensitive computer chip's electric charge to prepare it to receive a new image.

Photons from the subject hit that chip. It converts them to electrons, changes them to digital data (typically at least two million chunks of color and brightness data), and moves them to an interim storage location. From shutter press to image capture, up to two seconds elapse.

If you're ready to take another picture, you have to wait from two to five seconds while your digital camera recycles. The camera has to compress that digital informa- tion and store it before it's ready to take another photo.

Shooting action photos is just about out of the question, and expecting portrait sub- jects to hold that smile for a second and a half is asking a lot. No longer is it, "Three, two, one, click." Now it's "Three, two, depress shutter, one, click."

There is one way around this, though. You can spend a few thousand dollars for a professional digital camera, which uses one-click/one-shot, or **sequencing**, tech- nology.

But even then, depending on the camera, you might need to wait more than a sec- ond between photos. Also, you can't use the flash (it can't recycle fast enough), the photos might have lower resolutions than normal, and the color balance might be off.

So, if you use a digital camera, you'll need to make some adjustments. See the sec- tion "Compensating for Lag Time," later in this chapter.

Digital Camera Buying Tips

Other than convenience, I see no compelling reason to buy a digital camera specifically for a video or DVD project. If you need to use archived photos in any project—family history DVDs, for instance—you'll use a scanner to import them into your PC. Therefore, you can continue to rely on film.

But the demand for digital cameras continues to grow. Despite my reservations, you might want to buy one, or you might already own one and want to replace it—new technology is so tempting.

So, here are my digital camera buying tips:

▶ **Megapixels**—These are millions of picture elements or data points on the light-sensitive CCD chip (the charge coupled device) that I covered in the previous chapter. The higher the number, the more you can enlarge the printed image and not lose details. Two megapixels is the minimum to make an average-quality 5"×7" photo printout, three megapixels is the min- imum for an 8"×10" printout, and four megapixels is the minimum for an 11"×17" printout.

▶ **Storage capacity**—Larger megapixel images require more storage space. Note how much capacity comes with the camera and the cost for additional memory modules: CompactFlash, SmartMedia, Secure Media, or Memory Sticks. Don't buy cameras with floppy disk or CD storage because they're too slow.

▶ **Try before you buy**—The feel, size, and weight of the camera along with the location of its controls are important.

▶ **Optical zoom capability**—2X optical zoom capability is the minimum you should get, but 3X is much better. Ignore references to digital zoom; that just reduces the resolution of the image.

▶ **Rechargeable batteries and a charger**—These are a must. Buying them separately adds $30+ to the total price. NiMH (nickel metal hydride) rechargeable batteries are better than NiCad (nickel cadmium). Always keep a second set on the charger, and keep in mind that many rechargeable batteries tend to lose power over time.

▶ **Burst**—This is also called **sequence shooting mode**, and it compensates for shutter and shot-to-shot lag times.

▶ **Check out the software bundle**—Some cameras come with some excellent products, but most do not.

▶ **Color liquid crystal display (LCD) panel**—You use this to preview photos and determine whether exposure or color balance adjustments are necessary.

▶ **Macro function**—You use this to make extreme close-ups, from an inch or so away from the subject.

▶ **USB PC connectivity**—It's ubiquitous.

Three Rapidly Changing Digital Image Technologies

Digital camera technology does not stand still. Here are three recent developments:

▶ **CMOS versus CCD**—Most still cameras and video camcorders used CCDs (charge coupled devices) to capture images. Kodak and Canon have challenged that dominance with two ultra-high-resolution digital still cameras: the 14 megapixel Kodak DCS Pro 14n ($4,000) and the Canon EOS Digital line (from 6.3 to 11.1 megapixels and ranging in price from $1,000 to $4,000). Both use CMOS (complementary metal-oxide semiconductor) chips.

CCD chips with the same resolution would be more costly and bulky. And CMOS chips use far less power than CCDs. Another advantage is that the CMOS chip has the same frame size as 35mm film, meaning there is no need for owners of SLR (single-lens reflex) cameras to buy new lenses.

▶ **Digital focal multiplier**—That CCDs are smaller than 35mm film creates a sometimes expensive inconvenience for owners of digital SLR cameras using their 35mm film SLR (single lens reflex) lenses. The smaller image-capturing area effectively increases the focal length of any interchangeable lens used on a digital SLR camera. That boosts telephoto lens power—arguably a nifty benefit—but narrows the view of wide-angle lenses. Creating distortion-free wide-angle lenses is an expensive art—buying a new one just for a digital SLR camera can easily cost more than $1,000.

Olympus, Kodak, Panasonic, Fuji, and two other firms think they have an answer: the Four Thirds System (www.four-thirds.org/en/index_01.htm), a standardized lens-mounting scheme for digital SLRs. If enough companies sign on, this will resolve the digital focal multiplier issue (you'll still have to buy new lenses, though). It will also lead to smaller, lighter lenses and ensure uniform lens mounts across all brand lines, something that does not exist for 35mm SLRs.

▶ **Foveon X3 image sensor**—CCDs and CMOS technology pale in comparison to the image clarity of Foveon X3 (www.foveon.com). These new chips capture three times the color resolution, feature a simpler design, and offer higher overall performance for digital still and video cameras.

Standard digital camera chips use a mosaic pattern of pixels in groups of three red, green, and blue photodetectors. The resulting image, when viewed up close, looks like a checkerboard.

As illustrated in Figure 3.1, Foveon embeds three layered photodetectors in silicon at every pixel location to capture all colors within each pixel. The result is sharper images with more accurate color reproduction.

FIGURE 3.1
Foveon X3
Technology.
*Illustration ©2002,
Foveon, Inc.*

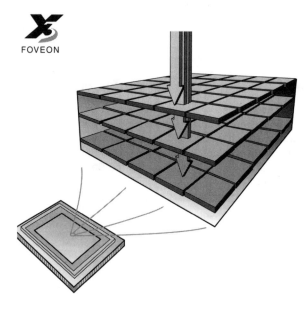

Three professional digital still cameras use Foveon X3 technology: Sigma SD9 ($750), Sigma SD10 ($1,200) and Polaroid x530 ($400).

Making High-Quality Photos—Tips and Tricks

Whether digital or film, here are some standard tricks and tips that will help you improve your picture-taking results.

Putting an End to Blurry Images

The biggest problem in amateur photos is blurry pictures. The principal cause is camera movement, but there are several other reasons, including the following:

- **Camera movement**—Figure 3.2 shows a classic example of the results of camera movement. Instead of gently pressing the shutter, many amateur photographers abruptly push it, shaking the entire camera. Digital cameras exacerbate this because shutter lag time leads many digital camera users to press down even harder.

FIGURE 3.2
When everything in an image is blurry, you can bet camera movement is the culprit.

- **Autofocus on wrong subject**—Autofocus usually sets the focus based on whatever is in the center of the viewfinder. If you're framing a scene with something in the foreground, as in Figure 3.3, the autofocus might "see" the frame, not the subject. Adjust the camera angle to place the subject at the center of the viewfinder, depress the shutter halfway to set the autofocus, compose your shot, and then press the shutter the rest of the way.

Composing Your Shots

Composition is critical, and for most photos only a slight change in camera angle or location will make the difference between a mediocre snapshot and an effective, pleasing photo. Here are some tips:

▶ **Get close to your subject**—Instead of typical tourist shots of family members off in the distance standing directly in front of some fountain, frame the fountain to fill your viewfinder and then have your family stand close to the camera and a bit off to one side of the frame.

By the Way

Depth of Field

If you put your family up close with the fountain some distance away and then focus on your family, will the fountain be out of focus? It depends. In daylight, the auto aperture (iris) will be very small, creating a deep depth of field. Foreground and background elements will all be in focus.

In low-light settings, however, the aperture is wide open and the depth of field is very shallow. Therefore, the fountain *will* be out of focus. Using a narrow depth of field well can lead to dramatic images.

- ▶ **Add a foreground element**—Adding something between you and your subject gives depth to your images.

- ▶ **Use the rule of thirds**—As shown in Figure 3.4, divide your image into thirds, vertically and horizontally, and place the object of interest at one of the intersecting lines. That creates much more visual interest. One quick and easy way to adhere to this rule is to keep your subject off-center.

FIGURE 3.4
This image has elements from each of the three previous tips: It has a foreground element, the subject is off-center, and it uses the rule of thirds.

- ▶ **Shoot at oblique angles**—As shown in Figure 3.5, instead of shooting straight on, shoot a subject from a nonperpendicular angle.

FIGURE 3.5
Use oblique angles
to add interest.

Other Photo-Taking Tips

Fuzzy photos and poor composition are the most frequent culprits in the picture-taking snafu department. Here are a few other tips you can follow to improve your photo-taking skills:

▶ **Watch backlit scenes**—As shown in Figure 3.6, your camera's autoexposure sets itself for the light behind your subjects, meaning they'll be silhouettes. Either set the autoexposure on them first and then compose the shot, or use fill-in flash—or do both.

▶ **Use fill-in flash**—Whenever you shoot outdoors, adding flash brings out the colors and details of your subject. Figure 3.7 shows how fill-in flash can overcome the silhouette effect of backlit shots.

Watch Out!

Flash Goes Only So Far

Flash has a very limited range, about 10–15 feet. Next time you're at a concert or nighttime sporting event, note all the fans with point-and-shoot cameras taking flash photos from 100 rows back. What they'll get is brightly illuminated backs of heads from a couple rows in front of them. Don't waste your time. The only way to use a flash is to get close to your subject.

FIGURE 3.6
When the sun is behind your subjects, silhouettes might be all you get.

FIGURE 3.7
Fill-in flash can overcome backlit scenes (getting your subjects to stop squinting takes much more effort).

▶ **Don't overexpose foreground objects**—As shown in Figure 3.8, when you're using flash, objects close to the camera will be over-illuminated. This is one time when adding a foreground element might not work.

FIGURE 3.8
The flash tends to illuminate the closest object, which might not be your desired outcome.

▶ **Avoid stiff poses**—Encourage your subjects to do something, such as walking, talking, pointing—anything to add interest.

▶ **Keep the background simple**—Distractions draw the attention away from your subject.

▶ **Use lines to add interest**—S-curves and diagonal lines, such as those in Figure 3.9, add visual interest.

FIGURE 3.9
Diagonal lines help draw attention to the subject (the backlit cloud of dust is a nice touch, too).

Compensating for Lag Time

Here are some tips to overcome lag time inherent to digital cameras:

▶ Turn on your camera before you need it but, if possible, keep the LCD viewfinder and flash turned off (they drain too much battery power).

▶ Get used to depressing the shutter release halfway to lock focus and exposure and then depressing the shutter all the way when you are ready to take the picture.

▶ When shooting action, switch to the burst or sequence mode. However, those modes typically create less-than-perfect images.

▶ If you let your subjects know when you're going to take the photo by counting down from three, press the shutter on "one."

▶ Anticipate action by shooting sooner than normal.

Importing and Scanning Images

Getting your digital images onto your hard drive is relatively easy. Scanning in photos takes a little more effort. In the latter case, you want to streamline the process (because scanning is time-consuming and tedious) to ensure you have a consistent look and to avoid last-minute fixes when editing them into a video or DVD.

Importing Digital Images to Your PC

Your digital camera probably came bundled with some image-capturing and editing software. But if that's not the case, you don't need commercial software to load digital images to your PC.

When you connect your camera to the PC (typically using an included USB cable) Windows detects that connection and then displays a window labeled Removable Disk (Windows considers your camera to be a storage device, like a hard drive). Select Copy Pictures to a Folder on My Computer and click OK to open the Scanner and Camera Wizard as shown in Figure 3.10.

Within the Scanner and Camera Wizard (shown in Figure 3.11), you can select photos you want to use in your project. After making your selections, click Next, select a file folder, and save the photos. At some point you might want to crop them or do some touch-up work. I give a brief overview of both techniques later in this chapter.

FIGURE 3.10
When you connect and turn on your digital camera, Windows pops up this Removable Disk screen.

FIGURE 3.11
Use the Scanner and Camera Wizard to select "keeper" photos to store on your hard drive.

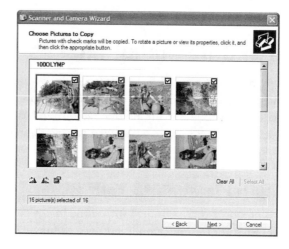

Selecting a Scanner for Your Video and DVD Projects

A scanner is a critical part of your video and DVD production toolset. You will frequently need to include printed photos, logos, graphics, or other hard copy in your projects. To do that, you need a scanner.

Now is a great time to buy either your first scanner or one to replace that old clunker in the corner. For $75–$150 you can get plenty of horsepower.

Scanner Buying Tips

Before heading off to the store or jumping online, take a look at the following shopping tips:

▶ **Dots per inch (DPI) and color depth**—1,200dpi is sufficient for video production work; 2,400dpi works well for high-end photo or prepress projects. 42- or 48-bit color depth is more than you'll ever use. Most image-editing software scales down to 24 bits—8 bits per color (red, green, and blue).

Which Way Is Up?

DPI is supposed to be noted as horizontal by vertical, as in 1,200×2,400. The horizontal number is the true resolution and refers to the density of sensors in the image chip. The vertical number equals the steps per inch that the scanner motor moves the scanner head. Some manufacturers flip the numbers, so pay close attention.

Watch Out!

▶ **CCD versus CIS**—Most scanners use CCDs, the same type of image sensor chips found in digital still and video cameras. At least one company—Canon—relies on contact image sensor (CIS) chips. CIS chips use less power and are more compact (making for some very trim and sleek scanner designs). However, they have trouble with books that don't lie absolutely flat on the scanner glass, they are slower than the norm, and they can't do transparencies. So stick with the industry-standard CCD scanners.

▶ **Scanning speed**—This varies greatly and changes with each new model. I suggest checking online at CNET or (reviews.cnet.com) or PC World (www.pcworld.com) for current bench test results. At last word Epson, HP, and Visioneer have the best scanning speeds for low-resolution (300dpi) scans—typically about 20 seconds.

▶ **Connection speed**—USB 2.0 scanners are becoming more popular (versus USB 1.1 or parallel connectors). If you have USB 2.0 capability, you will see speed improvements, but only for higher-resolution images. Otherwise, USB 1.1 is adequate.

▶ **Transparencies**—Most consumer scanners do not handle slides or negatives as a standard feature. You'll need an optional tray, which typically costs about $25.

▶ **Onboard buttons**—Some scanners give you several controls on the scanner itself, which can be convenient and helpful.

▶ **Bundled software**—Most flatbed scanners come with the excellent ABBYY FineReader optical character recognition (OCR) software and a barebones image-editing package. Even though all scanners these days are TWAIN compliant, meaning that products such as Microsoft Word and Photoshop can directly access and operate your scanner, the software bundle usually includes a rudimentary scanner control interface.

TWAIN Is Not Samuel Clemens

TWAIN, surprisingly, is not an acronym (some jokingly say it stands for "technology without an interesting name"). It is an industry standard describing how PCs communicate with image acquisition devices.

Explaining Scanner Settings

If you already have a scanner you probably don't give much thought to its settings. I'm guessing you select a standard mode—print, photo, web, file—click scan, and that is that.

What you generally end up with (depending on the original document size) is a fairly large file, perhaps 2,400×1,800 pixels or more.

The thing is, images used for video productions don't need to be anywhere near that size. Standard NTSC TV sets can't display more than 720×540 pixels.

In addition, you probably scan at a high resolution—600dpi (dots per inch) or more. The reason: Standard inkjet printers work at 600dpi or more and you want your printed photos to look sharp.

However, TV sets display only at 72dpi (PC monitors typically have a slightly sharper display: 96dpi). In general then, there is no reason to scan at a resolution greater than 72dpi. The exception is when you are scanning a photo smaller than 5"×7" (I'll explain the math behind that in a moment). The goal is to have even small images fill the TV screen and have them look sharp.

Using a dpi density much larger than 72 is a waste of hard drive space and time. The smaller the resolution, the faster the scanning process.

Resolving Resolution

Resolution, dots per inch, pixels, and **image size** are used interchangeably in PC parlance. This leads to some confusion.

Dots equal **pixels** (picture elements).

Resolution sometimes means image size and sometimes means dots (or pixels) per inch—**dpi.**

Most times, when referring to an image, resolution means dpi, such as 600 horizontal dpi and 600 vertical dpi (usually horizontal dpi and vertical dpi are equal; otherwise, you'd end up with a distorted or stretched image).

Sometimes resolution refers to image size in some number of pixels, as in 800×600 pixels. If you run Windows at 800×600, a 400×300 size resolution image takes up one-fourth of your screen. This is true no matter how large your monitor screen is.

But printed images work differently. For example, a digital image with a 600×600dpi resolution and a 400×300 size resolution prints out in postage stamp size, two-thirds of an inch by one-half inch (300 pixels—dots—at 600dpi equals one-half inch).

What this all means is that when you scan an image for use in a video or DVD, the only setting you'll need to worry about is dpi. You select a dpi based on the original size of the hard copy photo, document, or graphic. I give you some dpi settings later, in Table 3.1.

Scanning Images Using Manual Settings

Today's scanner software leans toward "idiot proof" status. That's not a good thing, because it gives you virtually no direct control over individual scans.

It's not the end of the world if you opt for the automated approach. But for consistent results, faster scanning, and smaller files, you might as well take a stab at the manual approach using Windows XP's built-in manual scanning option.

Before tackling this book's first Try It Yourself task, though, you need to do some calculating.

Selecting an Appropriate DPI

For consistent results, adjust your scanner's dpi setting based on the size of the image you're going to scan. In general, you set higher dpi settings for smaller images (less than 5"×7") to ensure they display cleanly on a TV set. You can set lower dpi settings for larger images.

The goal is to create an image with 72dpi or more (but not too much more) to ensure sharp reproduction on your TV while minimizing file size and speeding up the scanning process.

Calculating Correct Scanner DPI

Photos generally are either vertical format (portrait) or horizontal (landscape). Horizontal matches the general shape of a TV screen but usually does not exactly match the aspect ratio. Photos tend to be a bit wider.

The goal is to have horizontal-format photos fill the TV screen from left to right. That means the top and bottom will not quite reach the top and bottom of the TV screen, but you can fill those gaps with a color background.

With vertical format pictures, your goal is to have the top and bottom of the photo touch the top and bottom of the TV screen. That means the left and right sides will be well inside from the edges of the TV screen.

Table 3.1 gives you some general dpi settings for photos of various sizes.

Did you Know?

Higher DPI for Zooms and Pans

Some video-editing software lets you zoom in and pan across still images. Pinnacle Studio Plus, the NLE featured in this book has that effect.

If you plan to use an NLE's zoom/pan function, you should scan the photo at a higher dpi setting to ensure that the blown-up or panned photo looks sharp. The greater the planned zoom or longer the pan, the more you should increase the dpi setting.

In general, smaller photos require higher dpi settings and larger photos require smaller dpi settings. But, as listed in Table 3.1, never scan at less than 72dpi because your image will lose fidelity. And it's always a safe bet to round up your dpi numbers—that is, calculate the proper dpi and then round it up to a slightly higher, even number.

Again, this isn't rocket science. The purpose simply is to have consistent-looking images, faster scans, and smaller file sizes.

TABLE 3.1   Scanner DPI Setting Examples for Photos (NTSC)

Photo Size	Horizontal Format	Vertical Format
2''×3''	217dpi	163dpi
4''×6''	109dpi	82dpi
5''×7''	93dpi	72dpi (minimum resolution)
8''×10'' or larger	72dpi	72dpi (minimum resolution)

The Math Behind the DPI Settings

This section goes over the math behind how I arrived at the recommended scanner dpi settings. Feel free to skip it.

This is a two-part calculation that depends on your country's TV standard (NTSC or PAL), whether you're working in full-screen (4:3 aspect ratio) or wide-screen (anamorphic 16:9), whether you want to compensate for NTSC overscan, and the size of the document or photo.

Overscan is an NTSC issue (PAL and the other TV standard, SECAM, do not overscan). Most consumer NTSC TV sets enlarge the TV signal, pushing it beyond the edges of the TV tube. That means you frequently cannot see about 10% of the original video. For example, when watching *CNN Headline News*, you might not be able to read all the stock ticker data at the bottom of the screen.

If you're creating an image to play on a standard NTSC TV, you can ensure that viewers will see the image in its entirety—top to bottom or left to right—if you create your image using the overscan resolution noted in Table 3.1: 650×490 pixels (this is an approximation—overscan varies from TV set to TV set). You will later place that image within a 720×540 frame. In that way, overscan will cover part or all of the frame, but not the image.

You certainly can use the full resolution (720×540 pixels), but the edges of your image will not display on most NTSC TV sets. Figure 3.12 shows the approximate overscan area and the visible area, or the so-called **safe zone**.

Another Way to Compensate for Overscan

Did you Know?

Later in this chapter I show how you can put images, intended for display on NTSC TV sets, in a frame to ensure the edges of the TV screen do not truncate portions of the picture. If you don't want to do that extra work *and* your original image has some extra room around the edges, scan a larger area. The NTSC set will clip some of that extraneous stuff away but will leave the essential part of your image.

To compensate for these differences and ensure that your images retain their original aspect ratios, you should create graphics using the resolutions noted in Table 3.2.

FIGURE 3.12
When working with NTSC DVD projects, you should keep images within the safe zone to compensate for overscan.

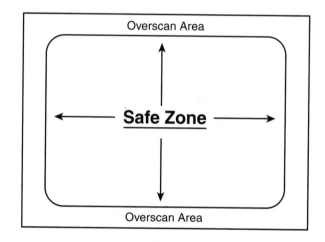

TABLE 3.2   Standard Image Resolutions—Sizes

TV Standard and Aspect Ratio	Full Resolution
NTSC 4:3	720×540 pixels or 650×490 pixels*
PAL 4:3	768×576 pixels
NTSC widescreen 16:9**	852×480 pixels
PAL widescreen 16:9**	1024×576 pixels

*To compensate for NTSC overscan resolution.

**Widescreen resolutions are for images only. Menus cannot display in the 16:9 widescreen format. Create all menus using the 4:3 resolutions for each TV standard.

Calculating the DPI Setting

For horizontal format photos, measure the width in inches and divide that into 650 pixels (the screen width compensating for overscan) for NTSC or 768 for PAL.

For example, with a 5"×7"photo, divide 7 into 650 to get 93dpi. When you scan a 5"×7" horizontal format photo, select a dpi setting of 93 or slightly more.

If you have a 5"×7" vertical format photo, you should divide 7 inches into the screen height, or 490. In this case, 490/7 = 70. That's less than 72dpi, so select at least 72dpi when you scan a 5"×7" vertical format photo.

Use the Windows Scanner Wizard to Customize Scan Settings

With Windows XP, you have at least one built-in manual scanning option, no matter how your scanner's bundled software works. In this book's first of many Try It Yourself tasks, you will use a Windows Wizard's manually adjustable settings to create manageable-sized images. Here's how it works:

1. You might find the Scanner or Camera Wizard under Start, Programs, Accessories. If so, start it that way; if not, locate it in your Control Panel. You might have a Control Panel icon on your desktop, or you can find Control Panel under Start, Settings. In either case, open Control Panel, double-click Scanners and Cameras, and double-click your scanner's name in that window (you might then need to double-click Printers and Other Hardware to find your scanner). The Scanner and Camera Wizard shown in Figure 3.13 opens.

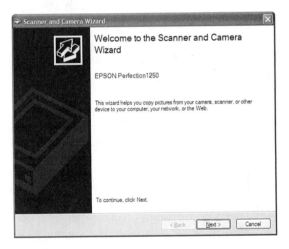

FIGURE 3.13
Use the Scanner and Camera Wizard to manually alter your scanner's settings.

2. Click Next, and you'll see the Choose Scanning Preferences screen shown in Figure 3.14.

FIGURE 3.14
Select Custom settings to adjust the dpi setting.

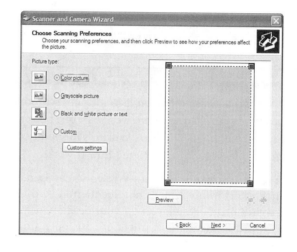

3. Select Custom settings to open the Properties interface. Here you select a dpi setting to match your image size. If it's a 4"×6" horizontal format photo, select 109dpi, as shown in Figure 3.15. Click OK to return to the Scanning Preferences interface.

FIGURE 3.15
Use Windows XP's Scanner Wizard Custom setting to select a specific dpi resolution.

4. If you need to do any cropping of your image, now is the time to do it. Click Preview (it might take about a minute for the scanner to make a preview image) to display your image in the cropping window, shown in Figure 3.16. Drag the highlighted box corners to the desired size, and then click Next.

FIGURE 3.16
Crop your image before completing the scan to get the best results later.

Get Your Crops in Early

Did you Know?

You should crop now rather than use image-editing software to do it after you've scanned your image. Doing it now ensures your image will have the proper dpi resolution, whereas cropping it later will lead to a lower-quality image because of reduced dpi (after you blow up the smaller cropped image to fill the TV screen).

You should also cut out large borders like those shown in Figure 3.16 and remove unwanted portions of the photo to save a cropping step later. If you plan to crop, don't include the cropped-out area in the measurement used to calculate dpi.

5. Click Next to open the Picture Name and Destination window shown in Figure 3.17. Name the picture, select a file folder, and choose an image type.

Selecting an Image Format

Did you Know?

BMP and TIFF are the best of the four image formats available in the Windows Scanner Wizard because they are uncompressed and retain all image quality. PNG does compress image data, but it only imperceptibly alters its quality. Do not use JPEG because it both compresses and reduces image quality. In any event, most video-editing and DVD-authoring products can handle any of these four image types.

6. Click Next to make the scan and store the image. It's now available for further editing.

FIGURE 3.17
Select any of the
four image for-
mats—BMP and
TIFF work best. The
video-editing and
DVD-authoring
software covered in
this book can
handle all or most
of them.

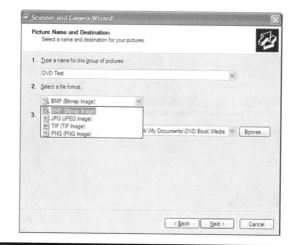

Formatting Images for Videos and DVDs

Few of your scanned images will exactly match the NTSC or PAL screen sizes or
4:3 aspect ratios needed for DVD menus and stills. Most software these days
(including Studio and MyDVD) keep your image in its original aspect ratio,
adjusting its size to fit the top and bottom or sides of the TV screen. But you have
no control over the color or other appearance of the gaps between the image and
the edges of the TV screen. Studio puts black there, MyDVD makes the gaps gray
for images used in menus, and black for images in slideshows.

Therefore, if you want to have control over the color or other appearance of those
edges, you need to place images on a template of the proper size, adding any
color frame or other graphic of your choice along the image sides or top and bottom to fill the screen.

Fun House Mirrors
If you use your photos without placing them over a background that matches the NTSC or PAL screen resolution you're working in, some consumer NLEs will distort the images' aspect ratios, forcing them to fill the TV screen (squashing or stretching them like fun house mirrors).

I've chosen my favorite, low-cost image-manipulation software, HyperSnap, to
perform this upcoming task. You can download a trial copy for free or the full
version for $35 from www.hyperionics.com. Or you can use any other image-
manipulation software.

Use Graphics-Editing Software to Create a Template for Images

Try it Yourself

▼

The goal here is to create a template that matches your country's TV standard resolution—NTSC or PAL. Then, in the next task, you'll crop and adjust the resolution size of your images and paste them on the template. Here's how to create a template:

1. Open HyperSnap (or your image-editing software of choice).

2. Click the New button, shown in the upper-left corner of Figure 3.18, or select File, New from the main menu. In HyperSnap, a default 400×300 pixel white rectangle displays. That's the correct 4:3 aspect ratio, but not the correct size.

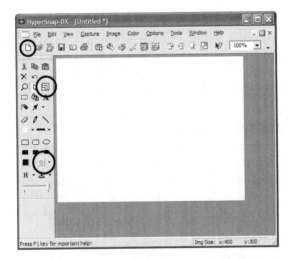

FIGURE 3.18
I recommend using HyperSnap to crop and resize your images.

3. Change that into a 720×540 (NTSC) or 768×576 (PAL) rectangle by clicking the Resize button shown in the center of the toolbar in Figure 3.18. Doing so displays the Bitmap Dimensions interface shown in Figure 3.19. Change the Width to 720 (or 768 for PAL) and the Height to 540 (or 576). Click OK.

FIGURE 3.19
Change the bitmap dimensions to match your country's video standard.

▼

4. Click the Background/Transparent Color button shown at the bottom of the toolbar in Figure 3.18 to open the collection of 40 color swatches, shown in Figure 3.20.

FIGURE 3.20
Use the Background/Transparent Color tool to set the template color to black (or a color of your choosing).

5. If you're creating a DVD for use on PAL TV sets, click the black swatch in the upper-left corner and go to step 7. If you are producing a video or DVD for NTSC (U.S. and Japan), you need to create an NTSC-safe color (see the following Watch Out!). Select More Colors (see Figure 3.20) to open the Color Selection window shown in Figure 3.21.

Watch
Out!

NTSC Rears Its Ugly Head Again

The NTSC TV standard has several drawbacks (versus PAL and SECAM). The one that affects the creation of this task's image frame is color.

To avoid tearing, bleeding, or smearing of colors, NTSC graphics must not be too bright, too dark, or too saturated. (Those who travel from the United States to Europe, for instance, usually notice how much richer the colors are on PAL or SECAM TV sets.)

To ensure that the black frame you create for your images is NTSC-safe, you need to keep the RGB (red, green, and blue) values less than 230 and more than 16. Step 6 explains how to do that.

6. To give your template, or frame, an NTSC-safe custom color, select the middle box (Sat—Saturation) shown in Figure 3.21 and type in **17**. Tab to the next box (Lum—Luminance) and type in **17** again. You'll note that the red/green/blue color numbers change to about 17 (the Hue number is inconsequential in this case). The Color|Solid box displays this new color (even though it's NTSC-safe, it still looks very black). Click Add to Custom Colors and then click OK to return to the main HyperSnap interface.

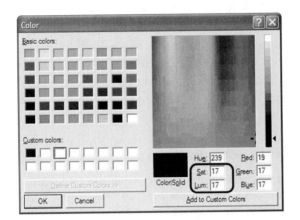

FIGURE 3.21
Select an NTSC-safe template color using this color selection dialog box.

More Than One Way to Be Safe

You can create NTSC-safe colors in HyperSnap and other graphics products using many methods. In the case of HyperSnap, you can create a color by inputting separate values that are greater than 16 and less than 230 in the Red, Green, and Blue boxes. You can also reduce the Contrast setting and increase the Brightness setting.

Did you Know?

---

7. Click New again, and your rectangle should turn black. This also sets a new default template that fits your TV standard size and aspect ratio. Now when you reopen HyperSnap and click New, you'll always get a 720×540 (or 768×576) black rectangle.

A Frame of a Different Color or Style

If a black frame does not look right with a particular still, you can change the background color. One approach is to place your image on the black background and use the eyedropper Color Picker tool to select a color from the image itself (perhaps along an edge). You can then use the Paint Can tool to apply the new color to the background, blending it more closely with the image and making it look less like a frame or border.

And if a solid color does not appeal to you, you can use any graphic as the backdrop for your template. Simply make sure it matches the screen resolution you're working in: NTSC or PAL.

Did you Know?

Use Graphics-Editing Software to Crop and Resize Your Images and Paste Them onto Your Template

Your goal when you scanned your images was to limit the dpi to no less than 72dpi and no more than is necessary to create a full-screen image. In this task, you'll adjust your images so they exactly fit into the 650×490 NTSC or 768×576 PAL viewable area. Then, you'll paste them onto your newly created template. Here's how:

1. In HyperSnap (or your own image-editing software) select Open (the icon next to New) and locate and open a scanned (or any other) image file.

2. During scanning, you should have cropped out any extraneous borders or unwanted portions of the original picture. Now you might want to fine-tune that process. Select the Crop tool (see Figure 3.22). Click and drag to define the region you want to keep; then click again within the workspace to tell HyperSnap you've completed setting the cropping boundaries.

Using Undo

If you don't like how you've cropped your image, select Edit, Undo (or use the standard Windows keyboard shortcut Ctrl+Z) to back up one step and start over.

FIGURE 3.22
Use HyperSnap's highlighted cropping tools to trim out unwanted edges from your image.

Slim Crops

If you crop too much now, you will end up with a fuzzy, out-of-focus image when you place it in your DVD project. When you made the scan, you limited the dpi to save disk space and speed up scanning. If you crop out a lot after saving the scanned image and then expand the image to fit the template, you will lose resolution. Use this last-minute cropping step solely to make minor fixes.

3. Scale the image to ensure it will fit exactly into the 650×490 NTSC or 768×576 PAL frame by selecting Image, Scale from the main menu. In the Scale dialog box shown in Figure 3.23, either change the width (for horizontal-oriented images) to 650 or 768 (NTSC or PAL) or change the height (for vertical images) to 490 or 576. Do not uncheck Keep Aspect (it keeps your image in its original aspect ratio) or Interpolate (it smoothes pixel-to-pixel color changes when you shrink or expand images). Click Done.

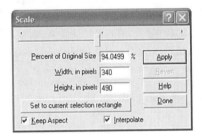

FIGURE 3.23
Use the Scale dialog box to ensure that your image fits into the template.

4. Copy your image by selecting Edit, Copy from the main menu (or use the standard Windows keyboard shortcut Ctrl+C).

5. Click New to open your 720×540 (or 768×576) black, rectangular template.

6. Paste the image onto this black background by selecting Edit, Paste (or use the keyboard shortcut Ctrl+V).

7. As shown in Figure 3.24, drag the image so it's centered over the template. When you're satisfied with its location, click outside the image to anchor it.

NTSC Leaves a Little Room

After you paste your image into the NTSC template, there should be a little room around the image to compensate for overscan. For the PAL template, the top and bottom of a vertical image will be flush with the top and bottom of the template, and the left and right edges of a horizontal format image will be flush with the left and right edges of the template.

FIGURE 3.24
Paste your image
onto the template
to complete this
process.

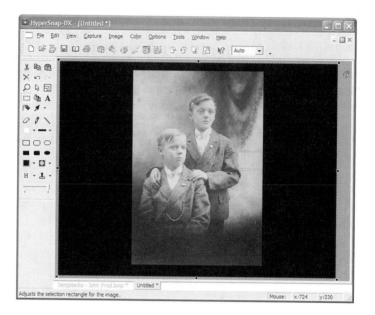

8. Save your image by selecting File, Save and choosing a name and file folder
   location.

Favorite File Formats

You have numerous image types from which to choose. BMP, GIF, JPG, and TIF (the
top four in the HyperSnap list) are your best options for compatibility and image
quality retention.

The end result of all this effort is a collection of images with dpi resolutions,
image sizes, and aspect ratios that will lead to a high-quality, consistent look for
all the stills and menu backgrounds in your video and DVD projects.

Editing Images with Adobe Photoshop Elements

If you're a graphics professional, you use Photoshop. It's a given. If you're an
entry- to mid-level video producer, you might already—or someday will—use
Photoshop. If Photoshop is not on your PC, try its younger, leaner sibling:
Photoshop Elements.

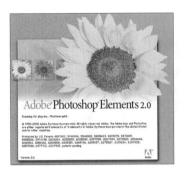

Photoshop Elements offers standard photo touch-up tools that are found in many consumer-level photo products. Some software bundled with digital cameras even has features on par with Photoshop Elements.

But Photoshop Elements goes beyond simple touch-up. It offers professional graphics-creation tools that can come in handy as you increase your video production and DVD menu creation skills.

I will give you only a brief overview of what this full-featured product has to offer. I strongly suggest you download and install the trial version and then follow along. You can find the trial version at `www.adobe.com/products/photoshopelwin/main.html`. Click the Tryout link under Downloads.

Photoshop Elements' opening interface, shown in Figure 3.25, eases users into this powerful program.

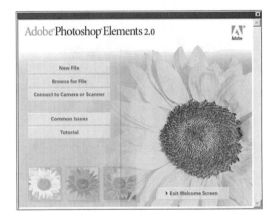

FIGURE 3.25
Photoshop Elements offers extra help not found in Adobe's professional product lines.

Fixing photos is its forte. Access its file browser by selecting File, Browse in the main menu. As shown in Figure 3.26, the file browser is an excellent way to preview photos while also viewing image data.

FIGURE 3.26
Photoshop Elements' file browser improves image access.

I chose an old photo full of imperfections. To make repairs, I selected Filter, Noise, Dust & Scratches in the main menu (see Figure 3.27).

FIGURE 3.27
Photo touch-up is a powerful feature.

I also used the Clone Stamp, which is accessible in the toolbox and shown in Figure 3.28. It grabs image data from a selected area and then lets you apply it over a flawed region in the photo to repair it. In that way you can select skin tone right next to a scratch on the photo and use that skin tone to repair the scratch.

FIGURE 3.28
The Clone Stamp lets you fix photos using other portions of the same image.

Other touch-up tools include

▶ **Sponge**—This tool subtly changes the color saturation.

▶ **Focus**—This tool sharpens or blurs an image.

▶ **Dodge and Burn**—These darkroom-style tools change the exposure in specific areas of an image.

▶ **Red Eye Brush**—This tool repairs that vampire glow caused by camera flashes reflecting off the back surface of your subjects' eyes.

▶ **Color and Contrast**

▶ **Straighten and Crop**

Photoshop Elements has several drawing tools, which you can use to create buttons for your DVD menus. As shown in Figure 3.29, I used the rounded rectangle tool, applied color, applied a bevel from the Style drop-down menu, and added text. The options are endless and readily accessible. You can create multiple identically shaped buttons in layers.

FIGURE 3.29
Photoshop
Elements provides
several tools to
create DVD menu
buttons.

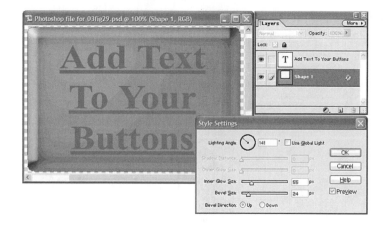

One other handy tool is the video frame importer shown in Figure 3.30. You can use it to capture an image from your video.

FIGURE 3.30
Use the video
frame importer to
grab freeze frames
that you can alter
and use as DVD
menus or back-
grounds for titles in
your video.

After saving the freeze frame, use Photoshop Element's tools to change its charac-teristics: Alter the color; replace or remove features; or apply any of the many fil-ters, some of which are shown in Figure 3.31. After you've altered it, the frame can make an excellent-looking DVD menu or background for a title.

FIGURE 3.31
Elements offers dozens of filters and effects that you can easily apply to images, graphics, or text. In this case, I used Sumi-e to create an abstract oil painting look.

Make Your Image Safe for NTSC Viewing

I mentioned earlier that your colors need to be "safe" for NTSC viewing. Photoshop has a simple tool to accomplish that. With your color frame selected, click on Filter, Video, NTSC Colors. Done.

Watch Out!

Summary

Still images play a vital role in DVD projects both as content and menu backgrounds. Digital cameras are a convenient way to create those images, but this new technology has too many drawbacks for it to replace film cameras. Consider buying a digital camera only as a supplement to your film camera.

Following some basic photo-shooting tips will ensure your images are of top quality.

Owning a scanner is a must. For $100 or so, you can get an excellent model that does everything you need.

Creating consistently sharp-looking and distortion-free images for a video or DVD project takes some extra effort. The process begins by scanning images using the proper dpi settings for the original image size. While scanning, you should crop your images to remove borders or unwanted areas around the edges. When creating projects for NTSC, compensate for overscan by calculating the scanner dpi using the NTSC safe zone 650×490 size resolution.

You need to create an image background template that fits your local TV standard: NTSC or PAL. You then can use image manipulation software—I recommend HyperSnap—to do some final cropping and size resolution adjustments to your images and then drop them onto the template.

This somewhat detailed process guarantees your images will maintain their aspect ratios and quality, which would be lost if the DVD-authoring software had to expand or shrink the images to fit its screen. If you want to ramp up your image editing skills I suggest you give Photoshop Elements a trial run.

CHAPTER 4

Acquiring Audio

What You'll Learn in This Chapter:

- ▶ Selecting the right mic for the job
- ▶ Connecting mics to your camcorder or PC
- ▶ Getting the most from your mics—expert audio tips
- ▶ Building a voice recording area
- ▶ Recording high-quality narrations

Audio is crucial. The best images will lose their impact if their audio is mediocre.

You'll need to acquire some of that audio—or "natural sound"—during on-location taping. Relying solely on your onboard camcorder microphone (or **mic**, for short) might lead to disappointing results. Choosing and using additional mics will sweeten your sound.

After you're back in your studio—be it at home or work—you'll likely add a narration. There's no need to rent an expensive audio studio—your camcorder or soundcard and a simple makeshift audio recording area will do the trick. Some professional narration techniques will help as well.

Finally, there's no need to hire a composer and musicians for noncommercial-use music: I show you various ways to obtain or create music in Chapter 5, "Making Marvelous Music."

Selecting the Right Mic for the Job

Your camcorder's onboard microphone takes the middle ground. It picks up sound from everywhere, including camera noise and wind. If you zoom in on a subject, onboard mics don't zoom with you. They don't focus tightly on a subject, they continue to pick up noise from all around you: crowd noise, sound reflecting off walls, the hum from the air conditioner, the zoom lens motor itself—as well as noise you create while handling the camcorder.

Your PC's mic (if it has one) is probably inadequate for you to use for voice narrations as you edit your videos. It has a narrow frequency range and picks up too much room and PC fan noise. Use it and your video will sound unprofessional.

What you need are some mics. Well, at least one that you can use with your camcorder and your PC (depending on the mic you select, you can use the same mic for both).

The second order of business: Get a headset—one that covers your ears to block out extraneous sound. You'll want to plug it into your camcorder or PC and use it to listen as you record. Later in this chapter I explain how important that is when recording your own narrations. In general, it's always a good idea to listen to what your mics "hear."

Low-Cost Mic Solutions

Finding a mic for your PC is as simple as visiting your local Radio Shack and spending $20 to $30 on a mic. You'll have two basic choices:

▶ **Dynamic mics** come in two models. One is combined with a headset. Gamers and those who use their PCs to make phone calls like this hands-free approach. The other is a long-neck version that sets on your desk, which minimizes extraneous noise.

▶ **Condenser mics** offer slightly better voice-over quality and require a battery. They typically are lavaliere style.

Buy a mic with a 1/8" (3.5mm) stereo minijack connection so that it can plug directly into your PC's soundcard or your camcorder's plug. I suggest bringing along your camcorder and testing the mic in the store. You might discover that your camcorder needs a powered condenser mic. If you opt for a professional mic, you'll need to use some other connection tools. I discuss those issues in the next section.

Figure 4.1 shows a typical soundcard rear panel. Plug the mic into the correct jack (usually marked Mic or with a mic icon) and not the Line-in jack used with amplified devices such as CD players and sound mixers.

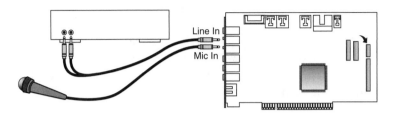

Figure 4.1
Plug your mic into the Mic jack on your soundcard's back panel. Use the Line-in jack only if you're using an amplified mixer with your mic.

While you're shopping, buy a simple headset. Test it on your camcorder before putting your money down. As I mention later in this chapter in "Voicing Solid Narrations," it's important to hear how the mic hears you.

Stepping Up to Professional-Quality Mics

If you want to make professional-sounding projects, you need some decent-quality external mics—specialized mics that serve narrow but useful functions. I've illustrated them in Figure 4.2. Here are the five basic types:

- Handheld
- Shotgun
- Wireless
- Surface mount
- Lavaliere

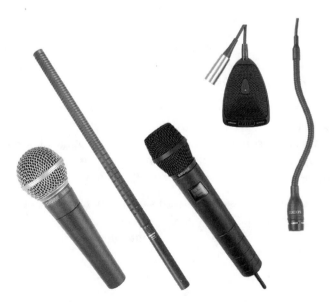

Figure 4.2
Five standard-issue mics: handheld, shotgun, wireless handheld, boundary, and lavaliere. (Products provided by Shure, Inc.)

Handheld Mic

If you own only one external mic, make it a handheld. They're the rugged work-horses of the audio industry. Built with internal shock mounts to reduce handling noise, you'll use these mics for interviews, place them on podiums to record speeches, and use them to create narrations.

Many handheld mics are **omnidirectional**, meaning that they pick up sound from all directions. Thus, they'll pick up ambient room noise as well as close-up audio. To minimize unwanted noise, keep the mic as close to your subject as practical—about a foot from the speaker's mouth works well.

A top-of-the-line, rugged, durable handheld costs from $150 to $250. Radio Shack offers handheld mics ranging from a bargain basement $30 to $60 for a Shure unidirectional mic.

Shure, Inc. (www.shure.com), the world's leading mic manufacturer, loaned me a handheld—as well as a lavaliere and a shotgun mic—to test. (A senior engineer with Shure provided the expert sidebar later in this chapter.) The Shure handheld SM63LB performed flawlessly within a wide frequency range, accurately capturing low and high voices. It retails for $225.

Most handheld mics use what's called a **dynamic transducer**. As Figure 4.3 illustrates, the transducer is a thin diaphragm attached to a tiny coil. As sound waves vibrate the diaphragm, the wire moves over a magnet, which converts that physical energy into an electrical signal. Dynamic transducer mics do not require any electrical power to operate.

Shure, Inc. notes that "Dynamic mics are rugged and can handle high sound pressure levels, like those delivered by kick drums, snare drums, and high volume guitar amps. They're also good for loud, aggressive vocals. Most people start out recording with dynamic mics because of their lower cost and high durability."

The other type of mic—the **condenser transducer**, also shown in Figure 4.3—needs "phantom" power to be provided by a mixer or batteries. It uses a thin, flat plastic or metal diaphragm layered over another piece of metal or metal-coated ceramic. This type of mic is typically very small and has an extremely weak signal that requires preamplification before sending it to your camcorder or a mixer.

Shure adds, "Condenser mics are more sensitive than dynamic mics and are very responsive to high frequencies produced by an acoustic guitar or cymbals on a drum-kit." Condenser mics are excellent for interviews, narrations, and performance or studio music vocal recordings.

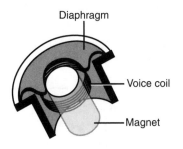
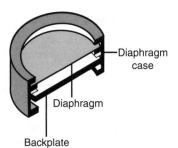

Lavaliere Mic

Most lavalieres use condenser transducer technology. They're perfect for formal, sit-down interviews. Their tiny size means that you can conceal them to minimize that "Oh, we're watching TV" disconnect. The downside is that most require batteries. As you know, batteries invariably fail at critical moments, so always use fresh, high-quality mic batteries. It *is* possible to power lavalieres directly from some mixers, but few budding video producers will use mixers.

I tested Shure's WL50B. The clear and crisp sound was a cut above the handheld and is reflected in its higher price: $316.

Shotgun Mic

So-named because it resembles a shotgun barrel, the shotgun mic's unidirectional barrel (called an **interference tube**) narrows the focus of the audio field to about 30 degrees.

A shotgun mic can handle a number of tasks. I picked up one idea from top freelance photojournalist John Alpert. He's a one-man band (cameraman and reporter) who ventures into uncomfortable and frequently dangerous situations and uses his affable demeanor to get some amazingly revealing sound bites. Instead of shoving a handheld mic into his subject's face—which frequently leads to "mic-stare" and other nervous reactions—he uses a shotgun mic tucked under his armpit. He leans his head away from the camera viewfinder and simply chats with his subjects in his unique, gee-whiz kind of way. It works like magic.

One thing shotgun mics don't do is zoom. As Chris Lyons, the Shure engineer who wrote the audio expert sidebar says, "They're more like looking through a long tube at someone." They narrow your "view" of the sound.

By the Way

A Telephoto Mic

The telephoto lens equivalent in the microphone world is a parabolic dish. You've seen networks use them along the sidelines of NFL games to get those great crunching hits.

Good shotgun mics will set you back about $1,000. I tried out Shure's superb SM89 ($1,180). This is a condenser mic and needs phantom power that a standard prosumer camcorder cannot provide. A $100 (list price) PB224 portable phantom power adapter from the Rolls Corporation (www.rolls.com) will take care of that.

Boundary or Surface Mount Mics

You'll use these very specialized mics to pick up several speakers at a conference table or on a theater stage. They're built to be placed on a flat surface and pick up sound waves in both the air and from the hard surface. A good omnidirectional boundary mic costs about $160. Radio Shack's lists for $40.

Wireless Systems

Wireless mics open a whole new spectrum of possibilities—a presenter at a trade show, the priest at a wedding, or a football coach working the sidelines. Wireless mics enable you to grab sound from a distance. After you've used one, you'll wonder how you got along without it. Professional wireless mic systems are a luxury, and good ones are priced to match. My Shure UP4 test unit, including receiver and an M58 mic with a built-in U2 transmitter, retails for $2,086 (see Figure 4.4).

Radio Shack and other outlets offer wireless mic systems starting at only $50.

Figure 4.4
The Shure UP4
wireless receiver
with a combo mic
and wireless
transmitter.

Connecting Mics to Your Camcorder or PC

Surprisingly, this is the place where most mic problems arise. Most consumer and prosumer camcorders do not have decent mic input connections. They use mini-plugs, whereas most professional mics use rugged, reliable, three-pronged XLR jacks. And they typically do not have enough amplification to "hear" standard handheld mics.

If you use a professional mic you might need a transformer with an XLR-to-mini-plug cable to increase the impedance and enable you to connect your mic to your camcorder. Such transformers are passive, meaning that they don't require electricity. Shure has just such a transformer—the A96F—for $54. If you use a powered mic such as a lavaliere, you might need only the XLR-to-miniplug converter cable.

Making the PC Connection

Pinnacle Studio, the video-editing software featured later in this book, makes it possible for you to add a narration track to your project, live, as you watch your video play. To do that, you need to connect a mic to your soundcard. (I cover that recording process in Chapter 12, "Audio Production with Studio Plus.")

Voice-overs created with mics connected to soundcards, generally can't sound as good as those recorded with professional equipment in a recording studio or even as good as those made using a mic plugged into your camcorder. But they still can sound good enough for basic production work.

As I mentioned earlier, the simple approach is to visit your local Radio Shack and check out their reasonably priced options.

Upping the PC Mic/Soundcard Ante

You can up the PC mic/soundcard voice-over ante. Buy two professional omnidirectional mics. Most come with 1/4" or the much larger XLR connectors. Connect them to a preamplifier and a mixer.

The preamp will improve the "color" of the sound. The mixer enables you to increase the stereo effect or sweet spot. To achieve that sweet spot, place the mics a few inches apart and then voice your narration into both of them. Doing so will better approximate the human ear spacing for stereo recording. You'll need an adapter to connect the mixer to the soundcard's 1/8" plug.

Radio Shack offers a simple mic mixer but I suggest you check out Mackie mixers (www.mackie.com), the leader in this field.

Getting the Most from Your Mics— Expert Audio Tips

When I considered whom I'd tap for audio expertise, only one name came to mind: Shure, Inc. Throughout my TV news and video production career, Shure mics have been the staple in our audio kits.

 This 80-year-old company is a world leader in microphone technology, playing a role in audio history from the Japanese surrender ending World War II and President John F. Kennedy's inaugural address to Woodstock and the 2002 Winter Olympics, where Shure's wireless systems captured all the opening ceremonies' audio moments. You heard Shure mics at the 2003 Montreux Jazz Festival, the 2003 Country Music Awards, and at the Rock and Roll Hall of Fame Museum.

Shure's "Elvis mic," the Unidyne, kicked things off when the company first introduced it in 1939. Frank Sinatra and the Rolling Stones field-tested the SM58—the world's best-selling, all-purpose vocal mic, which was introduced in 1966. And now groups such as N*SYNC and D'Angelo rely on Shure's Beta Series.

Shure put me in touch with Chris Lyons, a senior engineer in Shure's Applications Group. In his 12 years with Shure, he has served as technical liaison for Shure's broadcast customers and as product-line manager for Wired Microphones. Chris has presented hundreds of audio training seminars to broadcasters, educators, government agencies, and audio/visual production specialists. He has written and edited numerous articles and technical papers, including the booklet *Audio Systems Guide for Video Production*, available for free download at `www.shure.com/booklets/techpubs.html`.

Chris offers this expert advice:

▶ **Positioning the microphone**—Always place the microphone as close as is practical to the sound source. Every time the source-to-mic distance increases by a factor of two, the sound pressure level (SPL) reaching the mic decreases by a factor of four, making clear sound pickup progressively more difficult. This is called the **inverse-square rule**, and it applies whether the distance increases from 6 inches to 12 inches or from 6 feet to 12 feet. This means that the talker-to-mic distance must be cut in half to cause a significant improvement in sound quality.

▶ **How many mics**—Use the fewest number of microphones necessary for the situation. People sometimes have a tendency to over-mic a shot, using three or four microphones when one or two would be sufficient. Using excess mics means more background noise pickup, a greater chance of feedback or "tin can" sound, and more levels for the operator to keep track of. If additional mics don't make things sound better, they'll probably make things sound worse.

▶ **Handheld mic tips**—Whether held in the hand or mounted on a stand, place this mic about 6–12 inches from the talker's mouth, pointing up at about a 45-degree angle (see Figure 4.5). With some types of microphones, holding the microphone very close (3–6 inches) will cause additional emphasis of the lower frequencies (known as **proximity effect**), resulting in a warmer, bass-heavy sound.

▶ **Positioning a lavaliere**—For best results, clip a lavaliere mic on the outside of clothing, about 6–8 inches below the chin. You can clip the mic to the collar of a shirt or blouse, but sound quality in this position tends to be somewhat muffled because some high frequencies (which contain consonants) do not fully wrap around to the area under the chin.

Figure 4.5
Proper placement
for a handheld mic.
(Illustration cour-
tesy of Shure, Inc.,
2002.)

Figure 4.5
Proper placement for a handheld mic. (Illustration courtesy of Shure, Inc., 2002.)

▶ **Concealing a lavaliere**—Keeping the lavaliere hidden from view gives your production an extra level of quality. Make sure that you keep both the microphone and the first few inches of cable from rubbing against either the body or clothing, which will cause noise. Try taping the "lav" under the shirt collar near the opening in front. The cable can be routed around to the back of the neck, over the collar, and under the shirt. Alternatively, tape it to the interviewee's eyeglasses on the inside by the temple. Route the wire over the ear and down the back.

▶ **Setting up surface mics**—These are great for panel discussions and work best when positioned on a smooth, flat surface, such as a table or desk. A thin piece of soft foam rubber or a computer mouse pad underneath the mic helps minimize problems created by surface vibrations. Small surfaces—less than 3-feet square—reduce the pickup of low frequencies and might improve the clarity of deep voices by reducing "boominess."

▶ **Shotgun mic dos and don'ts**—Avoid aiming shotgun mics at hard surfaces such as tile floors, brick walls, and flat ceilings. These surfaces reflect background noise into the microphone or cause the sound to be slightly hollow. Place a heavy blanket on a reflective surface to provide some sound absorption. Shotgun mics are more sensitive to wind noise than standard microphones, so use a foam windscreen and don't move them too rapidly. A rubber-isolated shock mount will help control handling noise.

▶ **Low-impedance allows long cord length**—Low-impedance or "low-Z" mics (less than 600 ohms) enable you to use very long runs of cable (more than 1,000 feet) with negligible loss of sound quality. "High-Z" mics (greater than 10,000 ohms) lose high frequencies and begin to sound muffled with 20-foot cables. The impedance of a microphone should *not* match the impedance of the input to which it is connected. Matching the impedance causes significant signal-level loss. Always connect low-impedance microphones to higher-impedance inputs—preferably 5 to 10 times greater. Inputs on professional mixers typically have an impedance of 1,000 ohms or more.

▶ **Wireless setup tips**—Try to keep the distance from the transmitter to the receiver as short as possible. Always do a walk-around with the mic before the event. If dropouts occur, try moving the receiver a few feet and repeat the walk-around. Dual-antenna diversity receivers minimize dropout because it is unlikely that the signal to both antennas will be interrupted at the same instant. If possible, do your sound check at the same time of day as the event to discover whether there are any nearby users of your wireless frequencies. When using belt-pack-type transmitters, make sure that the antenna cable is hanging straight. Coiling it up in the wearer's pocket significantly reduces transmission distance. With handheld transmitters that have an external antenna, discourage users from holding their hands over the antenna to avoid reducing transmission range and increasing dropout.

▶ **Strike a balance**—Use balanced cables and connectors. Their metal shielding keeps the audio signal free of interference from things such as fluorescent lights, dimmer switches, and other audio or electrical cables. Use cables with braided or mesh shielding. They are more resistant than metal foil shielding to cracks or tears, which cause electrical shorts.

▶ **Plan ahead**—This is the most important thing you can do to improve the audio quality of your productions. When you set up your equipment, look for things that might cause a problem with your audio—air conditioning ducts, noisy doors, fluorescent lights, and so on. Check for things that you can use to your advantage—sound-absorbent carpeting or a built-in PA system. Experiment with different mic placements, but don't gamble an important project on a method you've never tried. Monitor your audio and listen carefully for anything that sounds unnatural. As the saying goes, "If you notice the sound, there's something wrong with it."

Building a Simple and Inexpensive Voice-Recording Area

To create your voice-over narration, you'll need a quiet, sound-absorbing location. I touched base with the industry leader in sound absorption material: Auralex Acoustics.

Auralex suggests that the easiest solution is to build a temporary recording area simply by hanging some thick blankets or fiberglass insulation on two joining corner walls. It is an old audio myth that egg cartons, carpeting, and foam rubber work well. Avoid them. If you can create something like a four-sided, blanketed cubicle, so much the better.

If you drape the blankets only in one corner, point the mic toward that corner, place yourself between the mic and the corner, and speak *away* from the blankets. It seems counterintuitive, but the mic is sort of like a camera. It "sees" what's in front of it (even if it is omnidirectional). In this case it "sees" your face and the hanging, sound-absorbing blankets.

If you want to take your voice-recording area quality up several notches, consider purchasing Auralex's studio foam sheets or a portable recording area kit. These kits range in price from $159 to $999. Figure 4.6 illustrates two of these **acoustic environments**, as Auralex calls them. The company emphasizes that these kits are not true isolation booths. Those are intended to keep sound out and require some serious construction. Visit www.auralex.com/ for product and dealer info, plus a contact phone number. Auralex is very customer-service oriented and will help you find a solution.

FIGURE 4.6
Acoustic environments from Auralex—MAX-Wall 420 (right) and MAX-Wall 1141VB (top of next page). (Photos courtesy Auralex Acoustics.)

Voicing Solid Narrations

Creating narrations is as easy as turning on your camcorder. If you have a hand-held mic (or some other external mic), plug it into your camcorder. Otherwise, you can use the built-in, onboard camcorder mic.

Before you record your voice-over, go over this checklist to make sure that you're ready:

▶ **Read your copy out loud**—Listen to your words. They should sound comfortable, conversational, even informal.

▶ **Avoid technical jargon**—That demands extra effort from your listeners, and you might lose them.

▶ **Short sentences work best**—If you find yourself stumbling over certain phrases, rewrite them.

▶ **Stress important words and phrases**—As you review your copy, underline important words. When you record your voice-over, you'll want to give those words extra emphasis—more volume and punch.

▶ **Mark pauses**—Go through your copy and mark logical breaks with short parallel lines. They'll remind you to pause at those points. Avoid overly smooth and constant pacing. That's characteristic of a scripted delivery and, once again, you don't want to remind viewers that this is TV. It's real life. It's conversational.

▶ **Break up your copy into shorter sentences**—Always be on the lookout for convoluted, wandering sentences. Too many modifiers can be unwieldy. Break long sentences into several shorter ones. Shorter sentences tend to have only one key point. It's easier to emphasize one key point in one sentence versus multiple points in a rambling speech.

▶ **Punch up your voice**—When reading copy, it's too easy to slip into a dull, monotone voice. Instead, add some zest and enthusiasm to your narration. As one consultant told me, "Pump up your projection." You want people to pay attention. You do that by speaking as if the subject truly interests you. On the other hand, you aren't trying to be a professional announcer. No need to put on airs or use a *basso profundo* voice.

▶ **Practice**—Record a couple narrations and listen. Have others listen. Most first-time narrators mumble or swallow words. Have you made yourself clear?

▶ **Use a wind screen**—Although you need to record close to the mic for best effect—12 inches away or so—getting too close can lead to "popping P's." As you say P-words, you project a small blast of wind at the mic. Using a wind screen minimizes that, as does not speaking directly into the mic.

▶ **Wear earphones**—In this case, the purpose is not to make sure that you're actually getting audio; rather, it's to hear yourself. That might seem a bit odd. You can hear yourself just fine without a headset. But you need the headset to see how the mic "hears" you. You'll also discover whether you're popping any P's or speaking with too much **sibilance**—an overemphasis on the S sound.

Summary

Audio is critical to a high-quality video production. Most important is the original footage and its "natural sound." Take some extra measures to ensure high-quality audio. Select the right mics for the job and turn to wireless audio if your budget allows.

Your narration is crucial. Building a personal voice recording area is the first step. Then, by following a few narration tips, you can add professional polish to your piece.

CHAPTER 5

Making Marvelous Music

What You'll Learn in This Chapter:

▶ Ripping music CDs

▶ Licensing music or buying royalty-free music

▶ Creating custom music with SmartSound Movie Maestro

▶ Introducing two high-end music creation and editing products

Music adds immeasurably to the overall quality of your video and DVD projects. But few of us have the chops to compose and create custom music.

The good news is that you can tap several resources to obtain or produce just the right piece to fit your project or set a mood.

As I explain in this chapter, the easiest is to rip a cut from a CD. Next up is to license a tune or buy a royalty-free song. In each of these instances you are using someone else's music. If you want a custom, unique, personalized style, you need to try another option.

Three products featured in this chapter allow you to easily create customized music to more closely suit your needs. I give you step-by-step instructions on one of them: SmartSound Movie Maestro.

This easy-to-use product has a library of songs in different genres and instrumentations created by seamlessly combining snippets of live performance music. You achieve a customized feel to your piece by choosing a genre, a tune within that genre, and then trying out a variety of opening and closing riffs. Movie Maestro then builds the tune to fit the length of your production exactly.

I introduce you to two other products that further refine customized music creation: Movie Maestro's bigger sibling—SmartSound Sonicfire Pro 3—and Adobe Audition.

Ripping Music CDs

The easiest source for video production music is next to your stereo: your personal music CD collection. All CD cuts are digital and easily **ripped**. Once ripped—converted from CD audio to a digital file on your hard drive—it's a simple matter to import CD music into your nonlinear video editor or DVD-authoring software.

Watch Out!

> ### Beware the Copyright Police
>
> Those tunes on your CDs are all copyrighted. I'm not an attorney and don't pretend to fully understand copyright law. That said, I'd suggest treading carefully when using someone else's music. Generally, if it's for personal use, it's considered **fair use** and there are no copyright issues. But just about any other use can step outside fair use.
>
> To be on the safe side, produce your own music or license or buy royalty-free music. I cover all three topics later in this chapter.

Try it Yourself

Use Windows Media Player to Rip CD Cuts

No, the book is not taking a violent twist. **Ripping** is just how some describe the process of transferring music from a CD to a PC.

Several products are available to do that. Pinnacle Studio, the nonlinear editor featured in this book, has a CD-ripping module. I show you how it works in Chapter 12, "Audio Production with Studio Plus."

In the meantime, there is one product that can rip CDs that is right at your fingertips: Windows Media Player. Here's how it works:

1. Open Windows Media Player. It's probably in the Start menu under Accessories. If not, its default location is `C:\Program Files\Windows Media Player\wmplayer.exe`. You can open My Computer, go to this location, and double-click `wmplayer.exe`. Doing so opens the interface shown in Figure 5.1.

Did you Know?

> ### Automatically Opening Windows Media Player
>
> You can open Windows Media Player another way. Simply insert a music CD into your DVD or CD drive and, depending on your version of Windows, either Windows Media Player automatically starts playing that CD or you're given an option of playing the CD with one of several programs that you have installed on your PC.

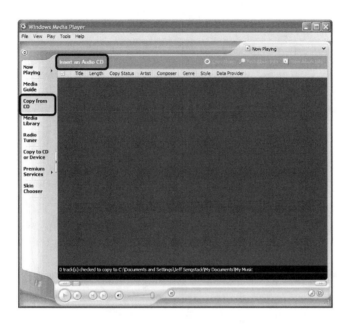

Figure 5.1
Use Windows Media Player to rip tracks from music CDs.

2. Click Copy from CD, as highlighted in Figure 5.1. That pops up a message asking you to insert an audio CD.

3. Insert a music CD. Either Windows will ask you which CD player you want to use (select Media Player) or Windows Media Player will automatically start playing the CD. Click the Stop button, as shown in Figure 5.2.

Online Album Details

If you're connected to the Internet, Media Player will display your CD's information—title, artist, and track names. This info is not on the CD; it's stored in a huge online repository.

Media Player retrieves that info using an unexpected method to identify the CD. You'd think each CD would have some kind of unique identification number, but they don't. Media Player generates an identification number for each CD by examining the CD's track times. It then sends that generated number through www.windowsmedia.com to www.allmusic.com, a massive database owned by All Media Guide.

As shown in Figure 5.2, click View Album Info (or, depending on your version of Windows Media Player, click Album Details or click the CD cover in the lower-right corner of the interface) for a full listing plus a review.

By the Way

Figure 5.2
Windows Media
Player's Copy CD
interface displays
information about
your CD retrieved
from the Internet
(to avoid any
possible copyright
conflicts, I created
a dummy screen-
shot using my
choir's material).

4. By default, all tracks are check marked for copying to your hard drive. You
   can uncheck any that you don't want to copy.

Did you **Know?**

Preview a Tune

If you want to preview a track, click it to select it, and then click the Play button.

5. The default copy location is C:\Documents and Settings\current user\My
   Documents\My Music. Windows Media Player creates a folder for the artist
   and a subfolder for the selected album. If you want to change that location,
   select Tools, Options from the menu bar. Doing so opens the Options menu,
   shown in Figure 5.3. Select the Copy Music tab and change the directory.

Did you **Know?**

Avoid Vocals for Background Music

When selecting music for use in video or DVD productions, instrumentals generally
work best. Vocals can step on your narration, natural sound, or voices in your
videos.

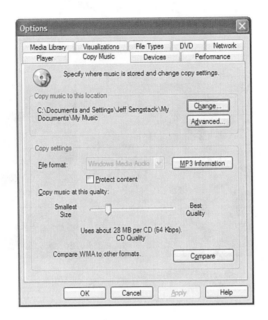

Figure 5.3
Use the Options interface to change the file folder storage location for your selected music tracks.

6. When you're ready to copy the tracks, click the Copy Music button at the top of the interface. That opens two dialog boxes: The first reminds you to not make illegal copies and the second asks you about setting the recording quality level. It's best to use the highest quality setting for tunes you'll use in a video project. When you're past the dialog boxes, Windows Media Player displays progress bars to let you know how things are proceeding.

Now that you've ripped a few tunes, you can use Media Player to burn a music CD. As shown in Figure 5.4, access that feature by clicking Copy to CD or Device, select the tracks you want to burn, place a recordable CD in your drive, and click the Copy button. This is a great way to create personalized CDs of your favorite tunes.

Figure 5.4
Use Windows
Media Player to
create personal-
ized, customized
music CDs.

Licensing Music or Buying Royalty-Free Music

For those who will venture beyond personal—noncommercial—DVD productions, you can avoid any copyright hassles by licensing or purchasing tunes. The Internet makes that remarkably easy.

Music licensing agencies abound. They offer song search capabilities geared to multiple parameters: music genre, mood, instrumentation, tempo, and so on. Most even have try-before-you-buy listening capabilities.

When you find what you like, you pay a fee based on planned usage and audience size and then download the music file. For most readers, that usage will be nonexclusive and for fewer than 5,000 DVDs. In that case, a license might cost $75–$300.

Another approach is to pay a one-time fee for a song and get the right to use it as often and in any way you want. That's a so-called **royalty-free** stock music service. In the pre-Internet days, stock music companies sent out boxes of music CDs to production houses. Most times they gathered dust until that one moment when a producer needed a special piece of music and had to slog through a mound of CDs to find it.

Now some stock music houses have put their products online with the same type of search and try-before-you-buy capabilities as the music-licensing houses offer.

I contacted both types of companies, selected three to use as examples, and will go through the process you can use to buy music.

Licensing Music

Anyone with any Internet savvy and a search engine—www.Google.com is my favorite—can track down music-licensing houses. The choices can overwhelm you, though. Here are two that take slightly different approaches.

Use LicenseMusic.com to Audition and Download Tunes   *Try it Yourself*

LicenseMusic.com, based in Copenhagen, Denmark, represents more than 100 content providers with more than 100,000 songs. It characterizes itself as the "foremost Web-based music licensing company," and I see no reason to dispute that. Here's how to use its service:

1. Navigate your browser to www.licensemusic.com. That takes you to the company's home page, shown in Figure 5.5. You can register if you want, and it's free.

FIGURE 5.5
LicenseMusic.com offers a full range of musical production possibilities.

2. Click Find Music. As illustrated in Figure 5.6, doing so opens a collection of drop-down menus that let you narrow your search. You have a choice between two main music sources: Pre-cleared and Production Library. Pre-cleared tends to be more pop oriented, whereas Production Library leans toward filling specific production needs. For this exercise, stick with the default setting: Music from Both Sources.

FIGURE 5.6
Use more than a dozen criteria to narrow your search for the best musical number to fit your DVD production.

3. Go through the drop-down lists and narrow your search. As you add parameters, note that the Tracks Found number decreases. If you refine things too much, it can drop to zero (for instance, selecting Country Rock as the genre and Oboe as the instrument). You don't have to make a selection from each list.

By the Way

Licensing Is Not Free

The Maximum Price menu displays from one to three dollar signs ($).The lowest-priced offerings for a limited distribution DVD typically license for about $75.

4. When you're done adjusting parameters, click Show Songs to display a list of songs. Clicking one, as shown in Figure 5.7, displays information about that tune and lets you listen to a 25-second excerpt.

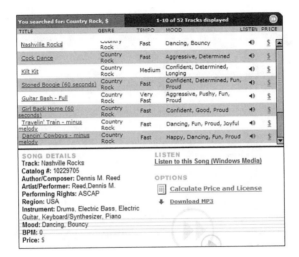

FIGURE 5.7
After you've narrowed your search, view and preview your music "hits."

5. You can download the selection (you have to be registered) at no charge on a try-before-you-buy basis. Right-click the Download MP3 link, select Save Target As, select a file folder location, and click Save.

Watermarks Track Music Ownership

LicenseMusic.com watermarks its MP3 files. As you download, the company embeds inaudible yet readable digital code into those MP3 files that identify you as the buyer.

If you later upload or transfer a LicenseMusic.com file to other users, the unique watermark can clearly identify the MP3 file's origins (you need the watermark manufacturer's software to do this). However, it does not prevent playback of that file.

By the Way

6. To check the licensing fee, click Calculate Price and License (you'll need to register to see the fee and other particulars). The page shown in Figure 5.8 opens. Your likely medium is Straight to Home Video/CD-ROM/Similar Media: Roll-Over (Limited # of Copies). Select it, and click Next.

7. You'll see a couple other options about the number of DVD units: whether it'll be the theme song, whether your budget is less than $100,000, and whether you'll use more than a prescribed amount of time (usually 45 seconds). The bottom line is that your license will likely cost about $100.

FIGURE 5.8
LicenseMusic.com
bases its fees on
your type of
production and its
audience size.

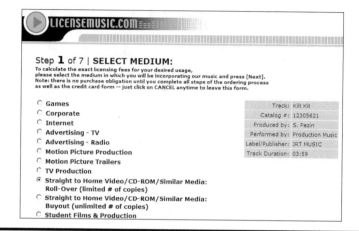

I'd suggest checking out at least one other music-licensing firm: Dittybase (www.dittybase.com), based in Victoria, British Columbia, Canada. It works similarly to MusicLicense.com in that it has a search engine and a try-before-you-buy option. Its selection is not as vast, but its service is more user friendly (see Figure 5.9).

FIGURE 5.9
Dittybase works
much the same
way as
LicenseMusic.com
but has a more
user-friendly
interface.

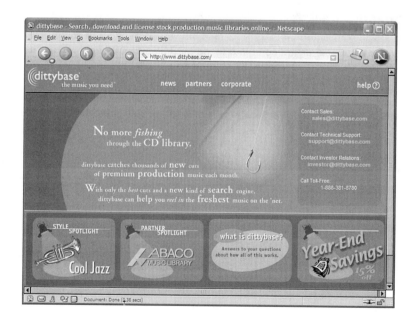

It bases its rates solely on your usage, in contrast to varying rates based on artist and publisher contracts. Typical business uses for a one-time, so-called "needle-drop" cost about $80, and uses for fewer than 10,000 copies of a DVD for retail sale cost about $150.

Using Royalty-Free Music

As with licensed music, so-called royalty-free music has hit the Internet. Only a few differences exist between the two business models. For royalty-free music, you pay a one-time flat fee for *unlimited*, nonexclusive use, whereas licensing agencies usually base their fees on a single use plus the expected sales or audience size and the type of production.

Royalty-free companies tend to be less broad-based than licensing firms. Frequently, they represent only a handful of artists or have limited genres. Theirs is a simpler, easier-to-manage business model. They typically cost much less than licensing, yet the quality of music can be just as good as licensed music.

One such royalty-free firm is Stock-Music.com (`www.stock-music.com`). Figure 5.10 shows its home page. This small, Utah-based firm at last word had 67 songs in seven categories.

FIGURE 5.10
Stock-Music.com is a small, royalty-free shop with several dozen tunes across a handful of genres.

When you purchase a tune from Stock-Music.com, you get three lengths: :15, :30, and the entire song (typically 3:00 or so). To try out songs from this company, visit www.stock-music.com. As shown in Figure 5.11, after selecting a genre, you can listen to brief excerpts and then purchase individual tunes or an entire collection.

FIGURE 5.11
Stock-Music.com offers straightforward music preview pages.

Creating Custom Music with SmartSound Movie Maestro

Even if you can't carry a tune, you can create professional quality music. SmartSound Movie Maestro helps you compose custom music that fits not only the style of your video production, but also its exact length. The $50 retail version comes with 26 customizable songs (additional music collections, with themes such as Sentimental, Sports, and Vacation, retail for $30).

Here's what sets Movie Maestro–created songs apart from any you'd receive from a licensing agency or royalty-free firm:

▶ SmartSound Movie Maestro can change the character of each tune to fit your needs by rearranging song segments in several distinct ways. Effectively, you get about eight songs for every one in the package.

▶ Using those same song segments and some smart software, Movie Maestro gives each song a clear, decisive ending right when you want it. There's no need to fade it out at your video's close.

By the Way

Movie Maestro Music Usage Restrictions

Songs you create with the demo and retail versions of Movie Maestro are for non-commercial use only—meaning for home or school. If you want to use Movie Maestro for other purposes, such as business promotions, DVDs for retail sale, or in-house training DVDs, you must purchase other, customizable music from SmartSound's Audio Palette or Edge series.

There are two ways to acquire the software needed to complete this upcoming task. You can buy the retail version or download the demo version of Movie Maestro from www.smartsound.com/moviemaestro/index.html.

By the Way

SmartSound Comes Free with Studio

Pinnacle Studio, the nonlinear video editor you will work with later in this book, ships with a SmartSound module. Functionally, it is virtually identical to SmartSound Movie Maestro. There is some duplication of content (they have 14 songs in common and a dozen others unique to each product). Despite the duplication, I suggest you download the Movie Maestro demo and do the following tasks because I will cover the SmartSound Studio module only briefly in Chapter 12.

Use Movie Maestro to Add Music to a Video

Try it Yourself ▼

The downloaded version works the same way as its retail big brother. Here's how to use it:

1. Install the Movie Maestro demo by double-clicking the following file: MovieMaestroDemo.exe.

2. Open the program by double-clicking the SmartSound Movie Maestro icon on the desktop. The main user interface opens and a small dialog box, shown in Figure 5.12, pops up.

3. Click Create Music for a Movie (as shown in Figure 5.12). Doing so opens a file selection window with a default location of My Videos. If you have a video there, feel free to use it; otherwise, navigate to Movie Maestro's file folder (the default location is C:\Program Files\Movie Maestro\ Documentation) and select Sample Movie.mov.

▼

Figure 5.12
You can use SmartSound Movie Maestro to create custom instrumental music in minutes to fit a particular video or as a standalone tune.

By the
Way

Try the Tutorial

Feel free to use Movie Maestro's built-in tutorial by clicking the Tutorial button on the left side of the screen. It, too, uses the Sample Movie.mov file to demonstrate the software's functionality.

4. Click the Add Music button in the lower-left corner of the main interface to open the dialog box shown in Figure 5.13. This screen offers several musical styles as well as other means to make a musical selection.

Figure 5.13
You can narrow your Movie Maestro music search using this interface. However, the demo version has only three songs, so don't expect too many choices.

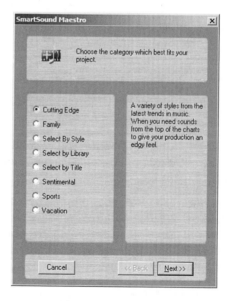

Demo Music Selection Limitations

It might appear that you have several choices in music, but this demo version has only three songs, so the various options don't have much meaning. If you click through the categories, you'll find little choice is available. If this were the retail product or the Premiere plug-in, there would be several tunes for each category, 26 in all.

5. Select a category and then select one of the three songs. Preview it by clicking the Play button at the bottom of the screen (see Figure 5.14). If it suits your needs, click Finish. Movie Maestro will automatically add it to the movie Timeline and set its length to match the video.

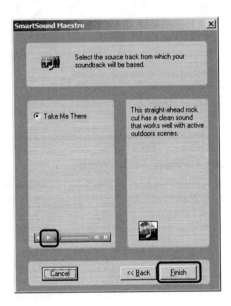

Figure 5.14
Listen to your selected tune by clicking the Play button.

6. Try your newly edited video (you might need to drag the Play Indicator to the start of the video—see Figure 5.15) by clicking the Play button. Notice that it has an obvious finish (instead of a fade) at the end.

Figure 5.15
Use this Timeline
interface to listen
to how well your
composition fits
the video style.

Did you **Know?**

Change the Length to Suit Your Needs

You can adjust the song's length by simply dragging and dropping its start and end-
points. As you move the cursor, the video moves as well, so you can fine-tune the
music to start or finish with a specific shot in your video. As you change the song's
length, Movie Maestro automatically makes internal changes to the tune to ensure
that it plays and ends smoothly and on time.

7. As the music is playing, try the variations by clicking the drop-down menu
   shown in Figure 5.15. Select any variation you want, and the video clip
   jumps back to the beginning. Each variation has a distinctly different start.

8. After you've chosen a variation, save your musical selection by clicking the
   Stop button and then click the Save Sound button in the upper-left corner of
   the screen. You have several save options: the sound file itself, as separate
   musical segments, or combined with the video. You also have three levels of
   audio: less than music CD quality (22KHz), music CD (44KHz), and digital
   video (48KHz).

Take Care When Saving with a Video

If you choose to save the combined movie and soundtrack, the Save window uses the original filename as the default saved filename. *Be careful*: You don't want to overwrite your original video file. Give this file a new descriptive name, such as `oldfilename with soundtrack.avi`.

Other Save Options

The Advanced Save button enables you to convert the original video file into several other video formats. Some selections give you more options than you might have believed possible. For instance, select Export Movie to QuickTime Movie and then open the Use drop-down menu. None of these options is particularly suited to Pinnacle Studio video production, but feel free to experiment.

Introducing Two High-End Music Creation and Editing Products

As I mentioned earlier in this chapter, you can rip music from a CD, but that raises the copyright infringement red flag. You can license prerecorded music. Or you can use SmartSound Movie Maestro (or its Pinnacle Studio module) to create music.

None of these solutions is ideal. Two options that *are* ideal are SmartSound Sonicfire Pro 3 and Adobe Audition.

- ▶ SmartSound Sonicfire Pro can create professional music that matches your project style and length.

- ▶ Adobe Audition enables you to take custom music creation further by offering 4,500 music loops that you can tap to create compositions. Plus it's loaded with professional audio-editing tools and high-end effects that go way beyond those available in Pinnacle Studio or other video-editing software.

Making Music with SmartSound Sonicfire Pro

This full-featured big brother of Movie Maestro from SmartSound (www. smartsound.com), shown in Figure 5.16, makes it possible for you to create highly customized soundtracks that exactly fit the style and length of your work. You can use multiple tunes within a project, edit them to fit certain segments, and build transitions between them if that suits your production.

Figure 5.16
Sonicfire Pro 3
enables you to
build customized
original sound-
tracks that exactly
fit the length and
style of your pro-
duction—and you
pay no additional
licensing fees.

Figure 5.16
Sonicfire Pro 3
enables you to
build customized
original sound-
tracks that exactly
fit the length and
style of your pro-
duction—and you
pay no additional
licensing fees.

Sonicfire Pro 3 works much like Movie Maestro in that all its music is recorded from real instruments (rather than using MIDI files). Movie Maestro transparently moves, adds, or removes little snippets of the song to make it fit a project length or user-selected style. Sonicfire Pro 3 offers those same features and enables you to select different phrases for dramatic effect and build your own arrangements by mixing and matching those snippets in whatever order and quantity suits you.

The **blocking** feature, shown in Figure 5.17, is a simple drag-and-drop process. Blocks that work well at the start, middle, or end of a song are easily identifiable.

Figure 5.17
Sonicfire Pro uses
original tunes
recorded by studio
musicians in such
a way that you can
add, remove, move,
and alter the length
of snippets of
music to fit your
video production
needs.

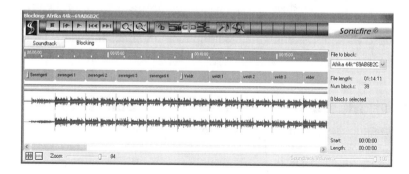

Sonicfire Pro 3 ($299) ships with 42 tunes at 44.1KHz (CD audio quality) and the Bundle Edition ($499) comes with 98 songs. Because you can edit them in uncountable ways, these songs open up a wealth of possibilities. You access those tunes directly or, as shown in Figure 5.18, narrow your search using criteria such as genre, instrumentation, and intensity.

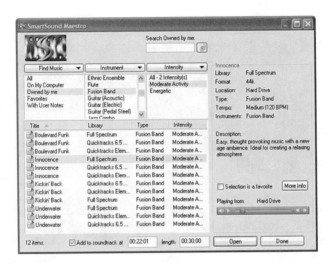

Figure 5.18
Access the SmartSound music library using Sonicfire's Maestro search tool.

You can limit your search to your existing collection or dramatically expand it by scouring the SmartSound collection on the company website. There you can preview and purchase tunes individually or select from several dozen themed CDs. CDs typically have 18 songs and retail for $100 (22KHz versions cost $50). Individual tunes sell for $20. Sonicfire Pro 3 is a great way to add a professional touch to your projects.

Introducing Adobe Audition

Adobe Audition ($299) is a complete, professional, 128-track recording studio that offers advanced audio mixing, editing, and effects processing. You'll want to use Adobe Audition for music productions, radio broadcasts, or to enhance audio for your Pinnacle Studio videos.

Audition started its life as Cool Edit, a high-end, professional audio editing tool from Syntrillium Software. In mid-2003, Adobe bought Syntrillium's technology assets and rereleased Cool Edit Pro 2 as Adobe Audition.

Although Adobe made no changes to the Cool Edit Pro 2 code, the company did add one tremendous feature: about 5,000+ music loops. The loops are like the song snippets in Sonicfire Pro 3 in that they are typically a few bars of an instrument playing in a certain musical style. As shown in Figure 5.19, you can layer multiple instruments in tracks to create an exciting mix.

Figure 5.19
Use Audition's 128-track professional mixer to layer loops to create a full, rich-sounding, tune.

What makes Audition much different from Sonicfire Pro is what you can do with those loops.

Here are some of Audition's features:

▶ **Change pitch and tempo without losing sonic fidelity**—Audition's beat-marking technology and superior stretch engine enable you to make pitch and tempo changes while retaining all the characteristics of the original instrument or voice.

▶ **Audio repair**—Noise reduction selectively removes room noise, hiss, hum, and even camera motors while retaining full audio quality. Automated and user-defined click and pop removal cleans up vinyl recordings.

▶ **Sound your best**—Adobe Audition supports files with sample rates up to 10MHz (that's 10 MEGAHertz! in contrast to the standard CD-audio sampling rate of 44 KILOHertz), so whether your destination is tape, CD, DVD, or DVD-Audio, Audition can handle the files. All processing is done at the maximum 32-bit resolution for the highest quality sound. All edits are sample-accurate, and short crossfades can be added for smooth, pop-free cuts every time.

▶ **Additional features**—It also offers real-time effects, loop creation, audio analysis tools, and video support.

Auditioning Audition and Sonicfire Pro

I suggest you download trial versions of Audition from the Adobe website (www.adobe.com/products/audition) and Sonicfire Pro from SmartSound's site (www.smartsound.com). If you download Adobe Audition, you'll want to download some "loopology" content as well. That content is divided into musical genres.

Summary

Music can make or break a production. It can set a mood and help hold viewers' interest. But unless you're a dedicated musician with some fairly sophisticated PC music hardware and software, you probably can't create original recorded music on your own.

Not to fret. Finding or fashioning music is fairly easy these days. You can rip tunes from music CDs, license or buy compositions, or create your own professional-quality songs using inexpensive software customizable, precomposed song snippets.

In this chapter I took you through all three areas of music creation and acquisition. Then I introduced you to two professional music production tools: SmartSound Sonicfire Pro and Adobe Audition.

CHAPTER 6

Story-Creation and Video-Production Tips

What You'll Learn in This Chapter:

▶ Creating your story

▶ Story-creation tips from NBC-TV correspondent Bob Dotson

▶ Writing in the active voice

▶ Mackie Morris's writing tips

▶ Storytelling with video—scriptwriting tips from two Hollywood screenwriters

▶ Video-editing tips from an expert—John Crossman

By choosing this book you've made a commitment to take your video production quality up several notches. To do that requires more than learning basic video-editing and DVD-authoring techniques.

You also need to hone your story-creation skills and writing style. This chapter addresses those issues.

In putting together this book, I've had the enjoyable opportunity to contact many of the people who have given me advice or from whom I have gained a lot of practical knowledge. Each agreed to provide expert tips focusing on his specialty.

You've already met KGW-TV chief photographer Karl Petersen in Chapter 2, "Shooting Great Videos." In Chapter 4, "Acquiring Audio," Chris Lyons, an audio engineer from the world's leading microphone manufacturer, Shure, Inc., offered up his expert advice.

For this chapter, I compiled columns from five experts. I think they all speak to enhancing your skills beyond the fundamentals of camera work, editing, and learning how to use a nonlinear video editor's toolset.

Creating Your Story

A lot more is involved in crafting stories than you might think. The best TV news and video production writers use clever techniques to grab and hold your interest. They create a story flow that pulls you along and makes you want to pay attention.

You, too, can use those tips and tools to your advantage. You might not write network-quality stories immediately, but as you gain experience and revisit your old stories, you'll continually increase the quality of your work.

Overall Story-Creation Tips

In my 15 years in TV news and video production, I received advice from some real pros, including NBC reporter Bob Dotson and noted TV news media consultant Mackie Morris, both of whom provide expert advice later in this chapter. Here are some of the tips I gleaned from those contacts:

▶ **Use people to tell your story**—Your pictures and words might be fascinating, but if you add a compelling or colorful character, your story will have much more impact. People add interest.

▶ **Tell as much of the story as you can without narration**—Tell it visually by letting the images move your story. Unlike a radio sports announcer, you don't have to do a play-by-play.

▶ **Give viewers a reason to remember your story**—What do you want them to take away from your piece? If your viewers can feel something about the story, or its subject, they will remember it.

▶ **Listen to other TV writers**—Bob Dotson is my favorite feature story reporter. And Andy Rooney (yes, that old curmudgeon on *60 Minutes*) is the dean of TV writers.

General Writing Tips

As you craft your videos, keep the following standard writing concepts in mind:

▶ **Keep your writing simple**—Short sentences work best. Write one thought to a sentence. Limit your story to only a few main ideas. Give the audience the best possible chance to understand the story.

▶ **There's no need to tell viewers what they already know or what the visuals tell them**—For instance, you don't need to tell viewers, "The children were ecstatic," when your video shows kids jumping for joy.

▶ **Write for the ear**—People will listen to your copy, not read it. Always read your copy aloud. How does it sound? Does it have a logical flow? Unlike the printed word, your viewers will not be able to reread a section that did not make sense.

▶ **Allow for moments of silence**—Stop writing occasionally and let two seconds or more of compelling action occur without voice-over.

▶ **Use natural sound**—Let your videos "breathe" by adding brief moments of "wild" sound: a gurgling brook, the crack of a baseball bat, or the sound of assembly-line equipment.

▶ **Add surprises to your piece**—They can be brief sound bites, exciting natural sound, or a clever turn of phrase. These moments build viewer interest.

▶ **Keep your interview sound bites brief**—Use them to add emphasis to your piece. Refrain from using sound bites as a substitute for your storytelling.

Specific Writing Tips

The following tips apply more to the mechanics of writing:

▶ **Write factually and accurately**—A standard newsroom admonition is, "When in doubt, leave it out." The corollary is, "Get the facts."

▶ **Write in the present or present perfect tense**—Immediacy is more interesting. When you use past tense, include a time reference—yesterday, five days ago, last year—to avoid confusion.

▶ **Write in the active voice**—Instead of writing, "This widget was made by our company," write, "Our company made this widget." This is a very important concept that takes some explanation. I tackle this in the next section, "Writing in the Active Voice."

▶ **Use of the "rule of threes" (not to be confused with the photo composition "rule of thirds")**—When writing, try to group items by threes, such as red, white, and blue; left, right, and center; over, under, and through. Saying things in groups of three always sounds more interesting.

▶ **Avoid numbers**—Listeners have trouble remembering numbers. If you do use numbers, simplify them. Instead of writing, "We reduced expenses from $240,000 to $180,000," write, "We cut expenses by 25%."

▶ **Avoid pronouns**—Many times listeners have difficulty connecting a pronoun with the correct individual. Instead of saying, "Bob kidnapped Bill. Police later found him," say, "Bob kidnapped Bill. Police later found Bill."

Story-Creation Tips from Bob Dotson

Bob Dotson, NBC-TV reporter.

NBC-TV *Today Show* correspondent Bob Dotson is, I think, the best human-interest feature-story TV reporter. Dotson has received more than 50 awards. The National Press Photographers Association award committee wrote, "Bob Dotson's reports help us understand ourselves a bit better. They show that all our lives are important and really matter. After all, this country was built not by great heroes or great politicians, but by ordinary people—by thousands whose names we don't know, may never know, but without whose influence America wouldn't exist."

Although you probably aren't a TV newsperson, you'll probably create human-interest stories—Dotson's forte. If there's a storyteller out there you should emulate, I think he's the one. During my TV reporting days I tried to watch all his stories, and when a station I worked for offered me the chance to attend one of his seminars, I jumped at it.

I've reproduced my notes, with his approval, here. I took many things away from his class. Three points stand out:

▶ **Give viewers a reason to remember the story.**

▶ **When interviewing people, try not to ask questions**—Merely make observations. That loosens people up, letting them reveal their emotional, human side to you.

▶ **Make sure that you get a closing shot**—Most video producers look for dramatic opening shots or sequences (and that's still a good thing), but your viewers are more likely to remember the closing shot.

Bob Dotson's Storyteller's Checklist

Dotson's Storyteller's Checklist inspired his book *Make It Memorable* (Bonus Books) and a companion videotape of all the stories in the book. He prepared his list (and book) with TV news reporters in mind, but his tips apply to professional, corporate, and home video producers as well:

▶ **Always remember that the reporter is not the story.**

▶ **Make sure the *commitment* is present**—Commitment is your description of the story, stated in one sentence—that is, what you want the audience to take away from the report. You should be able to state the commitment as a complete sentence with subject, verb, and object. "Outside money is altering the city's architecture," "This cow has never taken an order in her life," "You can't murder a pumpkin," and so on. You formulate this commitment to yourself to help guide the story creation. Then you use your images to prove the commitment visually. Very seldom will you state the commitment verbally in any story.

▶ **Write your pictures first**—Give them a strong lead, preferably visual, that instantly telegraphs the story to come.

▶ **The main body of the story should usually be no more than three to five main points**—Prove these points visually after you've identified them.

▶ **Create a strong close that you can't top**—Build toward the close throughout the story. Ideally, the ending is also visual.

▶ **Write loose**—Be hard on yourself as a writer. Say nothing in the script that your viewers would already know or that the visuals say more eloquently.

▶ **Throughout the story, build your report around sequences**—Film two or three shots of a guy buying basketball tickets, two or three shots of a husband and wife drinking coffee at a kitchen table, and so on. Sequences demand matched action.

▶ **Allow for moments of silence**—Stop writing occasionally and let two or three seconds or more of compelling action occur without voiceover. For a writer, nothing is more difficult to write than silence. For viewers, sometimes nothing is more eloquent.

▶ **Use strong natural sound**—Sound heightens realism, authenticity, believability, and heightens the viewer's sense of vicarious participation in the events you're showing. Some reports merely enable you to watch what happened. The best reports make it possible for you to experience what happened.

▶ **Tell your story through people**—People sell your story. Try to find strong central characters engaged in compelling action that is visual or picturesque.

▶ **Build in surprises to sustain viewer involvement**—Surprises help viewers feel something about the story; surprises lure uninterested viewers to the screen. Surprises can be visual, wild sounds, short bites, or poetic script. Always, surprises are little moments of drama.

▶ **Short sound bites prove the story you are showing**—Don't use sound bites as substitutes for more effective storytelling.

▶ **Address the larger issue**—"A trailer home burned down." Such a story fails to meet the "so what?" test. "The trailer home burned down because the walls are full of flammable insulation" describes the larger issue and meets the "so what?" test.

▶ **Finally, make your story memorable**—Can your viewers feel something about the story and its subjects? If feeling is present, it will stick in the viewers' minds.

Keep It Simple...and Short

As a coda to Dotson's advice, I'll add one more thing you need to remember: *this is only TV*. You need some mighty compelling or entertaining material to keep viewers glued to the tube for more than a few minutes. Think about whatever message you're trying to get across in your video project and consider what images, sound, and graphics will convey that message in the briefest, most effective manner. Then shoot with brevity in mind.

That's not to say that you don't grab unplanned video that looks great. Or that you cut interviews short even if you haven't heard some compelling sound bites. Videotape is expendable. Feel free to shoot plenty. Although it's true that you might have to wade through a lot to find the best shots, the advantage of DV is that after these shots have been logged, you can simply capture them individually to your hard drive and they become immediately accessible.

Writing in the Active Voice

It's a rare classroom experience that can cause a tidal change. One of those for me was a seminar with Mackie Morris (see the upcoming section). Morris makes his message clear: "Write in the active voice." For example, instead of writing

A bill was passed by the Senate.

Write this instead:

The Senate passed a bill.

Put the receiver of the verb's action after the verb. Instead of the passively voiced "John Doe was arrested by police" (Doe is the receiver of the action and is ahead of the verb), change that to "Police arrested John Doe."

Morris emphasizes that passive voice deadens, complicates, and lengthens writing. It's not ungrammatical, but it's more suitable for print than television copy. You use passive voice sparingly in everyday conversation, and you should use it sparingly in video productions. You're asking people to listen to your words, not read them. Make it easy. Make it active.

It takes some effort to make the shift from passive voice to active. Simply recognizing passive voice takes extra attentiveness. The biggest giveaway is some form of the *to be* verb in a verb phrase. The following sentences are all in the passive voice:

> The students were praised by the teacher.
>
> The unruly customer was told to leave by the maitre d'.
>
> The forest was destroyed by fire.

Make them active by moving the receiver of the action to after the verb:

> The teacher praised the students.
>
> The maitre d' told the unruly customer to leave.
>
> Fire destroyed the forest.

That one fundamental technique makes your sentences simpler and shorter.

Morris calls it **straight-line meaning**. The listener understands the copy better because it flows in a straight line. You know that when you read a newspaper you frequently go back and reread some sentences because something didn't add up. Video viewers don't have that luxury.

Besides switching the sentence around (*relocating the actor*, as Morris puts it), you can fix passive sentences in three other ways:

- ▶ **Identify the missing actor and insert it into the sentence**—Change "The airplane was landed during the storm" to "A passenger landed the airplane during the storm."

- ▶ **Change the verb**—Instead of writing "The bell was sounded at noon" write "The bell rang at noon." (Or tolled, pealed, chimed—using active voice fosters the use of more descriptive words.)

- ▶ **Drop the *to be* verb**—Change "The spotlight was focused on downtown" to "The spotlight focused on downtown."

Not all *to be* verb phrases are passive. "The man was driving south" contains a verb phrase and a *to be* helper. But the man was performing the action, not receiving it. Therefore, the sentence is active. A sentence is passive only if the receiver of the verb's action precedes the verb.

Writing in the active voice forces you to get out of your writing rut. Instead of saying the same old things in the same old *to be* passive way, select new active verbs and constructions. You'll write more conversationally and with a fresher and more interesting style.

That's not to say that you'll write exclusively in the active voice. You should write, "He was born in 1984," or "She was injured in the accident" because that's what people say.

Focusing on active voice makes your copy more interesting and easier to understand.

Mackie Morris's Writing Tips

Mackie Morris.

Few if any media consultants match Mackie Morris's 25-year record as a journalism and communications seminar leader, teacher, coach, and practitioner. Founder and president of Mackie Morris Communications, he works with a wide range of corporate and public service clients to enhance their communication skills.

Morris previously served as chairman of the Broadcast News Department at the University of Missouri School of Journalism. He later worked as a vice president and lead consultant for Frank N. Magid Associates, a major media-consulting firm, where he implemented a series of instructional workshops for broadcast professionals. It was at one of those seminars that I became a devotee of Morris's "active voice." Morris continues to be one of the most sought-after broadcast writing seminarians ever.

The Good Writer's Dazzlin' Dozen

At his seminars, Morris relentlessly hammers home his active voice message. But peppered throughout his presentation he interjects other useful writing tips. He calls them "The Good Writer's Dazzlin' Dozen":

> ▶ **Write factually and accurately**—The best technique and the finest form mean nothing if your copy is wrong.

- ▶ **Write in the active voice**—This technique makes your copy tighter, complete, easier to listen to, and more interesting. Do whatever you must to avoid the passive voice.

- ▶ **Write in the present or present perfect tenses**—They make your copy more immediate, and immediacy is more interesting. Avoid the word *today*. If you use past tense, make sure that you give a time reference to avoid confusion.

- ▶ **Keep your writing simple**—Choose positive forms over negative forms. Write one thought to a sentence. Don't search for synonyms; repetition is not a sin. Don't search for complicated, intellectual language. Give the audience the best possible chance to understand the story.

- ▶ **Be complete and clear**—In your quest for brevity and conciseness, don't omit necessary information.

- ▶ **Be creative**—Stick to the rules, but develop your own style. Try to say the same old thing in a different, new way. Make use of writing devices that make copy easier to listen to and more interesting, such as using the "rule of threes" (that is, grouping items by threes, such as red, white, and blue; left, right, and center; over, under, and through). Saying things in groups of three always sounds better. Pausing before saying the third item is even more effective.

- ▶ **Write to be heard**—Maintain a sense of rhythm in your writing. All life has rhythm, and rhythmic writing is easier to hear. Avoid potentially confusing homonyms. Always test your copy by reading it aloud.

- ▶ **Avoid interruptives**—Don't force the listener to make difficult mental connections. Put modifiers next to what they modify. And, if you split infinitives (verb phrases), make sure your sentence's meaning is clear.

  Incorrect: The attorney will, depending on the ruling, eventually decide.

  Correct: Depending on the ruling, the attorney will decide eventually.

  Incorrect: Doctors only gave him six months to live.

  Correct: Doctors gave him only six months to live.

- ▶ **Avoid commas**—A comma demands a hitch in reading, and the resulting jerkiness frustrates the listener. Avoiding commas also eliminates subordinate clauses. Such clauses kill the impact of copy, especially if they come at the top of a story or sentence.

- ▶ **Avoid numbers**—The listener has trouble remembering them.

- ▶ **Avoid pronouns**—If you must use a pronoun, make sure that the pronoun agrees with its antecedent and appears close to the antecedent. For example, "John Doe hit Bob Smith on the head and paramedics took him to the hospital." In this case, instead of *him* use *Smith*.

- ▶ **Write to the pictures, but not too closely to the pictures**—Remember that more specific video requires more general writing, and vice versa. Utilize the touch-and-go method, wherein you write directly to the video at the beginning of a sequence, and then allow the writing to become more general with background information and other facts as the video continues.

Storytelling with Video

This is what you do. You're a storyteller. In most cases, you might go out on a shoot with only a basic idea of what you're going to tape and how you're going to piece it together. That kind of approach will get you only so far.

As you up the ante in your work, there will be times when you'll want to work from a script. It may be as straightforward as a corporate safety production with employees doing the acting, or you may have aspirations to create a dramatic feature.

In either case, some fundamental scriptwriting skills will help you raise the bar of your production. I've tapped two of Hollywood's top writers to do the honors.

Stephen Black's and Henry Stern's Scriptwriting Tips

Stephen Black (left) and Henry Stern (right), TV scriptwriters and producers.

Stephen Black's and Henry Stern's TV scriptwriting and producing credits would fill this page. They forged new directions in episodic dramas with their work on *Dynasty*, *Falcon Crest*, *Flamingo Road*, *Matlock*, and *Knot's Landing*. Their work as head writers on *As the World Turns* and consultants for *One Life to Live* stirred things up and added sizzle to both of these long-running daytime staples. They've had a hand in a half-dozen TV movies, including the only TV film starring Audrey Hepburn, *Love Among Thieves*.

They got their start as a writing team doing comedies in the mid-1970s. Stern had been one of Broadway's youngest producers, and Black had written a couple plays. Despite failing to sell their first comedy script to *The Mary Tyler Moore Show*, they were given free access to the set, where they watched rehearsals and show tapings, all the while taking copious notes. That led to a brief stint writing for a new show called *The Love Boat* ("It paid the bills and got us in the Writers Guild") and finally landed them a job with Norman Lear Productions, the company behind *All in the Family*.

These days they're working on their second novel and a movie script. Here's their advice to aspiring scriptwriters:

- ▶ **The most important thing is that we like to tell stories.**

- ▶ **The most important thing in stories is the characters**—The best kind of character is one with the ability to surprise you. The audience is not dumb. You've got to come up with something unpredictable. You don't want a white hat or a black hat. You want people wearing gray hats—people you can't read. You want to be interested in what happens to them.

- ▶ **It's *not* a good idea to start your scriptwriting with a plot**—It's better to start with a theme. Know what you want to say, how you want to say it, and where you want to be at the end. The theme of our current film script is, "How does the death of someone affect his three closest friends?"

- ▶ **With the theme in hand, we next create the characters**—What is their arc and how will that change throughout the story? We invent detailed character bios. Where did they go to school? What were their parents like? What was their childhood like? We don't have to use all that in the script, but it's good for us to know to help craft the story.

- ▶ **Next, we sit down with a yellow legal pad and make 30 to 40 story points**—Points such as guy robs bank, hides in mother's house, falls in love with neighbor, and so on.

- ▶ **Then we write an extensive narrative outline**—30 pages or more. We include texture—the tone and detail. We take time to describe settings and characters. Instead of merely using physical descriptions of characters, such as Bob is 6'2" with the torso of a long-distance runner, we're more likely to write, "As John was driving up Canyon Avenue, he looked out his rain-spattered window and caught sight of Bob, one more time, running in the rain." That says a lot. We love doing that. It makes it easier to do the script.

- ▶ **It's really crucial that you learn how to structure a piece so that your story makes sense**—Know where your story is going and how plot elements and character elements will build on each other so they peak at certain points. An excellent film example of structure is *Two for the Road*, with

Audrey Hepburn and Albert Finney. Even though they use multiple flash-backs, you know that from beginning to end this is a story of a marriage on the skids.

▶ **Tell as much of the story as you can without dialogue**—Tell it cinematically. Don't give camera directions such as wide, tight, medium. That's the director's job and disrupts the story flow. But it's okay to script camera *angles*. We wrote a scene where a woman was about to tell her husband their son was killed in combat. The husband ran a steak house and happened to be in the walk-in freezer when his wife arrived. We directed the camera to look through the window and, without any dialogue, watch the woman tell the husband and see the reaction.

▶ **You can't write if you're not an observer**—We're constantly eavesdropping in restaurants. We're acutely aware of dialogue going on around us. Our characters have to speak in the vernacular of the time.

▶ **Dialogue is more than just writing down what two people say to each other**—Good dialogue is succinct, crisp, entertaining, and rich. It's a level above conversation.

▶ **Bury the "pipe."**—The **pipe** is the exposition, the conduit of information, the stuff that the audience needs to know to make sense of the story. Suppose the character has been divorced three times, has six kids with six different women, and runs a grocery. You don't come out and say that. You impart it to the audience in an interesting way.

▶ **Scriptwriting is collaborative**—Everyone has a hand in it. A screenplay will go through 10 to 15 drafts before shooting begins.

▶ **Writing is hard work**—To sit there in front of a blank computer screen knowing that you have to come up with compelling characters and stimulating plots week after week after week can be daunting. Back in 1970, we were working with Leon Uris on a musical production of his novel *Exodus*. After several tiring meetings with potential backers, Stephen asked Uris if he had any advice for aspiring playwrights. He said, "Put your ass in a chair in front of a typewriter." This was the most succinct, valuable information we were ever given.

Unblocking Creativity

Writer's block strikes us all. As Black and Stern noted, it's darned hard to sit down in front of a blank computer screen and start putting words in the computer.

Here are some ways to get the creative juices flowing:

- ▶ **Bounce ideas off others**—Simply talking about your project typically will give you a whole new perspective. Listening to questions posed to you about your work will help you focus your writing.

- ▶ **Change your work environment**—I have the luxury of going outside and sitting on a rocking chair overlooking a lovely valley. That moment in the fresh air helps bust loose a few cobwebs.

- ▶ **Scribble down some ideas**—Turn away from your computer and grab a yellow legal pad and a felt-tip pen. Connect the thoughts on paper.

- ▶ **Take a break**—Listen to a great tune. Take a jog. Then get back to work—you're on deadline!

Video-Editing Tips from an Expert—John Crossman

Forever seared in my brain is one edit. It was in my first "magazine" piece for KSL-TV in Salt Lake City. This was back in the mid-1980s. The national Radio and Television News Directors Association had just named KSL the TV news station of the year—an honor that KSL would win an unprecedented two years in a row. KSL had the highest-rated (by percentage of viewers) news shows in the country. It was a TV news powerhouse. I had just moved there from a medium-sized market and was in awe of the professionalism, the scope of the news operation, and the array of high-tech goodies.

 Buried deep in the editing bays was something akin to the command center of the Starship Enterprise. At its helm was John Crossman, KSL's chief editor. For me, having come from a station with *no* editors (the photographers did all the editing), this was a tad overwhelming. One of my first assignments was a long feature story on a local piano manufacturer. I'd never done a magazine-style piece and handed John a straightforward news-style voice-over. He barely batted an eye.

A couple hours later he called me into his realm wanting to show me how the piece was coming together. It sang. It danced. It had rhythm. I was confounded. The segment ended with a Billy Joel piano crescendo followed by a loud "clip" of a wire cutter snipping a piano string. I looked at John and at all his whiz-bang electronics and said one of the dumbest comments I've ever muttered in my TV career: "This equipment is amazing!" Fortunately, he forgave me my egregious error and we got on famously after that.

John spent eight years at KSL and now runs Crossman Post Production (www.crossmanpost.com) just outside of Salt Lake City. He provides video editing, graphics, and computer-generated animation for a lengthy list of corporate, educational, and broadcast clients. He's won five regional Emmys, 26 national Tellys, and a slew of other awards.

John is a wonderfully talented guy who has a true passion for the art of editing. Here are his editing tips.

To begin, good editors need certain basic talents:

- ▶ **Rhythm**—Life has a rhythm, so does editing. If you can't feel it, it's very hard to learn.

- ▶ **Visualization**—Good editors can see the completed project before they start. The actual editing is just the detail work. The images are already completely edited in their minds.

- ▶ **Patience**—Even when you can see it in your mind's eye, you'll have to make compromises on every project. The true test of an editor is whether he or she can make compromises work well. The best editors make it look like every single choice was the best choice.

- ▶ **Positive attitude**—Your attitude will go a long, long way toward determining your success. You'll spend countless hours editing in a small dark space, usually on a deadline, and always with budget pressure, client pressure, spouse pressure…you name it. And the better your attitude, the better the job will go.

- ▶ **Team player**—You're part of a team. Try not to criticize the other members. Remember, you didn't have your eye in the viewfinder when the bomb went off. Thinking you could have had that shot when you're looking at the tape hours and miles away is easy, but not productive. Let the producer say, "I wish he had gotten closer." You say, "Well, let's do it this way and it will still work." That's where editors earn their money, their reputation, and their loyalty.

To edit well, you need to do the following:

- ▶ **Use motivation and logic**—This is the most important concept in editing. Your editing should be motivated. You should have a reason for the shots you select and the order in which you select them. There should be a purpose to why you dissolve, why you use a wipe, as well as why you cut. Your goal is to communicate clearly what has happened. Your shot selection and the time spent on each shot should reinforce the narration while conveying information.

▶ **Plan as you digitize**—As you digitize the video (transfer it from your camera to your PC), you should see in your mind's eye how the pictures are going to line up to get you to where you want to be at the end. Is the shot a great scene-setter (beginning)? Is it incredibly beautiful (possible ending shot)? Is it self-explanatory or incomprehensible (possible cutting-room floor material)?

▶ **Build new skills**—If you're in the professional ranks, or want to be, you must budget a considerable amount of time and money toward keeping current. At the very least, you're going to need to learn about how to incorporate graphics, animation, compositing, and special effects into your editing to serve the demands of your clients.

▶ In the world of broadcast television, you are surrounded by people who know how to create good stories. In corporate production, you might be working with someone who has no clue. At this point, you become 90% teacher and 10% editor. Your attitude will win you a loyal client or lose you a lifetime customer.

▶ Like music in a movie, good editing helps communicate your message and shouldn't really stand out to the viewer. The editing is not the message, but the editing can make the message work, not work, or work better than it should.

Summary

By reading this book you are making a commitment to do something other than create vacation movies to show your (ungrateful) relatives. To up your production ante means improving your story creation, writing, and video production business acumen. The advice given here comes from folks who've been in the trenches for years. They know from where they're speaking.

By following this hour's writing tips, gleaned from experts in the TV news and video production business, your video productions should have an even greater impact.

PART II

Video Editing

CHAPTER 7

Capturing and Editing Video with Windows Movie Maker 2

What You'll Learn in This Chapter:

▶ Movie Maker 2—pros and cons
▶ Overview of video editing with Movie Maker 2
▶ Capturing video
▶ Gathering other assets
▶ Using the Storyboard to make a rough draft
▶ Splitting and trimming clips on the timeline

So how does that saying go? "Free is a very good price." Or is it "You get what you pay for"? With Windows Movie Maker 2, it's a bit of both. In this chapter I give a quick take on Movie Maker 2, warts and all.

I introduce you to nonlinear editing tools such as the Storyboard, Timeline, Preview window, and audio and video tracks.

I show you how to transfer or **capture** video from your DV camcorder to Movie Maker 2. I explain how to convert that captured video into clips, trim them, and turn them into a simple, **cuts-only** video. I save the cool stuff like transitions and video effects for the next chapter.

Movie Maker 2—Pros and Cons

If I had my druthers, this chapter and the next would be an appendix. I'd rather you skipped Movie Maker altogether and jumped with both feet into Studio. But, market research indicates a whole lot of video editors like to first dip their toes into Movie Maker.

That's understandable. It's free. And it does do pretty decent videos. Heck, there are whole books out there on Movie Maker, including a couple from Peachpit Press, an imprint of Pearson Education, the parent company of this book's publisher.

The quandary this puts me in is this: How much ink do I use in my Movie Maker chapters to explain some of the finer points of nonlinear editing when I plan to do that in the chapters on Pinnacle Studio? The answer is—not a whole lot, but enough to make it worth your while to read these two chapters.

A Minimal Run-Through

Let me make this clear. If your intention is to edit videos *only* with Movie Maker 2, then return this book to the store and buy either *Making a Movie with Windows XP—Visual QuickProject Guide* or *Microsoft Movie Maker 2: Visual QuickStart Guide*. Both are by *PC Magazine* writer Jan Ozer, and both do a fine job of taking you through everything Movie Maker 2 can do.

What I'm going to do is give you a minimal run-through of Windows Movie Maker 2.

Go Ahead—Give Movie Maker 2 a Try

You can skip these two chapters on Movie Maker 2 and proceed directly to Chapter 9, "Capturing Video with Pinnacle Studio Plus." But because I do introduce some editing concepts here that I won't re-explain in detail in the Studio chapters, I recommend that you follow the tasks in these two chapters and use Movie Maker 2 to test the waters of nonlinear editing. It is free, so what do you have to lose?

Heck, even when you do start working with Studio, you don't have to spend any money (for the time being). You can download the trial version and use it to do the many tasks to come, starting in Chapter 9.

Movie Maker 2—Pluses and Minuses

Pluses:

- ▶ It's free.
- ▶ It works more or less the way other nonlinear editors work.
- ▶ It offers a full complement of transitions and video effects.
- ▶ It has a text/titler tool.

Minuses:

▶ Audio limitations—It has only two audio tracks versus three for Studio and 99 (!) for Premiere Pro. It's a clumsy process to make a video with music *and* narration, ditto for some standard, news-style audio edits, and it has minimal volume controls.

▶ Only two primary video **output** formats (no MPEG, analog video or RealVideo) versus five output formats for Studio.

▶ No control over video effects.

▶ No means to overlay graphics on videos.

▶ Title tool has only a few options.

▶ Awkward file handling.

▶ No DVD-authoring tools.

▶ Slow playback of some DV files captured by software other than Movie Maker.

And there are others that would take too much time to explain. But Movie Maker 2 is a freebie and it does let you make reasonably good videos. So let's forge ahead.

Overview of Video Editing with Movie Maker 2

Nonlinear editors let you do things in whatever order suits your needs at the moment. However, because of some of Windows Movie Maker 2's limitations, it has a more-or-less standard workflow:

1. Capture video.

2. Gather other assets (video, audio, music, and stills).

3. Place and arrange clips on the Storyboard.

4. Split and trim clips on the Timeline.

5. Add video effects and transitions.

6. Add titles.

7. Add audio (narration, music, sound effects).

8. Export to DV tape or PC file.

Why Adding Audio Is the Final Editing Step

When using a professional NLE, most editors do not wait until finishing the video editing to add audio. They add audio in pieces as they work through a project. For example, when building a news story, editors typically lay down some of the reporter's narration, edit in video clips over that to match the points in the narration, add a sound bite or natural sound, then lay down more narration, and so on.

So why not follow the same procedure with Movie Maker? Turns out that each time you add a transition between two clips, Movie Maker (and other entry-level NLEs like Studio) *shortens* the overall length of the finished video by the length of the transition (usually one second). Professional NLEs *retain* the overall length. This happens because consumer NLEs tend to be idiot-proof (in this case they automatically slide the beginning of the second clip over the end of the first clip to perform the transition), while professional NLEs like Adobe Premiere Pro, give editors much more control.

In this chapter, I present tasks covering steps one through four. I save the remaining four steps for the next chapter.

Tour the Interface

First order of business: Download a copy of Movie Maker 2 from `www.microsoft.com/windowsxp/using/moviemaker/default.mspx`. If the file's 12MB size is more than your Internet connection can handle, that website has a link to order Movie Maker 2 on a CD. Install Movie Maker 2 by double-clicking that downloaded file: `mmenu20.exe`.

What About Movie Maker Version 2.1?

As we went to press, Microsoft had just released Movie Maker version 2.1. It has only a few minor bug fixes and does not have a different look or functionality from version 2.0. At press time the only way to get the upgrade was to get a copy of the Service Pack 2 (SP2) update to Windows XP. By the time this book ships you might be able to get that updated version as a single file download on the Microsoft Windows Movie Maker website.

I want to give you a brief tour of Movie Maker 2. Feel free to follow along. Fire up your copy of Movie Maker 2 by double-clicking its icon on your desktop or selecting Start, Programs, Movie Maker (you can drag its icon from the Start menu to your desktop to make it more readily accessible). Take a look at Figure 7.1. This is the default opening screen.

Task Window

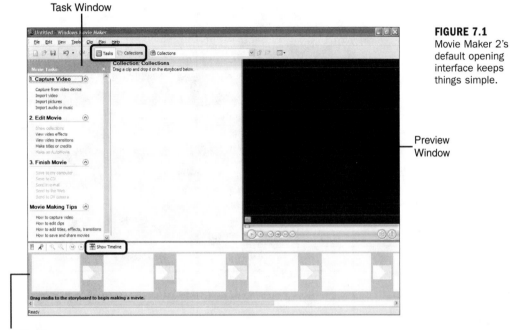

FIGURE 7.1
Movie Maker 2's
default opening
interface keeps
things simple.

Preview
Window

Storyboard/Timeline

▶ The Tasks list on the left side is kind of a workflow but it's missing some essential points, such as adding clips to a Storyboard or Timeline and trimming those clips. Click the Tasks button to close or open the Tasks view.

▶ The Storyboard is the collection of rectangles at the bottom of the screen. Click the Show Timeline button to switch to the Timeline view. I explain both editing methods at the end of this chapter.

▶ The Preview window is where you view your clips and edited video.

▶ The Collections window is where you access your video, audio, and image files. Click the Collections button twice to display the collections list on the left side. As shown in Figures 7.2 and 7.3, by clicking the Video Effects or Video Transitions icons, you can view the fun stuff to come in the next chapter.

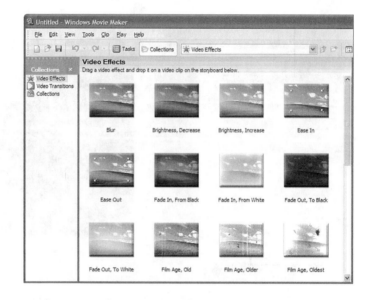

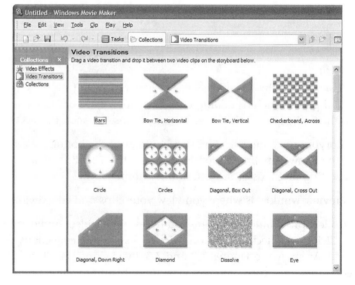

Capturing Video

If this is the first time you've transferred video from a DV camcorder to a PC,
you're in for a treat (if all goes smoothly). Movie Maker 2 and other NLEs let you
control your camcorder using a familiar remote control interface. The first time I
saw video from my camcorder pop up in a PC NLE video capture interface, it put
a grin on my face.

What About Analog Video Capture?

Movie Maker 2 lets you capture video from either a DV *or* analog camcorder. An analog camcorder requires a special capture card. I cover that topic in Chapter 9. If you have an analog capture card and want to use Movie Maker 2 to transfer video to your PC, select Help in the Movie Maker toolbar, and under Contents go to Using Windows Movie Maker, Capturing Video, To Capture Video from Tape in an Analog Camera or VCR.

By the Way

You can manually roll your tape (using the capture interface remote control) to a start point for a clip you want to transfer (or **capture**). Click Start Capture, watch the clip, and press Stop Capture at the end of the clip. But Movie Maker 2 is all about making it easy on users, so for this coming exercise, you'll take the automated approach.

Automated DV Capture

Try it Yourself

▼

You'll take Movie Maker's user-friendly approach and have it automatically detect scene changes and make a separate clip for each one. Here's how to do that:

1. Connect your DV camcorder to your PC by attaching the FireWire cable to the outlet on the camcorder and to the PC (typically the PC outlet is on the soundcard).

2. Plug your camcorder into an AC outlet (your batteries might die on you or the camcorder might go into **sleep mode**). Turn on your camcorder and switch to VCR or VTR mode (not Camera mode).

3. Switching on your camcorder should cause Windows to pop up the little dialog box shown in Figure 7.4. Select Take No Action and click OK.

FIGURE 7.4
When you connect your camcorder to your PC and turn it on, Windows detects the new device and asks you what you want to do. In this case select Take No Action.

▼

4. Open Windows Movie Maker 2. If the Movie Tasks list is not visible, click the Tasks icon in the toolbar.

5. Under the Capture Video main heading, click Capture from Video Device. That opens the Video Capture Wizard shown in Figure 7.5. Give your video a name and a hard-drive storage location and then click Next to open the Video Setting window.

By the
Way

Analog Video Capturers—Take Note

If you have an analog video capture card installed, you will see its name in the Video Capture Wizard window. To capture video from an analog camcorder or VCR, simply select your analog capture card and follow the prompts.

FIGURE 7.5
Use the Video Capture Wizard to give your video a name and a file folder location on your hard drive.

6. In the Video Setting window (shown in Figure 7.6) you choose from three quality settings:

   ▶ Best Quality for Playback on My Computer

   ▶ Digital Device Format (DV-AVI)

   ▶ Other Settings

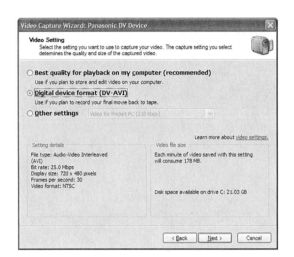

FIGURE 7.6
Movie Maker 2 converts incoming DV into one of two file types: WMV and DV-AVI. My recommendation: Stick with DV-AVI to retain the quality of your original video.

Best Quality and Other Settings both create WMV (Windows Media Video) files. Best Quality is more compressed than DV but still reasonably good looking. Clicking Other Settings lets you select from a lengthy drop-down list of presets, all of which have greater compression (and therefore lower quality) than the Best Quality selection.

My recommendation is to select Digital Device Format (DV-AVI—Digital Video, Audio Video Interleave). It keeps your video in its original DV quality. You can later **export** it at its full DV quality back to videotape or select a WMV export (output) preset to suit your display needs. The drawbacks to selecting Digital Device Format are larger file sizes and possibly slower playback on older PCs.

    7. Make your quality selection and click Next. That opens the Capture Method window shown in Figure 7.7. If you want to capture the entire tape, select Capture the Entire Tape Automatically. If you have only a section of tape you want to capture, select Capture Parts of the Tape Manually. If your PC is a klunker, uncheck the Show Preview During Capture box. Click Next.

    8. That opens the Capture Video window shown in Figure 7.8. This is the cool part. Check out the video player controls. If you want to cue up your video to a particular segment, go ahead and do that.

FIGURE 7.7
Whether you choose Capture the Entire Tape or Capture Parts of the Tape, you can later have Movie Maker automatically detect scene changes and create separate clips for each.

FIGURE 7.8
Here's where the fun begins. Use these controls to remotely operate your camcorder.

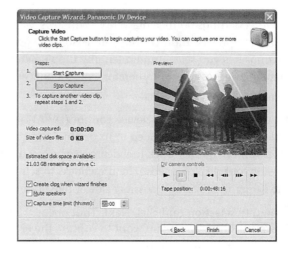

9. Click Create Clips When Wizard Finishes. That feature examines your original DV tape's Time Stamp for times when you pressed the Record/Pause button and creates separate clips for each instance.

10. If you know how much time you want to capture, note that in the Capture Time Limit window.

11. After you've set these few parameters, click Start Capture. Movie Maker 2 will cue up your tape, play it, and record the video to your hard drive.

12. If it completes the capture and stops automatically, fine. If the tape keeps on rolling past the stop point, click Stop Capture. As shown in Figure 7.9, at this point Movie Maker will close the Capture Wizard, switch to the Contents window, and display all the clips it created using scene detection. Note that Movie Maker names each clip with the date and time stamp recorded on the original tape.

FIGURE 7.9
After video capture is completed, Movie Maker 2 displays the clips it created using its scene detection feature.

Gathering Other Assets

In editor parlance, **assets** refers to the multimedia material you use to create your video or DVD: videos, natural sound, narration, music, other audio, images, and graphics.

Movie Maker 2's Collections window serves as the repository for your assets. You don't actually store your material in some additional hard-drive folder assigned by Movie Maker; rather, Movie Maker notes the locations on your hard drive where you've stored your assets and keeps that information in its Collections window.

To gather or **import** your assets, select a Collection (in which you will list your assets) from the drop-down list at the top of the screen and click any of the three Import options in the Movie Tasks window.

That opens the Import File window, shown in Figure 7.10. Depending on whether you selected Import Video, Import Pictures, or Import Audio or Music, those respective file types (that are compatible with Movie Maker) will display. Select any number of media files and click Import.

How to Select More Than One File

Use standard Windows shortcuts to select multiple files. You can click and drag to create what's called a **marquee** (a box that highlights multiple files), Ctrl+click various files individually to select a collection of files, or click one file and then Shift+click another farther up or down on the list to select those two files and all other files between them.

Awkward Collection Window Storage

When you import pictures, audio, and music, their names or icons appear in whatever collection you selected before clicking Import. That's a good thing.

But when you import videos that you captured using some other software or obtained in some other fashion, Movie Maker creates a different **collection** for each individual video. This is yet another idiot-proofing approach to ensure that you can divide each video into smaller clips and not lose track of them.

FIGURE 7.10
Clicking any of the three Import options in the Task window opens this Import File window.

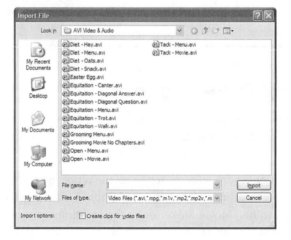

Now, when you look at your Collection, you will see a mix of images, audio, and video. As shown in Figure 7.11, all audio files—music, narration, sound effects—have a musical note icon. Images use a thumbnail. Videos have a filmstrip border.

FIGURE 7.11
A collection with (from top to bottom) video, image, and audio files. Note the different thumbnail styles representing each asset type.

Using the Storyboard to Make a Rough Draft

Movie Maker gives you two approaches to editing videos: Storyboard and Timeline.

Using the Storyboard is a fine way to ease into nonlinear editing, but you probably will outgrow it quickly. Eventually, with Movie Maker and other NLEs you'll rely exclusively on the Timeline.

Building Your Video on the Storyboard

Try it Yourself

You've probably seen storyboards. Film directors use them to visualize sequences and build something like visual rough drafts. Typically they consist of a collection of sketches pinned to a wall. They work well because it's easy to move, remove, add to, or replace the sketches. And it helps to see the big picture and overall story flow. Movie Maker's storyboard handles those tasks digitally. Here's how:

1. Adjust the Movie Maker interface to look like Figure 7.12. Do that by clicking the Tasks icon to hide the Movie Tasks list. If the Timeline view is open, click the Show Storyboard icon to switch to that view. Drag the left side of the Preview monitor to expand it.

FIGURE 7.12
To prepare to use the Storyboard, change the Movie Maker display setup to look like this. Click either highlighted Play button to view your video.

2. Looking over your clips, try to settle on a sequence that tells a story. Then drag those clips, one at a time, to the Storyboard, placing them in sequence from left to right.

By the Way

Storyboard Characteristics

Note that as you add a clip to the Storyboard, a little gray star appears in the lower-left corner of its thumbnail. Later, if you add a Video Effect to that clip, the star will change to blue. Apply more than one Effect (you can apply up to six per clip) and two overlapping blue stars appear.

The chevron between clips is the placeholder for a transition. When you drop a transition there, a blue representation of the transition fills that spot.

3. Play that sequence of clips by clicking either of the two Play buttons—the one toward the upper-left corner of the Storyboard or the one at the bottom of the Preview window. I highlighted both previously in Figure 7.12.

4. Move a clip to a new location on the Storyboard by clicking it in its placeholder thumbnail image, dragging it left or right, and dropping it into a new placeholder. As shown in Figure 7.13, a vertical blue bar appears as you drag the clip around, indicating the clip's new relative position. Note

that when you move a clip, all the other clips slide over and fill the gap to accommodate the changed position.

FIGURE 7.13
As you drag a clip to a new location in the Storyboard, a vertical blue line appears, noting where the clip will go relative to the other clips.

5. Remove a clip by clicking it to select it and then pressing Delete. Note that clips to the right of—*after*—the removed clip slide left to fill the gap made by the deletion. If you change your mind, select Edit, Undo Remove Clip (keyboard shortcut—Ctrl+Z) to bring it back.

Nondestructive Editing

As you build your video, you are not in fact creating a video. Movie Maker tracks your work with **pointers**. These simply are data noting the original asset file location, where that file is relative to other assets in your production, whether you've trimmed that asset (you'll trim clips in the next section), for how long a still image displays, and other characteristics.

If you delete a clip from your project, you are not deleting it from your hard drive. This is **nondestructive** editing. After you've completed your editing, you will have Movie Maker actually create—or **render**—a new video file.

By the Way

6. You quickly fill the placeholders visible in the Storyboard. To view more, either move the slider bar at the bottom of the screen or drag the top of the Storyboard down (making it shorter) to shrink the placeholders (see Figure 7.14). As you add clips to the Storyboard, Movie Maker adds more empty placeholders. You can't run out.

7. Now is a good time to save (and name) your project. Select File, Save Project, navigate to a file folder (My Documents/My Movies is the default location), give your project a name, and click Save.

FIGURE 7.14
To increase the number of Storyboard placeholders displayed on the screen, shrink the height of the Storyboard.

Splitting and Trimming Clips on the Timeline

Dropping a bunch of clips onto the Storyboard is just the beginning of the editing process. Most of those **raw** clips are probably longer than you want them to be in your finished product. Or they might have two or more elements in them that you want to put in different places in your final video.

Try it Yourself   **Splitting and Trimming Clips**

What you need to do now is to split and trim your clips. You'll do this work on the Timeline (you can't do this in the Storyboard). Here's how it works:

1. Switch to the Timeline view by clicking the Show Timeline button above the Storyboard. As shown in Figure 7.15, the Timeline is a series of parallel tracks representing the following:

   ▶ Video clips (and their associated audio)

   ▶ Transitions (I cover that feature and the following two features in the next chapter)

   ▶ Additional audio for music, sound effects, or a narration

   ▶ Title overlay—or text—track

FIGURE 7.15
The Timeline view. Use the highlighted Control Time Indicator to view any of the clips.

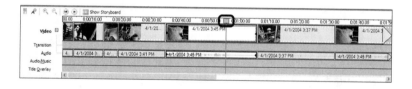

2. Click any clip's thumbnail in the Timeline and note that the clip's first frame appears in the Preview window.

3. Drag—or **scrub**—the Control Time Indicator (CTI), which was highlighted previously in Figure 7.15, through that clip and adjacent clips. This is an easy way to fast forward or rewind through a clip. Find a clip you want to split in two.

4. Use the CTI or the VCR controls to move the CTI to the exact spot where you want to make the split. When you're ready, click the Split Clip button highlighted in Figure 7.16. That creates two clips in the Timeline.

FIGURE 7.16
Split a clip by clicking the highlighted button.

5. Either drag one of the split clip halves to another location on the Timeline or delete it by selecting it and pressing Delete. Note that when you remove it or drag it to a new location, just as with the Storyboard, other clips slide to fill its gap and give it room at its new location.

6. You can use the same clip-splitting method to **trim** a clip, removing frames from its beginning or end. But I want to show you a different method. First, select a clip you want to trim by clicking it. Note that the clip box on the Timeline turns white when selected.

7. Move the cursor to the beginning or end of the clip. As shown in Figure 7.17, the cursor changes to a double-arrow (if you position the cursor over an unselected clip, the arrows won't appear).

FIGURE 7.17
Drag in the edges of a clip to trim it.

8. Now drag the cursor *into* the clip. If you placed the cursor at the head of the clip, you'll drag to the right. If you placed it at the end, you'll drag left. Note that as you drag the cursor, the video in the Preview window changes

to show your current position. When you find the place you want your clip to start or finish, release the mouse button. The portion you wanted to remove disappears and the remaining clips slide over to fill that gap.

9. Repeat this trimming process with your other clips to tighten up your project.

Summary

If you want to get into nonlinear video editing without spending any more money, Movie Maker 2 is the logical choice. Despite its limited features, you can use it to make a pretty darned good video.

In this chapter I used Movie Maker 2 to introduce you to the NLE process, starting with video capture and asset gathering, moving on to laying out your video in a Storyboard, and trimming it down to size in the Timeline.

As you likely noticed, none of these steps is all that difficult. Most are a mouse click-and-drag process.

From there you could simply output that video to a DV tape or a PC file. But I'm guessing you want to spice it up a bit with some special effects, transitions, titles, and extra audio. You'll tackle those topics in the next chapter.

CHAPTER 8

Jazzing Up Your Video with Windows Movie Maker 2

What You'll Learn in This Chapter:

▶ Adding video effects and transitions

▶ Working with titles

▶ Editing in extra audio

▶ Exploring some fun add-on packs

▶ Exporting to DV tape or PC file

In the previous chapter you created a cuts-only video. **Cuts-only** means you did not use any between-clip transitions such as dissolves, wipes, or sliding blocks. In addition, you did not apply any special effects to clips, such as giving them a sepia tone, putting them in slow motion, or fading them to black. You will add both types of features in this chapter.

You also will add text, be it an opening title, a **super** (to identify an interviewee), or closing credits. You'll edit in some extra audio (a narration or music), take a look at some add-on special-effects packs (some are free), and finally export your project to videotape or a file on your hard drive.

Adding Video Effects and Transitions

This is where budding video enthusiasts tend to go overboard—throwing transitions between every clip and sprinkling productions with video effects. The general rule is to use transitions and video effects with restraint.

I delve into the pitfalls of excess effects in upcoming chapters on Pinnacle Studio. For now, get to know the cool effects available for Movie Maker 2 (those that ship with it and those you can add on), and then think twice before using them.

Applying Transitions

Transitions smooth the change from one clip to the next or make it clear to your viewers that you are changing scenes or locations. Applying them in Movie Maker 2 is easy. Here's how they work:

1. Start Movie Maker and open your project by selecting File, Open Project, and then select your project and click Open.

2. Make sure you are in the Timeline view (you can add transitions in the Storyboard view but you can't change their length).

3. Select Transitions from the drop-down list at the top of the main toolbar (highlighted in Figure 8.1). Depending on your layout, that displays about a dozen transitions to the left of the Preview window. Use the scroll bar on the right side of the Transition window to view all the possibilities. There are 60 transitions in all.

FIGURE 8.1
With your project in the Timeline view, select Video Transitions from the highlighted drop-down list to display the transition icons.

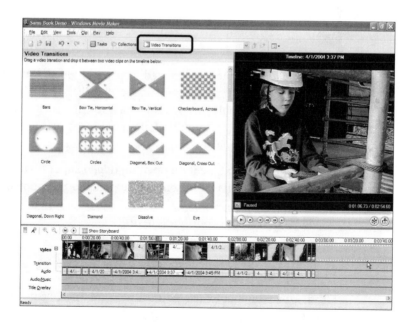

4. Click and drag a transition to the Timeline. As shown in Figure 8.2, note that a blue vertical line appears between clips. That line always appears

behind the clip to which you've dragged the transition. Release the mouse button and a transition box appears at that clip junction in the Transition track in the Timeline.

FIGURE 8.2
When you drag a transition to a clip on the Timeline, a vertical bar appears at the junction between the clip and the previous clip.

5. The CTI automatically should move to the clip before the transition. If not, move it there and play the transition. Depending on your choice of transition, it can look pretty wild. As shown in Figure 8.3, I chose the Star transition.

FIGURE 8.3
Play your transition to see how it works. This Star transition starts with a small star in the center of the screen and expands to reveal the next clip in the timeline.

6. Expand the Timeline view by clicking the plus (+) sign highlighted in Figure 8.4 until you can readily see the full width of the transition you just applied.

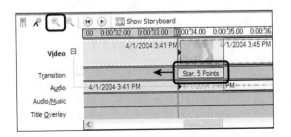

FIGURE 8.4
Expand your view of a transition in the Timeline by clicking the highlighted plus (+) sign. Lengthen the highlighted transition by dragging its left edge to the left.

7. Transitions, by default, are one second long. Lengthen yours by clicking the transition in the Transition track to select it, and then click and drag its left side to the left (Movie Maker does not let you drag it farther to the right).

8. Change to a different transition by dragging another transition to the same location on the Timeline. Movie Maker automatically replaces the old with the new.

By the Way

No Transition Audio Controls

When you view (and listen to) the transition, you might note that Movie Maker blends the audio from the two clips. You have virtually no control over the levels of the two clips. You can use the Audio Fade effect on each adjacent clip to fade one down and fade the next one in, but those effects happen very quickly and you have no control over their timing.

This is a real weakness of Movie Maker 2. Pinnacle Studio and other retail NLEs give you much more control over audio during transitions.

Give Your Clips Some Visual Special Effects

Movie Maker 2 ships with 28 video effects. You apply these to individual clips (in contrast to transitions, which go between clips).

Video effects fall into a few categories: Motion, Artistic, Fades, Hues, and Old Film. Again, judicial use is the order of the day.

Try it Yourself   **Using Video Effects**

Applying video effects requires only a simple drag and drop. You can apply up to six effects per clip, and you can access those effects in an easy-to-use menu window. Here's how it works:

1. Change your project view to Storyboard (you can apply effects in either Storyboard or Timeline, but Storyboard is more intuitive).

2. Select Video Effects from the drop-down list at the top of the main menu bar. Your interface should look like Figure 8.5.

3. Apply an effect to a clip by clicking the effect and dragging it to the clip's thumbnail image in the Storyboard. I suggest you use the Smudge Stick effect. As shown in Figure 8.6, it makes your video look like a soft chalk drawing. Note that adding an effect to a clip turns the gray star in the thumbnail blue.

FIGURE 8.5
Movie Maker 2 is set up to add video effects to your project.

FIGURE 8.6
Apply a video effect by dragging it to a clip. I applied Smudge Stick. Note that the highlighted star changes from gray to blue when you add an effect.

4. Drag the same effect to that clip again. In the case of Smudge Stick, the lines get thicker. You can apply the same effect up to six times to a clip. Note that two stars appear in the clip's thumbnail, indicating you have applied an effect more than once or more than one effect.

5. Remove that second effect by right-clicking the blue stars icon and selecting Video Effects. That opens the Add or Remove Video Effects window shown in Figure 8.7.

6. This is an intuitive means to edit effects. To remove the second effect, select that effect on the right side and click Remove. To add an effect, select it on the left side and click Add. When you're done working in this window, click OK.

FIGURE 8.7
Right-click a clip to open this nifty Add or Remove Effects window.

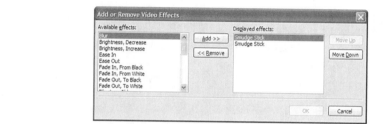

Try out some other effects, including these:

▶ **Change Clip Speed**—Do this in the Timeline view so you can see how changing clip speed alters the length of the clip. In the Timeline view, drag Slow Down, Half to a clip. Note that the clip doubles in length and a blue star appears in the clip on the Timeline. Remove that effect (right-click the blue star to open the Add or Remove Video Effects window) and add Speed Up, Double. That cuts a clip's length in half.

▶ **Fade In or Out**—Apply Fade In, From Black (or White) to the first clip in your project. That gives your project the professional look of starting black and fading up (in a half second—you can't change the fade-in time) to the first clip. Apply Fade Out, To Black to the last clip in your project. You can apply these effects at the end and beginning of adjacent clips for a nice transition.

▶ **Ease In or Out**—This zooms in or out of your clip for the duration of your clip. If you apply Ease Out, Movie Maker starts your clip zoomed in and gradually zooms out. Apply one of them more than once for a longer zoom. The more times you apply them, the longer the zoom.

Working with Titles

An opening title, a **super** used to identify an interviewee or location, and closing credits all add to your project's quality.

On one hand, Movie Maker 2 offers enough features to give you plenty of title creation options. But compared to retail NLEs, Movie Maker's Title tool is rudimentary at best. It does not let you position text on the screen, and you can't have multiple font colors or styles such as colored borders or drop shadows.

Create Titles

Try it Yourself

You do have some control. You can select a font from any you have on your PC; change its size; make it bold, italic, or underlined; give it any color you like; and animate it. Here's how:

1. Switch to the Title tool by selecting Tools, Titles and Credits. As shown in Figure 8.8, that displays something like a Title wizard.

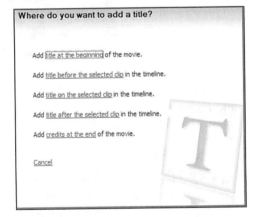

Where do you want to add a title?

Add title at the beginning of the movie.

Add title before the selected clip in the timeline.

Add title on the selected clip in the timeline.

Add title after the selected clip in the timeline.

Add credits at the end of the movie.

Cancel

FIGURE 8.8
Movie Maker 2 has something like a Title Wizard.

2. Your first choice is where to place this particular title (you can create as many titles as you want). In this case, select Add Title on the Selected Clip in the Timeline.

3. That opens the window shown in Figure 8.9. Type in some text and note that it does not appear over the clip you selected. Rather, it appears over a generic Windows landscape.

Only One Text Style Per Title

Movie Maker gives you two areas to add text. If you choose to add text in both boxes, you have fewer but distinctive text-animation options. But you cannot give those two sets of text different characteristics. If you want the top line to be red and underlined and the bottom line to be blue and bold, you're out of luck.

FIGURE 8.9
Add your text into one or both of these boxes. Using both gives you fewer but distinctive animation options.

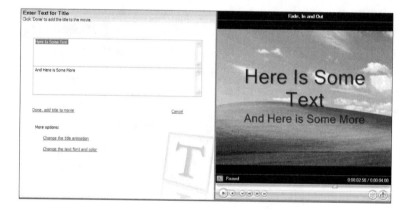

4. Click Change the Text Font and Color to open that window. Here you can change several things: the font (using a standard drop-down list); the text color; the size; whether it's bold, italic, or underlined; its transparency, and its justification: left, right, or centered. Make a few changes and see how they look in the Preview screen.

5. Click Change the Title Animation to open that screen. Here you have a plethora of options. I suggest you simply click through them one at a time and watch the animations play out in the Preview screen. Click the Play button if nothing happens when you switch animation styles. Figure 8.10 shows how the Scroll Perspective looks (it's reminiscent of the *Star Wars* opening text).

Background Color

If you choose an animation that has a background—News Banner, News Video, Wow!, or Sports Scoreboard—you can change that background color in the Change the Text Font and Color window. It's the small box next to the Text color icon. If you don't have a background, that box is gray and nothing happens if you click it.

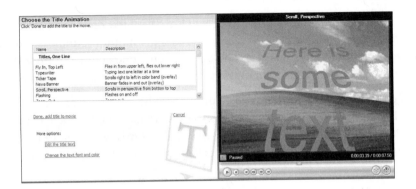

FIGURE 8.10
Movie Maker 2 has a full range of fun title animations. This Scroll Perspective animation is reminiscent of the opening scene in *Star Wars*.

6. When you're finished, click Done, Add Title to Movie. That adds a clip directly after the CTI line in the Title Overlay track of the Timeline (you cannot see titles in the Storyboard). You can drag that title clip anywhere in the project and change its length by dragging its ends. Changing its length also changes the duration and relative speed of any animations.

7. If you want to add an opening title, closing credits, or text between clips (they all appear over black unless you change the background color), click Tools, Titles and Credits, and select one of those options. As shown in Figure 8.11, Movie Maker lets you place credits over a video clip squeezed off to the left (or the top) of the screen. That does distort the image, but it's still a cool effect.

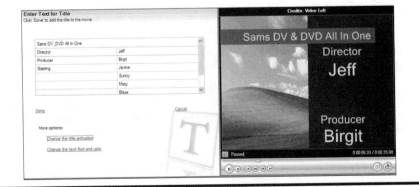

FIGURE 8.11
You can add rolling credits anywhere in your production, even having them display with your video off to one side.

Editing in Extra Audio

As I mentioned in the previous chapter, you have very few options when it comes to working with audio in Movie Maker 2. Besides the natural sound associated with your original videos, you can add audio to only one additional track. So if you want to add both narration and music, you have a tough row to hoe.

There are some clumsy workarounds, but my goal here is not to explain every possible way to work with Movie Maker. It's to introduce you to video editing on your PC using this freebie. After you've mastered it, I trust you'll move beyond Movie Maker to Pinnacle Studio. I start covering that product in the next chapter.

Try it Yourself   Adding Audio—Files or Narration

If you already have an audio file somewhere on your hard drive, adding that clip to your production takes not much more than a drag and a drop.

After you've added it to your Timeline, you can move that audio clip around, shorten it (you can't make it any longer than it already is), and fade it in or out. Making a narration is equally easy. Here's how you do both things:

1. To add an audio file, import that file into a collection and then drag and drop that clip on the Audio/Music track in the Timeline (you can't work with audio in the Storyboard).

Did you Know?   Using Audio Only from a Video Clip

If you want to add only the audio portion of a video clip to your project at a certain point, click that clip in the Collection window and drag it to the Audio/Music track.

2. You can adjust the overall volume of that specific clip (or any other audio clip) by right-clicking the clip and selecting Volume. That opens the Audio Clip Volume tool shown in Figure 8.12. This is an inexact science. You can't listen to the clip as you change the volume. Make your change, close the box (click the little X), listen to your clip, and if needed, reopen the Volume tool and make further adjustments.

FIGURE 8.12
The Audio Clip Volume tool lets you adjust the volume for any selected clip, but you can't listen to the clip as you make the changes.

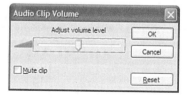

3. Split an audio clip in the same way you split a video clip. Position the CTI to where you want to make the split and click the Split Clip button in the Preview window. This comes in handy if you want to add a narration between musical interludes.

4. To avoid abrupt transitions between the music and the narration, add a Fade Out or Fade In to the audio clip by right-clicking it and selecting Fade In or Out (or both).

5. To add a narration, select Tools, Narrate Timeline. In the Narrate Timeline interface click Show More Options to display all the extra features shown in Figure 8.13.

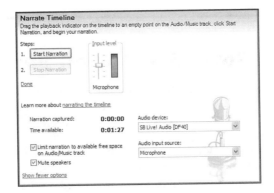

FIGURE 8.13
The Narrate Timeline interface has some helpful options to ensure that you won't cover up existing audio and that you avoid screeching audio feedback.

6. Position the CTI where you want your narration to begin. If you've added audio files to the Audio/Music track, it's best if you click the Limit Narration to Available Free Space check box. In addition, check Mute Speakers to avoid the screeching feedback that occurs when a mic is too close to the speakers.

7. Check your audio volume using the little Input Level meter. If you're in the red zone, lower the level.

8. Click Start Narration and do just that. You'll notice that if you checked Limit Narration, the Time Available lets you know how much time you have until recording stops.

9. Click Stop Narration. A Save Windows Media File window opens. Navigate to the file folder you want to use, give your narration a name, and click Save. The clip now appears on the Timeline at the CTI. Give it a listen.

10. Finally, you can adjust the overall volume balance between the two audio tracks. This is kind of a kludge because few projects lend themselves to this kind of global command. However, to do this select Tools, Audio Levels (or

click the little Audio Levels icon in the upper-left corner of the Timeline). That opens the Audio Levels tool shown in Figure 8.14. Make your adjustment, close the tool, listen to your project and, if needed, go back and adjust further.

Exploring Some Fun Add-on Packs

Movie Maker 2 has spawned something of a cottage industry in add-ons. They range from basic assets—sound effects, music, and title backgrounds (static and video)—to high-end, very cool video effects and transitions.

Microsoft offers three free Fun Pack downloads and one retail CD that include Movie Maker 2 material. SoundDogs.com has four sound-effect and music files available for free download as well as many retail audio collections that you can use with any nonlinear video editor. And Pixelan Software has several retail collections of some very nifty Movie Maker toys.

Microsoft Fun Packs

Surprisingly, Microsoft does not provide a link to the Movie Maker 2 Fun Packs on its main Movie Maker web site. Instead, you'll find them at the PowerToys and Add-ins web site: www.microsoft.com/windowsxp/downloads/powertoys/default.mspx.

Scroll down the page to locate the three Fun Packs:

- **Creativity Fun Pack** (creativity_mmfull.exe—25MB—April 2003): www.microsoft.com/windowsxp/downloads/powertoys/mmcreate.mspx.

- **Winter Fun Pack** (mm2funpack.exe—14MB—December 2002): www.microsoft.com/windowsxp/downloads/powertoys/mmholiday.mspx.

- **Winter Fun Pack 2003** (WinterWMM2Pack.msi—15MB—November 2003): www.microsoft.com/windowsxp/downloads/powertoys/mmfunpack.mspx.

Creativity Fun Pack

This has four mini-fun packs: one for Movie Maker and three others for digital photography, Windows Media Player, and PowerToys for Windows XP.

The Movie Maker fun pack gives you an extra set of title backgrounds (video and static) plus some sound effects and music from SoundDogs.com, a major provider of film and video production music and sound effects.

Did you Know?

> ### SoundDogs Has More Movie Maker 2 Audio
>
> Visit www.sounddogs.com/htm/mm2.htm to download four free collections of sound effects, looped music tracks (audio files you can place end to end to create a seamless tune of any length), and production music. This website is not accessible from the SoundDogs.com home page.

After installation, access the Creativity Fun Pack items from Movie Maker 2 by selecting File, Import into Collections and then navigating to My Documents/My Videos/Creativity Fun Packs. You'll see four collections: Music Tracks and Music Transitions, Sound Effects, Static Titles, and Video Titles and End Credits.

Music Tracks are orchestral tunes or brief snippets you can use as transitions. The 54 sound effects cover a lot of possibilities. The Static Titles are very basic. You can use a simple graphics or greeting card program and come up with better stuff. The Video Titles are kind of cool, but there's not much call for countdowns like the one shown in Figure 8.15.

FIGURE 8.15
The Creativity Fun Pack has a few useful goodies, but you probably won't get much use out of video countdowns like this one.

Winter Fun Pack (2002)

Like the Creativity Fun Pack, this, too, is four packs in one. SoundDogs.com provided 48 seasonal sound effects and 8 holiday songs (including *Jingle Bells* and *Silent Night*). In addition, you get a dozen graphical backgrounds, as shown in Figure 8.16.

FIGURE 8.16
The Winter Fun Pack (2002) includes these 12 full-screen holiday graphics.

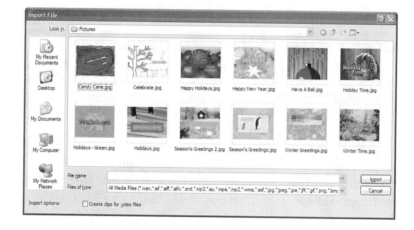

The seven videos included in this Fun Pack are much more useful than those in the Creativity Fun Pack. They can serve as great opening or closing greetings for your holiday video cards.

Winter Fun Pack 2003

In addition to a larger-than-usual collection of assets, Microsoft upped the ante with the Winter Fun Pack 2003 by adding three Movie Maker plug-ins: two transitions and a video effect.

By the Way

What Are Plug-ins?

Plug-ins are mini programs that work within a program. In the case of Movie Maker plug-ins, they generally are video effects or transitions. The three plug-ins provided with the Winter Fun Pack 2003 are all from Pixelan Software. I cover their retail Movie Maker plug-ins later in this section.

Again, this Fun Pack includes four mini fun packs. The Movie Maker portion (you'll find it under My Documents/Movies/My Videos/Windows XP Fun Pack/Winter 2003) has 10 static graphics for use as backgrounds, 8 videos (but 6 are included in the Winter 2002 Fun Pack), and a ton of sound effects—92 in all!

The exceptional items are the two transitions and the video effect. To see them you need to close and then reopen Movie Maker 2 after installing the Winter Fun Pack 2003.

Open the Video Effects Collection and check out the newly added Snowflake effect (see Figure 8.17).

FIGURE 8.17
This is the only Fun Pack with a video effect. Snowflake animates a lovely snow storm over your video.

Now switch to the Transitions Collection and track down the two new entries: Snow Burst and Snow Wipe. Figure 8.18 gives you an idea of how Snow Burst looks.

Microsoft Plus! Digital Media Edition

This huge collection of goodies is available from Microsoft on CD only for $20.
Visit www.microsoft.com/windows/plus/dme/dmehome.asp to learn more about it.

Whereas Winter Fun Pack 2003 gave you a taste of what a few extra video effects
and transitions can do, consider that Plus! DME has 50 such goodies.

Take a look at Figure 8.19. That's a sampling of the 25 video effects that ship with
Plus! DME. All are from Pixelan Software, the company I feature next.

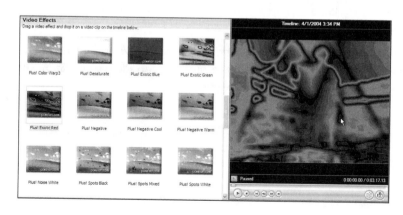

Same story for the Plus! DME Movie Maker 2 Transitions. It has 25 unique and exciting ways to move from one clip to the next. In Figure 8.20, I featured the snazzy Fire Iris transition.

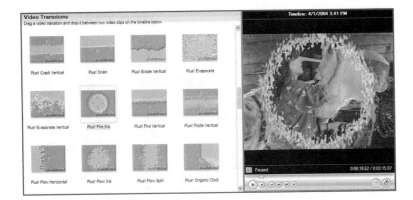

FIGURE 8.20
The Plus! DME transitions give you some wild ways to ease from one clip to the next. Fire Iris looks like a growing circle of flames.

Pixelan SpiceFX

It was after swapping emails with Pixelan Software's president Michael Feerer that the huge popularity of Movie Maker 2 became fully evident. He said, "We did our SpiceFX add-ons as more or less just a fun project to do with our NW neighbors Microsoft, but those add-ons have turned into a major part of our business."

Visit www.pixelan.com/mm/intro.htm (see Figure 8.21) to get a sense of just how major those add-ons have become. As we went to press, Pixelan offered 8 packs with more than 350 transitions and effects (more than 400 if you buy the entire collection at once).

Many of the transitions let you do something that's usually available only with NLEs that have more than one video track: create a Picture-in-Picture. I demonstrated that in Figure 8.22.

If you plan to do more than simply rudimentary work with Movie Maker 2, it's worth your while to check out the Pixelan Software SpiceFX packs. You can download a demo that lets you use some of the goodies, but each will have the Pixelan logo in them.

FIGURE 8.21
The Pixelan
SpiceFX website
lets you see all the
transitions and
effects in each
package.

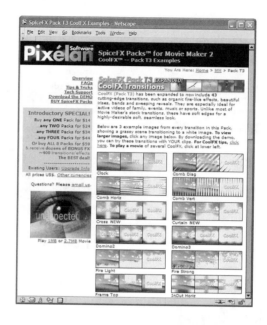

FIGURE 8.22
Pixelan Software's
SpiceFX packs offer
more than 400
video effects and
transitions like this
Picture-in-Picture (I
added a border
around the PiP for
emphasis).

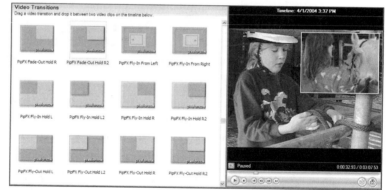

Exporting to DV Tape or PC File

After you add the finishing touches, it's time to export your project. Movie Maker
gives you five output choices, but when you cut through the verbiage, it comes
down to two basic choices: videotape or file.

Export Your Project to a File

You can access the export options via the Task List or the main menu. In this case you'll use the menu. Let's get started:

1. Save your project by selecting File, Save Project.

2. Start the export process by selecting File, Save Movie File (yes, this is an awkwardly named command). That opens the Save Movie Wizard shown in Figure 8.23.

FIGURE 8.23
Use the Save Movie Wizard to export your video project to a PC file or to DV videotape.

3. The Save Movie Wizard gives you five options. Four create WMV (Windows Media Video) files. The fifth—DV Camera—exports directly to your camcorder. In this case, select My Computer and click Next.

Other Export Options

The first four options create WMV files but do some hand-holding along the way. If you choose Recordable CD, Movie Maker first checks that a recordable CD is in the drive and ready to record. Choosing E-mail automatically creates a low bit-rate file (you have no control over its compression rate). The Web takes you to the same settings window you work with when you select My Computer or Recordable CD.

By the Way

4. Give your video a name and the hard drive file folder storage location and click Next. That opens the Movie Setting window shown in Figure 8.24.

FIGURE 8.24
Use this window to
select a quality—or
video compres-
sion—setting.

5. Here's where you choose your output quality. WMV files come in many compression modes. The more compression, the lower the video and audio quality. Click Other Settings; then select a setting from the drop-down list to suit your needs. I chose High Quality Video (Large). You also can select Best Fit to File Size, select a file size (you might want to fit the video file on a 650MB CD) and Movie Maker will set a compression to match your choice. Click Next.

6. That will start the **rendering** process. This takes those file pointers and other data I referred to earlier and uses them to create an actual video file. Depending on the speed of your PC and the number of transitions and video effects, the rendering process can take several times as long as the actual length of your finished video.

7. When rendering is completed, Movie Maker asks you if you want to see your video.

Export Your Project to a DV Videotape

This method has fewer options but still goes through the same rendering process. Here's how it works:

1. Connect your DV camcorder to your PC via the FireWire. Using AC power, turn your camcorder on and switch it to VCR (or VTR—not Camera).

2. Select File, Save Movie File. In the Movie Location window select DV Camera and click Next.

3. As shown in Figure 8.25, Movie Maker will note that it has detected your camcorder and then tells you to cue the tape up to where you want to start recording your finished video. You need to use the controls on the camcorder to do that.

FIGURE 8.25
Making a DV recording of your project is a straightforward process.

4. Click Next. Movie Maker warns you that it will overwrite anything on your DV tape. Click Yes if that's okay.

5. As it did when it created a file, Movie Maker first will render your project—in this case as a DV-AVI file. This too will take a while, about the same time it took to create the file in the previous Try It Yourself task, because a DV-AVI file is larger than a WMV file but requires no processor-intensive compression.

6. After the project is rendered, Movie Maker will automatically record the finished video project to your DV camcorder. When it completes, you simply close the wizard.

Summary

Movie Maker has a solid collection of video effects and transitions. You add them to your project by dragging them to a clip or to a juncture between two clips. You can adjust the length of a transition but cannot change how a video effect works.

What you can do with video effects is use them up to six times on a clip. In that way you can zoom in farther, for example.

Movie Maker's Title tool has its limitations but is flexible enough to satisfy the expectations of an entry-level video editor. Especially cool are the fun animations.

Audio editing is Movie Maker's biggest weakness. With only one spare audio track, you have to take some extra care when adding both music and a narration. You can not have both playing at the same time.

Movie Maker's popularity has spawned a cottage industry for add-ons. Two companies in particular—SoundDogs.com and Pixelan Software—have produced products that are worth checking out. Microsoft's free Fun Packs have a few cool goodies.

Finally, Movie Maker gives you two output options: DV videotape or a WMV (Windows Media Video) file. WMV files come in many flavors to suit your display needs. In either case, output or export is easy, but rendering the video can take a while.

CHAPTER 9

Capturing Video with Pinnacle Studio Plus

What You'll Learn in This Chapter:

▶ Video editing: from engineers to artists

▶ Getting acquainted with Pinnacle Studio Plus

▶ Looking over the Studio Plus user interface

▶ Checking out Pinnacle Systems' video capture hardware

▶ Capturing digital or analog video and still images

Video editing has come a long way from massive tape machines operated only by engineers to today's desktop PCs offering anyone an opportunity to enjoy the art of video editing. In this chapter I give you a brief history.

Then it's on to Pinnacle Studio Plus, my pick as the best all-around entry- to intermediate-level NLE. At first glance it might not look all that different from Windows Movie Maker 2, but after you check under the hood, you'll be amazed at all the cool things you can do with Studio Plus.

In this chapter we'll revisit a topic I introduced in the Movie Maker chapters: video capture. I expand on the Movie Maker tasks by going over analog video capture and grabbing still images.

I cover other editing topics, such as Studio's SmartMovie automated editing tool, cuts-only editing, transitions, and effects in the next few chapters.

Video Editing: From Engineers to Artists

Pinnacle Studio and other nonlinear editors have opened new opportunities. Anyone with a PC, even a laptop, now can do broadcast-quality video editing. What was once reserved for high-end video production studios and well-equipped TV stations has reached the mass market (at least for those willing to spend $600 and up for a DV camcorder and NLE software).

Old-Fashioned Editing

To gain some perspective on the video-editing process, a little history is in order. In the early days of TV, engineers did the editing. They had to. They were trained to deal with unruly, bulky, and complex tape machines. They had to monitor things such as color framing, sync timing, and blanking.

Here's how John Crossman, a long-time editor and friend of mine, puts it (see "Video-Editing Tips from an Expert—John Crossman" in Chapter 6, "Story-Creation and Video-Production Tips"):

> *The logic was that the same people who pushed the "record" and "playback" buttons in the tape room should be the ones to run the editing machines. Videotape editing then was considered a very technical job, not an artistic job.*

Microprocessors eventually resolved and automated many of those technical issues, and nonengineering people—folks with an eye for editing—started populating the editing bays. However, prohibitive costs limited access to those machines.

As recently as a few years ago, whenever I created a video that called for some special transitions or video effects, I worked **offline**; that is, I used low-resolution copies of my original master tapes on a lower-priced editing system to create an edit decision list (EDL). Figure 9.1 shows one example.

By the Way

EDLs—On Their Way Out

Studio Plus has something like an EDL option, but I doubt that you'll use it. I'll point it out later just as a point of reference and to give you an idea of how Studio Plus keeps track of edits.

Not only is working with EDLs more or less a thing of the past, the standard EDL format is losing favor with those few editors who use EDLs. Its biggest drawbacks are that EDLs are text-only and have limited transition and effect options.

These days, those editors who use EDLs typically turn to professional NLEs such as Adobe Premiere Pro that use an emerging cross-platform EDL technology called AAF—Advanced Authoring Format. AAF resolves those two drawbacks and offers additional features.

There's even an AAF Association (www.aafassociation.org). Here's their description of their technology: "AAF is a multimedia file format that enables content creators to easily exchange digital media and metadata across platforms, and between systems and applications. The AAF simplifies project management, saves time, and preserves valuable metadata that was often lost when transferring media between applications in the past."

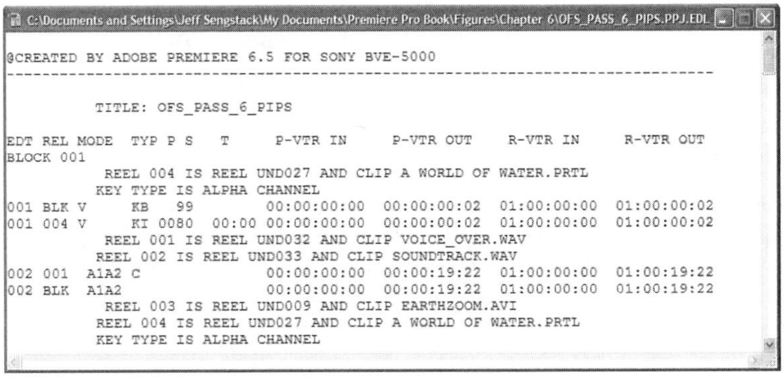

FIGURE 9.1
An EDL created for a Sony editing machine.

Then I took my original raw footage and that EDL data file, with all the transition commands built in, to an expensive online facility that could handle the high data throughput necessary to do special video effects and transitions. That production studio automatically (with some manual labor) cranked out a polished product. That process, although more time-consuming than working online from start to finish, saved a ton of money.

Today the pendulum has swung to the opposite extreme, and you're riding that pendulum. Anyone can work solely **online**—that is, use the *original* video footage from start to finish and incorporate any number of exciting special effects and transitions. No longer do video producers need to rely on high-priced production houses. Heck, now you can do it at home. The purpose is to do it well, and that starts with getting to know your NLE.

Getting Acquainted with Pinnacle Studio Plus

Pinnacle Studio Plus is the latest iteration of the world's top-selling video editor. This success is not a fluke. Its popularity is justified.

Because you've worked with Movie Maker, I think you'll appreciate what Studio Plus has to offer:

> ▶ **Video Capture**—Four automated clip-creation and scene-detection modes, as well as true 16:9, widescreen support.

▶ **Video Overlay Track**—Gives you the option to create picture-in-picture effects and blend two clips using a chroma key (just as TV stations do with weathercasters).

▶ **Apply Motion to Still Images**—You can zoom in, zoom out, and move still images. Ken Burns did this so much in his various PBS series that many editors now refer to this as the "Ken Burns Effect."

▶ **Transitions**—More than 200 transitions (16 in 3D) versus 60 for Movie Maker.

▶ **Video Effects**—Twenty effects, from Slow Motion and a Strobe stop action style to giving your video the look of an old film or stained glass. Most have customizable parameters that let you adjust the effect's look or actions. In addition, Studio Plus comes with very useful color correction, video noise reduction, and image stabilization effects.

▶ **Audio**—Four audio tracks (versus two in Movie Maker), flexible audio editing, powerful audio effects (hiss/noise reduction, equalization, and reverb), precise volume control, stereo panning, surround-sound editing, a built-in CD ripper, and a SmartSound music creation module.

▶ **Titling**—There is no limit to what you can create with Studio's version of Pinnacle Systems' TitleDeko professional titler. The dozens of included styles, plus whatever custom "looks" you create, will fill all your text and graphics needs.

▶ **Output**—Multiple output modes: DV (4:3 and 16:9 aspect ratios), analog video, RealVideo, and MPEG.

▶ **DVD Authoring and DVD Burning**—A solid, feature-packed DVD-authoring module that lets you record a DVD with menus and other features that can play in your living room DVD player.

▶ **SmartMovie**—This is an automated video editor that takes a few user-selected parameters and whips out a music video in minutes. What makes this work well is that you can fine-tune those edits later.

▶ **Plug-ins and Add-ons**—Pinnacle updated Studio Plus version 9 with what's called **open plug-in architecture**. That means Pinnacle and third-party providers can program tons of exciting and useful audio and video effects and transitions. As we went to press, Pinnacle offered packages with about 1,000 such add-ons.

Studio Plus Pricing and Packages

Pinnacle Systems is marketing Studio Plus as an advanced version. I strongly recommend that you purchase Studio Plus rather than its slightly older (and $20 less expensive) sibling. Studio Plus offers an additional video track for picture-in-picture and other cool effects, lets you put images in motion (a la Ken Burns), and has a so-called **chroma key** (or **green screen**) effect that lets you turn any solid color transparent.

Upcoming Tasks Work for Both Products

In this and the next few chapters, I will take you through tasks to help you get up to speed in Studio and Studio Plus. Virtually all the tasks apply to both products. Only when I discuss two-track editing, picture-in-picture, chroma keys, and putting still clips in motion will that apply only to Studio Plus.

By the Way

Rather than go through all the various packages offered by Pinnacle for both products, I will focus only on Studio Plus. It comes in three basic flavors: with or without video capture hardware or in a bundle with several other media editing products. Sans hardware, the list price for Studio Plus is $99 (you can buy it online at several outlets for about $75).

Pinnacle also offers Studio Plus bundled with one of two Pinnacle Systems video capture hardware solutions (I cover these products in the section "Checking Out Pinnacle Systems Video Capture Hardware" later in this chapter).

If you buy Studio Plus with a capture card or break-out box, you also receive Hollywood FX Plus (a $50 value): 300 video effects and transitions (I go over HFX Plus and several other add-on packs in Chapter 13, "Advanced Editing Techniques, Add-Ons, and Exporting"). The video capture hardware and Hollywood FX Plus bundle adds between $100 and $150 to the price.

Finally, Pinnacle packages Studio Plus in a full suite of media editing and DVD creation tools called Studio MediaSuite ($129). To get a clearer picture of all the packages, visit www.pinnaclesys.com/studioplus.

Try Out Studio Plus for Free

You can download a trial version. When you get to the Studio web page, look for a link to Try It Now! There you can download the 214MB file. After installation, the trial version of Studio Plus will be fully functional for 30 days.

There are only two differences between the trial version and the full retail version:

▶ The trial version displays only in 1024×768 resolution. The retail version also offers 800×600.

▶ The trial version has only 3 SmartSound QuickTracks tunes versus 25 in the retail version.

Looking Over the Studio Plus User Interface

Installing the retail version of Studio Plus is a two-step process:

1. Insert the software CD, install it, and restart your PC.

2. Upon restarting, a little screen will pop up telling you to put in the other disk—Bonus Content DVD.

Go ahead and install this DVD. The upside is that it adds a bunch of extras such as transitions and DVD menus. But it also loads your hard drive with all sorts of cool, fun stuff, none of which will work unless you buy **unlocking keys** online. The entire Studio install consumes an incredible 3.7GB!

I cover that extra content and a passel of other great add-ons and plug-ins in Chapter 13.

Fire It Up

When you start Studio Plus for the first time, it asks you if you want to take a guided tour (see Figure 9.2). Even though I'm about to give you just such a tour, you might as well try Pinnacle's. Click Don't Ask Me Again if you want to avoid seeing this splash screen over and over.

View Guided Tour Later

By the Way

In previous versions of Studio Plus, you could always access the Guided Tour by selecting Help, Take Guided Tour. That option was not available in my copy of Studio Plus.

If that's true for your copy as well, all is not lost. Open My Computer, navigate to `C:\Program Files\Pinnacle\Studio 9` (or wherever you installed Studio Plus), open the Guided Tour folder, and double-click Tutorial.exe.

As you proceed on the tour, you'll note a lot of similarities to Movie Maker. As shown in Figure 9.3, Studio's Storyboard looks similar to Movie Maker's but has the added feature of more screen real estate: three parallel Storyboard placeholder tracks instead of only one.

Make the Update and Register for Free Stuff

Upon completing the tour, reopen Studio Plus. Depending on when you purchased your product, you might get the prompt shown in Figure 9.4 that lets you know about an update. This is an essential upgrade because it repairs a bunch of bugs that irritated a whole lot of users. If you don't see this window, you probably have version 9.1.x or later (Studio Plus was known to beta testers as version 9.3) and you're set. To check your version, select Help, About Pinnacle Studio. If it's 9.0, go to www.pinnaclesys.com and track down the upgrade.

FIGURE 9.2
Take the tour. It's worth your time.

FIGURE 9.3
You'll travel through some familiar territory during your tour. Studio Plus uses the same Storyboard approach you worked on in Movie Maker.

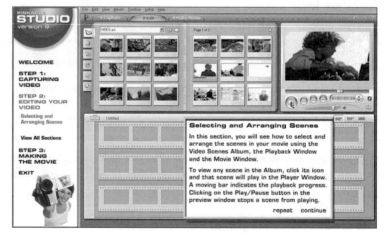

If you need to download the 46MB update, Pinnacle will get your registration information along the way. In any event, there is a registration incentive: 16 free Hollywood FX Transitions. Simply go through the registration process (no need to answer all the probing marketing questions), download the file, close Studio Plus, navigate to the downloaded HFX file on your hard drive, and double-click to install this extra content.

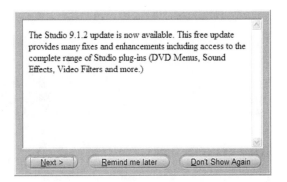

The Studio 9.1.2 update is now available. This free update provides many fixes and enhancements including access to the complete range of Studio plug-ins (DVD Menus, Sound Effects, Video Filters and more.)

Next >   Remind me later   Don't Show Again

FIGURE 9.4
If you don't have version 9.1 or later, upon opening Studio Plus for the first time, you'll see this prompt to download the update.

Unlock Strobe and Speed

When you get to the update site, you'll see more than one file you can download. In addition to the Studio 9.1.x patch, download the Unlock Strobe and Speed zipped file, unzip it, and double-click it to make those two effects available to you.

By the Way

Fire It Up Again

Now you're really ready to go. Double-click the Studio Plus icon. Studio Plus opens with a sample video project ready to edit. The thumbnail images represent clips from the photo shoot for the retail box and starting splash screen.

Take a look around the interface. In Figure 9.5 I've noted the three principal workspaces: Album, Player, and Movie Window.

The Album

Start with the Album and its collection of tabs shown in Figure 9.6. These give you access to assets, transitions, and effects.

I cover each of these features in more detail later in this and subsequent chapters. For now, just click through the following tabs to get an idea of what's available:

▶ **Videos**—The top tab displays thumbnail images of video clips you've selected for a video project. This is where you'll access your own video clips a bit later.

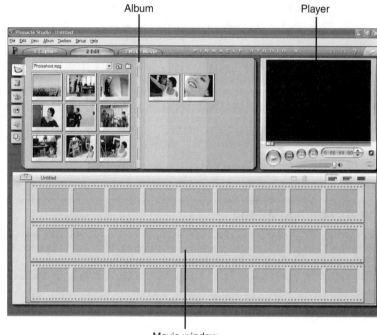

Album   Player

Movie window

FIGURE 9.5
Studio Plus opens with a sample project loaded up and ready to edit. I've pointed out the three main work areas.

FIGURE 9.6
The tabs open pages in Studio's Album.

Videos
Transitions
Titles
Still Images
Sound Files
DVD menus

By the Way

Play a Clip

If you click a thumbnail, it pops up in the TV preview monitor (Pinnacle calls it the **Player**) on the upper-right side of the screen. Use the VCR controls at the bottom of the Player window to play the clip. When it reaches the end of the clip, it moves seamlessly to the next clip in the Album window (each collection of videos in any single Album window is actually one long clip divided automatically by Studio Plus into smaller clips based on scene changes). Note that clicking the Play button switches it to a Pause button. Click Pause to stop the video playback.

▶ **Transitions**—This tab displays a collection of transitions you can use to move from one scene to another. Studio Plus offers more than 200 transitions plus demos of dozens more (the number of demos depends on whether you installed the extra-content DVD).

Try Some Transitions—Unlocked and Locked

Try it Yourself
▼

Take this opportunity to check out some transitions. The process is simple but there is a little extra feature about how to unlock some effects. I show you both **unlocked** and **locked** effects in this task. Here's how to do it:

1. Depending on whether you installed any extra content, you might have many transition groups from which to choose. At this point, only the first three—Standard Transitions, Alpha Magic, and Hollywood FX for Studio (and HFX Extra FX if you registered your product and downloaded those transitions)—should be unlocked. Select Standard Transitions.

2. Click a transition. As shown in Figure 9.7, when you click a transition, Studio Plus gives a little demo of how it works in the Player window TV monitor. I selected Push Up. In this case, the "B" scene (the next scene in the project) would push the preceding "A" scene up and off the top of the screen.

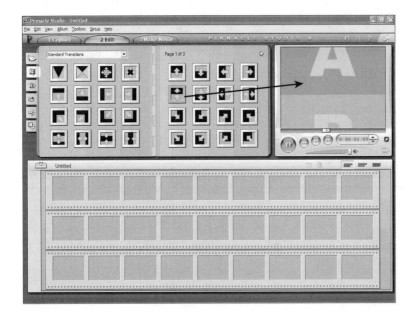

FIGURE 9.7
Studio Plus displays a preview of a transition in the monitor, or player screen.

▼

3. Select any of the HFX groups (they're all locked). I chose HFX Complex Shapes (it has some really wild transitions). As shown in Figure 9.8, they all have little lock icons and the page on the right has a link that states Click Here to Unlock.

FIGURE 9.8
All the HFX transition groups are *locked*. Each transition thumbnail has a padlock icon and the display in the Player window has a Pinnacle Systems watermark.

4. You can click Click Here to Unlock. I would suggest waiting until Chapter 13 to do that. Just so you know, if you do click it, Studio will open a browser window like that shown in Figure 9.9. There you can buy that one set of transitions (or audio clips, title styles, DVD menus, or video effects). Before plunking down your credit card number, Pinnacle's E-Shop will offer up many more packs with substantial discounts for quantity purchases.

FIGURE 9.9
To unlock any of the dozens of add-ons and plug-ins for Studio Plus that installed via the Content DVD, you need to access Pinnacle's E-Store via Studio's Album pages.

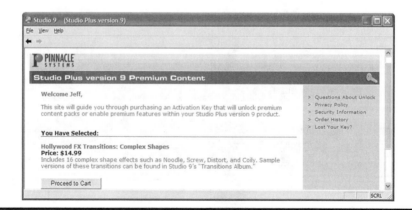

▶ Titles—This opens a collection of **templates**: 26 helpful tools that simplify adding text to your video. As shown in Figure 9.10, when you click one, it shows up in the TV monitor window.

FIGURE 9.10
The title page offers 26 templates that you can alter to fit your project.

To see Studio's title editor—or character generator—drag a template to the Storyboard—Movie Window—and double-click it. That opens Studio's version of Pinnacle's professional TitleDeko (shown in Figure 9.11). TitleDeko has a lengthy and impressive pedigree with roots in broadcast TV character generation. The version included with Studio Plus has 40 preset type styles, each with an additional selection of colors for each style (hover your cursor over a style to see those extra versions). It also comes with 66 graphical backgrounds (click the little cactus/desert scene icon to see them) and dozens of buttons (click the doorbell icon) that you can use in your videos or for DVD menus. As you can see, there's a lot to Studio's version of TitleDeko. I cover it in Chapter 11, "Enhancing Your Video with Transitions, Effects, and Titles."

FIGURE 9.11
Studio's Title Editor (a subset of Pinnacle's professional TitleDeko), is loaded with presets and features.

- ▶ **Photos and Frame Grabs**—Studio DV displays two images that come with the program. You access your still images via this tab.

- ▶ **Audio Files**—Studio Plus fills this Album page with its own collection of sound effects, but you can add narration, music files, and other sound effects here for use in your project. Check out a few sound effects by double-clicking them.

- ▶ **DVD Menus**—Studio Plus has a solid DVD-authoring module. As part of that package, it ships with enough DVD menu templates to fill most of your needs as you become more proficient in DVD authoring.

The Movie Window—Storyboard or Timeline

Now check out the Movie Window, which is the filmstrip-like interface at the bottom of the screen. This is where you piece together a rough cut of your video. You'll start doing that in the next chapter. For now, though, note the three icons in the upper-right corner of the Movie Window (see Figure 9.12).

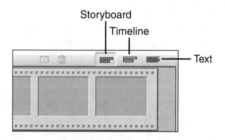

FIGURE 9.12
These icons access three Movie Window editing interfaces: Storyboard, Timeline, and Text.

The default view is the filmstrip-like Storyboard. As I mentioned in the Movie Maker chapters, for first-time video editors, this can be an intuitive way to approach editing.

Roll your cursor over the middle icon, and note that the pop-up ToolTip tells you it's for the Timeline view. Click it to switch the Movie Window's editing section to the Timeline view shown in Figure 9.13.

Did you Know?

Turn ToolTips On or Off

If you hover your cursor over a button or icon and nothing happens, ToolTips is turned off. ToolTips are those little messages that appear when you roll your cursor over a screen object. To switch them on or off, select Help, Display ToolTips.

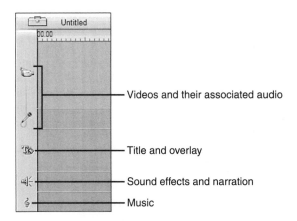

Videos and their associated audio

Title and overlay

Sound effects and narration

Music

FIGURE 9.13
The Studio Plus Timeline view with each track identified.

Look at the left side of the Timeline view and note that, at first glance, Studio Plus has one more track than Movie Maker (it actually has three more tracks—one additional video and two more audio tracks—more on that in a moment).

The icons that identify each track's function should make sense in light of your experience with Movie Maker. In Figure 9.11, I annotated each one. Despite the different audio icons, you can put any kind of audio in any of the audio tracks.

New to Studio Plus: An Overlay Video Track!

For years my main complaint about various iterations of Studio was that it didn't have a second video/audio track. Missing that extra **overlay** track meant there was no easy way to do a picture-in-picture effect as well as other effects that combine two video clips. Other NLEs, most notably Ulead VideoStudio 8, offer that option and for some video editors that extra feature was enough to eschew Studio.

Checking Out Studio's New Overlay Video Track

Try it Yourself

Pinnacle fixed that one drawback in Studio Plus, an update released in September 2004. Pinnacle chose to make that change in a subtle and user-friendly way. Developers hid the second video/audio track, revealing it only if a video editor chooses to use it. To see that Overlay Track, do one of two things (you have to have Studio Plus to see this):

1. Right-click in the Timeline view (on any nonaudio track) and select Always Show Overlay Track. That adds the second Overlay Track shown in Figure 9.14.

Feel Free to Experiment a Bit

You will work extensively with the Timeline in coming chapters, but if you want to experiment now, that's fine. Drag a video clip to that Overlay Track and click Play in the Player window. Now drag another clip to the main video track (the top track) directly above the clip you placed in the Overlay Track. Click Play again and note that only the clip in the Overlay Track is visible. It covers the clip in the main video track. I show you how to reveal that covered clip using the picture-in-picture effect as well as other two-layer effects in Chapter 13.

FIGURE 9.14
The Studio Plus Timeline view with the Overlay Track switched on and highlighted.

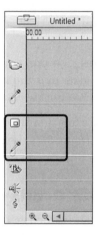

2. For now, hide the Overlay Track by right-clicking in the Timeline view again and deselecting (unchecking) Always Show Overlay Track. If you added clips to that track, remove them first—that will hide the track as well.

3. Here's the other way to open that hidden Overlay Track: Drag a video clip from the Album to the Title Track. That automatically opens the Overlay Track and places that clip on the Overlay Track, not the Title Track.

Title Track's New Functionality

In previous versions of Studio, you could use the Title Track to overlay graphics but not video (Pinnacle used to call it the Title *Overlay* Track). If the graphic had a solid color background, Studio would automatically make that color transparent and show only the graphic—a logo for example—over the video.

Now, if you put a graphic with a solid color background on the Overlay Track, Studio Plus will *not* automatically remove that color. That is a good thing. You might want to keep that color. Or you might want to use a more precise method to remove it, called **chroma keying**. Studio Plus has an excellent Chroma Key video effect to do just that.

In the meantime, you still can put a graphic in the Title Track and Studio Plus will automatically remove the background color.

Finally, open the Movie window's Text view by clicking its icon on the far upper-right side of the Movie Window. As shown in Figure 9.15, this displays something like an Edit Decision List, EDL, that I mentioned earlier in this chapter.

This is not a true EDL in that you can't save it as a text file and use it in a production facility to automate editing. It's simply a way for you to see how Studio Plus keeps track of your work.

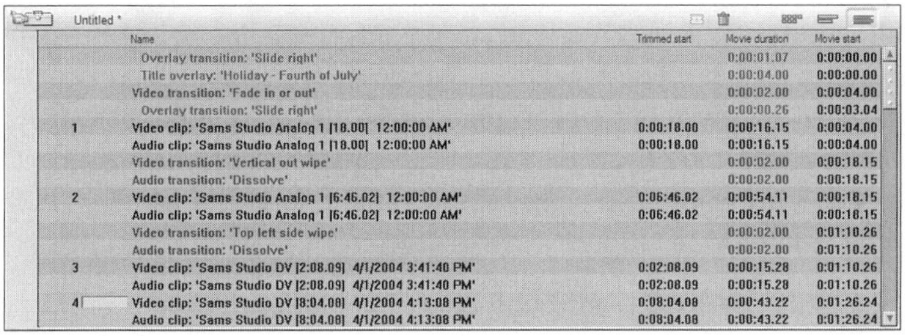

FIGURE 9.15
The Text view lets you see how Studio Plus tracks clips, transitions, effects, and titles.

Checking Out Pinnacle Systems Video Capture Hardware

Before you open the Capture interface, I want to go over your choices in analog video capture hardware.

One of the very powerful competitive advantages that Pinnacle Systems brings to the DV market is its own analog video capture hardware. The company offers two basic types—external break-out boxes that connect to your PC via FireWire or USB cables or an internal PCI card with a break-out box. Each is an excellent solution for those who need to import analog video.

There is a handful of other video capture card options out there. The primary players are Pyro, Canopus, and Matrox. I won't go over any of those companies' offerings because two of Pinnacle's hardware products come bundled with Studio Plus. But if you want to check out what's available, a good place to start is Videoguys.com at www.videoguys.com/vidcap.htm.

Two Video Capture Options

Figure 9.16 shows the two analog video capture hardware options available from Pinnacle Systems: Studio MovieBox and Studio AV/DV.

FIGURE 9.16
Pinnacle Systems' two analog video capture hardware options that ship with Studio Plus are Studio MovieBox (left) and Studio AV/DV (right).

Studio MovieBox Deluxe   Studio AV/DV

MovieBox comes in two versions: USB or FireWire. In both cases you do not need to install an internal video card. You simply attach the MovieBox break-out box to your PC via a USB or FireWire cable. Windows XP recognizes the MovieBox as a digital video device. You then can plug an S-Video or Composite Video cable to it (as well as audio cables), click a button to tell MovieBox which connector to activate, and start your video capture using Studio Plus or any other NLE that can handle analog video input.

Studio AV/DV is a PCI video card and break-out box combo. To install it, you need to open your PC and insert the video card into an open PCI slot. Then you connect the break-out box to the card to do analog capture. The card has an external FireWire connection for DV capture.

Both types of setups have video/audio **output** enabling you to display your video on a TV monitor or record it to an analog VCR or camcorder.

I tested the MovieBox FireWire version and it worked without a hiccup. It's so simple that no manual is needed. Just make sure you activate-click the Select button until it illuminates the LED above the video-in plug you're using: S-Video, Composite Video, or Digital Video.

MovieBox FireWire is not bundled with Studio Plus—you need to buy it separately from Pinnacle for about $100. It does come bundled with Studio 9 for $199 (and you can upgrade to Studio Plus for $30—you get some extra goodies taking that route). MovieBox USB and AV/DV come as Studio Plus bundles for $250 and $200, respectively.

USB Does Not Have Device Control

Watch Out!

The USB version of MovieBox comes with a caveat. USB has no DV device control. That is, unlike FireWire, you *cannot* operate your DV camcorder remotely from within Studio Plus via a USB connection. This defeats one of the cool aspects of DV and can become darned inconvenient.

There are two reasons to use a USB box to capture DV: to save $50 versus the FireWire hardware or if your PC does not have a FireWire connector. If you buy the USB version of MovieBox and your PC does have a FireWire connection, use FireWire to transfer DV and use the MovieBox to capture only analog video.

Composite Video Versus S-Video Versus Component Video

Did you Know?

Most consumer analog camcorders give you two ways to output video: Composite and S-Video. As shown in Figure 9.17, Composite uses a single RCA plug, the same type of plug you use for your two audio connections. S-Video uses a special four-pin plug, and Component video uses three RCA plugs.

You find Component output only on high-end camcorders. It divides the TV video signal into its three constituent parts—brightness and two color signals—and is the best quality of these three. S-Video has two elements: brightness and a combination of the two color signals. It is only slightly lower in quality than Component. Composite combines all three video elements into one signal; thus it is the lowest quality.

Therefore, if your camcorder has an S-Video out jack, use it rather than the Composite plug. If you have a camcorder with a Component out, you are in a distinct, high-end minority, and you'll need a specialized Component video capture card to use that output format.

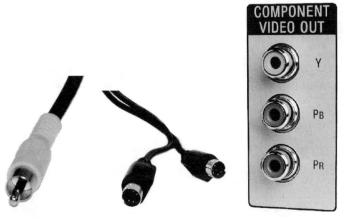

Composite   S-Video   Component

FIGURE 9.17
Three analog video format connectors from left to right, lowest quality to highest: Composite (single RCA jack), S-Video (four-pin connector), Component (three RCA connectors).

Capturing Digital or Analog Video and Still Images

Now it's time to get back to work and tackle a couple tasks. First up: DV capture. Even if you have only an analog camcorder and analog capture hardware, read through this task because DV capture shares several functions used in analog video capture.

DV capture using Studio Plus is very user friendly and has some extra features not found in Movie Maker.

By the Way

What to Do If You're Not Ready to Capture Video

You don't have to capture video to complete any of the tasks in subsequent chapters on Studio Plus. As you might have noticed, Studio Plus ships with a sample movie called Photoshoot.mpg. I explain how to work with it in the next chapter.

Try it Yourself

Using Studio Plus to Capture DV

This works virtually the same way Movie Maker handles DV capture. The exception is that Studio Plus offers three additional ways to automatically create clips as you capture:

1. Plug your camcorder to your PC using the FireWire cable. Using AC power, switch it to VCR or VTR mode. Windows will detect your camcorder and pop up a Digital Video Device window. Select Take No Action and click OK.

2. Open Studio Plus and click the Capture tab. That opens the interface shown in Figure 9.18.

Watch Out!

What Can Go Wrong

When you click the Capture tab, you might see the Device Initialization Error message shown in Figure 9.19. This means that either you have not properly connected or turned on your DV camcorder, or you are using an analog camcorder and capture hardware and need to tell Studio Plus about both. I cover analog capture in the next task.

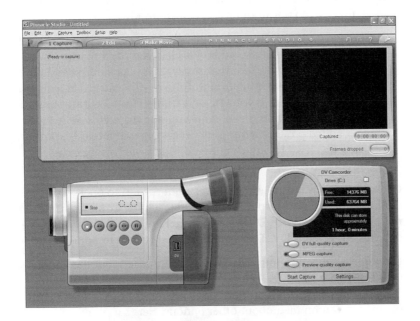

FIGURE 9.18
The Studio Plus video capture interface has the familiar look and feel of a camcorder.

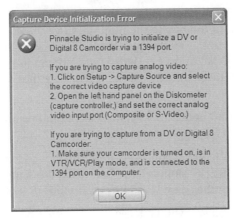

FIGURE 9.19
This Device Initialization Error message pops up when Studio Plus cannot detect your camcorder.

3. Studio Plus offers three capture file formats:

   ▶ **DV**—Retains the original quality of your digital video. I recommend that you always capture in DV mode. That way you retain full quality and can always output to MPEG or some other lower bit rate and lower-quality mode later.

▶ **MPEG**—Create an MPEG file with user-set parameters. Use this if you plan to save your final project *only* in an MPEG format.

▶ **Preview-Quality Capture**—This is a holdover from the era of slower PCs and offline editors. Studio Plus lets you capture in a low-resolution (Preview-Quality) format that saves disk space and speeds up editing. When you finish editing and want to create your video, you plug your camcorder back into your PC and Studio Plus recaptures, in full DV or MPEG, only the portions of your original video you've included in your edited project. With faster processors and larger hard drives, using Preview-Quality Capture adds an unnecessary extra step for most video editors.

4. Click the Settings button (in the lower-right corner) to open the Setup Options dialog box shown in Figure 9.20 (click the Capture Format tab if it's not already open). With DV selected, you'll note you have no user-selectable options. DV is DV is DV. There's nothing you can do to adjust its quality.

5. For a quick education into video compression, check out the various settings (you'll switch back to DV before exiting this Setup box, so don't worry about messing things up by scrolling through all the various options). This is simply to give you an idea about other options. Here's a rundown:

▶ **MPEG**—As highlighted in Figure 9.17, select MPEG from the drop-down list. In the box to the right are three presets for specific media: DVD (MPEG-2), SVCD (Super Video CD—lower resolution MPEG-2 that plays on CDs), and VCD (Video CD—VHS quality MPEG-1 video). As you scroll through those three presets, note that other parameters—MPEG Type, Resolution, Quality—change.

Select Custom and note that you can select from several resolutions and change the data (higher creates better video quality).

▶ **Preview**—Here you can select from three so-called MJPEG compression presets. MJPEG—Motion Joint Picture Experts Group—compression comes from the same standards group that brought us MPEG.

Select Custom and you will be faced with several Codec (Compression/ Decompression) options. There are reasons to use one over another, but video compression Codecs are technology esoterica, and I won't cover them in this book.

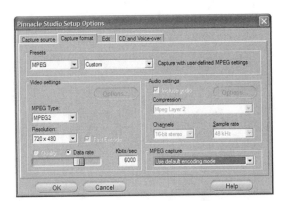

FIGURE 9.20
The Setup Options dialog box lets you make video quality adjustments when you opt to capture in MPEG or Preview Quality.

6. Select DV from the Presets list and click the Capture Source tab. Because you're working with DV, your Video and Audio sources will be DV Camcorder. The purpose for this window is to select a Scene Detection option. Choose from one of the four shown in Figure 9.21:

   ▶ **Automatic Based on Shooting Time and Date**—Checks the Time Stamp for when you pressed the Record/Pause button on your camcorder. This is the same technique used in Movie Maker.

   ▶ **Automatic Based on Video Content**—Examines each scene for any obvious changes. Creates new clips for each Time Stamp change plus notes when you've suddenly moved the camera to a new scene without pressing the Record/Pause button.

   ▶ **Create New Scene Every (fill in the blank) Seconds**—Not much call for this, but if you recorded a timed event with things happening at regular intervals, this is a great way to automatically break that into clips.

   ▶ **No Auto Scene Detection—Press Space Bar to Create Scene**—This is a slick tool. As you watch the video capture in progress, press the spacebar when you want to make a new clip.

7. Just for grins, click the Test Data Rate button to check the performance of your hard drive. 10,000KB per second is the speed you need. Most hard drives these days easily exceed that.

8. Make your Scene Detection selection and click OK.

9. Use the camcorder controls in the Capture window to cue up your videotape to where you want capture to begin.

▼

FIGURE 9.21
In the Capture Source tab, make a Scene Selection choice. You have four options (versus only one for Movie Maker).

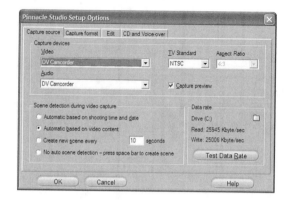

10. That opens the Capture Video dialog box shown in Figure 9.22. Give your video a name and file folder location, indicate for how long you want the capture to go on (Studio Plus calculates), and click Start Capture.

Did you Know?

Setting the Stop Capture Time

Studio Plus calculates how much room you have on your hard drive and displays that as the default setting in the Stop Capturing After window. You can change that time if you want the capture to stop before getting to the end of the tape or the end of whatever portion you recorded. After it gets to an unrecorded section, Studio Plus automatically stops capturing.

FIGURE 9.22
In the Capture Video window, give your video a name, file folder location, and (if you choose to do so) set a time limit for capture.

▼

11. As shown in Figure 9.23, as it captures, Studio Plus displays a thumbnail of the first frame from each video clip it creates. The capture process will stop automatically when it reaches the Stop Capture time, the end of the tape, or the end of the recorded portion of a partially recorded tape (you also can press Stop Capture anytime you want).

12. Save your project by selecting File, Save Project, giving it a name and file folder location, and clicking Save.

Deleting a Captured Video

Sometime you might want to remove an entire captured video from your project. For instance, you might have captured the wrong piece of video or started the capture at the wrong place on the tape. To remove it from the hard drive and from the Album, click the Capture tab to open that interface and then select Capture, Delete Captured Videos. Studio Plus will display a list of your captured video files from any folders or drives you captured to. Make your selection and click Delete.

Did you Know?

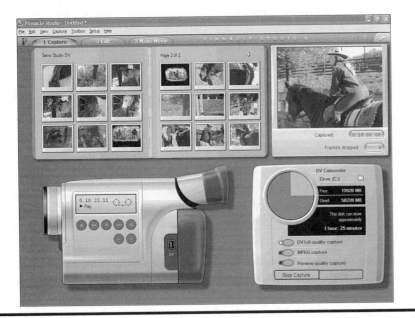

FIGURE 9.23
How your capture interface will look (with a scene detection mode switched on) after you've transferred a few minutes of video.

Analog Video Capture

This is for those of you with analog video hardware: a camcorder (or VCR) and a capture device. The main differences between analog and digital video capture are

▶ You cannot control the camcorder via the Studio Plus interface.

▶ Analog tape does not have a Time Stamp recognizable by Studio Plus (so that means of scene detection won't work).

▶ You have the option to adjust video quality—Brightness, Contrast, Hue, and Color Saturation—and audio levels and stereo panning.

 Analog Video Capture

Although you need to go through a couple extra steps to do analog video capture, many of the options are the same as DV. Here's how you do it:

1. Connect your camcorder to your analog capture hardware. Choose the highest-quality connection format available. Component is best, then S-Video, and then Composite. Also connect your two audio cables, making sure the colors (typically red and white) match the output and input connections, respectively, on your camcorder/VCR and PC hardware.

2. Open Studio Plus and click the Capture tab. The Capture Device Initialization Error message shown back in Figure 9.19 should pop up. Not to worry. Studio Plus merely is looking for a DV camcorder (if you've done some analog capturing already, this message might not appear). Click OK to close it.

3. Click Settings down in the lower-right corner (or select Setup, Capture Source) to open the Setup Options window. Click its Capture Source tab. As shown in Figure 9.24, select your analog capture device from the drop-down list and click OK. That opens the Analog Video Capture interface shown in Figure 9.25.

4. Click the two icons shown in Figure 9.25 to open the video and audio adjustment slider control fly-out panels. Select the Video Input: Composite or S-Video.

5. Play your video using the controls on your camcorder. The video will display in the capture interface. Try out the video quality settings—Brightness, Contrast, Hue, and Color Saturation—and test the audio sliders—volume and panning. If you need to make adjustments, do so. (Note: The number of quality settings varies depending on the hardware capture device.)

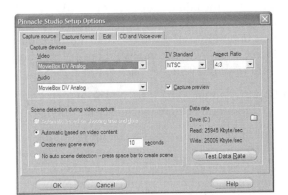

FIGURE 9.24
Open the Capture
Source section of
the Setup Options
dialog box to select
your analog video
capture hardware.

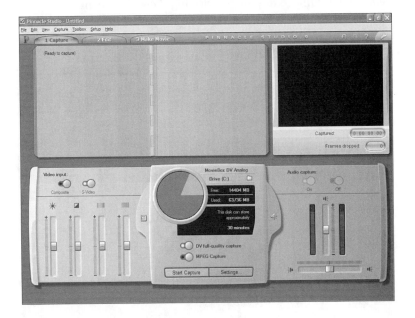

FIGURE 9.25
Studio's analog
video capture inter-
face. Click the two
highlighted icons to
open the video and
audio adjustment
fly-out panels.
(Note: The icons
sometimes disap-
pear when you
open those slider
control windows.)

DV Capture with a USB Connection

If you purchased the USB version of MovieBox and are using it to transfer from your
DV camcorder (you would do this only if your PC does not have a FireWire connection
or to save a few dollars) you will have no device control. That is, as with typical analog capture, you'll need to cue your tape up and start playing it by using the controls
on the camcorder. If your PC does have a FireWire connection, use it for your DV
camcorder.

*Watch
Out!*

6. Select other settings referred to in the previous Try It Yourself, "Using Studio Plus to Capture DV," including Capture Format (DV or MPEG or others, depending on your analog capture hardware) and Scene Detection. The first scene-detection option that uses the DV Time Stamp is disabled—Automatic Based on Video Content will accomplish more or less what checking for the DV Time Stamp would have done. Click OK to close Setup Options.

7. Click Start Capture, name your video, and set a Stop Capturing After time (you can stop it manually before reaching that time).

8. Using the controls on your camcorder, cue up your tape to a few seconds before where you want to start capturing, press Play on your camcorder, and immediately click Start Capture. When done, either click Stop Capture or let Studio Plus stop capturing based on time expired. Your interface should be full of clip thumbnails like Figure 9.26 (I switched to the Comment view for the thumbnail image display by selecting View, Comment View).

FIGURE 9.26
I used Comment view to see details about the clips as Studio Plus added them during analog capture.

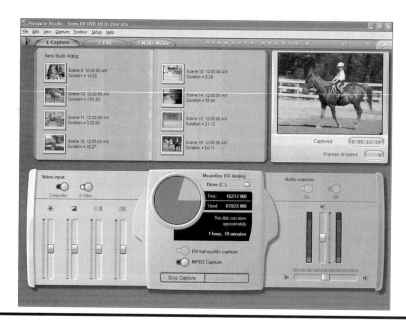

Capturing Still Images from Your Camcorder

Frequently, you'll want to grab a still image from a videotape. There are two ways to do this:

▶ **Directly from the camcorder**—Typically used when you would rather grab that single image instead of an entire clip.

▶ **From a clip you already captured**—If you plan to grab the still from a clip you already captured, there's no need to grab it separately from the tape.

This works for both analog and DV camcorders with one caveat: You can pause a DV camcorder right on the image you want to grab and get a perfectly sharp shot. But analog camcorders do not pause on a single frame (they typically have stretch marks), so you have to put the analog camcorder in the Play mode and grab the image on-the-fly.

Grabbing Stills

Try it Yourself

Even though this works a lot like video capture, you do it in the Edit interface using the Video Toolbox. We'll start by grabbing a still directly from a videotape and then move on to using an existing clip as the still image source. Here's how:

1. As you did with video capture, connect your camcorder to your PC, plug it into AC, and switch it to VCR/VTR.

2. Open Studio Plus and click the Edit tab.

3. From the Main Menu select Toolbox, Grab Video Frame. That opens one of the two interfaces shown in Figure 9.27—DV (with its camcorder controls) on top or analog (no controls) on the bottom. If the wrong interface shows up, select Setup, Capture Source, and select the correct camcorder.

Other Ways to Open the Toolbox

Did you Know?

There are at least two other ways to open this frame-grab toolbox. Roll your cursor over the left side of the little Toolbox icon in the upper-left corner of the Movie Window and click the Camcorder icon that pops onscreen. That opens the video toolbox. Click the Frame Grab button (the hand icon, fourth from the top). The keyboard shortcut is ALT+T and then G (no ALT needed).

---

4. With DV, cue your tape to the frame you want to grab, and then click Grab and Save to Disk. You can also click Add to Movie to drop it onto the Timeline or Storyboard.

5. With Analog Video, you need to find the image you want using the controls on the camcorder. When found, rewind a bit, press Play, and when you see that frame, click Grab. Save it and, if you want, add it to your Movie Window.

6. To grab a frame from a previously captured video clip, you need to drag it to the Storyboard (or Timeline) and then open the Frame Grab interface. Use the Player controls to find the frame you want and click Grab. Save it.

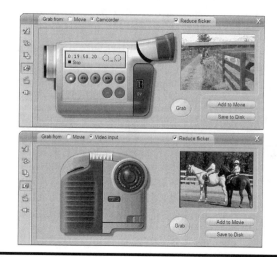

FIGURE 9.27
When you open the Frame Grab window (and you have a camcorder connected to your PC), your interface will indicate whether you're working with a DV camcorder (top) or analog (bottom).

Summary

Video editing has gone from engineers to artists. In days of yore, engineers pushing buttons on huge machines were considered editors. Now it's no longer restricted to the technically savvy. Nonlinear editing is for anyone with a little creative flair, a camcorder, and a PC.

You got a taste of nonlinear video editing when you worked with Movie Maker in the two previous chapters. As I think you began to see in this chapter, Pinnacle Studio Plus goes far beyond the limited functionality of Movie Maker.

In this chapter I gave you an overview of its interface and touched on its deep functionality. Specifically, on the video and still image capture front, I noted that it has many more options and scene detection features.

As we continue to work with Studio Plus in the next few chapters, I think you'll enjoy its ease of use and the many nifty tricks it can do.

CHAPTER 10

Editing Cuts-Only Videos with Studio Plus

What You'll Learn in This Chapter:

▶ Assembling your assets

▶ Creating an instant music video with SmartMovie

▶ Using a storyboard approach

▶ Editing your cuts-only video on the Timeline

It's time to start editing a video. You took your first stabs at this using Movie Maker. Now we'll up the ante a bit, although in these early stages, the process is very similar.

At its most basic level, creating a video involves assembling your assets in an easily accessible location, dragging and dropping video clips and stills in a desired order onto the Storyboard, and then trimming clips to remove unwanted material and to create Match Action edits.

Cuts-only means all edits are straight cuts, with no transitions such as dissolves or fancy spinning boxes. You'll play with those fun tools in the next chapter.

You do get to have some fun creating an instant (well, it does take a few minutes) music video using Studio's SmartMovie. It's not elegant, but it gives you an idea of some of Studio's features.

Assembling Your Assets

As a reminder, **assets** are the media files—video, audio, images, and graphics—you use to create your finished, edited product. Studio Plus organizes them behind their associated tabs in the Album.

Studio's designers made assembling your assets a little too user friendly, in my view. I show you what I mean in the sidebar "Clumsy File Handling."

Try it Yourself ▼

Importing Assets

Studio Plus uses the term **Open** to describe bringing or importing assets into a project. In fact what's really happening is that you are placing **pointers** to the asset file folders and files in Studio's Album.

In addition, as you import or open your video assets, Studio Plus automatically uses its scene detection feature to divide them into clips. Here's how to do all of this:

1. Open Studio Plus to the Edit tab (that's the default opening screen). Click the Show Videos tab to open that page of the Album (that, too, is the default view, so it probably is open already). As shown in Figure 10.1, clips from your most recently captured video should display in the Album.

By the Way

What to Do If You Haven't Captured Video Yet

As I mentioned in the previous chapter, you don't have to capture any video to complete the tasks in this and subsequent chapters on Studio Plus. Simply use the video file that came with Studio Plus: Photoshoot.mpg.

If you don't see that video in your Album (Studio Plus removes it the moment you add any kind of file to a project), you'll find it in a fairly obscure and otherwise difficult to track down location: `C:/Documents and Settings/All Users/Shared Documents/Shared Video`. I explain how to add it, and other files, to a project in step 3.

---

2. You probably see only thumbnail images of your scenes. I recommend that you switch to the Comment view (shown in Figure 10.1) by selecting View, Comment View. This displays the thumbnails along with their associated clip names and durations.

▼

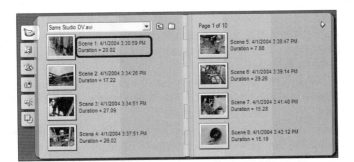

FIGURE 10.1
When working with videos in the Album, I like to use the Comment view to see the length of each clip.

Checking Out Clip Names

Did you Know?

With Comment view selected, you'll see that Studio Plus has automatically given your clips (created during scene detection) generic names numbered sequentially, as in: Scene 1, Scene 2, and so on. Clips captured from DV have the original Time Stamp date and time information added to the Scene name. Clips captured from analog tape have 12:00:00 AM following each numbered scene. Studio Plus also displays the duration of the clip in hours:minutes:seconds:frames (NTSC video plays at 30 frames per second, PAL is 25).

To change a clip name, click it twice to highlight it, drag your cursor over the portion you want to change (changing the duration will not change the clip's actual length), and type in a new name (with or without a duration).

3. To add other videos already stored on your hard drive to your Studio Plus project, click the little blank file folder in the Album window, highlighted in Figure 10.2. That opens what Studio Plus calls the Open window. Navigate to the video file you want, select it, and click Open. You're actually adding the entire contents of that file's file folder—see the sidebar "Clumsy File Handling" for an explanation.

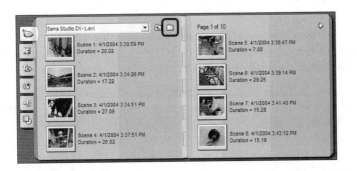

FIGURE 10.2
Click the little file folder icon to add videos from another folder on your hard drive.

Clumsy File Handling

In my view, Studio Plus handles asset files in a nonintuitive fashion.

The reasoning behind the file-handling approach is to make Studio Plus idiot proof. But, in this case, Pinnacle went *way* overboard. Here's how that file handling works and what I think is wrong with it:

1. When you open a file (video, audio, or still), Studio Plus not only adds that file to the Album, but also adds all other like files in that selected file's file folder to the Album.

2. In addition—and this is especially irksome—if that file is in a subfolder, when you add that file, Studio Plus adds all other associated subfile folders and their contents to the Album. This creates a horribly cluttered mess.

3. When you add a video file, Studio Plus automatically splits it into clips based on scene changes. That, too, can create unnecessary clutter.

4. After you've added a file to the Album, there is no way to remove it. This means that as you edit more and more projects, your Album drop-down list becomes loaded with files that you don't need for whatever project you're working on.

5. If there are some clips (scenes within a video file) that you know you'll never use, you can't remove them from the Album.

So, what to do?

1. If you have a bunch of clips (scenes selected via the scene selection process) that you know you'll *never* use, select them by Ctrl+clicking them individually. Then select Album, Combine Scenes, and Studio Plus will turn that group of clips into one clip, with one thumbnail (it automatically renumbers all other clips that still have their original "Scene #" name). Name this new combination clip something like **Discarded scenes**, and you've at least cleaned things up a bit.

2. If you want to remove an entire file—video, audio, or still—from the Album, navigate to it in My Computer and either move it to a new file folder or delete it (remember, if you delete it from your hard drive, it's really gone). If you simply rename it without moving it to a new file folder, Studio Plus will check that file folder and display that renamed file in the Album using its new name.

This file handling methodology is a kludge but not a deal killer. I still like Studio Plus more than any other entry- to intermediate-level NLE.

4. To add other assets—audio and still images—click their respective tabs, click the Open button, and add those files. (Actually, as noted in the sidebar, you're adding their file folders and all media-related contents.)

5. As shown in Figure 10.3, with additional file folders added to the Album, when you select a file folder name in the drop-down window it displays the files in that file folder. In the Audio or Video pages, those files have icons noting whether they are DV, MPEG, WAV, or MP3 files. Double-clicking a Video filename opens the Album page to that video file's collection of scene selection clips.

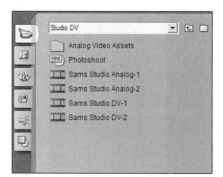

FIGURE 10.3
Selecting a file folder in the Album's Video page drop-down list displays that file folder's video files using different icons to represent DV or MPEG.

6. One other way to access files via the Album window is simply to navigate through your hard drive in My Computer fashion. To do that, click the little Move Up One Level file folder highlighted in Figure 10.4. As you move up a level, Studio Plus will display all file folders at that level. Double-click one to view any of its contents that match the file type of the Album page—video, audio, or still.

FIGURE 10.4
The other way to add files to the Album is to navigate through your hard drive in the same way you would if you had opened My Computer. I highlighted the Move Up One Level icon.

Creating an Instant Music Video with SmartMovie

In the next section I begin to go over the nuts and bolts of video editing, including adding clips to the Storyboard and trimming clips on the Timeline.

But that level of editing can feel like work. How about a little fun first? SmartMovie automates the video editing process.

That easy automation comes with a caveat: SmartMovie is fraught with unknowns. I am no fan of automated video making. It's more a gimmick and marketing tool than a practical means to make a video. For example, depending on the style you select, your opening title and closing credits might be tiny text running over your video clips or massive text on a purple backdrop. And after you've built an automated music video, if you try out different styles on it, expect some strange results.

Try it Yourself   Feeling the Beat with SmartMovie

Despite the drawbacks, SmartMovie lets you get your feet wet in Studio Plus video editing. To do it, simply select your video clips, input a few parameters, and voila—a darned near instant music video. Here's how you do it:

1. Start Studio Plus and click the Edit tab. Click the Show Videos tab in the Album. This is the default opening display, so you might not need to do anything to get to this point. You can dive right into SmartMovie by selecting Toolbox, Create SmartMovie. But the first step within that interface is to go to the Album to select your video clips.

2. Using the Photoshoot.mpg clips or any you've captured, drag and drop clips to the Storyboard. You can use standard Windows multiclip selection techniques: Ctrl+click to select scattered clips, click and then Shift+click to select contiguous clips, or drag a marquee. As shown in Figure 10.5, I selected all the clips and dragged that collection to the first placeholder in the Storyboard. That filled the first 11 placeholders with clips.

3. Select Toolbox, Create SmartMovie from the main menu. That opens the SmartMovie interface shown in Figure 10.6.

Did you Know?   Other Routes to SmartMovie

As you would expect, there are other ways to access SmartMovie. Here are two:

Hover your cursor over the left side of the little toolbox in the upper-left corner of the Movie window to display the Camcorder icon. Click it to open the Toolbox and then click the Scene Clapper icon (fourth from the top).

Or press Alt+T, and then C and C again and then Return.

4. You can uncheck Use Clips in Random Order to keep them in the sequence in which you placed them on the Storyboard.

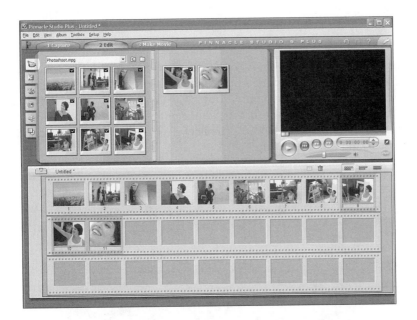

FIGURE 10.5
To use SmartMovie to create a music video, first drag a bunch of clips to the Storyboard (or Timeline).

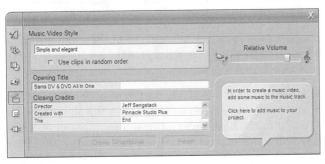

FIGURE 10.6
The SmartMovie interface guides you through the automated music video creation process.

5. Move the Relative Volume slider to mix natural sound from the clips and music. If you want only music, move the slider all the way to the right.

6. Give your video an opening title that will display at the beginning (sometimes over video, sometimes over a backdrop, depending on the Music Video Style) by typing your video title in the Opening Title box. Add some closing credits. Use Figure 10.6 earlier as a reference.

7. Select a Music Video Style. Studio Plus does not give you any explanation for these styles. Each has a different look and feel with varying video effects, transitions, brief or long clips, and plain or elaborate credits. Remember, SmartMovie is a gimmick, not a true video-production tool.

8. You can have SmartMovie rip a tune from a CD, grab an audio file from your hard drive, or use its SmartSound module to create music that automatically fits the length of your project. In this case, use SmartSound. To do that, click Click Here to Add Music to Your Project.

9. In the next window select A Song Created by SmartSound and then click OK. That opens the SmartSound interface shown in Figure 10.7. I will go over SmartSound in detail in Chapter 12, "Audio Production with Studio Plus." So for this exercise, accept whatever Style/Song/Version comes up (probably Blues/"Blues to Go"/The Pocket—or—Classical/Bach Guitar/Calm) by clicking Add to Movie.

FIGURE 10.7
Use the SmartSound module to create music to fit the length and nature of your video. I will discuss this nifty production tool in detail in Chapter 12.

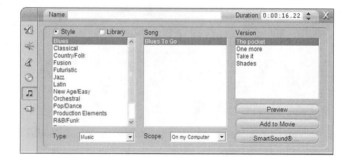

10. SmartSound instantly creates the song to fit the calculated length of the SmartMovie and then displays Click Here to Return to SmartMovie at the top of the Storyboard. Click that.

11. Now click the Create Smart Movie button in the SmartMovie interface. After a short while, your new video will appear in the Storyboard. As shown in Figure 10.8, it might have several transitions, titles, or ending credit scenes and some video effects. And it probably will be quite a bit shorter than the original length of your assembled clips because of transitions and some edits made by SmartMovie.

FIGURE 10.8
After it is completed, your SmartMovie might have several transitions, title screens, and special video effects applied.

12. Play the movie in the Player window. You can save it by selecting File, Save Project. Or you can start over by clicking Reset in the SmartMovie interface.

Reset Does Not Remove Audio

Reset is only a partial means to start over. It does not remove the audio. So if you selected a SmartSound tune, its length won't change to accommodate a new video style. You might start with a dozen video clips and SmartMovie will turn them into a video with only two or three clips.

Using a Storyboard Approach

As you've seen, automated video production leads to less-than-desirable results. To do it right, you need to do a little manual labor.

As I mentioned in the Movie Maker chapters, the Storyboard is an intuitive way to get started. It lets you build your story as if you were posting scene sketches or stills on a bulletin board. If you think a clip (or scene) belongs somewhere else or should be deleted, you move it or remove it. Simple.

Edit a Video Using the Storyboard   *Try it Yourself*

You'll use the sample video provided with Studio Plus to create your first video with Studio Plus. Here's how:

   1. Click the Edit tab at the top of the screen to return to the Storyboard interface and the Photoshoot sample video thumbnail images.

Roll Your Own   *Did you Know?*

You can use your own video instead of Photoshoot. To do that, click the file folder icon shown in Figure 10.9, locate your video, and click Open. Studio Plus performs an automatic scene detection and displays thumbnail images of each scene.

FIGURE 10.9
Use the highlighted file folder icon to access your own videos for editing.

2. Drag and drop the first scene to the first placeholder in the Storyboard by clicking the scene, holding down the mouse button, and dragging the scene to the filmstrip. Repeat that for the rest of the scenes. Remember, you can select multiple clips by dragging a marquee around them or using the Ctrl+click or Shift+click methods. When you're done, your screen should look similar to Figure 10.10.

FIGURE 10.10
Drag and drop video clips to the Storyboard to begin editing a video. Use the highlighted Go to Beginning button to go to the start of the project.

3. Play this rough-cut video by clicking the Go to Beginning button (Keyboard shortcut=Home) highlighted in Figure 10.10 and then clicking Play. You can scrub through this collection of clips by dragging the slider highlighted in Figure 10.10.

4. If you don't like a scene (the second clip—where the model comes in the front door doesn't work for me), remove it from the Storyboard in one of three ways:

 ▶ Right-click it and select Delete.

 ▶ Click it to select it, and then press the Delete key.

 ▶ Select it and click the Trashcan icon above the Timescale.

By the
Way

Studio Plus Is Nondestructive, Too

I mentioned in the Movie Maker chapters that nonlinear editing is nondestructive. That is, removing a clip from your Storyboard does not remove that clip from the Album page or from your hard drive. You can still use that removed clip elsewhere in your video.

5. Rearrange your video clip sequence by dragging one scene to a new location between two other scenes and dropping it there. As shown in Figure 10.11, the cursor changes to an arrow with a rectangle and a vertical stripe appears between the clips where that clip will go.

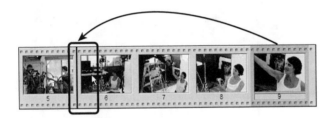

FIGURE 10.11
Move a clip to a new location in the Storyboard by dragging it between two other clips. Note that the cursor changes to an arrow, and a box and a vertical line (expanded and darkened for emphasis in this figure) notes where it will go when you release the mouse button.

6. Insert a scene by dragging it from the Album to the Storyboard and placing it between two clips, at the beginning of your video or the end. As shown in Figure 10.12, that same vertical line appears, but this time the cursor has a little plus sign icon (+) to indicate that you are adding a clip.

By the
Way

Out with the Linear

The removal, rearrangement, and insertion processes demonstrate just how much easier and faster nonlinear editors are than traditional, linear, videotape systems.

FIGURE 10.12
When you drag a new clip to the Storyboard from the Album, that same vertical line appears between clips, and this time the cursor has a little plus sign.

7. You can trim individual clips in the Storyboard. To do so, double-click a clip in the Storyboard (I chose the third clip, Scene 3, because it's a bit too long). That opens the Clip Properties interface within the Video Toolbox shown in Figure 10.13.

Did you
Know?

Other Ways to Access Clip Properties

Double-clicking a clip is an easy way to open the Clip Properties interface. You can also open it by hovering the cursor over the left side of the Toolbox icon in the upper-left corner of the Storyboard and then clicking the Camcorder icon that appears. Click the top icon in the Video Toolbox to open Clip Properties. Or select Toolbox, Modify Clip Properties. After it is open, you can trim any clip within Clip Properties by clicking a clip in the Storyboard or Timeline.

FIGURE 10.13
Move the in and out points to trim clips in the Video Toolbox.

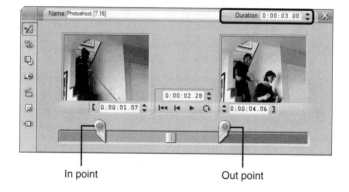

In point   Out point

8. Drag the in and out points to change when the clip begins and ends. As shown in Figure 10.13, Studio displays the changing duration of the clip as you move the edit points. Three seconds is a comfortable length for a video scene.

9. Trim other scenes by double-clicking them in the Storyboard and using the Video Toolbox to make adjustments.

10. Save your project by selecting File, Save Project; then select a file folder location and name.

You can view how your edits have worked to this point by clicking the Go to Beginning (Home) button in the Player/Monitor window and then clicking Play.

Editing Your Cuts-Only Video on the Timeline

Your piece could probably use some fine-tuning. The Timeline is the best means to that end.

As you might have noted back when working with Movie Maker, at first, the Timeline might not be as intuitive as the Storyboard. But I think you will come to rely on it. It's the standard interface used by countless video editors.

Switch to the Timeline view by clicking the Timeline icon at the upper-right of the Storyboard filmstrip. This opens the Timeline interface shown in Figure 10.14.

FIGURE 10.14
The Timeline interface displays additional tracks—three for audio and one for placing text and graphics over your videos—that are not readily accessible in the Storyboard view. Studio Plus has one additional hidden Video/Audio track. Use the highlighted Timeline Scrubber to move quickly through your project.

The Timeline displays more than simple thumbnail images. It also shows the overall length of your video across the top and the relative length of each clip (based on the rectangular box size associated with each clip's thumbnail image). Plus, as noted in Figure 10.14, it displays the audio track associated with your original video clips (sometimes called **natural sound**) and gives you places to add text, a narration, sound effects, or music.

Adjusting the Ruler Timescale

Your edited video probably does not fill the full width of the Timeline. Some short duration clips might be nothing more than thin, vertical lines. As shown in Figure 10.15, you can expand the project view by moving your cursor over the Timeline's Timescale Ruler (it turns into a clock cursor with double arrows). Then click and drag to the right to expand—or zoom in—and to the left to contract—or zoom out.

FIGURE 10.15
Use the double-arrow cursor to adjust the scale of the Timeline view to fit your project into the Timeline window or expand a portion of it to enable more precise editing.

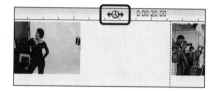

Did you Know?

Ruler Adjustment Shortcuts

Here are some other ways to adjust the Timescale Ruler.

The equal sign (=) key expands the view (meaning each clip takes up more space on the Timeline), and the minus sign (–) key shrinks the project view.

As shown in Figure 10.16, right-clicking the Ruler displays several time increment options. Selecting an increment, such as 30 seconds, means that the 30 seconds of your project will fill the entire width of the Timeline window. You can scroll through your project using the scroll bar at the bottom of the Timeline window.

A very cool right-click option is to select Entire Movie. That fills the width of the Timeline with your entire project, giving you an instant overview of your work.

FIGURE 10.16
Use a right-click menu to expand the Timescale and get a better view of your clips.

Drag the Timeline Scrubber through your project (refer to Figure 10.14). Note that each clip's box on the Timeline turns blue as you scrub through it.

Arranging Clips on the Timeline

You can insert, remove, and rearrange clips on the Timeline just as you did in the Storyboard. In addition to using the Clip Properties interface to trim a clip, you can both trim and slice a clip on the Timeline. I take you through trimming in the next Try It Yourself.

In this Try It Yourself, I want you to use the Photoshoot.mpg file that ships with Studio Plus. I want to give you a couple editing tips and need to refer to some specific clips. Here's a quick run-through of cuts-only editing on the Timeline:

1. You should be in the Timeline view with some clips already in place. For this exercise, I want you to start with a clean slate. To remove all the clips from the Timeline, drag a marquee around them. Do that by clicking below and to the right (or left) of all the clips and dragging up and to the left (or right) to select all the clips. They should all turn blue (showing that you've selected them). Click the Delete key.

2. Switch to the Album to Comment view by selecting View, Comment View from the main menu. This way when I refer to a particular clip scene number, you can locate it.

3. Place Scene 1 in the Main Video Track by dragging it from the Album to the top track of the Timeline. Note that it automatically snaps to the beginning—00:00—of the Timeline.

What Happens on Other Tracks

Did you Know?

If you drag and drop your clip on the Title Track, that will open the hidden second Video Overlay Track and place the clip there. If you drag it to either of the two audio tracks at the bottom of the Timeline window, that will place the natural sound from your clip there, but not the video portion.

---

4. Drag Scene 2 to the Main Video Track. Note that two vertical green bars appear on the Timeline indicating where that clip will go—directly to the right of the first clip—when you release the mouse button.

5. Drag Scene 3 and attempt to drop it in the middle of Scene 2. As shown in Figure 10.17, a red bar and a universal "no" symbol display, as well as a text message above the Time Ruler stating Can Only Insert Between Clips. Drag your cursor to the right until the green bars appear indicating a legal insertion point.

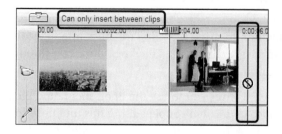

FIGURE 10.17
If you attempt to place a clip within another clip, a vertical (red) bar with the universal *"no"* symbol appears, along with the highlighted message telling you where you can place your clip.

6. Select the rest of the clips in the Album by Ctrl+clicking each in turn (you'll need to move to the second page in the Album to get all of them) and then dragging that collection to the point after Scene 3 in the Timeline. Adjust the Timescale Ruler to display the entire project within the width of the Timeline (remember, you can right-click the Ruler and select Entire Movie).

7. Rearrange your clips by clicking one in the Timeline and dragging it to a new location.

Deselect Collection Before Rearranging

If you drag more than one clip to the Timeline, Studio will note that you've selected these clips by turning them blue. If you try to drag one of the clips within this collection of blue-tinted clips, you will end up moving the entire collection. This can be a good thing under some circumstances. But in this case, deselect that collection by clicking in the Timeline and somewhere outside those clips.

8. Remove a clip (I recommend Scene 2—it's an awkward shot) by selecting it, right-clicking, and selecting Delete (or click it to select it and press the Delete key).

9. At this point you can save this project so that you can come back to it later to complete the next task. If that's the case, select File, Save Project As. If you want to move right to the next task, there's no need to save.

Trimming and Match Edits

Trimming clips on the Timeline is easier than opening the Clip Properties interface. If you worked with Movie Maker, this will seem like old hat. But you might notice a few wrinkles that make it go more smoothly.

Trimming Clips On the Timeline

In the next few steps you will remove some extraneous footage using frame-accurate trimming, and you will create an edit to match action. Here's how:

1. Trim the last clip—Scene 10. It has a few extra frames (a close-up of the model) at the end. Drag the Timeline Scrubber (highlighted in Figure 10.18) to just before that scene change.

2. Click the Forward One Frame and Back One Frame triangles (also highlighted in Figure 10.18) to find the exact frame that precedes that scene change (in my case, that's at 49 seconds and 20 frames). Doing so will move the Timeline Scrubber to that exact spot. You will use that Scrubber line to help you make a frame-accurate edit.

3. Place your cursor on the right edge of the final clip in the Timeline. A left-arrow cursor will appear (as you drag it left, it will turn to a double arrow indicating that you can add frames you've removed).

4. Drag that cursor left (which shortens the clip) until the edge of the clip arrives at the Timeline Scrubber line. The cursor will linger there a little bit. Release the mouse button and voila, you've made a frame-accurate edit.

Select a Clip to Trim It

Make sure you actually select a clip by clicking it; otherwise, you won't see the clip-trimming arrow cursor. Also be sure to select only one clip (you can select more than one by holding down the Ctrl key while clicking other clips). By selecting two clips, you change the in point of one clip and the out point of the other.

5. Now you'll make a Match Action edit. Start by putting Scene 9 (the medium shot of the model holding up the camcorder) *ahead* of Scene 8 (the wider shot of the same action). To do so, click and drag Scene 9 in front of Scene 8.

6. Play those two scenes and notice that the model reaches up in both. What you want to do is cut from Scene 9 to Scene 8 just as the model completes that action. Look at the two images in Figure 10.19 for reference. The left shot is the final frame that you should trim to in Scene 9 and the right shot is the first frame you should trim to in Scene 8 (your time codes will be different because I removed other clips from the Timeline).

▼

FIGURE 10.18
Drag the edge of a
clip to trim it.

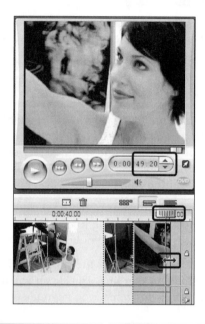

FIGURE 10.19
To create your
Match Action edit,
you want to trim
Scene 9's out-point
(left) and Scene
8's in-point (right)
to match these
shots.

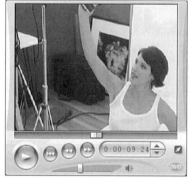 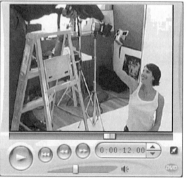

7. Drag the Timeline Scrubber to the point in Scene 9 just as the model reaches as far as she can. She kind of pulls back a bit. Make sure you cut just before that. Place your cursor on the right edge of that clip and drag to the Scrubber line to make that edit. You'll note that the clip to the right—Scene 8—slides to the left as you trim Scene 9.

8. Drag the Timeline Scrubber into Scene 8 to the point where the photographer lifts his hand above the camcorder. Trim that clip's starting point by

▼

placing the cursor on the left edge and dragging it to the right to the Scrubber line. When you release the mouse button, the clip will jump left, directly adjacent to Scene 9.

9. Play those two clips. If all went smoothly, just as the model's arm extends to its full length, the scene will cut to a wide view with her arm straight up and the photographer just moving his hand into view. You have made a Match Action edit.

Feel Free to Use Clip Properties

Just as you did in the Storyboard, you also can trim clips by double-clicking a clip to open the Video Toolbox and using its Trim Calipers to drag in the ends.

Did you Know?

10. You can split a clip in two as a means to insert another clip between the two pieces. Select a clip and move the scrubber to the point at which you want to cut the clip. Click the Razor Blade icon, shown in Figure 10.20. You now have two separate clips, between which you can drag another clip.

FIGURE 10.20
Use the Razor Blade icon to slice a clip in two.

Oops. Fix Bad Edits Via Undo

You can always undo a bad edit. If you split a clip in the wrong place or insert a clip in the wrong location on the Timeline, press Ctrl+Z or click the Undo button (see Figure 10.21). You can undo as many steps as you like, but you cannot selectively undo one thing you did several steps back without undoing everything that came after it. The Redo button, next to the Undo button, restores whatever you just undid. Get it?

FIGURE 10.21
Use the Undo command to take back one or more edits. Use the Redo command (the other curved arrow icon) to redo what you undid.

Summary

Studio Plus (and its older sibling Studio 9) is the real deal. This is a powerful non-linear video editor with a full suite of tools that allows you to create professional-looking videos.

In this chapter you used SmartMovie to create a nearly instant music video and discovered this process' shortcomings along the way.

Then I showed you how to gather your assets, place clips in a Storyboard, and trim them in the Clip Properties interface.

You switched to the Timeline—the editing workspace with which you will become comfortable in a short while. There you did some extra fine-tuning of your project, including slicing and trimming clips as well as creating a Match Action edit.

In coming chapters, you'll work with still images, audio, transitions, special video and audio effects, and delve into advanced editing techniques and the scores of add-ons and plug-ins available for Studio Plus.

CHAPTER 11

Enhancing Your Video with Transitions, Effects, and Titles

What You'll Learn in This Chapter:

▶ Using Transitions with restraint

▶ Adding transitions

▶ Using special video effects

▶ Putting still images in motion

▶ Using **supers** to help tell your story

▶ Adding titles to your videos

Applying transitions between clips—dissolves, page wipes, spinning screens, and others—is a nice way to ease viewers from one scene to the next or to grab their attention. Studio gives you more than 200 transitions to play with. But I urge you to not overdo it.

Studio's video effects give you many ways to jazz up your video and dazzle viewers. You can put clips in motion and change their speed, color, and overall appearance.

New to Studio Plus is the capability to zoom in or out on still images and put them in motion. This can add some real life to old family photos, for instance. I show you how it works in this chapter.

Finally, Studio's TitleDeko character generator is such a full-featured product that you might never fully tap its potential. With TitleDeko, you can create simple text, rolling credits, and colorful shapes. You can use any font stored on your PC; your text can be any color (or multiple colors), any degree of transparency, and throw drop shadows in any direction you choose. TitleDeko is an engaging and powerful tool.

Using Transitions with Restraint

Watch TV news stories, and you'll notice that most edits are cuts—quick jumps from one scene to the next. No transitions, such as dissolves, wipes, or pushes, are used. The reason is that viewers expect cut edits. They know they're watching news, not a feature film, so they expect the stories to move quickly from one scene to the next.

The principal reason for the dearth of transitions is that they can be distracting. If a TV news editor uses one, it's for a purpose. Transitions typically take what would have been a jarring edit—such as a major jump cut—and make it more palatable. An oft-heard newsroom phrase applies: "If you can't solve it, dissolve it."

Transitions with a Purpose

On the other hand, consider the *Star Wars* movies. Remember all the highly stylized transitions? Obvious, slow wipes for example. George Lucas knows what he's doing. Each of those transitions has a purpose. In general, they are reminiscent of old serialized movies and TV shows. Specifically, they send a clear message to the audience: "Pay attention. We're transitioning across space and time."

The possibilities that Studio offers are truly endless. During this chapter, I encourage you to experiment with all that Studio has to offer.

But here's the caveat: Editors new to Studio's wealth of transition possibilities might opt to overuse them. I strongly suggest restraint.

Studio's transitions look very cool. You'll probably be tempted to use a different one between each scene of your video, but resist that urge. Transitions tend to be distracting, so use them judiciously.

What Transitions Can Do

Studio Plus ships with more than 200 transitions. Some are subtle and others are "in your face." The more you experiment with them, the more likely you are to use them well.

For example, transitions can work with your video to add visual interest:

▶ Take a shot of a car driving through the frame and use a Wipe (in Studio's Standard Transitions group), synchronized with the speed of the car, to move to the next scene.

▶ Use the Blinds 2 Wipe (like Venetian blinds—Standard Transitions) as a great way to move from an interior to an exterior.

▶ The STB-Page Peel (Hollywood FX for Studio group) works well with a piece of parchment. It curls/rolls back to reveal the next clip.

▶ Start with a tight shot of a clock (analog, not digital) and use the aptly named Clock Wipe (Standard Transitions)—a line centered on the screen sweeps around to reveal another image—to move to another setting and time.

▶ Using a Push transition (Standard Transitions) along with some planning and experimentation, you can videotape someone pushing against a wall while walking in place and use the Push Right transition to have that person "slide" the old scene offscreen.

Transitions can add whimsy. Studio comes loaded with all sorts of wild, offbeat transitions. And hundreds more are available in retail add-on packs. Here are a few examples using transitions that ship with the retail version of Studio:

▶ Start on a tight shot of a diploma, then use the STP-Scroll 2 transition (in the Hollywood FX for Studio group). For example, you can have the diploma roll up like a two-handled scroll to reveal a college campus.

▶ When editing a children's birthday party video, use STB-Balloon (Hollywood FX for Studio). It takes one clip and turns it into an inflated balloon, then spins and flies it offscreen, revealing the next clip.

▶ The BlackHole transition (Alpha Magic group) is great when transitioning from one water scene to another. It looks like you've dropped a pebble into water. The ripples reveal the next scene.

▶ The Hive (Alpha Magic) works on anything with scales: tight shots of reptiles or butterfly wings, for instance.

▶ The HFX Extra FX pack of 16 transitions that you receive when you register is loaded with amazing, colorful effects. The 70s transition has swirling, psychedelic colors and stars. Squarespots floats your first clip in space with rings dropping over it, then flips to the next clip. And Stretch n Squash does what its name implies. It's a *video* effect that demands a "booing" *sound* effect.

Adding Transitions

Applying a transition between two clips starts with a simple drag and drop. That might be enough for many transitions, but Studio lets you change the duration of a transition and its direction (for example, instead of sliding left to right, you can have the transition move right to left).

In the following Try It Yourself tasks, I introduce you to the various transition groups, demonstrate a simple transition, and then explain the extra options.

Try it
Yourself   **Getting Acquainted with Studio's Transitions**

I think it's important to see what Studio has to offer before diving into the process of adding a transition and adjusting its characteristics. So first up, a brief transition tour:

1. Open Studio to the main Edit tab (the default opening view) and click the Transitions tab (the lightning bolt) in the Album (see Figure 11.1).

2. Studio automatically begins displaying in the Player window how the highlighted Fade In Or Out transition works. It uses two solid color screens labeled A and B to represent the two clips the transition will go between. In this case, Clip A fades to black and then Clip B fades up from black.

FIGURE 11.1
Click the Transitions tab to access Studio's many transitions.

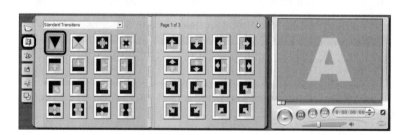

3. Hover your cursor over several transition icons in turn. Note that with ToolTips turned on (select Help, Display ToolTips), Studio displays the name of each transition. Click Center Out Wipe (the third from the left in the top row—highlighted in Figure 11.2) to select it. Note that it now displays in the Player window. The transition gradually reveals Clip B as an expanding rectangle.

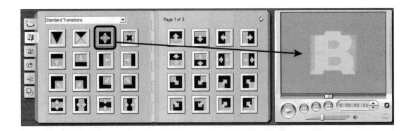

FIGURE 11.2
Click a different transition (Center Out Wipe in this case) to have it display in the Player window.

4. Take a look at some more transitions in the Standard Transitions group. Note that in addition to the Fade and Dissolve (the first two transitions), there are three basic transition types (I've highlighted samples in Figure 11.3):

   ▶ **Wipe**—A moving edge reveals the next clip behind the current clip.

   ▶ **Slide**—Slides one or both clips on or off the screen. One clip might slide off revealing another beneath it, or a clip might slide over the current clip.

   ▶ **Push**—The next clip appears to push the current clip offscreen.

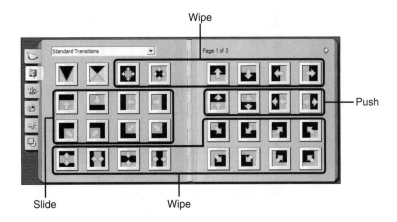

FIGURE 11.3
Most transitions fall into three basic types: Wipe, Slide, and Push.

5. Click the Next Page arrow (upper-right corner of the Album) to view other transitions within the Standard Transitions group. There are 74 in all. Figure 11.4 shows the group on page 2. All are Wipes. Click a few to see how they work. Some are pretty wild.

FIGURE 11.4
The Standard
Transitions group
has 74 transitions
in all. You can see
that some transi-
tions are
whimsical.

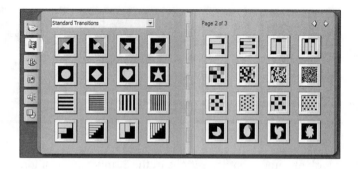

6. Take a look at the Transitions drop-down list shown in Figure 11.5. There are more than 40 transition groups. Most are locked. That is, you have to purchase an unlocking key online to use them. You'll look at some in a moment. The unlocked groups are Standard Transitions, Alpha Magic, Hollywood FX for Studio, and HFX Extra FX (the group you unlocked when you registered Studio).

FIGURE 11.5
Studio ships with
hundreds of transi-
tions in a couple
dozen collections.
Most of these are
locked; you need to
purchase an
unlocking key to
use them.

7. Select the Alpha Magic group (second on the list) and click BlackHole, the transition I referred to earlier and highlight in Figure 11.6. This ripple-wipe transition is indicative of the quality and style you can expect in the Alpha Magic group.

Alpha Magic's Lineage

Alpha Magic goes back to 1999 and was co-created by Harald Heim and Hollywood FX. Heim, of Nuremberg, Germany, is one of the leading developers of plug-ins and is the driving force behind The Plugin Site (http://thepluginsite.com). His site contains a massive collection of plug-ins for several video- and image-editing products. Pinnacle acquired Alpha Magic when it bought out Hollywood FX in 2000. Pinnacle now includes some of the Alpha Magic transitions in Studio and sells Hollywood FX Pro as a standalone video-effects and transitions editing-and-creation tool (www.pinnaclesys.com—look in the Advanced Video section).

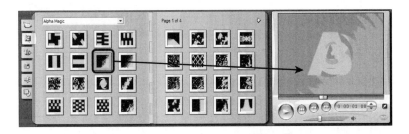

FIGURE 11.6
Alpha Magic transitions tend to be wild wipes.

8. Take a look at the two other unlocked transition groups: Hollywood FX for Studio and HFX Extra FX. Hollywood FX for Studio twists, turns, and rolls Clip A to reveal Clip B. HFX Extra FX adds lots of extra bells and whistles. I recommend that you look at the wildly colorful 70s transition that I mentioned earlier (see Figure 11.7).

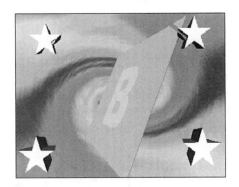

FIGURE 11.7
The 70s transition from the HFX Extra FX group is a very colorful (yes, I know this is a black and white image) and zany transition.

9. Finally, click any of the other transition groups. As shown in Figure 11.8, when you do, you'll see two things: Studio asks you if you want to buy that collection, and a Pinnacle Systems watermark will appear in the transition. The only way to remove that watermark is to buy and install the unlocking key. I cover the locked transitions in greater detail in Chapter 13, "Advanced Editing Techniques, Add-ons, and Exporting."

FIGURE 11.8
When you select any of the locked transition groups, Studio asks if you want to purchase that group and displays a watermark on the transition until you make that purchase.

Try it Yourself   **Working with Transitions**

You add transitions to a project in much the same way as you add clips: Use a simple drag-and-drop method. After you've applied transitions, you can change their duration and direction. Here's how to do that:

1. To see how this works, I want you to start with a clean slate. Open a new project by selecting File, New Project. Switch to the Timeline view (you can apply transitions in the Storyboard view, but the Timeline view gives you more control).

2. Add two clips to the Timeline. If you're using the Photoshoot.mpg clips, select longer clips, such as Scenes 5 and 8.

3. Trim both clips (by dragging them in from the right side) to an equal length. If you are using Photoshoot.mpg Scenes 5 and 8, trim them to 8 seconds each so that your overall project length is 16 seconds. As shown in Figure 11.9, use the time display in the Player window as your guide when you make those trims.

4. Expand the Timeline view (zoom in) so that the two adjacent clips take up most of the space (refer to Figure 11.9). Remember, you can right-click the Timescale Ruler and select Entire Movie or place the cursor over the Ruler and drag the double-arrow/clock cursor to the right. You're doing all this setup work so that you can see later how adding a transition shortens your project.

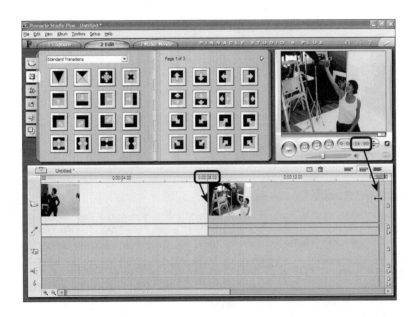

FIGURE 11.9
How your Timeline should look after adding and trimming two clips and zooming in on the Timeline.

5. Open the Transition Album page and drag and drop the Center Out Wipe transition (top row, third from the left) to the edit line between the two clips. As shown in Figure 11.10, you'll know that you've positioned it correctly when a thin green line appears at the edit point as well as another line 2 seconds into the B clip. The cursor has a little plus (+) sign indicating you are adding something to your project. Releasing the mouse button adds the transition, noted by a blue rectangle (see Figure 11.11).

Why Center Out Wipe?

You can choose any transition you want. I chose Center Out Wipe because it's the first Standard Transition displayed that has a Reverse function. You'll test that in a moment. The only Standard Transitions that do not have a Reverse function are Fade In or Out and Dissolve.

By the Way

Storyboard? Same Story

Adding transitions to the Storyboard is just as easy: Drag and drop a transition to the placeholder between two images on the filmstrip. To change the transition's duration and put it in reverse, double-click the transition icon between the two clips in the Storyboard to open the Clip Properties window. However, it's still best to use the Timeline because you can drag the ends of the transition to adjust duration without opening the Clip Properties window.

Did you Know?

FIGURE 11.10
When you drag a transition to the Timeline, Studio lets you know you've found a legal insertion point by displaying two vertical green lines.

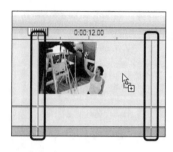

By the Way

Automatic Audio Cross-fade

After you've added the transition, take a close look at the audio track beneath the transition in the Timeline (see Figure 11.11). The two blue lines that form an X show an audio cross-fade. When you add a transition, Studio automatically smoothly fades down the A clip audio and fades up the B clip audio to avoid an abrupt sound change during what is a gradual visual change. The only exception is the Fade In or Out transition. In that case it fades the first clip's audio out and then fades up the audio of the next clip.

FIGURE 11.11
Adding a transition automatically creates an audio cross-fade.

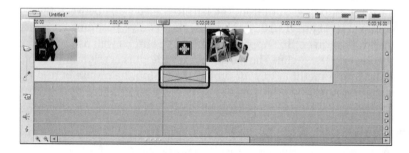

6. Take a look at the Timeline Timescale Ruler. Note that your project is now 2 seconds shorter and the transition starts 2 seconds before the end of the first clip. See the sidebar, "Studio's Consumer-Oriented Transition Behavior," for an explanation.

7. Double-click the transition icon on the Timeline to open the Clip Properties window, shown in Figure 11.12. Here you can change the length of the transition or, if available, have it move in reverse (in this case, instead of a box appearing in the center of the screen, Clip A starts full screen and shrinks to a small box in the center of the screen).

FIGURE 11.12
The transition Clip Properties toolbox lets you fine-tune your transition (I added a border to the transition for emphasis).

8. Close the Clip Properties window and change the duration of the transition by clicking the transition in the Timeline to select it and then dragging its left or right edges. Note that if you increase its duration by 1 second, that will shorten the overall length of your production by 1 second (again, see the sidebar for an explanation).

9. To replace the current transition, drag a different transition from the Album to the transition on the Timeline that you want to replace. Studio immediately swaps them (and updates the icon in the Timeline to indicate that).

10. You can make your video start with a fade-up from black and end with a fade-down to black. As I've done in Figure 11.13, add dissolve transitions to the start and finish of your video.

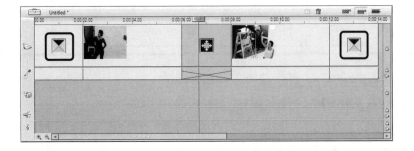

FIGURE 11.13
Use a dissolve transition at the start and end of your video to fade up from black and fade down to black.

11. The default transition duration is 2 seconds. Most video editors prefer 1 second. Although you can change each transition manually, I suggest changing the default transition time to 1 second. To do that, select Setup, Edit, and change the Transition time (highlighted in Figure 11.14) to 01:00. A reminder: The time is noted in seconds:frames (NTSC—30 frames equals 1 second and PAL—25 frames equals 1 second).

▼

Use Hardware 3D Acceleration

If your PC has a 3D graphics accelerator card—NVIDIA, ATI, and others—enabling Hardware Acceleration will speed up the display of 3D transitions (Hollywood FX) and video effects. To do that, select Setup, Edit, and, as shown in Figure 11.14 in the Rendering section, select Use Hardware Acceleration. That will pop up a warning saying that making the switch might cause Studio to crash. My PC has a standard NVIDIA GeForce card, and switching to Hardware Acceleration caused Studio to close every time I selected a 3D effect. I had to uninstall and reinstall Studio to get it to run properly. So gird yourself for that.

FIGURE 11.14
Use the Edit dialog box to change the default transition duration and enable Hardware Acceleration (if you have a 3D graphics card) to speed up display of 3D transitions and video effects.

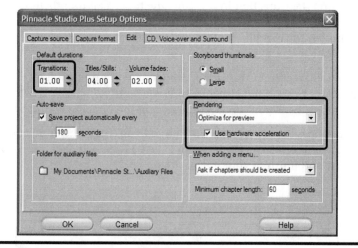

▲

Studio's Consumer-Oriented Transition Behavior

Studio is a consumer-level product and has a default transition behavior geared to that market. It's counterintuitive to me because I'm used to professional-level editors such as Adobe Premiere Pro. But this might be a nonissue for you, depending on how you create videos.

In Studio, every time you add a transition to your video, it shortens the overall length of your project by the length of the transition. This is true for most consumer-level editors.

In general, transitions overlap adjacent clips by blending the end of the A clip with the start of the B clip. Studio accomplishes this by sliding the B clip (along with all subsequent clips) to the left by the length of the transition (the default time is 2 seconds).

Higher-end NLEs, such as Adobe Premiere Pro, use extra footage from the original video clips—tailroom and headroom—to let that overlap happen without shifting the B clip (and all subsequent clips) to the left on the Timeline.

This is important for professional editors because they frequently edit in the narration first and then choose video clips to match the audio. If each transition shortened the video, that narration would fall out of sync with the images.

Studio's programmers assume you will lay down your video clips, insert transitions, add titles and music, and then perhaps add a narration.

The bottom line is that you should either narrate your video as the last step or give clips extra tailroom and headroom at edits where you plan to insert a transition.

Using Special Effects

Studio offers several special video effects. They affect the appearance of a clip, put it in motion, layer it over another clip, or change its playback speed.

You can combine effects. For instance, you can apply slow motion to a clip and add water droplet waves. It's a cliché, but it applies—the only limit is your imagination.

To see what Studio has to offer, place a clip in the Timeline (or Storyboard) and double-click that clip to open the Video Clip Properties toolbox. Click the Plug icon (as in plug-in, get it?) to open the Video Effects toolbox (see Figure 11.15).

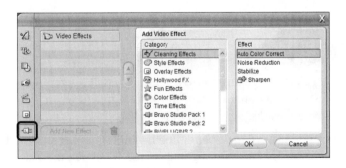

FIGURE 11.15
Use the Video Effects toolbox to change the appearance of a clip.

Studio ships with dozens of video effects. Only 20 are unlocked and ready to go. The rest are Pinnacle Systems or third-party plug-ins available for an extra charge. I will cover several of them in Chapter 13.

Studio divides the available video effects into six categories:

▶ **Cleaning**—Auto Color Correct fixes poor white balance, Noise Reduction reduces visual "noise" usually due to low-light situations, and Stabilize reduces camera shakiness. These are very useful tools.

▶ **Style**—Five cool effects: Blur softens a clip's look, Emboss makes it look like a notary public paper stamp, Mosaic breaks clips into blurry rectangles, Old Film gives your clips a sepia tone with film scratches, and Stained Glass breaks your clips into just what the name implies.

▶ **Overlay**—These require two video tracks. Chroma Key lets you key out a single color background (usually Chroma Key Green) into which you can place another video or still. Picture-in-Picture lets you place one video in a box on top of another video. I cover these effects in Chapter 13.

▶ **Fun**—Lens Flare simulates something you usually try to avoid, Noise gives your clips a grainy feel, Pan and Zoom lets you get in tighter on a clip and move it around, and Water Drop makes your clip look like a pool of water into which you dropped a pebble.

▶ **Color**—Black and White does what it says; Color Correction lets you manually adjust Brightness, Contrast, Hue, and Saturation (kind of like what you might do with a TV set); Posterize reduces the color palette to give your clip an Andy Warhol graphic look; and Sepia gives your clips that old-fashioned photo look.

▶ **Time**—Speed lets you speed up or slow down your clips, and Strobe makes your clip look like a stop-action film.

Try it Yourself   Adding Video Effects and Changing Parameters

Applying a video effect is relatively easy. What makes it interesting is how you choose to adjust an effect's parameters and what happens when you combine effects. Here's how it works:

1. To repeat the instructions given at the beginning of this section, drag a clip to the Timeline (or Storyboard), double-click it to open the Video toolbox, and click the Video Effects (Plug) icon to open the Video Effects toolbox.

Other Ways to Access Video Effects

There are three other ways to access the Video Effects section in the Video toolbox.

▶ Hover your cursor over the left side of the Toolbox icon in the upper-left corner of the Timeline/Storyboard window to reveal a camcorder icon. Click it to access the Video toolbox, and then click the Plug icon.

▶ Select Toolbox, Add Video Effects.

▶ Press ALT+T, V, and Enter.

Did you Know?

Choose a Simple Scene

For this exercise, I selected Photoshoot.mpg Scene 4 because it's a simple composition with only one subject.

By the Way

2. Because none of the Cleaning Effects makes much of an obvious change to well-lit, properly white-balanced video (which is the case for the Photoshoot.mpg video), click Style Effects (the second group). As shown in Figure 11.16, that displays five unlocked effects: Blur, Emboss, Mosaic, Old Film, and Stained Glass.

FIGURE 11.16
First check out the Style Effects. In particular, Emboss looks for edges in your clip's images and gives them a raised, 3D look.

3. Click each of the five video effects in turn and note that Studio immediately displays in the Player window how that effect will look. You can fine-tune how each effect works using parameters unique to each effect. So, when you try Stained Glass and note that not much happens, don't worry.

4. Double-click Stained Glass to add it to the Video Effects list and to open its Settings window (as shown in Figure 11.17). When that Video Effects list is open, you can click Add New Effect to return to the Add Video Effects list.

FIGURE 11.17
Double-click an
effect to add it to
the Video Effects
list for the currently
selected clip.
Changing the
Stained Glass
parameters dis-
plays how this
video effect works.

5. Make some changes to the slider settings (or parameters) and note the results (use Figure 11.17 as a reference). If you change Joint to something other than its default setting of zero, you will get a better idea of how this effect works. The settings numbers (in the case of this specific effect) denote size. So a large horizontal number means each stained glass piece will be very wide.

By the Way

Check Out the Icon in the Timeline

When you add an effect to a clip, Studio adds an icon to that clip's thumbnail in the Timeline (it does not do this in the Storyboard—yet another reason to stick with the Timeline). That icon (shown in Figure 11.18) is the same one used for that effect's group—for example, a palette for Style Effects, a star for Fun Effects, and a Broom/Dustpan for Cleaning Effects.

By the Way

Background Rendering

Both when you add a video effect and change its parameters, Studio attempts to display immediately how that effect will look. But most effects require some inten- sive calculations, and many PCs will need some time to complete them. Studio does that rendering process in the background. That is, it doesn't just come to a screech- ing halt while it renders; it allows you to still work within Studio while it renders. It keeps you updated on its progress via the Timescale Ruler. It changes the color (to light green) above any clip being rendered (refer to Figure 11.18). Gradually, it changes that to dark green to note the rendering progress until rendering is complet- ed; then the Ruler color returns to its default yellow.

If rendering is overwhelming your PC, you can limit or eliminate background rendering by selecting Setup, Edit and changing Rendering to No Background Rendering. In that case, Studio will show your effect or transition at a lower resolution and/or frame rate.

FIGURE 11.18
Studio uses the Timescale Ruler as a background rendering progress bar. Note also that when you add an effect to a clip, the icon for that effect group appears in the clip thumbnail.

6. Remove that effect from the clip by clicking the Garbage Can icon next to the Add New Effect button.

7. Click Add New Effect and double-click Blur. In its settings/parameters window, select Horizontal Blur from the Presets drop-down list. As shown in Figure 11.19, that makes it look like the model is moving quickly across the scene. Most video effects have presets. They help you zero in on a particular look. Then you can fine-tune the parameters to suit your needs.

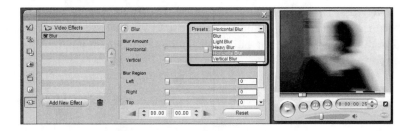

FIGURE 11.19
Use effect Presets to help you find general effect parameters to suit your needs.

8. Note that Blur has six parameter sliders. As you move through the Presets, note the new parameter values. Adjust a few to see how they work. If you get too far from your desired look, click the Reset button to return to ground zero.

9. Studio gives you the very cool option of adding an effect gradually over time. Do that using the Fade In and Fade Out windows at the bottom of the Effect Settings window (highlighted in Figure 11.20). In this case, Studio takes 1 second to reach the full vertical blur preset, holds that for a while, and then uses the clip's final second to fade back to an unblurred look. You can apply different fade-in or fade-out times to any effect applied to a clip.

FIGURE 11.20
Gradually apply or remove an effect to or from a clip using the Fade In or Fade Out time settings.

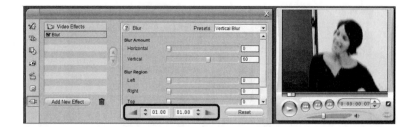

10. Add another effect to this clip (on top of Blur). Click Add New Effect, select the Fun Effects group, and double-click Water Drop.

11. In the Player window, play your clip and note how Water Drop is an animated effect. It changes over time. In this case, you might also note that the waves are in sharp focus but your image is blurred. That's because, being the last effect applied, it changes what's above it on the Video Effects list.

12. To get Water Drop to look "right," click it in the Video Effects list to select it, and then click the Move Effect Up triangle (highlighted in Figure 11.21) to move Water Drop above Blur. Now the waves are blurred, as you'd expect, because the Blur effect (being lower on the Video Effects list) changes anything that has been applied above it. The order in which you apply effects is important.

FIGURE 11.21
Combining two effects can dramatically alter the look of your clip. And order does count. With Blur applied last (at the bottom of the Video Effects list), the Water Drop ripples look blurred. To change the order, use the highlighted Move Effect Up or Down triangles.

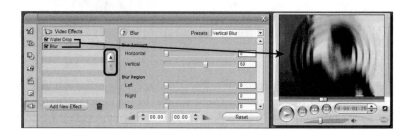

Checking Out Specific Effects

I gave you a brief explanation of all the effects earlier. There's no need to give detailed explanations of all 20. But some warrant explanation:

▶ **Stabilize**—Smoothes jerky camera movement (different from smoothing action within the scene). To do that, it zooms in about 20% (thus removing the edges of your clip), and then examines the overall clip for motion and attempts to counter that. The zoom does add some graininess to the clip, as is the case when you use digital zoom on a video camcorder.

▶ **Lens Flare**—This takes some real experimentation and you should use it sparingly (refer to Figure 11.22). Apply it only when there is a bright light in the scene (for example, sunny exteriors or interiors with a spotlight) and typically only if there is a camera pan or zoom. Lens Flare is an animated effect that moves smoothly across the scene. Generally, you should have the lens flare move in the opposite direction of your camera movement.

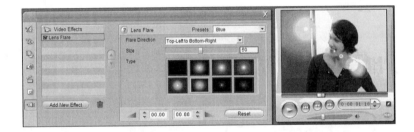

FIGURE 11.22
Lens Flare is effective but works best if there is smooth camera movement and a bright light source.

▶ **Pan and Zoom**—This, too, takes some experimentation to master. It gives you a start and end location and zoom factor (I cover panning and zooming still images—the controls are very similar to the video effect—in the next section).

You can use the Fade In and Fade Out settings to start and/or end with your clip at full-screen size. Or you can start zoomed in or out and end using different parameters.

Take a look at Figure 11.23, for an example. In this case I set Fade In and Fade Out values to 1 second each. I set the Start parameters to make the clip shrink to quarter-screen size (its smallest setting) in the upper left. I set the End position to quarter screen in the lower right.

When –100 Equals 25%

I don't understand the reasoning behind the numerical values in Studio's Pan and Zoom video-effect settings. If you set Zoom to its smallest setting, –100, you'd think that would mean a tiny dot. But the smallest zoom setting displays the clip at 25% of its original size. And the Horizontal and Vertical numerical values do not represent Cartesian—X and Y—coordinates. A Vertical Position of +100 puts the *center* of a fully zoomed-out image (–100 Zoom value) at the top edge of the screen. But if you leave the zoom set to zero, a Vertical Position of +100 moves the *entire* clip off the top of the screen. Basically, you need to use the sliders and then eyeball the results.

What happens in this case is that the clip starts full screen but immediately starts shrinking and moving. At 1 second into the clip, it has finished its move to the upper-left corner. It then immediately starts moving to the lower-right corner and arrives there with 1 second left in the clip. Then it returns to full screen by the end of the clip.

FIGURE 11.23
Pan and Zoom settings that have the clip start and end at full screen. The clip shrinks and moves to the upper left, slides down to the lower right, and then expands back to full screen.

▶ **Water Drop**—I mentioned earlier that this is an animated effect. It starts as if you've dropped a pebble into a calm pool; then the ripples spread and dissipate at the end of the clip (or the time you've allotted between Fade In and Fade Out points). As shown in Figure 11.24, you can set several parameters, including where to locate the center of the ripples, the number of waves, and the size of the waves.

FIGURE 11.24
Water Drop parameters let you set its center and wave characteristics.

▶ **Speed**—This lets you put your clip in slow motion (down to one-tenth its regular speed) or speed it up (five times regular speed). It does that by either repeating frames or cutting frames and then attempting to smooth the differences between frames to avoid jumpy, stop-frame action (use Strobe for that).

Changing Speed Changes Clip Length

As you move the Speed slider, you might notice that the selected clip's length changes. Speeding up a clip shortens it, whereas slowing down a clip lengthens it. After changing a clip's speed, you might want to change how you trimmed it to compensate for the new length.

By the Way

Putting Still Images in Motion

Thanks to Ken Burns's PBS documentaries, zooming in on or panning across stills for dramatic effect or to emphasize something or someone has become ubiquitous. A basic slideshow of static images is simply boring.

New to Studio Plus is a tool to emulate what editors now call the Ken Burns effect. And on top of this, you can apply just about any video effect to still images as well.

Moving Images

Try it Yourself

You do your image editing in the Video toolbox, Clip Properties interface. But Studio recognizes that you're working with a still image, so it opens a vastly different-looking window than what you saw in the Video Clip Properties window. Here's how it works:

1. Either start a new project (File, New Project) or clear all the clips from the Timeline. In the Album, click the Photo and Frame Grab tab to reveal the two photos that ship with Studio. Drag one to the Video Track. That still image will have whatever length you've set in the Edit menu (4 seconds is the default setting). You can drag its end to extend or shorten it.

Other Tracks

You can drag a still image to any of three Timeline tracks: the Main Video Track, the Overlay Track, or the Title Track. Stills work the same in each of those three locations. I want you to use the Main Video Track for this exercise.

By the Way

Use Higher Resolution Stills If You'll Zoom In

In general, if you plan to zoom in on or pan across a still image, you will want to use an image with a resolution greater than the standard NTSC 720×540 or PAL 720×576. Otherwise, when you zoom in on that clip, it will look grainy. Any still you grab from a video clip will be at that TV standard's resolution. Keep that in mind if you want to put it in motion. Zooming out shrinks the image, so resolution is not an issue.

2. Double-click the image to open the Still Clip Properties window shown in Figure 11.25. Note that if you move the cursor to that image, a four-arrow cursor appears. I've highlighted it in Figure 11.25. Unlike the Pan and Zoom Video effect, Pan and Zoom for still images lets you grab the image and drag it to a new position. Move the image around to get a feel for this.

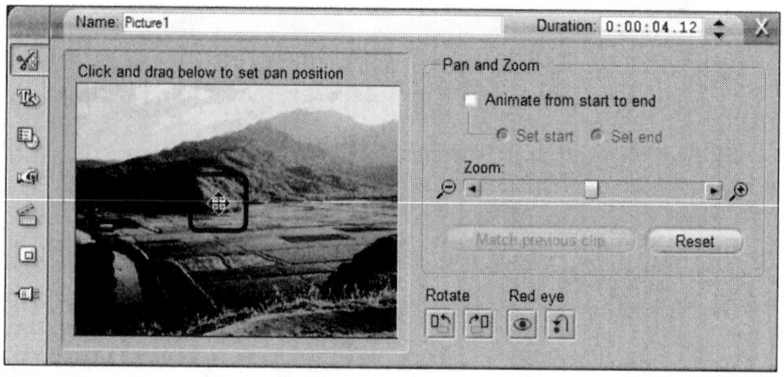

FIGURE 11.25
Unlike the Pan and Zoom Video effect, the Still Image Pan and Zoom lets you drag the image to a new location using the highlighted, four-arrow cursor.

3. Zoom out to the smallest setting (quarter screen) and drag the image to the upper-left corner. If you play the clip in the Player window, it'll stay in its new location.

4. Give your still image some motion by clicking the Animate from Start to End button. Click Set Start and use the current upper-left, zoomed-out parameters (you don't need to change anything). Click Set End and drag the clip to the lower right. Now play the clip and it should slide from the upper left to the lower right, all the while maintaining its quarter-screen size.

5. Many times you'll want to zoom in on an image, hold that position for a while, then zoom back out. You do that by using the same image three times. Start by working with the single image you've already added to the Timeline. Click Set Start, click Reset (that will display the still at full screen), click Set End, and zoom in on the image (in my case I zoomed in on the river).

6. Close the Clip Properties window (click the X in the upper-right corner) and drag the same still image to the Video Track two more times. Double-click the second clip to reopen the Still Image Properties window. Your project should look like Figure 11.26.

FIGURE 11.26
To put an image in motion and then hold that position, you need to add another instance of the image to the Timeline.

7. With the middle still-image clip selected, click the now-activated Match Previous Clip button in the Clip Properties window (it was grayed-out before because there was no "previous clip"). That will set the zoom and place-ment parameters for the second clip to those of the last frame of the previous clip. Don't animate this clip.

8. To zoom back out to the original clip size, select the third clip, click Match Previous Clip, click Animate from Start to End, click Set End, and click Reset. That will set the ending value to a regular full-screen view. Play your three clips and the image should zoom in, hold the zoom, and then zoom back out.

9. Finally, you can place one image over another. I cover this in more detail in Chapter 13. For now, try some experimentation. Go back to the Album and add a different still image to the Title Track.

10. The Title Track, by design, plays on top of the Main Video Track so this new clip covers up whatever is on the main track. To reveal what's in the Main Track, zoom out of the still image on the Title Track. Figure 11.27 shows how I zoomed out of both clips on the Main and Title Tracks. You can take this one step further and open the Overlay Track (right-click in the Timeline and select Always Show Overlay Track), add another still to that track, and move it around so you can see all three images.

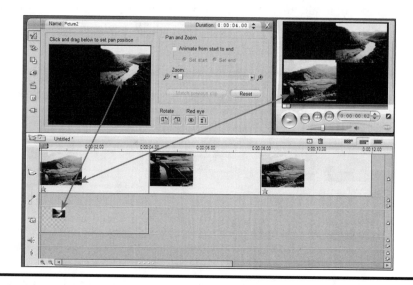

FIGURE 11.27
You can combine still images in a scene by placing images on more than one track and zooming and panning on each one.

Using Supers to Help Tell Your Story

Consider this opening sequence: A telephoto shot of scorched desert sand with rippling heat distorting the scene. Dry, desiccated, lifeless sagebrush. A lizard slowly seeking shade beneath a small stone. And a small plume of dust in the distance. Attention-getting stuff.

Now a narrator intones, "The summer heat beats down on the Bonneville Salt Flats." Effective. But what might work better is a **super** (superimposed, onscreen text)—something such as "Bonneville Salt Flats." Then, as the plume of dust moves toward the camera, add another super: "Speed Trials—Summer 2003." Then a rocket-shaped vehicle screams through the scene.

Rather than interrupt the building suspense with a dulcet-toned narrator, save him for later. Instead, simply slap on a couple supers to set up your story.

Onscreen text helps tell your story. Using a location super sets the scene and saves the narration for other relevant points. Displaying an interviewee's name and title at the bottom of the screen reminds viewers who this person is. Using onscreen bulleted points reinforces the message you're trying to get across. Or you can give your production a title screen or rolling credits at the end.

Here are a couple other sample instances in which text can be an effective alternative to voice-overs:

▶ Instead of using a voice-over to say "John Jones, president of the XYZ Association for the Preservation of Salient Sayings," put that information in a super at the bottom of the screen.

▶ Instead of saying a collection of statistics, such as 12 drummers drumming, 11 pipers piping, 10 lords a-leaping, and so on, use a collection of bulleted points that you pop onscreen with each new numbered item. If you have small graphical images of each element, you can add them along with the text.

Text strengthens your project.

Adding Titles to Your Videos

Studio's Title Editor—a derivative of Pinnacle's well-regarded, professional video text product TitleDeko—is an outstanding feature. No other NLE in this price range matches its high quality.

To explain it in detail would consume an entire chapter of this book, so I'll just present some highlights.

Explore Studio's Title Editor   *Try it Yourself* ▼

To demonstrate what the Title Editor can do, let's step through a few brief exercises. I'll start with selecting a background:

1. Either start a new project (File, New Project) or clear all the clips from the Timeline.

2. Open the Title Editor by double-clicking anywhere in the Title Track in the Timeline. Figure 11.28 shows the screen that appears, which has several features, including Title Types, Templates, Backgrounds, and Object Tools.

Another Route to the Title Editor   *Did you Know?*

As you'd expect, there's another way to open the Title Editor: Select Toolbox, Create Title and then click Edit Title in that interface.

FIGURE 11.28
The full-featured
Title Editor packs a
lot of muscle for a
video editor in this
price range.

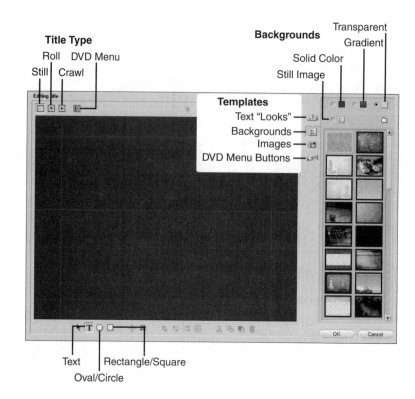

3. The text Background tools are in the upper-right corner, and Transparent is
the default setting (see the following By the Way for an explanation). Select
Still Image (the small cactus icon) and use the slider on the right to check
out all the available graphics. Note the checkerboard pattern in several of
the graphics (see Figure 11.29). This indicates that that portion of the background is transparent—it lets the video clip show through.

By the Way

Built-In Backgrounds

Normally, when you use text with a video, it appears on the video clip. By default,
Studio gives your text a **transparent** background to let that video appear behind the
text. Sometimes, though, you'll want text to appear over a still image or graphical
background; that's where Studio goes the extra mile—it gives you all sorts of text
background options.

FIGURE 11.29
Studio offers dozens of background graphics. Those with checkerboard patterns (highlighted) work like frames. The checkerboard areas are transparent and let the video show through.

4. To create a solid-color background, click the Solid Color swatch. That opens the color selector interface. As shown in Figure 11.30, you can select a color using the crosshair tool and adjust the color intensity using the slider on the right side. I want you to create a gradient background, so for now, click Cancel.

Create Transparent Tints

You can adjust any background color's opacity, meaning you can give it some transparency to let the video clip show through. In this way you can place a transparent color on top of a video clip (or still image) to give it a tint and then apply text over the video and the tint. That's a great way to emphasize the text without obliterating the video. To give a selected background color some transparency, in the Color selection screen, move the opacity slider and then return to the Title Editor window to check the results (see Figure 11.30).

Did you Know?

---

5. Select Gradient to open the Gradient box shown in Figure 11.31. Note that you can change colors in each of the four corners. Click one of the corner boxes to open the Color Selection tool and select a color. You'll use this gradient background for your text. So, select colors for each corner and give your gradient some transparency (you adjust that individually for each corner). You won't see your results until you close the gradient box.

FIGURE 11.30
Use the Color Selection tool to create a solid or gradient back-ground. Use the highlighted Opacity slider to make your background trans-parent.

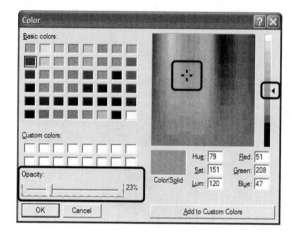

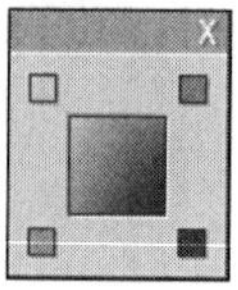

FIGURE 11.31
Use the Gradient tool to make your background more interesting.

6. Click the Text Tool icon (T). Click somewhere in the upper-left portion of the Text Editor window and drag down and to the right to create a text bounding box (see Figure 11.32). Start typing. The text style that appears is the default selection from the Styles list.

Did you Know?

Add Transitions Between Stills and Titles

You can apply transitions between stills and titles. As you might expect, you can apply transitions between any kind of clip that resides on either of the two video tracks. In addition, if you have two adjacent titles or graphics on the Title track, you can drag and drop a transition there. It works the same way as a transition on any of the video tracks.

7. Click the bounding box to let Studio "know" you want to edit the entire text segment (you can click and drag your cursor to highlight a portion of your text). Doing so will thicken the border and add some **handles**.

8. Click the text Looks button (the Aa icon) shown in Figure 11.32. Scroll through the type styles and click a few. Note how the text in the Title Editor immediately changes to the new style. Select a style that appeals to you. Figure 11.32 shows my selection.

FIGURE 11.32
Use the Title Editor and its template Looks collection to create text for your video project. Use the highlighted standard text tools (Font, Size, and other characteristics) and Justification tool (the tic-tac-toe icon) to align your text.

9. You can change the typeface, font size, and other characteristics such as Bold, Italic, or Underline. To do that, drag your cursor over the text to highlight it, use the standard text tools at the top of the Title Editor to make your changes, and use the Justify tool (the tic-tac-toe icon) at the bottom to arrange your words (refer back to Figure 11.32).

NTSC Safe Zone

The intersecting dashed red lines in the Title Editor window delineate the NTSC safe zone. Most TV sets display less than a full-screen view by truncating the edges of the original video. This is the **overscan** issue I covered back in Chapter 3, "Creating Compelling Still Images." By keeping your text within the red rectangle, you'll guarantee that all your words will appear on all NTSC TV screens. PAL does not have this inconvenience.

Watch Out!

Other Fun Tools

You also can manipulate the text box by changing its size, moving it, and rotating it. Move your cursor around in the text box to see how it changes depending on the function it can perform in each location. A four-arrow icon means you can move the entire box; a double-arrow means you can slide a border; and an arrow in a circle (this appears only over the handle above the frame) means you can rotate the text box.

Did you Know?

10. Change your text look to the style in the upper-left corner. Do that by high-lighting the text or clicking the bounding box, and then clicking the text style. This is the simplest style and lends itself to the most customization.

11. Click the Custom tab, shown in Figure 11.33. Its interface lets you fine-tune your typeface.

FIGURE 11.33
The Custom interface gives you detailed control over the look of your text.

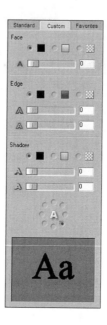

Did you Know?

Create Your Own Text Looks

In the Custom interface, the Face (typeface) option lets you change the text color, make it a gradient, or make it transparent. You also can give it an out-of-focus look. The Edge option has similar features and lets you change the edge width and add a glow. The Shadow option works the same way and lets you set the direction the shadow falls by using the dial in the lower-right corner.

Explaining all the options in the Custom interface could take many more steps. Instead, I suggest you experiment with the controls. Give your text a gradient look or apply an edge (drag the slider to the right a bit) and make the text transparent. You can add a drop shadow that is a gradient so that it shows through the transparent text (this is a wild effect).

12. When you've created a custom title style you like, you can save it as a Favorite. To do that, click the Favorites tab and click the Suitcase icon (as shown in Figure 11.34) to add your customized look to that collection.

13. When you're done adjusting your text and background, click OK to put the title on the Timeline. You can change its length by either dragging the start or end or dragging it to another location on the Timeline. You can also view it by playing your video at that point. If you want to re-edit it, double-click it.

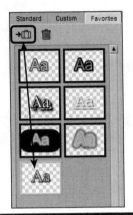

FIGURE 11.34
Save your newly created custom style within the Favorites folder by clicking the Suitcase icon.

Using the Shape Tools

You can make ellipses, circles, rectangles, and squares using the Title Editor. These are great for title backgrounds or for highlighting a portion of your video.

To create them, open the editor again by double-clicking the title track. Click the Add Ellipse tool (see Figure 11.35). Then click in the Title Editor window and drag to create a shape. As with text, you can change a shape's characteristics, including color (with gradients), border, and drop shadow, by opening the Custom interface.

Creating Circles and Squares

To create a circle, hold down the Ctrl key as you drag the Add Ellipse tool. The same method applies when using the Add Rectangle tool to make a square. If you want to change the size of a square or circle, hold down the Ctrl key as you drag a handle.

Did you Know?

I created three shapes, rotated them a bit, and used colors and gradients (with some transparency thrown in) to give the feeling of depth. Then I add text over one to show that you can use a shape as a backdrop for a super.

FIGURE 11.35
Use the Shape Object tools to create ellipses, circles, rectangles, and squares. Rectangles make good backdrops for supers.

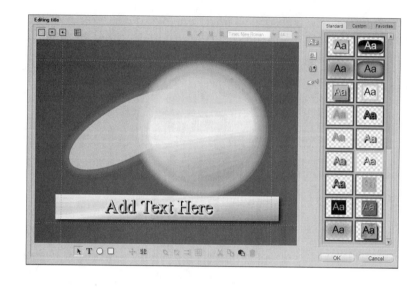

Did you Know?

Move Multiple Objects

Adding text on top of a rectangle makes a more visually interesting super. After you do that, you might need to adjust their location to fit a scene. Moving the rectangle and then trying to reposition the text can be tedious. Save some time and effort by clicking the Select arrow and then dragging a border around both objects. Now you can drag them as a unit around the screen.

You can move these shapes from front to back or vice versa by selecting one and accessing the Title Menu: Title, Layer, and then select from one of the four options shown in Figure 11.36.

FIGURE 11.36
Move shapes from front to back, or reverse, using this menu.

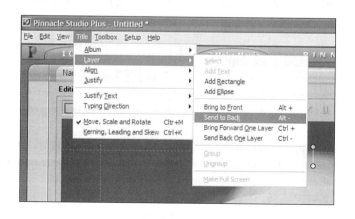

Realistic Drop Shadows

When using transparent colors with an object or text, be sure you reduce the opacity of its shadows as well. To maintain a realistic look, set all the shadows in the same title screen in the same direction. The distance can vary, giving the impression that some objects or text are farther above the background than others.

Did you Know?

Finally, you can access the Title Editor in a couple other ways:

▶ Use any of the title templates that ship with Studio. In the Album, click the Show Titles tab to reveal the Standard Titles (the only unlocked set available). Double-click any template to drop it into the Timeline. Double-click that Timeline clip to open the Title Editor and select the Custom tab to see how Pinnacle's graphic artists created this look. Sometimes Title Template Edge and Shadow attributes are disabled (meaning you can't change them). However, if you change the look, you usually can access those characteristics.

▶ Double-click any clip to open the Clip Properties window, click the Create or Edit Title tab, and then choose between Title Overlay (adding a title over that selected clip) or Full Screen Title (a title with its own background).

Summary

Straight, cuts-only editing works well for most circumstances. But some videos cry out for some extra fun stuff. Transitions help ease viewers from one scene to the next, or they are so jarring that viewers will know that something just happened. Video effects, including slow motion, putting clips in motion, and changing clip colors and other visual attributes—can help set a mood or draw attention to a video clip or still image.

Studio Plus comes filled to the gills with plenty of cool transitions and effects and makes it easy to add them to your project and adjust their attributes.

Studio's developers tapped one of Pinnacle Systems's high-end products: TitleDeko. The subset of that powerful character generator used in Studio is a full-featured suite of text-creation tools. Make text with borders, transparencies, drop shadows, gradients, and any of the fonts on your PC. Add some geometric shapes to spice up supers. Studio's Title Editor is chock-a-block with possibilities.

CHAPTER 12

Audio Production with Studio Plus

What You'll Learn in This Chapter:

- ▶ Voicing narrations and adding music
- ▶ Adding and editing other audio
- ▶ TV news–style editing
- ▶ Working with audio effects
- ▶ Adjusting audio levels and surround sound with the mixer

Audio is almost as important as video. Viewers might not notice your careful audio edits but if you do them well, they'll dramatically enhance your project. In this chapter I show you how to record a narration, create music, and edit in all sorts of audio. I explain how to add TV news–style cutaways and edit J-Cuts and L-Cuts.

Studio ships with six audio effects, and you can find dozens more on Studio's content DVD and online. You can use these effects to dramatically alter and improve your audio. Finally, Studio's audio mixer gives you real-time control over clip and track volume, balance, and lets you place any clip anywhere you want in 2D space using the surround-sound controller.

Voicing Narrations and Adding Music

Most professional video editors build a video in chunks. They might begin by laying down part of the narration or music, covering it with video to match the announcer's words or the music's beat, adding a snippet of video with audio, and then laying down another narration segment. That's not the approach used by most entry-level editors, however. Typically, adding audio—a narration or music—is the *last* step.

Studio's designers created their NLE with that fact in mind, which is why they included a built-in real-time narration tool and a music creation module that builds tunes to exactly fit the length of your finished piece.

As I mentioned in the previous chapter, "Enhancing Your Video with Transitions, Effects, and Titles," this is why those developers have no qualms about Studio's transition process that shortens the overall length of the video with each added transition. They fully expect that you will edit your video and then use the built-in narration tool to voice your piece as you watch it play or use the SmartSound music tool to create a soundtrack that matches your project's duration.

Voicing a Narration

Depending on your audience, you might want to write a script or simply improvise. In either case, you should view your edited project and take some notes before building your voice-over.

Try it Yourself ▼   **Use Studio's Voice-over Tool to Narrate Your Video**

Studio makes recording your voice directly onto your edited video surprisingly easy. Here's how you do it:

1. Open Studio to an edited project by selecting File, Open Project, and then locating an edited video and clicking Open.

2. As shown in Figure 12.1, click the Audio Toolbox icon in the upper-left corner of the Storyboard or Timeline (whichever you're using).

By the Way

> **Say "Adios" to the Storyboard**
>
> After you start adding audio to your projects, you should forego the Storyboard and use the Timeline exclusively. The Storyboard simply does not give you the access you'll need to the various audio tracks.

FIGURE 12.1
Click the Audio Toolbox icon to access the Voice-over tool.

3. In the Audio toolbox, click the Microphone icon, shown in Figure 12.2, to open the Voice-over tool. Speak into your PC's microphone and check your Volume Unit (VU) level on the right.

Don't Pin Your Needle

Some recording studios still use mechanical VU meters. They have a little metal arrow that sweeps out an arc. At the end of the arc is a little pin that keeps the needle from moving too far and possibly breaking the meter. Hitting that pin—that is, cranking the volume up too high, is called "pinning" or "pegging" the needle.

The equivalent of pinning the needle in the case of Studio's electronic VU meter is to record with the VU meter in the red zone. That leads to **over modulation**, a rough, scratchy, muffled voice-over. Try to keep the narration level in the yellow zone. Also, avoid popping your Ps by moving the mic a little off to one side, away from the puffs of air you make when you say P words.

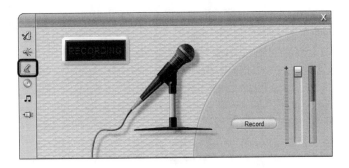

FIGURE 12.2
The Voice-over tool lets you create real-time narrations. Access it by clicking the Mic icon in the Audio toolbox. Use the slider and the VU meter to set levels.

4. Move the Timeline Scrubber to wherever in your video you want to start your narration. If you want to start at the beginning, click the Go to Beginning button (keyboard shortcut: Home) in the Player window or drag the Timeline Scrubber to the beginning (refer to Figure 12.3).

Record Multiple Narration Snippets

You can record narration snippets by starting and stopping in one location and then moving the Timeline Scrubber to another spot in your video and recording a narration there.

5. Studio lets you record only to the Sound Effect Track (the one with the Speaker icon). It has to be clear of any audio for the time frame in which you want to record (Studio will **gray out**—deactivate—the Record button if the Timeline Scrubber is in a location where audio already exists on that track). When you're ready to record, click the Record button. Watch the countdown, shown in Figure 12.4, and when the Record light comes on, begin your narration. When you've finished, click Stop.

FIGURE 12.3
Move to the beginning of your piece by clicking the Go to Beginning button in the Player window.

FIGURE 12.4
Watch the countdown to begin recording your narration.

6. Listen to your recording by playing the video from where you started your narration.

If you don't like what you hear, you can delete your narration segment and start over. However, the only way to do this is in the Timeline. As shown in Figure 12.5, your narration snippets appear in the sound-effect/voice-over track. To delete a narration segment, click it to select it and press Delete.

By the Way

Move Your Narration

You can slide your voice-over segment to another Timeline location. Roll your cursor over the narration clip and, when the cursor changes to a hand, click and drag your clip. Note that the cursor also turns into a blue speaker that lets you grab the blue Volume Adjustment Line and drag the clip volume up or down. I'll cover more on that later in this chapter.

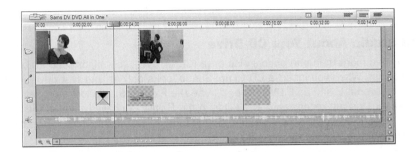

FIGURE 12.5
The only way to
delete or move
your narration seg-
ments is in the
Timeline.

Adding Music

Studio gives you two ways to add music to your project: You can rip a tune directly from an audio CD or use the SmartSound module included with Studio. I
briefly covered SmartSound Movie Maestro (which is very similar to the module
in Studio) in Chapter 5, "Making Marvelous Music," so this might seem like
déjà vu.

Ripping Tracks from CDs

Try it
Yourself

Using Studio's CD Audio tool, you can rip music from a CD and add it to your
video. Here's how:

1. Open the Audio toolbox by clicking its icon in the upper-left corner of the
   Timeline.

2. Open the CD Audio tool by clicking the CD icon, shown in Figure 12.6.

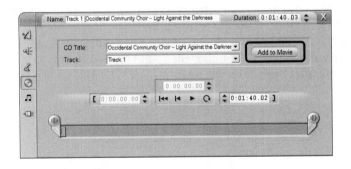

FIGURE 12.6
Use the CD Audio
tool to rip songs
from CDs.

3. Place a music CD in your DVD drive. Studio might ask you for the CD's
   name, or it might find it automatically online.

Watch
Out!

Tell Studio About Your CD Drive

If you have more than one optical disc drive (CD or DVD), you might need to tell Studio that. When you insert a CD to rip, Studio looks only at your first drive. In my case, I have an E and an F DVD drive. If I use the F drive, Studio looks only at the E drive and does not recognize that a CD is in the F drive. To have it look at the F drive, select Setup, CD, Voice-over and Sound and, as shown in Figure 12.7, change the Drive Letter.

4. Select the track you want to use and click Add to Movie.

FIGURE 12.7
If you have more than one CD/DVD drive, use the Setup window to tell Studio which one has the audio CD in it.

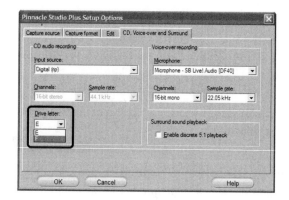

5. Studio does not immediately add that audio to the movie. Rather, it displays the standard rectangular clip in the Music Track (the one with the Treble Clef icon). Only when you attempt to preview your video does Studio actually rip that track. If the CD is still in the drive, Studio lets you know it's ripping that tune by displaying the progress bar shown in Figure 12.8. If you've removed the CD, Studio tells you to place it back into the same drive as before, and then it rips the tune.

FIGURE 12.8
Studio needs you to preview your project; then it lets you know it's ripping the music track from your CD.

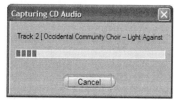

Move Your Audio to Any Audio Track

After you have ripped a tune, recorded a narration, added SmartSound music (see the next Try It Yourself, "Making Music with the SmartSound Module"), or added any other kind of audio, you can move that audio to any other audio track. Studio has four audio tracks, two associated with video (Video Track and Overlay Track) as well as the Sound Effect Track and the Music Track. To move audio to either of the Video Tracks requires the extra step of **locking** the video portion of those tracks.

Making Music with Studio's SmartSound Module

I explained SmartSound Movie Maestro in Chapter 5. The SmartSound module in Studio is very similar. Basically, it's a collection of songs recorded by musicians using a variety of instruments. They are not simply tinny-sounding MIDI tunes.

Each song is made up of discrete segments that can be moved around. In that way, one song can have a half-dozen different beginnings, verses that are arranged in various orders, and different endings. And SmartSound will create each tune to fit the exact length of your project. If you have SmartSound add a tune to your piece, and then you change the length of your project, you simply double-click the SmartSound tune and have it automatically change the length to fit.

Making Music with the SmartSound Module

SmartSound is a fun and easy-to-use tool. Basically, you complete your project and then scroll through SmartSound's 25 musical offerings to find one that matches the mood you want to set. Select a version of that tune that works for your piece and click Add to Movie. In your Timeline, you can change that tune's length or cut it into smaller chunks—all of which will sound like complete tunes with a beginning, a middle, and an end. Here's how to do it:

1. Access this module using the Audio Toolbox—click the music note icon shown in Figure 12.9.

2. You can select tunes based on Styles or directly by title from the Library list. For now, scroll through the Style types and note that each Style has some number of tunes within it. Some have only one song; others, like Classical, have quite a few. If you switch to the Library view, you'll note there are 25 songs that ship with Studio.

FIGURE 12.9
SmartSound is a
fun module that
lets you add music
that fits your video
project's mood and
exact length.

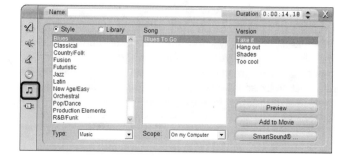

3. Select "Kickin' Back." It's in the Fusion Style (you can select any song you want—I will show the options available for "Kickin' Back" in this Try It Yourself).

4. As shown in Figure 12.10, "Kickin' Back" has eight versions. SmartSound builds each version from the same collection of song segments. It arranges them differently, typically by altering the opening and closing segments as well as the order of some other elements. Scroll through the various versions and click Preview to try them out.

FIGURE 12.10
Each SmartSound
tune has several
variations from
which you can
choose to fit how
your piece begins
and ends.

5. Select one and click Add to Movie. SmartSound instantly adds that music clip to the Music Track. Note that it's exactly as long as your project.

Watch Out!

Unexpected Behavior

If the Music Track already has audio in it, SmartSound will still add a tune to that track, but it likely won't be the proper length and it will move the clip in that track to the right. So make sure the Music Track is clear before working with SmartSound.

6. To see how SmartSound handles changes to your project, go back to the Album, add a still or a video clip to the end of your project, and then drag the right end of the SmartSound audio clip to the new end of the piece.

7. Move the Timeline Scrubber to just before the end of the newly added clip and press Play in the Player window (keyboard shortcut=spacebar). Studio will pause for a moment while SmartSound extends the music clip; then it will play and you'll note that the music clip is now longer and ends at the new ending point of your project. Neat.

Other SmartSound Tricks

Here are two other nifty SmartSound tricks. You can drag the end of any SmartSound clip to make it as long or as short as you like. It doesn't have to match the length of your project. SmartSound will adjust its formatting accordingly. You also can cut SmartSound clips at any point. SmartSound will then reformat and create two complete clips, each with a beginning, a middle, and an end and will make each one as long as you choose. In that way you can use the same style music in more than one location in your project.

Did you Know?

Adding Other Audio

With Studio's four audio tracks, you have enough locations to place all the audio you'd expect to add to most video productions.

What would be ideal is to have five audio tracks—two for the two video tracks plus three for the narration, music, and other audio clips such as sound effects. But it takes only a small amount of juggling to add a full spectrum of audio material within the four available tracks.

However, Studio exhibits what I consider to be unexpected and unpredictable audio-editing behavior, and you do need to exercise some care when adding audio to tracks where you already have audio in place.

Adding and Arranging Audio

Try it Yourself

As with video clips, adding audio is not much more than a drag-and-drop affair. But adding audio to either the Main or Overlay Video Tracks takes a couple extra steps. Here's how:

1. Start a new project: File, New Project. Add a video clip (that also has audio) to the Main Video Track. Add a brief narration and create a SmartSound

tune. Display the Overlay Track by right-clicking in the Timeline and select-ing Always Show Overlay Track. Your project should look like Figure 12.11.

FIGURE 12.11
For this Try It Yourself, set up your project along these lines: Open the Overlay Track, add about 30 sec-onds of video (with natural sound) to the Main Video Track, and include a narration and music.

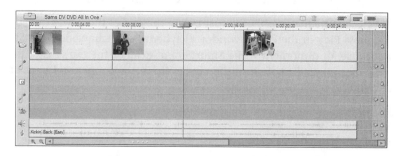

2. In the Album, click the Show Audio Files tab. That opens the Sound Effects collection shown in Figure 12.12. If you have your own collection of audio files, this is where you'd access them. For now, select any sound effect by double-clicking a category and finding an effect (that sound will play auto-matically in the Player window).

FIGURE 12.12
Studio Plus ships with dozens of sound effects that you can add to any project.

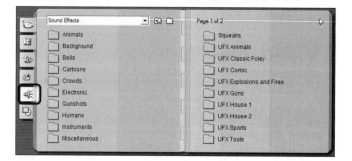

3. This step will serve more as an experiment. You'll see what you can and cannot do and check out what I think is a bizarre little Studio audio-editing quirk. Drag the sound effect to the Timeline (but don't release the mouse button just yet). Move it over each audio track. You'll note that Studio dis-plays that universal No symbol for all tracks. For the moment, you cannot add audio to either of the audio tracks associated with the two video tracks, nor can you ever add audio on top of existing audio (your narration and music). This runs counter to professional nonlinear editors that let you drop audio (or video) anywhere you want.

4. The best place to add a sound effect or other extra audio is on the Overlay Audio Track. To do that you need to **lock** the Overlay Video Track. Do that

by clicking the padlock icon highlighted in Figure 12.13. Note that Studio displays diagonal lines on any locked track.

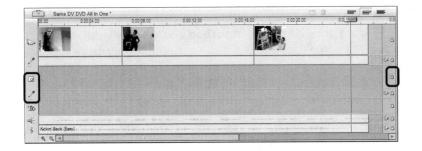

FIGURE 12.13
The best place to add small audio snippets is in the Overlay Audio Track.

5. Now drag a sound effect to the Timeline and drop it anywhere in the Overlay Audio Track. As shown in Figure 12.14, Studio displays those two parallel green lines and the "+" cursor that you've seen before, indicating that this is a legal location to place a clip. Move the Timeline Scrubber to that point and play your project to hear how that sound effect works in your piece.

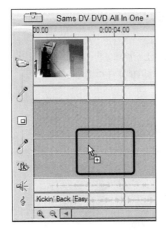

FIGURE 12.14
If you drag an audio (or video) clip to the Timeline, two parallel green lines let you know you've found a *legal* loca-tion to add a clip.

6. If you want to add an audio clip to a track that already has audio in it, you need to make room for that clip. Do that by cutting your SmartSound music clip. Click it to select it, move the Timeline Scrubber within it somewhere, and then click the Razor Blade icon at the top of the Timeline.

7. Now drag either the right or left music segment to one side (first you need to select whichever segment you want to change by clicking it) to open a space

for a sound effect. But for this exercise, make it smaller than the actual length of the sound effect you've already used.

8. Now drag the sound effect you added earlier from the Overlay Audio Track to the newly opened location (just move your cursor over it until it turns into a hand, then click, drag, and drop it to the new location). As shown in Figure 12.15, you'll see those parallel green lines you saw in step 5. They define the length of the selected audio clip. That's a given, but what happens next is not so clear. Here's how adding audio in a space that's too small for your clip works:

   ▶ The green lines do not delineate where the clip will go. They show what portions of the audio clip Studio will truncate. If the lines are on top of existing clips, Studio will truncate those portions of the newly added clip.

   ▶ If you line up the beginning of the new clip at the end of the preceding audio clip, Studio will truncate the end of the newly added audio clip. If you line up the end of the new clip with the beginning of the next clip, Studio will cut off the beginning of the new audio clip.

   ▶ You cannot add audio ahead of an existing clip. Unlike adding a video clip, you cannot insert an audio clip and have that shove all other audio clips to the right.

   ▶ If you place the clip at the end of your project but do so with the left green line inside the preceding clip, Studio will truncate the beginning of the newly added audio clip.

FIGURE 12.15
Inserting an audio clip that's longer than the opening on a track leads to some unexpected (but consumer-friendly) results.

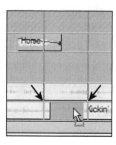

9. That Studio simply truncates an audio clip is a consumer-friendly thing. Generally, audio already edited into a project is tied to video in some fashion—as natural sound with the original video, music, or narration. So you don't want to willy-nilly shove it around. But there is a way to make some adjustments using the Audio Clip Properties window. Double-click the newly added (and truncated) sound effect to open the Audio Clip Properties window shown in Figure 12.16.

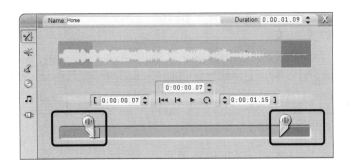

FIGURE 12.16
Use the Audio Clip Properties window to see, and possibly adjust, the truncated portions of your clip.

10. Note that the truncated portions are colored green (on the left) and red (on the right). If you drag either Trim Caliper (highlighted in Figure 12.16) to lengthen the clip, it will encroach on the adjacent clip and truncate it instead.

SmartSound Automatically Adjusts If Truncated

If you extend a clip you've fit next to an existing SmartSound music clip (thereby shortening that music), SmartSound automatically updates the music to fit the new length. If you truncate any other clip, the extended clip covers the truncated portion.

By the Way

▲

TV News–Style Editing

TV news editors (and other professional editors) use two editing techniques day in and day out: **cutaways** and **J-** and **L-Cuts**. With the addition of an Overlay Track in Studio Plus, it's now much easier to do both.

Cutaways do just that. They briefly cut away from the current action or interview. If it's a sporting event, they might show a crowd reaction to a touchdown. In interviews they generally show the interviewee listening intently.

In the case of an interview, they can cover an edit where you spliced two sound bites together. Without the cutaway, you'd see a jump cut at the edit point between the two bites.

To A/B or Not to A/B?

Pinnacle Systems refers to this style of editing as A/B editing. I think they should have avoided this moniker.

A/B editing is old-school, film-style editing. Film editors frequently use two reels of film: an A-roll and a B-roll, usually duplicates made from the same original. The two-reel approach permits nice, easy-on-the-eyes cross-dissolves, gradually fading down the images from one reel while fading up the other (see sidebar: "Still 'Grabbing B-Roll' After All These Years").

Adobe, Inc. incensed a whole segment of its professional video-editing market when it chose to drop A/B editing from Premiere Pro. Previous versions of Premiere gave editors the option to divide the first video track (out of 99 total) into A and B tracks. That let editors, used to the idea of A- and B-roll, work in that configuration.

Their reasoning behind the change was to "bring Premiere into the 21st century." So I would have preferred that Pinnacle not even bring up this outdated editing concept. For its part, Pinnacle says that those who use Studio Plus (rather than the single video-track Studio) will know about A/B editing and will relate to it.

Still "Grabbing B-Roll" After All These Years

In the TV news business—back when everyone used film and didn't have time to make duplicate reels—the A-roll typically was the interview and the B-roll was everything else. They relied on two reels because the audio and images were not synchronized in the same place on the film. Older film projectors use a soundtrack that is 20–26 frames (about a second) ahead of the associated images because the sound pickup in the projector is not in the lens. If you've ever threaded a film projector, you know how important it is to get just the right size loops to ensure that the sound synchronizes to the images.

So, in the old TV news film era, to get a sound bite to play audio at the right time, that clip had to play behind the B-roll for about a second to allow enough time for the sound to reach the audio pickup device. Only then would a director cut to the A-roll image to play the interview segment and then would cut back to the B-roll after the sound bite ended. Despite this now-outmoded means of editing or playing back news stories, news photographers still say they're going to go "grab some B-roll" (that is, some extra footage to go along with some sound bites).

When stations began switching to ENG (electronic news gathering) video gear, there was no longer a need to use A/B-rolls. Audio and video were on the same place on videotape, but the only way to do those smooth cross-dissolves was to make a copy of the original videotape (leading to some quality loss), run it on a second VCR, and make the cross-dissolve with an electronic switcher. That was a time-consuming and

> cumbersome process fraught with timing problems. Older VCRs frequently were not frame accurate and you ended up with spasmodic-looking dissolves.
>
> DV changes that. No more dubbing, no more generation loss, no more timing problems, and no more need to edit using ancient A/B-roll methods.

Adding Cutaways

Editing in cutaways in Studio Plus is now a simple affair. You simply drop whatever video you want to use as a cutaway on the Overlay Track and adjust its location to fit the video it's covering.

Editing in a Cutaway

Try it Yourself

You can use the Photoshoot.mpg video that shipped with Studio to see how a cutaway works. There aren't any true cutaway shots—reaction shots, views from behind the model, tight shots of her hands, or shots of the photographer—but you can use the exterior shot as a cutaway between two shots. Here's how:

1. Start a new project: File, New Project. If the Overlay Track is not open, right-click in the Timeline and select Always Show Overlay Track.

2. Drag Scene 6 and Scene 7 to the Timeline. Note that in Scene 6 the model is wearing a black blouse. In Scene 7 she's wearing white. Without a cutaway between these two clips (or at least an obvious transition) you'd have a clumsy jump cut.

3. Drag the exterior shot—Scene 1—to the Overlay Track. For the moment place its center someplace near the edit point between Scene 6 and Scene 7. Your project should look like Figure 12.17.

Cutaway

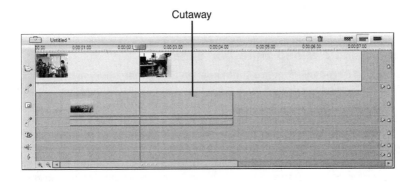

FIGURE 12.17
A basic view of how a cutaway looks on the Timeline.

4. Play the Timeline: Click the Go To Beginning button (keyboard shortcut: Home) in the Player window and then click Play. Note that the exterior in the Overlay track covers the end and the beginning of the two interior scenes. Also note that the exterior shot's audio is as prominent as the interior audio. I show you how to fix those audio levels in the final section of this chapter, "Adjusting Audio Levels and Surround Sound with the Mixer."

By the Way

Nonintuitive Overlay Track Placement

Studio's Developers chose to put the Overlay Track *under* the Main Video Track. This is counter-intuitive because anything in the Overlay Track covers whatever is in the Main Video Track when you play the Timeline.

I asked Studio's product manager about this. He conceded that I might have a point but said they chose to arrange the tracks like this because of two "established paradigms":

▶ In Studio the title track (formerly called the Title Overlay Track) has always been below the video track. They did not want to change this.

▶ Studio's editing behavior is based on the concept that the video track is the master track, and tracks below it are subordinate to it, so that editing the video track affects the tracks below.

5. Adjust the location and length of the cutaway. My general tip for cutaways is that they should either start at the end of a sound bite or a shot or end at the beginning of a sound bite or a shot. And they should be short—two seconds, max. In this case, the first Scene 6 is already fairly short, so move the cutaway so that it starts at the end of Scene 6.

6. Trim the end of the exterior-scene cutaway so that it's no longer than 2 seconds. You can drag the end of the clip and approximate a two-second length. Or, in my case, as shown in Figure 12.18, I used the Clip Properties window to trim to that exact length.

By the Way

Duration and Elapsed Time Don't Match

In Figure 12.18, you might notice that Duration time in the upper-right corner of the Clip Properties window is one frame more than the calculated duration below the right video window. They're always off by a frame. That's because Studio's developers chose to call the beginning of a clip frame zero. So frame 29 is the 30th frame played. Yes, it's nit picking, but you'd be amazed at the number of emails I've read on beta test sites about what to call the beginning of a clip (is it frame one or zero) and what the programmers should choose to display when you jump to an edit point (the first frame of the next clip or the last frame of the previous clip). And these are only two of many discussions along these lines. Nothing is cut and dried.

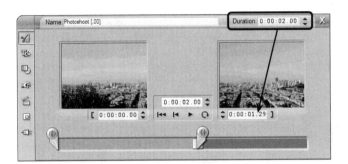

FIGURE 12.18
You can trim your
cutaway in the Clip
Properties window.

Working with J-Cuts and L-Cuts

J-Cuts, sometimes called **audio lead cuts**, quietly play the audio of the next clip under the video and audio of the previous one for a short time, as a means to let their audience know that someone is about to say something or that a transition is coming. **L-Cuts**, on the other hand, let the audio trail off under the next video clip.

These effects work best if you do both an audio cross-fade and a video dissolve. However, Studio's consumer-oriented transitions shorten clip lengths and create synch problems for audio placed on separate tracks. So skip the video transitions (unless you do some real careful editing) and do the audio cross-fades manually. I show you that latter process in the coming Try It Yourself.

Using a Single Track for J- and L-Cuts

Try it Yourself

There are ways to use both audio and video transitions in J- and L-Cuts and I urge you to experiment. I had the good intention of attempting to explain those processes here, but they ended up taking way too many steps, so I decided to keep it simple. Here now is a basic overview of J- and L-Cuts:

1. Start a new project: File, New Project. Make sure the Overlay Track is visible (right-click in the Timeline and select Always Show Overlay Track).

2. A J-Cut works well to ease the transition from an exterior shot to an interior shot (or vice versa). In this case the interior audio will fade up under the exterior video (and audio), and then you'll cut to the interior shot. To start, drag Photoshoot.mpg Scene 1 (the exterior) to the beginning of the Main Video Track on the Timeline.

3. Drag Scene 4 next to Scene 1 on the Main Video Track (you'll drop it down to the Overlay Track in a moment). Trim one second from the beginning of Scene 4. You're shortening the clip to give it some **headroom** (some extra video at the beginning) so you can have the audio from that headroom play under the preceding clip. Your project should look like Figure 12.19.

By the Way

What's Going On?

To trim the clip, I double-clicked it and used the Clip Properties window. But you can accomplish the same thing by dragging the left end of the clip to the right one second. In either case, the trimmed clip automatically slides to the left to fill the gap, which is why I had you put it on the Main Track for now. It wouldn't do that on the Overlay Track.

FIGURE 12.19
How your project should look before you create the J-Cut. Shorten the second clip by a second to give it some *headroom*.

4. Drag that shortened clip directly down to the Overlay Track, making sure it remains lined up with its former position.

5. Lock the Overlay Video Track by clicking the padlock highlighted in Figure 12.20.

6. Drag the start of that audio to the left so it will run under the preceding clip. Do that by selecting the audio clip on the Overlay Audio Track, hovering the cursor over the left end of the clip until the double arrow appears, and then dragging that audio segment to the left as far as you can. If you set it up right, that will be one second. Your project should look like Figure 12.20.

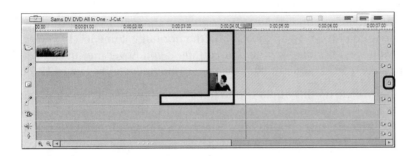

FIGURE 12.20
A J-Cut. I've high-
lighted the second
clip's audio seg-
ment to show why
it's called a J-Cut.
Note that I locked
the Overlay Video
Track to keep it
from moving as I
moved the audio
portion.

7. You need to reduce the volume of the audio clip in the Overlay Audio Track
   for the time it runs under the exterior shot. Then fade it up quickly when
   you cut to the interior. To do that, you use the clip's Volume Adjustment
   Line (see the following By the Way). Click that clip to select it. That displays
   its Volume Adjustment Line—the blue horizontal line.

What's a Volume Adjustment Line?

The audio Volume Adjustment Line (see Figure 12.21) is the thin, horizontal blue line
that runs through all audio clips (visible when you select that clip or after you've
adjusted the volume using the Adjustment Line). It's a visual representation of audio
volume. The default setting is about two-thirds of the way up the clip rectangle. To
change volume using the Adjustment Line, hover your cursor over it. It'll change into
either a light blue or dark blue speaker. Dark blue means you can click there, drag
the Adjustment Line to a new location, and create a **handle** in the process. Light
blue means you've moved the cursor over a handle or the beginning or end of the
clip. After you've placed a handle on an Adjustment Line, you can drag that handle
up, down, left, or right. Setting volume levels this way is an inexact science. The
Audio Mixer that I cover at the end of this chapter gives you more precise control.

By the Way

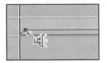

FIGURE 12.21
Adjust audio levels
using the Volume
Adjustment Line
(enlarged here for
clarity).

8. Hover your cursor over the Volume Adjustment Line at the beginning of the
   J-Cut until it turns into a light blue speaker. Click the Volume Adjustment
   Line to grab it and drag it all the way down. That drops the volume for the
   entire clip.

9. Hover your cursor over the Volume Adjustment Line right at the beginning of the audio clip until it turns into a dark blue speaker. Dark blue means you can add a handle here. Click and drag the Volume Adjustment Line one-third of the way up (about half the normal volume level). Your clip will now have a handle—a little blue square. If you hover the cursor over that handle, it will be a light blue speaker. It should look like Figure 12.21.

10. Finally, fade up this audio clip to full volume just before the video cuts from the exterior shot to the interior. Do that using the Adjustment Line. You'll need to make two handles—one that starts the fade up and the other to finish it. Use Figure 12.22 as a reference.

11. To fine-tune this J-Cut, you can use the same Volume Adjustment Line method to quickly fade out the volume in the first clip, just before it ends. That smoothes the transition. Your audio clips should look like those in Figure 12.22. Play your project to see how that J-Cut looks and sounds.

FIGURE 12.22
How your project's J-Cut Volume Adjustment Line audio levels should look for both audio clips. Note that the first clip's audio drops just as the audio for the second clip quickly fades up.

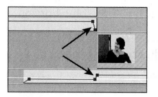

12. Build an L-Cut by unlocking the Overlay Video Track, shortening the interior scene by about a second (the audio should not move, leaving enough **tailroom** to have the audio play under the exterior shot), and putting the exterior shot on the Main Video Track directly after the end of the video portion of the clip on the Overlay Track. Now use the Volume Adjustment Lines to adjust the audio. Use Figure 12.23 as a reference.

By the Way

Another Adjustment Line: Balance

You can pan audio (it's called Balance in Studio) by placing it all the way left or right or somewhere in between using the Panning Adjustment Line. To access it, right-click any audio clip and click Select Balance Display. That turns the clip green, signifying that the Adjustment Line on display now controls Panning. Up pans left. Down pans right.

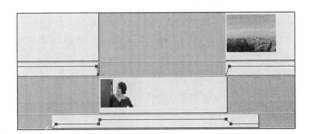

FIGURE 12.23
A project with both a J-Cut (left) and an L-Cut (right). Note the Volume Adjustment Line audio levels.

Working with Audio Effects

You've applied effects to your video, and typically the results are obvious: Mosaic, Sepia, and Lens Flare for example. You can do something similar (but generally not as obvious) to your audio.

Studio ships with six audio effects (as we went to press, Studio also shipped with 23 additional locked, third-party plug-in audio effects):

- ▶ **Noise Reduction**—The only effect in the Studio Effects group. Noise Reduction can reduce background hum and wind noise.

- ▶ **Equalizer**—You've seen this in high-end stereos. It lets you control volume levels of specific frequency ranges. Typically, editors use this to pump up or reduce bass or treble. Equalizer and the remaining four effects are all in the VST group. VST is a special audio plug-in technology that I explain a bit later in this section.

- ▶ **Grungelizer**—Normally you want clean, static-free audio. Grungelizer lets you add noise. To each his own.

- ▶ **Karaoke**—This is an effect that is good in theory but rarely good in practice. Its purpose is to remove vocals from music so you can use the instrumental portion as a karaoke number.

- ▶ **Leveler**—If your audio has very loud and very soft passages, it's darned hard to find an overall level that works well. Apply this to compress high volume and amplify low volume.

- ▶ **Reverb**—This might be your most frequently used effect. Use it to make music sound like it was recorded in a cathedral or give your narration some extra presence.

Apply Audio Effects

The way you add audio effects to your clips is similar to how you deal with video effects. The difference, in this case, is that VST effects tend to have their own unique controls. Here's a look at a few effects:

1. Start a new project: File, New Project. In this case there's no need to display the Overlay Track. To close it, right-click in the Timeline and deselect Always Show Overlay Track.

2. Add two pieces of audio to your project. I suggest you add a narration and vocal music with an instrumental backup. If you use Studio to rip a tune from a CD and record your narration, then each audio clip will automatically appear in its respective track in the Timeline.

3. Double-click the narration clip to open the Audio Clip Properties window in the Audio toolbox.

4. Open the Audio Effects window by clicking the Plug icon highlighted in Figure 12.24. The interface looks the same as the Video Effects window. The only difference is the effect names.

FIGURE 12.24
The Audio Effects window looks and works just like the Video Effects window.

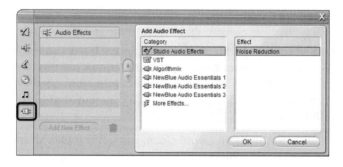

5. Double-click Noise Reduction (the only effect in the Studio Audio Effects Group) to open its interface. It has a few parameters. If you recorded your narration next to your computer, there might be some hum in it from your PC's fans. Noise Reduction will remove that hum.

6. Mute the Music Track by clicking its speaker icon highlighted in Figure 12.25. In this way you can hear exactly how these effects work.

7. Play your clip, and then start making changes to the Noise Reduction parameters. You should get more or less immediate feedback. If you recorded in a quiet setting, you might notice that the noise reduction makes your audio sound tinny.

8. Click the music clip to select it (and display an empty Audio Effects list), mute the narration and unmute the music track, click Add New Effect, open the VST group, and double-click Equalizer. That opens the interface shown in Figure 12.26.

FIGURE 12.26
The Equalizer effect has the look and feel of the equalizer you might have on your home or auto stereo.

9. Play your clip and then open the Presets drop-down list and sample a few. Note how the frequency range sliders change positions. This is a fun effect. Feel free to adjust the sliders manually and check out how things sound.

10. Remove Equalizer, click Add New Effect, and double-click Karaoke. It attempts to remove the center of a clip (usually where studio engineers place vocals). Play your music clip where there are vocals and note how well (or not) Karaoke removes them. Adjust the slider to find a sweet spot.

11. Click the narration clip to select it, mute the music track, and unmute the narration track. Remove Noise Reduction and add Reverb. This cool effect can really kick up a narration or solo vocalist. Scan through the Presets drop-down list and check out all the cool "locations."

12. Remove Reverb and add Grungelizer. Doing that displays a little button, Edit Grungelizer. Click it to open the separate—and very cool-looking—interface shown in Figure 12.27. This is a third-party, VST plug-in (see the next section for more on VST). Play with these analog-looking controls to make your audio sound like an old, scratchy 78RPM vinyl album (ask your parents what that is).

FIGURE 12.27
The Grungelizer is a third-party, VST (Virtual Studio Technology) effect. In general, such effects run in their own interface. Grungelizer can make your audio sound like an old, crystal radio (ask your grandparents).

VST Effects—New to Studio Plus

This sudden appearance of a rack of control knobs signals your first look at a VST third-party plug-in. These are custom-designed audio effects that adhere to a standard set in 1996 by Steinberg audio (purchased by Pinnacle Systems in 2003). Pinnacle Systems added VST's open plug-in architecture to Pinnacle Studio and Studio Plus.

Karl Steinberg—Audio Visionary
To learn more about VST, I suggest you check out the Steinberg website: www.steinberg.net. One other resource is an interview with Steinberg, the man behind VST, who is still an audio innovator: http://streamworksaudio.com/contents.php?id=103.

Invariably, those who create VST audio-effect plug-ins want them to have a unique look and offer some very specialized audio effects. A treasure trove of VST plug-ins is available on the Internet. I suggest you start your quest at www.kvr-vst.com. Check out its Quick Effect Links for a lengthy listing of VST audio effects, all of which should work with Studio Plus.

Most of these VST audio-effect plug-ins cost something, but there are a few freebies. In particular, check out Little Duck. Figure 12.28 shows how it appears in Studio Plus. It emulates a classic analog filter bank.

Little Duck's developer, Land of Cockaigne, offers several other free VST plug-ins featuring an older, analog look at its website: www.funkelectric.com/~cockaigne/.

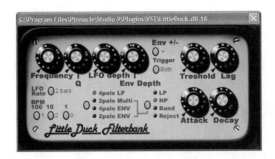

To add a VST plug-in to Studio Plus, download the plug-in (usually a .DLL file) and paste it into the Studio Plus VST Plug-ins file folder. The default location is `C:\Program Files\Pinnacle\Studio 9\Plugins\VST`. The next time you open Studio, that new plug-in should be in the VST group list.

Adjusting Audio Levels and Surround Sound with the Mixer

Your video might have audio from the original raw video, narration, music, and sound effects. You can bring order to this cacophony with Studio's Audio Mixer.

Use the Audio Mixer to Blend Audio Tracks

Try it Yourself

The Audio Mixer lets you adjust each track's sound level in real-time, creating a mix that's pleasing to the ear. Here's how it works:

1. Using the audio project you just worked on, add several clips to both video tracks. In this way you have audio on all four available audio tracks.

2. Open the Audio Mixer by clicking the Audio Toolbox icon in the upper-left corner of the Timeline and then clicking the Speaker icon shown in Figure 12.29. Note that it has sliders and other controls for each audio track, as well as a window to create surround sound. Here's a brief rundown:

   ▶ **Track Master Control**—Use this to set the volume level for an entire track.

   ▶ **Specific Volume Control**—As the video plays, you can move the slider to change volume levels within a specific clip on a specific track. You'll see those volume level changes in that clip's blue Volume Adjustment Line. You can fine-tune those changes by dragging and moving Volume Adjustment Line handles.

▶ **Fade In and Fade Out**—Click to gradually increase or decrease volume starting or ending at the Timescale Scrubber line.

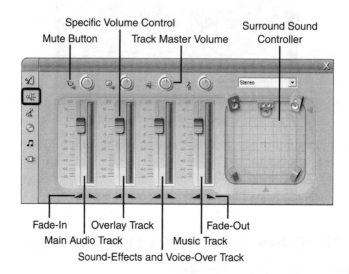

3. Drag the Timescale Scrubber to the beginning of the video (or press the Home key). Click the Fade-in button (the left triangle) for the Main Audio Track. Do this for the Overlay, Music, and Narration tracks as well. Your project should look like Figure 12.30.

By the Way

Volume Adjustment Line Visual Feedback

Take a look at Figure 12.30. As you click the Fade In button for any track, note that Studio displays the diagonal Volume Adjustment Line for that track denoting that fade in. Two seconds is the default Fade In and Fade Out duration. You can change that (I think one second is better) by selecting Setup, Edit and changing Volume Fades to whatever time you want. You also can click the handle created at the end of the fade in and drag it left or right to shorten or lengthen its duration.

4. Next, play your video by clicking the Go to Beginning (Home) button and then clicking Play. Note that the volume increases gradually as the video begins.

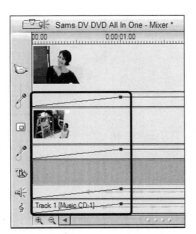

FIGURE 12.30
Blue Volume
Adjustment Lines
show the fade-in
audio-level changes
for each track.

Setting the Fade Location

Did you Know?

When using the Fade-in or Fade-out tool, where that volume change takes place depends on the location of the Timescale Scrubber when you click the fade buttons. When using the Fade In control, the fade starts at the Scrubber line by dropping the clip audio at that point to silence and then gradually fading up to full volume. When using Fade Out, the fade ends at the Scrubber line and jumps to full volume at the beginning of the fade. This is kind of unexpected behavior (you would think that a clip with the volume set to zero would not jump to full volume) so watch the clip Volume Adjustment Line to make sure what you want to happen is what actually happened. To fade out at the end of a clip, move the slider to the end of the video and then click Fade-out.

5. Experiment with the real-time volume adjustments by playing the video and moving the sliders. Isolate a track by clicking the mute buttons for the two other tracks.

6. Switch to the Surround Sound controller by clicking the drop-down list shown in Figure 12.31 and selecting Surround. Surround Sound is new to Studio Plus and is a very slick feature.

7. Click any audio clip. Note that the icon for that clip's audio track appears at the center of the Surround Sound controller. Play that clip and drag the icon around in the controller. The Panning—or Balance—changes show up in that clip's Balance Adjustment Line.

FIGURE 12.31
The Surround
Sound controller
works on each
track individually.
The highlighted
icon denotes the
selected track.

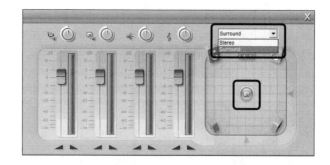

8. Switch to that clip's Fade Adjustment Line by right-clicking that audio clip and clicking Select Fade Display. Your clip will turn orange and the Fade Adjustment Line will show the movement of your clip's audio relative to the front and back of your room.

Fade Has Two Definitions

Video-editing terminology can be confusing. You just used the Fade In and Fade Out options in the Mixer. And now you are accessing the Fade Display. Fade In and Fade Out refer only to changing a clip's volume over time. The Fade Display refers to the audio's location relative to the front and back of a room.

9. If you have a Surround Sound speaker setup for your PC, you will hear all these changes in real-time. Feel free to move all your tracks anywhere in 2D space.

Summary

Audio is a critical part of your editing mix. Imagine a balloon bursting with muffled sound. Or a racecar speeding by with barely a whimper. Studio gives you detailed control over audio placement and quality. Its mixer lets you pan that racecar's engine noise from left to right (or from in front of you to behind you) and lets you crank up the volume as it passes. You can use the Equalizer effect to pump up the lower frequencies.

A J-Cut will let viewers know that the next shot will be of a speeding auto. And an L-Cut will ease viewers to the next scene of a racecar designer at a workstation.

Most audio effects go unnoticed by viewers. The best audio editors are the unsung heroes. But some extra attention to audio editing using Studio will turn an average video into a great product.

CHAPTER 13

Advanced Editing Techniques, Add-ons, and Exporting

What You'll Learn in This Chapter:

▶ Advanced two-track editing techniques

▶ Examining Studio's premium transitions

▶ Testing third-party audio effect plug-ins

▶ Reviewing third-party video-effect plug-ins

▶ Overview of Studio's RTFX packages

▶ Exporting your finished product

Studio has hidden powers only marginally available in other nonlinear editors in its price range. The addition of a second video track along with the inclusion of two powerful effects—Picture-in-Picture and Chroma Key—put Studio at the top of this market niche.

In addition, Pinnacle Systems has a treasure trove of Studio-compatible special effects that exist largely because of the company's suite of professional video-editing tools. Now that Pinnacle Studio and Studio Plus have so-called open, plug-in architecture, Pinnacle Systems has increased its premium content offerings, and third-party developers have flocked to the party. These add-ons and plug-ins bring some real value to Studio. In this chapter, I give you an overview of what's available.

Pinnacle also offers a very useful tool that lets you customize many of its effects. It is equivalent to what Studio's designers use to create the effects and transitions in the first place. So, if you want to give your videos a look that no one else can match, the HFX Filter is worth your time.

Finally, when you've wrapped up your project, you'll need to export it to whatever medium works for you. Your options include videotape, a PC file, the Internet, or a DVD. In this chapter I cover the full spectrum, except for DVDs, which I cover in Chapter 18, "Authoring DVDs Using Studio's DVD Module."

Advanced Two-Track Editing Techniques

Studio Plus has a second video track: the Overlay Track. Anything you put in the Overlay Track will cover up whatever is in the Main Video Track. As I mentioned earlier in the book, I think it would be more intuitive to put the Overlay Track *above* the Main Video Track in the Timeline to represent its behavior. That issue aside, just remember that Overlay trumps Main.

Having an Overlay Track means you now can layer video and stills, meaning you can combine two clips, one over the other, so you can see all or parts of both. Studio Plus gives you four ways to do that:

▶ Shrink or crop the clip in the Overlay Track to create a Picture-in-Picture—PiP—effect.

▶ Crop the clip to create a Split-Screen effect.

▶ Reduce the opacity of the Overlay Track clip to blend the two clips.

▶ **Key out** a color (make a selected color transparent) in the Overlay clip to reveal whatever is on the Main Track in that space where you've removed that color.

Using the Picture-in-Picture Tool

This is such a standard part of professional editors' repertoires that it's almost an afterthought. But for Studio editors, this is new (to Studio Plus) and a big deal. You can take any video clip (or still image), reduce it in size, and place it anywhere on another clip. You can give it a border and a drop shadow. And using any of a number of transitions, you can animate it onto and off of the screen.

Try it Yourself   **Testing the Picture-in-Picture Tool**

There's a lot to the Picture-in-Picture tool. It's actually three video effects in one: PiP, Cropping, and Opacity. This Try It Yourself will focus only on PiP:

1. The setup for this task is simple. Start a new project (File, New Project) and open the Overlay Track (right-click in the Timeline and select Always Show

Overlay Track). Using Photoshoot.mpg, place Scene 1 on the Main Video Track and Scene 4 on the Overlay Track directly below Scene 1.

Did you Know?

PiP Shot Selection

I chose Scene 1 (the exterior) to be the background and Scene 4 (the close-up of the model) to be the PiP for some specific reasons. PiPs work well if you use a wide shot for your background and tight shots for the PiPs. The wide shots generally have no specific detail you want to emphasize (so it's okay to cover up parts of them). And because you shrink the clips you use for the PiPs, they should be tight shots so that the subject remains prominent enough for your viewers to see what's going on.

2. You apply the PiP effect to the clip in the Overlay Track, so double-click that clip to open the Clip Properties window and then click the Overlay icon highlighted in Figure 13.1 to open the Picture-in-Picture tool.

Tool or Effect

Pinnacle Systems calls the interface shown in Figure 13.1 the Picture-in-Picture *tool*. The reason, I guess, is because there is also a Picture-in-Picture video *effect*. The effect does the same thing as the tool but lets you input numeric parameters rather than simply rely on sliders. To see the PiP effect, click the Effect tab (the Plug icon) to open the Video Effects window, select the Overlay Effects group, and double-click Picture-in-Picture.

FIGURE 13.1
Access the Picture-in-Picture tool using the highlighted tab and Enable it to display it in the Player screen. This interface gives you detailed control over the PiP size, placement, border, drop shadow, and opacity.

3. Click Enable Picture-in-Picture to activate this effect.

By the Way

PiP Points

Three things to note:

▶ As shown in Figure 13.1, the default PiP effect (quarter-screen in the upper-right quadrant) shows up in the Player monitor screen.

> ▶ The checkerboard background in the PiP interface indicates the area that will be transparent.
>
> ▶ When you use any Overlay Effect (PiP, Transparency, Cropping, or Chroma Key), the Overlay icon appears in the clip.

4. Open the Presets drop-down list and click a few. They are good to get you started, but you probably want to select a specific location and size for your PiP within your background video clip or still image.

5. To select the location for your PiP, hover your cursor over the PiP image (as shown in Figure 13.2, the cursor turns into the four-arrow cursor you saw in the Still Image Pan and Zoom window). Click and drag your PiP to a new location.

FIGURE 13.2
The four-arrow cursor lets you know you can click and drag your PiP to a location of your choosing.

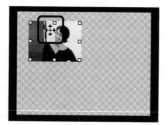

6. Change the PiP's size by moving your cursor over one of the frame handles and clicking and dragging to make the change.

Did you Know?

Maintain Aspect Ratio—or Not

Dragging a corner of the PiP will maintain the original aspect ratio. Dragging a side or bottom will stretch or squash your clip.

---

7. Add a border. To do that, select a border color (white is the default color), give it some width by dragging that slider, and experiment with the transparency and softness of the border. As shown in Figure 13.3, as you make changes you get immediate feedback in the Player window (unlike the PiP interface window, which displays only size and placement).

Did you Know?

Find a Matching Color with the Eyedropper Tool

The Eyedropper tool located next to the Border (and Shadow) color swatch lets you select a Border (or Shadow) color from the video clip. In this way your border's color won't clash with your image. To select that color, click the Eyedropper tool (your cursor changes to an Eyedropper), move the cursor to your clip in the PiP interface, and click a color in your clip that suits you. The new color will show up in the color swatch and in the Player monitor screen.

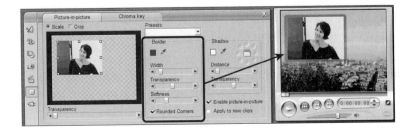

FIGURE 13.3
As you use the Border controls, your changes show up in the Player window.

8. Now apply a Drop Shadow. Select a Shadow color (white is the default), a direction that it falls away from the clip (select one of the eight circles around the white rectangle, adjust its distance (how far you want it to be from the PiP), and give it some transparency.

Shadow Characteristics

Shadows in real life have two characteristics that might not be immediately apparent: color and transparency.

Few shadows are only shades of gray. Generally shadows pick up some color from the background. Consider selecting a shadow color that more or less matches the background clip in the Main Video Track. Shadows are not opaque. Give your shadows some transparency to let some of the background clip show through.

Finally, keep in mind that if you use a border that has some transparency, the shadow will reinforce that. It, too, will have a border, with more transparency—less opacity—than the rest of the shadow, and you will be able to see the shadow through the PiP border. I've highlighted that characteristic in Figure 13.4.

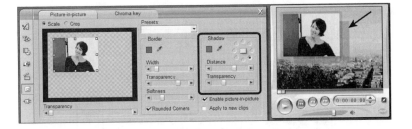

FIGURE 13.4
Use the Shadow controls to add a drop shadow. Note that if your PiP has a border with transparency, the shadow reinforces that. The shadow also shows through the transparent border.

Spicing Up Your PiPs

If you play the PiP you just created, the background clip will start with the PiP displaying wherever you placed it. That's kind of jarring and boring. There are some better ways to use PiPs:

▶ You can use a transition to have the PiP fade up or fly onscreen and then spin it or fade it off screen.

▶ For still images, you can use the Pan and Zoom tool to slide a PiP onscreen, hold it in position for a time, and then slide it off. Studio won't let you use the Pan and Zoom on a PiP video, but you can use the Slide Transition to do more or less the same thing.

▶ An effective way to make PiPs stand out is to put the background out of focus.

▶ Having more than one PiP onscreen works well, too.

PiP Tips

I want to show you how to do all of these. But instead of a Try It Yourself series of steps, here are some PiP tips:

1. A comfortable way to ease into a PiP is to use the Fade In or Out transition to bring your PiP onscreen and off. To do that, drag that transition to the start and end of the PiP clip on the Overlay Track. Figure 13.5 shows an example.

Watch Out!

Downside to Transitions and PiPs

The caveat to using a transition at the beginning or end of a PiP is that it also affects the clips that come before or after it on the Timeline. So, PiP transitions work only if there is a gap between clips on the Overlay Track. This might take a little planning, but usually won't present a problem. And you need only a very small gap between clips to accomplish this.

FIGURE 13.5
Fade In and then Fade Out your PiP using that transition. Note the Overlay icon in the clip shows that you're using that family of effects on this clip.

2. To slide the PiP onscreen, hold it in position and then slide it off, using the applicable Slide Transition—Up, Down, Left, Right, and so on—at the beginning and end of the clip.

3. Instead of gently easing in a PiP, use one of the many wild transitions that ship with Studio. The STB-FlyOff in the Hollywood FX for Studio works well.

4. Pan and Zoom lets you slide a PiP **still image** onto the screen, hold it for a while, and then slide it off. You need to take several steps to do that. Click the Picture-in-Picture Apply to New Clips check box to ensure that each new still has the same PiP characteristics as the preceding one. And in the Still Image Properties window, click the Match Previous Clip button to have the beginning Pan and Zoom characteristics of a still image match the ending Pan and Zoom characteristics of the clip that precedes it.

Watch Your Audio

Keep in mind that when you create a PiP or combine clips in any other fashion, you also are blending their audio. Most times I think you should use the audio from only one clip when layering video clips. As I mentioned in the previous chapter on audio, you can change clip audio levels using the blue Volume Rubberband or the Audio Mixer.

Did you Know?

---

5. Have your PiP clip stand out even more by putting the background out of focus. It usually works best if you start in focus and then **rack** out of focus using the Blur effect and the Fade In parameter. You want to time that rack focus to match the appearance of your PiP onscreen.

6. As shown in Figure 13.6, you can put more than one PiP over the background by creating a single PiP, saving it as a video file, using it as a background for another PiP, and so on. This is venturing into the final topic of this chapter: exporting your project. But this is fairly simple. Open a new project and create a single PiP clip. Apply any transitions, Blur, or any other effects. Then click the Make Movie tab, select AVI, and click Create AVI File. Use that file as a PiP background and add another PiP to it, and so on, for however many PiPs as you care to make.

FIGURE 13.6
Create multiple
PiPs by saving a
single PiP as an
AVI file and then
using it as a back-
ground for
another PiP.

Two Other Picture-in-Picture Effects

As I mentioned earlier, the Picture-in-Picture tool is like three effects built into
one. In addition to creating PiPs, you also can blend two clips using the tool's
Transparency slider and create a split-screen effect using the Crop effect.

Split screen is kind of a misnomer. You don't have to fill the screen with two
equal-sized rectangles left and right or top and bottom. You can crop and scale
your clips to any size and place them anywhere. If there's a gap around any clips,
Studio fills it with black. And you can add a third clip (a still only) in the Title
Track.

Try it Yourself   Blending and Cropping Multiple Clips

▼

When blending clips, your only option is to reduce the opacity of the clip in the
Overlay Track to reveal the image in the Main Video Track. You crop clips to create a so-called split screen or to arrange them on the screen. To do that, you need
to crop all clips, scale them, and place them in the screen. Here's how to do both
effects:

1. Set up a Timeline with two clips, one directly above the other in the Main
    and Overlay Video Tracks. I chose Scene 5 for the Overlay Track and Scene 4
    for the Main Track (see Did You Know? "Transparency—An Inexact
    Science").

Did you Know?   Transparency—An Inexact Science

▼

Reducing the opacity of a clip to reveal a clip below it sometimes leads to some
less-than-ideal results. In general, you want to use a clip that has a large area of
white in it so when you apply transparency to it, the clip beneath it tends to show

through more obviously in that white area. That's why I chose to apply some transparency to Scene 5.

2. Double-click the clip in the Overlay Track to open the Clip Properties. Click the Overlay icon to open that window.

3. The default view puts the Overlay Track clip as a PiP in the upper-right corner. Switch that to full screen by dragging a corner of the clip to expand it and dragging the entire clip to center it onscreen. Or open the Presets drop-down list and select Full Screen.

4. As shown in Figure 13.7, move the Transparency slider to the right and watch the results in the Player window. Note that after you make any change to Transparency, a check appears in the Enable Picture-in-Picture check box.

FIGURE 13.7
Blend two clips by applying some transparency to the clip in the Overlay Track.

5. Again, if you want to ease in or ease out of this transparency, apply a transition to it. The caveat is that there needs to be a gap between it and adjacent clips in the Overlay Track.

Use Scale and Crop with Transparency

I cover Cropping starting in step 5 (you used Scale when you created PiPs). But in the case of the clips in Figure 13.7, I did some cropping and clip stretching to put the wide shot of the model a bit to the left and the tight shot a bit to the right to avoid overlap.

Did you Know?

---

6. To crop clips to create a Split-Screen effect, set up your Timeline with two video clips directly above each other on the two video tracks. There's no need to worry about which clip goes on which track, because they will appear side-by-side.

7. Double-click either clip to open the Clip Properties window and click the Overlay icon to open the Overlay interface.

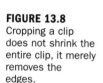

8. Click the Crop button and use the bounding box handles to trim away the edges of your clip. As shown in Figure 13.8, this does not shrink the clip—it crops it, in the same way a photographer crops a photo.

FIGURE 13.8
Cropping a clip does not shrink the entire clip, it merely removes the edges.

9. You can now scale and place that image by clicking Scale and then changing its size and placement. You can also add a border. I did all of the above in the clip in Figure 13.9.

10. Click the other clip to display it in the same Overlay interface. (Note that whatever border you just applied to the first clip will be applied to this one.) Crop and scale it to fit next to the first clip. As shown in Figure 13.9, you use the Player window to adjust placement.

FIGURE 13.9
How your Split-Screen effect might look. Note that I added borders and used the Scale effect to adjust both clips' overall size and position.

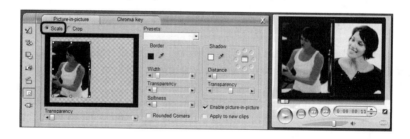

11. Add a third clip (it has to be a still image) to this twosome by dragging a clip to the Title Track below both video tracks.

Track Order Counts

If you look at Figure 13.10, you'll see that the still image is above the wide studio shot, which is above the tight shot of the model. That's because the Title Track (despite being on the bottom of the Timeline) covers whatever is in either video track. There's good reason—the Title Track is where you put text generally and you want that to appear over all your video clips. Next in line is the Overlay Track. It covers the Main Video Track.

Did you Know?

12. It should show up in the Overlay interface (if not, double-click it and select Overlay). As shown in Figure 13.10, crop and scale it and the two other clips to make a nice three-image arrangement.

FIGURE 13.10
You can crop and scale up to three clips (one has to be a still image) using the Overlay tool.

Even More Cropped Clips

I mentioned earlier in this chapter that if you want to have more than one PiP, you need to save your first PiP as an AVI file, then apply another PiP to it, and so on. The same concept applies here. If you want to crop more than two video clips (or more than some combination of three video clips and still images) create your first group, leave room for any other clips you want to add, save that as an AVI file, use that as a background for a PiP and add more cropped clips that way. It's not elegant, but it works.

Did you Know?

Keying Out Parts of a Clip

You might know that TV weather folks do not stand in front of weather maps. As shown in Figure 13.11, they stand in front of solid-color—usually lime green—walls.

They use strategically placed studio monitors (including one in front of the camera lens—it's a one way mirror) to see how those graphics look, so they can point at the right place. If you've ever been in a TV studio during the weather, it looks mighty weird to see the weather guy pointing at a blank green wall.

As shown in Figure 13.12, technicians electronically **key out** that solid color, turn it transparent, and replace it with weather graphics.

Studio Plus offers a Chroma Key effect as part of the Overlay tool. It's a cool effect but it comes with a very prominent caveat: **It's darned hard to get a clean chroma key.**

There are two basic reasons for that:

1. Consumer and prosumer camcorders use what's called DV25. That's the bottom end of digital video quality. It has one-fourth the data of a full, top-end DV signal.

   That lower data rate means the video images are not as sharp as those you see on broadcast TV. They still look great, but when you start working with chroma keys, for example, you begin to see their weaknesses.

2. It takes some very careful lighting to create an evenly lit, solid color background. Any slight deviations in the light intensity can create **bleed** or a **halo** effect—kind of a fuzzy edge around the subject. See the sidebar, "Making Blue and Green Screens Work," for more on this.

The best solid color backgrounds are Chroma Key Blue or Chroma Key Green (two very specific, industry-standard colors). The Studio Plus Chroma Key effect comes with two presets for those colors.

However, you don't need a true chroma key green or blue screen to use the Chroma Key effect. Any solid color backdrop will work. No matter what color background you work with, make sure the color does not match anything in your subject that you don't want to key out; otherwise, your subject will have transparent holes.

Making Blue and Green Screens Work

Setting up chroma green or blue backdrops can be a royal pain—especially on location. About 12 years ago I hired one of Portland's top production companies to do a fairly involved chroma blue screen shoot at a local college. They lit the heck out of that blue screen, got the dolly rails and the trucking move down perfectly, and rolled and recorded.

When we got back to the studio, try as we might, we could not completely key out the blue screen without creating some transparency in the actor. We ended up building an elaborate moving matte (it had to fit the actor's shifting silhouette). What a time-consuming hassle!

As someone once said, "It's not easy being green" (or blue). Here are some tips:

- ▶ Blue and green screens require "flat" lighting—no hot spots. If you can set up your screen outdoors, overcast days work best (even lighting and fewer shadows). No need to overdo the lighting. Simply make it even.

- ▶ The actor's lighting does not have to be flat. Controlled spotlights or lights with "barn doors" work well. Using soft lighting with umbrellas and reflectors is less dramatic but also is effective. A so-called "key" backlight aimed at the actor's head helps more clearly illuminate hair to eliminate or at least minimize blue or green screen halos. The actor's wearing a hat will eliminate that hair halo altogether.

▶ If you plan to key in an outdoor background, try to re-create outdoor lighting on your subject. If you're working with live actors, further enhance the illusion by using a fan to blow their hair around a bit.

▶ Avoid the dreaded blue or green spill. Actors' skin will pick up the reflected color of the backdrop if they're too close to it. Move them at least a few feet away. One other way to minimize this is to use a backlight.

▶ Stay far enough away from the backdrop to avoid having the actor's shadow fall on it. That's not a horrible problem, but your life will be easier if you don't have to worry about adjusting the chroma key effect to compensate for shadows.

▶ Tight shots work better than full-body shots. The closer you are to your subject, the more realistic the finished product.

▶ If there is fast-paced action in your shot, you may have trouble keying right to the edges of your subjects.

▶ Set your camcorder to Manual and open the iris (you'll probably need to increase shutter speed to avoid overexposure). A wide-open iris—1.8 or so—limits the focal plane to your subject and throws the green screen a bit out of focus, making it easier to key out.

▶ To build a backdrop on a budget, consider using unofficial chroma blue or green paint (the real stuff retails for about $40 a gallon). Grab a paint sample collection, videotape it, and then use Studio's blue screen or green Chroma Key preset on it. Find a color that keys well and buy a gallon. Paint that on a large piece of plywood and you have a portable studio.

Alternatively, you can use chroma key fabric or wide rolls of chroma key paper. Both run about $10 a square yard ($20 with foam backing). One source is www.Filmtools.com.

▶ Which color to use? With chroma green you have reasonable assurance no one will have clothing that matches and therefore will key out. Chroma blue works well because it's complementary to skin tones. The kind of scene you key in may be the determining factor. If you will have your actors keyed in to a scene with a blue sky, use a blue screen. In this case, the dreaded blue spill could be a nice feature.

 Using the Chroma Key Effect

The Chroma Key effect takes some trial and error. Even when working with industry-standard chroma key green or blue backdrops, you still might need to tweak the settings a bit to expand the width of the keyed-out color and to soften the edge of the subject to reduce halo. Here's how Chroma Key works:

1. Pinnacle Systems provided a green screen video to demonstrate this effect. Check your Album drop-down list and see if Chroma_key.mpg is there with Photoshoot.mpg. If not, click the Select Videos button in the Album and track it down. Its default location is `C:\Documents and Settings\All Users\Documents\My Videos` or `Shared Video`.

2. Chroma_key.mpg is nearly two minutes long. I think you should use two clips: Scene 1 (a close-up) and Scene 5 (a wide shot with some action). Drag Scene 1 to the Overlay Track and trim it to about 9 seconds. Then drag Scene 5 next to Scene 1 and trim it to 9 seconds or so. Remember, you're placing these clips in the Overlay Track because you will key out the chroma key green color, making it transparent to show what's behind/beneath it on the Main Video Track.

Chroma_Key.mpg Poor Video Quality

By the Way

You might notice that Chroma_Key.mpg is of poor video quality, especially when compared to the other sample video: Photoshoot.mpg. The reason? When Pinnacle Systems converted the original digital video—DV—to MPEG, they reduced its size to quarter screen. Studio automatically blows up that video to full screen, leading to resolution loss and causing the chroma key green color to "bleed" around the edges of the model. You will see how these fuzzy edges lead to a halo effect in a moment.

---

3. Lock the Overlay Track by clicking the Padlock icon at its right end (this overcomes a bug in Studio that changes the length of a clip in the Overlay Track when you change the speed of a clip in the Main Video Track).

4. Switch to the Photoshoot.mpg clips and drag Scene 1 (the exterior) to the Main Video Track. To make it fit the length of the two green screen clips (about 16 seconds) apply slow motion to it. Using Figure 13.13 as a reference, do that by double-clicking it to open the Video toolbox, clicking the Effects icon, opening the Time effects group, and double-clicking Speed. Change the speed parameter to .20 (one-fifth normal speed) and your clip will more or less fit the length of the green screen clips.

5. Unlock the Overlay Track by clicking the Padlock icon at its right end (otherwise you cannot apply the Chroma Key effect to it).

6. Click the Chroma_key.mpg clip in the Timeline to switch to it in the Video Effects window. Switch to the Overlay interface by clicking its icon.

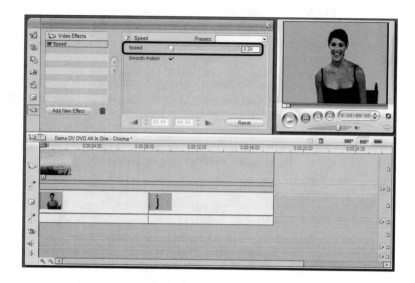

7. In the Overlay interface, click the Chroma Key tab and then select Green Screen Key from the Preset drop-down list (that automatically puts a check in the Enable Chroma Keying check box). As shown in Figure 13.14, that also puts **mask** in the Overlay tool screen. Black represents the transparent region; white is opaque. And you get immediate feedback on how the model will look over your background image in the Player screen.

By the Way

She's Got the Jaggies

Take a look at the model's face. Because of the poor quality of the original Chroma_Key.mpg video, the edges around the model are not distinct. That leads to those jagged, unnatural lines and the halo effect, the white gap between the model and the background. I'll say it again, chroma key is an inexact science. Don't expect perfect results the first time you try it.

8. Try to remove some of the jaggies and the halo effect using the four sliders. In this case, color tolerance won't have much of an effect because the background has such a distinctive, saturated color. Try Softness and Spill Suppression to at least do some repair work.

9. Switch to Scene 5 (the second Chroma_Key.mpg clip in the Overlay Track) and click Enable Chroma Keying to switch that effect on. Play that clip. Because the model is shot from a distance, getting a clean key is even more difficult to accomplish.

Jaggies

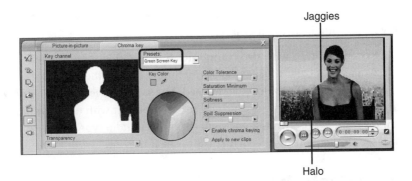

Halo

FIGURE 13.14
Selecting the Green Screen Key from the drop-down list switches on the Chroma Key effect, displays a mask to the left, and shows how the effect will look to the right.

10. Use the Chroma Key effect on a non-green or non-blue screen video. Add Scene 4 from the Photoshoot.mpg video to the Overlay Track, beneath a portion of the Background video on the Main Track.

11. Apply the Chroma Key effect to it. As shown in Figure 13.15, click the Eyedropper tool and use it to sample a color from the clip that you want to remove (to turn transparent). I suggest the red door. Note that keying out that color also turns part of the model's face transparent because her skin has some red tones. This demonstrates that you need to select a background color that does not match anything in your subject (unless putting holes in your subject is the effect you want).

FIGURE 13.15
You can use the Chroma Key effect on any scene, with or without a chroma key screen. In this case, selecting the color red from the door causes transparencies to show up in the model's face.

Testing Third-Party Audio Effect Plug-Ins

New to Studio 9 and Studio Plus is VST (Virtual Studio Technology) plug-in architecture. I covered this in the previous chapter. This means that most VST plug-ins will work with Pinnacle Studio 9 or Studio Plus.

There are tons of such plug-ins scattered around the Internet. And as I mentioned earlier, you can purchase them online.

Pinnacle Systems worked with two companies that updated some of their VST effects to work specifically with Studio 9 and Studio Plus (if they had not altered them, they probably still would have worked, but would have run in their own interfaces). To try them out, I suggest you set up a project with a narration, sound effect, and music so you can test each effect on each audio type. I urge you to do this. It's very simple to listen to each effect to see if they are worth buying.

Unlock Effects for Use in Projects

Those effects are on the Content DVD that shipped with Studio. Installing that DVD loaded those plug-ins on your hard drive and made them available in the Audio toolbox, Audio Effects window.

To use them in a final project, you need to buy an unlocking code. Otherwise they beep or produce some other audio hiccup. I mentioned in Chapter 9, "Capturing Video and Cuts-Only Editing with Pinnacle Studio Plus," that to unlock an effect, click on the Click Here to Unlock button. It takes you to Pinnacle's **upsell** site where it displays the order form for that particular effect. After you've made a selection, the site offers other products before taking you to the checkout page.

I briefly explain every premium audio effect, but I won't do the same in the upcoming video-effects section. The main reasons are that I can show you how video effects look (I present a representative cross-sample) but I need to explain what the audio effects do. And there are many more video effects, some of which are deeply detailed. To explain them all would take several chapters.

One other note: I state product prices but they are subject to change.

Algorithmix Effects

Algorithmix (www.algorithmix.com) offers two of its fun effects (compared to its high-end, professional—and expensive—effects available on its website).

▶ **Alien ($19)**—Creates what we've all come to think of as the voice of some alien from outer space. Sliders make it sound like a chorus of little green men.

▶ **RoboVoice ($19)**—Have you seen the 1960s "Lost in Space" TV show? Meet its robot. RoboVoice has two robot voices—that metallic/electronic style popular culture has embedded into our brains.

NewBlue Audio Essentials

NewBlue (www.newblueinc.com/home.html) has provided 21 effects in three groups, each retailing for $39 ($99 for all three).

NewBlue Essentials 1

▶ **Background Fader**—Reduces background noise by reducing the volume of quieter sounds.

▶ **Bass Boost**—Does what it says: increases loudness of low frequencies.

▶ **Compactor**—Sort of a one-sided compressor in that it increases loudness of soft sounds while not changing loud sounds. The downside is that this can raise the level of background noise, which means you probably need to use a noise-reducing filter, too.

▶ **Distortion**—Creates what NewBlue calls a "nasty, grungy" effect.

▶ **Echo**—What you'd expect. Figure 13.16 shows that it has a number of presets and parameters that allow for some really fun effects. You can set the delay (the amount of time before you hear the echo) to up to one second. A high intensity will repeat the echo clearly several times.

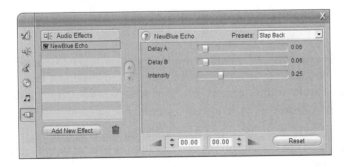

FIGURE 13.16
NewBlue Essentials Echo is one of those effects that you'll use over and over and over and over...

▶ **Flange**—This is one of those you've got to hear to comprehend. Just a quick rundown on the presets—Laser, Aliens, and Waterpipes—gives you an idea of the variety of possibilities. It works by delaying the sound and mixing it to varying degrees with the original audio.

▶ **Insectoid**—Your preset choices: Gnat, Fly, and "Swamp Thing" tell the tale here. Select any one and you'll be greeted with a buzzy, irritating, and bizarre sound.

NewBlue Essentials 2

▶ **Auto Mute**—This removes annoying, low-level background noise during what would otherwise be silent moments. It has a Decay parameter that lets you determine how quickly the volume drops completely to avoid unnatural, instant roll-offs.

▶ **Chorus**—This makes one voice sound like many. Basically it duplicates the original audio and plays it back with a very small delay. It also, by design, adds some reverb, which I found disconcerting.

▶ **Crisper**—This increases the volume of the higher frequencies. You can accomplish more or less the same thing using the equalizer.

▶ **Hum Remover**—This is a very specialized effect that removes hum created by electrical power. That hum falls right on 60Hz in North America and 50Hz everywhere else. So if you hear that hum, select your country's preset. I've worked with other so-called **Notch Filters**, and the presets on this one removed more audio than they should.

▶ **Phone**—Makes audio sound like it's coming from a cheap speaker in a telephone.

▶ **Sound Expander**—Whereas a compressor (NewBlue Compactor) lifts low-volume audio and cuts high volume, the Sound Expander does the opposite: It makes quiet sounds quieter and loud sounds louder. It increases the dynamic range.

▶ **Wind**—You've seen those TV reporters doing stand-ups in the middle of a hurricane. That's what the Wind effect sounds like (refer to Figure 13.17). Just remember that when you voice your narration, you make your voice sound stressed. Calm and desultory don't cut it when facing down the Santa Ana winds. Shout!

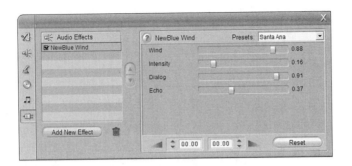

FIGURE 13.17
Wind's presets
include Gale,
Blizzard, and
Santa Ana.

NewBlue Essentials 3

▶ **High Only**—Removes low-frequency sounds.

▶ **Low Only**—Removes high-frequency sounds.

▶ **Noise Reduction**—As simple, one-slider noise reduction effects go, this one works very well. For example, it takes care of motor noise and fluorescent light hum.

▶ **Parametric EQ**—This is a work horse of the audio engineer. It increases or decreases volume of a specific, user-defined frequency range. For example, this lets you beef up a thin vocal. You can apply Parametric EQ multiple times to the same clip.

▶ **Resonator**—This gives a strange metallic sound to your clip. It works by boosting a narrow tone—creating a ringing effect.

▶ **Robot Fog**—Consider any sci-fi film. Robot Fog fits. Its three presets—Dark Menace, Shredding Metal, and Steel Cave—demonstrate the versatility of this effect. It creates reverberations with so much variety that you need to play with the sliders to see all it can do.

▶ **Wah**—Ever seen a trumpet player use a wah-wah mute? He holds a rubber cup (looks like a toilet bowl plunger) in front of the trumpet's bell and moves it back and forth. As in "wah-wah." That's what this effect does.

Help Is Only a Click Away

Some third-party effects come with instruction manuals. Figure 13.18 is one example from NewBlue Audio. Access these help files by clicking the question mark icon (?) in the upper-left corner of each effect's settings interface. Note: Some effects have no help files. And some effects are standalone products with help files accessible from the main menu.

By the Way

FIGURE 13.18
Many third-party plug-ins—audio and video—come with help files like this one. Access those files by clicking the question mark icon (?) in the effect's Settings interface.

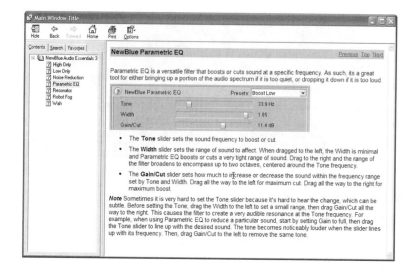

Reviewing Third-Party Video-Effect Plug-Ins

This is a much bigger deal than audio plug-ins. Four companies provided 70 video-effect plug-ins for the debut version of Studio Plus. By the time this book ships, there might be more.

In addition, Pinnacle Systems offers two bundles of video-effect plug-ins: RTFX Plus (16 effects) and RTFX Mega (includes 16 Plus effects and 7 more).

Most of the effects do something simple and fun, such as adding a stroke of lightning to a clip or making your clip look like a funhouse mirror. Some are immense. Adorage, in particular, has scores of amazing effects! You absolutely must take that product for a test drive.

Even though I gave overviews of all the audio effects, that would be impractical for the video effects. I will cover each group and highlight a few real attention getters.

Bravo Studio Packs 1 and 2

This wide-ranging collection of 32 fun effects (priced at $59 each or $99 for both) is from Virtix (www.virtix.com), a computer-aided design and video application production company (refer to Figures 13.19 and 13.20).

Tunnel

Lightning

Funhouse

Witness Protection

FIGURE 13.19
Bravo Studio Pack 1 has 14 effects, including Tunnel, Lightning, Funhouse (our apologies to the model for that one), and Witness Protection (more apologies).

Most of the Bravo Studio effects are fun and easy to use. Typical parameters let you set the position onscreen for the effect as in Lightning, Tunnel, and Witness Protection. The one caveat: Some of these effects would work better if you could have them follow the action onscreen (that is, have the Witness Protection mask cover the face of someone moving through the scene) but they can't do that. That kind of **keyframing** is available only in higher-priced professional editors such as Adobe Premiere Pro and Pinnacle Liquid Edition.

BWPLUGINS and BWPLUGINS 2

BWPLUGINS ($19.95 each) are the product of two men who work together in the northeast U.S. but who live hundreds of miles apart—proving, as they say, that "modular software design can be done from anywhere on earth that has access to the Internet."

Their two effect packs have distinctly different themes. BWPLUGINS has two effects—Lighting and Video Cleansing—that can improve poorly lit scenes (like Studio's Noise Reduction video effect but with more parameters). The third effect—Theme Styles—lets you create a "look" for your clip from eight selections. Figure 13.21 shows the Edge White look along with an example of Lighting and its parameters.

FIGURE 13.20
Bravo Studio Pack 2 has 18 effects, including Bubbles, Crosseyed, Dream Border, and Sparkle By Color. The latter applies sparkle on selected colors within your clip.

 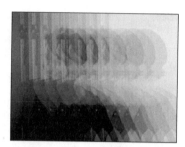

Bubbles   Crosseyed

Dream Border   Sparkle by Color

FIGURE 13.21
BWPLUGINS has three effects. Lighting (top) and Video Cleansing (not shown) repair poorly lit clips, and Theme Styles (bottom) lets you change the overall "look" of your clips.

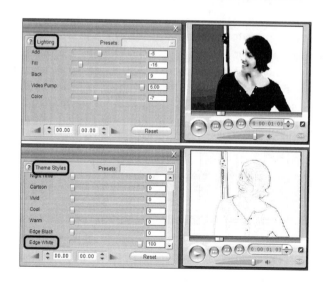

BWPLUGINS 2 has three effect types: Acid Rain (7 variations), AutoRoto, and Fade From or To Color. Figure 13.22 shows an Acid Rain sample (the six other Acid Rain effects have the rain falling in different directions).

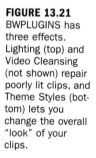

AutoRoto highlights a selected color while turning other colors into grayscale. You've seen something like this in advertisements where only one object has color. Because this book's images are black and white, I can't show it here, but using it on the tight shot of the model, I could retain the door's red color and turn all other elements into grayscale. Very cool.

Fade From or To Color is not just a simple fade (see Figure 13.22). It gradually changes the colors on the clip either from their normal color to the selected color (ending in a full-screen solid color) or from the selected color to normal.

FIGURE 13.22
Acid Rain (left) gives clips an urban, *Blade Runner* feel, whereas Fade From or To Color (right) gradually shifts colors in the clip to the selected color.

Dziedzic's Effects Packs 1 and 2

Michael Dziedzic, a Boston-based programmer, has created eight effects in these two packs ($19.95 each) that are all very useful, and I think they should be on every editor's palette.

Pack 1 has four basic but very practical effects: Flip Horizontal, Flip Vertical, Negative (see Figure 13.23) and Reverse (backward motion). The Flip effects alone give you more composition options when creating split screens or PiPs, for example. And with Reverse—the possibilities are endless.

Pack 2 also has four simple but useful effects: Standard Screen in 16:9 Aspect Ratio and Wide Screen in 4:3 Aspect Ratio let you edit wide-screen and standard-screen clips in the same project and not lose the original aspect ratios.

Video Camera makes it look like you're viewing your clip through a camcorder viewfinder. This simple-looking effect has 16 (!) parameters that let you control the specific details in the display, such as date, frame counter, and battery life indicator.

And Ghost works the same way Echo works for audio. It displays the original action in your clip as well as a delayed version. You can select the number of ghosts, how ghostlike they are, and the length of the delay.

FIGURE 13.23
Three of Michael
Dziedzic's eight
effects: Negative,
Video Camera, and
Ghost. I think
these two packs
are "must buys."

Negative   Video Camera   Ghost

eZedia eZeMatte and eZeScreen

These effects come from eZedia (www.ezedia.com). Although they both do their jobs well, you should not purchase eZeScreen ($49) because Studio's Chroma Key Video Effect does as good a job in fewer steps, and eZeMatte ($29) works only marginally better than placing a graphic on Studio's Title Track.

By the Way

eZedia Explains eZeScreen

I was surprised that a third-party plug-in provider would sell something that Studio Plus already does and does better. I asked eZedia about that and they acknowledged that Studio's Chroma Key effect works better. Basically, they were left out of the loop. "Studio came out not long after eZeScreen came out," says eZedia's multimedia development manager. "Unfortunately, we were not informed that they were working on a chroma-key filter when we were developing eZeScreen for Studio."

Figure 13.24 shows how eZeMatte works. It lets you layer a graphic over your video. In that way you can give your video a border or some other graphic element like a logo.

FIGURE 13.24
eZeMatte lets you
layer a graphic over
your video.

This is not unlike what happens when you place a graphic with a solid color background on the Title Track and automatically have the Title Track remove whatever color is in the upper-left corner of the graphic.

The difference is that eZeMatte works with Photoshop, PNG, and other graphics that have transparency. The Title Track makes a solid color transparent (sometimes leaving a disconcerting solid color edge along your graphic); eZeMatte displays only the graphic. It also lets you adjust the size of the graphic and give it some transparency. eZeMatte ships with 10 graphics and you can download 20 more for free from their website.

PE CameraPOV

PE CameraPOV (price had not been set when we went to press) works like Michael Dziedzic's Video Camera effect in that it simulates what a camcorder viewfinder displays. The difference is that you have a whole lot more camera styles with CameraPOV (Figure 13.25 shows several samples displayed on the corporate website—www.profoundeffects.com).

FIGURE 13.25
Clicking any of these sample PE CameraPOV effects on the Profound Effects website opens a brief demo of all the parameters available on high-end editors such as Adobe After Effects.

Check out Generic Camcorder. Profound Effects calls it "Generic" not because it's simple. Rather, it has so many options—22—you can make it look like just about any camcorder's viewfinder.

PE CamcorderPOV includes a suite of 12 effects. I highlighted three in Figure 13.26: a night-vision camera (it has a green tint), a black and white security camera, and an SLR (single-lens reflex) still camcorder viewfinder that lets you put the subject out of focus or simulate taking a bunch of shots (you need to add the sound effects).

FIGURE 13.26
Three of the PE CameraPOV effects: Night Vision Camera, Security Camera, and High-End SLR.

Night Vision Camera   Sercurity Camera   High-End SLR

These effects are derived from some high-end (and much more expensive) effects created by Profound Effects for professional video products like Adobe After Effects and Avid editing systems. I suggest you visit the Profound Effects website and take a look at the CameraPOV section. Click any of the samples shown earlier in Figure 13.25 to see an Adobe After Effects interface and get an idea of the level of detail in a motion graphics product like that.

proDAD Adorage and Heroglyph

These are absolutely amazing products. Adorage is a collection of scores of effects! $39 makes this an unbelievable bargain. If scores of effects aren't enough, proDAD would be happy to sell you thousands (yes, 1,000s) more. 8,000+ in all are available at www.prodad.de in seven groups. The site is worth a visit just to play with all the samples.

And Heroglyph ($59) is a full-featured character generator with tons of special effects, moves, and animations thrown in. (You can buy both proDAD Adorage and Heroglyph for $89.)

Figure 13.27 shows the Adorage interface. In that case the video clip zoomed down to fit in the frame.

As shown in Figure 13.28, other effects let you place a clip inside an animated object, add waving flags to a clip, zoom in on a book as it opens to reveal your clip inside, and slide beveled frames across your clip to reveal and later cover it. In addition, you can fly objects such as planes and wedding rings across your clips; add flames, snow, or explosions; and place your clip in a bouquet of flowers. Adorage has a wealth of possibilities.

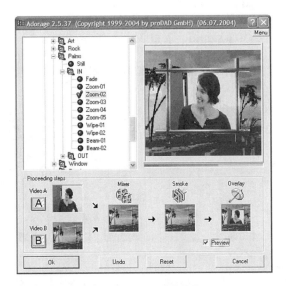

FIGURE 13.27
Adorage has dozens of effects. This one zoomed the video down into the frame.

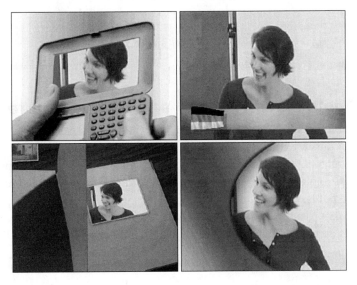

FIGURE 13.28
Four Adorage effects out of the many available.

Heroglyph, shown in Figure 13.29, is a professional title editor that goes way beyond what you worked with in Studio's version of Pinnacle Systems' TitleDeko character generator. In addition to creating text using all the bells and whistles you'd expect, you also have a wealth of animations that let you spin, bounce, fly, twist, and stretch characters. Plus you have numerous backgrounds and special effects at your disposal. It's a huge and powerful product.

FIGURE 13.29
ProDAD's Heroglyph Title Filter is a full-featured character generator and animator, loaded with special effects.

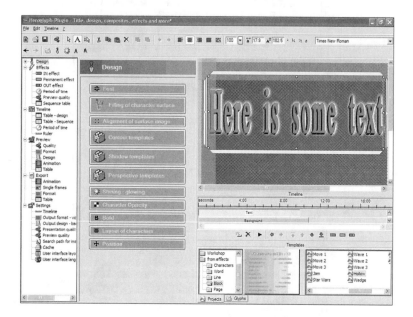

StageTools MovingPicture and MovingPicture LE

MovingPicture puts still images in motion, much like Studio's Pan and Zoom effect. What puts MovingPicture several cuts above Pan and Zoom is that you can work with huge (8,000×8,000 resolution) images, define curved motion paths (instead of a single, straight line), rotate and zoom the images as they move along those paths, and add motion blur. It works within its own interface shown in Figure 13.30. Even with those extra features, the price ($199) might scare away most Studio users. And the $69 LE version is essentially the same as Studio's Pan and Zoom.

FIGURE 13.30
MovingPicture lets
you zoom in and
out, rotate, and put
still images in
motion on smooth
curved paths.

Overview of Studio's RTFX Packages

In addition to offering a few dozen video-transition packs, Pinnacle Systems offers
two effects packages for Studio called RTFX Plus and RTFX Mega as well as a 3D
effects editor.

RTFX Plus

This package ($49) includes 15 effects: Sharpen, Invert, Shift Channels, Threshold,
2D Editor, Fractal Fire, Framer, Hall of Mirrors, Magnify, Water Wave, Old Film
Advanced, Stained Glass Advanced, Mirage, Replicate, and Watercolor. You can
find these effects scattered among several of Studio's effect groups.

I've highlighted a selected sampling in Figure 13.31.

RTFX Mega

RTFX Mega ($99) has all 15 of the RTFX effects plus 9 more: Lens Flare Advanced,
Water Drop Advanced, Magnify Advanced, Fractal Clouds, Fractal Tunnel, Motion
Blur, Turbulence, Bevel Crystal, Minmax, Radial Blur, and Video Feedback.

Old Film Advanced   Stained Glass Advanced

Mirage   Hall of Mirrors

As shown in Figure 13.32, some of the RTFX Mega effects are absolutely amazing. Lens Flare Advanced offers some extraordinary looking, colorful, glowing orbs. Fractal Tunnel spins flames around your clip. And Bevel Crystal looks like Mosaic in 3D.

HFX Creator

HFX Creator ($39)—also known as HFX Filter and Hollywood FX for Studio—is an amazingly versatile effect editor. You can take any Studio HFX video effect or transition and make it do exactly what you want in terms of location, rotation, movement, angles, colors, opacity, and shadow. In addition, you can use any graphics of your choice (including corporate logos or photos) to build custom effects and transitions.

Figure 13.33 shows its interface with only one of several options panels open. If you want to give your effects unique characteristics, $39 makes this a steal.

Lens Flare Advanced

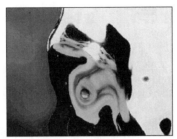

Turbulence

Bevel Crystal

Fractal Tunnel

FIGURE 13.32
RTFX Mega has nine additional and feature-rich video effects, including Lens Flare Advanced, Turbulence, Bevel Crystal, and Fractal Tunnel.

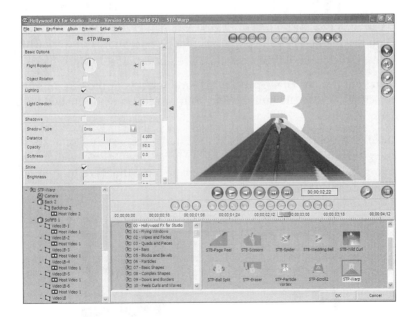

FIGURE 13.33
HFX Creator (aka Hollywood FX for Studio and HFX Filter) opens the door to uncountable effect and transition creative possibilities.

Exporting Your Finished Product

You have several ways to output—or **export**—your finished video:

- ▶ PC file for use on a PC: AVI or MPEG.

- ▶ PC file for use as streaming video on the Internet: Windows Media or RealVideo.

- ▶ Output a highly compressed file to your personal web page on Pinnacle Systems's MyStudioOnline site.

- ▶ Videotape: Analog or Digital Video—DV.

- ▶ Optical Disc: DVD, VCD (Video CD), or S-VCD (Super Video CD). I cover outputting to DVD in Chapter 18.

Try it Yourself   **Output to a File**

The easiest process is to convert your project into a file. There's no need to connect your PC to a camcorder or VCR. Simply select a file type, adjust a few parameters, and sit back while Studio does the work.

The one caveat is that if you captured your video in Preview mode (I urged you not to), you need to attach your DV camcorder (Preview does not work with analog) and insert the original videocassette. Here's how to create video files:

1. Open your project: File, Open Project, and select your project—or select your project by clicking File and clicking your project name at the bottom of that menu.

2. Click the Make Movie tab to open the interface shown in Figure 13.34. It opens with AVI file type selected. AVI (Audio/Video Interleaved) has several flavors, but its primary purpose is to create a file that is as high in quality as your original DV tape.

FIGURE 13.34
Clicking the Make Movie tab opens this interface to the default AVI file setting. The highlighted Diskometer lets you know if your hard drive has enough room for this file.

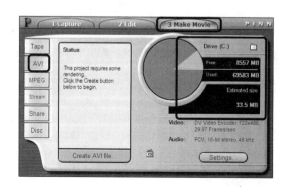

3. Click Settings to open the dialog box shown in Figure 13.35. Here you can select an encoder/compression type. If you select something other than the default DV Video Encoder, that will compress your video causing anywhere from virtually no quality loss to significant quality loss, depending on the settings you choose.

Codecs—Only for the Brave

Studio comes with eight Codecs—video COmpression/DECompression schemes. Your PC might have several more loaded on it. You can see all that you own by clicking the List All Codecs check box. The primary reason you'd use a Codec is to create an AVI with a smaller screen resolution and lower frame rate (and consequently reduced file size) than the original DV. When you select a Codec other than DV Video Encoder, Studio will open some or all of the options windows.

By the Way

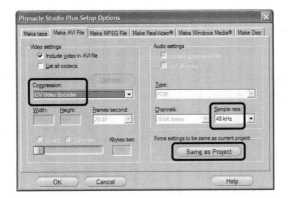

FIGURE 13.35
Use the Setup Options to select a Codec or an Audio Sample Rate. Clicking Same as Project is your best bet.

4. Note that with DV Video Encoder selected, you have only one option: Audio Sample Rate. The difference between your choices—32 or 48kHz—is minor. Generally, select whatever you recorded your original audio at (generally 32kHz if you recorded two stereo channels—48kHz if you recorded a single stereo channel). Your best bet is to click the Same As Project button. Click OK.

5. Back in the Make Movie interface, check the Diskometer (highlighted earlier in Figure 13.34) to make sure you have enough hard drive room.

6. Click the green Create AVI File button. That opens the standard save file interface shown in Figure 13.36. Select a file folder, give your video a name, and click OK.

FIGURE 13.36
Click the Create AVI File button to open this standard save file interface.

Watch Out!

Saving CD Ripping to the Last Minute

If you used Studio's CD track ripper to add music to your project, Studio did not actually rip that music (convert it to a file and store it on your hard drive). Only now, when you actually output/export your project, does something like that happen. So when you click OK in the Save window, Studio will tell you to insert whatever CD or CDs you used to add music to your piece so it can actually rip those tracks directly to your DV AVI file.

7. Studio will start rendering your project—converting it to an AVI file. It displays a progress bar, shown in Figure 13.37. When done, it simply states The Current Project Has Been Rendered as an AVI File. You can return to Studio's Edit interface, locate that file, and play it.

FIGURE 13.37
Studio displays a progress bar in the Player window as it renders your project.

8. Follow a similar process to create an MPEG file. You want to make MPEG files to save space (they're usually smaller than AVI files) or to create a DVD or CD (see Did You Know, "Which Flavor of MPEG is Right?"). Click the MPEG tab in the Make Movie interface and click Settings to open the Setup dialog box shown in Figure 13.38. Note that there are a dozen MPEG presets, including Custom. MPEG has many flavors, but if you want to ultimately create a DVD, select DVD Compatible. Note that the VHS Preset is actually MPEG-1. Select a Preset, adjust any parameters, and click OK to start encoding.

Which Flavor of MPEG Is Right?

With a dozen Presets it appears it can be difficult to choose. MPEG-1 will play on any Windows PC going back to Windows 95. MPEG-2 requires an MPEG software player such as Sonic Solutions Cineplayer. Video CD and S-VCD are MPEG-1 and a low-end MPEG-2 format, respectively. You can record them to a CD that will play in most consumer set-top DVD players. If you want to create a Video-CD or an S-VCD (rather than creating an MPEG file that you can later burn to a CD), use the Disc option in the Make Movie interface. And MPEG-4 is a relatively new MPEG flavor favored by Apple Mac users.

Did you Know?

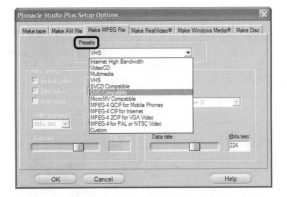

FIGURE 13.38
MPEG offers multiple settings; your choices depend on where you want to play your project.

9. To make streaming video for Internet playback, click Stream in the Make Movie interface. Your choices are Windows Media and RealVideo files. The process is similar to making MPEG or AVI files. Select either Windows Media or RealVideo and click Settings. The issue here is selecting a Playback setting to meet your expected audience's Internet or Network connection speed. As shown in Figure 13.39, with Windows Media you can select Custom and choose from a couple dozen narrowly defined presets. RealVideo works similarly.

FIGURE 13.39
When making a
Windows Media or
RealVideo file, your
primary concern is
the Internet or
Network connection
speed that your
audience uses.

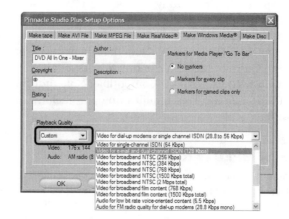

10. To use Pinnacle Systems' StudioOnline site to share your video with the world, click Share in the Make Movie interface. There you can change the thumbnail image by clicking the check mark highlighted in Figure 13.40 and moving the Timeline Scrubber to a frame that suits you.

Watch
Out!

Thumbnail Selected from Main Video Track

A heads-up: There appears to be a bug in the Thumbnail image tool. It grabs the thumbnail from the clip in the Main Video Track even if you have a clip in the Overlay Track. One other note: The little Pinnacle House icon highlighted in Figure 13.40 takes you to the StudioOnline home page.

FIGURE 13.40
It's easy to upload
your videos to
Pinnacle Systems's
StudioOnline site
where you can
invite friends and
family to view your
projects.

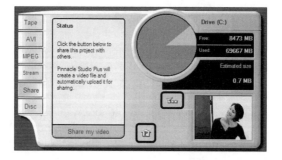

11. Click Share My Video. Studio will make a very compressed version of your video and will then take you to the StudioOnline site, shown in Figure 13.41, where you'll need to create an account. After you've signed up, you

can store up to about five minutes of videos. You can email family and friends and give them your StudioOnline address so they can enjoy your work.

FIGURE 13.41
Create an account on Pinnacle Systems' StudioOnline site to post your clips online.

Record to Videotape or CDs

Try it Yourself

I've combined these two areas into one task because there aren't that many steps for either. You can record to DV or analog camcorders or VCRs. Or you can use Studio to burn a VCD (Video CD) or an S-VCD (Super VCD). Here's how:

1. To record to videotape, start by clicking the Tape tab in the Make Movie interface and click Settings to open the dialog box shown in Figure 13.42.

2. Your Video output choices will depend on your video capture/playback hardware: analog and/or DV (you can choose VGA if you want to simply output full screen to a PC monitor). If you have DV, check the Automatically Start and Stop Recording check box. Make your selection and click OK.

3. Back in the Make Movie interface, click Create. That starts the rendering process. When completed, Studio will tell you to Click the Play Button on the Player Window to Output Your Video to Tape. If you have an analog VCR or camcorder, put it in record mode first and then click the Play button. If you have a DV recording device and you selected Automatically Start and Stop Recording, click the Play button and Studio will take care of everything.

FIGURE 13.42
Select your hardware—analog or DV—from the Video drop-down list.

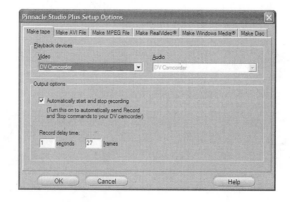

4. To make a VCD or an S-VCD, click the Disc tab in the Make Movie interface. Click the Settings button (it's in the upper-right corner of this interface) to open that now very familiar Setup Dialog box shown in Figure 13.43.

FIGURE 13.43
Return to the Setup dialog box to select parameters for your Video or Super Video CD. If you opt for a VideoCD, most options become unavailable.

5. Here you select the type of Video CD and some other parameters. Note that CBR and VBR stand for Constant and Variable Bit Rate, respectively. CBR works well if you plan to use this file on the Internet, but high action scenes lose some quality. VBR works well when played in a PC or DVD set-top player. When ready, make sure you have a CD in your CD/DVD recorder, click OK, and Studio will burn a VCD or an S-VCD.

Summary

Studio has a lot going on under the hood. The recently added extra video track with its two exciting effects—Picture-in-Picture and Chroma Key—upped the ante. Adding open plug-in architecture for audio and video effects opened the flood gates for third-party developers who offer some genuinely powerful, practical, and eye-catching effects.

After you've created your video project—taking advantage of all of Studio's cool and creative features—Studio offers a panoply of output options: videotape, PC file, streaming Internet files, or optical discs. The one optical disc I did not cover in this chapter—DVD—gets full coverage in Chapter 18.

CHAPTER 14

Two Additional Recommended PC Editing Products

What You'll Learn in This Chapter:

- ▶ Overview of the video editing market
- ▶ Touring Adobe Premiere Elements—things look different here
- ▶ Taking Adobe Premiere Pro for a test drive

Studio is not the only player in the nonlinear editing software game. At its $100 price point (or less) you can find several worthy competitors. And after you get comfortable with Studio, you might want to step up to a professional-level NLE.

In this chapter I give you an overview of Adobe Premiere Elements, the one $100 NLE that outshines Studio in some areas and takes a substantially different and, some might say, riskier approach to this market niche.

Finally, I briefly cover the professional NLE offerings and give you a hands-on walkthrough of Adobe Premiere Pro, my choice as the best product in the $500 and up price range.

Overview of the Video Editing Market

You've been working with Studio for the past five chapters (and you'll create DVDs with it in Chapter 18, "Authoring DVDs Using Studio's DVD Module"). I chose to feature Studio in this book because I think it's the best overall NLE at its $100 price point.

When I first proposed this book, this choice was a close call. I gave serious consideration to featuring Ulead VideoStudio 8 (see Figure 14.1).

FIGURE 14.1
Ulead VideoStudio 8 is nearly Pinnacle Studio's match, but improvements to Studio Plus caused Pinnacle to stay on top.

At that time Pinnacle Systems had not announced Studio Plus (with its additional video track and its still-image motion-control features). From my perspective back then, Studio's lack of a second video track and the picture-in-picture, chroma keying, and layering that would have gone along with that was an issue.

Ulead VideoStudio 8 offered that extra track as well as a user-friendly approach similar to Studio's. What tipped the scales to Studio back then were all its extra, cool features, its terrific Title Editor, and its excellent DVD-authoring module.

Nevertheless, I planned to give VideoStudio 8 some substantial coverage in this chapter. Now, I've changed my mind—for two reasons.

Studio Plus and Premiere Elements Raise the Bar

After I had written two chapters on Studio, Pinnacle sent me a prerelease copy of Studio Plus. That led to a significant rewrite of those chapters, plus some changes to earlier chapters and a rewrite of this book's table of contents.

Concurrently, Adobe sent me a prerelease version of Premiere Elements, a brand new $100 NLE based on Adobe's superb, professional-level NLE, Premiere Pro.

After taking Premiere Elements through its paces, I concluded that Adobe had thrown down the gauntlet. With the release of Premiere Elements, it challenged similarly priced NLEs to step up to its flexible and powerful editing.

Changed Plans

At any event, two things became clear: VideoStudio 8 no longer warranted additional coverage and Premiere Elements did. True, Premiere Elements is not as consumer-friendly as Studio, but I think Premiere Elements is a sign of where this entry-level market is going.

Folks like you who are relatively new to video editing are becoming more computer savvy. You expect more power in your PC products and are willing to take some time to learn to use them well.

From my perspective, Premiere Elements might just be the next logical, entry-level NLE evolutionary step that takes this market in a whole new direction.

As a result, in this chapter I give you an overview of Premiere Elements instead of VideoStudio 8. I also present some hands-on tasks using its older, more sophisticated sibling: Premiere Pro.

Other Entry-Level NLEs

▶ **CyberLink PowerDirector ($80—www.gocyberlink.com)**—PowerDirector features a plethora of special effects, but that offering does not overcome its overly simplified timeline interface and limited DVD-authoring tool.

▶ **Nova Development Video Explosion Deluxe ($80— www.novadevelopment.com)**—Video Explosion Deluxe is the newest entrant in this field. Its interface is a bit confusing but it matches up reasonably well against VideoStudio.

▶ **Roxio VideoWave Professional ($50—www.roxio.com)**—VideoWave used to be MGI VideoWave. Roxio bought this product a while back but has done little to bring it up to today's standards. Its strength is its huge library of special effects, image editing, and digital animation tools. As this book went to press, Sonic Solutions was seeking regulatory approval to purchase Roxio's video-editing and DVD-creation business. A likely scenario is for Sonic to incorporate VideoWave into the MyDVD Suite.

▶ **Ulead VideoStudio**—VideoStudio gives Pinnacle Studio a run for its money in some areas. It has a full range of transitions, a detailed text tool and an extra video track that enables you to create a very simplified picture-in-picture. However, the VideoStudio interface has many quirky usability issues, and its DVD-authoring module is inadequate.

Professional NLEs

Professional video-editing software lets you do things on your PC that only a few years ago required very expensive hardware and a degree in engineering (well, sort of).

Now, a PC with a Pentium 4 or Athlon 64 processor (or better), 512MB of RAM, and a decent 3D graphics card (along with plenty of hard-drive storage) can create broadcast-quality video productions.

Here are the four principal offerings at this level for Windows-based PCs:

▶ Adobe Premiere Pro—$699—www.adobe.com

▶ Avid Xpress DV—$695 or $1,795 for the Pro version—www.avid.com

▶ Pinnacle Liquid Edition—$499 or $999 for the Pro version—www.pinnaclesys.com

▶ Sony Vegas—$560—http://mediasoftware.sonypictures.com

I have worked with all four at one time or another. All are tremendous products that offer video editors just about everything they need.

What sets them apart tends to be subtle differences in how they handle special effects, title editing, putting clips and graphics in motion, high-level audio-editing tools, and interface features. For me to take the time to differentiate among them would mean delving into esoterica.

What I suggest then is this: If moving into this editing realm interests you, download trial versions or read online reviews.

Premiere Pro is my pick for the best professional-level NLE for Windows-based PCs. And with the release of Premiere Elements, it is the only NLE at this rarified level that has an easy upgrade path for entry-level editors who want to ramp up their skill set.

Along those lines, I introduce you to Premiere Elements in the next section and then take you through some tasks using Premiere Pro. You can follow along using the trial versions of both Premiere Elements and Premiere Pro.

By the Way

Full Disclosure

Several years ago I reviewed most of the major NLEs for *PC World Magazine*. Adobe Premiere completely impressed me, such that I immersed myself in it and became an Adobe Certified Instructor in Premiere. I have written *Sams Teach Yourself in 24 Hours* books on both Premiere 6.5 and Premiere Pro.

Touring Adobe Premiere Elements— Things Look Different Here

Adobe released Premiere Elements (see Figure 14.2)—a subset of Premiere Pro—in October 2004. This came a couple years after Adobe released Photoshop Elements, a simplified version of the photo-and-graphics editing industry's leading product.

Although Photoshop Elements has the look and feel of Photoshop, it falls well shy of providing all the tools available in its hugely popular, graphic-industry-standard sibling.

FIGURE 14.2
Adobe Premiere Elements ($100 retail) offers only slightly fewer than all the features available in Premiere Pro ($700). It attempts to set a new direction to the nonlinear video-editing market.

Not so with Premiere Elements. I am amazed (yes, *amazed*) that Adobe has given entry-level video editors so much to work with. Premiere Elements is only a few degrees removed from Premiere Pro. You get a lot of power for only $100.

I won't list those differences (because I have not introduced Premiere Pro to you). Rather, I want to show you how Premiere Elements is different from every other (yes, *every* other) entry-level, nonlinear editor.

What Makes Premiere Elements So Different

First, take a look at the Premiere Elements interface shown in Figure 14.3. About the only concessions to the entry-level market are the highlighted task icons and the How-To section. The rest of the interface—the Monitor, Timeline, and Media windows—all have the clean, professional look of Premiere Pro.

Premiere Elements' professional appearance is not a radical departure from the rest of the entry-level NLE market. However, 99 video and 99 audio tracks are.

FIGURE 14.3
Premiere Elements
features an inter-
face with only a
couple entry-level
features.

Take a look at Figure 14.4. You recall that I raved about Studio's extra video track.
Figure 14.4 shows Premiere with six video and six audio tracks open (remember,
there can be as many as 99 video and 99 audio tracks). The layering possibilities
are endless. The audio mixing opportunities are mind boggling.

FIGURE 14.4
Premiere Elements
can have up to 99
video tracks and
99 audio tracks.
The creative possi-
bilities can be over-
whelming.

One immediate benefit of all these tracks is the capability to make multiple pictures-in-picture without having to export and then record over the same clip several times. Figure 14.5 shows a PiP I made in a couple minutes using five layered video clips.

FIGURE 14.5
All those video layers make it easy to create PiPs with multiple clips. You can apply video effects, such as Bevel Edges, to each PiP.

Premiere Elements gives you direct control over each clip's motion path, size, rotation, and timing. You can move them on all at once or one at a time and then have them fly off together or separately. You can fade them on and off. Or any combination of the above.

As shown earlier in Figure 14.5, you also can apply any effect you want to each individual PiP clip. Note that I used Bevel Edges to give all of them a 3D look.

Minutely Detailed Control

Figure 14.6 shows another professional-level editing tool: direct control over transitions. You recall with Studio that every time you add a transition, you shorten the overall length of your production by the length of the transition.

The reason: Studio automatically slides the beginning of the second clip over the end of the first. The purpose is to ensure that there are enough head and tail video frames to complete the transition.

That's not the case with Premiere Elements. Instead, Premiere Elements places the transition where you tell it, and if there isn't enough extra footage at the end or beginning of the two clips, Premiere Elements lets you decide how to handle that. You can change the transition duration, move its start and end, or use freeze frames for the missing head or tail frames.

FIGURE 14.6
Premiere Elements gives you direct control over every aspect of a transition: duration, where it starts and ends, and how it deals with insufficient head or tail frames.

You also have other options that depend on a particular transition's characteristics. In the case of the Spin Away transition in Figure 14.6, you can add a border of any width and any color.

The same level of control applies to video effects. Premiere Elements (and Premiere Pro) uses something called **keyframes**. I've illustrated a few in Figure 14.7 as I applied them to a Lens Flare effect.

FIGURE 14.7
Using the highlighted keyframes gives you absolute, precise control over this Lens Flare effect.

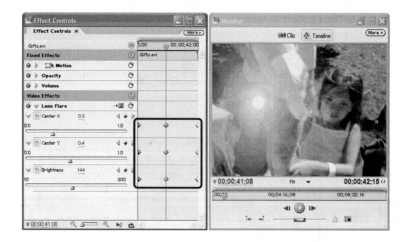

The little triangles and diamonds highlighted in Figure 14.7 are points of reference. Basically, you tell the effect what its behavior—or parameters—will be at each keyframe and then have it change gradually between keyframes. You can even control the acceleration of the changes using what are called **Bezier** curves (high-level controls typically found only in professional, motion graphics products such as Adobe After Effects).

Professional But Not Impenetrable

Adobe does offer up some concessions to its intended entry-level video-editor audience. One very cool video-capture feature resolves a complaint I have about Studio, and it saves users a lot of time. The issue is what happens to video after you capture it or add it as a file to your project.

Video capture takes place in the very simple and clean interface shown in Figure 14.8. One thing that's clear about Adobe is that it doesn't do consumerish things like put camcorder controls inside a camcorder-like interface.

FIGURE 14.8
You capture video in this very straightforward interface.

What happens next is what I like. It involves two windows. In the Media window (the equivalent of the Album in Studio), all media are in the same window. As shown in Figure 14.9, you can tell them apart by their icons or their Media Type designations. Studio stores different media types on individual Album **pages.**

Another big difference between Premiere Elements and Studio is that Elements does not display every file in a file folder when all you wanted to do was add a single file to your project. Nor does it use scene detection to divide entire videos into clips and clutter up your Media window with them.

Instead, when you do video capture, Premiere Elements takes your entire video and drops it directly into the Timeline and divides it into clips there. It gives you the best of both worlds.

FIGURE 14.9
Unlike Studio,
Premiere Elements
displays all media
in a single window
and does not split
them into clips or
load every file into
a file folder.

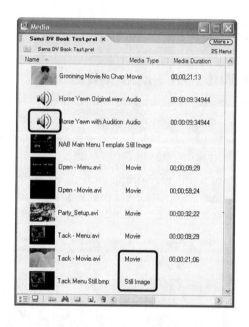

Another helpful concession to the entry-level market is the help section and its
tutorials (refer to Figure 14.10). They are very thorough, well written, and, well,
helpful.

FIGURE 14.10
Premiere Elements
has an excellent
help file and tutori-
al collection.

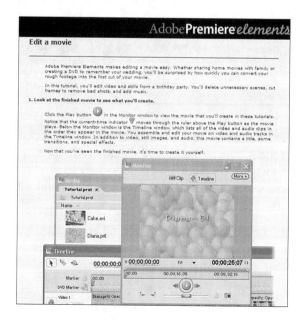

How Do Studio and Premiere Elements Compare?

There are two parts to this question:

▶ Do Premiere Elements's offerings, in toto, outshine Studio's?

▶ Will Premiere Elements's many possibilities and opportunities overwhelm (and possibly turn off) its intended customer base?

The answer to the first question is—not yet. All the features I've shown so far do work better than those you find in Studio. Where Premiere Elements loses a little ground is in its Title Editor, shown in Figure 14.11. It's basically on par with Studio's, but it does not have anywhere near the number of styles and templates that Studio has, nor can you use it to create DVD menus.

FIGURE 14.11
Premiere Elements's Title Editor has more or less the same features as Studio's but nowhere near as many styles and templates.

And Premiere Elements's DVD-authoring capabilities are woefully inadequate. Figure 14.12 shows its DVD menu setup screen. It comes with more than 50 templates, but you cannot edit them. If the name you give a button is too long, it'll overlap the adjacent button and you can't move those buttons to make them fit. You have to shorten the name.

Adding scene markers is clumsy and nowhere near as elegant as the method used in Studio. To really compete in this marketplace, Adobe will have to strengthen Premiere Elements's DVD-authoring tools.

FIGURE 14.12
Premiere
Elements's DVD-
authoring module
offers only a few
options and does
not begin to meas-
ure up Studio's.

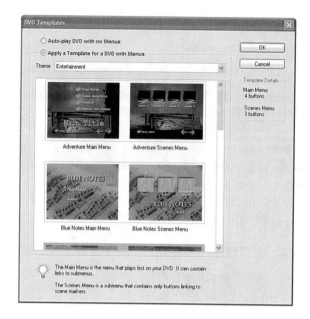

Premiere Elements Charts a New Course

Now for question number two. For years, Pinnacle's approach has been to keep things simple and consumer-friendly. Its philosophy has been that entry-level video editors do not want to deal with the arcana of transition placement and video-effect keyframes.

Its take on transitions has always tended toward what Pinnacle believes consumers want: the wild and wacky using objects like stars, planes, and champagne glasses. The company's many HFX transitions add-on packs are chock-a-block with that kind of stuff.

And their editing paradigm has always been that if entry-level video editors narrate a project, they do it as an afterthought.

Premiere Elements will have none of that. Professional editors know that stuff like excessive transitions and adding audio after completing a project gets old real fast. And Adobe's marketplace until now has been prosumer to professional only.

So Adobe has applied that same philosophy to Premiere Elements. I think they are on the right track. Premiere Elements might very well take this entry-level video-editing market to a new level.

Taking Adobe Premiere Pro for a Test Drive

You can take Studio and other entry-level NLEs only so far. If you want to raise your video-editing bar, you need to step up to a professional-quality editor. Premiere Pro is my top pick.

Premiere Pro's many options mean your video projects are limited only by your creativity, time, and energy.

As with Premiere Elements, Premiere Pro lets you layer, or **composite**, up to 99 video tracks. Its high-end audio tools and 99 audio tracks let you sweeten and mix audio to suit your most exacting expectations. And you can change the characteristics of its audio and video effects gradually over time using keyframes.

I suggest you download the Premiere Pro trial version from www.adobe.com to get the most value out of the rest of this chapter. To find it, go to the Premiere Pro page and click Tryout to go to the link for the 170MB download.

Demonstrating Premiere Pro's Power

I want to demonstrate Premiere Pro's power and give you some hands-on time with it. Because this book is geared to entry-level video editors, I won't dive too deeply into Premiere Pro's many features.

I'll offer only a few detailed, hands-on, step-by-step tasks and fill in the gaps with some bare-bones demonstrations.

As for the demos, do what you can to follow along. Because I leave out some details and gloss over some steps, something might come up as you try to follow along that will stump you. Not to worry—Premiere Pro is a powerful product that takes a lot of effort to master.

And no matter how many problems arise, experimenting with Premiere will open your eyes to its potential.

Exploring Premiere Pro's User Interface

The first time you open Premiere Pro, as shown in Figure 14.13, it asks you what kind of project you're going to make. The options appear to be very limited: PAL or NTSC, Standard aspect ratio (4:3) or Widescreen (16:9), and 32KHz audio or 48KHz.

FIGURE 14.13
The first of many collections of options. In this case, select the preset that matches your video (instead of a Custom Setting).

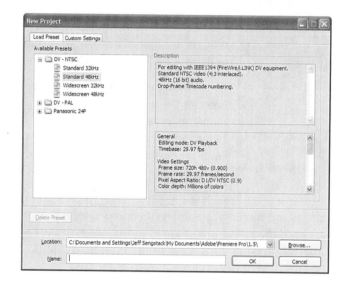

Before making your selection, click the Custom Settings tab just to get an idea that there are many more possibilities. Switch back to the Load Presets tab and select a preset that matches your project; then give your project a name and click OK to open Premiere Pro's editing workspace.

By the Way

> **Audio Quality**
>
> The 32KHz and 48KHz refer to audio quality. Many DV camcorders let you choose between a single stereo track recorded at 48KHz or two tracks recorded at 32KHz. That said, it's generally better to select a high setting at the outset. You always can reduce the audio—and video—quality when you later record your edited project to a DVD, videotape, or other media.

As shown in Figure 14.14, Premiere's interface has some familiar elements, including the standard NLE timeline, a Project window for media storage, and two monitor windows (Source and Program). Two monitors let you view your unedited source videos on the left and your edited program videos on the right.

Select a Workspace to Suit the Occasion

If your Premiere workspace is not as neat and tidy as the one in Figure 14.3, Premiere Pro can fix that. From the main menu select Window, Workspace, Editing.

Project Window　　　　　Monitor Window

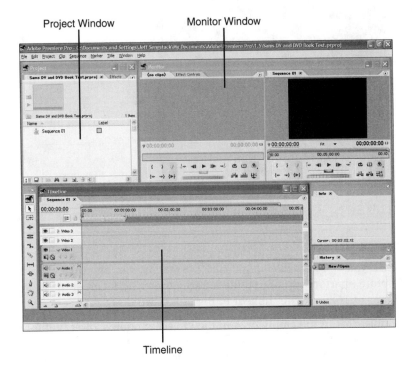

FIGURE 14.14
Premiere's interface has some standard NLE elements.

Timeline

Start a New Project

You'll need to load some media into Premiere Pro to try some of its features. You begin by importing video from your camcorder and putting media files in the Project folder. Here's how:

1. Select File, Capture to open the Capture window shown in Figure 14.15. You will note that it is loaded with more goodies than you encountered in Movie Maker or Studio.

2. Connect your DV camcorder to the PC and turn it on to VCR. To simplify things, just cue up your tape, note whether the highlighted Scene Detect feature is checked (your choice), give your tape and clip a name, and click the highlighted record button.

FIGURE 14.15
The capture interface offers extra automation features and controls versus entry-level NLEs.

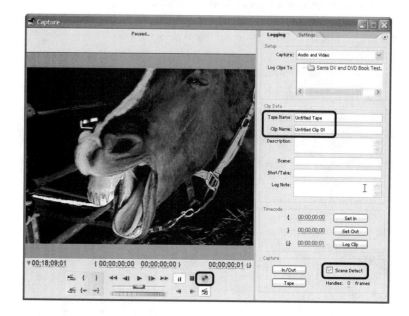

3. When you've recorded enough, click the Stop button and then close the Capture interface by clicking the X in the upper-right corner. As shown in Figure 14.16, your clips appear in the Project window.

4. Double-click in the empty area in the Project window's lower half (or select File, Import) to open the Import window. Navigate to wherever you've stored other videos, stills, or audio; select any files and click Open. Those files will show up in the Project window.

By the Way

What's "Sequence" Doing in the Project Window?

Premiere Pro lets you use multiple timelines in a single project. It calls each of those individual timelines "sequences." The advantage is that you might want to apply an effect to multiple edited clips or use an edited sequence in several places or projects. To do that, simply edit that segment as one sequence and then place that sequence in another sequence just as you would place a clip there.

5. Drag the right edge of the Project window to the right to see all the information Premiere tracks here (refer back to Figure 14.16).

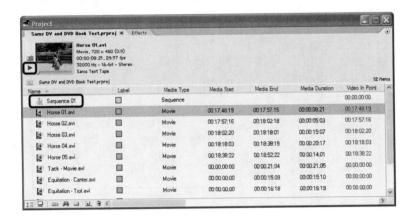

FIGURE 14.16
Captured and
imported clips
show up in the
Project window.
Preview them in the
little monitor. Note
that a Sequence is
the equivalent of a
Timeline within the
Timeline window.

All-in-One

One big difference between Premiere Pro and Studio is that in Premiere, all media types—videos, stills, audio, and graphics—are accessible in one window instead of as pages in an album.

By the Way

6. Select a video or audio clip in the Project window and click the Play button in the lower-left corner beside the little monitor screen highlighted earlier in Figure 14.16. This lets you easily preview your clip.

7. Drag a video clip to the Video 1 track on the Timeline. In the Timeline, click the clip to select it, press the Home key, and click the Play button in the Program Monitor screen (the screen on the right). This should all seem mighty familiar. The only difference is the second monitor on the left. You use it to preview and trim clips before adding them to the Timeline/Sequence.

Looking at Layering

As I mentioned earlier, Premiere Pro lets you work with as many as 99 video tracks and 99 audio tracks. Figure 14.17 shows how the Timeline looks after you add some additional tracks.

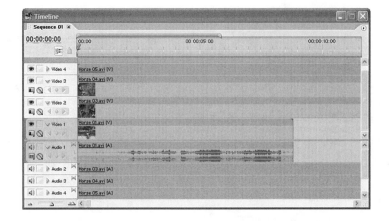

On the video side, those extra tracks let you layer video. The following sections present a few brief demos of what that entails.

Try it Yourself — Compositing Clips

This task is a collection of several bare-bones demos. Despite this, I think you still can complete this and other upcoming demos without any problems. I first explain how to use opacity to blend two clips into one. Then I move on to Picture-in-Picture, Split Screen, and finally, Chroma Key. Here you go:

1. As shown in Figure 14.18, drag one clip to the Video 1 track and another directly above the first on Video 2. Click the clip in the Video 2 track to select it.

By the Way — Logical Layering

Unlike Studio, in Premiere Pro, the clip in the uppermost track covers all clips below it. Premiere Pro gives you multiple means to reveal what's beneath a clip: reduce its opacity, shrink it, crop it, or key out part of it.

2. Switch to the Effect Controls window by clicking its tab above the left screen in the Monitor window (I've highlighted it in Figure 14.19). Click the highlighted twirl-down triangles to reveal the Opacity slider.

3. Move the Opacity slider to something less than 100%. Note that the Program Monitor screen displays the changes as you make them (refer to Figure 14.19).

FIGURE 14.18
Place two clips on separate tracks to begin the layering process.

Gradually Apply Opacity Changes with Keyframes

Did you Know?

Look to the left of the word "Opacity" in the Effect Controls window. You'll see a little stopwatch. If it's activated (a little minute hand appears) each time you change the opacity setting for some point in the video clip, Premiere Pro will add a keyframe there. In this way you can gradually change the opacity of the top clip over time. I explain keyframes in more detail later in this section.

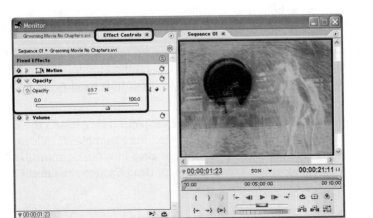

FIGURE 14.19
Access the Opacity effect by clicking the highlighted tab to open the Effect Controls window. Opacity is a **fixed** effect, one that is always available in the Effect Controls window.

4. To create a PiP, start by turning off any Opacity settings you made by clicking the little "f" next to "Opacity." Alternatively, you can move the Opacity slider to 100% or click the Reset button to the right of "Opacity." If you added keyframes, click the Keyframe stopwatch to remove them.

5. Twirl down the Motion disclosure triangle (highlighted in Figure 14.20) to reveal its settings.

FIGURE 14.20
Use Premiere Pro's Motion settings to create a PiP. Clicking the clip in the Program Monitor screen switches on its handles and a little "x" in a circle (emphasis added in this figure), that let you move it and change its size.

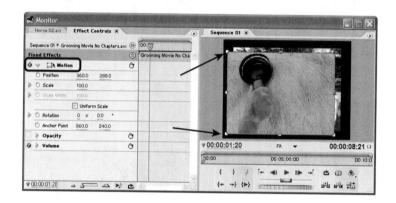

6. Click the clip image in the Program Monitor screen. That switches on the clip's handles (highlighted in Figure 14.20). Drag the clip to a new location using the x in the circle in the center and shrink it using a handle. Take a look at the numerical parameters in the Effect Controls window and watch them change as you move the clip around.

7. You can rotate it by moving the cursor slightly to the clip's right or left and watching for the cursor to change to a curved double arrow. Note that you also can use keyframes for each motion setting, letting you bring the clip on from offscreen, hold it for a while, and move it somewhere else or offscreen, all the while spinning it or changing its size.

8. You can use the Motion settings to create a split screen or use the Crop effect. To get this process started, switch off the Motion settings by clicking the little "f" next to Motion in the Effect Controls window (or click the Motion Reset button).

9. As shown in Figure 14.21, locate the Crop effect by clicking the Effects tab in the Project window. Twirl down the disclosure triangles for Video Effects and Transform (alternatively, you can type **crop** into the Contains box at the top of the window to locate this effect). Drag Crop to the Effect Controls window (or to the clip on Video Track 2).

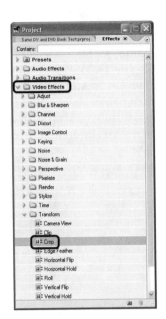

FIGURE 14.21
Locate the Crop video effect by clicking the Effects tab in the Project window.

10. As shown in Figure 14.22, in the Effect Controls window, click the word Crop to display its four handles on the clip in the Program Monitor screen. Move them to crop out part of the clip. You can select the clip on Video Track 1 and crop and move it if you like.

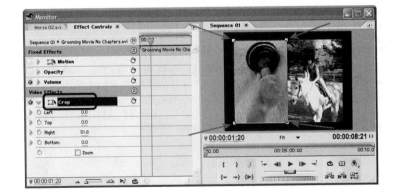

FIGURE 14.22
Create your split screen by dragging in any of the four corners of the clip in the Program Monitor screen. You can click anywhere in the cropped clip and slide the cropping rectangle over the clip.

11. Now to try Chroma Keying. Select File, Import and add the Chroma_Key.mpg video you worked with in Studio to your Project window. You should find it in the Shared Documents/Shared Video folder.

12. Drag it to Video 3 track (if there is no Video 3 track, drag and drop the clip to the blank space above Video 2 and Premiere Pro will automatically create a new video track. Click the newly placed clip to select it.

13. What you see in the Program Monitor screen might surprise you. Your screen should look like Figure 14.23. When Pinnacle compressed the original DV version of Chroma_Key to MPEG, it did it to quarter screen. That's one reason it looks so fuzzy when blown up to full screen. Studio, being consumer-friendly, automatically blows it up to full screen. Premiere Pro, being professional, displays it at its original size.

FIGURE 14.23
After adding the Chroma_Key.mpg video to your Timeline, you'll note that it is not a full-size clip.

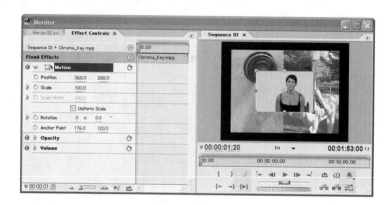

14. Because it's quarter-screen size, you can blow it up to full-screen size in one of two ways: manually or mathematically. You can click it in the Program Monitor screen to select it and then drag a corner until it fills the screen. Or twirl down the Motion disclosure triangles in the Effect Controls window, click the Scale figure, and change it to 200%.

15. Locate the Green Screen Chroma Key effect by clicking the Effects tab in the Project window, twirling down Video Effects and Keying, and then dragging Green Screen Key to the Effect Controls window. It immediately turns the green screen transparent, revealing the two clips below it on the Timeline. Twirl down its disclosure triangle. Your project should now look like Figure 14.24.

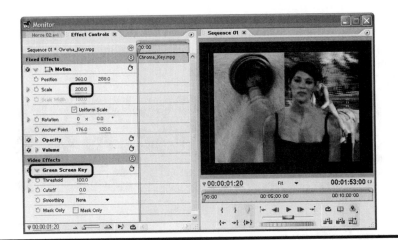

FIGURE 14.24
How the
Chroma_Key.mpg
clip should look
after expanding it
to 200% of its orig-
inal size and apply-
ing the Green
Screen Key to it.

Playing Clips Slower, Faster, or Backward

Right-click any clip in the Timeline and select Speed/Duration. As shown in
Figure 14.25, you have five choices: Speed (in percentage of original clip speed),
Duration (you can change that to match a space you need to fill with a clip that's
too short or long), Reverse Speed, Maintain Audio Pitch (plays back the original
audio to match the new speed without changing pitch—a very powerful feature),
and a Link/Unlink tool to change speed without changing the clip length.

FIGURE 14.25
Clip
Speed/Duration
lets you play a clip
in reverse and at
virtually any speed
you want. Note that
you can maintain
audio pitch (a very
powerful feature)
and retain the origi-
nal clip length by
clicking the Link
icon.

Changing Video Effects Over Time—Using Keyframes

Studio offers 20 video effects, whereas Premiere Pro has 135.

In Studio, when you apply a video effect, it changes the clip equally for its entire
duration. You can fade it in or out, but otherwise you have little control. Premiere

Pro and Premiere Elements let you use **keyframes** to change the effect over time—a very useful and creative option.

Figure 14.26 shows this process in action using the Mosaic effect. The first frame has only a minimal amount applied, the next has a slight change, and the third has a more obvious change.

FIGURE 14.26
Changing a video effect over time is an effective creative technique.

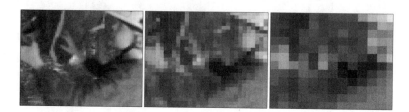

Try it Yourself

Applying Keyframes

This is an example of how to use keyframes. For first-time video editors, this can be fairly daunting. I will try to ease you into the concept with a very basic demo:

1. Delete the clips on the Timeline by selecting them one by one and pressing Delete. Add a new clip to the Video 1 track.

2. Locate the Solarize video effect by clicking the Effects tab in the Project window and twirling down the Video Effects and Stylize disclosure triangles. Drag Solarize to the clip on the Video 1 track, click that clip to select it, open the Effect Controls window, and twirl down the Solarize disclosure triangles. Your Effect Controls window should look like Figure 14.27.

By the Way

Solarize—A Single Parameter Effect

I chose Solarize for this demo because it has only one parameter (it shifts a clip to its negative image). Applying keyframes to a single parameter is relatively easy. Some effects have more than a dozen parameters. Just for grins, apply Lightning (from the Video Effects/Render group) to a clip and open its disclosure triangles in the Effect Controls window. It has 25 parameters!

3. The Effect Controls window should have space—like a mini-Timeline—between the effects list and the Program Monitor screen in which you add keyframes. That space might be closed. To open it, click the chevron icon at the top of the Effect Controls window, highlighted in Figure 14.27.

4. Press the Home key to take you to the clip's first frame. Move the Threshold slider to zero. Click the Keyframe (*Toggle Animation*) stopwatch to switch on

keyframes. A little triangle should appear on the left side of the mini-Timeline.

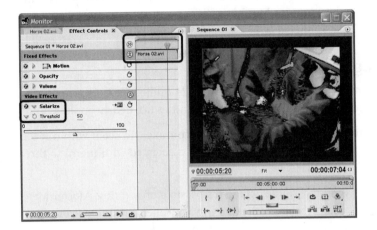

FIGURE 14.27
How a clip should look with Solarize applied to it at its default 50% setting. If the highlighted mini-Timeline is not open, click the chevron icon at the top of the Effect Controls window.

5. Move your Current Time Indicator (like the Timescale Scrubber in Studio) in the mini-Timeline to the center. Move the Threshold slider to 100 (full application of the effect).

6. Press the End key and the Back Arrow key once to go to the final frame of this clip. Move the Threshold slider back to zero. Your Effect Controls window keyframes should look like Figure 14.28.

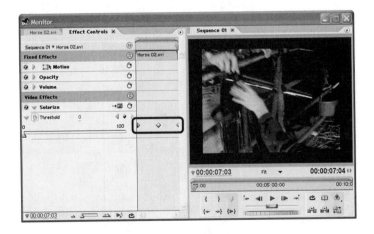

FIGURE 14.28
Changing parameters with Keyframes activated adds little markers in the Effect Controls window's mini-Timeline.

7. Play this clip by pressing the Home key to return to the first frame and the spacebar to begin playback. Watch as the Threshold slider moves from left to right and back to the left and watch the effect change over time on the clip in the Program Monitor screen.

Editing Audio

With Premiere Pro's 99 audio tracks and 24 audio effects (versus Studio's 4 tracks and 6 effects) your audio-editing opportunities are nearly endless.

As with Studio, Premiere Pro uses an audio mixer. To see it with a few tracks visible, first add some clips (that have audio associated with them) to three or four video (or audio) tracks.

Then select Window, Audio Mixer. It's possible only a tiny, Master Meters window will open. If that's the case, click its wing-out menu triangle (in the upper-right corner) and click Audio Mixer (your only option).

As shown in Figure 14.29, Premiere Pro's Audio Mixer displays controls for every audio track on which you've added audio, as well as a list of available audio effects.

FIGURE 14.29
Premiere's Audio Mixer gives you greater creative control over all your audio tracks and lets you apply effects from the drop-down list to entire tracks.

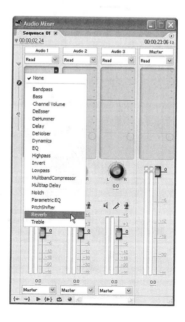

One of Premiere Pro's strengths is the capability to apply audio effects, volume, panning, and surround-sound placement to an entire track instead of to only a clip. And you can **gang** audio tracks and apply those same audio characteristics to groups of tracks.

Like Studio, Premiere Pro works with VST audio plug-ins. Unlike Studio, Premiere ships with a full suite of incredibly useful effects.

To check out a few, follow these steps:

1. Click the Effects tab in the Project window and twirl down the disclosure triangles for Audio Effects and Stereo.

2. Drag EQ (or any other effect) to an audio clip on the Timeline. If you try to apply it to the video portion of a clip that has audio, nothing will happen.

3. Open the Effect Controls window and twirl down the EQ and Custom Setup disclosure triangles.

4. To see all of this effect's controls, you'll need to close the mini-Timeline (click the chevron at the top of the Effect Controls window) and expand the Monitor window by dragging its left or right edges. The EQ controls should look like those in Figure 14.30.

5. If you aren't blown away by this just yet, scroll down the page and twirl down Individual Parameters. There is very little you cannot do with the Audio Effects and Mixer in Premiere Pro.

FIGURE 14.30
EQ is one of many audio effects that give you full control over virtually every aspect of your sound.

This EQ audio effect lets you change volume levels in narrow frequency bands to add more bass oomph or cut the treble range. Other effects remove specific frequency ranges to reduce hum, bring down ambient noise while increasing the volume of quiet passages, and add reverb to create the feeling of being in a giant cathedral.

Adding Text with the Adobe Title Designer

In something of an ironic twist, Adobe's Title Designer, shown in Figure 14.31, replaced Pinnacle's TitleDeko that Adobe bundled with previous versions of Premiere. Access the Title Designer by selecting File, New, Title.

FIGURE 14.31
The Adobe Title Designer gives you total control over text; it comes loaded with styles and templates and offers plenty of shape-creation tools.

With this module you can do just about anything you can think of with text. Scores of graphical templates and text styles are available, as well as customizing tools that let you fine-tune your text to the *n*th degree.

It's worth checking out a template just to see all that's involved in higher-level text design. To do that, click the highlighted icon above the upper-left corner of the Title Designer's display window.

That opens the Templates window shown in Figure 14.32. Twirl down Title Designer Presets and Lower Thirds (or whatever group you choose) and click any template. It will show up in the Preview window. Now arrow down through this group of templates to get an idea of what you can create with the Title Designer.

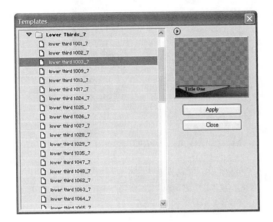

FIGURE 14.32
The Adobe Title Designer ships with dozens of templates that you can customize to suit your production needs.

Select a template. I recommend "lower third 1003_7" because it has several elements worth further examination. Click Apply to return to the Title Designer window.

Trial Version Might Not Have Templates

As this book went to press, the trial version of Premiere Pro did not have any Title Designer Templates.

By the Way

Uncheck Show Video (highlighted in Figure 14.33) to get a clearer view of this template. Click the Selection tool (in the upper-left corner). Use it to select each layer of this template and spread them out as I did in Figure 14.33.

Take a look at the Object Style section on the right side of the Title Designer. As you click each object, the Style parameters change. Just to see some of these elements in action, feel free to change some parameters. Any changes you make show up immediately in the Title Designer window.

When done, close the Title Designer window by clicking its X in the upper-right corner.

FIGURE 14.33
Each template is a collection of several editable elements.

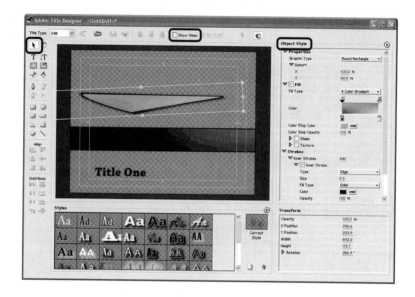

FIGURE 14.33
Each template is a collection of several editable elements.

Summary

For years, Studio has dominated the entry-level NLE marketplace. Ulead VideoStudio has been its primary challenger. By adding a second video track to Studio Plus along with still-image motion control, Studio has lengthened its lead and continues to justify its immense success—10 million units sold.

However, Adobe Premiere Elements might change that market dominance. At the very least it aims higher and might cause others in this niche to rethink their view of their target audience.

At some point you might grow frustrated with the limitations inherent in entry-level NLEs. If you want to raise your video-editing bar, you need to step up to a professional-quality editor. Four products dominate the Windows-based NLE market, and of them, Premiere Pro, is my top pick.

Its many options mean that your video projects are limited only by your creativity, time, and energy. It lets you composite videos, change video and audio effects over time, and create text that rivals the best TV broadcast–quality titlers.

PART III

Entry-Level DVD Authoring

CHAPTER 15

What DVDs and DVD-Authoring Software Can Do for You

What You'll Learn in This Chapter:

▶ Enhancing your media with DVDs

▶ Delving into DVD projects—personal to professional

▶ Discovering what DVD-authoring software can do for you

▶ Overview of DVD-authoring products

DVDs offer countless possibilities. Yet they represent such new technology, few PC owners have begun to exploit DVDs' potential. In this chapter I offer a taste of what DVDs can do for you, your business, or your profession. I relate four anecdotes about how others have used DVD-authoring applications, from consumer-level to commercial production.

The whole concept of DVD authoring remains shrouded in mystery. I demystify that process to prepare you for what's to come in this book's remaining chapters.

Enhancing Your Media with DVDs

As I mentioned in Chapter 1, "Digital Video and DVDs—Getting Acquainted," DVDs have multiple benefits:

▶ Interactivity

▶ You can use multiple media file types

▶ Easy customization

▶ Better audio and video quality than VHS tapes

▶ Instant access to media

You can see all those characteristics when you put a Hollywood movie DVD into your living room DVD player. First, you probably see that oft-ignored FBI warning. Then a brief video sequence might play, followed by a menu that might have video playing behind it along with music from the movie. As you navigate your remote through the menu's various choices, each button or text item becomes highlighted in turn.

One button might take you to a setup screen that allows you to select subtitles, dubbed foreign languages, or Dolby digital audio. Another might open a scene selection menu with buttons displaying thumbnail images of various scenes in the movie. Still another might take you to a collection of "extras": movie theater trailers, behind-the-scenes clips, actor photos and bios, outtakes, deleted scenes, or director's comments. Finally, yet another button starts the movie. Not only will the video and sound be distinctly better than videocassettes, you won't see those video defects caused by stretched or worn-out tapes.

DVDs Improve the Viewing Experience

DVDs have changed the way we view movies at home. It used to be that we rented a video, watched it, and returned it. Now, all these extra features make it worth our while to take a second look.

Some DVDs' extra features create compelling reasons to own a movie. Directors' comments alone can be the equivalent of college filmmaking coursework.

DVDs have made Hollywood filmmakers rethink the entire creative process. The same holds true for home video enthusiasts, professional videographers, and corporate media producers. DVDs have expanded the creative possibilities.

Delving into DVD Projects—Personal to Professional

As you begin to create DVD projects, you'll quickly discover that this medium's potential is endless. In the following four sections, I present about a dozen uses for DVDs along with four anecdotes. Those stories show you some real-world examples of persons using DVD technology to enhance their media and their viewers' experience.

Home DVD Projects

Your first DVD projects will probably start at home. A homemade DVD can be as straightforward as a simple recording of a video or as complex as a family tree project with multiple menus and media. I suggest getting your feet wet creating some of the following DVD projects before moving on to more demanding efforts:

- ▶ Video recording or archival storage
- ▶ Holiday greeting cards
- ▶ Vacation videos and slideshows
- ▶ Sports team season highlights
- ▶ Family tree history

Video Recording or Archival Storage

Some software and hardware products let you transfer one or more videos or TV shows directly to a DVD. I cover that process in Chapter 19, "Stepping Up to MyDVD 6."

Holiday Greeting Cards

Using a DVD for those annual family updates sent to friends and relatives adds several new dimensions to what you might now consider to be passé word processor printouts. Figure 15.1 shows how you can mix videos, photos, and your favorite seasonal music into one appealing, memorable, and long-lasting greeting.

FIGURE 15.1
Use video clips, photos, and music to turn those annual family update letters into holiday multimedia extravaganzas.

Vacation Videos and Slideshows

As shown in Figure 15.2, you can give your vacation videos some interactivity by using menu buttons to let viewers jump to specific activities. Viewers can click buttons to view particular segments of the vacation or a slideshow complete with music and transitions. Viewers can watch to the end of those clips, and the DVD automatically will return them to the opening menu screen. Or they can exit a video at any time and return to the main menu by pressing the Menu button on their remote control.

FIGURE 15.2
Add simple interactivity and ease of access to your vacation videos and still images using a DVD menu.

Sports Team Season Highlights

The approach demonstrated in Figures 15.3 and 15.4 offers viewers more interactivity. In this case, clicking a menu button takes viewers to a **nested** menu (a commonly used DVD-authoring technique that puts a menu within a menu). The nested menu can offer stats for that season or other menu buttons to play specific season highlights.

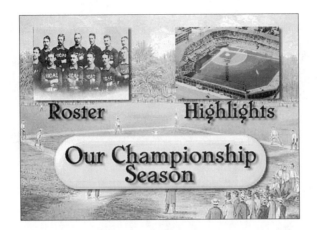

FIGURE 15.3
Sports DVD menus have extra flair when you give viewers options.

FIGURE 15.4
Use a nested menu to offer access to statistics, highlights, and more.

Family Tree History

The family tree DVD illustrated in Figures 15.5–15.7 shows how you can take the nested menu approach a bit further. The opening menu in Figure 15.5 gives viewers options to view an overall family history video or take a tour of specific family lines and so on. The nested menu in Figure 15.6 lets viewers access the portion of the material that applies to that line, and the third menu in Figure 15.7 uses thumbnail images to give viewers access to those family photos.

FIGURE 15.5
A family tree history DVD opening menu might look like this.

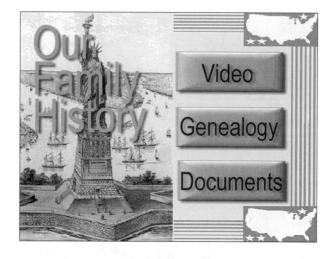

FIGURE 15.6
A nested menu, or submenu, provides access to a specific branch of the family tree.

FIGURE 15.7
Accessing the next menu level lets viewer see photos of individuals within that branch of the family tree.

A First-Time DVD-Authoring Experience

"Exciting" is how Leonard Broz describes burning his first DVD. "I waited my whole life for this moment," he adds with a smile. When he shows family video albums and "mini-travelogues" to relations and friends, they are "elated" with the results.

Leonard Broz teaches video editing to seniors.

The former technology and industrial arts teacher from suburban Chicago winters in Arizona, where he teaches computer-based video- and photo-editing techniques to other seniors in his community.

Broz uses Sonic Solutions MyDVD to convert his still photos and digital video into crowd-pleasing DVDs as shown in Figure 15.8.

He edits 90 minutes of raw video down to 10 minutes, converts his digital images into a slideshow with transitions, and then adds a narration and music. He uses MyDVD's custom styles to personalize attributes such as the font, text size, and background images of his menus; then he saves that updated style for use later.

FIGURE 15.8
Broz creates trave-
logues combining
videos and digital
photos with a nar-
ration and music.

Besides travelogues, Broz produced a DVD of his son's wedding as shown in Figure 15.9. He used photos from the prewedding showers, the ceremony, and the honeymoon, along with a video from the reception, and put them all together on a DVD.

FIGURE 15.9
Broz's son's wed-
ding DVD was a big
hit.

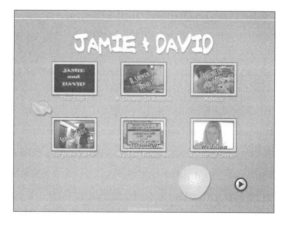

His next task will be to create "the story of our life on DVD" from the many family photos and the 300 or so videotapes he has shot over the years, starting with his wedding day.

Videographer DVD Projects

Professional videographers, many of whom work as one-man bands, need something to give them a competitive edge. DVDs do that. They turn formerly linear event videos—weddings, concerts, and panel discussions—into interactive, enjoyable projects. Here are some DVD ideas that might enhance your products:

▶ Interactive event videos

▶ Client rough cuts

▶ Demo reels

Interactive Event Videos

Weddings are the bread and butter of event videographers, so competition in this market niche is fierce. Adding DVDs to your product offerings makes you stand out above the crowd. Figure 15.10 demonstrates how you might create a wedding DVD.

This one gives viewers instant access to specific wedding day highlights and uses a nested menu to jump to individual greetings from the guests. You could create DVDs using Sonic Solutions' OpenDVD format (see Chapter 19) to let you or your clients later add honeymoon vacation highlights.

FIGURE 15.10
Wedding videos, the videographers' mainstay, have more sizzle when delivered on DVD.

Client Rough Cuts

Frequently, clients like to play "what if." DVDs let you present customers with all the optional takes or special video effects they request. Place those clips on a DVD with a simple menu, and let clients view them at their leisure.

There's no need to make the client cue up a bunch of tapes or have them sit down in your editing room to fast forward and rewind through a project. Rough-cut DVDs let clients view their editing options on their home or office TV, in an environment that can duplicate how others will see their videos.

Demo Reels

If you want to give clients a true taste of what you can do, use a DVD. You no longer need to rely on videotape and hope that potential clients will take the time to sit through that linear experience. In addition, if you use tape, you usually must rely on VHS as the lowest common denominator, thus using something that by design does not equal the visual and aural quality of your original material.

Instead, use a DVD. Give your clients a variety of material and let them choose to view what they want, for however long they want.

DVDs send a message that you're on top of things.

Using Prosumer Techniques on Personal Projects

This next story demonstrates the power of DVDs. Not only are they a media repository, but they also preserve memories. In addition, their interactivity and ease of use mean your DVDs' viewers will want to share those memories again and again.

The Peoria, Arizona Hockey Mites on DVD

Ed Loeffler and his (then) eight-year-old hockey-playing son, Taylor.

Ed Loeffler had a surprise for the Peoria, Arizona Junior Polar Bears hockey team. The group of eight- to ten-year olds and their families had gathered for their season-ending party at a home with a large-screen TV.

Loeffler, the team historian, popped in a DVD and for the next two hours, the gathered families clicked back and forth through menus (see Figure 15.11) and videos, reliving the highlights of their travels all around the Southwest. What they saw "amazed them," says Loeffler. "They loved it."

When completed, Loeffler handed out 25 copies of that DVD (he burned them one at a time on his PC), giving each family "a lifetime of memories," he says. "I saw joy on each person's face."

FIGURE 15.11
Loeffler's opening menu organizes the season by each road trip.

Those DVDs are the distillation of a lot of digital video and 3,000 (!) digital photos. Using Sonic Solution's DVDit!, Loeffler created nested menus to ease access to the individual clips. The opening menu has links to each road trip, and each of those menus has links to the game and other family fun. He used photos and graphical software to create custom menu backgrounds and then added text links as shown in Figure 15.12.

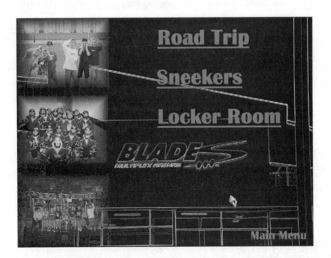

FIGURE 15.12
Loeffler used photos to create menus.

Loeffler is already making plans for next year. He wants to step up to a full-featured authoring product such as Sonic DVD Producer that lets him create animated menus and buttons, work in Dolby audio, and use wide-screen features. "It's addictive," he says. "I want to do it even better next time."

Business DVD Projects

DVDs can change the way businesses operate. Instead of the usual PowerPoint demonstrations, arm your roadshow warriors with DVDs loaded with videos, graphs, and data. Promote your products, secure in the knowledge that your clients will be able to play your production on their home and office TVs. Here are some business-related DVD ideas:

▶ Marketing/promotion

▶ Training and product demonstrations

▶ Catalogs

Marketing/Promotion

No longer do you need to worry whether your laptop will fail. Now marketing presenters need only attach a DVD player to a projector and use the remote to easily and quickly navigate to the marketing material that suits the occasion.

Using rewritable DVDs, those same presenters easily can add to or change their presentations. If you can't get to your clients, send them a DVD. Real estate developers who want to show out-of-town customers their properties—complete with model home virtual tours—will find that DVDs make a positive impact.

Training and Product Demonstrations

DVDs resolve most problems associated with interactive training on a PC. For example, your training videos can run full screen, the menus (see Figure 15.13) allow for true interactivity, and you don't need to tie up a PC or worry about compatibility issues.

Catalogs

Instead of static images of products in a printed book, send clients a DVD that lets them search for products by category and then view their functionality. This applies to any type of company: Music publishers can excerpt individual works, manufacturers can show their wares at work, and service companies can demonstrate their offerings.

FIGURE 15.13
Use DVDs to enhance your corporate training videos.

Designing a Business-Oriented DVD

DVDs' interactivity, excellent video quality, and capability to include data files make them the perfect media for corporate training, marketing, and meeting-presentation tools. The latter use is particularly powerful.

Consider the following MGM Mirage story as a case in point. Instead of thinking of DVDs as a collection of media with some data assets thrown on for extra measure, the Mirage corporate executives make presentations using web browsers peppered with HTML links. At any point in their presentations, they can click a link that starts a software DVD player and then quickly access the DVD menu and its many high-quality videos—a very slick tool.

MGM Mirage Has DVD Vision

Randy Dearborn was there at the beginning. As multimedia director for MGM Mirage's massive casino empire, he has led the charge to DVD. Six years ago, he began replacing the company's unwieldy, expensive, and unreliable laser discs with DVD players. Now all the laser discs are gone, and DVD and MPEG-2 videos are on display throughout the MGM Mirage resorts nationwide as shown in Figure 15.14.

FIGURE 15.14
MGM Mirage uses
DVD-based kiosk
displays to promote
its resort offerings.

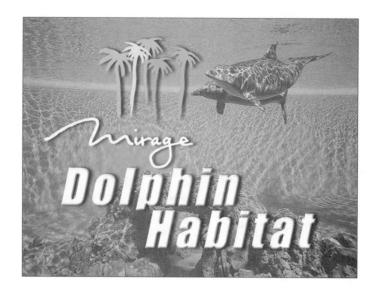

Dearborn and his Mirage Resorts team use professional-level Sonic Solutions'
DVD-authoring applications to create point-of-sale video displays, exterior sig-
nage, corporate archives, and "back of the house" communications with the company's 10,000 employees (see Figure 15.15).

FIGURE 15.15
Mirage retail store
customers use
touch screens con-
nected to DVD play-
ers to sample video
and audio prod-
ucts.

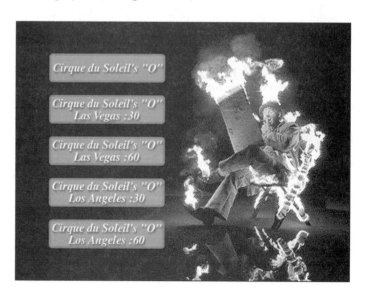

The resorts use Pioneer professional DVD players that have built-in software that allows playback by clips directly to the giant reader boards on the casinos' towering marquees on Las Vegas Boulevard and through interaction with touch screens. Some interactive touch-screen kiosks let customers select music CDs and listen to specific tracks.

MGM Mirage corporate executives supplement their investor road shows with DVDs (see Figure 15.16). They click a button in an HTML page to bring up the DVD menu and they jump instantly to an MPEG-2 video to further amplify a point.

FIGURE 15.16
Corporate executives eschew PowerPoint and use DVDs linked to HTML pages as the AV tool for their road show presentations.

Dearborn's latest efforts are to transfer the entire video archives of the company to DVD, categorizing clips and creating menus that let users outside the department easily access the material.

Commercial/Professional DVD Projects

You might consider turning your growing DVD-authoring expertise into a business. High-end production firms take DVDs to new levels, using professional DVD-authoring applications to explore the arcane realms of the DVD specification to find new ways to entertain. The following story is a case in point.

Creating Interactive DVD Fun for Children

The Chicago Recording Company, one of Chicago's leading music and advertising recording studios, is a DVD pioneer. In 1999, the company started using Sonic DVD Creator to create DVDs for music groups—repackaging archival audio tapes and videotapes of concerts and television appearances.

The company's recent DVD products are light years beyond those early pioneering efforts, says CRC's DVD-authoring specialist, Sean Sutton. "We are pushing the envelope of the DVD specs."

As shown in Figure 15.17, CRC's latest efforts have focused on creating innovative and interactive DVDs for children. Working with Big Idea Productions, developers of *Veggie Tales* and other children's products, CRC has produced DVD movies with kid-friendly mazes, trivia quizzes, and other fun activities.

FIGURE 15.17
CRC creates Big Idea Productions' *3-2-1 Penguins!* DVDs as well as *Veggie Tales* and *Larryboy*.

The challenge is to use "a technology designed only to play nice-looking pictures and good sound," says Sutton, "to somehow make games that are fun and accessible to children who may not yet be able to read." Navigating the maze in Figure 15.18, for instance, requires only the use of the arrow keys on a DVD remote control. Each button click seamlessly displays a new screen showing the changed location. It takes 300 such images and some horribly tedious coding of if-then statements to create this maze.

FIGURE 15.18
It took 300 stills to fashion this maze.

The deceptively straightforward-looking Penguin quiz in Figure 15.19 takes advantage of part of the standard DVD specs that allow randomizing—a bit like hitting random play on your music CD player. Sutton exploited that function to display questions in different sequences each time children play the DVD.

Other elements create additional DVD design complexity, including

▶ Fashioning a way to get the DVD to respond to wrong answers by returning to the original question

▶ Having it not repeat previously asked questions

▶ Getting it to keep track of a child's score

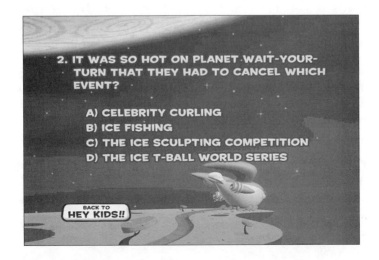

FIGURE 15.19
Official DVD specifications include a randomizing feature used to keep this quiz fresh.

As shown in Figure 15.20, creating the Veggie Tales Voice Swap, which lets kids give characters the voices of other characters in a variety of settings, required 96 separate video clips.

FIGURE 15.20
This mix-and-match character and voice activity required 96 video clips.

Clearly, it's no longer enough to simply slap a 30-minute video on a DVD. CRC fills each Big Idea product to the limit.

Discovering What DVD-Authoring Software Can Do for You

To create DVDs, you need DVD-authoring software. Depending on how many features you want to include on your DVDs, that software can range in price from free (bundled with a DVD recorder), to a few hundred dollars for prosumer-quality products, to $10,000+ for Hollywood-style software.

You also could opt to use DVD-authoring modules included with virtually all the latest video-editing software products. However, none of the entry- to mid-level video-editing software titles, including Pinnacle Studio Plus, offers a full range of authoring tools.

Starting with Chapter 19, you will work with two standalone DVD-authoring products from Sonic Solutions: MyDVD 6 and DVDit! 5. I chose those from the dozen or so DVD-authoring products in their price range because I think they are the best at each of their respective price points.

That's not to say that you won't want to try a different DVD-authoring product at some point. In this section I want to give you a basic idea of the range of features you can find in DVD-authoring products: from entry-level to professional:

▶ Menu creation and functionality

▶ Button and text features

▶ Playback options

▶ Special features

▶ Output and video encoding

▶ DVD burning

▶ Compliance with DVD specifications

Menu Creation and Functionality

What sets DVDs apart from videotapes is their interactivity and immediate access to media deep within the DVD. DVD menus foster that functionality. Authoring products offer varying degrees of menu creation capabilities.

Lower-priced products limit you to automated templates with few options for menu, button, and text styles or placement. Higher-priced products frequently offer graphics toolsets, letting you create custom menus with animated or video backgrounds and music. Other features that some entry-level applications and many prosumer products offer include

▶ **Full menu navigation controls**—These control what happens when a video ends or the viewer presses Next on the remote.

▶ **Timed events**—Still images or menus that automatically move to a default video or another menu if the viewer does nothing with the remote.

▶ **First-play option**—Lets you choose what happens when viewers insert the DVD into a player (the default First-play is the main menu). This could be a brief video, previews of coming attractions, or an animated logo.

▶ **Chapters**—Those scene-selection screens in Hollywood DVDs actually do not take you to separate videos of those individual scenes. Rather, clicking a scene's button takes you to that point in the original movie. Some authoring products let you set points like that—called **chapters** in DVD parlance. One other feature is the capability to use chapter point button thumbnail images selected from the chapter scenes.

Button and Text Features

Buttons and text usually are the links to media or other menus on your DVD. Authoring products can offer a wide range of options:

- ▶ Changing a button's visual characteristics such as shape, color, size, placement, and drop shadows.

- ▶ Text-creation tools that allow extra features, such as borders and gradient colors.

- ▶ Adding text to a button.

- ▶ Transparency option for buttons and text.

- ▶ Multiple button **states**. (As viewers use the remote to navigate among the buttons, the buttons change color or animate differently.)

- ▶ Letting editors use Photoshop-created graphics with multiple layers that alter their appearance depending on user actions. For example, rolling the cursor over a button or clicking that button changes the button's appearance.

- ▶ The capability to link text to media and menus. Most DVD-authoring products let you link only buttons to media and menus.

- ▶ Animated or video buttons.

- ▶ User-selected video frames for buttons, typically when linking buttons to video chapters.

By the Way

> ## Managing Button, Menu, and Media Behaviors
>
> Higher-level authoring products let you specify certain behaviors for buttons, menus, and other media. That might seem a bit obtuse, so I'll offer plenty of practical applications later in the book. For now, here's one example: Most DVD remote controls have Menu and Title buttons. What happens when viewers press them depends on how you created the DVD. Consumer DVD-authoring products tend to set those parameters automatically. Higher-end products expect you to manually set those functions.

Playback Options

Most DVD feature films offer several extras ranging from subtitles to Dolby digital surround sound. At first blush, you might think you won't tap these features, but they offer several creative options:

▶ **Extra audio tracks**—Higher-quality Hollywood DVDs offer extra sound-tracks of varying quality or content, from simple stereo to Dolby digital surround sound, as well as director's comments and foreign language dubs. The *Monsters, Inc.* DVD uses this feature uniquely: Its developers added a sound effects-only track. Higher-priced DVD-authoring products let you lay in those multiple tracks.

▶ **Subtitles**—Most higher-level authoring tools let you add subtitles that you create in a word processing program or within the authoring software and place them exactly to match the movie dialogue. You can also use subtitles in educational DVDs as tips to teachers. Those teachers can use a special code to access the subtitle tip mode and then turn that off when students view the DVD.

▶ **Widescreen or 16:9 aspect ratio**—Puts your video into a letterbox on a standard TV set or expands it to fit a widescreen display. No entry-level authoring applications have this functionality.

▶ **Links to URLs**—Give PC users viewing your DVD direct access to associated web pages. This is a great way for businesses to tie their DVDs to their website promotions.

▶ **Multiple camera angles**—This rarely used option can enhance a DVD movie. For instance, the feature film *Moulin Rouge* has some dazzling dance numbers that use rapid-fire edits and multiple camera angles. To give viewers a different feel for those scenes, the DVD's producers let viewers choose one or more camera angles.

Special Features

Some of the following options might seem like afterthoughts, but they can make or break a DVD project:

▶ **Slideshows**—The best DVD-authoring products let you add transitions between still images, such as dissolves (a surprisingly complex technical feat on a DVD), and add music or narration.

▶ **DVD-ROM files**—This is a powerful option that lets users with PC DVD-ROM drives access data files, word processing documents, spreadsheets, PowerPoint presentations, or even the original video and image files used on the DVD. Only some prosumer-level products offer this option.

▶ **A flowchart or timeline project layout**—Instead of using only a collection of menus, this makes producing a DVD more intuitive. No entry-level product uses either of these toolsets.

- ▶ **Video capture**—This lets you bypass an NLE and go directly from your camcorder to DVD authoring.

- ▶ **Video-editing tools**—No DVD-authoring product offers anything approaching a full-featured video NLE like Pinnacle Studio Plus. But some give you the option to trim, combine, or split clips as well as add transitions such as wipes and dissolves. If your project needs are simple, these features let you circumvent the NLE editing process.

- ▶ **Still frame capture**—This enables you to use any video frame as a menu background.

- ▶ **DVD/CD jewel box and disc label creation tool.**

Output and Video Encoding

Only two types of video will play back from DVDs on your set-top box: MPEG-1 and MPEG-2. Most DVD-authoring products will convert your media into MPEG video files.

> **Missing MPEG Encoders**
>
> Somewhat surprisingly, the most expensive DVD-authoring products sometimes do not offer MPEG-conversion tools. The reason is that at that production level, DVD-creation studios prefer using expensive hardware or software MPEG encoders. These perform in-depth analyses of source videos and create sharper-looking and better-sounding MPEG-2 videos than you can get from lower-cost software-only encoders.

The level of user control over that conversion process is what sets the top authoring products apart from the rest of the field. Here are some other options to consider:

- ▶ **User adjustable encoding output quality settings, such as bit rate**—This gives you more latitude when creating your DVD. If you find your project will not completely fill a DVD, you can increase the quality settings to improve the overall look of your vides and still stay within the DVD space limits.

- ▶ **Dolby digital stereo encoding**—Top-end DVDs offer Dolby AC-3 5.1 discrete six-channel surround sound (two front speakers, two rear, a center, and a subwoofer). Or viewers can choose from other standard, uncompressed or minimally compressed audio streams, such as PCM or LPCM (linear pulse code modulation).

▶ **Audio sampling rate conversion**—Changes various quality audio files to standard DVD 48KHz quality.

▶ **Output formats**—These include video CD (VCD), super video CD (SVCD), or VR (rewritable CDs/DVDs that allow later reauthoring).

Open DVD Format

Sonic Solutions has begun shipping DVD products that incorporate the company's new Open DVD format. DVDs created with Open DVD–compliant products can be opened in other Open DVD–authoring software and completely reworked.

By the Way

▶ **Multiple media formats**—These include all recordable DVDs (DVD+R/RW, DVD-R/RW, and DVD-RAM), all recordable CDs, and digital linear tape (DLT), as well as DVD images created on the hard drive.

▶ **Dual-layer recording capability**—Some newer DVD recorders let you record to dual-layer discs. I discuss these in the next chapter. Basically, they let you record nearly twice the data as a single layer disc—8.5GB versus 4.7GB for a single-layer disc. That means MPEG-2 videos longer than two hours can run from a single-sided disc with no obvious pause as the DVD player shifts to the second layer.

Burning DVDs and Making Masters for Mass Production

All DVD-authoring software products **burn** DVDs, meaning they take your DVD-authored project—media and menus—and record it to a recordable DVD.

Some give you extra options, such as letting you add data files or create CDs that mimic DVDs when played in a PC CD-ROM drive.

Some even let you take your authored DVD on a test drive before burning it to make sure all buttons lead to their expected destinations. For the most part, this is a fairly straightforward process, but ease of use and quality do vary from product to product.

Until recently, if you wanted to use the services of a mass replicator to make multiple copies of your DVD, you needed higher-priced authoring tools and a digital linear tape recorder (DLT). Replicators now typically use the DVD you create as the recording "master." I offer tips on dealing with replicators, take you through a simple online mass duplication process, and explain basic DVD-burning procedures in Chapter 27, "Burning DVDs and Dealing with DVD Duplicators."

Compliance with DVD Specifications

All DVD-authoring products work within the DVD specification to ensure that your finished DVD meets those specs and runs on *most* DVD set-top boxes. Some work better than others. One reason I chose to feature Sonic Solution products in this book is that they have a proven track record of creating DVDs that work with the widest range of DVD players.

> ### Noncompliant Older DVD Players
>
> Some older DVD set-top players do not handle all aspects of the DVD spec—thus, the caveat is that not all your DVDs will work on all DVD players. Also, three basic types of DVD recordable media exist: DVD-R (dash-R), DVD+R (plus R), and DVD-RAM. The dash and plus formats also offer rewritable (RW) formats: DVD-RW and DVD+RW. Some players work with some formats and not others. I explain more about what some call the "format wars" in the next chapter.

Higher-priced DVD-authoring products have correspondingly higher-level functionality that pushes the DVD spec to its limits—allowing things such as games on DVDs. The first *Harry Potter* movie DVD is a good example—it "remembers" your previous answers despite working in a DVD set-top that has no memory.

Overview of DVD-Authoring Products

In the competitive PC software universe, you usually get what you pay for. In the DVD-authoring sphere, at the entry level at least, you get more. Even though entry-level products don't offer much flexibility or customizability, they still produce impressive-looking DVDs.

You can find entry-level products packaged as modules with nonlinear editing software or as standalone products.

The DVD-authoring market is in constant flux. For example, as I was writing this, Sonic Solutions announced the purchase of Roxio, its major competitor in the entry-level DVD-authoring market. Any listing of products will likely be out of date and prices will have changed by the time this book arrives in stores. So I recommend that you use the following lists only as a basic reference and check around online for current reviews:

Entry-Level Video Editors with DVD-Authoring Modules

None of the entry-level nonlinear video-editing products on the market today have DVD-authoring modules that match the features, depth, and flexibility found in the standalone DVD-authoring product Sonic Solutions MyDVD 6.

▶ CyberLink PowerDirector ($70)—www.gocyberlink.com

▶ Pinnacle Studio Plus ($100)—www.pinnaclesys.com

▶ Roxio VideoWave Professional ($80) (purchased by Sonic Solutions)—www.roxio.com

▶ Ulead VideoStudio ($100)—www.ulead.com

Standalone Entry-Level DVD-Authoring Software

This market segment is another example of industry consolidation. Dazzle DVD used to be a standalone product. But Pinnacle Systems purchased it and no longer sells it. Pinnacle also discontinued its entry-level, standalone DVD-authoring product—Expression. That leaves five entry-level products that I know of as of early 2005:

▶ Ahead Software Nero Ultra ($100)—www.nero.com/us

▶ MedioStream neoDVD ($50)—www.mediostream.com

▶ CyberLink PowerProducer ($70)—www.gocyberlink.com

▶ Sonic Solutions MyDVD Studio ($70) and Studio Deluxe Suite ($150)—www.sonic.com

▶ Ulead DVD MovieFactory (regular edition—$50, Disc Creator Edition—$65)—www.ulead.com

Standalone Prosumer DVD-Authoring Software

There is minimal competition as you move into this wide open market niche. Pinnacle discontinued its prosumer product, Impression, in 2004. Prices tend to reflect relative levels of features and functionality.

- ▶ Adobe Encore DVD ($550)—www.adobe.com

- ▶ Sonic Solutions DVDit! ($300) and ReelDVD ($250)—www.sonic.com

- ▶ Ulead DVD Workshop ($395) and DVD Workshop Express ($200)—www.ulead.com

Summary

You are about to embark on what I think is an exciting and creative adventure. Finally, all the technological elements are in place to let you create a multimedia experience that meets your imagination and talents.

DVDs present you with myriad possibilities in terms of how to present your media. I presented about a dozen ideas in this chapter along with four real-world DVD-authoring stories. As you work with DVD-authoring software, you will come up with many additional exciting project ideas.

DVD-authoring software lets you make truly interactive DVDs with menu access to video clips, images, music, and data. Higher-end DVD-authoring tools give you many menu and button creation options. You can add multiple language tracks, various audio quality options, and subtitles. They offer numerous output and video-encoding options and make burning DVDs a remarkably straightforward process.

CHAPTER 16

Getting Your Gear in Order—DVD Recorders and Media

What You'll Learn in This Chapter:

- ▶ Clearing up the DVD recording format confusion
- ▶ Selecting a PC DVD recorder
- ▶ Evaluating three DVD software movie players
- ▶ Using Sonic Solutions CinePlayer to test drive your DVD recorder

You can author DVDs to your heart's content, but without a PC DVD recorder, only you can view your masterpiece and only on your PC. If you don't own a recorder, read this chapter and then go out and buy one. If you already have a DVD recorder, check out my overview of the latest industry developments and decide whether you need to upgrade.

The format wars within the DVD recorder industry have created confusion over which recordable medium is most compatible, fastest, or most useful. I do what I can to clear the air and fill you in on one development that I think has put an end to the bickering.

One way to give your DVD player a test drive is to use it to play a DVD movie. To do that, you need DVD player software. In this chapter, I present an overview of the three top DVD software players and take you through the features of one.

Clearing Up the DVD Recording Format Confusion

Recordable DVD drives and media come in a confusing variety (and combination) of three basic flavors: dash R/RW (DVD-R/RW), plus R/RW (DVD+R/RW), and DVD-RAM. The news media have called this the **format wars** and likened it to the bloody and brutal VHS versus Betamax quagmire in the early days of home VCRs.

By the Way

> ### R, RW, and RAM
>
> R stands for record-once media and RW means rewritable. It's the same nomenclature used for CD-recordable drives. RAM, on the other hand, stands for what it has always stood for: Random Access Memory. This despite this particular use as a moniker for a recordable DVD format.

In that case, Sony's Betamax format lost out to VHS—but only after years of acrimony, bad blood, lawsuits, and marketing miscues.

Sony's Betamax was first to market by a year, momentarily held several technological edges, and was priced competitively. But the company waited more than a year before licensing its technology to another manufacturer—Zenith (eventually seven companies manufactured Betamax VCRs). VHS started with more manufacturers, originally allowed for longer recording times, and by sheer timing was not included in a lawsuit filed against Sony by the movie industry.

The bottom line is that no one can say with certainty why VHS won. Call it serendipity, timing, or luck of the draw. Essentially, consumers settled those format wars.

By the Way

> ### Betamax/VHS Myths
>
> Many misconceptions exist about those Betamax/VHS days. The biggest is that Sony failed to license Betamax. If you want to delve into the history, visit `http://tafkac.org/products/beta_vs_vhs.html`.

As for the DVD-recordable format wars—*surprise*—Sony is playing the role of peacemaker (see the sidebar titled "Sony Ends the Format Wars," later in this chapter).

Dash R/RW Versus Plus R/RW Versus DVD-RAM

Those three DVD-recordable flavors continue to create consumer confusion. But clarity is coming (I explain why in the next section).

Much of that confusion is a result of the plus R/RW camp that came late to the game, promising better performance and a simple upgrade path from early rewritable-only drives to rewritable/record-once combo drives.

The plus R/RW camp attempted to crash the party of a 230-company group called the DVD Forum. That major industry group formed in 1997 and supported two DVD-recordable formats: DVD-R/RW (dash R/RW) and DVD-RAM.

DVD-RAM's original focus was largely massive data backup. DVD-RAM is rewritable up to 100,000 times (versus 1,000 times for DVD-RW), is more expensive than DVD-R/RW, and initially required a special disc holder tray.

The DVD-R/RW format serves multimedia and home/business PC users. Pioneer broke that market wide open in 2001 with the release of its $1,000 DVR-A03 DVD-R/RW CD-R/RW drive. The PC and Mac community (the original Mac SuperDrive was the Pioneer A03) embraced the DVD-R/RW (dash) format, and the consumer DVD player industry followed suit, ensuring that its set-top boxes could play back movies recorded to DVD-R discs.

By the Way

DVD-R (Dash-R) for Mass Duplication

If you plan to have a replication firm mass-produce your DVD project, recording your project to a DVD-R (as opposed to DVD-RW, DVD+R, DVD+RW, or DVD-RAM) is your best bet.

Most replicators recognize the ubiquity of DVD-R and recently have developed means to use that medium to create duplication masters in addition to the previous standard digital linear tape.

I cover dealing with commercial replicators in Chapter 27, "Burning DVDs and Dealing with DVD Duplicators."

DVD+R/RW—Better, But with a Bitter Aftertaste

Philips, Sony, Hewlett-Packard, Ricoh, and others formed a splinter group called the DVD+RW Alliance and developed a slightly different format—DVD+R/RW (plus R/RW).

It promised better performance and improved set-top player backward compatibility, but this technology not only arrived late to the rapidly growing DVD-recordable scene, but also arrived half baked.

This group's first drives (all using the same Ricoh mechanisms) were DVD+RW (rewritable) only. They had no write-once DVD+R capability. Early on, customers were led to believe that they could later do a simple firmware update (see the following note) to convert their DVD+RW drives to DVD+R/RW combo drives.

How Firmware Upgrades Work

Firmware is software electronically inserted into a confusingly named **erasable programmable read-only memory (EPROM)** or **electrically erasable programmable read-only memory (EEPROM)** chip within the DVD drive.

In older computing days, a ROM was just that: **read-only** memory. Then along came PROMs, which allowed one-time burning of instructions and saved manufacturers the expense of building an integrated circuit from scratch.

Nowadays, with easy access to downloadable code on the Internet, most manufacturers use EPROMs or EEPROMs to allow consumers to automatically perform bug fixing or performance-improving firmware upgrades simply by downloading a small program and running it.

The DVD+RW alliance later discovered it could not use a simple firmware fix to upgrade its rewritable-only drives to +R/RW status. It informed customers that the only way they could make write-once +R discs was to buy a second-generation DVD+R/RW drive that began shipping in mid-2002. That decision created a lot of rancor among early DVD+RW adopters.

In the end, the DVD+ camp failed to connect, and the companies involved, for the most part, stopped manufacturing or marketing DVD-recordable drives.

Selecting a PC DVD Recorder

Until October 2002, this was a true consumer conundrum. What would it be, DVD Plus or DVD Dash? Back then, clarity arrived in the form of Sony's new multiformat, DVD±R/±RW and CD-R/RW DRU-500 drives (see the following sidebar, "Sony Ends the Format Wars," for a report on my hands-on evaluation).

By early 2005, several other DVD-recordable drive manufacturers had released competing multiformat drives.

One other recent development has improved offerings for consumers: dual-layer-capable recorders. Many Hollywood film DVDs are recorded on dual-layer discs with capacities nearly twice the size of standard, single-layer DVDs.

That allows film companies to put more than two hours worth of material on one side of a DVD. Typically, for films that run longer than two hours, the end of the film is recorded on the second layer.

Two Hours of Video—Not a Hard–and-Fast Rule

When Hollywood studio executives envisioned DVDs, their goal was to create a technology that would allow for two hours of sharp video on a single disc. They chose to use MPEG-2 for the video compression. But that compression scheme allows for a wide range of quality settings such that if you have a three-hour video, you can reduce the compression bit rate (thereby reducing visual quality) to enable you to fit it onto a single-layer DVD. The caveat is that it won't look as good as full-bit rate MPEG-2 video.

As you watch that film, your DVD player should move more or less seamlessly between the layers. DVD-authoring and burning software that can work with dual-layer discs usually lets you select the location where the transition takes place to avoid any obvious stutter (the goal is to avoid placing the transition in the middle of a scene).

Until late in 2004, there were no consumer-priced DVD recorders that were dual-layer capable. That, too, is rapidly changing as several companies now include dual-layer capability in their standard PC DVD recorders.

Narrowing Your Search

What's happening, then, is that DVD-recordable drives are becoming commodities, similar to what has happened with CD-R/RW drives. As drive performance becomes less of an issue, the primary ways to differentiate drives are increasingly limited only to price, software bundles, technical support, and brand-name awareness. The latest models typically retail for around $150. Recently discontinued models (that are perfectly acceptable) can be had for about $80.

I suggest you start your search at CNET's review site: reviews.cnet.com. There, look for the Drives and Burners section. Here are the general options I think you should consider:

▶ **Single format (Dash or Plus) or Multiformat**—Most drives these days are multiformat. As manufacturers phase out single-format drives, you might still pay a small premium of about $30 for a multiformat drive versus a single-format drive.

▶ **Dual-layer capable**—Typically, this adds about $20 to the retail price.

▶ **Internal connector type: EIDE (ATAPI), ATA, or Serial ATA**—Serial ATA is the fastest connection and costs $10 to $20 more.

▶ **External drives**—These connect to your PC via FireWire or USB connectors and generally cost $50 to $100 more, but they are a heck of a lot easier to install, and they're portable.

▶ **Bundled software**—This is where you might do some real comparison shopping. What you should expect to get at the very least is a DVD-authoring product (Sonic's MyDVD is the favorite), a DVD software player, and DVD-burning software.

▶ **Read and write speeds**—This is where **specmanship** can get in the way of value. Write speeds of 8X (allowing you to record a full, two-hour DVD in about 10 minutes) are about the norm. Higher speeds—16X was the top speed as we went to press—might be worth the premium price if you burn a lot of DVDs.

Multiformat DVD±R/±RW Drives

This is the high end of the PC DVD recorder market (see Figure 16.1). The major players are Pioneer, Sony, and Plextor.

FIGURE 16.1
Pioneer's multiformat, dual-layer DVR-108 is the latest drive from the de facto industry leader.

Pioneer ignited the PC DVD recorder business in 2001 when it released its DVD-103 DVD-R/RW drive (or A03), which was also Apple's original SuperDrive. Its latest offering, the DVR-108 (or A08), is capable of writing at speeds up to 16X. As we went to press, 16X-capable media were not yet available, but Pioneer uses what they call "over specification technology" to record at higher speeds with certain selected media. The drive's dual-layer technology extends data storage capacity on DVD-recordable discs from 4.7 gigabytes to 8.5 gigabytes.

Sony Ends the Format Wars

If you can't beat 'em, join 'em. That seems to be Sony's take on the DVD-recordable media format war.

Its solution, back in late 2002, was to be first to market with a multiformat R/RW DVD-recordable drive that supported both the dash R/RW and plus R/RW as well as CD-R/RW. DVD-RAM is not part of this equation, but that format serves only a narrow market niche—data backup.

This was a big shift for Sony. It was one of the original members of the DVD+RW Alliance and, like Philips and Hewlett-Packard, relied on a Ricoh drive mechanism for its first- and second-generation DVD+RW drives.

Now, Sony builds its multiformat drives from the ground up and makes the drives, optics, motors, and key-integrated circuits. The company worked for more than a year to bring its first multiformat drive to market.

Sony's current DVD+R/±RW iteration, the DRU-710A (shown in Figure 16.2), is an internal EIDE (ATAPI) drive that sells for about $150 (down from $350 two years ago). Sony's external USB 2.0/FireWire drive sells for about $200.

FIGURE 16.2
Sony's DRU710A is the latest iteration of the olive branch that is ending the DVD format wars.

Hands-On Testing

Back in 2002 when Sony announced it was working on a multiformat drive, they loaned me a prerelease engineering sample for testing. I came away impressed on several fronts.

The DRU500 (internal, ATAPI/EIDE) looked and installed just like any other internal DVD or CD drive. I placed the jumper (a tiny clip) on the proper pins (slave or master, depending on the PC setup), opened the PC, slid the drive into a free bay, attached the ATAPI cable and power plug, and turned on my PC. Windows noted the presence of this new drive, identified it as a DVD-R drive, and gave it a new drive letter.

That Sony engineering test drive outperformed all other drives on the market back then. It was the first to offer 4X DVD-R record speeds (equivalent to about a 36X CD-R record speed) along with 2X DVD-RW and 2.4X DVD+R/RW record speeds. Its 24X CD-R and 10X CD-RW record speeds put it at the top of that category as well.

Its latest drive, shown earlier in Figure 16.2, matches the Pioneer DVR-108 16X speeds and records CD-R discs at up to 48X.

> Sony still includes a comprehensive array of bundled software with its DVD-recordable drives, including Sonic Solutions MyDVD with Arcsoft's ShowBiz video editor, CyberLink's PowerDVD movie player, two data recording utilities, and a music recorder/organizer.

Single-Format DVD-R/RW and DVD+R/RW Drives

Pioneer, um, pioneered the DVD dash market. But Pioneer now sells only multi-format drives. There are a few off-brand products in the dash niche. One known entity is Toshiba. Its SD-R5112 retails for only $60 (see Figure 16.3).

FIGURE 16.3
Toshiba is one of the last "name" brand drive makers still manufacturing a single-format, DVD *dash* R/RW drive: SD-R5112.

Hewlett-Packard, Philips, and Ricoh were the original DVD Plus Alliance members. But none makes DVD+ drives anymore and none has a strong market position in the DVD recorder field.

Philips is out of the drive-manufacturing business altogether (sticking instead to recordable media). HP has an internal, dual-layer, multiformat, 16X drive—HP DVD writer 630i—that retails for less than $130 (see Figure 16.4). And Ricoh has never had much of a U.S. market presence.

FIGURE 16.4
Hewlett-Packard is the last of the DVD Plus group still manufacturing DVD-recordable drives for the U.S. market. This 630i multiformat, dual-layer unit competes toe-to-toe with Pioneer, Sony, and Plextor.

DVD+R/RW drives generally did perform better than DVD-R/RW, but consumer acceptance was slow, and they failed to catch on before Sony opened the door to multiformat drives.

DVD Dash R and DVD-RAM Combo

Panasonic's DVD Burner II Multi drive, released in November 2002 and updated since then (shown in Figure 16.5), is an attempt to attract both camps from within the DVD Forum—DVD-R/RW multimedia enthusiasts and DVD-RAM data storage folks.

FIGURE 16.5
Panasonic's LF-D521 DVD Burner II covers both DVD Forum bases.

After Sony's breakthrough multiformat drive, Panasonic's is the second drive to market that offered 4X DVD-R record speeds. It also features 3X DVD-RAM and 2X DVD-RW and supports CD-R/RW. At $250, it's priced to compete with the high end of the DVD recorder market. It is a niche product, oriented toward those who do regular backups to the same DVD (the real appeal of DVD-RAM).

Panasonic is the only DVD-RAM recordable drive manufacturer. Toshiba used to build a DVD-RAM-only recordable drive and Iomega built the only all-format drive. But both companies have discontinued those products.

Evaluating Three DVD Software Movie Players

Most DVD-recordable drives wear several hats: DVD-ROM, DVD-recorder, CD-ROM, and CD recorder. On the ROM or playback side of things, running DVD movies smoothly is their most fascinating use.

To view movies on your PC, you need DVD movie player software. That software typically includes an MPEG decoder—software that converts an MPEG video data stream into a video signal playable on your PC monitor—as well as DVD remote control-like buttons and extra control features not found in standalone, DVD set-top players.

The three major competing products are Cyberlink PowerDVD, Intervideo WinDVD, and Sonic Solutions CinePlayer. After discussing these, I'll take you through the features of CinePlayer, the movie playback software included with the retail version of MyDVD, or as a standalone retail product.

By the Way

WinDVD Takes Top Honors

WinDVD is the industry leader and my top pick of these three DVD software players. But CinePlayer is nearly as feature rich and is included with some versions of MyDVD. Because you're going to be working with MyDVD later in this DVD-authoring section of the book, I chose to highlight CinePlayer in this DVD player section of this chapter.

Cyberlink PowerDVD

PowerDVD (www.gocyberlink), shown in Figure 16.6, is a worthy competitor to CinePlayer but is my third choice in this group. It offers most of the same features, but its graphical user interface is too small and some of the icons' meanings are unclear.

FIGURE 16.6
PowerDVD's interface is too small, and some icons are indecipherable.

One advantage of playing DVDs in your PC, instead of in a standalone player in your living room, is the access to a full menu of features. That holds true for PowerDVD. All you need to do to access those features with this and other software DVD players is to right-click in the video display to pop up a menu like that shown in Figure 16.7.

FIGURE 16.7
PowerDVD's right-click menu offers myriad, easily accessible choices.

The right-click menu offers a time-saving feature. It lets you directly step through items such as subtitles and foreign language dubs instead of making you step through several actual menus on the DVD to make your choice. But the right-click menu fails to offer the most logical right-click menu item: opening the graphical interface. This is an issue when you are viewing the video full screen on your PC and forget what keyboard command you need to display the user interface.

Another nice feature of PowerDVD is bookmarks, which let you easily return to specific scenes. Similar to CinePlayer, PowerDVD has a fly-out number pad. PowerDVD is available for $50 ($70 if you want DTS surround sound). You can download a trial version at www.gocyberlink.com.

Intervideo WinDVD

WinDVD (trial version available at www.intervideo.com), shown in Figure 16.8, is the de facto industry standard and my top pick. It has every feature imaginable, along with a few surprises.

FIGURE 16.8
The feature-rich WinDVD6, with its multipurpose pop-out menus, is my selection as the top DVD player.

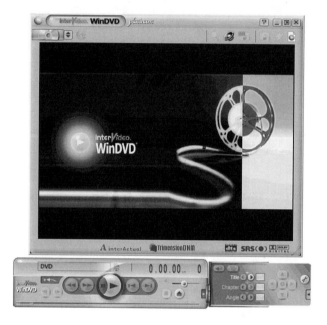

For instance, not only can you bookmark movie scenes, but you can also open a panel with thumbnail images of your bookmarked scenes. WinDVD's pop-out window offers seven sets of tools, including controls for color/hue; multiple audio options; and easy navigation through chapters, subtitles, and foreign language dubs. I also like that if you choose to use the video viewing window, you then have ready access to several video controls.

I would, however, prefer a larger interface with more clearly defined icons because it's not immediately apparent how to get from a full-screen movie view to a windowed view. Minimizing the interface minimizes the video as well. Niggling inconveniences aside, this $50 product ($70 for *Platinum* edition) has every bell and whistle imaginable.

Sonic Solutions CinePlayer

You will get a chance to see CinePlayer's features in detail in a moment. In the meantime, my basic take is that it's a fine product with deep customizability and control over any DVD movie you play. The interface, shown in Figure 16.9, is clean, the icons are large, and the settings and other menus are readily accessible and intuitive.

FIGURE 16.9
CinePlayer's interface has larger icons and easier-to-read controls than its competition.

However, it doesn't have the extra features that set WinDVD apart from the field in this three-horse race. For instance, CinePlayer has no bookmark thumbnail display capability, but it does automatically return to where you left off when last viewing a particular DVD.

At $30 (basic version—$50 for *Surround*), it's the bargain-priced product in this group. Considering that you might even get it for free in a hardware/software bundle, you can't go wrong with CinePlayer.

Using Sonic Solutions CinePlayer to Test Drive Your DVD Recorder

PC power users love benchmarks—overclocking motherboards or graphic cards is their forte. But there's not much you can do to change the performance of a DVD recorder other than providing it with the best blank media it can handle.

Nevertheless, just to ensure that your DVD drive is up to snuff, you might want to take it for a couple of test runs. This chapter covers only the playback side of things. Chapter 17, "Burning Data DVDs," covers the recording side of the equation.

Test Your DVD Drive

Over the course of several years, I tested dozens of CD and DVD drives for several magazines. In each case I relied on benchmarking tools from Simpli Software (formerly TestaCD Labs). As we went to press, Simpli had discontinued DVD Tach but promised to release a new version soon (it still offers a hard-drive test product). If you want the absolute best storage device benchmark software (anything they have is available for free download for noncommercial use), visit www.simplisoftware.com.

By the Way

Try it Yourself   Play a DVD Movie

Go through the following steps to play a DVD movie. I am featuring Sonic Solutions CinePlayer software, but other DVD players have very similar controls. And your fallback can be Windows Media Player. If your version is relatively new (version 9 or later), it should be able to play DVD movies:

1. If you accept the defaults when installing CinePlayer (or another DVD movie player), CinePlayer will become the default DVD movie player on your PC. That means when you insert a movie DVD into your PC's DVD player/recorder, Windows should detect it (this is not a certainty), automatically start CinePlayer, and start playing the movie DVD (probably by taking you to that DVD's main menu).

By the Way   One Reason to View DVD Movies on a PC

Most people prefer viewing DVD movies on a TV versus a computer monitor. But using a PC has at least one advantage: Monitors have sharper images than TV sets. Movies therefore look crisper and clearer on a PC than on a standard TV. And because TV-out jacks are now available for many video cards and portable PCs, the PC is frequently used as a DVD movie player.

2. Place a DVD movie in your DVD recorder/player. Depending on your version of Windows, either it will automatically open CinePlayer (or some other DVD movie player software you have installed on your PC) or you'll see the screen shown in Figure 16.10.

FIGURE 16.10
The Windows Autoplay feature pops up this screen when you insert a DVD movie into your DVD drive.

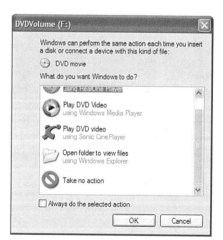

3. If you see the screen in Figure 16.10, select Play DVD Video Using Sonic
    CinePlayer or your DVD movie player of choice.

You should now see the interface in Figure 16.11. It has the instantly familiar
look and feel of a set-top DVD player. Most of the buttons are self-explanatory,
but I'll explain some special features in a moment. For now, use Figure 16.11 as a
guide to try the standard DVD playback buttons.

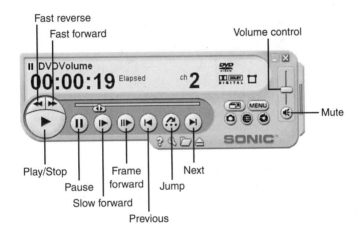

FIGURE 16.11
Sonic CinePlayer's
user interface has
the look and feel
of a set-top DVD
player.

In particular, check out the Fast Forward and Fast Reverse buttons. Note that with
each click, the speed increases—to 1.5X, 2X, 4X, 10X, and 20X.

The Slow Forward button also operates in increments: 1/4X, 1/2X, 3/4X, and full
speed.

Previous and Next move from one part of the DVD to another—that is, from a
menu, movie, graphic, or still image to another such element on the DVD,
depending on how the DVD was authored.

Jump opens a submenu that lets you move directly to a specific chapter or to a
time within the current video segment.

Examine CinePlayer's Extra Features
Try it Yourself

Most PC DVD movie players offer extra features beyond those available in a standard set-top, standalone DVD player. CinePlayer's offering tops this category.
Follow these steps to get a taste of the options at your fingertips:

1. Using Figure 16.12 as a guide, click the Question Mark icon to open the Help menu. The opening help screen explains all the buttons in Figures 16.11 and 16.12. Sonic Solutions uniformly has the best help screens I've encountered for *any* software. Feel free to explore them. They cover CinePlayer in depth, so I will touch on only a few items.

FIGURE 16.12
CinePlayer's extra feature options.

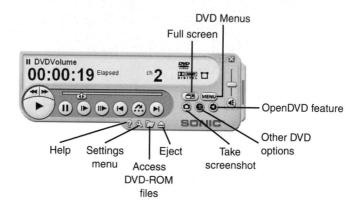

2. Close out of the help screen, click the Menu button, and select your DVD's Main or Chapter menu. Click the Expand/Collapse button circled in Figure 16.13 to open the Navigation/Keypad Button menu. These buttons duplicate the functions of a remote control and let you navigate around the menu buttons or type in a chapter number. However, using your mouse and clicking an onscreen button or chapter is much easier.

FIGURE 16.13
Because using a mouse is a much better way to control CinePlayer, its pop-out Navigation/Keypad Button menu is kind of superfluous.

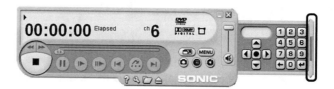

3. Click the Wrench icon to open the Settings menu. As illustrated in Figure 16.14, you have more options than you probably imagined would be available in a simple DVD movie player.

FIGURE 16.14
CinePlayer's Settings menu accesses myriad options.

4. Click through the various tabs (I explain a few in the next steps). Note that the General tab gives you some control over CinePlayer's behavior. OSD is for onscreen display characteristics, and Parental Control gives you password-level control over who sees this DVD.

5. Under the Video tab, the Decoding section gives you two options: Enable Hardware Acceleration and Use VMR (Video Mixing Renderer). Normally, you want to take advantage of your graphic accelerator, so keep that enabled. VMR is available only for Windows XP users. If you have XP, click VMR and click OK.

6. Depending on your video card, CinePlayer might pop up a box asking whether it's okay to close your movie to switch on VMR or Hardware Acceleration. Click OK. Moments later you'll return to where you left off in the movie.

7. VMR might not make an obvious difference in image quality. However, one clear change is that it lets you adjust the Closed Captions Opacity option. Reopen the Settings interface (using the Wrench icon), select the Video tab, and note that the Opacity slider in the Closed Captions section is no longer grayed out. With your DVD movie playing, select Always Show "Closed Captions" if Available, move the Opacity slider, and note how the captions change in real-time onscreen.

A Quick PC Info Window

A handy way to get a fix on your PC's hardware setup and current DVD software is to select the Information tab in the Settings window.

8. Now select the Screen Capture tab, which lets you grab any frame from any DVD movie. Here you set the file type and naming convention for each time you click the Take Screenshot button. This is a valuable tool because grabbing screenshots using image editing (or your keyboard's PrintScreen button) sometimes doesn't work. The reason: DVD movies run in a DirectX Overlay. CinePlayer, however, makes it simple.

By the Way

Screen Capture Formats

You have two screen capture image format choices: Windows Bitmap (BMP) or JPEG. BMP is a standard Windows uncompressed format. JPEG is a picture format from the Joint Photographic Experts Group. It uses a sliding scale of 0–100 to define picture quality. Anything less than 50 is unacceptable to most people, so the CinePlayer slider, although it doesn't have a numeric scale, actually ranges from 50 to 100.

By the Way

Grabbing at the Right Aspect Ratio

Most DVD movies are enhanced for wide-screen TVs, meaning they're stored on the DVD in a 4:3 standard TV aspect ratio and then are stretched to fit a 16:9 format. Selecting Correct Aspect Ratio guarantees your screen grab will look similar to what you see on the monitor.

9. Close the Settings interface and use the Take Screenshot camera icon to capture an image from your movie. If you selected the Audio Feedback on Success check box, you'll hear a camera shutter sound effect. Your screenshot will be in the designated file folder.

10. Finally, reopen the Settings interface and select the On Screen Display Options illustrated in Figure 16.15. This lets you add a time display or change the characteristics of the Events display: the words that confirm user actions, such as "Play," "2X FastF," "Pause," and the like.

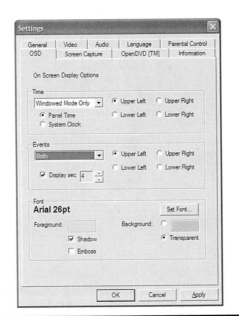

FIGURE 16.15
CinePlayer's
Onscreen Display
Options interface
lets you fine-tune
CinePlayer's visual
feedback.

Right-Click Menu Features

Use CinePlayer's handy right-click menu. Right-click anywhere on the video screen or
control interface and up pops a menu similar to the one in Figure 16.16. The
options that are accessible and those that are grayed out depend on features available on the DVD movie you've selected. This is a slick and easy way to quickly
change DVD playback settings or move quickly to other menus.

Did you know?

Summary

The DVD format wars are still fresh in many DVD users' minds. But clarity has arrived in the form of multiformat drives. Sony started the charge and the rest of the DVD drive industry has followed suit. If you're in the market for a new drive, start your quest by looking at DVD±R/±RW drives.

Choosing media is easier. Stick with non-DVD drive manufacturer brands or better, and don't buy 8X DVD-R-rated media when your drive can handle only 2X.

One of the benefits of a PC DVD recorder is its capability to play DVD movies on your PC. Not only does most DVD movie-playing software perform MPEG decoding, but it also offers features no set-top DVD player can provide. Your DVD recorder probably had a DVD movie software player that came with it. If not, consider any of the three players I covered in this chapter.

CHAPTER 17

Burning Data DVDs

What You'll Learn in This Chapter:

▶ Selecting recordable media
▶ Using Windows XP's My Computer to copy files to a CD
▶ Burning a DVD
▶ Taking a quick tour of Roxio's Easy Media Creator

I know you're itching to venture into DVD authoring. But before heading off in that direction, I want to make sure you've at least burned a **data** DVD (and CD). This is not DVD authoring; rather, it's a simple file transfer.

This chapter starts with a brief overview of recordable DVD media. Then I move to a hands-on run-through of Windows built-in optical media disc burning module. Its one drawback is that Windows My Computer doesn't do DVDs. So I want you to use it simply to cut a CD first.

Following that, I take you step-by-step through a well-known DVD creation product—Sonic Solutions RecordNow!—that's equal to, or at least very similar to, any you're likely to find bundled with a PC DVD recorder.

Finally, this chapter details the highlights of the latest update to the de facto DVD creation software industry-standard product: Roxio Easy Media Creator.

Selecting Recordable Media

Deciding which DVD blank recordable media to purchase is similar to selecting an audiocassette. You end up buying based on brand identification, hardware compatibility, and price.

In the case of DVD-recordable media, your choices come down to drive manufacturer–branded discs from Pioneer, Sony, HP, and so on; name-brand generic media from Verbatim, Memorex, Maxell, Mitsui, and TDK; and house brands.

Just about any DVD-recordable media retailer on the Internet offers its own house brand of the more popular DVD media formats. User reliability reports vary on these nonname-brand products from noting inconsequential differences between them and name brands to fairly high failure rates for house-brand DVDs. I suggest the middle ground: name-brand generic.

Be sure you buy media to match your drive; that is, don't use plus-R discs in a dash-R drive.

Finally, DVD-recordable media recently took a giant leap forward. As we went to press, 8X DVD-R and 4X DVD-RW media were available (16X recordable DVDs were on the horizon). If you have a drive that can record at those speeds (or faster), you might want to pay the small premium for the time savings they offer.

Typically, record-once media—DVD-R and DVD+R—cost about two-thirds of what their RW (rewritable) counterparts cost. Dash-R discs run about a dollar apiece in bulk (8X is slightly more expensive). Plus-R is harder to find and costs a little more. Dual-layer discs are much more expensive, typically selling for more than $10 each in bulk.

Did you Know?

Comparison Shopping at My Simon

To check the latest disc prices, visit `http://www.mysimon.com/` and search on "DVD blank media."

By the Way

When a Gigabyte Is Not a Gigabyte

When you check out those recordable DVDs, they will invariably say their capacity is 4.7GB (gigabytes) for single-layer discs and 8.5GB for dual-layer.

Those numbers are inaccurate and misleading. Although it's true that a single-layer DVD holds 4.7 billion bytes, that does not translate to 4.7 gigabytes. Rather, 4.7 billion bytes equals 4.37 gigabytes. And 8.5 billion bytes equals 7.95 gigabytes.

The problem is that the prefix **giga** normally represents a billion or 10^9. But when used in the computer world to measure bytes, giga refers to powers of 2, specifically multiples of 1,024 (1,024=2^{10}=kilobyte, 2^{20}=megabyte, and 2^{30}=gigabyte). When referring to RAM, hard drive capacities, and file sizes, Windows lists amounts in "true" megabytes and gigabytes, not millions and billions of bytes.

On the other hand, most DVD capacities are based on multiples of 1,000, in spite of using notation such as GB and KB that traditionally have been based on multiples of 1,024.

This is not a trivial distinction. If you create a DVD project or select files to copy to a DVD that approach 4.7GB, you will discover either before you attempt to burn your disc or after (depending on the quality of your DVD-burning software) that you've exceeded the capacity of your 4.37GB recordable DVD.

Different DVD Sizes and Capacities

There are several types of recordable-DVD media including combinations of single- or double-sided media and single or dual layers. The most popular are single side and either single layer (called DVD-5) or dual layer (DVD-9). Following is a list of the *actual* capacities for those two varieties as well as for CD-R/RW:

CD-R or RW 650-700MB—.64-.69GB or 0.68-0.75 billion bytes

DVD-5 (single layer) 4.37GB—4.70 billion bytes

DVD-9 (dual layer) 7.95GB—8.54 billion bytes

By the Way

Using Windows XP to Copy Files to a CD

One of my goals in writing this book is to help you create full-featured, interactive, multimedia DVDs. In this chapter you take the first steps in that direction, beginning by burning data files, first to a CD and then to a DVD.

It might seem a bit mundane to use a DVD for normal data storage, but DVDs, with their 4.7GB capacity (actually 4.37GB—see the previous sidebar, "When a Gigabyte Is Not a Gigabyte"), are excellent data backup media. And your PC's DVD recorder also can record to CD-R and CD-RW discs.

We'll discuss those CD-recordable discs first because Windows's built-in optical disc recording software *cannot* handle DVDs. Those of you with older versions of Windows—Windows Me, 2000, 98, and earlier—that don't have any CD-copying features built in will want to purchase bundled software to burn a DVD.

Burn Data Files to a CD-R or CD-RW Disc

Try it Yourself

With Windows, your PC DVD recorder can behave much like a massive floppy disc drive: You simply copy and paste files to it. Here's how:

1. You'll need a CD-R or CD-RW disc. Insert a blank, recordable CD into your DVD recorder, and the screen in Figure 17.1 probably will pop up (if you've already installed CD/DVD recording software and it's set to be the default recorder, it should start automatically). You can select the Open Writable CD Folder option or click Cancel. In this case click Cancel because you don't need to go to that folder just yet.

FIGURE 17.1
The Windows
Autoplay feature
notes when you've
inserted a record-
able CD into your
DVD drive and asks
what you want to
do with it.

2. Open My Computer by double-clicking its icon. Depending on whether
   you've adjusted any My Computer Views settings, it'll look similar to Figure
   17.2. Note that after you've inserted a CD-R or RW disc, the Total Size and
   Free Space values for that drive will be equal. In the case of my CD-RW disc,
   both those values are 702MB (megabytes).

FIGURE 17.2
How My Computer
should look after
you've inserted a
recordable CD into
your DVD drive.

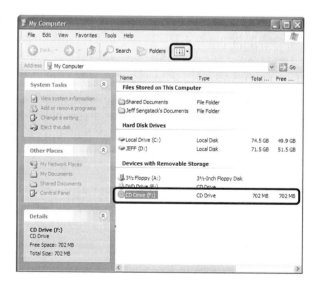

Changing the My Computer Default Display

I do not like the default Windows XP, My Computer icon-oriented settings; I much prefer the Details view. To switch to this format, click the Views icon (circled in Figure 17.2 at the top of the screen) and select Details from the drop-down list.

Did you Know?

Windows XP lags behind the DVD technology curve. My Computer demonstrates that.

With no recordable CD or DVD inserted into your DVD drive, My Computer refers to that drive as DVD-R (or DVD-RW) Drive (F:)—*CD Drive*. As highlighted in Figure 17.2, after inserting a CD-RW disc, Windows updates the My Computer display by renaming the DVD-R/RW drive CD Drive (F:).

If you insert any recordable DVD into your DVD drive, Windows XP refers to it as a CD. If you try to write to a DVD-recordable disc, you'll probably get an error message similar to the one in Figure 17.3. Windows XP does not have a DVD recorder module. You need third-party software for that task.

By the Way

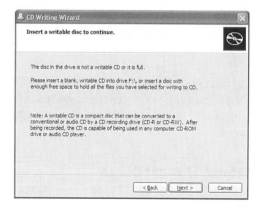

FIGURE 17.3
Using My Computer to try to write to a DVD-recordable disc leads to this error message. I believe the message should read My Computer cannot write to recordable DVDs.

3. Select the files you want to add to your recordable CD.

How to Select More Than One File

To select groups of contiguous files, either click the top file and then Shift+click the bottom file, or click just to the right of the top file and drag your cursor down and to the left to create a *marquee* around a group of files. To select scattered files in the same window, click one file and then use Ctrl+click to select each subsequent file. The same process works for folders.

Did you Know?

4. After you've selected a file, folder, or group of files or folders, you need to copy them. I like to use right-mouse-click shortcuts, so here's how I do it. As illustrated in Figure 17.4, right-click one of the selected files/folders (if you have more than one selected, right-clicking one applies to all those you've selected) and select Copy from the drop-down menu.

FIGURE 17.4
Use the right-click window to simplify the file-copying process.

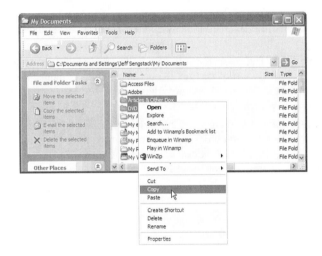

5. Navigate back to the opening My Computer screen (use the Backspace key as a shortcut). Right-click the DVD-recorder drive and select Paste. Depending on the size of the selected files, a pause might occur as Windows creates temporary files.

By the Way

Using Menus Instead of Right-Clicks

If you do not care for the right-click approach to Windows file management, feel free to use the menu-driven approach. There are two ways:

After you've selected some files or folders to copy, the Files and Folders Tasks window in the upper-left corner of My Computer will offer an option labeled Copy the Selected Items. Click that to open the Copy Items dialog box. Select the DVD drive, and then click Copy.

Or, after selecting some files, select Edit, Copy, navigate back to the DVD drive, click it to select and highlight it, and then select Edit, Paste.

When you're ready to burn your files or folders, go to step 6.

6. When you've copied and pasted all the files and folders you want to transfer to the recordable CD in your DVD drive, double-click its icon. Your screen should look similar to Figure 17.5. Note the highlighted window in the upper-left corner. Click Write These Files to CD.

Do Not Exceed Disc Capacity

Make sure your selected files don't exceed the capacity of your CD disc, which is usually about 650MB–700MB. You're on your own in this regard because Windows does not display your total file size as you add files and folders to the queue for later writing to the CD.

FIGURE 17.5
Use the CD Writing Tasks window to copy selected files and folders to your recordable CD.

7. The CD Writing Wizard shown in Figure 17.6 opens. Name your CD, click Next, and watch as Windows burns the files to your CD. When it's done, your CD will eject.

Pop the CD back in to make sure all went well. My Computer should display the name you gave it in the CD Writing Wizard.

FIGURE 17.6
The CD Writing Wizard simplifies the final CD recording steps.

> ### Getting Burned
>
> In 1994, I was the principal writer for the now defunct *CD-ROM World Magazine*. (*Multimedia World Magazine* bought it out in 1995, and *PC World* absorbed *Multimedia World* shortly thereafter.)
>
> *CD-ROM World*'s parent company organized a trade show that fall, and I was one of the presenters. One of my sessions covered the then-breakthrough technology of recordable CDs. Knowing how finicky they could be, I gave the trade show computer supplier detailed specs for my demonstration PC.
>
> They almost got it right; the only minor deviation from my specs was a slightly different model video card that created an irresolvable conflict that killed my demo. I still could go through all the steps to prepare the data for recording to the CD-R drive, but when it came to actually burning a disc, the CD-R drive refused to function.
>
> I let the audience know well in advance that the drive was not going to work. Many in attendance had had similar experiences, though, and I noted a sea of sympathetic expressions.
>
> These days, bugaboos still abound; they just take on different forms. For instance, you might run into conflicts over competing DVD-recordable standards—dash R, plus R, and DVD-RAM. It's always something.

Burning a DVD

PC DVD recorder drives typically ship with a collection of reasonably good software: a movie player, DVD authoring, and a DVD-burning application. The three principal products in this latter market niche are: Sonic Solutions RecordNow!, Roxio's Easy Media Creator, and Ahead Software's Nero.

In this section, I give you a step-by-step walk-through of RecordNow! because it's frequently bundled with DVD-recorders and works much like other DVD-burning software. A trial version is also available at www.sonic.com.

In the next section, I present an overview of Roxio's Easy Media Creator. It's the Swiss Army knife of this market niche.

RecordNow!—A Bundling Favorite

RecordNow! has a long lineage. Its roots go back nearly 30 years to an Italian firm, Prassi. That company, which moved to California in the mid-1990s, created Easy-CD Pro (later acquired by Adaptec) and DVD-Rep (bundled with the early Pioneer DVD-R drives). Later it produced PrimoDVD, which was *the* de facto standard DVD burner well into 2003. Veritas bought out Prassi along the way and Sonic Solutions bought out Veritas in December 2002.

Veritas improved on PrimoDVD when it released RecordNow!. Sonic Solutions has made a couple updates and continues to market RecordNow! on several levels: to drive manufacturers to bundle with their products, as a module within MyDVD Studio Deluxe, and as a standalone product ($30—www.sonic.com).

If your PC shipped with a DVD recorder or if you bought a recorder separately, it probably came with some kind of DVD-burning software. RecordNow! is a likely candidate as is Ahead Software's Nero. In any event, this next task uses RecordNow! to show, in general, how to make a data DVD. If you don't have RecordNow!, whichever DVD-burning product you do have will take a very similar approach. Or you can download a copy of RecordNow! from www.sonic.com.

Using RecordNow! to Record Data to a DVD

Try it Yourself

▼

RecordNow! uses simple task-oriented icons to access its three main modules. Clicking one opens a familiar window and gets you rolling. Here's how to use RecordNow! (or a similar DVD burner) to burn a data disc:

1. RecordNow!'s task icons, shown in Figure 17.7, give you three primary choices: Audio CD, Data Disc, and Exact Copy (you also can create a Video Disc—see the "Making VideoCDs" By the Way). You'll create a Data Disc in this example. Click that button to open the Data Disc window.

Making VideoCDs

By the Way

RecordNow! and most other optical disc recording software let you make VideoCDs. These use video files recorded in MPEG-1 format (they have a lower quality and lower data rate than MPEG-2). They play on most PC CD and DVD drives and many newer DVD set-top players. In RecordNow!'s case, clicking the Video Disc option opens MyDVD, which then lets you choose between making a DVD or a VideoCD.

2. As shown in Figure 17.8, you can add individual files or folders. Click the Add Files and Folders button, and select from the Windows Explorer–style window. You can select more than one file or folder at a time by using the Ctrl+click or Shift+click shortcuts I explained earlier. Click OK to place the files or folders in the Data Disc list.

▼

FIGURE 17.7
Sonic Solutions
RecordNow! offers
three main task
icons to step you
through the DVD
creation process.

Did you Know?

RecordNow! Updates Disc Space Used

As you add files, RecordNow! lets you know how much space you're going to use on the DVD. It does that in two ways: in the gray arc in the upper-left corner and in the number readout in the upper right. I highlighted both items in Figure 17.8.

Did you Know?

Drag and Drop Instead

You don't have to use the Add Files and Folders button. You can drag and drop files and folders directly from My Computer to the Data Disc window.

FIGURE 17.8
RecordNow!'s Data Disc creation interface lets you select multiple files folders, keeps you apprised of disc space used, and lets you access Options (click the Wrench icon).

3. When you're ready to record, you can click the Burn button and let 'er rip. But in this case, check out a few things first. Click the Wrench icon (highlighted earlier in Figure 17.8) to open the Options window shown in Figure 17.9.

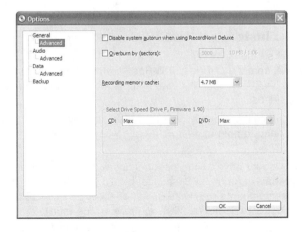

FIGURE 17.9
Under most circumstances, there's no need for you to check under the hood. But if tweaking features is in your blood, click the RecordNow! Wrench icon to access this Options collection.

4. Click General, Advanced, and note that you can change record speeds. You might need to do this if the media is not rated as high as your recorder's maximum rate. Check out the options under Audio and Data, then click Cancel (or OK to accept any changes you want to make).

5. Click the red Record button. RecordNow! will start recording your DVD (noting the time remaining to complete the task). When completed, the DVD drive will eject the disc. Insert the newly recorded disc again and check in My Computer to make sure it recorded properly.

Did you Know?

No Testing Required

RecordNow!'s older sibling, PrimoDVD, offered an option to test the DVD recorder before burning. These days it's less critical to test before doing the actual DVD (or CD) burning. Most DVD recorders are fast enough and have large enough data buffers (Sony's new DRU-710A has a 2MB buffer) to avoid those nasty buffer under-run errors that have created many useless coasters.

Testing Your DVD Drive's Speed

As you make data CDs and DVDs, you might want to test the performance of your DVD recorder.

In RecordNow!, before clicking the red Record button, note the Total Size on Disc figure in MB or GB. Start recording and note two times: how long it takes to get to 100% and how long it takes to finalize the disc.

Drive manufacturer's specs for DVD recorders state top recording speeds. For example, 24X for CD-R and 8X for DVD-R.

Those Xs can be confusing. 1X for a CD means 150KB per second (KBps). That's the original speed for audio CDs.

On the other hand, 1X for a DVD is 1.25MBps, or more than eight times the data transfer rate of a 1X CD. Double that rate is the speed necessary for smooth playback of MPEG-2 videos.

Data are packed much more tightly on a DVD disc, so when the DVD drive reads a DVD, it does not need to spin as fast as it does when reading a CD to get the same data throughput.

When you calculate your drive's write performance with a CD-R, divide the rate you come up with (probably around 3MB/second) by .15 (150KB) to get the "X factor." In this case, 3MB/sec amounts to a write speed of about 20X (3÷.15=20). If you factor in the time it takes to finalize a CD-R, you have a true rating.

You can do the same testing with a CD-RW, DVD-R, or DVD-RW. RW (rewritable) speeds will be slower than their R (one-time recordable media) counterparts.

Keep your decimal places in mind. Your total file size might be some number of MB or GB even though you might be dividing by KB.

RecordNow! has some other features of note: Exact Copy and Audio CD creation. Exact Copy works well with CDs, especially if you have two optical drives (CD or DVD). Even if you have only one drive, RecordNow! handles that with aplomb by copying the contents of a CD or data-only DVD (see the following caution) to a temporary location on your hard drive, prompting you to place a recordable CD or DVD in the DVD recorder, and then recording to it.

> **DVD Copy Protection**
> If you try to record a DVD movie, you'll probably run into some roadblocks. Hollywood studios have come up with copy protection schemes for most of their DVD movies, and RecordNow! does not let you make duplicates of your favorite movies.

Watch Out!

Making audio CDs (DVDs won't play in your music CD player) is easy. The only issue is knowing how to **rip**—or copy—songs from your personal music CD collection to your hard drive. I explained that in Chapter 5, "Making Marvelous Music."

Taking a Quick Tour of Roxio's Easy Media Creator

Roxio (www.roxio.com), a spin-off from Adaptec, is the industry leader in optical disc creation software. Its Easy Media Creator is the de facto industry standard. Microsoft uses Roxio software in the Windows CD recording module you might have tried at the beginning of this hour.

By the time this book ships, Sonic Solutions should have completed the purchase of Roxio's video and disc burning business (Roxio will retain ownership of its Napster products). No word on what eventually will become of Easy Media Creator, but it's such a widely known and respected product, Sonic likely will continue selling it in some form.

The latest version, Roxio Easy Media Creator 7 ($70—shown in Figure 17.10), is head and shoulders above previous iterations which either tended to ignore DVDs (version 5) or were a hodgepodge of loosely connected modules of variable quality (version 6).

FIGURE 17.10
Roxio's Easy Media Creator 7 is a neatly integrated collection of five general functions, seven applications, and a dozen tools.

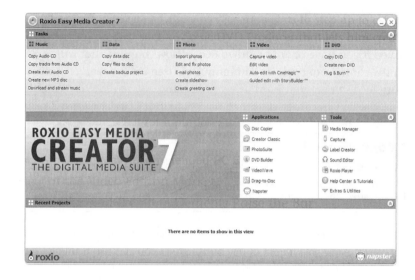

As illustrated in Figure 17.10, Easy Media Creator's opening interface—sort of a command console—gives you easy access to its five primary functions and myriad applications. In addition to CD and DVD recording modules for Audio, Data, and Video, it includes full-featured image and video-editing modules (Figure 17.11 is its nonlinear video editor—VideoWave 7) and numerous applications and tools.

FIGURE 17.11
Easy Media Creator comes with a full-featured nonlinear video editor, VideoWave 7, that approaches Pinnacle Studio Plus in quality and features.

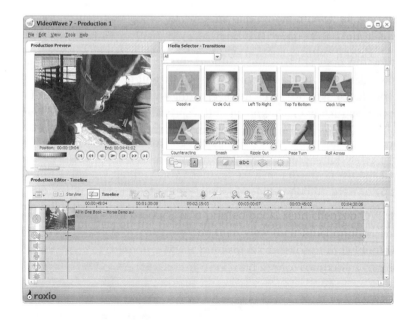

The lengthy list of possibilities is a bit misleading. Most listings lead to only a handful of modules. For instance, clicking Copy Audio CD, Copy Data Disc, or Copy DVD takes you to the Disc Copier application shown in Figure 17.12.

Disc Copier couldn't be easier to use. As shown in Figure 17.12, you open the Disc Copier module, tell the program the source and destination drives, and then click the Roxio logo Copy button on the right side to start copying. You can copy using one DVD/CD drive or two. It's *easy*, just as the name says.

FIGURE 17.12
You access this simple and effective Disc-to-Disc copy interface by clicking one of three options: Copy Audio CD, Copy Data Disc, or Copy DVD.

Most of the other data-copying options take you to the true core of Easy Media Creator: Creator Classic shown in Figure 17.13.

Creator Classic is the real workhorse of this five-function collection. Its clear and remarkably easy-to-use Windows Explorer (or My Computer) style drag-and-drop interface and simplified setup for a wide variety of disc types makes working with this module a snap.

I really like that the project size display at the bottom notes when you've exceeded the capacity of a disc, but then simply lets you know that Creator Classic will put that excess capacity on another disc. That is a very clever twist on the old out of disc space message other products use.

Finally, DVD Builder, illustrated in Figure 17.14, is a major step up from Roxio's previous stabs at DVD authoring. Although still rudimentary, it is a simple and easy way to get your videos and images on a DVD.

FIGURE 17.13
Creator Classic is the core of Easy Media Creator. It has the familiar look and feel of Windows Explorer.

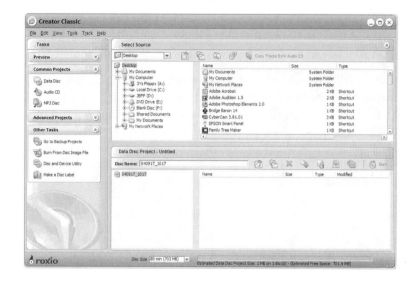

FIGURE 17.14
If you're seeking a quick way to get your videos and images on a DVD, DVD Builder will fill your needs.

DVD Builder has a good-size collection of menu templates (complete with animated video backgrounds and music as shown in Figure 17.15). Using simple drag-and-drop techniques, you can add buttons to a menu so viewers can access your videos and images. But DVD Builder does not measure up to the DVD-authoring module included in Studio Plus, and it's a far cry from a standalone DVD-authoring product such as MyDVD.

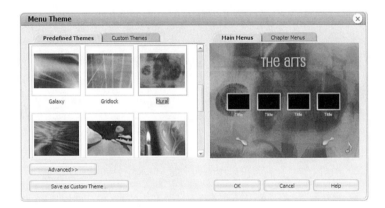

FIGURE 17.15
DVD Builder offers a good-size collection of menu templates complete with animated backgrounds and music beds.

Summary

The next few chapters will get you up to speed on DVD authoring—creating enjoyable DVDs that take advantage of all that technology has to offer. To get there, I think it's a good idea to take care of a few fundamentals. Topping that list is taking a look at recordable media and then having you use your DVD recorder to create data CDs and DVDs. Windows XP has a built-in CD recording module created by optical recording industry leader Roxio. But that module does not work with DVDs.

Recording data to DVDs requires DVD-creation software. Most PC DVD recorders come bundled with rudimentary DVD burning software. Veritas's (now Sonic Solutions) RecordNow! is a commonly used product and readily dispatches most DVD-recording chores. Moving up to a full-featured product such as Roxio's Easy Media Creator means added functionality and features.

CHAPTER 18

Authoring DVDs Using Studio's DVD Module

What You'll Learn in This Chapter:

▶ Overview of Studio's DVD-authoring process

▶ Creating a single-menu, single-button DVD

▶ Higher-level DVD authoring and menu editing

▶ Burning your DVD project

Studio's DVD-authoring module is a great way to take your first stab at DVD creation. Its collection of menu templates and buttons lets you produce some eye-popping DVDs with motion menus and animated buttons.

Its tools simplify and streamline the DVD creation process, and it offers enough options to let you go beyond basic DVD creation.

Unlike most other nonlinear editors with DVD modules, Studio uses the same interface you use to edit your video. You build your DVD on the Timeline, edit the menu in the Title Editor, and burn your DVD in the Make Movie interface.

Its one drawback does not lie in its functionality. Rather Pinnacle's consumerish, nonintuitive explanation of how to author DVDs with Studio fails to present this powerful and exciting module in its proper light. I do what I can to fix that in this chapter's various tasks.

As a result, I think you will end up creating professional-looking DVDs.

Overview of Studio's DVD-Authoring Process

DVDs are interactive. But Studio's DVD-authoring process is linear. That might be a disconnect for you, but there's something to be said for having the DVD-creation process take place in the same interface you used to create your video.

Figure 18.1 gives you a basic overview:

▶ After finishing a project, you place a menu or menus at the head of your Timeline on the Main Video Track.

▶ Or place menus in the Main Video Track and then add entire edited videos or collections of still images following the Menus on the same track.

▶ Edit menu characteristics in the Menu Properties interface.

▶ Preview your DVD's behavior in the Player window using the DVD option.

FIGURE 18.1
You use the familiar Studio video-editing, Timeline interface to author your DVD. The only obvious difference is the addition of a Menu Track at the top of the Timeline. Access the DVD Player controls by clicking the high-lighted DVD logo.

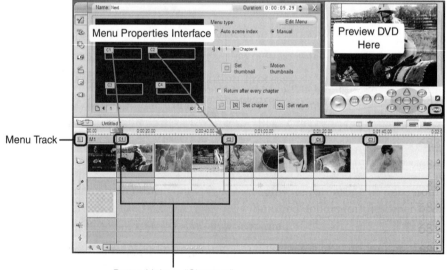

Button Links to "Chapters"

Take a look at the top of the Timeline in Figure 18.1. There's a new Menu Track. It appears automatically when you drag a menu to the Timeline.

Studio "knows" you've added a menu to your project for one of two reasons: You dragged a menu template from the Menu page in the Album to the Timeline or, when you created a title in the Title Editor, you clicked the Menu Button to **flag** that title as a menu.

Essentially, menus are no different from any other text and graphics assembled in the Title Editor. When you use a Title in a video project, you put it over a static or video background. The same thing is true for menus. The difference is that you tell Studio this Title is a Menu by clicking the Menu button in the Title Editor sometime while building the title. (I explain this in more detail later in this chapter.)

Menu Track Characteristics

The addition of that Timeline Menu Track leaves a place to display **flags** noting the presence of links between the buttons displayed in the Menu Properties interface and clips, images, and videos on the Timeline.

Those flags don't show up all that clearly in Figure 18.1, so I've enlarged a couple portions of that screenshot in Figure 18.2 to highlight them.

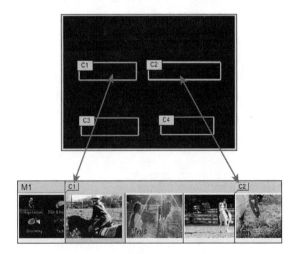

FIGURE 18.2
The Menu Track displays flags that denote links between menu buttons and clips (or other menus) on the Timeline.

Basically, the way DVD menus work is that the viewer uses the remote to click a menu button. That action then starts playing whatever the DVD author linked to that button.

In the case of Figure 18.2, when the viewer clicks Button 1 (C1 in the Menu Properties interface), the first video clip will play. And in this case, the viewer will end up seeing the entire Timeline unless he/she presses the Menu button on the remote. Clicking Button 2 (C2) will start playing the Timeline at the beginning of the fourth clip and will play until the end of the Timeline unless the viewer takes some other action.

Other DVD-Authoring Options

There are a few other options available to you in Studio's DVD-authoring interface (refer to Figure 18.3):

▶ **Set Thumbnail**—Use thumbnail images of video clips inside menu buttons. Set Thumbnail lets you select an image other than the default first frame of a clip or still image.

▶ **Motion Thumbnails**—Have Studio put those thumbnails in motion (that is, have thumbnail-sized videos play in the menu buttons).

▶ **Return After Every Chapter**—Instead playing to the end of the project each time you click a button to start playing a clip, you can play them as individual videos and return to the Main Menu after each one. This is the standard Studio DVD-authoring model or paradigm, and I explain why I don't think you should do this later in this chapter.

▶ **Set Return**—This allows you to manually determine where during a clip or entire video playback you should take viewers back to a menu. This is a feature you will use a lot in coming tasks.

▶ **Auto Scene Index** or **Manual**—Auto Scene Index assigns menu buttons to match the order of the clips in your project, even if you rearrange the clips after creating the menu. Again, I think the Manual approach is much better and more predictable.

FIGURE 18.3
Menu Properties options give you extra control over the behavior of buttons and links in your DVD menus.

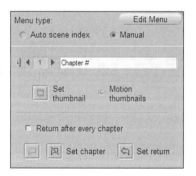

What About DVD Chapters?

I believe that you and other entry-level video editors are aiming higher than those who came before, and NLE developers are trying to meet increased expectations. But Studio's manual writers (and, to some degree, developers) haven't quite made that shift in how they present Studio's DVD-authoring module.

They apparently believe that you will limit yourself to creating only the simplest of DVDs. I don't think that's what you and the rest of this market are about.

Pinnacle's viewpoint is evident in Studio's DVD-authoring paradigm. It assumes you are creating a project with only one main menu (you might have a series of "main" menus if you run out of room on one screen for all the buttons). And you use that main menu to link to **chapters**—scenes or segments—of your project.

The general approach behind Studio's DVD-authoring process is the belief that your project's viewers will go to a chapter, watch it, and then the DVD will automatically return them to the main menu where they can select a different chapter or scene.

That's why the links I showed you earlier in Figure 18.1 are labeled C1, C2, and so on. Those stand for Chapter 1, Chapter 2, and so forth.

My approach in the rest of this book's chapter will be to assume that DVD chapters are only a *part* of the DVD-authoring process. I believe that you also will want your menu buttons to link to entire videos or slideshows or to other menus (in addition to chapters—scenes—within a project).

I don't expect you to jump right into multimenu projects, but that is where we're going to go.

Creating a Single-Menu, Single-Button DVD

Many times the only thing you want to do with a DVD is put a video or slideshow on it. No chapters. No fancy buttons. No links. Just have your viewers pop the DVD into their set-top player, click one onscreen button, and sit back and watch the entire video or slideshow.

Author Your First DVD

Despite this being a 13-step task, making a single-menu, single-button DVD is relatively easy. These instructions are long, but I spend several of the upcoming steps explaining some DVD menu concepts. Basically, this authoring process amounts to adding a menu to the Timeline and linking a button in that menu to the first clip of your project. Here's how to do that:

1. Set up a new project (File, New Project). Using Photoshoot.mpg, select every clip and drag them to the Main Video Track on the Timeline. To select all of them, drag a **marquee** around them or use Ctrl+click on each one. You don't need to use the Overlay Track, so close it—right-click in the Timeline and deselect Always Show Overlay Track.

Create a Multiclip Project

I want you to use all the clips from the Photoshoot.mpg video for this project because you will use this project in upcoming tasks and I refer to specific clip numbers at various points. However, you *can* use your own clips. Use at least a dozen to ensure that you can follow along during the upcoming tasks.

2. Open the Menus page of the Album by clicking the Show Menus tab. As shown in Figure 18.4, select Standard Menus from the drop-down list (all other menu groups are premium and require unlocking).

DVD Menu Collection

A couple points: When you open the DVD Menu Album page, it'll probably take a fairly long time to display all the thumbnails. They are hefty files and require some processing to display. And you'll see a yellow icon in the lower-right corner of some menu thumbnails. Those menus have video backgrounds.

3. Check out some of the menus:

   ▶ The top-left menu (it should display by default in the Player screen) has three frames. These are button placeholders for thumbnail images from the clips that you will link to them.

   ▶ Note that in the bottom-left corner of that first menu there are two words: "Prev" and "Next." If you have a series of menus, these buttons take viewers to the Previous or Next menu in the sequence. As I mentioned earlier, using a series of menus because you have too many links to put on one menu is kind of a kludge, so I will show you how to remove these items later.

▼

▶ The third menu in the top row has an icon in its lower-right corner indicating it has a video background. Click it to play it in the Player window. For this chapter's tasks, I suggest you do not work with menus that have video backgrounds, because they can substantially slow down your PC.

▶ That third menu does not have frames for buttons. It uses normal buttons that do not display thumbnails of the clips you link to them.

FIGURE 18.4
Access the DVD Menu collection by clicking the highlighted Show Menus tab. Note the little icon in the lower-right corner of some Menus. Those menus have video backgrounds. The top-left corner menu should display in the Player screen.

4. Drag the top-left corner menu (or any other nonvideo background menu with video thumbnail, frame-style buttons) ahead of the clips in the Main Video Track of the Timeline.

Menus Must Be at the Beginning

You can place menus anywhere among your clips, but they will become part of your video and behave as a video or a still clip instead of a menu. Whatever number of menus you end up using, you need to put all of them *ahead* of your clips.

Watch Out!

5. That will pop up the dialog box shown in Figure 18.5, asking if you want Studio to automatically place chapters at the start of each video clip. I much prefer adding chapters manually, so click No, I Will Create Chapters Manually and then click OK.

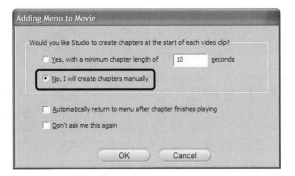

FIGURE 18.5
When you add a menu to your Timeline, Studio pops up this dialog box. I think it's best to create chapters manually, so for now select that option.

6. Studio should automatically open the Menu Properties interface and add a Menu Track in the Timeline (if the Menu Properties interface does not open, double-click the menu in the Timeline). Your project should look like Figure 18.6.

FIGURE 18.6
Adding a Menu to the Timeline opens the Menu Properties interface and adds a Menu Track to the Timeline.

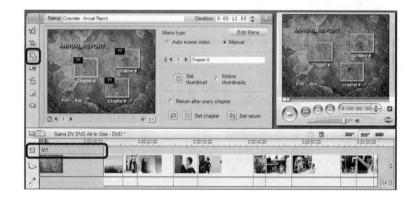

7. Check out the Menu Properties interface shown in Figure 18.6.

   ▶ Roll your cursor over the button frames in the interface screen and note how the frames change color. These are so-called Selected Highlights. As viewers use their remotes to navigate around your DVD menu, the Selected Highlights let them know which button they've moved to.

   ▶ Click a frame in the Menu Properties screen and note that it changes to a different color. This is the Active Highlight that appears briefly after a viewer clicks a button.

   ▶ Note that as you click different frames, the number to the right of the Menu Properties screen changes, indicating which button number you've clicked.

   ▶ You can switch off the display of chapter—more properly **button**—numbers by unchecking the tiny check box below the lower-right corner of the Menu Properties interface. I thinks it's best to display those button numbers to help keep track of things.

8. Create a link between a button and the first clip by clicking that clip and dragging it to a button frame. As shown in Figure 18.7, that adds a thumbnail image (the clip's first frame) to the menu button frame, changes the double question marks to C1 on that frame (meaning Chapter 1) and adds a C1 flag in the Menu Track above the first frame of the first clip.

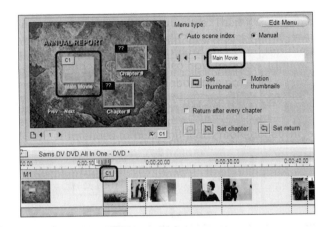

FIGURE 18.7
Drag a clip to a button to create a link from that button to that clip. Type in a new name for the button in the highlighted space.

9. Change the name of the menu button from "Chapter 1" to "Main Movie" by typing it into the space highlighted in Figure 18.7 and pressing Enter. It will show up in the Menu Properties screen.

10. Preview your single-menu, single-button DVD by clicking the DVD button in the Player screen (I've highlighted it in Figure 18.8) to open the DVD controls. Click the highlighted Main Menu button to switch to the menu.

11. Note that Studio has done a few very cool things:

   ▶ Your menu now has only one button (Studio removed the unused buttons).

   ▶ The Prev and Next buttons are gone because Studio noted that you don't have other menus in a sequence.

   ▶ The Main Movie button is already **selected** because it's the only button available to click.

12. Click that Main Movie button; your video should play until the end and then return to the Menu. Slick.

13. Save this project: Click File, Save As, and give it a name, such as **DVD Project**.

FIGURE 18.8
Preview your DVD project by clicking the highlighted DVD button to open the DVD controls (I've enlarged this figure for clarity). Then click the Main Menu button to jump to the menu and click the Main Movie button.

Main Menu

Higher-Level DVD Authoring and Menu Editing

Now you'll step up from a single-menu, single-button project. You have several possibilities.

Sometimes you want to put only a single video on a DVD, but you want viewers to be able to jump to scenes (chapters) in that video.

As you create larger projects, the more likely scenario is for you to give viewers access to several full videos or slideshows as well as individual scenes. That requires some additional **scene selection** menus.

You will likely need to make some changes to your menus: adding buttons or changing their characteristics, updating the text, or altering the Selected and Active colors and opacities.

Studio lets you do all of the above, and it gives you some surprisingly useful and clever tools to do that. Despite this being what amounts to a free module in a nonlinear editor, Studio's DVD-authoring software is fairly robust and logical.

Upping the DVD-Authoring Ante—More Links and Attributes

Interactivity and DVDs go hand-in-hand. It's good to give viewers options to jump around within a video or move to a different video. That takes additional links and linking attributes. I cover both in this task. I go over basic menu layout editing and multimenu projects in upcoming tasks. Here's how to work with extra links and their characteristics:

1. Open the saved DVD project you worked on in the previous task. Double-click the menu in the Timeline to open its Menu Properties interface.

2. Create two chapter links by dragging two clips (one at a time), about one-third and two-thirds of the way into your project, to the remaining two buttons on your menu. That will add thumbnail images to the button frames in the menu and put **chapter flags** in the Menu Track on the Timeline. Your project should look like Figure 18.9.

Easy to Change Links

If you want to link a different clip to a button, merely drag it to a button with an existing link and Studio will change links.

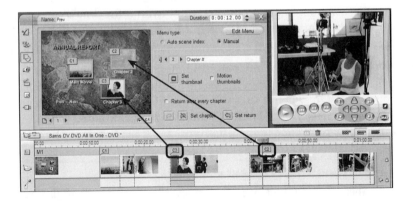

FIGURE 18.9
Dragging two additional clips individually to two separate buttons puts thumbnails in those buttons and adds chapter flags in the Menu Track on the Timeline.

3. Change the names of your buttons by clicking them one at a time, typing in a new name, and pressing Enter (the same as you did earlier with the Main Video button). I suggest you use "Scene A" and "Scene B" as shown in Figure 18.10.

Scene A = Chapter 3 = Button 3

This is where Studio's chapter-oriented DVD-authoring paradigm becomes confusing. C3 (which stands for Chapter 3) is now associated with Scene A. So, instead of thinking C3 means Chapter 3, just think of it as *Button 3*, which links to a clip of your choice, named anything you want to name it.

FIGURE 18.10
Change button names in the Menu Properties interface. (Note the little number next to the changed button name notes you are updating Button 3.) Use the two other highlighted items to change button thumbnail images and/or use videos in the button frames.

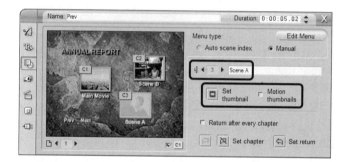

4. The thumbnail image for each button is its clip's first frame. Change one or more thumbnail images by clicking a button to select it, moving the Timeline Scrubber to any frame you want (within the linked clip or in any other clip before or after it), and then click the Set Thumbnail button highlighted in Figure 18.10.

5. Instead of static thumbnails, you can have Studio play video clips in your menu buttons' frames. Click the Motion Thumbnails check box (refer to Figure 18.10) to switch that on. To save rendering time (see Watch Out! "Motion Buttons: Four Caveats") I shortened my menu to 5 seconds by dragging its right edge to the left.

Motion Buttons: Four Caveats

Caveat 1: When you click the Motion Thumbnails check box, Studio begins background rendering of that video. Motion buttons are actually a collection of full menu frames. Your menu's default 12-second duration means Studio needs to create 360 frames (12 seconds×30 frames per second). So rendering takes a while. That means you won't see the video buttons in the Player preview screen until rendering is completed (when the green Timescale Ruler rendering bar turns yellow).

Caveat 2: Studio starts playing the video button at the thumbnail frame you've selected (or the default first frame of the clip). That motion button will play for the duration of the menu (default—12 seconds). If there are not 12 seconds left in the clip, the button video will play to the end of its clip and then jump back to the thumbnail frame and start over. This can be mighty disconcerting if you select a thumbnail near the end of a clip.

Caveat 3: Any changes you make to the menu length (you can drag its ends just like a regular video clip), its contents (new buttons or changing button placement), or its thumbnails causes Studio to rerender the entire menu.

Caveat 4: After you change the thumbnail, there is no way to know exactly what frame you selected other than eyeballing the thumbnail in the button frame. This isn't a deal-breaker, but sometimes it's nice to know which frame you used.

6. Preview your project in the Player window by clicking the DVD symbol, clicking the Main Menu button (at that point your screen should look like Figure 18.11), and then clicking either of your new chapter buttons. Note that when you jump to a scene, Studio plays that scene and continues playing the project to the end or until you click either the Main Menu or the Return to Previous Menu button.

Watch Timeline Scrubber on Menu

When you switch the Player screen to its DVD Preview mode and click the Main Menu button, the Timeline Scrubber starts moving across the Timeline Ruler. Studio is playing the menu. And when it gets to the end of the menu, it goes back to its beginning and keeps cycling until you (or your DVD's viewer) clicks a button. It exhibits this behavior whether the menu uses a still image or a video as its background.

By the Way

FIGURE 18.11
Preview your DVD project by clicking the DVD symbol in the Player screen to switch the DVD controls.

Editing Menus

If you want to add a fourth link—or **chapter**—to your three-button menu, Studio's DVD-authoring paradigm would expect you to open a second three-button menu and create that fourth link there (see Did You Know? "Following the Studio Linked–Main Menu Paradigm" for an explanation of how you do that).

This string of main menus is not a good thing in my view. Especially if you're adding only a small number of additional chapter links. The better solution is to manually add one or more buttons to your present menu.

To add another button, you need to edit your menu in the Title Editor. There you can do many other things to your menus: Change buttons, change colors, edit text, and change the Selected and Active Highlight colors and opacities.

Did you Know?

Following the Studio Linked–Main Menu Paradigm

You don't have to do things my way. You can follow the Studio DVD–authoring paradigm. If you want to create more links than the number of available buttons in whatever menu you selected from the Album (most menus have three or four buttons; one has eight) click the little triangle highlighted in Figure 18.12 to move to a second menu. Studio automatically opens a menu that looks exactly like the first one, naming it M2 (Menu 2). Then create one or more links in the same way you did before, by clicking a clip and dragging it to a button.

Note that when you preview your project, the Next text button will appear in the opening Main Menu. Clicking it will take you to the second menu, which will have a Prev link to take you back to the opening Main Menu.

FIGURE 18.12
To follow the Studio DVD–authoring paradigm, click the highlighted triangle to open a new menu using the same background and button styles.

Customizing Menus in the Title Editor

Studio comes with an industry-leading Title Editor. By now you should have taken it for a test drive or two. One usage I have not discussed is how it works with DVD menus. For instance, adding additional buttons is very easy. It has some elegant tools that handle some arcane and complex DVD issues smoothly and simply. Here are a few things you can do with it:

1. You will add a fourth button to your menu in a moment. First, I want you to check out the DVD menu-editing elements in Studio's Title Editor. To do that, open your Menu in the Menu Properties interface and click Edit Menu in the upper-right corner to open the Title Editor shown in Figure 18.13. Note that the highlighted Menu icon at the top of the Editor window is active, indicating you are working on a menu rather than a basic title.

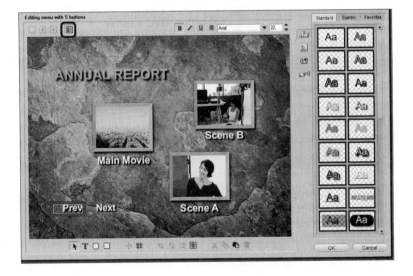

FIGURE 18.13
Studio's Title Editor opened to a menu. Note that Studio has automatically selected the Menu icon, meaning that Studio will recognize that this title page constitutes a menu, rather than a simple graphic.

2. Take a look at a few items in the Title Editor. Start by clicking the Buttons icon to display all the buttons that ship with Studio (refer to Figure 18.14).

3. Scroll through the button graphics. Note that there are two basic types: thumbnail (those with frames) and normal. The thing is, even though *you* can see the difference between a thumbnail and a normal button (a thumbnail has a rectangular placeholder for the thumbnail image), Studio can't tell the difference unless you tell it. I explain that next.

FIGURE 18.14
Studio ships with dozens of buttons. You can add them to any menu template; change their size, aspect ratio, and color; and use them to create custom menus from scratch.

4. Look at the highlighted drop-down list window in Figure 18.14 as you click the Prev, Next, and Main Menu buttons. Note that the word/phrase in the drop-down list window changes to indicate the type of button selected.

By the Way

Other Button Types

That Studio lets you identify a button as a certain type is a clever programming trick. The DVD specification allows for these various button types, and some other programs don't make it so easy to differentiate among them.

Studio offers three other button types (besides Thumbnail, Previous, and Next):

▶ **Root**—Studio automatically links any button with that designation to the DVD's main menu.

▶ **Normal**—A non-thumbnail button.

▶ **Not a Button**—You can add a button as a graphic with no DVD functionality by selecting Not a Button from the drop-down list.

Did you
Know?

Switching Button Roles

If you were to click on one of your menu's thumbnail buttons to select it and then select Normal Button from the drop-down list, that would change the button type. The thumbnail image would remain in the Title Editor for the moment, but when you closed the editor and returned to the Menu Properties interface, there would be no thumbnail in that frame and you would not be able to drag one there.

5. Add a button by clicking any thumbnail button, select Edit, Copy (keyboard shortcut—Ctrl+C), and then select Edit, Paste (keyboard shortcut—Ctrl+V). As shown in Figure 18.15, that adds another thumbnail in the menu.

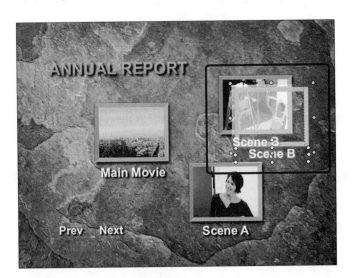

FIGURE 18.15
Selecting a button and then copying and pasting it adds a duplicate (sans thumbnail image) to the menu.

6. Before arranging these four thumbnail buttons, select and delete the Prev and Next text buttons. You don't have to do this, as Studio will remove them automatically if you don't have any other main menus in a sequence, but deleting them gets them out of the way.

Did you
Know?

Changing the Background Is Fine

As with any full-screen Title, you can change the background of a DVD menu at any time. Click the Background icon to display the 50+ backgrounds that ship with Studio (or find one of your own) and drag it into the Title Editor screen. It will replace whatever is in there without affecting any buttons, graphics, or text.

7. Now click and drag the four buttons to arrange them. Make sure none of their borders (the handles that are visible when you click them) overlap, because that causes unpredictable behavior when a viewer clicks one of them. You can use the menu alignment tools to help (Title, Align). And you can drag the "Annual Report" text toward the top of the menu to make more room. When you're done, your menu should look like Figure 18.16.

By the Way

Check Out a Couple Things

The new thumbnail button does not have an image in it. That's because you have not linked it to a clip yet. And try to keep your buttons and text inside the red dashed lines (they are barely visible in Figure 18.16). They delineate the NTSC safe zone I've mentioned earlier. Anything outside the lines might not be visible on an NTSC TV set.

Did you Know?

Checking for Overlap

Selecting all the buttons is a good way to check for overlap. To do that, select Edit, Select All. If you see some button handles touching or overlapping other button handles, either spread the buttons out a bit or reduce them in size. With all of them selected, you can reduce one button and all the others will change as well (including any selected text or graphics). You can deselect nonbuttons before making the changes by Ctrl+clicking them individually.

FIGURE 18.16
How your four-
button menu
should look after
some house-
cleaning.

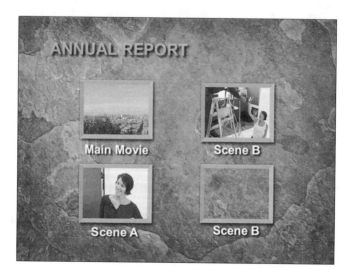

8. I want you to change the Active and Selected Highlight colors for these buttons. The current highlight colors are in the two boxes above the button graphics (I've highlighted them in Figure 18.17). Click any thumbnail button and note that the color matches either the Active or Selected Highlight color (because the default opacity setting is 50%, it won't be a solid, opaque color).

Minor Studio Miscue

Did you Know?

There should be some way to tell whether the Active or Selected color will be the one that shows up when you click a button. But there isn't. And the only way to switch views from Active to Selected (or vice versa) is to click one of those color boxes (which opens the Color Selection window) and then close that box by clicking OK. A cumbersome process.

FIGURE 18.17
These two color swatches denote the Selected and Active Highlight color for your buttons.

9. Change the Active color by clicking any button and then clicking the Active color box. That opens the familiar Color selection window shown in Figure 18.18. Select a color, adjust the opacity (100% is opaque, 0% is invisible), and click OK. Now when you click that or any other button, the entire thumbnail should take on that new tint. Do the same for the Selected Highlight color.

One Color and One Size Fit All

Did you Know?

Studio lets you use only one Active and one Selected Highlight color for all the buttons in a menu. This is a typical consumer-level product limitation. Professional products let you use several colors per menu. The other limitation is the shape of the highlight. It exactly matches the shape of the button. Higher-level DVD-authoring products let you create highlights of any shape that don't even have to appear on or near the button. Those extra options open doors to more creative possibilities.

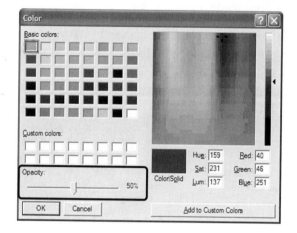

FIGURE 18.18
Use the familiar
Color selection win-
dow to choose
Active and Selected
highlight colors and
opacities.

10. Change the text from "Annual Report" to "Main Menu" by clicking Annual Report, dragging the mouse over the text to highlight it, and typing in the new **Main Menu**.

11. Close the Title Editor by clicking the X in the upper-right corner. That returns you to the Timeline, but not to the Menu Properties interface.

Did you Know?

Create Custom Menus from Scratch

You can use the Title Editor to create custom menus. Use it the same as you would when creating titles, except either click the Menu icon at the top of the editor or drag a button into the editor. Either action alerts Studio that the graphic you are creating is now a DVD menu. That means that when you close the Title Editor interface, Studio automatically adds that menu to the Timeline Main Video Track ahead of any clips and after any other menus.

12. Double-click the menu in the Timeline to open the Menu Properties interface.

13. Drag a clip to the newly created thumbnail frame button and give it a new name. **Scene C** would work well in this case.

14. Preview your project in the Player screen and then save it.

Using Multiple—*Nested*—Menus

This is the kind of DVD you should aspire to. I introduced the concept of nested menus in Chapter 15, "What DVDs and DVD-Authoring Software Can Do for You."

Nested menus are menus you access from other menus. For instance, a Family Tree DVD might have an opening main menu with buttons linking viewers to other menus that have links to various photo collections, documents, videos, and oral histories.

Because you probably don't have a bunch of edited videos and collections of old family photos already loaded up on your PC, we can simulate how you'd create a Family Tree DVD using the project you worked on in the previous tasks.

Working with Multiple Nested Menus

Try it Yourself ▼

Your goal is to change the first menu so that one button links to a main movie and the other three buttons link to other menus: a scene selection menu, photos, and interviews. Then you need to edit those menus and create links to specific clips. To explain every step would take way too long, so I will give you some general instructions:

1. Return to the DVD project you've been working on. From the Menu page in the Album, drag the same menu you've been working with to the Timeline three times. Place each one after the main menu and ahead of the clips. Studio will ask about automatically creating chapters—answer No each time or answer No and click Don't Ask Me This Again. Shorten each menu so they are all about the same length (five seconds is fine). The beginning of your Timeline should look like Figure 18.19.

New Menu Appearance

By the Way

Studio uses a different color and name—M2, M3, M4—to help differentiate each new menu. As you add links, the chapter flag colors match their menu's color. This is a very nifty little feature.

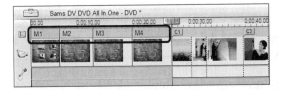

FIGURE 18.19
How your Timeline should look after adding three more menus to it.

2. Because this is a simulation, I want you to consider that the first four clips are an entire video. The second menu will be a scene selection menu that will have buttons to access clips 2 through 4 in that group. To start that process, make sure there are no chapter flags on those three clips. If there are, click and drag them to the right to other clips.

Studio Treats Edited Videos as Clip Collections

There is one fly in this higher-level DVD-authoring ointment. When you create a project of this type, you use videos you've edited and converted into separate video files (typically AVI or MPEG-2). When you add those files to your Album, Studio's scene detection feature automatically divides them into separate clips. So you either have to select all those clips and drag them en masse to the Timeline's Main Video Track to keep them in their original order, or you can select them all and select Album, Combine Scenes to convert them back to one video file.

3. Double-click the second menu to open it in the Menu Properties window and drag each clip (2 through 4) in turn to the three buttons. Rename them Scene 1, Scene 2, and Scene 3.

Place a Scene Link Anywhere in a Clip

Dragging a clip to a button causes Studio to automatically place the button link at the first frame of that clip. Later, you can drag that link flag (above the clip in the Menu Track) anywhere within any clip. That means you can have multiple chapter—or scene—links within a single clip.

4. Click Edit Menu, delete the Next text button, change the text in the Prev button to **Main Menu**, and use the button type drop-down list and select Root Button (when viewers click it, they'll go back to the Main Menu). Change the Menu title from "Annual Report" to **Scene Selection**. Check the Active and Selected Highlight colors to make sure they work right (Studio's default colors sometimes don't work well on text). Close the Title Editor and double-click Menu 2 to reopen the Menu Properties interface.

5. Here is a new concept: You need to make sure that when viewers reach the end of the fourth clip, the DVD returns them to the Main Menu. Do that by double-clicking the Main Menu to open it in the Menu Properties interface. Click that fourth clip in the Timeline (it should have a C3 chapter flag over its first frame) and then click the Set Return button in the Menu Properties interface. A little M1—Menu 1—flag should appear at the end of clip 4. Your Menu and Timeline should look like Figure 18.20 (I've highlighted the Set Return button, but note that I set it when the Main Menu was open, not the Scene Selection menu shown in Figure 18.20).

Or Return to the Scene Selection Menu

You can change a clip's Set Return, or **end action**, after setting it. In the case of playing to the end of the fourth clip and then returning to the Main Menu, you might want to send the viewer to the Scene Selection menu instead. To do that, right-click the M1 flag in the Timeline, Menu Track and select Delete to remove that Set Return (End Action). Open the Scene Selection menu in the Menu Properties interface, click that clip in the Timeline to select it, and click Set Return. That will put a little M2 flag above its last frame.

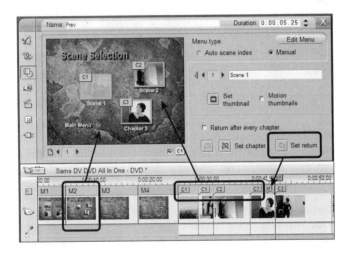

FIGURE 18.20
How your second Scene Selection menu and its Timeline links should look (I've enlarged the image for clarity).

6. Now, here comes a very cool feature. You need to link a button in the Main Menu to the Scene Selection menu. With the Main Menu open in the Menu Properties interface, click the Scene Selection menu in the Timeline and drag it (just as you would drag a clip) to the top right button in the Main Menu in the Menu Properties interface. A little M2 will appear on that button in the Menu Properties interface showing that new link.

7. Click that newly linked button and change its name to **Scene Selection**. Your Main Menu should look like Figure 18.21.

Menu As a Thumbnail

The Scene Selection thumbnail image is that menu. You can change it the same way you changed the thumbnail to a clip. Click the Scene Selection button, move the Timeline Scrubber to a video frame you want to use, and click Set Thumbnail. For the figure I show at the end of this task, I changed all the thumbnail images.

FIGURE 18.21
How your Main Menu should look after linking a button to the Scene Selection menu. Note the Scene Selection menu button has its menu as its thumbnail image.

8. Follow the same procedures for the third and fourth menus. Call the third menu Photos, and link its three buttons to each of the next three clips. Call the fourth menu Interviews, and link its three buttons to three of the final four clips.

9. Make sure you add a Set Return for the last clip in each sequence by double-clicking the menu to open it in the Menu Properties interface, clicking the clip, and clicking the Set Return button. Also add a Root button in each of the Menus to allow viewers to return to the Main Menu from any of the three nested menus.

10. For the simulated Photos and Interviews menus, each clip should stand alone because the purpose is to access the "photos" and "interviews" individually. So set a return for each of those clips back to their respective menus.

11. When completed, your Main Menu and Timeline should look like Figure 18.22 (I broke the screen into pieces and expanded the Timeline to better highlight the chapter and menu flags).

12. Preview your project in the Player screen. Try all of the following:

   ▶ Start at the Main Menu by clicking that button in the DVD controls.

   ▶ Click the Main Movie button to watch those three clips. When the clips have completed, the Player should automatically jump back to the Main Menu.

▶ Click the Scene Selection button to go to that menu. Click any scene. It should play to the end of the final clip and return to the Main Menu.

▶ Click the Photos button to go to that menu. Click any Photo and it should play only that clip and return you to the Photos menu. When you're done looking at the photos, click the Main Menu (Root button) to return to the Main Menu.

▶ Follow the same procedure for the Interviews menu.

FIGURE 18.22
How your finished project's Timeline and its many flags should look.

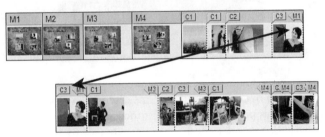

13. Make note of anything that needs fixing. Most fixes are very simple. For example, if you need to change a link, drag a new clip to a button.

14. Save your project.

Burning Your DVD Project

Congratulations. You've authored a relatively complex project. Now it's time to burn it to a DVD. You've done most of this before in Chapter 13, "Advanced Editing Techniques, Add-ons, and Exporting." The primary difference this time is that Studio will convert your entire DVD project into MPEG-2 files and will then burn them onto a DVD.

▼   **Burning Your Project to a DVD**

You don't have to have a recordable DVD to follow most of the upcoming steps. But burning your first DVD project to a recordable DVD and then running to the nearest set-top DVD player to watch it on TV is pretty darned exciting. So, if you've got the gear, this is the time to use it. Here's how:

1. Open the DVD project you worked on in the previous task.

2. Click the Make Movie tab. As shown in Figure 18.23, Studio switches to the Make Movie interface with the Create Disc option already selected. Note how much time the project uses versus the time available on a DVD. In the case of the Photoshoot.mpg task you just completed, it'll consume only a minute or so.

FIGURE 18.23
With your DVD project open, clicking the Make Movie tab opens the Create Disc interface. Note the amount of time your project consumes versus the space available on the DVD.

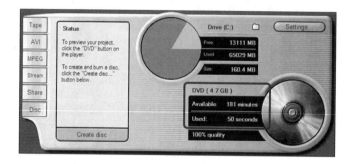

3. Click Settings to open the Setup Options dialog box. As shown in Figure 18.24, Studio has preselected all the standard MPEG-2 settings. Under Video Quality/Disc Usage, select Best Video Quality (see By the Way, "Selecting Video Quality").

By the Way ▼

> **Selecting Video Quality**
>
> Video Quality—Both Automatic and Most Video On Disc use the same slightly lower-quality MPEG-2 video compression that can store up to three hours of video on a single DVD. Best Video Quality has a 76-minute limit. Most Hollywood DVDs fall somewhere between the two compression levels—consuming about two hours per DVD.
>
> Custom gives you wider control over the level of compression. You select the **bit rate**. The highest rate is 8,000Kbits/sec (just about the most a DVD player can handle). The lowest is 3,000, or low-end VHS quality.

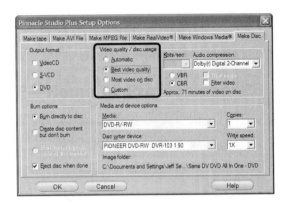

FIGURE 18.24
The Make Disc Setup Options interface opens with all the standard MPEG-2 options preselected. For a small project like the one in this task, select Best Video Quality.

4. You have three output format types: VideoCD, S-VCD, and DVD. Because you're making a DVD, stick with that (see Watch Out! "VideoCD and S-VCD Are Dinosaurs"). Accept the rest of the defaults by clicking OK.

VideoCD and S-VCD Are Dinosaurs

VideoCD and S-VCD (Super VideoCD) were bridge technologies developed a few years ago when DVD burners and media were rare and expensive. They let you burn MPEG videos to a CD using a format that many set-top DVD players can play. These days, there's no practical reason to use them.

Watch Out!

---

5. That takes you back to the Make Disc interface. Click the green Create Disc button. That starts rendering your video (converting it to MPEG-2). I've highlighted the rendering progress bar in Figure 18.25. This is a nice feature in that you get a very specific update on the exact clip-by-clip rendering progress.

Two-Pass High-Quality MPEG Compression

If you selected the Best Quality MPEG option, Studio will do what's called two-pass compression. It will examine each clip twice as it calculates the best way to compress the video while retaining as much of the original quality as possible.

By the Way

FIGURE 18.25
Studio notes the rendering progress in the Player screen.

6. After Studio completes rendering, it moves right into burning the DVD. No extra input from you is required. Again, Studio gives you something of an update, shown in Figure 18.26, but this one is less informative than the rendering progress bar. Despite the lack of a progress bar, you can estimate burning time to be somewhere in the vicinity of real-time—that is, it'll take as long as your project's playing time plus a couple minutes to put some finishing touches on your disc.

FIGURE 18.26
After giving you a nice rendering progress bar, when actual DVD burning begins, Studio shifts into a less-helpful display.

7. When burning is complete, the DVD drive ejects the disc. Hustle it over to your nearest DVD player and watch it on TV. It should work like a charm. Do check that all links work as expected, that all Selected and Active Highlights display the way you wanted them to, and that clips that are supposed to return to their originating menus do just that.

Summary

I've worked with many DVD-authoring products—both standalone and modules within other products. Studio's DVD module is a pleasant surprise. It uses a Timeline approach (which can be nonintuitive at first) but it has several features that make it easy to create professional-looking DVDs. I especially like how it creates links, lets you change thumbnails, edit highlight colors and opacities, and how it differentiates among button types.

My only real complaint is the approach that Pinnacle takes in presenting this module. They assume you will use it only to create a DVD with one video and a bunch of scene selection menus that play discrete clips instead of the entire video. This DVD module can do much, much more than that.

I did my darnedest to explain its undocumented, higher-end attributes in this chapter.

Burning a DVD is remarkably easy. In fact, if you accept the defaults, it takes all of one click.

You can access some options that can help you fit a large project onto a DVD by reducing the overall MPEG compression quality. Otherwise, choose Best Video Quality.

CHAPTER 19

Stepping Up to MyDVD 6

What You'll Learn in This Chapter:

▶ Introducing MyDVD 6
▶ How MyDVD 6 stands up to Studio
▶ Checking out the MyDVD interface and feature set
▶ Capturing video with MyDVD
▶ Editing video with MyDVD

I chose MyDVD as the primary consumer-level DVD-authoring software to feature in this book because it's the best product in its entry-level category. And it has much more utility, versatility, and depth than the DVD-authoring module in Studio.

In this chapter I go over its features, highlighting some that are new to version 6, which was released in September 2004. Its interface is remarkably user-friendly yet still gives you detailed control over such things as menu button placement and MPEG compression levels.

MyDVD comes in three versions ranging in price from $70 to $150. I explain the differences and go over the data, audio, and disc copying tools available in its two higher-priced versions.

Finally, I cover video capture and editing with MyDVD 6: two strong attributes for a product with the primary goal of authoring DVDs.

In the next two chapters I explain MyDVD's DVD-authoring and DVD-burning tools. I finish the MyDVD section with coverage of Sonic's Style Creator: a miniprogram that lets you customize MyDVD menus in ways that go well beyond what you can do in MyDVD.

Introducing MyDVD 6

MyDVD is the best entry-level DVD-authoring product. I reached that conclusion after testing a half-dozen such products along with several nonlinear editing software DVD-authoring modules.

MyDVD lets you create DVD projects with ease. It has built-in templates and wizards that step you smoothly through the DVD-authoring process. The numerous menu and button styles give you all the options you need to cover most of your DVD production needs.

As you gain expertise, you can substitute your own graphics, images, and audio during menu creation. Using a **plug-in** (a miniprogram inserted into another program to perform a specific function), you can use Adobe Photoshop or Photoshop Elements to create menus with built-in buttons and import them directly into MyDVD. (I cover that in Chapter 22, "Creating Custom MyDVD Templates with Style Creator.") As you increase your skills, you might want to build customized DVD templates and post them on the Sonic Solutions website (more on that in Chapters 21 and 22).

MyDVD Flavors

MyDVD 6 comes in three flavors: MyDVD Studio ($70), Studio Deluxe ($100), and Studio Deluxe Suite ($150).

All three have the full version of MyDVD, which is a full-featured DVD-authoring and burning product with a solid video capture and nonlinear editing module.

The Deluxe and Deluxe Suite versions add things like RecordNow! capability including CD-audio ripping to MP3 files and CD disc copying and recording. In addition, they have some higher-level backup features. To see a feature comparison chart, go to www.sonic.com/products/mydvd/mydvd/whatsnew.asp.

I suggest you also visit the Sonic website to download a trial version of MyDVD. Sonic said it would post the trial version to its website by the time this book ships. Go to www.sonic.com/go/sams/ and click the link to the trial version there.

MyDVD 6 Features

MyDVD 6 is a lot like Studio and the rest of the entry-level NLE products I've mentioned earlier in this book. It's an integrated suite of video-editing and DVD-authoring tools. Its greatest strength is on the DVD-authoring side of the equation. But its video editor is good enough that you can use it instead of Studio if you are creating only basic video projects.

Figure 19.1 shows its default opening interface. What you might notice right off the bat are two features you wouldn't expect in a DVD-authoring product: Edit Disc and Watch Movie.

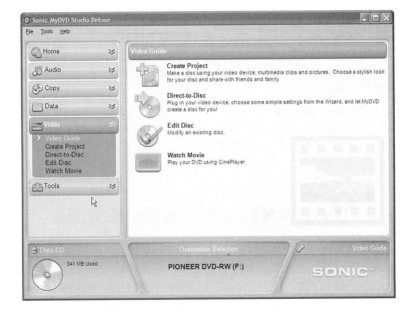

FIGURE 19.1
MyDVD's opening interface is the first indication of how streamlined and simplified this entry-level DVD-authoring process can be.

- ▶ **Edit Disc**—This uses OpenDVD, a Sonic Solutions technology to take menus, videos, slideshows, and audio from a completed DVD created with an OpenDVD-compliant authoring tool and do additional authoring. You can add more menus and assets to an existing project and then burn that to another disc. This is a great way to create and update archives without having to keep the original files on your hard drive.

- ▶ **Watch Movie**—This is a link to Sonic's CinePlayer software DVD player I featured in Chapter 16, "Getting Your Gear in Order—DVD Recorders and Media." CinePlayer is included in all versions of MyDVD 6.

Other features common to all MyDVD 6 versions include a printed disc labeler, the capability to burn a video directly to a disc, thorough tutorials, and slideshow creation tools (using up to 1,000 images).

The two Deluxe versions of MyDVD 6 offer RecordNow! capability: audio CD creation, direct disc-to-disc copying, and data disc creation. And the Deluxe Suite has a very useful, and fully automated, back-up-to-disc utility.

Some Features That Are New to MyDVD 6

▶ **Fit-to-DVD**—This is a great feature that takes the worry out of MPEG compression settings. Select Fit-to-DVD and MyDVD chooses the MPEG compression that works best for your project size and media capacity.

▶ **MPEG Compression by Project and Video**—You can set an overall project MPEG compression level for menus, videos, and audio, but you can override that for specific videos. You might want to play a short video at the best possible quality but compress a longer video to make it fit better.

▶ **Some other new features**—There are many, including freeform menu button placement, dual-layer DVD+ support, many additional video transitions, the capability to capture photos directly from cameras, true anamorphic 16:9 support, and MPEG-4 compression.

How MyDVD 6 Stands Up to Studio

Studio is a clear winner in the video- and title-editing battle. MyDVD 6 is the winner in DVD authoring, video capture, scene detection, and in file handling.

▶ Studio is first and foremost a nonlinear video editor. MyDVD's editing module is for the casual user only or for very basic projects.

▶ Studio's title editor is the best of any product in this price category. MyDVD's is rudimentary at best.

▶ What makes MyDVD stand out is how easy it is to make menus and nested menus, create chapter markers, and test the finished product.

▶ Sonic's DVD so-called **authorscript** engine is the best in the business and gives you the greatest likelihood that a DVD burned using any Sonic authoring product will play on the widest range of set-top players—old and new.

▶ MyDVD's video capture interface is more professional looking, the capture options are more useful, and scene detection has more user-adjustable, automated controls. Studio's automatic scene detection needs an "off" switch.

▶ File handling might seem like a low-level thing, but Studio's is clumsy. Its Album lists all files in a file folder when all you're interested in is one file. MyDVD's file handling is much more user friendly.

Checking Out the MyDVD 6 Interface and Feature Set

To fully appreciate all that MyDVD 6 has to offer, I strongly suggest you download and install the trial version of MyDVD Studio Deluxe (www.sonic.com/gosams) and then follow along with the following Try It Yourself tasks.

Tour MyDVD's Interface   *Try it Yourself*

MyDVD's interface is logically laid out and very user friendly. Here's a basic run-through to give you an idea of its features and what's to come in upcoming chapters:

1. Start MyDVD by double-clicking its icon on your desktop. Alternatively, if the installation process failed to place an icon there, select Start, Sonic, MyDVD. Doing so opens the main interface. Click the Home button highlighted in Figure 19.2.

Big Button Options   *By the Way*

If you click the buttons on the left you will see lists of options within each major task. But when you click the links at the bottom of the Home page, MyDVD displays those options anyway.

---

2. Take a look at the Quick Links, highlighted in Figure 19.2. Your choices are fairly straightforward: make an audio CD, do a disc-to-disc copy, create a data disc, or author a DVD. We'll go through them in order. Click Audio CD to open the interface shown in Figure 19.3.

FIGURE 19.2
MyDVD's opening interface is the first indication of how streamlined and simplified this entry-level DVD-authoring process can be.

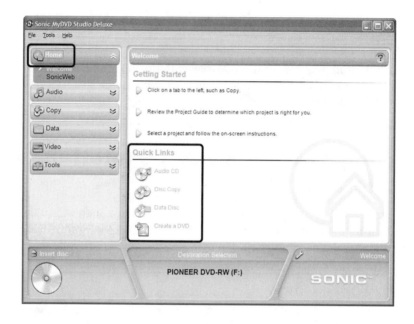

FIGURE 19.3
Use the highlighted Add Music or Quick Find (as well as Windows Explorer) to select a variety of music files and have MyDVD make a standard Music CD, a Jukebox CD, or have MyDVD convert CD music tracks into MP3 files.

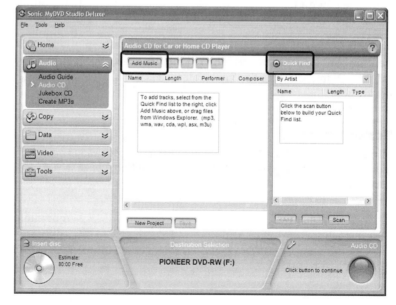

What's a Jukebox CD?

A **Jukebox CD** is not a standard music CD. It's a CD that can play only in a PC or in music players that can read MP3, WMA (Windows Media Audio), or WAV (Windows Audio/Video) files. The advantage is that the compression schemes used for WMA or MP3 files mean that you can store many more songs on a Jukebox CD than on an audio CD.

3. It's a simple matter to gather up music of several file types to make an audio CD that will play in your car or home stereo. MyDVD offers three ways to add files: Quick Find locates by Artist, Genre, and so on; Add Music lets you track down files individually; and you can drag and drop files from the standard Windows Explorer/My Computer interface. You might note that the audio interface looks familiar. It is representative of MyDVD's RecordNow! functionality. The same holds true for the Copy and Data tasks.

4. Click Copy to open the interface shown in Figure 19.4. This lets you make direct disc-to-disc copies. It also works with **disc images**. These are files created by DVD-authoring software that match how they would be stored on a DVD.

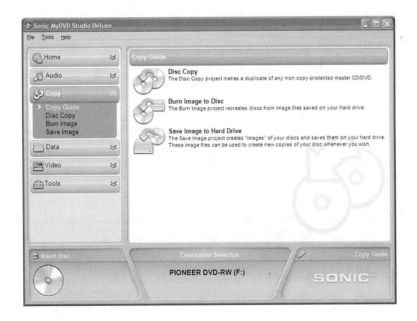

FIGURE 19.4
Copy is another RecordNow! element that lets you make direct disc-to-disc copies; it also works with DVD disc images.

5. Click Data to open that interface and then click the Easy Archive link to access the interface shown in Figure 19.5. What is very slick about this archive feature (found only in the Deluxe Suite version of MyDVD) is that it lets you store massive amounts of data on multiple DVDs and creates an index to help you track down files.

FIGURE 19.5
Easy Archive facilitates storage of many files across multiple discs and creates an index to track down files later.

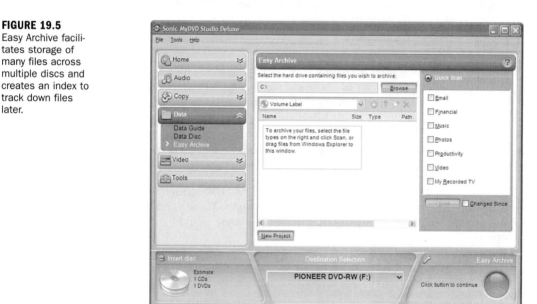

6. Skip the Video button for a moment and click the button below it—Tools. As shown in Figure 19.6, Tools offers four options: Erase Disc, Finalize Disc, Disc Information, and Label Disc. Click Disc Information to learn more about your DVD drive and the media you have in it. If you burned a DVD using Studio's DVD-authoring module (or created any other kind of DVD), put it in your drive and check out the Disc information.

7. Click Label Disc to open the Sonic Express Labeler shown in Figure 19.7. This is a third-party plug-in licensed by Sonic from MicroVision Development (www.surething.com).

Did you Know?

Disc Labeling Limitations

The SureThing plug-in has some real limitations. It works only with paper labels purchased from SureThing, it comes with only six backgrounds and six fonts, and you can't use your own image as a background. Spending $20 will resolve all those shortcomings. Click the Upgrade button to go to the SureThing upsell website.

FIGURE 19.6
Disc Information displays your recordable DVD drive data and information on any disc in that drive.

FIGURE 19.7
MyDVD's licensed DVD/CD labeler offers up only a handful of fonts and backgrounds, but many more are available for purchase online.

8. Close the Express Labeler by clicking Quit, and then click the Video button. It should open to the Create Project task. If not, click that option to open the interface shown in Figure 19.8. You have three main choices: DVD, DVD+VR, and VCD.

▶ **DVD**—This is what MyDVD is all about: authoring DVDs. You start that process by clicking this link.

▶ **DVD+VR (Video Recording)**—This is a specialized DVD format used by set-top DVD *recorders*. It is not compatible with standard set-top DVD *players*. There are some strict limitations: DVD+VR discs can contain only videos (no slideshows), only silent and static menus and buttons, no submenus (nested menus), and you can record them only to DVD+R/RW discs.

▶ **VCD (Video CD)**—VCD is the original video disc format that preceded DVD. It uses MPEG-1 video (VHS quality) but does have higher-quality audio. It's popular in Asia but, with low-cost DVD recorders and media, its popularity elsewhere is waning.

FIGURE 19.8
MyDVD's Create Project selections include DVD+VR. This is a special format for set-top DVD recorders.

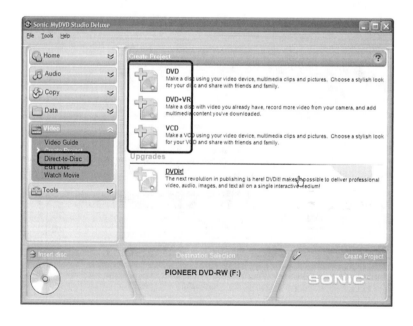

DVDit! Upgrade Info

The last link in the Video interface is to the Sonic e-Store site where you will see the offer for DVDit! 5 shown in Figure 19.9. This is Sonic's prosumer DVD-authoring software that I cover in this book's final chapters. Even though the link says Upgrades, there is no special upgrade price for MyDVD users.

Did you Know?

FIGURE 19.9
Clicking the DVDit! upgrade link takes you to this Sonic upsell site. DVDit! is the prosumer authoring product I feature in this book's final chapters.

9. You will begin the DVD-authoring process (by doing some video capture and editing) in the next tasks. Before going there, take a look at one more interface: Direct-to-Disc (shown in Figure 19.10). Access that by clicking its link below the Video button (highlighted earlier in Figure 19.8).

10. I cover the Direct-to-Disc task in Chapter 21, "Authoring DVDs with MyDVD 6: Part 2." For now, note that after you give your project a name and insert a recordable DVD into your drive, the Next button will become active. Clicking it will take you to the Video Capture interface where you will transfer your video directly to a DVD. Click Cancel to return to the Main interface.

FIGURE 19.10
Direct-to-Disc is a
quick and easy way
to record a video
straight from your
camcorder to
a DVD.

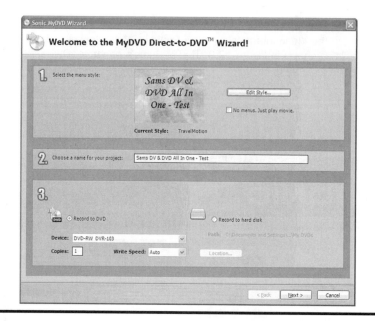

Capturing Video with MyDVD

The final two sections of this chapter take you through some familiar territory:
video capture and video editing.

Because you now are an old hand at this, I don't go over too many details, and I
try to avoid repeating material from previous chapters—such as how to connect a
camcorder to your PC.

Why Capture or Edit Video with MyDVD?

Because you already know how to use Windows Movie Maker and Pinnacle
Studio to capture and edit video, you might wonder why I take the time to
explain it yet again.

MyDVD is like Studio in that it is a full suite of video- and DVD-production tools.
Its strength lies in its DVD authoring. That's why I've included it in this book. But
its other features are strong enough to stand on their own if your video-editing
needs are basic.

The workflow that exploits the strengths in both Studio and MyDVD is to *edit* videos in Studio and *author* DVDs using those videos in MyDVD. In that case, you'd skip video capture and editing.

My guess is, though, that there will be many instances when you want to do all of your work—from video or still-image capture to DVD—in MyDVD. Here are some examples:

▶ If your only goal is to transfer DV raw footage directly to DVD, MyDVD is the product of choice.

▶ If you want only to trim down some raw video clips into something a bit more manageable and presentable and then create a DVD with a menu or two, MyDVD will take care of that more gracefully than Studio.

▶ Creating DVD slideshows from collections of image files or directly from a digital camera is a breeze in MyDVD.

Capturing Video and Using Scene Detection

Try it Yourself

So let's start with video capture. You know the basic process. One twist with MyDVD is that its Scene Detection process has a couple more options. Here's how capture and scene detection work:

1. Open MyDVD to its main interface (the default view should be Video), click Create Project, and click DVD to open the main MyDVD-authoring interface shown in Figure 19.11 (if you get an error message about DMA, read the next Watch Out! "Your DMA Setting Probably Is Fine"). Take a look at its main options:

   ▶ **Add Files**—This is the MyDVD equivalent to Studio's Album. But the Add Files process is much more intuitive and predictable.

   ▶ **Capture Video**—We'll go here in a moment. This also takes you to the Scene Detection options.

   ▶ **New Slideshow**—Creating a collection of images set to music and with nice transitions is easy in MyDVD.

   ▶ **New Sub-Menu**—Unlike Studio, MyDVD is geared to higher-level DVD projects that invariably use nested—or sub—menus.

FIGURE 19.11
MyDVD's main authoring interface gives you ready access to all elements of your DVD project.

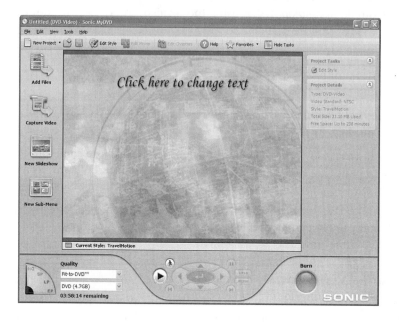

*Watch
Out!*

Your DMA Setting Probably Is Fine

When you first open MyDVD's main authoring interface, you might get the Alert shown in Figure 19.12. DMA—Direct Memory Access—is a feature of most hard drives. And most of the time it's on by default. MyDVD 6 has a bug that sometimes reports DMA is turned off when it's on.

To check your DMA setting you need to open your Device Manager. One way to do that is to open your Control Panel, double-click System, click the System Properties Hardware tab, click Device Manager, click the plus sign (+) next to your IDE controllers line, and as shown, right-click Primary IDE Channel and select Properties. As shown in Figure 19.12, click the Advanced Settings tab and make sure the Transfer Mode is set to DMA If Available.

FIGURE 19.12
If you get the DMA Alert on the left, go to the Device Manager (center) to access the Primary IDE Channel (right) to check whether DMA is enabled.

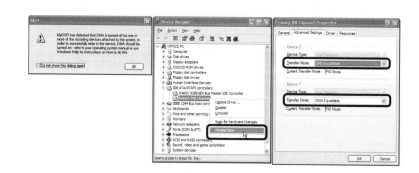

2. Click Capture Video to go to the interface shown in Figure 19.13. Note a few things:

▶ **Record Settings**—Set the quality of the video file created during video capture. Your choices are DV or three flavors of MPEG. As always, DV is your best choice because it preserves the quality of your original digital video.

▶ **Set Capture Length**—Capture for a specific amount of time.

▶ **Automatically Add a Chapter Point**—This is a little confusing. If you opt for any kind of Scene Detection in the next section, MyDVD automatically creates a chapter point at each new scene anyway. Selecting the Automatically Add a Chapter Point applies only if you want to add chapters at regular intervals irrespective of scene changes.

▶ **Scene Detection Settings**—MyDVD offers the same settings as Studio, plus two extra automatic scene detection settings (I show them to you in a moment). You can have MyDVD automatically create chapter (Scene Selection) menus as it detects scenes. You can also switch off the automatic scene detection and press the space bar to alert MyDVD to a new scene (if you want to split your captured video into scenes).

▶ **Grab Frame**—This is where you capture stills from your camcorder.

FIGURE 19.13
MyDVD's Video Capture interface has a full range of features.

3. Click Scene Detection Settings to open the dialog box shown in Figure 19.14. Note that MyDVD takes Studio's automatic scene detection two steps further: You can change scenes when the timecode changes or the content changes, *or both*. And the Detection Sensitivity slider adjusts how carefully MyDVD looks for content changes. Make your selection and click OK.

FIGURE 19.14
Automated Scene Detection has some extra options compared to what you've seen before.

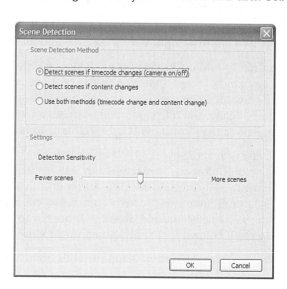

4. For the purposes of this exercise and the DVD-authoring tasks in the next two chapters, leave the Chapter Points box unchecked and select Use Automatic Scene Detection.

By the Way

Truly Helpful Help

Sonic Solutions has the best context-sensitive help files of any product I've seen. Note that each major item in the Capture interface has a little question mark (?) in the upper-right corner. Click the Chapter Points (or Scene Detection) help icon to open the screen shown in Figure 19.15. If you ever wonder how something works in MyDVD, click a help icon. When you're finished, close that window.

5. Cue up your tape and click the big red Start Capturing button (the button name changes to Stop Capture). When you've captured enough video, click that Stop Capture button.

6. That will open a Save As window. You can navigate to a file folder of your choice and then give your video a name. That returns you to the Capture interface. Cancel to return to the MyDVD main authoring interface.

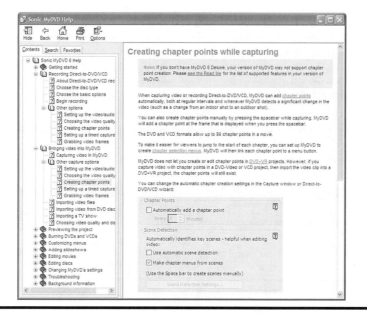

FIGURE 19.15
Most PC users eschew help files because they are so darned unhelpful. Not so for those found in Sonic Solutions products. Check them out.

Editing Video with MyDVD

Overall, MyDVD's video editor is about on par with Movie Maker. The downside for MyDVD is that it has only one audio track (versus two for Movie Maker), no title overlay track (it does have a text tool) and only a storyboard (no timeline). The plus side is its well-designed interface and easily accessible tools (and Movie Maker has no DVD authoring).

MyDVD offers a full slate of entry-level video-editing functionality. You can trim, delete, or rearrange scenes. It has a solid collection of transitions, numerous video effects—such as embossing, sepia, and mosaic—and you can add music or a narration to the entire video.

Using MyDVD's Video Editor

Because you've edited on a timeline before, I won't go over all the nuts and bolts. But I do want to point out a few things as you proceed toward DVD authoring. Here's how to use MyDVD for video editing:

1. Continuing from the previous task, you should be back at the main MyDVD-authoring interface with a single button in the center of the window (refer to Figure 19.16). If you captured more than one time, each set of clips will have a single button. If you opted to create automatic chapter menus, those buttons will access those menus.

By the Way

Forgo Adding Files for Now

At this point you could click Add Files to get some other video clips, but my assumption is that any files you get you will have already edited. In any event, I save gathering assets for the next chapter.

FIGURE 19.16
How MyDVD's authoring interface should look after capturing one video. Access the video editor by clicking the highlighted link.

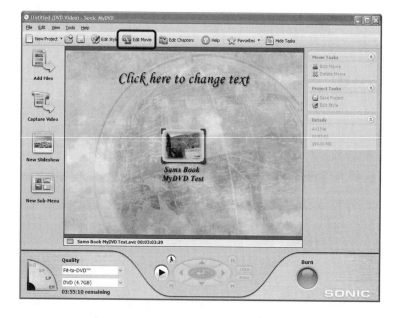

2. Access the video editor by double-clicking the button on the screen or by clicking the Edit Movie button highlighted in Figure 19.16. That interface, shown in Figure 19.17, opens with your clip in its Storyboard and its first frame in the monitor screen.

3. At this point you could trim the entire clip manually to create scenes or display all the scenes that MyDVD detected during capture. Because you used automated scene detection during capture, start there. Click the Find Scenes link highlighted in Figure 19.17. That opens the Mark Scenes for Editing window shown in Figure 19.18.

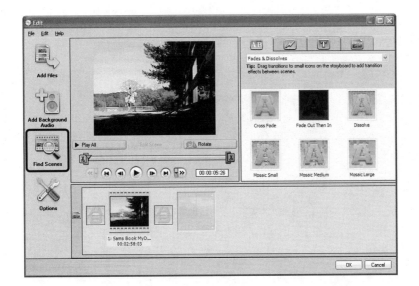

FIGURE 19.17
MyDVD's video edi-
tor uses a
Storyboard editing
model and features
a logical and easy-
to-use layout.
Access your auto-
matically detected
scene collection by
clicking the high-
lighted Find Scenes
button.

FIGURE 19.18
Use the Mark
Scenes for Editing
interface to remove
scenes from your
project or redo the
scene detection
process.

4. You can have MyDVD reanalyze the video to attempt to create more or
   fewer scenes by using the slider at the bottom-right of the screen (highlighted in Figure 19.18). And you can uncheck scenes you don't want to include
   in the edited video. When ready, click Add to Storyboard. That returns you
   to the Edit interface.

5. As shown in Figure 19.19, all your clips will show up sequentially in the Storyboard. Click a clip and use the highlighted trimming tools to tighten it up. What's nice about this is that, unlike in Studio, you don't have to open a separate window to do the trimming.

FIGURE 19.19
Use the trimming tools to slice away unneeded footage from individual clips.

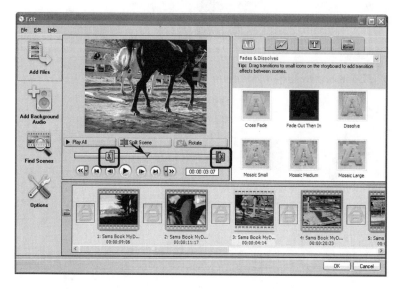

6. You've worked in storyboards before. The same basic drag-and-drop rules apply here. To move a clip from one placeholder to another, click it and move it left or right. A vertical black line indicates where it'll go.

7. You can split a clip by dragging the gray triangle, pointed to by the red arrow in Figure 19.19, to wherever you want to make the split and clicking the Split Scene button. That will place another thumbnail in the Storyboard and shove all the following scenes to the right.

8. MyDVD has 85 transitions. To view them, click the Transitions tab, highlighted in Figure 19.20. They are organized by type (a good thing). They have no parameters, such as duration or direction. Drag one to a transition placeholder between two clips and click Play in the monitor window to watch it. Click Pause to return to the editing mode.

Did you Know?

Fade Up from or Down to Black

Use the Fade Out Then In transition at the beginning or end of your project to fade up from black or down to black.

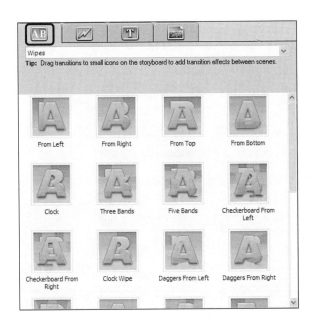

FIGURE 19.20
MyDVD is loaded to the gills with transitions. The only drawback is that they have no options, such as the capability to set duration or direction.

9. Even though you have no control over an individual transition's duration, you can change the default duration that MyDVD applies to all transitions. Doing that is a little awkward. Click OK to close the Edit interface and return to the DVD-authoring interface. Select Tools, Options, click the Video Editing tab, and, as shown in Figure 19.21, change the Transition Defaults Duration setting.

10. Access Video Effects by clicking the tab highlighted in Figure 19.22. There are 75 effects, but most are variations on a theme: tint, zoom, and brightness compose the bulk. And, again, they have no parameters. What you see the moment you apply one to a clip is what you get. The Frames collection is a bit out of the ordinary and worth a look.

11. The Text tool (refer to Figure 19.23) is basic at best. You can choose from any font (using only a few preset font sizes) on your PC, but your only editing options are (from left to right in Figure 19.23): justification, bold, italic, underlined, a barely visible drop shadow, and color. And all these attributes apply to the entire phrase you place over a particular clip. For example, you cannot underline only one word out of several.

FIGURE 19.21
To change the
default duration for
all transitions, use
this Options dialog
box (rather than the
Options menu in
the Edit interface).

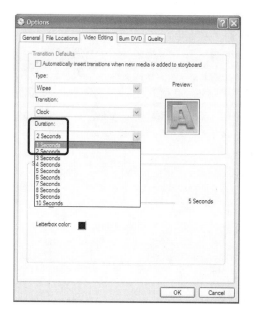

FIGURE 19.22
MyDVD appears to
have a lot of Video
Effects, but most
fall into only a
handful of cate-
gories.

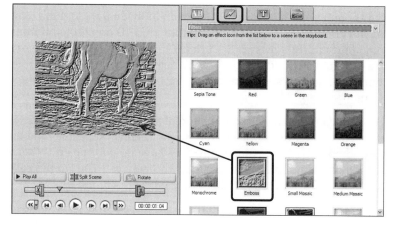

12. Finally, MyDVD ships with a few dozen graphical backgrounds over which
you can place some simple text (refer to Figure 19.24). You can use them as
opening titles or within a project. To do so, drag one to the Storyboard to
insert it between two clips. If you drag it directly on top of a clip, it will go
in front of that clip.

FIGURE 19.23
MyDVD's Text options are minimal.

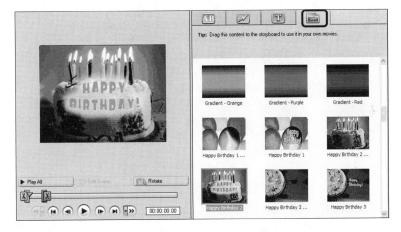

FIGURE 19.24
Use any of these 80-plus graphical backgrounds for opening titles, credits, or between clips.

13. Add audio (music or some other audio file) to your project by clicking the large Add Background Audio button on the left side of the interface, track down your file, and click OK to open the Movie Options dialog box shown in Figure 19.25. Here are a few of its features:

> ▶ **Add**—You can place more than one audio clip in your project. MyDVD will play them consecutively in order from top to bottom. Note the Movie and Audio Duration figures.

> ▶ **Fade In, Fade Out, Loop Audio**—Standard audio fades ease in or out of your audio. If your tune is shorter than your project, you can have MyDVD loop it.

▶ **Audio Levels**—This is MyDVD's very basic audio mixer used to blend the natural sound on your original video clips with the music, narration, or other audio you add in this interface. It affects the entire project (in contrast to one clip at a time) and it works only through trial and error. You can't listen as you adjust the slider. You make your fix, close Movie Options, listen to your project, and if you need to adjust the mix, reopen Movie Options by clicking the large Options button to make further adjustments.

14. Now you can make a basic video and view it by clicking the first placeholder in the Storyboard and clicking Play All in the Monitor window. When you finish editing your project, click the OK button in the lower-right corner of the screen. That takes you back to the main MyDVD-authoring interface.

15. Save your project. Select File, Save As, give your project a name, and click Save. You will continue the DVD-authoring process—asset gathering and menu building—in the next chapter.

FIGURE 19.25
You can add audio to your project by selecting a background audio track in the Movie Options dialog box.

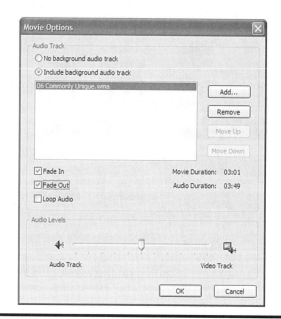

Summary

You've taken a close look at MyDVD's features. It's much more than a straightforward consumer-level DVD-authoring product.

For example, its design is user-friendly yet still gives you enough control to truly customize your work. As you'll learn in the next two chapters, you can place buttons and text where they suit you and it's very easy to build a project with multiple, nested menus.

It comes with a video capture option with customizable scene detection settings. MyDVD's easy-to-use video-editing module offers a multitude of transitions and video effects, an additional audio track, and a text function.

Although MyDVD is essentially on par with Movie Maker, there are some real advantages to doing an entire DVD project from scratch within MyDVD.

CHAPTER 20

Authoring DVDs with MyDVD 6: Part 1

What You'll Learn in This Chapter:

▶ Assembling video assets

▶ Adding chapter markers

▶ Adding a slideshow

▶ Organizing assets into menus

It's time to use MyDVD 6 to author a DVD with a full range of features. In this chapter you complete a series of tasks using MyDVD 6 to assemble your assets and automatically create menus and buttons. You place chapter points in a video, automatically create associated menu buttons, and add a slideshow to your DVD. At the conclusion of this chapter you build a four-menu project from start to finish.

In the following chapter, you'll edit the menu style, background, and buttons, and then finally burn your project to a recordable DVD. You can take the Direct-to-Disc route or create a full-fledged, menu-driven DVD.

And in Chapter 22, "Creating Custom MyDVD Templates with Style Creator," you will create custom menu templates and learn how to share them online.

Assembling Video Assets

Unlike Studio, MyDVD uses a predictable video asset gathering methodology. It places only what you've selected into your project. And when you import a video file, it automatically performs scene detection in the background but does not divide your video into clips. It gives you the option to do that later.

This is as it should be.

There are two ways to gather video assets:

▶ Import them as individual videos that viewers will access via separate buttons (one for each). You can later use Scene Detection as a means to place chapter markers in them so viewers can access clips within them via scene selection menus.

▶ Build a single video using each imported video as a single clip. This is a great way to combine a collection of clips into a single file. Later, as I mentioned in the previous paragraph, you can add chapter markers to use in a scene selection menu.

Try it Yourself   Gathering Assets

The gathering of assets—in both the main DVD-authoring interface and the video editor—is fairly straightforward. Here's how to do both tasks:

1. Open MyDVD to its main interface. Under Video, select Create Project, DVD to open the main DVD-authoring interface shown in Figure 20.1.

By the Way   A Fresh Start

You can use your saved project and add files to it. But I prefer that you start with a clean slate. The purpose of this task is to assemble a collection of video files with the goal of combining them into a full-featured DVD with multiple menus including scene selection nested menus.

2. Click the large Add Files button, highlighted in Figure 20.1. That opens a standard Windows Explorer style window shown in Figure 20.2. This is one reason why I prefer MyDVD's approach to file handling. It's familiar. Navigate to any video files you want to add to your project, select them (if you can, select more than six separate video files), and click Open.

3. When you add a video or videos to a MyDVD project for the first time, MyDVD automatically creates a main menu and adds one button to that menu for each video you add to the project. It lets you know about this by popping up the New Menu Alert shown in Figure 20.3. Click Do Not Show This Dialog Again and click OK.

4. Your project should look something like Figure 20.4. If you gathered more than six files, there will be a little button in the lower-right corner. I've highlighted it in Figure 20.4. This is a link to another menu that will have up to six more buttons that link to six separate videos. Double-click that triangle to check out the next menu.

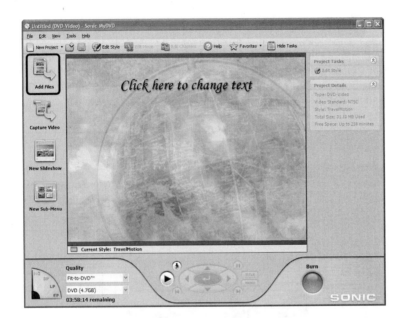

FIGURE 20.1
The familiar main MyDVD-authoring interface. Click the Add Files button to gather your assets.

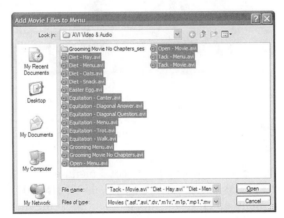

FIGURE 20.2
The familiar Windows Explorer makes it easy to gather assets for your project.

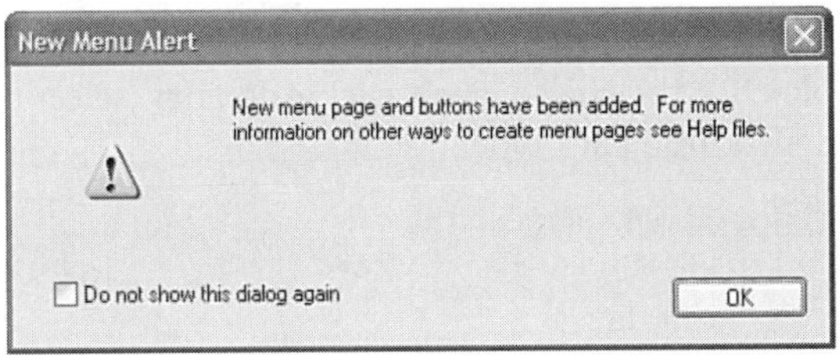

FIGURE 20.3
This New Menu Alert lets you know MyDVD has created separate buttons for each new asset and placed them in a collection of menus.

▼

By the Way

A Button for Each Asset

That MyDVD automatically creates a button for each asset is a good thing. This is why MyDVD is more intuitive than Studio. Studio is designed to work with only one asset with chapter points to gain access to clips within it. In Chapter 18, "Authoring DVDs Using Studio's DVD Module," I showed you how to override that paradigm by adding separate video files and creating separate menus, but MyDVD does that kind of process as its default behavior.

FIGURE 20.4
Adding video files populates your DVD-authoring interface with button links to those files. Each menu can hold no more than six buttons. If you add more than six videos, MyDVD creates an additional menu. You access that menu via the highlighted Next Menu button.

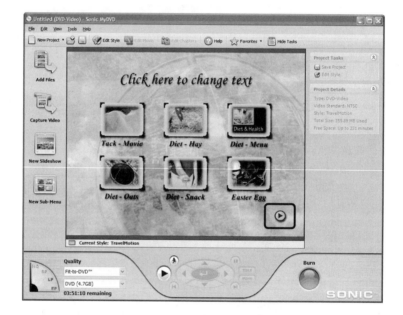

5. If you have more than 12 files, that second menu will have a link to a third menu, and so on. As shown in Figure 20.5, it will also add a link back to the previous menu and a Home link to take you to the main menu (which, in the case of only two menus, is the same as the previous menu).

6. You can combine files into one single video. To do that return to the Home menu (double-click the Home icon), click Add Files, select the clip you want to have play first, and click Open.

▼

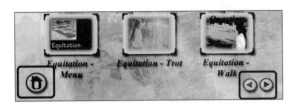

FIGURE 20.5
If you add enough assets to fill more than one menu, MyDVD automatically adds some buttons to those extra menus plus a Previous Menu button (the highlighted left-facing triangle), a Next Menu button (if you have even more linked menus), and a Home button to take viewers back to the main menu.

7. That adds a button to the last main menu page (if the number of buttons you had previously was a multiple of six, this new file will cause MyDVD to add yet another main menu page). Double-click that newly added button to open its Edit interface.

8. In the Edit interface, click Add Files and select all other files you want to add to this new video compilation and click Open. As shown in Figure 20.6, each video file will appear in the Storyboard.

Filenames and Clip Numbers

Look below each thumbnail in the Storyboard in Figure 20.6. You'll note that each has a label with the clip number, filename, and clip length. If you rearrange clips—that is, move clip 2 to placeholder 3—its number will change to 3, but the rest of its information will remain intact.

By the Way

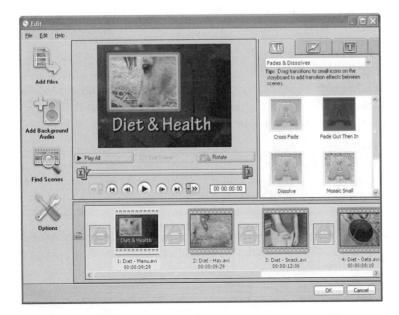

FIGURE 20.6
You can use MyDVD's video editor to combine several video clips into one single video. Later you can add chapter—scene selection—markers at the beginning of each clip.

9. If you want to add transitions, now's the time. Keep in mind that if you later plan to add chapter points at scene changes, you probably do not want those scenes to start playing within a transition.

10. When you're done adding and rearranging clips along with transitions, video effects, text, or even inserting some graphics from MyDVD's library, click OK to return to the main DVD-authoring interface.

11. Save your project by selecting File, Save or Save As.

Adding Chapter Markers

Now that you have added assets to your project, you might want to create a scene selection menu or two. MyDVD automates a large part of the process via the Scene Finder and Edit Chapter tools.

Each time you add a video clip to your project, MyDVD performs a background process: It automatically marks scenes but does not display them unless you ask it to.

That means you can manually adjust, remove, or add scenes and then add chapter markers. Or you can go directly to the Edit Chapters interface and have MyDVD place markers at each of the automatically selected scenes.

From there, you can have MyDVD automatically build scene selection menus to give viewers direct access to those scenes. I believe this approach is elegant and intuitive.

Try it Yourself   Adding Chapter Markers

I will show you both paths along the Scene Detection and Chapter Marking route. In both cases, MyDVD keeps the chapter marking process simple, making the scene detection process worth your time. Here's how it works:

1. MyDVD has already divided all imported clips into scenes. In many circumstances you'll never need to be concerned about that. But if you want to create a scene selection menu and if you might want to do some tweaking of scene breaks, you need to open that clip in MyDVD's Edit interface. To do that, double-click that clip's button.

2. In the Edit interface, click Find Scenes to open that interface. As shown in Figure 20.7, MyDVD automatically locates scenes based on your previous scene-selection criteria.

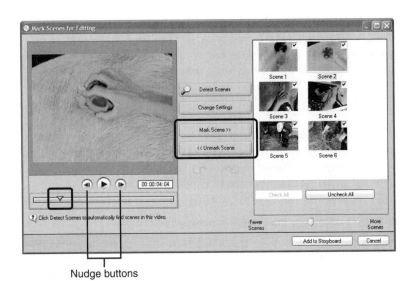

FIGURE 20.7
Use the Mark Scenes for Editing interface to automatically and manually select scenes. Use the highlighted scrubber triangle to move to a scene and the Nudge buttons to find the exact frame.

Nudge buttons

3. If you want to add a chapter point at a scene that MyDVD did not mark, drag the gray triangle under the monitor screen to the unmarked scene and click the Mark Scene button. Use the Nudge buttons, highlighted in Figure 20.7, to find the exact frame.

Unmarking Versus Unchecking

If you uncheck a scene, MyDVD will not display it in the video-editing Storyboard and will remove it from the video.

If you select a scene and click the Unmark Scene button, that clip will remain in the video. It will show up in the Storyboard as an extension of its previous clip. The main reason to unmark a scene is because you don't want to have your Scene Selection menu have a button to access that particular spot.

Did you Know?

4. After you've marked the scenes that you want to use for chapter points (and unmarked or unchecked the rest), click Add to Storyboard to return to the Edit interface. Click OK in the lower-right corner of that interface to return to the main DVD-authoring interface.

Did you
Know?

Incremental Jumping—Keyboard Shortcut

You can use the Skip Backward or Skip Forward button below the Edit monitor screen to move through a video clip in one-second increments, or try the keyboard shortcut of holding down the Ctrl key while pressing the right- or left-arrow keys. Either method is useful for getting to the vicinity of a scene change without having to use the Nudge button to step through every frame.

5. To add chapter markers to those newly selected scenes (and to automatically create a scene selection nested menu or submenu), click that clip's button in the Menu window to select it, and then click the Edit Chapters button at the top of the interface (highlighted in Figure 20.8).

Watch
Out!

MPEG Clips—Scene Detection Issue

MPEG videos (in contrast to AVI or QuickTime MOV files) have inherent technical issues that sometimes lead to less-than-accurate manual scene selection. The fault does lie with MyDVD, but the reason lies in how MPEG files are compressed and encoded. That's why, as you scrub through an MPEG video, you might notice the Mark Scene button switch on and off. Only when you've scrubbed to a selectable or editable frame can you actually mark a scene change.

FIGURE 20.8
To add chapter markers to the scenes in a clip, click this button.

6. That opens the Chapter Points interface shown in Figure 20.9. Here are its features:

   ▶ Click Add Chapters at Scenes to put markers at each scene you just selected.

   ▶ You can jump to each scene using the two highlighted buttons.

   ▶ You also can add a chapter by dragging the triangle to any frame and clicking the Add Chapter button.

   ▶ Remove a chapter by jumping to that chapter and clicking Remove Chapter.

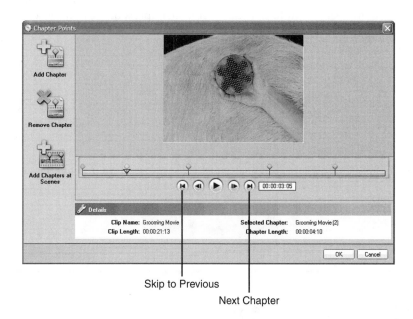

FIGURE 20.9
Use the Chapter Points interface to automatically add markers at scenes or to manually add or remove chapter markers.

Skip to Previous

Next Chapter

7. When you finish adding, deleting, and updating chapter locations, click OK. MyDVD pops up a message asking Do You Want to Display a Button for This Movie in the Current Menu? That button will serve as a link to what will become a Scene Selection menu. So, in this case, click Yes.

Possible Error Message

When you click Yes, you might receive an error message that states: Menu Editor Is Not Valid—37003. The message does not describe the problem. What's really going on is that MyDVD has run out of hard drive space.

MyDVD needs about 20GB (!) of temporary storage for all the menus, buttons, videos, and other material used in a full-featured DVD. If your project is fairly robust or you have limited hard drive space, that message pops up and the program crashes (freezes).

To get out of the program, do the so-called three-fingered salute—Ctrl+Alt+Delete—select Task Manager, click the Applications tab, select MyDVD, and click End Task. Next, delete stuff from your PC to free up room or reduce the size of your project and try again.

Watch Out!

---

8. As shown in Figure 20.10, when you return to the main DVD-authoring interface, the button label for the video you just worked on will have

changed. It now shows the video filename along with "Chapters." Double-click it to open the automatically created Chapters or Scene Selection menu.

9. Save your project: Select File, Save or Save As.

Adding a Slideshow

I want you to add one more asset to your project: a slideshow. MyDVD lets you add a collection of still images that can play with background music or a narration. You can place transitions between each image. New to MyDVD 6 is the capability to have up to 1,000 images in a show (versus 99 previously).

You can import those images directly from a digital camera or import existing image files directly into your project.

Another nifty feature is the option to add the separate image files to your DVD to let those who view it on a PC access those files for viewing or editing.

Try it Yourself   **Add a Slideshow to Your DVD Project**

In this task, you add a slideshow of stills to the existing menu you've created. Here's how:

1. Return to the main DVD-authoring interface. If you were looking at the Chapters submenu you created in the previous task, double-click the little Home icon in the lower-left corner to return to the main menu.

2. Click the New Slideshow button in MyDVD's main authoring interface, which opens the Create Slideshow interface shown in Figure 20.11.

3. Click the Add Files button and locate some images on your PC. Select whatever number suits you and click Open.

What If You Have No Images?

If you can't track down any images, first try looking in My Documents/My Pictures. There should be two sample images there. Two images don't make much of a slideshow, so if you want more, use MyDVD to make them. Open a video in the Edit interface, move the Playhead (gray triangle) to a frame you like, and select File, Export Current Frame As. That will open a Save window. Save the frame as an image file. You have five file types to choose from. I recommend BMP because it retains the full original image quality.

FIGURE 20.11
Use the Create Slideshow interface to add a collection of stills to your DVD.

4. Take a look at the Create Slideshow interface. It has several useful options:

   ▶ **Get Pictures**—If you have a digital camera, connect it to your PC and click this button. MyDVD will add selected images to the Create Slideshow interface.

   ▶ **Rotate**—Turn any selected image 90 degrees clockwise. You can do this more than once to hit 180 and 270 degrees.

▶ **Set Button Image**—Select an image that you think is representative of the entire slideshow, click Set Button Image, and that image will become the thumbnail image in its button on the main menu.

▶ **Options**—Open this to set the slide duration, add music, change—or switch off—transitions, change the color that fills gaps of images that do not match the standard video aspect ratio (see Figure 20.11 earlier for an example of a vertical format image with black gaps on each side), and opt to include the images as separate files on the finished DVD. I cover this in more detail in step 7.

▶ **Filmstrip, Thumbnails, Details**—This changes how you view the images, the same as it would in the Windows Explorer interface. Filmstrip is the most intuitive, but Details comes in handy if you need to navigate through a lot of images.

5. Use the two triangles at the top of the interface to step through the images.

6. Rearrange the display order of the slides by clicking and dragging images to other locations in the slide timeline.

7. Change the image that will display as a thumbnail on the menu button by clicking one of the stills and then clicking the Button Image icon. As shown in Figure 20.12, doing so adds the Set Button Image icon next to the newly selected image.

FIGURE 20.12
Use this interface to rearrange images and change the menu button thumbnail image.

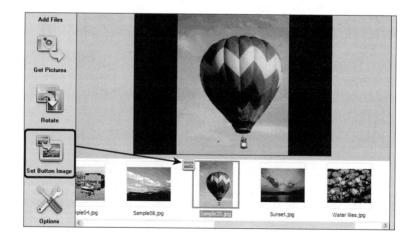

8. Open the Options interface by clicking that button. As shown in Figure 20.13, there are two tabs:

   ▶ **Basic tab**

      ▶ Change the slide duration.

      ▶ Add audio (this works the same way as adding audio in the video-editing interface).

   ▶ **Advanced tab**

      ▶ Change the transition between the slides (including a random setting that uses a variety of transitions).

      ▶ Change the letterbox color (that option is covered up in Figure 20.13 by the Transitions drop-down list).

      ▶ Save the images as data files on the DVD to make them accessible to PC users. This is one of several reasons why MyDVD is a cut above other entry-level DVD-authoring applications.

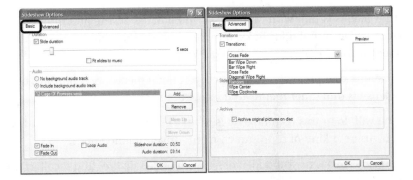

FIGURE 20.13
Slideshow Options has five sets of options, including altering the slide duration, adding audio, and three others in the Advanced tab.

9. Click OK in the Options dialog box to accept any changes you made. Click OK to exit the Create Slideshow interface. Your main menu now has an additional button called Untitled Slideshow. Your menu should look similar to Figure 20.14. Save your project by selecting File, Save.

FIGURE 20.14
How your project's
main menu should
look. Note that one
button links to a
video, another to a
chapter (scene
selection) menu,
and the other links
to a slideshow.

Organizing Assets into Menus

MyDVD uses an **asset**-driven approach to creating DVDs. Prosumer and professional products use a **menu**-driven approach.

What that means is that with MyDVD, as you add assets, the program automatically creates menus and adds links to those assets and to other menus. This is a consumer-friendly approach to building DVDs.

With prosumer and professional products you build menus, add buttons, and then link assets and other menus to those buttons. That's a menu-driven model.

What you will do in this coming task is to take charge of MyDVD's asset-driven process by using a kind of a prosumer, menu-driven methodology.

In the previous tasks, as you added assets, you ended up creating a collection of connected Main Menus with links to videos, a Scene Selection (Chapter) menu, and a Slideshow. In this section I want you to take a more deliberate and planned approach.

Try it Yourself   Building Menus from Scratch

In the following Try It Yourself you will build a four-menu project. You will create this project from scratch using the techniques covered in this chapter's previous tasks. Here's how:

1. As shown in the diagram in Figure 20.15, your project will have a main menu with links to two nested menus. One nested menu will give viewers access to a main movie, that movie's scene selection submenu, and a slideshow. The other submenu will let viewers access individual videos.

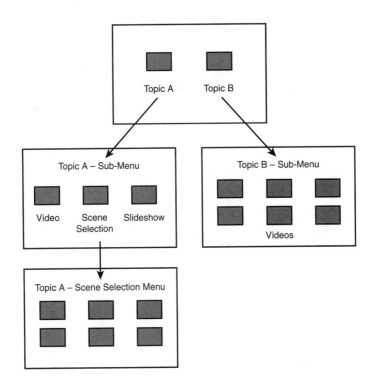

FIGURE 20.15
The basic design of
the DVD you create
in this upcoming
Try It Yourself fea-
tures a main menu
and three sub-
menus.

2. Start MyDVD and open it to the main DVD-authoring interface (select
   Create Project, DVD). It should open to a blank menu. If you already have
   MyDVD open to an existing project, save it—click File, Save—and then
   select File, New, DVD Project.

Other Menu "Looks"

Up until this point (and for the rest of this chapter) you have worked with MyDVD's
default menu style, with its associated buttons, text font, and music (it does have
music—you need to preview your project to hear it). In the next chapter you will give
this project a different look, add descriptive text, change the menu music, and add a
video background.

*By the
Way*

3. Start by adding a single video to this blank menu. You've done this before.
   Click Add Files, select a video file, and click Open. MyDVD will place a button on the menu that links to that video. You will later move that button
   (taking its link with it) to the Topic A—Sub-Menu.

4. Now you'll create the Topic A—Sub-Menu. Start that process by clicking the New Sub-Menu button highlighted in Figure 20.16. This will add a button to your main menu labeled Untitled Menu 0.

By the Way

Sub-Menu Buttons Look the Same

By default, when you're working with MyDVD menu templates, submenu buttons all look alike. They all have that curved arrow, shown in Figure 20.16, which points to a menu icon.

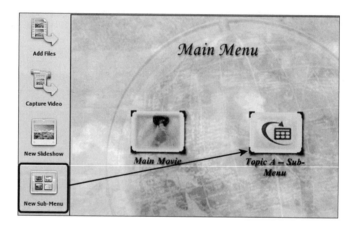

FIGURE 20.16
The Main Menu with a newly added link to the Main Movie (you'll move that button in a moment) and to the Topic A—Sub-Menu.

5. To help keep track of which menu and buttons are which, name your menu and the two buttons. To do that, click twice on each text string to highlight each in turn and, as shown in Figure 20.16, type in `Main Menu`, `Main Movie`, and `Topic A – Sub-Menu`.

6. You want to have viewers link to the Main Movie via the Topic A—Sub-Menu (instead of via the Main Menu as it's set up now). You do that by moving the button that links to that video *from* the Main Menu *to* the Topic A—Sub-Menu. Here's how: Right-click the Main Movie button and select Cut, double-click the Topic A—Sub-Menu button to open that blank menu, right-click anywhere inside that menu, and select Paste. The Main Movie button should appear in that menu.

By the Way

Characteristics of the New Submenu

Take a look at a couple things in this new submenu shown in Figure 20.17. The menu title, Topic A—Sub-Menu, is the same title you gave its button in the Main Menu. That's how MyDVD tracks submenus and their links. Also note the two buttons in the lower-left corner: Home and the curved arrow Return to Menu button. Both have different functions that happen to have the same end results here. Home takes viewers to your project's opening menu (the Main Menu in this case) and Return to Menu takes viewers to the previous menu—the menu they came from to get to this submenu (also the Main Menu in this case).

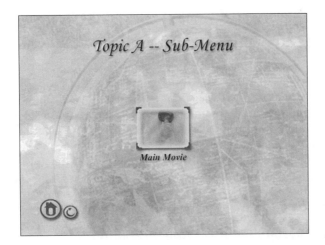

FIGURE 20.17
The newly added Topic A—Sub-Menu, with its Main Movie button link and its Main Menu and Return to (previous) Menu button.

7. Add a Scene Selection menu to the Topic A—Sub-Menu by clicking the Main Movie button to select it, clicking Edit Chapters to open that interface, adding some chapter markers, clicking OK, and clicking Yes when asked if you want to add a chapter menu button.

8. The little surprise awaiting you in the Topic A—Sub-Menu is that MyDVD has replaced your Main Movie button with a Main Movie *Chapters* button. You need to add another button and link it to the entire Main Movie. To do that, right-click the Main Movie Chapters button, select Copy, right-click again (even in the same place), and click Paste. A Copy of the Main Movie Chapters button appears.

9. As shown in Figure 20.18, turn that button into a link to the Main Movie by right-clicking it and selecting View as Movie Button. That changes its name to Copy of Main Movie. Edit that text to read `Main Movie` by clicking it twice and typing in the new text.

▼

FIGURE 20.18
Change a duplicate
chapter menu but-
ton back into a link
to a video by right-
clicking it and
selecting View as
Movie Button.

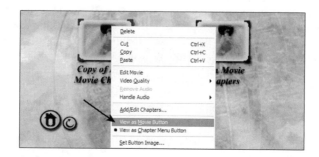

10. Now add a slideshow to the Topic A—Sub-Menu by clicking the New
    Slideshow button, adding some images, adjusting parameters in Options
    (slide duration, transitions, music, and so on), setting a button image, and
    clicking OK. Change the two buttons' text to match that in Figure 20.19 by
    clicking the button titles (one at a time) to highlight them and then type in
    the new text. Your updated Topic A—Sub-Menu should look like Figure
    20.19.

**By the
Way**

All Chapter Menus Must Be Named Chapters

No matter what name you give the button that links to the chapters menu, MyDVD
will always append it with the word *Chapters*. It's yet another example of that overly
helpful, consumer approach common to products built for the entry-level market.

FIGURE 20.19
This is how the
Topic A—Sub-Menu
should look. It has
three buttons,
which link to the
Main Movie, the
Scene Selection
menu, and to a
Slideshow.

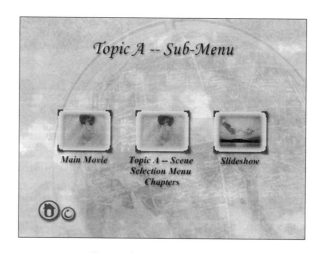

11. Now you will add the Topic B—Sub-Menu for buttons that link to a collection of video clips. To do that, double-click the Home Main Menu icon in the Topic A—Sub-Menu to return to the Main Menu. Click the New Sub-Menu button and name that newly created button **Topic B – Sub-Menu**.

12. Double-click the Topic B—Sub-Menu to open a blank menu page.

13. Click Add Files, select up to six video files (more than six would create more than one menu), click Open, and as shown in Figure 20.20, MyDVD places buttons on a menu that links to those videos.

14. Save your project—File, Save. You will use this DVD session in the next chapter.

Previewing Your Work

You have set up a main menu and three submenus or nested menus. At this point, you can preview your project. I explain that process in detail in the next chapter, but if you want to experiment a bit now, feel free. Click the Preview button (highlighted in Figure 20.20) and click menu buttons to see what happens. You should be able to navigate around the four menus and view the videos, chapters, and slideshow. You might note that when a clip selected from the Topic B—Sub-Menu ends, it automatically starts playing the next clip. You will fix that behavior in the next chapter.

By the Way

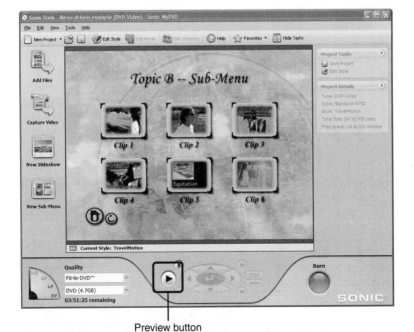

Preview button

FIGURE 20.20
This is the Topic B—Sub-Menu, a collection of buttons that each link to individual videos (I have changed the titles for this figure). Click the Preview button to see how your project will look when played off a DVD.

Summary

This chapter introduced you to the MyDVD-authoring process. The first step is gathering your video assets. Doing so creates at least one menu.

You added chapters to your video and opted for MyDVD to create a separate scene selection submenu. And you created a slideshow with its associated menu button.

At the conclusion of this chapter, you switched from the consumer-friendly asset-driven menu-building model to a more prosumer/professional approach of building menus and then adding assets. You will take that customized approach much further in the next two chapters.

CHAPTER 21

Authoring DVDs with MyDVD 6: Part 2

What You'll Learn in This Chapter:

▶ Previewing your work in progress

▶ Adding a First Play video and fixing some links

▶ Editing the menu style

▶ Introducing custom templates

▶ Recording videos direct-to-disc

▶ Burning your full DVD project

In this chapter, you'll start by testing the DVD navigation—using your mouse as a remote control to click to various menus and media—making sure things work as you'd expect. You'll discover that they won't, so I'll show you how to fix that and how to add what's called a **First Play**.

Then you'll edit the appearance of the menu backgrounds, buttons, and text. I give you a brief overview of custom templates (I cover them in depth in the next chapter) and describe how to find them online.

Finally, you'll take your DVD on one last test drive before burning it onto a DVD. You'll also see how to make a direct-to-DVD recording with or without a menu. With the newly recorded disc in hand, you'll then run down the hall, place it in your set-top DVD player, and view your work.

Previewing Your Work in Progress

MyDVD lets you test your project, reproducing the experience viewers will have when they play it in a set-top DVD machine. The only difference is that you get to use your mouse to click buttons onscreen and buttons on a simulated remote control.

Preview Your DVD Project

As you build menus and add elements, you might lose track of how everything is connected. Use the Preview mode to clarify that. Here's how to do it:

1. Return to the main MyDVD interface. Open your DVD project by selecting File, Recent Projects and clicking the project you completed in the previous chapter.

2. Preview your project by clicking the Preview button at the bottom of the main MyDVD interface (see Figure 21.1).

FIGURE 21.1
Access MyDVD's Preview feature by clicking the high-lighted button below the menu window.

3. The Information screen, shown in Figure 21.2, pops up and notes that ani-mated menus will not display. Click OK. That takes you back to the main screen; you'll hear music playing and note that all the menu navigation buttons next to the Preview button are not **active**.

> **Yes, You Can See the Menu Animations**
>
> During preview, you *can* see the animated/video menus, but it requires some time to **render** (convert the menus and buttons—with their video thumbnails—into new video clips).
>
> To see the motion menus and animated button in action, click the Build Motion Menu button (the little runner) next to what was previously the Preview button but is now the Play button. MyDVD will pop up a little render progress bar and will render that menu only. You need to render a menu only once to have it animate when you preview it later. If you change the menu in any way, you'll need to rerender it.
>
> If you want to see other menus in action, you need to click the links to those menus and click the little Render Runner for each menu.

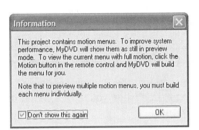

FIGURE 21.2
Before entering Preview mode, MyDVD lets you know that any animated menus and buttons will remain static.

Looks Almost the Same—Behaves Much Differently

Upon entering Preview mode, your MyDVD main interface changes a bit. As shown in Figure 21.3, the previously grayed-out DVD "remote" control buttons are now activated, whereas the various menu-building and video-editing buttons at the top and left side of the screen are grayed out. Also, the Main Menu music plays in a continual loop.

By the Way

Inactive Functions

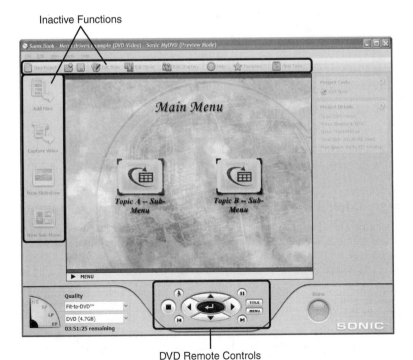

DVD Remote Controls

FIGURE 21.3
After clicking the Preview button, the MyDVD main screen changes, activating the DVD "remote" control buttons and graying out the menu/video editing icons.

4. Before beginning the preview process, take a look at Figure 21.4. It identifies the various buttons you can use to simulate a remote control. You can, however, forgo the remote control buttons and click the DVD menu directly.

Stop Means Return to Menu Editing Interface

If you click the Stop button, you exit the Preview mode and return to the main DVD-authoring interface. Clicking Pause when you're in a Menu mode stops the music but keeps you in the Preview mode.

FIGURE 21.4
Use these controls to take your DVD for a test drive.

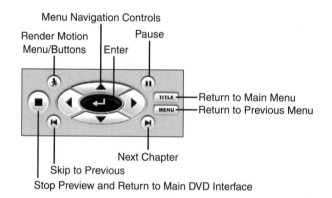

Menu Navigation Controls
Render Motion Menu/Buttons   Pause
Enter
TITLE ——Return to Main Menu
MENU ——Return to Previous Menu
Next Chapter
Skip to Previous
Stop Preview and Return to Main DVD Interface

5. Start previewing your DVD project using either of two methods:

   ▶ Use the Menu Navigation Control buttons to highlight the Topic A— Sub-Menu button and then click the Enter (crooked arrow) button.

   ▶ Click the Topic A—Sub-Menu button directly in the menu screen (something you can't do with a DVD remote control).

A Single-Click'll Do Ya

Unlike when building a menu, in Preview mode you don't need to double-click to go to another menu. A single click is all you need, the same as when using your remote control.

6. In the Topic A—Sub-Menu, click the Main Movie button and that video will play. You can then do one of two things:

   ▶ You can let it play to the end, in which case MyDVD automatically starts playing whatever the next button in the menu links to. This is a consumerish kind of DVD-authoring behavior and is not the way standard DVDs are supposed to work. I show you how to fix that in the next section.

▶ While the video is playing, you can click the Menu button in the remote control section to return to the Topic A—Sub-Menu. Clicking the Title button takes you back to the Main DVD menu.

7. Return to the Topic A—Sub-Menu by clicking the Menu button. Click the Scene Selection Menu button to open that menu and click any scene to go to that point in the video. Stop the video playback (the default behavior is to play the entire video from that chapter point) by clicking the Menu button in the remote control section. Doing so takes you back to the Topic A—Sub-Menu.

Even More Unexpected Consumerish Behavior

If you select a clip from the Scene Selection menu and let it run to the end of the entire video, it will not return you to the Scene Selection menu or to the Topic A—Sub-Menu. Instead it will start playing whatever the next button in the Topic A—Sub-Menu links to—in this case, the Slideshow. This is yet another example of consumerish DVD-authoring behavior that you will put the kibosh on in the next section.

Did you Know?

---

8. Click the Topic A—Sub-Menu Slideshow button. The music should change and the still images should display in succession for 5 seconds each (or whatever time you set). Let the slideshow play to the end; it returns you to the Topic A—Sub-Menu.

Drawback to Narrating a Slideshow

DVDs are interactive. Viewers know that. So, as they're watching your slideshow they might want to skip past some images (by clicking the Next Chapter button) rather than have them play for however much time you set in the Slideshow Options.

The problem with that is the music or narration restarts at its beginning each time they jump to the next scene. So, if you carefully crafted a nice narration to match the displayed slides, all that work will be for naught the moment a viewer presses the Next Chapter button.

Prosumer and professional DVD-authoring software lets you wrest that control away from the viewer by limiting certain actions while viewing selected assets. You know how some DVDs won't let you skip the FBI warning or the film company's animated logo. That's because the DVD's author switched off things like Fast Forward, Next Chapter, and Jump to the Main Menu for those assets.

Watch Out!

---

9. Return to the Main Menu by clicking the Home icon in the lower-left corner of the submenu or the Title remote control button.

10. Click the Topic B—Sub-Menu button to go to that menu. Click any of the video buttons you added to this menu. The video plays and does that irksome, consumerish thing of automatically playing the next video in the menu.

11. Click the Stop Preview Mode button to terminate the Preview mode and return to the main MyDVD interface.

Adding a First-Play Video and Fixing Some Links

Most Hollywood movies on DVD do not open with the Main Menu. They start by playing that darned FBI warning, perhaps a preview or two, a corporate logo, photos of the producer's pet gerbil, whatever.

In DVD parlance, that opening video is called **First Play**. MyDVD has a built-in feature that lets you do their version of First Play, called...well...Play First.

An Imperfect First-Play Methodology

Unfortunately, MyDVD's Play First mode is a less-than-ideal implementation of the First Play concept. In a MyDVD project, the Play First video can be only whatever video is linked to the first button in the Main Menu.

Normally, First Play videos are *not* accessible from within a menu. They simply play and the viewer does not have the option to see them again. In general, there'd be no reason to.

However, it is kind of cool to have a video play right after the viewer places a DVD in the player. In case this idea resonates with you, the next Try It Yourself explains how to do it.

The coming task also shows you how to resolve the consumerish behavior of your current DVD project. As it works now, when one video ends, instead of returning to a menu, MyDVD automatically starts playing the video associated with the next button in the menu. Fixing that is easy.

Try it Yourself   **Add the First-Play Feature and Fix Some Links**

Instead of using your existing Main Movie as the First Play (it's probably a bit too long to use as an introduction to your DVD), you will add another brief video clip to your Main Menu, move its button to the head of the line, and then make it the

First Play (or is it Play First?) asset. I also show you how to switch off the Play All mode that I've been complaining about. Here's how to do all that:

1. Open your project to the Main Menu. Click Add Files and track down a short video clip. Click Open. As shown in Figure 21.5, that adds a third button to your Main Menu (I renamed it First Play Video in Figure 21.5).

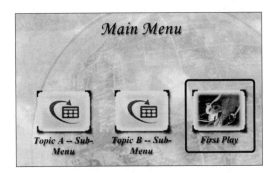

FIGURE 21.5
Adding a video asset with your Main Menu open automatically adds a button link to that asset after the two other buttons.

2. To make this video Play First, you first need to place it ahead of the other buttons (MyDVD looks for the first video in the opening menu when you switch on its Play First option). That's easy. Click, drag, and drop it ahead of the other buttons. As you drag it, a transparent version of the button and a flashing vertical line (both highlighted in Figure 21.6) display, showing you where the button will go.

FIGURE 21.6
It's a simple matter to drag and drop a button to change its position in a menu (I enlarged the vertical positioning line for emphasis).

3. To have MyDVD set that newly placed video as its First Play asset, click the Edit Style link at the top of the main DVD-authoring interface. That opens the interface shown in Figure 21.7.

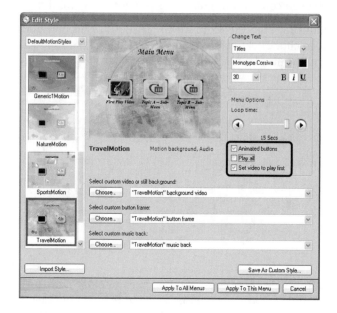

FIGURE 21.7
The Edit Style inter-
face is where you
change the look
and behavior of
your DVD's menus.
In the case of this
task, switch on Set
Video to Play First
and switch off
Play All.

4. I will explain this interface in detail in this chapter's next section, "Editing the Menu Style." To switch on MyDVD's Play First option, click the check box highlighted in Figure 21.7.

5. To switch off the consumerish behavior that I've referred to now several times, uncheck the Play All check box (also highlighted in Figure 21.7). Now, at the conclusion of video or slideshow, instead of playing the asset associated with the next button in the menu, MyDVD will return you to the menu and await your viewer's next remote button input.

Did you Know?

Chapters (Scenes) Should Still Play Through

Switching off the Play All mode should not change chapter viewing behavior. When you go to the Scene Selection menu and click a scene, MyDVD should play that scene and all others that follow it in the main video. At that video's conclusion, MyDVD should return you to the Scene Selection menu.

6. To complete the process, click either Apply to All Menus or Apply to This Menu. It doesn't matter which one you select because these two functions are applied to the entire project anyway.

7. Preview your project by clicking the Preview button. Your First Play video should start the show, and then the Main Menu should appear. Check out whether clips now behave as they should by clicking one in the Topic B— Sub-Menu. At its conclusion, MyDVD should return you automatically to that submenu.

8. Exit the Preview mode and save your project: Click File, Save.

Editing the Menu Style

Until now, you've been working with a default menu style—background, audio, buttons, and text—as well as **placeholder** wording: Click Here to Change Text, Untitled Menu 1, and so on. It's time to move beyond default settings and personalize your project.

Making Menu Style Changes

Try it Yourself

In MyDVD's Edit Style section, you can change text characteristics, menu and button graphics, menu music, and a couple other items. Here's how:

1. At the conclusion of the previous task, you ended up in the main MyDVD interface. If you're not there at this point, return to that location. Click the Edit Style button to open the interface you worked with in the previous task (I've highlighted some of its functions in Figure 21.8).

My Drop-Down List Has More Options Than Yours

By the Way

Figure 21.8 shows that I have nine Styles in my drop-down list. You probably have fewer. I have more because I've added some styles from Sonic's website and have created a couple of my own. I explain both means to beef up your Style selections later in this chapter and in the next chapter.

2. Take a quick look around the Edit Style interface shown in Figure 21.8. Clockwise from the upper left, it offers drop-down lists to change the menu style, menu title and button text characteristics, animated menu/button options, and customized menu/button selections.

3. Click the Menu Styles drop-down list (in the upper-left corner) and select Default Styles (MyDVD opens with Default Motion Styles selected). As shown in Figure 21.9, this updates the scrollable collection of menu templates so it now offers more than 25 menu styles that use static backgrounds. Scroll through them and click some to get an idea of how they look. As shown in Figure 21.9, when you select one, it appears in the Main Menu window.

▼

FIGURE 21.8
The Edit Style interface lets you change the look and feel of your DVD.

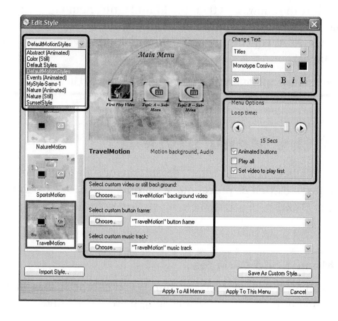

Check Out Changing Parameters

After selecting a Style from the Default Style group, note how the parameters in the Edit Style interface change. Beneath the Main Menu display MyDVD states that this menu has a still background with no audio. By default, it also unchecks Animated Buttons, but you can turn them back on. You can also add audio. (I cover both topics later in this Try It Yourself.)

4. Switch back to the DefaultMotionStyles menu backgrounds, scroll through the 10 motion menu backgrounds, and click SportsMotion (see Figure 21.10). Note that its parameters state it has a Motion Background and Audio.

5. There are three text-editing options in the Change Text drop-down list shown in Figure 21.11: Titles, Buttons, and All Text. Change the Title text style for the entire project (you cannot change text on an individual-menu basis) by selecting Titles from the Change Text drop-down list and then selecting whichever font, size, and other features (such as bold, italic, underline, and font color). In the example shown in Figure 21.11, I chose Team MT font style (MyDVD displays all the fonts you have installed on your PC), 52-point type, and Bold. As you make changes, they appear in the menu window.

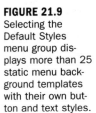

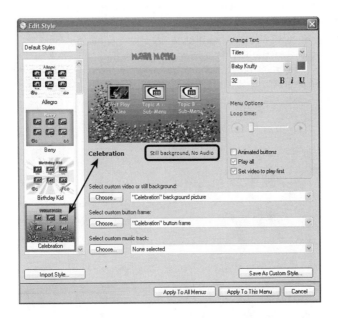

FIGURE 21.9
Selecting the
Default Styles
menu group dis-
plays more than 25
static menu back-
ground templates
with their own but-
ton and text styles.

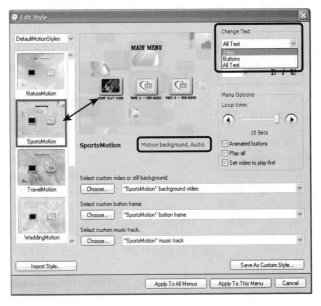

FIGURE 21.10
Choose
SportsMotion as a
best-fit template
for this chapter's
DVD project.

Change Button Font Style

You also can change the button font style using the same process. To do so, select Buttons from the Change Text drop-down list. Normally you'll want to make the title text larger than the button text, but if you want both the button and the title text to have the same characteristics and size, select All Text from the Change Text drop-down list and make your changes.

FIGURE 21.11
Use the Change Text features to alter your text's appearance. Use the highlighted Color selection window to change your font color.

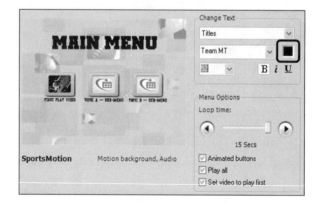

6. Change the font color by clicking the black box circled in Figure 21.11 to open the Color selection window shown in Figure 21.12. This is the standard Windows color selection tool. Click the Define Custom Colors button to gain a wider range of color options. Use the custom palette to select a color that suits you and click OK.

Working with Colors

Experiment with the Color selection palette. Click around in the large box on the right to select a hue and then drag the slider on the right to set its brightness (or luminance). Note how the numeric values in the six boxes change as you move the slider and crosshairs around. After you've selected a new color, click an empty Custom Colors box and then click the Add to Custom Colors button. Your new color will appear in the selected Custom Color box. Click OK to set that as your new font color.

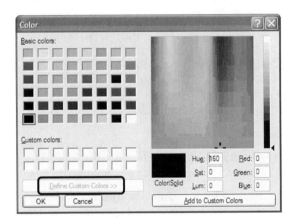

FIGURE 21.12
The Color selection box lets you select from a default palette of colors or create your own color. Click the highlighted Define Custom Colors button to open that extra palette.

7. Check out the Menu Options section shown in Figure 21.13. You've already dealt with two of them: Play All and Set Video to First Play. Here are brief reminders of those two, plus an explanation of the other two:

   ▶ **Loop Time**—How long the menu animation will play before restarting. Its maximum length is 15 seconds.

Changing Video Backgrounds Changes Animation Length

The menu animation default—and maximum—time is 15 seconds only because that is the length of the video used in MyDVD's default motion menus. If you replace a menu background (motion or static) with your own video, the menu and button animations will run for the length of your video background clip—up to one minute. I explain swapping out backgrounds a little later.

By the Way

   ▶ **Animated Buttons**—Checking this box means all the buttons created with video thumbnails will play when this menu is open. Keep this in its default checked condition.

   ▶ **Play All**—For your DVD to behave in a standard fashion, uncheck this box.

   ▶ **Set Video to Play First**—Because you've added a First Play video to this project, make sure this button is checked.

FIGURE 21.13
The Menu Options section gives you an extra level of control over your menu display.

8. At the bottom of the Edit Style interface are the three drop-down lists shown in Figure 21.14. Here's a list of what you can do with them:

   ▶ **Select Custom Video or Still Background**—This lets you choose a menu background still image or video from your own collection. If you use a video, MyDVD will play no more than 60 seconds before it starts looping it. It will play less if you adjust the loop time accordingly.

Did you Know?

Menu Background Aspect Ratio and Resolution

If you use a still image for a menu background, it should be in a 4:3 aspect ratio. If not, MyDVD will distort it to fit the TV screen. This is not the case for slideshow images. As you've seen, MyDVD adds frames to fill any gaps of images that are not in a 4:3 aspect ratio.

If your menu background image is less than 720×540 pixels for NTSC or 768×576 pixels for PAL, MyDVD will expand it to fit the menu, thereby reducing its quality.

   ▶ **Choose Custom Button Frame**—This offers 15 button frames that ship with MyDVD. As shown in Figure 21.15, you can use any of them to replace the frames used throughout your DVD project or on a menu-by-menu basis.

   ▶ **Select Custom Music Track**—This lets you select any compatible audio file (AC3, MP3, WAV, MPA, WMA, ABS, AIF, or AIFF) and use it with your menus (static or animated).

9. Feel free to change any of your project's attributes. You can start by changing the Style (Motion or Static) and changing the button frames, text font characteristics, and background. The Edit Style interface is a powerful feature of MyDVD.

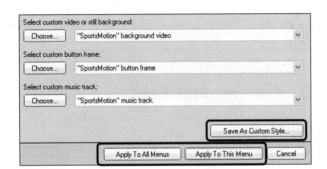

FIGURE 21.14
Use these three
options to further
customize your
project. The high-
lighted buttons let
you save your
changes as a cus-
tomized style and
apply your changes
to all menus or
only to the menu
displayed in the
Edit Style interface.

FIGURE 21.15
You can replace
the default button
style with one of
these custom
frames.

10. When you complete your customization, you can click the Save As Custom
Style button, highlighted earlier in Figure 21.14, to make this style immediately accessible in future projects. This can come in really handy if you have
a certain look you intend to use regularly.

Edit Style Customized Items

As you customize your project by adding customized backgrounds and music, those
items will show up in the drop-down lists. That's a nifty feature that speeds up
access to items you use regularly. Because you probably have not added custom
items yet, those drop-down lists likely have only the MyDVD SportsMotion default
motion menu items in them.

By the Way

11. You can choose to apply your menu changes to the currently displayed menu or to every menu in your project by clicking either of the two buttons highlighted earlier in Figure 21.14. Clicking either of those buttons closes the Edit Style.

Fixing Two Other Project Features

Stepping out of the task mode, I'll wrap up the menu-editing process by taking you through two additional items: changing thumbnail images and manually rearranging menu buttons.

Selecting Different Thumbnail Images

All the menu buttons that lead to videos use the first frame of each video as the thumbnail image on the button. However, you can select different frames that better represent each video.

Go to the Topic A—Sub-Menu. Probably the thumbnails for the Main Movie and the Topic A Chapters menu are the same. To remedy that redundancy, as shown in Figure 21.16, right-click a thumbnail and select Set Button Image.

FIGURE 21.16
Right-click a video button and select Set Button Image to change the thumbnail.

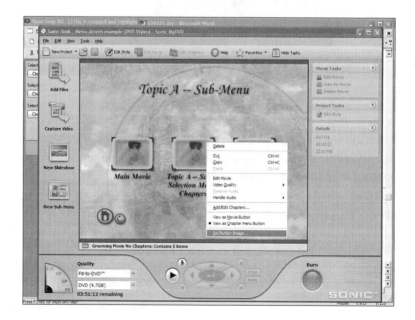

The screen shown in Figure 21.17 opens. Move the slider to a video frame that suits you and click Set. This returns you to the submenu with the new thumbnail image in place. Feel free to do that for some or all of the video clips and chapters in your project.

FIGURE 21.17
Use the slider to find a more representative button thumbnail image and then click Set.

Default Submenu Button Appearance

I mentioned earlier that buttons that link to submenus have the same default thumbnail image—a swooping arrow pointing to a collection of buttons. As you might have noticed, that's not the case for buttons that link to Chapter—or Scene Selection—menus. They use the first frame on the first scene in that submenu.

In any event, you cannot change that default swooping arrow, submenu thumbnail within MyDVD. You can, however, change the frame around it in the Edit Style interface. And you can change the swooping arrow thumbnail graphic by using Sonic Solutions Style Creator. I briefly explain that product later in this chapter in "Introducing Custom Templates." And I take you through some tasks about working with the Style Creator Photoshop plug-in in the next chapter.

By the Way

Arranging Buttons Manually

Earlier you moved a button to have its linked asset become the Play First video. That process is very simple. If you want buttons to appear in a different order, click the button you want to move and drag it ahead of its new location.

New to MyDVD 6 is the capability to place buttons anywhere you want on a menu. To do that, select View, Arrange Buttons Manually. You won't see anything change, but with that feature selected you now can drag and drop buttons anywhere you want.

Figure 21.18 shows how I rearranged the six buttons in the Topic B—Sub-Menu of individual clips. There are a few manual placement considerations:

▶ With the Manual Button Placement option turned on, you can have up to 12 buttons per menu (instead of 6 for automatic placement).

▶ MyDVD will not allow you to overlap buttons. So as you drag them around, you sometimes will not be able to move them.

▶ Auto-Arranging applies only to a single menu or a chain of menus, not to the entire project. A **chain** is a collection of linked menus created automatically by MyDVD when you add more than six buttons in a single menu.

▶ If, after manually adding more than six buttons to the menu, you switch back to Automatic Button Arranging (select View, Arrange Buttons Automatically), MyDVD will rearrange the buttons on all the menus in the current chain of menus and will add menus to ensure that no more than six buttons are on any single menu.

FIGURE 21.18
New to MyDVD 6 is the option to manually place buttons on a menu.

Introducing Custom Templates

As you increase your DVD production skills, you might want to create your own DVD menu styles and perhaps share them with others on the Sonic Solutions website. I'll give you a brief overview of the process here and go into greater detail in Chapter 22, "Creating Custom MyDVD Templates with Style Creator."

In general, to create a custom style, you use a plug-in (a small program within a program) called Sonic Solutions Style Creator. That plug-in works with Photoshop Elements ($99) and Photoshop 6 and 7. It does not work with Photoshop CS ($649), the current version, but Sonic Solutions plans to update the plug-in for the next release of MyDVD.

Even if you're not familiar with Photoshop Elements, it's not all that difficult to use it and the Style Creator plug-in to build new menu elements (typically button thumbnails and frames) to meet your project needs.

All you need to do is follow a few naming conventions and then Style Creator automatically builds a template, assigning certain characteristics to graphics with particular names.

Visit the Sonic Solutions MyDVD Styles website at `http://styles.mydvd.com/default.asp`, shown in Figure 21.19, to get a feel for how this works.

FIGURE 21.19
You can download MyDVD user-created menu templates at the Sonic Solutions MyDVD Styles website.

Even if you don't post any templates, you can download all the styles from the MyDVD Styles website at no charge.

Importing a Style

To add a downloaded style to your MyDVD collection, go to the Edit Style interface and click the Import Style button (in the lower-left corner of Figure 21.20), locate the Style on your hard drive, and click Open.

MyDVD will pop up a little Import Style dialog box. But your only "option" is to Create a New Style Category (MyDVD won't let you add styles to the two default style groups). Click Import.

As shown in Figure 21.20, the new template shows up on the left side, ready for immediate use.

FIGURE 21.20
Use the Edit Style, Import Style feature to add new menu templates. I added the Cinema Demo style that I downloaded from the MyDVD Styles website.

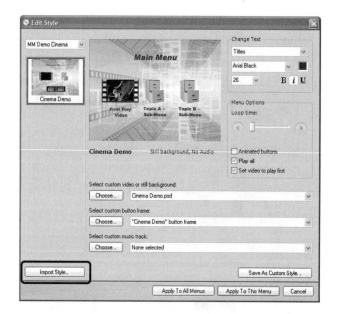

Recording Videos Direct-to-Disc

You know what a pain it is to use your camcorder to view a video on your TV. You have to connect the cables and then fast forward or rewind to find a clip that interests you.

A more elegant viewing approach is MyDVD's Direct-to-DVD option. This feature lets you capture video and transfer it directly to a DVD. You can add an opening menu and a chapter menu, and you can have MyDVD automatically select chapter points or you can select them manually.

After MyDVD burns the DVD, it's simply a matter of viewing your DVD with your set-top DVD player. You don't have to hassle with extra cables, and you can skip quickly to your favorite scenes. Plus, this is an easy way to archive videos.

Taking the Direct-to-DVD Route

Try it Yourself

▼

If you've used MyDVD's video capture module, this DVD burning procedure will be remarkably easy. If not, I think you'll still find that it's pretty effortless. Here's how to do it:

1. Connect your camcorder to the PC and turn it on to the VCR mode.

2. There are two ways to access the Direct-to-DVD module. Use one of the following to open the interface shown in Figure 21.21:

   ▶ In the main DVD-authoring interface, select Tools, Direct-to-DVD (MyDVD will ask if you want to save the current project before proceeding).

   ▶ In the MyDVD opening interface, click the Video button and then select Direct-to-Disc.

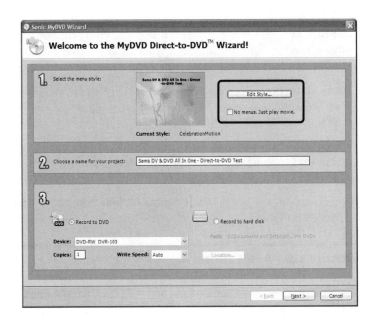

FIGURE 21.21
Using MyDVD's Direct-to-DVD option is a quick and easy way to archive and play back your videos.

▼

3. The MyDVD Direct-to-DVD Wizard, shown in Figure 21.21, gives you two options: You can select a menu style to suit your taste, or you can opt to *not* have a menu, instead having the DVD play your video automatically. In this case, select a new style.

4. You must name your DVD; otherwise, MyDVD won't let you go to the next step.

5. Place a recordable DVD in your drive.

6. If you have more than one DVD recorder, select the correct one. You can record the video directly to your hard drive as an MPEG file instead. After you've made your selection, click Next. That opens the familiar Video Capture interface shown in Figure 21.22.

7. The Video Capture interface presents several options. Here's a brief run-down:

   ▶ **Record Settings**—You can accept the default, highest-quality video compression setting or click this button to access a drop-down list of two lower-quality settings (as you adjust the quality, MyDVD updates the Record Time Available in the Details window at the bottom of the screen).

   ▶ **Capture Length**—Normally, you'll stop recording manually. If you have a specific duration in mind, you can have MyDVD stop recording automatically by setting a time limit here.

   ▶ **Scene Detection**—If you want MyDVD to create a chapter menu for your DVD, you can have MyDVD automatically detect scene changes or you can do it manually.

   ▶ **Scene Detection Settings**—If you select Automatic Scene Detection, this button becomes accessible. You've seen its interface before. It lets you set the scene change detection sensitivity.

8. When you're ready, use the VCR-like controls to cue your tape. Then, click the red Record button.

Did you Know?

Analog Recording—Add Preroll

If you are recording from an analog camcorder/VCR, rewind to a few seconds before your record start point, start playing the video, and then click the red Record button when you want to start recording.

---

9. When you're done, either click the red button to stop recording or watch as MyDVD does that automatically. MyDVD then transcodes the video and burns the disc.

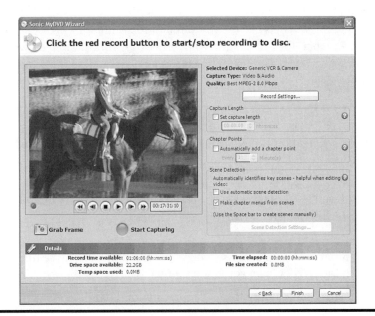

FIGURE 21.22
Add chapters and
adjust the video
quality of your
recording using the
MyDVD Video
Capture Wizard.

Burning Your DVD Project to a Recordable Disc

Before tackling the final step in the DVD production process, take your DVD on one more preview test drive.

To do that, return to the main DVD-authoring interface, select File, Recent Projects, and then click your project name.

Click the Enter Preview Mode button. This time you might choose to render some or all of the animated menus. To do that, click the Create Menu Animation Runner icon for each menu.

Rendering Time

The time to render depends on the length of the loop time. If you use a long video clip, it will take much longer to render your motion menu.

By the Way

Check all your buttons to make sure they go where you expect them to go. Click the Menu and Title buttons to make sure they work correctly. And play some video and slideshow assets all the way through to ensure that their **end actions**, what happens when they finish, are what you expected. Usually you want to return to a menu, but when a chapter concludes, it should go to the next clip in the original video.

Try it Yourself   **Burn Your DVD**

When you're satisfied that all your menus look and act as you expected them to, it's time to burn your DVD project to a recordable disc. Here's how:

1. Adjust the overall MPEG video compression quality of your project using the drop-down list Quality in the lower-left corner of the main interface, highlighted in Figure 21.23. Here are your choices:

   ▶ Fit-to-DVD reduces the overall quality of longer projects to ensure they fit on a DVD. Otherwise, you can select from a list of settings that match VHS tape recording terminology.

   ▶ HQ—High-Quality (least compression and best looking).

   ▶ SP—Standard Play.

   ▶ LP—Long Play.

   ▶ EP—Extended Play (highest compression and lowest quality).

FIGURE 21.23
Use this tool to set the overall project MPEG compression quality setting. Higher video quality means less compression with better-looking video and more space consumed per minute of video on the DVD.

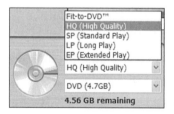

2. You might want to set individual videos to a quality setting that does not match the overall project quality setting. Suppose, for instance, you want your main video to run at the highest setting but other videos to be lower to ensure they all fit on the DVD. To do that, as shown in Figure 21.24, right-click the video's button, select Video Quality, and then select the quality from the list shown.

FIGURE 21.24
Adjust an individual video's quality setting using this right-click menu.

3. Insert a recordable DVD into your DVD recordable drive. That likely will open the window shown in Figure 21.25. Click Cancel.

FIGURE 21.25
Inserting a recordable DVD into your DVD recordable drive usually pops up this window.

4. Return to the main MyDVD interface and click the Burn button. It's the big red button at the bottom of the main interface. (See Figure 21.26).

FIGURE 21.26
Click the Burn button to start the DVD recording process.

5. The Make Disc Setup window, shown in Figure 21.27, opens. You have very few options (higher-level DVD-authoring products typically offer several more). In this case, you probably will want to accept the defaults and click OK.

A Couple DVD Recording Options

If you have more than one DVD recordable drive, you'll need to tell MyDVD which one to use. And if you want to make more than one DVD, you'll need to change that number. If you do make more than one, MyDVD prompts you when it's time to insert a new, blank DVD recordable disc.

FIGURE 21.27
The MyDVD Make Disc Setup window has very few options.

6. You can watch your progress at the bottom of the main MyDVD interface, and you can stop the recording by clicking Cancel.

In a few minutes you'll have a finished DVD. When completed, insert it into your nearest DVD set-top player and see how it has turned out. Unless you encounter a rare compatibility problem with an older player, your DVD should play back without a hitch. The first time I created a DVD and saw how smoothly it worked on my home TV, I realized that this was "it." Suddenly the possibilities were (and are) endless.

Summary

This chapter took you through the final stages in the MyDVD DVD-authoring process. You started by previewing your project to see how the menu buttons link to assets and other menus, and you viewed the videos and slideshows in action.

Then you used the Edit Style interface to fine-tune your project's look and feel. Even in this consumer-level product, you have detailed control over the menu backgrounds (static or video), button frames, text styles, and menu music.

Outside the Edit Style interface, you edited your menu title and button text, changed the button thumbnail images, dragged and dropped to rearrange the button placement, and switched on Arrange Buttons Manually to place them where they work best for you.

Finally, you tried the Direct-to-Disc DVD production option and then burned your complete project using the streamlined and simplified process in MyDVD. You successfully (I'm guessing) played the resulting DVD on your home DVD set-top. Congratulations!

CHAPTER 22

Creating Custom MyDVD Templates with Style Creator

What You'll Learn in This Chapter:

▶ Introducing Sonic Solutions Style Creator
▶ Taking a close look at the plug-in
▶ Changing a template background
▶ Setting text boundaries and font characteristics
▶ Examining button characteristics
▶ Editing buttons and button elements
▶ Testing your template edits in MyDVD

MyDVD ships with numerous menu templates that give you a wide range of DVD project options, from a family-friendly look to several corporate styles.

At some point, you might want to create a project with a more customized look and feel. Sonic Solutions offers Style Creator, a menu template creation tool that helps you craft entire menus that work in MyDVD. In effect, Style Creator turns a consumer-level DVD-authoring application—MyDVD—into a prosumer product.

In this chapter I introduce Style Creator's powerful functionality and show you how to make changes to an existing template and how to create graphics from scratch for use in a template.

Introducing Sonic Solutions Style Creator

I mentioned in the previous chapter, "Authoring DVDs with MyDVD 6: Part 2," that Sonic Solutions offers a Photoshop plug-in you can use to create menu templates or styles for MyDVD.

By the Way

> **Macros Automate Processes**
>
> Style Creator is a **macro**. Those who have worked with macros in word processors, for instance, know they duplicate some number of user-defined steps. The same holds true for this plug-in. When you save a template using it, you'll see it perform various functions (very quickly) as it converts your graphics into a template file that will work within MyDVD.

Templates are a great way to give DVDs with similar themes a consistent look. For instance, a production company that specializes in weddings can use a template to simplify its workload while giving clients a product that matches any demos they've viewed.

Those templates can have static or animated menus and buttons as well as customized button highlight features. The highlights can change color or shading as viewers navigate their remotes to them or select them.

How Style Creator Works

Style Creator takes a carefully formatted and named set of graphics you've created in Photoshop or Photoshop Elements and converts it to the style template file type that works within MyDVD.

Style Creator started (and continues) its life as a tool for Sonic Solutions software engineers and artists to create menu templates or styles to ship with MyDVD (and now for retail sale in Style Template Packs). Each template has very specific rules about where buttons appear on MyDVD menus and how large they can be. In the meantime, Sonic Solutions realized the value that Style Creator gave its users, so it released it to the public on its website.

Visit the Sonic Style Creator website at `http://styles.mydvd.com/default.asp` to download both the plug-in and, at no charge, a collection of custom styles created by MyDVD users.

As we went to press, Sonic was about to release a number of MyDVD Style Packs for retail sale. Details about pack contents and pricing were not available. Check out Sonic's website for an update—`www.sonic.com`.

Taking a Close Look at the Plug-in

Style Creator works only if you create a layered Photoshop graphic that follows specific rules. Figure 22.1 shows a listing of Photoshop Elements layers with some of the naming conventions used by Style Creator.

I Mean Photoshop *and* Photoshop Elements

Later in this chapter I present several tasks on how to use Style Creator to build MyDVD templates. Style Creator works in both Photoshop Elements and the full, professional version of Photoshop (only with older versions 6 and 7, not the current CS version). I use Photoshop Elements for those tasks because it retails for only $99 versus $649 for Photoshop (you can download a trial version of Photoshop Elements).

So, from now on, when I note how something looks or works in Photoshop Elements, the same thing applies to the full version of Photoshop (versions 6 and 7). Both products use the same layering approach to graphics and have very similar functionality and interfaces.

By the time Sonic Solutions releases the next version of MyDVD, it plans to have updated the Style Creator plug-in to run in Photoshop CS. When that updated version is ready, Sonic will post it on its Style Creator website: http://styles.mydvd.com/default.asp.

By the Way

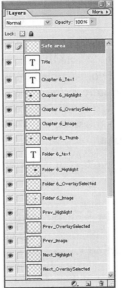

FIGURE 22.1
You must exactly follow the Style Creator layer naming conventions for it to work.

By the
Way

Style Creator's Rulebook

A full explanation of all that Style Creator offers along with all its rules would consume much more than one chapter. I've limited this chapter's discussion to an introduction and a basic explanation.

For more details, read through the 65-page Style Creator Tutorial. You'll find it on the
Sonic Solutions Style Creator website: `http://styles.mydvd.com/createastyle.`
`asp`. You'll need the industry-standard document viewer Adobe Acrobat Reader to
read it; it's available for free download at `http://www.adobe.com`.

Style Creator recognizes each layer name and treats whatever graphic it finds in
each layer according to its intended use.

For instance, the **Home_Image** layer is the button that returns viewers to the
DVD's main menu. When you import a Style Creator Style template into MyDVD,
the DVD-authoring application automatically creates a link from whatever
graphic is in the Home_Image Photoshop layer to the DVD project's main menu.

All templates that ship with MyDVD place that Main Menu (house icon) button
in the lower-left corner of the menu. One advantage of Style Creator is that you
choose where to place that graphic and how it will look.

Each MyDVD button graphic (with the suffix _Image) has up to four other graphic types associated with it: Highlight, Selected, Activated, and Text.

- ▶ The Highlight layer defines the **hotspot zone**, which is the area in which
  the button resides (hotspot zones cannot overlap).

- ▶ The Selected and Activated graphics display when the viewer navigates the
  remote control to a button (Selected) and then presses Enter (Activated) on
  the remote. These typically are simple highlights. In the templates that ship
  with MyDVD, they are usually rectangles or circles around the perimeter of
  a button or frame. Although the Style Creator puts them in different layers,
  they have to have exactly the same shape to work properly. The only difference is their highlight color.

- ▶ The Text layer defines where text appears relative to its associated button.

By the
Way

Start with Photoshop File—Finish with MyDVD Style

After you've created or changed a Photoshop PSD file or template, you use the Style
Creator Photoshop plug-in to convert it to a style for use in MyDVD. I explain that
later in the chapter, in the section "Editing Buttons and Button Elements."

Installing Photoshop Elements

Installing the Style Creator plug-in is done in one of two ways: for Photoshop 6 or 7, it's done automatically using an executable file that searches your hard drive for the Photoshop folder and adds two files to two Photoshop subfolders. For Photoshop Elements, you need to manually Copy/Paste two files to two different file folders (Sonic Solutions plans to make this an automatic install with the release of the updated version of Style Creator).

Before you install Style Creator, you need to have installed Photoshop Elements. If you have a copy, great. If not, download the trial version of Photoshop Elements. Locate it at the Adobe website at `www.adobe.com`; look under Products, Digital Imaging, and click Tryouts to track it down.

To simplify things, when you install Photoshop Elements, accept the default location: `C:\Program Files\Adobe\Photoshop Elements 2` (or 3—Adobe had just released version 3 as we went to press but was using version 2 on the Tryout site).

---

30 Days and Out

The trial version of Photoshop Elements is equivalent to the full version, but it expires 30 days after you install it.

By the Way

Installing the Style Creator Plug-in

If you have Photoshop 6 or 7, download the Style Creator plug-in and two other files—a sample template Photoshop file and a tutorial—from the Sonic website: `http://styles.mydvd.com/default.asp`. Double-click the .EXE file to automatically load the plug-in into the appropriate Photoshop file folders.

If you have Photoshop Elements, the *executable* install file does not work, so you need to download its two constituent parts: SonicHidden.8BF and SonicStyleCreator.8LI. Also download the other two files available on the site: ExampleSonicStyle.psd and Style Creator Tutorial.pdf.

To install the plug-in for Photoshop Elements, follow these two steps:

1. Copy SonicHidden.8BF and paste it into the `C:\Program Files\Adobe\Photoshop Elements 2\Plug-ins\Filters` folder.

2. Copy SonicStyleCreator.8LI to the `C:\Program Files\Adobe\Photoshop Elements 2\Plug-ins\Automate` folder.

To ensure that all went well, open Photoshop Elements (or Photoshop). You'll see the splash screen shown in Figure 22.2. Note that it tracks how many days you have left in your trial period.

FIGURE 22.2
The trial version of Photoshop Elements times out in 30 days.

Click Try to open the user interface. Check to see that the plug-in loaded properly by selecting File, Automation Tools and then noting whether Create Style for Sonic MyDVD is listed as an option (see Figure 22.3). If not, check the two file folders noted previously and make sure you copied and pasted the proper files to those respective folders.

FIGURE 22.3
Check Photoshop Elements to see whether the Style Creator plug-in loaded properly.

Changing a Template Background

In the next four sections, you'll use Photoshop Elements to edit an existing Photoshop PSD file set up to be a MyDVD menu. Then you'll run the Style Creator plug-in to convert that PSD file to a MyDVD Style.

PSD—Photoshop Document

PSD—Photoshop Document—is the standard file extension for Photoshop files. The PSD MyDVD Style Creator template file you downloaded from the Sonic website is a straightforward, layered Photoshop file. After you've made some changes to it, you'll convert it to a style using the Sonic Solutions Style Creator Photoshop plug-in.

By the Way

This is the easiest way to get an overview of the template-creation process, to take a look at the precise nomenclature required for the plug-in to work properly, and to see how button highlight layers work.

An Introduction Only

The purpose of the coming tasks is to introduce you to what Photoshop Elements can do to help you create customized menus and buttons. Because this is not a book about Photoshop Elements, sometimes I'll combine several steps into one task item and minimize the explanations of the associated features.

By the Way

Replace a Background

Try it Yourself

Even if you've never worked with Photoshop Elements, you can make Style Creator menu-style templates. Templates require very specific layer names, so you should take this first stab at creating a menu style template by editing an existing, conforming layered graphic. We'll start simply—by changing the graphic menu's background. Here's how to do that:

1. With Photoshop Elements open, select File, Open, and navigate to wherever you stored the Style Creator sample file. Select ExampleSonicStyle.psd and click Open.

Why Change the Background?

MyDVD lets you add any background in any existing template, so why do that inside Photoshop Elements? If you change a background in MyDVD for an existing template, that's all you've changed. The buttons and other menu elements remain unchanged. The purpose of this chapter's tasks is to take an existing template that has properly named layers and show you how you can **convert** it into a completely updated template that you want to use.

By the Way

2. The goal now is to make your workspace look similar to Figure 22.4. You do that by minimizing (or closing) the How To and Hints folders. Then click and drag the Layers tab from the upper-right corner to the workspace to open it (or select Window, Layers). Drag its lower edge to make it taller and display more layers.

FIGURE 22.4
Arrange your Photoshop Elements workspace along these lines.

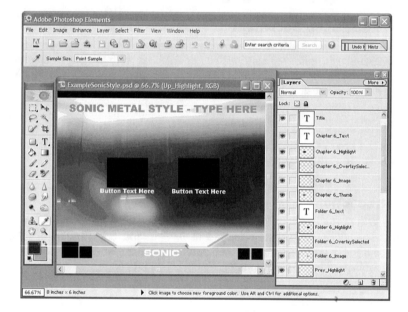

3. Each of the boxes in the Layers palette represents one layer of the image. Turn off the eyeball for every layer except the last one, Background. You can click them one at a time to turn them off individually or click the top eyeball—Safe Area—and hold down the mouse button as you drag it down that column of the layer palette, leaving the last eyeball (Background) turned on. Your image and Layer palette should look similar to Figure 22.5.

4. You will replace the Sonic Solutions background with a simple pattern. I show you three ways to do that:

▶ Pasting in a graphic or image

▶ Using the Paint tool

▶ Using the Gradient tool

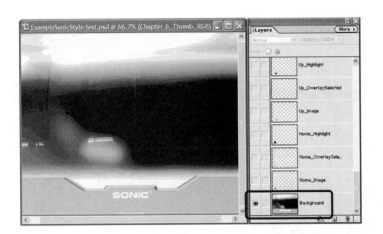

5. To paste in a graphic, select File, Open; track down and select the image you want to use (I selected a sample photo from the My Pictures folder) and then click Open. That opens a new file in the Photoshop interface and makes it the **active** file (the one you are working on currently).

6. Copy that graphic by selecting Select, All (keyboard shortcut—Ctrl+A) to highlight the entire graphic (you'll see a dashed border around the graphic) and then select Edit, Copy (or Ctrl+C) to copy it.

7. Click the MyDVD ExampleSonicStyle.psd file to make it active (check the Layer list to see that the word Background is highlighted—if not, click Background), select Select, All (that places a dashed border around it), press Delete to remove the entire Sonic Solutions background, and then select Edit, Paste (or Ctrl+V). Your interface should look something like Figure 22.6.

Background Graphic Resolution Issues

When making menus using the Style Creator plug-in, you should use background graphics that are 768 pixels×576 pixels. The Style Creator plug-in scales all non-768×576 background images to 768×576. This shrinking, expanding, or skewing of graphics that don't match this resolution or its 4:3 aspect ratio results in distorted or lower-quality graphics. You might note later when you open a new Photoshop Document that 768×576 is a standard Photoshop PAL preset, but it works fine in NTSC as well.

By the Way

FIGURE 22.6
To replace the MyDVD Style template background with an existing graphic, use the Copy/Paste method.

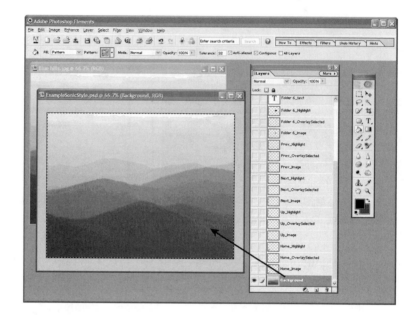

8. To use the Paint Can tool to create a new background, start by deleting the current background. To do that, click Background in the Layers palette to make it the active layer, Select, All, and press Delete.

9. Select the Paint Can icon shown in Figure 22.7, click the Fill drop-down list at the top, select Pattern (the only other choice is Foreground), and select a Pattern from the palette to the right of the word Pattern (I chose a brick pattern). Now, as shown in Figure 22.7, move your cursor over the ExampleSonicStyle.psd window (it turns into a paint can) and click. The window fills with the selected pattern.

10. To use the Gradient tool, start by removing the newly created Paint layer. Click Background in the Layers palette to make it the active layer, select Select, All, and press Delete.

11. Select the Gradient tool, highlighted in Figure 22.8, click its drop-down display to select a gradient, and then click and drag a line within the ExampleSonicStyle.psd window to add a gradient background.

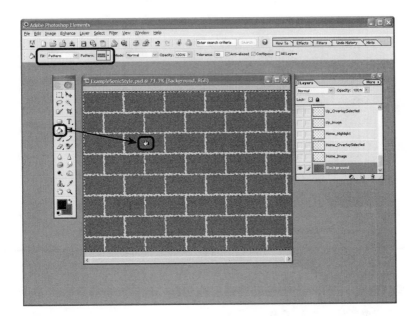

FIGURE 22.7
Use a Photoshop pattern and the Paint Can tool to create a new background for your style template.

Gradient Tool Tips

If you click Edit (in the Photoshop Elements Main Menu bar) or double-click the gradient pattern to the left of the Edit button, that will open a Gradient Editor. There you can customize the gradient.

The length, placement, and angle of the line you drag across the ExampleSonicStyle.psd window determine the direction, flow, and relative color amounts of the gradient.

You can click and drag that line as many times as you want until you create a "look" you like.

---

12. Save your project by selecting File, Save As; then navigate to a file folder of your choice (the Photoshop Elements file folder is a logical location), give your project a new name, such as **ExampleSonicStyle-test**, and then click Save. This creates a Photoshop PSD file, not a MyDVD Style Template. You'll do that later.

FIGURE 22.8
Use the Gradient tool to add a colorful background to your MyDVD Style template. The characteristics of the line you drag and drop in the window—length, angle, and placement—determine the gradient's appearance. I enlarged that line for emphasis.

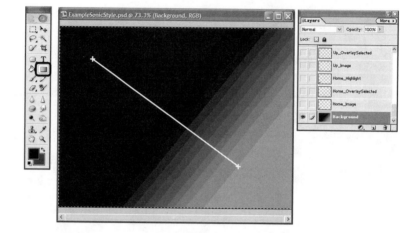

Setting Text Boundaries and Font Characteristics

At first glance, Style Creator has one nonintuitive feature. No matter what you write in the Text layer, MyDVD ends up putting something else there when you first display this template in the Menu Editor. For example, as shown in Figure 22.9, the edited sample template's Title layer reads, This Is Where Text Will Go in a MyDVD Project. But, were you to import that template as is into MyDVD and view it in the Menu Editor window, that line would read, Click Here to Change Text.

The same concept holds true for buttons with Text labels. No matter what you write within the template's Text layer, MyDVD automatically replaces that with the name of the asset to which that button links.

FIGURE 22.9
No matter what text you put in the title line, MyDVD will replace it with Click Here to Change Text. Use the highlighted Text tool to highlight your text and then use the Text options to change font characteristics.

Text Features

Placing text in your Style Template does three things:

▶ Delineates the location and maximum width of the text line, be it Title or Button text.

▶ Sets the font, color, size, and alignment (although you can change these characteristics within MyDVD's Edit Style interface).

▶ Denotes an area in which MyDVD will not allow users to place any buttons.

To change text characteristics within Photoshop Elements is easy. Here's a quick explanation about how to change the Title text (I cover Button text later in this chapter):

1. Select the Title layer by clicking it in the Layers palette.

2. Click the Text tool, highlighted in Figure 22.9, and drag it across the Title text to highlight it.

3. Change the font face, size, and color. To change the space in which MyDVD will let you place a title within this template, add or remove letters (it doesn't matter what letters you use). Press Enter if you want to increase the height of the text boundary (keeping in mind that you are taking away space for buttons).

Examining Button Characteristics

What really sets customized menus apart from the crowd is their buttons and button highlights. Each button has an associated hotspot zone—called Highlight in Style Creator. In addition, it might have a thumbnail video-still locator—called Thumb—and up to two associated highlight graphics, Selected and Activated. Style Creator lets you give your buttons and their associated graphics virtually any look you want.

Try it Yourself   Checking Out Button Features

Before making changes to the buttons in the sample template, you should look at the various button types and see how their associated elements work together. Here's how you do this:

1. Turn off all the eyeballs in your ExampleSonicStyle layer listing. Using Figure 22.10 as a reference, scroll to the Chapter layers and switch on the Chapter 6_Image and Chapter 6_Thumb eyeballs. Here's what those two elements are all about:

   ▶ When MyDVD sees the word *Chapter* in a style template, it knows it's a button that will take viewers to a video, a slideshow, or a Chapter (scene selection) submenu. It also will have a thumbnail image (or video clip) inside its frame.

   ▶ Chapter 6_Image is the frame that surrounds that thumbnail.

   ▶ Chapter 6_Thumb is a blue rectangle that defines where the video or still image thumbnail will appear.

   ▶ The number 6 refers to the maximum number of buttons that can appear on a MyDVD menu that uses this particular template. If you add more than six menu buttons (in this case), MyDVD automatically creates another menu. But if you use the manual button placement option within MyDVD, you can place as many buttons in a menu as you can fit.

FIGURE 22.10
The Chapter 6_Image and Chapter 6_Thumb graphic layers define the appearance and functionality of this button.

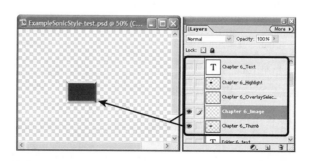

2. Turn on the other three associated eyeballs in this order: Chapter 6_OverlaySelected, Chapter 6_Text, and Chapter 6_Highlight. As you step through these three chapter button elements, you'll see how they work (Figure 22.11 has all but the Highlight layer switched on):

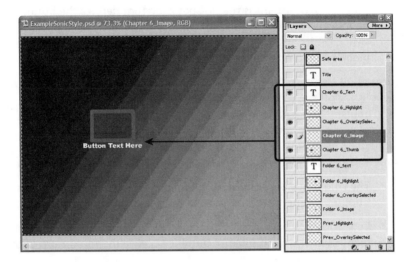

FIGURE 22.11
Additional button elements: OverlaySelected and Text.

▶ Chapter 6_OverlaySelected is a red box that displays when the viewer navigates the remote control to that button.

Overlay Graphics Can Be Any Color and Opacity

Did you Know?

You'll discover that all the OverlaySelected graphics in this example template are red. That means when a viewer moves the remote to that button, a red border will appear indicating that button is selected. You can select any color for the Overlay graphics—Selected and Activated.

The only caveat is that you need to use that color on all overlays of the same type. That is, if you use blue for one OverlaySelected graphic, you need to use blue on the rest of the OverlaySelected graphics. You'll want to use a different color for the OverlayActivated graphics so viewers will see something different when they click the remote on a button.

You also can use any opacity setting on Overlay graphics so your background and/or button shows through.

▶ This template does not have an OverlayActivated layer (the highlight when the viewer clicks on a button). You will add one later in this chapter.

▶ The Chapter 6_*Text* defines a placeholder for whatever text you want to add there later in MyDVD. In this template the text is white and hard to see on the checkerboard background. To see it, as shown in Figure 22.11, click the Background eyeball.

▶ Chapter 6_Highlight is the hotspot zone that defines the button's boundaries (button highlights or hotspot zones cannot overlap). If you switch on its display (by displaying that layer's eyeball) you'd see a black rectangle that would cover the entire button.

3. Turn off all those eyeballs. Using Figure 22.12 as a reference, turn on the eyeballs for all the remaining button_Image layers: Folder 6_Image, Prev_Image, Next_Image, Up_Image, and Home_Image. You also can turn on the OverlaySelected layers to see how they look. Turning on the black Highlight layers (that define each button's hotspot zone) will cover up each button. Each of these buttons has a specific function in MyDVD:

▶ The Folder button links to all submenus, with the exception of a Chapter submenu, which uses a Chapter button.

▶ Prev and Next take viewers to the previous or next menu in a chain of menus (when the number of buttons exceeds the maximum allowed by the Style template).

▶ Up takes viewers from a submenu to its parent menu.

▶ Home takes viewers to the main opening menu.

By the
Way

Gone with the Standard DVD Function Buttons

All menu templates that ship with MyDVD use the same graphics—triangles in circles, swooping arrows, and the small house icon—for their respective standard DVD functions: Previous and Next, Submenu (Folder), and Main Menu (Home).

The cool thing about Style Creator is that you can use it to completely change those, and any other, buttons that will appear in projects created using MyDVD. Style Creator lets you create customized, professional-looking DVDs with a consumer-priced product.

4. Experiment with these button types by clicking their associated elements on and off. You'll see that the Highlight hotspot zones vary in size, depending on the size of the button and that the OverlaySelected graphic is always a red box or circle. As I mentioned earlier, you can make any set of Overlay graphics whatever color you choose.

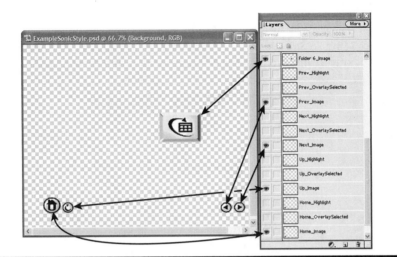

FIGURE 22.12
Each familiar button type in the Style Creator template has a different standard DVD function.

Editing Buttons and Button Elements

A button is not a simple thing. It consists of several layers:

▶ The button graphic itself (the Image layer)

▶ Its overlay layer(s) (Selected and/or Activated)

▶ Its Highlight (hotspot) zone

▶ The Thumbnail area (for buttons with images or videos playing in them)

There are certain rules that apply to buttons—such as, Highlights can't overlap and Overlays must equal the size and shape of the button graphic.

Despite the caveats, after you get the hang of working with graphical creation tools in Photoshop Elements, you'll readily create buttons for MyDVD templates that match your DVD production needs.

Creating a Button

Try it Yourself

Creating a button from scratch or editing one in an existing template means adding or changing graphics on several layers. You'll start with the button graphic itself and then tackle its hotspot and overlays in the next task.

It's sometimes easier to create a new button as a separate graphic and then paste it into a template. Here's how to do that:

1. Open a new blank image by selecting File, New. As shown in Figure 22.13, select 768×576 Std. PAL from the Preset Sizes drop-down list. Click the button next to Transparent in the Contents section and then click OK.

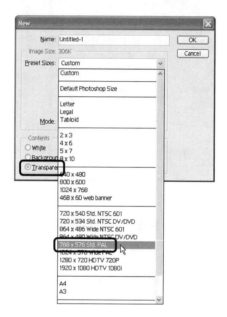

2. Using Figure 22.14 as a guide, create a new button graphic by selecting the Shape Drawing tool from the toolbar and selecting the Rounded Rectangle (or a shape of your choice). Then click and drag a shape in the bottom-left corner of the screen, give it a style by using the Style drop-down menu (click its wing-out menu and choose a style group and individual style—I chose Bevels, Simple Inner), and select a color from the Color swatch.

3. To add text to the button, click the Text tool (see Figure 22.15). Then select font characteristics (I chose Times New Roman, 36 Point, Bold, light blue), position the cursor over the left side of the button to ensure your text fits on the button, and type `Main Menu`.

4. Adding text to a Photoshop graphic automatically creates a new text layer called, in this case, Main Menu. If you didn't properly position the text on the button graphic, you can use the Move tool (shown in Figure 22.15) to change the text's location.

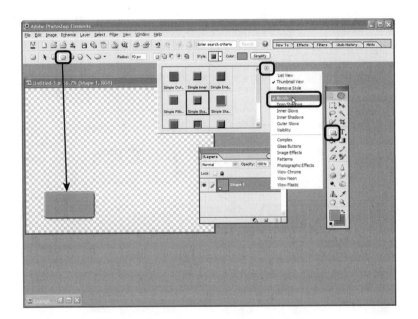

FIGURE 22.14
Use the Photoshop Elements Shape Drawing tool and its associated styles and colors to create a new menu button.

Move Tool   Text Tool

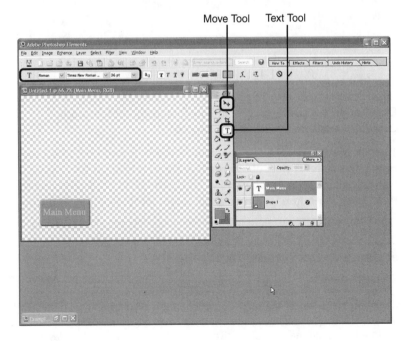

FIGURE 22.15
The Text tool is a simple way to clarify your button's function. Use the Move tool to fine-tune your text placement.

5. You need to merge the text and shape layers into one layer before adding the button to your menu template. As shown in Figure 22.16, from the main menu, select Layer, Merge Visible (depending on circumstances, your only option might be Merge Layers—that'll work too).

FIGURE 22.16
Merge layers by selecting Layer, Merge Visible (or Merge Layers).

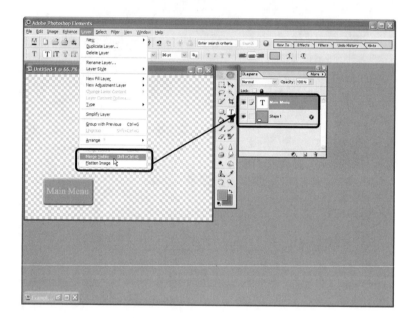

6. To add that newly merged Main Menu button to your template takes a few steps. Start by selecting Select, All (Ctrl+A) from the main menu. Select Edit, Copy (or press Ctrl+C) to copy the merged layer, and return to ExampleSonicStyle by clicking its window.

7. Turn off all the ExampleSonicStyle layer eyeballs and then select the Home_Image layer (just above the Background layer at the bottom of the list) by clicking its name. As shown in Figure 22.17, it displays the return-to-main-menu house icon used in all menu templates that ship with MyDVD.

Did you Know?

Selecting a Layer Versus Displaying It

Clicking a layer's eyeball displays whatever is in that layer but does not select the layer. If you want to edit a layer, you must click its name to select it, which also displays it. If you fail to select the layer and attempt to do some editing in the graphic's window, you'll end up changing a different layer or adding a new layer. If you inadvertently add a layer (and thereby fail to give it a Style Creator recognized layer name), the Style Creator plug-in might not be able to save the PSD graphic as a template.

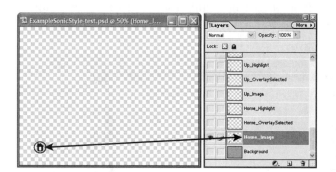

FIGURE 22.17
The Home_Image layer is the familiar MyDVD, return-to-main-menu house icon button.

8. Select the Home_Image layer by clicking its name in the Layers palette.

9. In the Photoshop Elements main menu, select Select, All (Ctrl+A) and then delete the house icon graphic by pressing Delete.

10. From the main menu, select Edit, Paste (or press Ctrl+V) to drop the new button in the middle of the workspace.

This Is Only the Beginning

Did you Know?

To fully exploit the benefits of the Style Creator, you need to go beyond simply changing this single button. One likely scenario would be for you to create a set of duplicate buttons to perform the four principal DVD menu functions: main, previous, next, and up. The only difference among the buttons would be the text on each one.

To create those four similar buttons, select the graphic window where you created the Main Menu button, undo the merge by using Photoshop Elements's Step Backward command—select Edit, Step Backward or press Ctrl+Z. Then either highlight the text to replace it or click the Text tool to create additional text layers. Add each new text object to your existing button and merge and copy each one in turn to the proper layer in the ExampleSonicStyle graphic.

---

11. To properly position this button and any subsequent buttons, do three things:

   ▶ From the Photoshop main menu, select View, Grid to add grid guidelines to the workspace.

   ▶ Scroll to the top of the ExampleSonicStyle layer palette and turn on the Safe Area layer eyeball. In Figure 22.18, I dragged that layer name from the top line to directly above the Home_Image layer for ease of reference.

▶ Select the Home_Image layer and then use the Move tool to adjust the location of your new button so that it doesn't fall outside the Safe Area.

FIGURE 22.18
Use the Photoshop Elements grid and the Style Creator Safe Area to align your buttons.

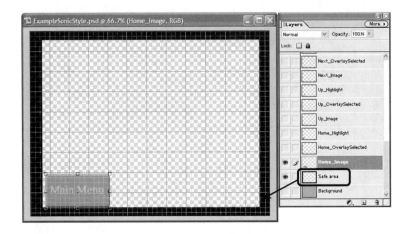

Did you Know?

Safe Area for NTSC

As mentioned earlier in the book, the black Safe Area box defines the portion of the NTSC TV signal that might fall outside the edges of most TV sets. You want your graphics to fall inside that perimeter to ensure that viewers can see them.

When you later save this PSD file as a Style Creator template, Photoshop Elements will display a message stating that it doesn't recognize the Safe Area layer. That's OK. It's only in the template to help you place objects so they will be visible on NTSC TV sets.

12. Finally, you should do a bit of housekeeping. Your new button is probably smack dab on top of the Up button. Move it and its associated elements out of the way. Using Figure 22.19 as a reference, turn off the grid, select each of the three Up layers in turn, and use the Move tool on each graphic to slide them just to the right of the Main Menu button. Reassemble them into one button.

13. Save your graphic file by selecting File, Save.

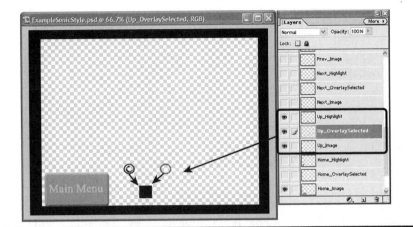

FIGURE 22.19
To avoid having the Up button show up on top of your newly created Main Menu button, move it and its elements off to one side.

Working with Other Button Layers

You might note that one button element is missing from all the layers in the ExampleSonicStyle file: OverlayActivated. None of the templates provided with MyDVD includes this element, although MyDVD can handle Activated Overlays. Therefore, the next task explains how to change all the existing button elements and shows you how to add a layer for the OverlayActivated element.

The purpose, simply, is to introduce you to this process, not to create a completely revamped template. To do that, you'd need to duplicate these steps several times. I do suggest you try to make a complete, personalized template after completing this chapter's exercises.

Change Button Elements

Try it Yourself

After you change the shape or size of a button, you need to change its associated elements to ensure that they all work together properly. In this task you change the highlight hotspot zone, edit the OverlaySelected graphic, add a new OverlayActivated layer, add the OverlaySelected graphic to it, and change its color. Here's how:

1. Click the Home_Image eyeball and select the Home_Highlight layer by clicking its layer name. Your screen should look similar to Figure 22.20.

FIGURE 22.20
Here's how your screen should look with the Home_Image graphic displayed and the Home_Highlight graphic layer selected.

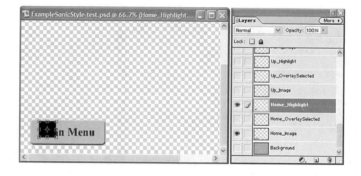

2. Click the Move tool and then grab the handles on the black highlight square to move and expand it to completely cover the Main Menu button. You should end up with a rectangle just like the one in Figure 22.21.

FIGURE 22.21
Here's how your Home_Highlight hotspot zone should look after moving and expanding it to cover the Main Menu button.

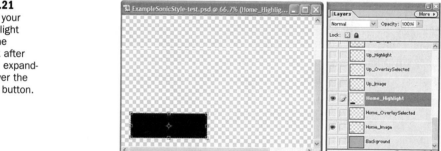

3. To simplify this next step, you'll use a graphic from the ExampleSonicStyle file. Unclick the Home_Highlight eyeball (so you can see the Main Menu button again) and select the Home_OverlaySelected layer; a red circle appears.

4. From the main menu, select Select, All (Ctrl+A); then press Delete to remove the Home_OverlaySelected circle.

5. Select the Folder 6_OverlaySelected layer. As shown in Figure 22.22, it's a rectangle (and therefore will work better as a Highlight for your rectangular Main Menu button). From the main menu, select Select, All; then select Edit, Copy or press Ctrl+C.

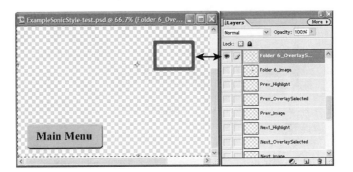

FIGURE 22.22
Use the rectangular overlay graphic from a different layer to serve as the Home_Image Selected overlay.

6. Unclick the Folder 6_OverlaySelected eyeball and select the Home_OverlaySelected layer. Select Edit, Paste (Ctrl+V) to drop the red rectangle into that layer.

7. Use the Move tool to slide the rectangle over the Main Menu button, and then use its handles to change its size and proportions to cover the perimeter of the Main Menu button. Your graphic should look similar to Figure 22.23.

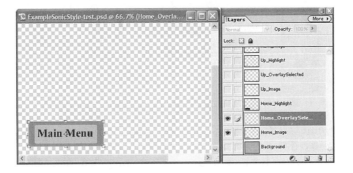

FIGURE 22.23
Use the Move tool to fit the red rectangle around the outside edges of the Main Menu button.

8. To add an Activated Highlight to your button, you need to exactly duplicate the OverlaySelected graphic you just created. To do that, right-click the Home_OverlaySelected name in the Layers palette, and select Duplicate Layer. As shown in Figure 22.24, in the Duplicate Layer dialog box, name this new layer **Home_OverlayActivated**. Be sure you use the exact spelling, capitalization, and underscore—otherwise, the Style Creator plug-in will not recognize it as a button layer.

FIGURE 22.24
To give a button an activated highlight, duplicate that button's OverlaySelected layer and name it `Home_Overlay` `Activated`.

9. Click the Set Foreground Color swatch to open the color selector (see Figure 22.25).

FIGURE 22.25
Double-click the highlighted Set Foreground Color swatch (left) to open the Color Picker (right).

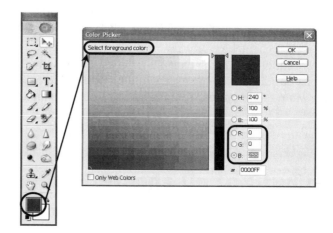

10. Using Figure 22.25 as a guide, use the Color Picker to change the rectangle color from red to any color of your choice. I chose pure blue by setting the blue value to 255 (its maximum) and red and green to 0. Click OK.

Highlight Color Rules

The Style Creator plug-in won't let you use more than three colors for all the overlays in a template. In this case, all *Selected* overlays are red and all *Activated* overlays are blue. If you choose more than one color for the same overlay layer (Selected or Activated), MyDVD selects the most commonly used color in your template for all the elements in that category.

11. Complete the color change process by clicking the Paint Can icon, checking to see that the Fill setting (in the Main Menu bar) is set to Foreground, and clicking its cursor on the rectangle border (not the interior, or you will change the color there instead).

12. Select File, Save.

Testing Your Template Edits in MyDVD

The purpose all along has been to show you how to use Style Creator to create templates that will work in MyDVD.

I limited this chapter's tasks only to changing the background, text boundaries, and characteristics, and a button and its elements, so when you test this edited style in MyDVD, it won't look very impressive. But I think you'll see how these elements all work together.

MyDVD has rigid rules about button locations (MyDVD 6 does let you manually relocate buttons), and you can't separate out button elements. But if you want to create a simplified and consistent template for use by several employees or students, for example, Style Creator and MyDVD make a great partnership.

Test Your Style in MyDVD

Try it Yourself

Because you worked with MyDVD in the three previous chapters, much of this task will be routine. What's of interest here is how MyDVD handles the changes you made to the ExampleSonicStyle file. Here's how to view those changes:

1. In Photoshop Elements, convert your graphic to a Sonic Solutions Style by selecting File, Automation Tools, Create Style for Sonic MyDVD. This opens the window shown in Figure 22.26.

2. Set the Source to Current Document, select Create New Style Pack in the Destination window, and select a file folder. Then give your style a name, click Save, and click OK. The plug-in will turn on its macro, perform a few dozen functions (it might take about 30 seconds), and then let you know the export has been completed successfully.

FIGURE 22.26
The Style Creator
plug-in interface.

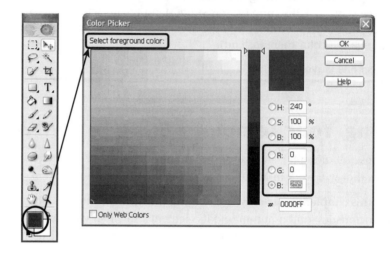

Error Messages

As the plug-in steps through its various functions, it might display one or more error messages. Most of these are inconsequential, and if you followed the previously mentioned steps, none of the messages should cause the plug-in to not complete its task. One message notes the presence of the Safe Area layer, which is not part of the style format; therefore, the plug-in merely alerts you about it and ignores it after you click OK. Other messages typically refer to possible overlay color conflicts, but MyDVD usually resolves them automatically. Simply click OK if any error messages appear.

3. Open MyDVD. Go to the main DVD-authoring interface and click Edit Style to open that interface.

4. In the Edit Style window shown in Figure 22.27, click Import Style.

5. In the Import Style dialog box, select Create New Style Category.

Only One Import Option

In the Import Style dialog box shown in Figure 22.28, the Import Style into Current Category option button might be grayed-out (disabled). The specific reason is that MyDVD does not let you import a style into its default style collections: Default Styles, DefaultMotionStyles, Abstract, Color, Events, and Nature. This forced choice occurs if you have not yet imported a style into MyDVD or if you have one of the default style packs selected.

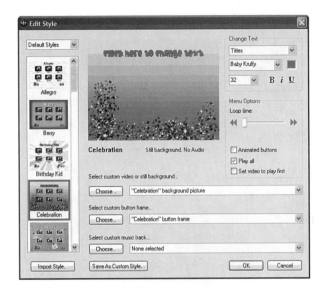

FIGURE 22.27
Import your style
by clicking that but-
ton in the Edit
Style window.

FIGURE 22.28
You might have
only one option in
the Import Style
interface, depend-
ing on whether
you've already
imported a style
into MyDVD.

6. Navigate to the style you created in the previous tasks, highlight that file, and click Open. It will load into the Edit Style window. As shown in Figure 22.29, click your edited style to display the background and the default menu text. Click OK in the bottom-right corner to return to the main MyDVD interface.

7. Click Add Sub-Menu two times to place two menu buttons on the main menu screen.

8. Switch to Preview mode by clicking the Preview button.

9. In the Preview window, shown in Figure 22.30, check out the button behavior by clicking one of them. It should turn blue (or whatever color you selected for the activated layer) and take you to a submenu.

FIGURE 22.29
After importing your edited style, click its thumbnail image to display it.

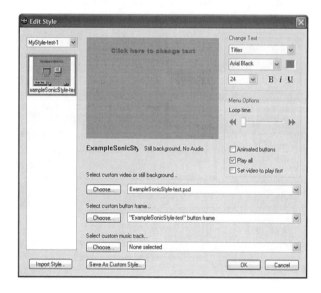

By the Way

Activated Highlight Color

Because you used Style Creator to add an OverlayActivated layer to this style (giving it a color other than red), all other buttons in the template gain that Activated Highlight color feature automatically.

FIGURE 22.30
In Preview mode, note that when you click your buttons ("activating" them) your buttons now display an Activated highlight color.

10. In the submenu shown in Figure 22.31, move the cursor back and forth between the Main Menu button and the Up button to see their respective red Selected Highlight graphics display.

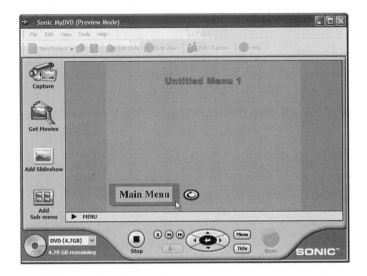

FIGURE 22.31
The Main Menu button now has rectangular Selected and Activated Highlights, whereas the round Up button has only a Selected Highlight layer (because you did not add an Activated layer to it).

Check Out Other Button Changes

The Main Menu button will display the red rectangle you swapped for the red circle, and the Up button will be in the new location you specified in Style Creator.

By the Way

11. Finally, click either button and note that the blue activated highlight displays.

12. Click the Stop button and then close MyDVD.

Summary

As you create more DVDs, you might want to create customized menus and buttons. Sonic Solutions's Style Creator is an excellent way to accomplish this task. It uses specifically named Photoshop and Photoshop Elements layers that, when imported to MyDVD, ensure that your graphics match the appearance and functionality you envisioned for them.

Although it takes a while to get up to speed with Style Creator, after you get the hang of it, you might come to rely on it as the primary means to personalize DVDs made with MyDVD.

PART IV

Intermediate-Level DVD Authoring

CHAPTER 23

Introducing DVDit! 5

What You'll Learn in This Chapter:

- ▶ Planning your project
- ▶ Presenting your media in the best light
- ▶ Organizing your DVD's menu structure
- ▶ Introducing DVDit! 5
- ▶ Checking out the DVDit! 5 interface

I've organized this book to build to this point. Up to now, you've created content, edited it in Movie Maker and Studio, and did some entry-level DVD authoring using Studio's DVD-authoring module and My DVD 6.

In this and most of the next four chapters, you'll work with DVDit! 5, Sonic Solutions's prosumer DVD-authoring application and the best DVD-authoring application you'll find at its $300 price point. You can work with the trial version available for download at www.sonic.com/go/sams/.

The reason you would make the move to a prosumer product such as DVDit! 5 is to improve the look and functionality of your DVD projects. Those higher-level goals usually require some project planning. I start this chapter by offering some general organizational concepts. Then we take a first look at DVDit! 5.

Planning Your Project

In this and the next four chapters, my objective is to let you see firsthand what DVDit! 5 can do and help you achieve a comfort level when working with this prosumer-quality authoring tool. After that is accomplished, it'll be much easier to design and create DVDs to suit your specific project needs.

In my view, when beginning to plan your project, you need to ask only two questions: "What's the message?" and "Who's the audience?"

What's the Message?

By message, I mean what are you trying to accomplish with your DVD? Will you archive videos, create video vacation albums, educate employees, or sell a product?

In each case, you'll need to take a different approach. For instance, if your goal is only to archive videos, you'll probably use just one simple opening menu with buttons linking viewers to each separate video. On the other hand, if you're trying to sell something—real estate, wine, travel, and so on—you'll want to increase your production values by adding music and animation to your menus; creating custom highlights for buttons; and giving viewers virtual tours, fast-paced edits, and many choices.

Who's the Audience?

Who will view your DVD and what are their needs and sophistication level? The beauty of DVDs is that just about anyone can use them. You stick them into a DVD set-top player and, with remote control in hand, sit back and enjoy.

However, you still need to create an intuitive flow to your project as a means to direct viewers to areas you want to emphasize. And if you want viewers to use PCs to access data files, you need to ensure that they'll have the means and resources to access those files.

On the other hand, if you're creating a review of your child's soccer team's season, consider that parents and kids will view your DVD. They'll want to jump directly to individual games, specific highlights, and player statistics. To make that work well, you'll need to create a logical organization for your DVD.

Presenting Your Media in the Best Light

By purchasing this book, you've made a commitment to do more than throw media onto a DVD. You want to create a quality product—something that will have an impact, send a message, or create an impression. Something you can be proud of.

Keep It Simple

In general, at this relatively early stage in your DVD production development, I'd suggest that you keep it simple. Avoid busy menu backgrounds and too many buttons. Keep the number of menus down to a manageable size and ensure that the navigation of your project is intuitive. That is, at the completion of a video clip, take viewers to what would logically follow that clip—for instance, the main menu or the menu from which they accessed that clip.

Keep It Short

Look at your video and image assets, and think in terms of keeping things short. If you absolutely insist on including every second of video you took at a wedding, do two things: First, edit a highlights video and let users access it through the main menu. Second, set chapter points in the original, unedited video and let viewers jump directly to those specific wedding moments using a scene selection submenu.

Take It for a Test Drive

Test your final product on a colleague, a friend, or your spouse. If you plan to mass produce your DVD, burn a single copy and play it on a set-top device. If you will make only one or a small number of DVDs, let your PC be your test bed.

In any event, you want your test subjects to navigate through and view your DVD without prompting from you. Then ask them what they think you were trying to accomplish. You'll want to note whether they had any trouble moving through the menus or making media selections.

This peer review can be an uncomfortable process for you. Nevertheless, it gives you a chance to step back from your work and take a viewer's perspective. I find that when I do this, I almost always see glaring issues that need repair. Something that made perfect sense when working on it fails to resonate with my test subject—and usually for good reason.

Organizing Your DVD's Menu Structure

DVDs are interactive. That's one of their real fortes. You should, therefore, organize your DVDs to exploit that strength. To do that, use nested menus, intuitive navigation, and clearly labeled buttons.

Nested Menus

Nested menus, as I explained earlier in this book, are menus within menus. If you worked through Chapters 18–21, you've already encountered nested menus. You built DVDs with a main menu that had buttons that linked to chapter menus and submenus—menus within a menu.

Consider a family-history DVD. Its main menu might have button links to a video overview, specific family lines, immigration stories, photos, documents, and living history interviews. The link to the video overview could take viewers to a scene selection—chapter—menu. Each of the other subcategories also could have its own menu.

Use a Flowchart

To ensure a logical flow to your DVD, organize it using a flowchart similar to the one in Figure 23.1. This follows the basic family-tree DVD structure I touched on in Chapter 15, "What DVDs and DVD-Authoring Software Can Do for You."

The main menu gives you access to submenu topics, which in turn might give you further access to additional submenus or nested menus. In this case, your viewers would be able to drill down quickly to a specific area of interest or take a more linear and leisurely stroll through the DVD's contents.

FIGURE 23.1
One possible DVD menu flowchart for a family history DVD.

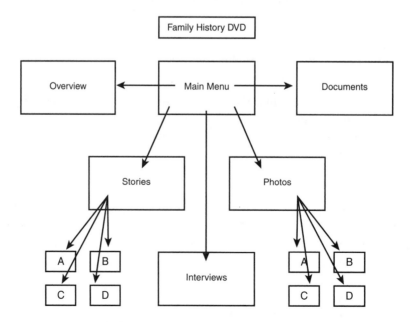

Buttons Should Do What They Say

This might seem like I'm stating the obvious, but I've seen too many DVDs that don't make sense. It's unclear what will happen when you press a button or where a click will take you. Many times, DVD authors try to use only icons for buttons. Although they make sense to the author, they might not make sense to the viewer.

One advantage of DVDit! is that not only can you place text on or near a button, but you also can use that text as a link to the same media as its associated button. The bottom line is that clear navigation trumps clever artwork.

Introducing DVDit! 5

Sonic Solutions released DVDit! 5 in June 2004. Sonic Solutions built DVDit! 5 from the ground up. It replaces DVDit! 2.5 (there was no version 3 or 4), a product that worked well but its interface was kind of nonintuitive and it didn't offer as many button- and menu-creation and navigation options as in DVDit! 5.

DVDit! 5 is loaded with features and functionality. Its focus is to make it easy to create higher-level DVDs. Those DVDs will have attributes not found in DVDs created with Sonic MyDVD or Pinnacle Studio's DVD-authoring module.

► DVDit! 5 uses tabs to let you navigate quickly to assets such as Menus, Buttons, and Media and features such as Links, Text, and DVD-ROM data files.

► DVDit! 5 lets you directly control the menu and movie navigation properties, button and text placement, and the appearance of text and buttons, including setting color and drop-shadow characteristics.

► In MyDVD you had virtually no control over so-called Overlay Highlight colors—the colors that display when viewers navigate to a button and then click it. In DVDit! you have total control over colors and even the shape of the highlight.

► DVDit! 5 is compatible with a wide range of video, audio, and image file formats, including Microsoft AVI, Windows Media WMV and WMA, Apple QuickTime MOV, as well as MPEG-1, 2, and 4.

► Its MPEG transcoder (the software that converts media files into MPEG) works in real-time (on faster PCs) and produces high-quality output.

▶ DVDit! 5 works with SAP (Second Audio Program) audio. These typically are TV programs with a dubbed-in second language track. DVDit! 5 lets you choose which audio track to use in your finished DVD.

▶ You can customize menu **end actions** allowing you to have slick intro and **outro** videos that lead into or from your menus.

▶ You've heard of **Easter Eggs**? Those hidden assets in Hollywood DVDs? DVDit! 5 lets you create them on your DVDs.

▶ It can burn your project to dual-layer DVD+R discs.

▶ You can add data, image, video, and other files to the disc.

Take a look at DVDit! 5's authoring interface shown in Figure 23.2. I am a real fan of DVDit!'s tab-based navigation system. Within the authoring interface you can easily access menu media (via the tabs in the upper-left portion of Figure 23.2) such as background images, buttons, thumbnail frames, and graphical elements such as text background banners.

In addition, below the Menu window (on the right side of Figure 23.2) another collection of tabs open menu-related functions like button links and button navigation.

FIGURE 23.2
DVDit! 5 uses a tab-based navigation system that gives you ready access to all DVD-authoring elements.

Figure 23.3 shows a couple other very nifty features of DVDit! 5. You might recall that in MyDVD the so-called button Overlay Highlights were built in to the template. Unless you created a new template using the Style Creator Photoshop plug-in, you had no control over the color, opacity, and shape of those Overlay Highlights.

As shown in Figure 23.3, DVDit! 5 gives five choices when it comes to button Overlay Highlights (DVDit! 5 uses the correct DVD-specification term: Subpicture Overlay). No other DVD-authoring application I've seen at this price point gives you this much built-in Subpicture Overlay Highlighting flexibility.

The other cool feature in DVDit! 5's Links menu is Button Routing. This is the order in which buttons highlight as the viewer navigates through a DVD menu. Consumer DVD-authoring applications automatically set this routing. DVDit! 5 offers a manual option.

FIGURE 23.3
DVDit! 5's Links tab has two very slick and well-implemented features: Five Subpicture Overlay styles (one is grayed out in this figure) and manual Button Routing.

DVDit! 5 has a very close connection to the industry-standard graphics program Photoshop and its much-less expensive and younger sibling: Photoshop Elements. Figure 23.4 gives you an example. You can take any graphic created in Photoshop and have DVDit! 5 convert it into a button. You can add Subpicture Overlay Highlight layers that look dramatically different from the original button or use DVDit! 5's Subpicture Overlay options. DVDit 5! gives you a full slate of readily available button customization features.

Another nice feature is the Preview Project interface (see Figure 23.5). You can jump here at any time from any menu in your project and either preview your entire project from the First Play asset or start your previewing from whichever menu you were working on. That latter feature is a great time-saving tool.

FIGURE 23.4
These are basic, single-layer graphics with transparent backgrounds created in Photoshop. It's a simple matter to import them into DVDit! 5, which automatically converts them to buttons complete with Subpicture Overlay Highlight layers that can exactly match these buttons' borders.

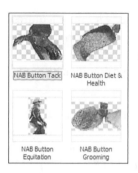

FIGURE 23.5
DVDit! 5's Preview Project feature not only lets you see how your entire project will look and behave, but also gives you the option to check out whichever menu you had open when you jumped to Preview.

What's Missing in DVDit! 5

There are some things that you might expect to see in DVDit! 5 that aren't there. The reason? DVDit! 5's market is prosumer and professional DVD editors. The basic assumption made by Sonic and other DVD-authoring application developers is that this market will do video editing in a separate application such as Studio or Premiere and that DVD authors will create custom menus, buttons, and other graphics in products such as Photoshop.

As an indicator of that development philosophy, take a look at DVDit! 5's Edit interface, shown in Figure 23.6. There are no video-editing tools besides clip trimming. That's because this is not a video editor per se. Although you can trim the beginning and end of a clip and you can add, move, or swap audio, you cannot combine clips to make a longer video or do any other kind of video editing, such as adding transitions or effects.

You use the DVDit! 5 Edit mode primarily to add chapter points to a video and grab video frame screen shots to use as graphics or backgrounds in your menus. That's it.

FIGURE 23.6
The DVDit! 5 Edit interface is not a video editor. Its primary function is to set chapter points.

There also is no full-featured text editor. Again, the assumption is that you will create your text in your nonlinear video editor or in Photoshop.

DVDit! 5 does not ship with any menu templates like those in MyDVD, nor does it work with MyDVD templates. But you can import any MyDVD menus you made using its templates into DVDit! 5 and after they are imported, all the elements, such as text and buttons, are editable.

And there is no video capture mode. Again, the assumption is that you have other means to accomplish that task.

Checking Out the DVDit! 5 Interface

DVDit! 5 is a prosumer-quality DVD-authoring application with some consumer-friendly features. It offers some of the power and flexibility found in professional products that expect a higher level of expertise on menu creation from the user, but it eases users into authoring by offering plenty of menu graphical elements, an organized workflow, and easy access to customization tools.

Touring DVDit! 5's Interface

You'll venture into actual authoring in Chapter 24, "Creating Menus with DVDit! 5." Before taking that step, I want you to examine the four DVDit! workspaces as a means to get comfortable with the workflow to come.

DVDit! 5 divides your authoring tasks into four basic steps:

▶ **Assemble Your Assets**—You can do this in the Edit and Author interfaces. In the Edit mode, you typically import videos that need trimming or videos that you want to add chapter points to or grab screenshots from. In the Author mode you gather up the remaining video, audio, and image files and add any menu graphical elements such as backgrounds and buttons.

▶ **Edit**—Trim video clips, add chapters, and grab still images from video clips.

▶ **Author**—Build menus using backgrounds (video or still), audio, and buttons. Link the buttons to their respective assets: media or menus. Adjust Subpicture Overlay Highlight colors and opacities, and manually alter the button navigation.

▶ **Finish**—Preview your project, looking for broken links or **end actions** that take viewers to the wrong place. Make fixes and then burn your DVD.

Routine drag-and-drop methods simplify most of these steps. You'll drag menu backgrounds to a window, drag buttons onto that background, add text (adjusting its location and other characteristics), and drag movies and chapters to those menus, creating buttons and links in the process.

Try it Yourself   **Examine DVDit! 5's Interface**

▼

Your work in the next chapters will go more smoothly if you first get acquainted with the workspace. To do that, follow these steps:

▼

1. Download the DVDit! 5 trial version from the Sonic Solutions website—www.sonic.com/go/sams/.

DVDit! 5 Might Crash When You First Start It Up

Watch
Out!

As we went to press, DVDit! 5 had a known problem that showed up when users had several Sonic Solutions products on their hard drives. Because you have been working with so many Sonic Solutions products throughout this book, you might experience it.

The problem is that after starting DVDit! 5, an Application Error or a Debug message displays. In either case, DVDit! 5 will not run. There's an easy fix that works most of the time and a more difficult fix that requires changing the Windows Registry. The easy fix is to go to your Control Panel, open Add/Remove Programs, and remove Sonic Update Manager and every other Sonic Solutions product including DVDit! 5. Restart your PC and reinstall DVDit! 5 (you can reinstall the other products later). If that doesn't fix things, contact Sonic tech support for an explanation of the other, longer fix.

2. Start DVDit! 5 by double-clicking its icon on the desktop or selecting Start, Programs, Sonic, DVDit! 5, Start DVDit!. You might see a splash screen asking you if you want to register. After you opt in or out, the interface shown in Figure 23.7 appears.

Slick Concept

By the
Way

DVDit! 5 offers a cool little means to avoid the egregious error of altering a project you intended to use as a standardized palette for multiple projects. Clicking New from an Existing Project opens an existing project, but when you go to save it, the Save option will be grayed out. Your only choice will be to Save As, thereby ensuring you don't alter your DVD template.

3. Click New Project. That opens the dialog box shown in Figure 23.8. The only option (besides your project name and file-folder location) is the TV standard drop-down list. Up to this point in the book, the only TV standards you've encountered have been NTSC and PAL. DVDit! 5 offers those plus SECAM (Systeme Electronique Couleur Avec Memoire) the TV standard in France, the Middle East, and most of Eastern Europe. No need to open a project just yet. Click Cancel.

FIGURE 23.7
The DVDit! 5 opening menu. New from Existing Project is a helpful little option.

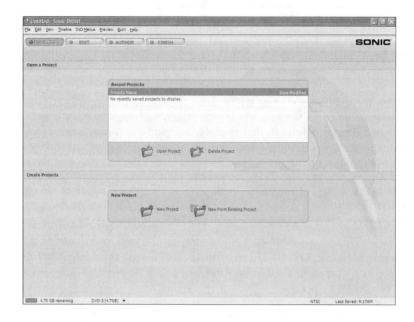

FIGURE 23.8
The New Project dialog box offers one additional TV standard: SECAM.

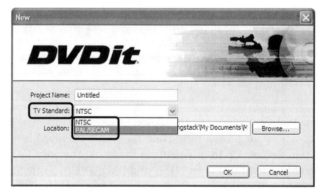

4. Click the Edit button to open the interface shown in Figure 23.9. This interface is intuitive. You click the highlighted file folder to import video files and drag to the filmstrip icon any video that you want to trim, add chapters to, or grab screenshots from.

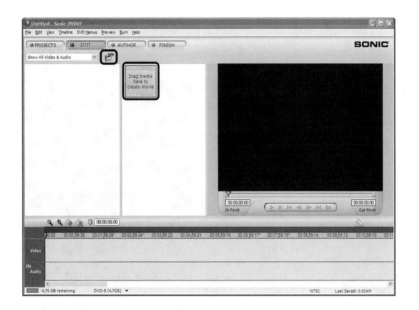

FIGURE 23.9
Use the Edit inter-
face to import
assets (click the
highlighted file fold-
er), trim clips, add
chapters, and for
frame grabs.

5. Click the Author button to open that interface (shown in Figure 23.10).
Check out the various graphical elements that ship with DVDit! 5.

▶ **Images**—As shown in Figure 23.10, DVDit! 5 ships with several static
graphics that you can use as menu backgrounds. These images also
show up automatically in the Buttons/Images group.

▶ **Media**—Any media assets you added in the Edit interface or in this
Author interface will show up here.

▶ **Buttons**—Click the Buttons tab and the drop-down list to check out
the three button types: Images, Objects, and Navigation buttons.
Objects are graphical elements that work well as text backgrounds.
Navigation buttons, shown in Figure 23.11, are useful to go from
menu to menu or to play all clips in a single menu.

▶ **Frames**—These are for video buttons. The video frame or animation
appears inside the frame. Some have banners for use as text **beds**—
pleasing backgrounds for button labels.

FIGURE 23.10
The DVDit! 5
Author interface
displays back-
ground images,
media, buttons,
and frames.

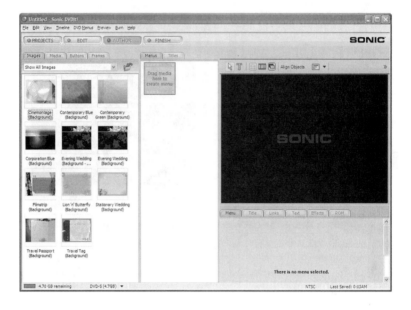

Adjustable Screen Real Estate

DVDit! 5's interfaces all have adjustable windows. Click a window edge/border and drag to expand or contract a window. This is a great way to get the big picture about available graphics or to expand the menu-editing screen.

FIGURE 23.11
DVDit! 5 ships with
several dozen navi-
gation buttons (I
dragged the edges
of the button win-
dow to show more
selections).

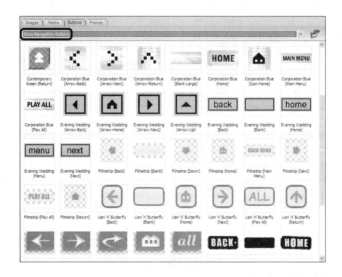

6. To be able to see some of the options available behind the tabs below the menu editing screen, you need to start working on a menu. To do that, click the Images tab and drag and drop any background to the filmstrip icon—Drag Media Here to Create Menu.

7. With a menu background in place, note that all sorts of options show up in the Menu tab shown in Figure 23.12:

   ▶ **Menu Type**—Can be an infinite still, a timed still, or a motion menu. Timed stills play for however long you choose and then go to another menu or asset. If you dragged a video to the menu editing window, the Menu Type would be Motion Menu.

   ▶ **Forced Selection**—Usually button number one is highlighted (Selected) when a viewer first opens a menu. Then whichever button was clicked is the Selected Highlight when the viewer returns to that menu. Forced Selection lets you assign a particular button to always be the one highlighted when returning to a menu.

   ▶ **Subpicture Colors**—You can choose from three sets of colors that you define and use on all buttons in any particular menu. This ease of access and the simple color and opacity editing in DVDit! 5 are a real plus over its competitors.

   ▶ **Select Audio**—You can have any audio clip play as your menu displays.

   ▶ **End Action**—A prosumer DVD-authoring feature that lets you dictate what happens when a video or timed still menu "times out."

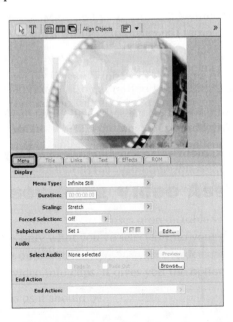

FIGURE 23.12
Adding a menu background switches on numerous options in each of the menu editing tabs.

8. Check out the other Menu Editor tabs:

   ▶ **Title**—This shows characteristics of a particular asset, such as duration and End Action.

   ▶ **Links**—Here you can adjust links between buttons and assets and menus, select a Subpicture style, and manually route button navigation.

   ▶ **Text**—A basic text editor on par with the one in MyDVD.

   ▶ **Effects**—Here you can give drop shadows and adjust opacity levels for individual buttons or text or for all buttons and text in a project.

   ▶ **ROM**—If you want users of your DVD to be able to access some files— images, videos, data, or other documents—add them here.

9. Finally, do two things to expand the view of the Menu Editor screen: Drag the right edge of the Image/Media/Button window to the left and drag the left side of the menu window to the left. Expand far enough to see all the icons at the top of the menu editing screen shown in Figure 23.13 (if you don't expand far enough, you can still access them by clicking the chevron on the right side of the icon bar). Following is a rundown of what those tools do:

   ▶ **Selection Tool**—Click this when you want to select an object, such as a button, to move it or change its linking characteristics.

   ▶ **Text Tool**—The standard means to create and edit text.

   ▶ **Add Sub-Menu**—Click this to add a Sub-Menu and place a link to that Sub-Menu in the currently opened menu.

   ▶ **Add Movie**—If you have not imported a video via the Edit or Author interfaces, this will add a video (or audio) clip to the Media collection and place a thumbnail button in your menu.

   ▶ **Add Slideshow**—Opens the same slideshow interface you worked with in MyDVD.

   ▶ **Object Alignment**—This very handy feature lets you line up buttons or text horizontally, vertically, or relative to the top, bottom, left, or right sides of your menu.

▶ **Create Solid Color Menu Background**—Another cool tool. A simple way to create a solid color menu background.

▶ **Display Safe Areas**—Shows dashed lines defining the two NTSC Safe zones: Title Safe (to ensure viewers can read your text) and Picture Safe (or Action Safe).

▶ **Display Grid**—Very useful when aligning objects.

▶ **Snap to Grid**—As you move an object around in the menu, this will snap the edge of that object to a grid line, making it easier to align objects.

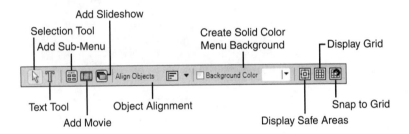

FIGURE 23.13
The Menu Editor toolbar is loaded with cool features that help you create professional-looking menus.

10. Finally, click the Finish button to open the interface shown in Figure 23.14. That the preview interface (with its large viewing screen) is only a click away is a very nice feature. You have the extra option of starting your preview from your current position (in addition to starting from First Play). Your Finish Disc options (in addition to Burning a DVD) include the following:

▶ **Write Disc Image**—This is a very useful feature. A DVD Disc Image creates a single file that you can then record to a DVD using software such as Sonic's RecordNow. This way you can save your finished work and remove all the associated media files from your hard drive.

▶ **Write DVD Volume**— A DVD Volume contains the same files that go on a DVD disc, but they are created in a folder on your PC's hard disk instead of on a recordable disc. Then you can use a software DVD player like Sonic's CinePlayer to test your project. This is a more thorough way to check your DVD than using DVDit! 5's Preview mode.

FIGURE 23.14
The Finish interface has extra features not found in entry-level DVD-authoring products, such as preview from the Current Position and Write DVD Volume.

Summary

In Chapters 18–22 you worked with two purposely consumer-friendly DVD-authoring applications: Pinnacle Studio's DVD-authoring module and Sonic Solutions MyDVD. Both make taking your first steps into DVD creation easy.

On the other hand, DVDit! 5 gives you much more control over your DVD production. You can create menus, buttons, and navigation that exactly suit your DVD design.

In this chapter, I gave you an overview of that process, suggesting ways to think through your DVD's navigation and introducing you to DVD flowcharting and layout. I took you through the DVDit! 5 authoring workflow and briefly explained how DVDit! 5 gives you direct access to button and menu attributes.

I think you'll find that DVDit! 5's tab-based navigation, easily accessible menu-editing tools such as Subpicture characteristics, and manual button routing will make it easy to create professional-looking DVDs.

CHAPTER 24

Creating Menus with DVDit! 5

What You'll Learn in This Chapter:

- ▶ Adjusting preference and project settings
- ▶ Trimming videos and adding chapter points
- ▶ Gathering assets and creating a slideshow
- ▶ Laying out menus and submenus

DVDit! 5 is a prosumer authoring application. It gives you much more control over how your DVD looks and behaves than an entry-level authoring application does. It affords you the opportunity to create DVDs that match your creative vision.

In this chapter you will start producing a DVD using graphics that ship with DVDit! 5 and videos you've created. You will adjust a few project settings, trim a clip, add chapter points, gather up all media assets, including images and graphics, and revisit the slideshow process you worked on in Chapter 20, "Authoring DVDs with MyDVD 6: Part 1."

After you've assembled and updated your assets, you will add a number of blank menus to your project and then fill them in with text, graphics, and buttons in the next chapter.

Adjusting Preference and Project Settings

Before starting your first project, you should take a look at the handful of user-selectable preferences and project settings available in DVDit! 5. In general, you'll likely accept the defaults, but I think you'll want to see what's under the hood.

You can use the Preferences window (shown in Figure 24.1) to customize settings in DVDit! 5. It's a good idea to review these settings before starting a project because you can't apply some of them to open projects.

FIGURE 24.1
DVDit! 5 organizes Preference settings to match its workspaces: General (Projects interface), Edit, Author, and Finish.

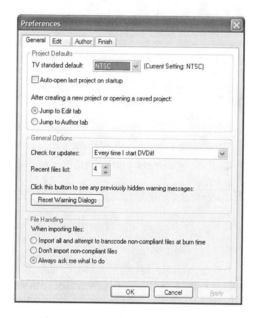

Four Preference-Setting Categories

Access Preferences by selecting File, Preferences. As shown in Figure 24.1, Preference settings fall into four categories that match the four main DVDit! 5 workspaces: General (Projects window), Edit, Author, and Finish. Following is a quick rundown:

▶ **General**—Sets some overall project default behaviors:

    ▶ **Project Defaults**—Each of the three defaults saves you only one button click apiece. Set the TV Standard Default to whatever standard you work in most frequently. This saves you a step at startup. Auto-Open Last Project on Startup skips the opening screen and jumps to your project. Select Jump to Edit Tab or Jump to Author Tab, depending on where you do most of your work.

    ▶ **General Options**—Check for Updates automatically checks the Sonic Solutions website for bug fixes. You can switch that option off. Recent Files List lets you display between zero and nine recent projects in the opening window. DVDit! 5 occasionally displays warning messages with check boxes. Clicking a check box keeps them from popping up again. Reset Warning Dialogs lets you see those warning messages again.

▶ **File Handling**—You can choose to have DVDit! 5 import all media files whether they comply with DVD specs, not import noncompliant files, or ask you what to do with each file. In general, letting DVDit! 5 import everything and then having it transcode files when it finishes your project works well.

▶ **Edit**—Gives you only two options. One involves what's called Drop Frame format. Rather than explain this arcane element of the NTSC standard, I recommend that you accept the default Non-Drop Frame. The other option is Show Chapter Labels. If your chapter labels are cluttering up the Timeline, uncheck this.

▶ **Author**—Sets several defaults for the Author window:

▶ **Palette Options**—You can set which Palette tab will display when you first open the Author window and whether similar file types will be grouped together.

▶ **Default Menu Background Color**

▶ **Button Options**—Select the default button subpicture style and button size for each button created automatically when you add a video or a link to a submenu to an existing menu. Maintain Aspect Ratio applies when you make adjustments to the default button size. And Scale Smaller Images expands small buttons up to the standard size.

▶ **Finish**—Notes the temporary storage folder for files created while working in DVDit! 5. You can choose to not delete those temporary files when you exit the application. Under Effort Control, you determine the general MPEG-2 transcoding (or encoding) speed. This does not affect the transcoding bit rate you set within the Finish window or in Project Settings. There are three speed settings: slower transcoding leads to better-looking MPEG-2 video.

Select Temporary Storage Drive with at Least 20GB

DVDit! 5 needs up to 20GB of hard drive space for all the temporary files needed when creating one 4.7GB DVD project. If you select a drive (the default is your C: drive) that doesn't have enough space, DVDit! 5 might not be able to finish your project. So choose a drive with enough free room.

Watch Out!

Changing Project Settings

Access the Project settings by selecting File, Project Settings (keyboard shortcut—Ctrl+E). That opens the tabbed window shown in Figure 24.2.

FIGURE 24.2
Project Settings offer only a few options—primarily the transcode (MPEG compression) quality, the file folder location of your project, and the PC file folder (ROM Data) you've added to the project.

The Project Settings window displays basic information about the project, such as its file folder location, size, and television standard. This window lets you change the bit rates used when transcoding (compressing) video to MPEG-2 and audio to Dolby Digital. Here's a rundown of the various settings:

▶ **General**—Shows your project's file folder location. If you have not opened a project yet, this will show the default location for your project and its temporary files. It also displays the project's present size, TV standard, the ROM Data file folder (see Did You Know? "ROM Data Can Be Only One File Folder"), Transcode settings, and when you created, modified, and last accessed the project.

Did you Know?

ROM Data Can Be Only One File Folder

If you choose to add PC files—called **ROM Data** in DVDit! 5—you can do so only by selecting a single file folder from your hard drive. I cover this in Chapter 26, "Advanced DVDit! 5 Authoring Techniques." Basically, you need to gather up all such data files into one file folder (it can have subfolders in it) and add that to your project in the Author interface ROM window.

▶ **Transcode**—DVDit! 5 **transcodes** (converts your asset files into MPEG video files) when you burn your finished project. The MPEG codec (compression/decompression technology) allows for a wide range of compression levels from VHS quality (relatively small file sizes) to Hollywood movie DVD quality (larger file sizes). You make those settings choices here. You can select from eight presets from the Encode Set drop-down list or customize a set of compression parameters. Here's a rundown of those options shown in Figure 24.3:

> ▶ **Video Bit-rate**—This sets the quality level for all video (including motion menus). Higher bit rates (maxing out at 8,000Kbps) produce better quality video, but require more disc space.

> ▶ **VBR (variable bit rate) or CBR (constant bit rate) encoding**—I explain this in Chapter 27, "Burning DVDs and Dealing with DVD Duplicators." Basically, VBR saves space because it reduces the bit rate for scenes with minimal action.

> ▶ **Audio Format**—You have two choices: PCM (uncompressed and a waste of DVD disc space) or Dolby Digital. So Dolby it is. The caveat is that DVDit! 5 supports stereo Dolby audio only (not surround sound).

> ▶ **Audio Bit-rate**—You can choose from five Dolby stereo audio quality settings or bit rates between 64 and 384Kbps (192Kbps is normal) depending on the desired sound quality. You cannot change the PCM audio bit rate.

> ▶ **Convert All Compliant Video and Audio Files**—Check this box to have DVDit! 5 re-encode MPEG files as well as non-MPEG files. You might want to do this if you used MPEG videos but your overall project size is too large to fit on a disc. In that case, you can have DVDit! 5 encode all the files at lower bit rates.

Re-encoding = Reduced Video Quality

Generally, it's not a good idea to re-encode MPEG videos. That almost guarantees video quality degradation, especially if the video was already encoded using a low bit rate.

Watch Out!

▶ **Summary**—You can enter information about the project here. This does not appear anywhere on the final DVD; it's more for your convenience or to remind you about certain project management characteristics.

Trimming Videos and Adding Chapter Points

DVDit! 5's Edit interface is less an editor and more a chapter insertion tool. Some DVD authors might not even use this interface because some higher-level nonlinear video editors let you add chapter points while editing your videos. And if those video editors follow industry standards, those chapters will show up in any video you import from them into DVDit! 5.

But skipping that step and using DVDit! 5 to add chapters might make more sense.

Why Add Chapters While Editing Your Video?

Because it's so convenient to use DVDit! 5 to add chapter points, you might think there are no reasons to add chapter points while editing your video.

Not quite. One reason is if you convert your project (transcode or encode it) to MPEG *before* importing it into DVDit! 5. Because MPEG compression does not save every frame from the original video (it calculates differences between sets of frames and removes those it doesn't need) the frame you want to use for a chapter point might not exist as a distinct frame in the compressed MPEG video.

However, the MPEG encoder will make sure that any frame you selected as a chapter point ends up as a full video frame in the final MPEG video.

The other three reasons to use DVDit! 5's Edit interface are for frame grabs (capturing still images from a video frame), to trim clips, and to add, replace, and move audio.

Working in the Edit Interface

Try it Yourself

▼

Because you have used Studio, you probably won't use DVDit! 5's trim option nor its audio functionality. But it is a convenient means to trim single video clips that would take too much time to deal with in an NLE. On the other hand, grabbing freeze frames and adding chapters are two very useful features. I cover all three functions plus audio features in the following steps:

1. Open DVDit! 5 and click New Project. In the New Project dialog box (shown in Figure 24.4), give your project a name, select the TV standard, and select a file folder (keep in mind you need 20GB of hard drive space for a full project). Click OK.

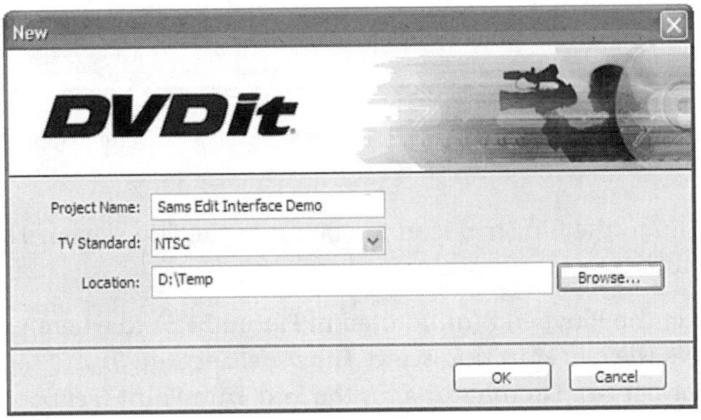

FIGURE 24.4
The New dialog box pops up when you select New Project in the opening interface.

2. DVDit! 5 will open to either the Edit or Author interface, depending on what you selected in the Preferences, General window. If DVDit! 5 takes you to the Author interface, click the Edit button to display the interface shown in Figure 24.5.

3. Add one or more video clips that you can trim to this interface by clicking the Import Media file folder icon highlighted in Figure 24.5, selecting your clips, and clicking Open.

▼

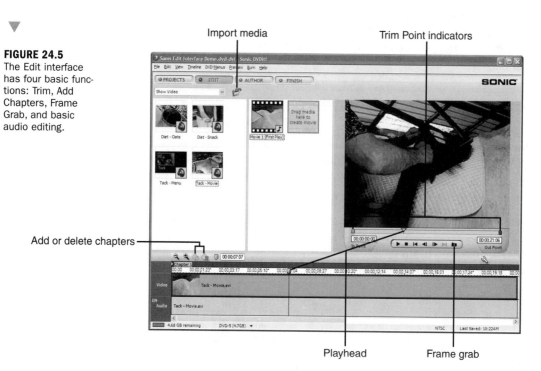

FIGURE 24.5
The Edit interface has four basic functions: Trim, Add Chapters, Frame Grab, and basic audio editing.

Import media

Trim Point indicators

Add or delete chapters

Playhead   Frame grab

4. Drag a clip to the filmstrip icon to open it in the Edit screen. There are two ways to trim it:

  ▶ Drag the Playhead (annotated in Figure 24.5) to where you want to have the clip start and select Timeline, Set Start Trim Point (keyboard shortcut—I). Do the same for the End Trim Point (keyboard shortcut—O).

  ▶ Drag the Trim Point Indicators (annotated in Figure 24.5) to the desired trim positions.

5. Drag another clip to the filmstrip icon to add it to the active media collection. You can select it and trim it. But in this case, drag the Playhead to a frame you want to use as a menu background and click the Grab Frame button (annotated in Figure 24.5). That opens a Save Picture As window. Give your image a name, select a file format, and click Save.

6. Add another clip to the active media collection. Drag the Playhead to a point where you want to add a chapter. There are two ways to add a chapter (in each case DVDit! 5 will add a numbered chapter marker and a vertical blue line to the Timeline):

- ▶ Click the Add Chapter button highlighted in Figure 24.6.
- ▶ Right-click the Timeline Ruler and, as shown in Figure 24.6, select Add Chapter.

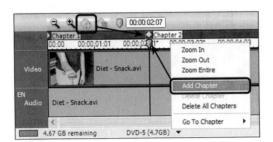

FIGURE 24.6
Add chapters by clicking the high-lighted Add Chapter button or by right-clicking the Timeline Ruler and selecting Add Chapter.

7. To remove a chapter, click the Chapter icon (or name) in the Timeline and click the Delete Chapter button (to the right of the Add Chapter button) or right-click and select Delete Chapter.

Add Chapter Points While Viewing Video

Instead of dragging the Playhead to chapter points, add them while watching the video. As the video plays, press the Insert key to add a chapter point. If it's off by a few frames, fix it later by dragging it to the proper frame.

Did you Know?

---

8. If you work with videos recorded on some DVD+VR recorders that work with SAP (Second Audio Program), you need to select which track to use (you can use only one of the two tracks). To do that, select Timeline, Audio Options (or right-click the audio clip in the Timeline and select Audio Options), and, as shown in Figure 24.7, select the Enable Bilingual Audio Support check box and select which track you want to use (see By the Way "SAP—How It Works with DVDit! 5").

SAP—How It Works with DVDit! 5

SAP (Second Audio Program) has a main audio channel (that could be stereo or Dolby surround) and a second channel (typically a dubbed-in second language track that also can be full stereo or surround). If you use a DVD+VR recorder to record an SAP program, the DVD+VR machine converts those two channels into separate right and left monaural channels. When you add a DVD+VR SAP video to DVDit! 5, you need to choose which of those two audio tracks to use (otherwise you'll hear one language coming from your left stereo speaker and the other from the right).

By the Way

FIGURE 24.7
For those who use
DVD+VR SAP
recordings, DVDit!
5 lets you choose
which audio track
to use in your DVD.

9. The DVD format lets you indicate the language of each audio track for each video. In this way, DVDs can automatically select the viewer's preferred language (if it's one of the languages offered). DVDit! 5 has taken a small step toward implementing this DVD feature (see By the Way "Audio Track Language Issues" for an explanation). You can use the dialog box shown in Figure 24.7 to select whether your project is in Japanese or English (there are no other language options and DVDit! 5 offers only one audio track per video). The abbreviation for the selected language shows up to the left of the audio track in the Timeline (see Figure 24.8).

*By the
Way*

Audio Track Language Issues

Higher-level DVD-authoring products let you have up to 16 audio tracks associated with any video. Typically, you use them for foreign language dubs or director comments. DVDit! 5's developers have created what amounts to a placeholder for that feature, which they will implement in version 6 of DVDit! For now, DVDit! 5 offers only one audio channel per video clip and only the option of choosing Japanese or English as the default language.

10. Finally, you have a few audio options at your disposal. With a video in the Edit screen, select Timeline, Audio—or, as shown in Figure 24.8, right-click the audio clip in the Timeline—and note that you have four options: Mute, Fade In, Fade Out, and Volume. Selecting Volume displays the dialog box shown in Figure 24.9.

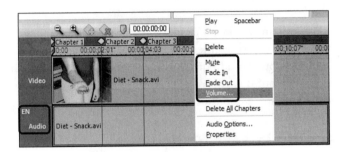

FIGURE 24.8
DVDit! 5 offers a
modicum of audio
controls: Fade In,
Fade Out, Mute,
and clip Volume.
Note that "EN"
means that English
is this clip's audio
language.

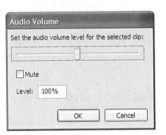

FIGURE 24.9
Selecting Volume
from the four audio
options opens this
simple dialog box.

Audio Offset

DVDit! 5 offers something called Audio Offset. The only circumstance I can think of
when you would use this is if you create or work with so-called Elementary Audio
and Video Streams.

Some editors create these when they compress video into MPEG. Instead of creating a single audio/video file, they create an MPEG-2 video-only file and a separate
audio file. If the original video started with a period of silence, the editor might have
compressed only the portion of the audio track with sound (to save some space).
Under that circumstance, you'd need to add the audio to the video in the filmstrip
icon, right-click the audio clip in the Timeline, select Audio Options, click the Offset
Audio Later By option button (shown earlier in Figure 24.7), and select a time for
that offset.

By the Way

Gathering Assets and Creating a Slideshow

In entry-level products such as MyDVD, your only assets are video and audio
clips. In addition, you can add still images to slideshows and can swap out a
menu background for a graphic of your choice. In general, you don't place assets

in a palette for ready access, you merely add them directly to menus or slideshows. That's the entry-level, hand-holding paradigm.

DVDit! 5 ups that ante in two ways. First, you can place all your assets (including background images) in one convenient location for placement in menus or slideshows later. And you can add graphical elements for use in building menus. Those graphics can be buttons you've created in Photoshop specifically for DVDit! 5 projects (I show you how to do that in Chapter 26.

Adding Assets in Edit Mode

Add any video or audio clips that you need to do rudimentary editing on in that interface. Any assets you add here will show up in the Author interface Media palette. Any Assets you actually do any editing to also will show up in the Author interface in both the Media palette and the Titles palette.

Adding Assets in Author Mode

Several asset issues are in this interface, and I'll run through them one at a time. Open DVDit! 5 to the Author interface to follow along.

- ▶ **Media Palette (tab)**—As shown in Figure 24.10, clicking the Media tab and selecting Show Video in the drop-down list displays video clips you added to your project in the Edit interface. To add more clips to this Media palette, click the Import Media file folder icon. You can use these clips as menu backgrounds by dragging them to the Menus palette or as media by dragging them to the Titles palette.

- ▶ **Titles Palette (tab)**—This displays any of the Media assets you added to the editing queue in the Edit interface. You need to place assets in the Titles palette before you can link a button to them or drag them to a menu, which automatically creates a thumbnail button.

- ▶ **Images Palette (tab)**—Add menu background graphics and slideshow stills here (it is easier to add images directly to a slideshow rather than store them here). To add graphics to the Images palette, click its tab and click the Import Media icon. Any background image you add here also will show up in the Buttons/Show Button Images palette (and vice versa).

FIGURE 24.10
In the Author interface, you access all assets needed to create menus as well as add any buttons and links to those assets.

Adding Assets

You can add graphics to the Images, Buttons, and Frames palettes in the same way you added Media assets to its palette. Click a tab, select a subcategory (if applicable) from the drop-down list, and click the Import Media button. Images can be any of the seven graphics formats DVDit! 5 works with. Buttons and Frames must be Photoshop PSD graphics only.

You cannot add menus or titles to those two palettes (to the right of the Images/Media/Buttons/Frames tabs) using the Import Media button. Instead, you create menus by dragging background images or videos to the filmstrip icon in the Menus palette. And you add so-called titles (actually videos or slideshows) to your project by dragging videos or images (respectively) to the Title filmstrip icon.

Did you Know?

▶ **Buttons**—There are three Buttons categories: Images, Objects, and Navigation buttons. Image buttons are the same as the images located in the Images palette. The only difference is that when you drag an Image button to a menu, DVDit! 5 creates a Thumbnail button. Objects and Navigation buttons are all Photoshop graphics with two layers named Image and Overlay. The Objects that ship with DVDit! 5 are all rectangles with some graphical element. The Navigation buttons are useful to link back to the Main Menu or the Next menu. You can change any of these buttons in Photoshop. I cover that in Chapter 26.

▶ **Frames**—These are thumbnail image buttons just like those used in MyDVD. They are Photoshop graphics with three layers: Image, Overlay, and Thumb. If you worked with Style Creator in Chapter 22, "Creating Custom MyDVD Templates with Style Creator," you know that the Thumb graphic defines the rectangle in which the video thumbnail image or animation will go. The Image is the border and the Overlay is the Subpicture.

Creating a Slideshow

The Slideshow module is virtually the same as that used in MyDVD 5 (the predecessor to MyDVD 6 that allows up to 99 slides, compared to 1,000 for MyDVD 6). Open that interface in one of two ways:

▶ Select File, Add Slideshow.

▶ Drag an image to the filmstrip placeholder in the Titles window (the placeholder will display a name like Slideshow #) and double-click that placeholder.

Taking the latter route opens the Slideshow interface (shown in Figure 24.11) with that image in the show and selected as the thumbnail image (it'll have the Button Image icon in its upper-left corner).

By the Way

Dragging an Image to a Menu Placeholder

If you drag an image to a Menu placeholder filmstrip icon (instead of to a Title placeholder), that will *not* open the Slideshow. It will open a new menu with that image as its background.

Add a few images to the Slideshow and click OK. Unlike MyDVD, DVDit! 5 does not automatically add a button to the menu. It merely returns you to the Author interface. If you drag the Slideshow placeholder thumbnail image to a menu background in the Menu screen, DVDit! 5 will add the thumbnail image you selected to the menu as a button.

Did you Know?

Creating an Instant Slideshow

Here's a rapid-fire slideshow creation tip: Import all your slideshow images into the Images palette, select them en masse (use Ctrl+click to select scattered images or click one at the top of the list and Shift+click one at the bottom to select those two and all in between), and then drag and drop them to a Titles palette's Drag Media Here to Create Title placeholder. That creates a slideshow instantly. To edit the slideshow, double-click its thumbnail in the Titles palette.

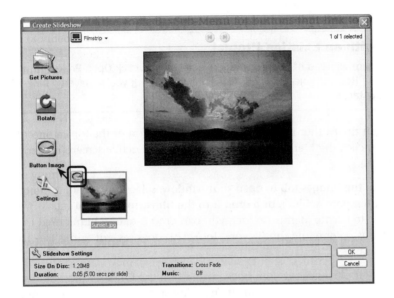

FIGURE 24.11
The Slideshow interface will look familiar if you worked with MyDVD.

Laying Out Menus and Submenus

Remember, changing to a prosumer DVD-authoring product means changing your DVD-authoring workflow. Instead of the MyDVD paradigm of automatically creating menus, buttons, and links as you add assets to a project, with DVDit! 5 you first create sufficient menu backgrounds to start your project (you can always add more menus as you proceed), add buttons and text to those menu backgrounds, and then create links and set other navigation attributes.

DVDit! 5's other major departure from entry-level authoring is its lack of menu templates and styles. Creating menus in DVDit! 5 is a free-form process. That process begins with menu backgrounds.

Create Menu Backgrounds

Try it Yourself

Your menus are the foundation of your DVD project and set its tone. In this task I show you how to add static and animated menus, change backgrounds, and work with non-4:3 aspect ratio backgrounds. I cover buttons, links, audio, and other menu-editing topics in the next two chapters. To create menus, follow these steps:

1. Open DVDit! 5, select New Project, give your project a name, select a TV standard and file folder storage location, and click OK.

By the Way

Work with an Existing Project

In the future, instead of clicking New Project, you can click Open Project (at the bottom of the Recent Projects window) to access any work you've saved during the upcoming tasks.

2. Open the Author interface by clicking its button at the top of the screen and then click the Menus tab to make sure it's the active screen (instead of Titles).

3. Click the Images tab to open that window, select any background (I chose Contemporary Blue), and drag it to the filmstrip icon that reads Drag Media Here to Create Menus (in fact, you can drag it to any blank area in the Menus palette and that'll work, too). This does several things (see Figure 24.12):

   ▶ It places the chosen background into the filmstrip placeholder, names it Menu 1, and assigns it First Play status (the big green triangle is the First Play graphical reminder).

   ▶ It displays the background in the Main Menu editing screen.

   ▶ It adds a new blank filmstrip icon placeholder in the Author window.

FIGURE 24.12
Dragging a background to the filmstrip icon placeholder also opens it in the main Author screen.

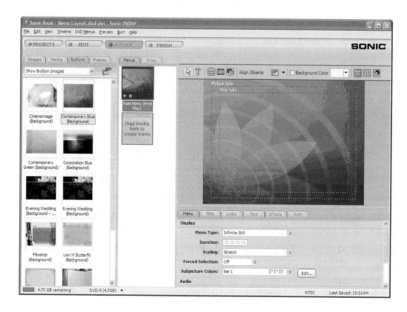

First Play—Menu or Video

By default, DVDit! 5 assigns **First Play** status to the first menu you create, which means that menu will be the first thing viewers see. But you can change that.

You might recall that MyDVD's implementation of First Play was kind of a kludge, limiting it to either a menu or the first video clip on the opening menu. In DVDit! 5, you can have any video clip (or series of video clips linked by **End Actions**—see Chapter 26 for more on that) or menu be the First Play asset. And, unlike MyDVD, that asset does not have to be in a menu. I explain First Play's various options in the next chapter.

4. Give your menu a descriptive name. To do so, click Menu 1 below the small thumbnail placeholder screen to the left of the main screen. This highlights the Menu 1 name. Type in something such as `Main Menu` and press Enter.

Create Multiple Menu Backgrounds at Once

To save time, you can create many menus in one step. Select multiple images in the Images palette and drag them to the Menus palette's Drag Media Here to Create Menu placeholder. DVDit! 5 will create one menu background for each image you dragged in.

5. Replace that background with a different image. In this case, use an image that does not have a standard TV 4:3 aspect ratio. To make the swap, add an image to the Images window using the Import Media button (I chose a sample image from the `My Documents\My Pictures\Sample Pictures` folder). Then drag it to either the Main Menu placeholder or the Author screen (if you drag an image from the Buttons tab, you'll add a button instead). As shown in Figure 24.13, the default action is to stretch the image to fit the 4:3 aspect ratio Author screen.

Customize Your Menus

The goal with DVDit! 5 is for you to use your own graphics to create menus. I strongly suggest you use whatever you have on your hard drive just to get used to that approach. DVDit! 5 supports the following graphic file types: BMP, JPEG, PSD, PNG, TARGA, and TIFF. DVDit! 5 also works with QuickTime's PICT file types, but that is an unsupported and undocumented attribute. Both PICT and TARGA require QuickTime version 6 (free download from `www.apple.com/quicktime`).

To import your background graphics to DVDit! 5, open the Images palette, click the Import Media file folder icon button, navigate to your graphics file(s), select one or more, and click Open.

For best results, your image should have a 4:3 aspect ratio. To avoid quality loss due to stretching, expanding, or contracting images, have them match the PAL TV standard: 768 pixels×576 pixels (this works well for the slightly lower-resolution NTSC standard, too).

FIGURE 24.13
Replace a menu background by dragging it to the placeholder or the Author screen. If your image does not have a 4:3 aspect ratio, you can adjust how DVDit! 5 displays it using the Scaling setting.

6. Use the Scaling option (highlighted earlier in Figure 24.13) to change how DVDit! 5 displays this non-4:3 image. Try them all. Note that Letterbox will display the full image and fill in the gaps with black.

Did you know?

Sharp Graphics Flicker

This might seem counterintuitive, but you want to avoid using background images that are too sharp. Clearly defined, high-contrast edges and fine horizontal lines might flicker when viewed on a television. If available, apply a blur filter in your image-editing application to remove hard edges.

7. Use a different method to add a menu. Select DVD Menus, Add Menu (keyboard shortcut—Ctrl+M) and, as shown in Figure 24.14, a solid-color screen will appear in the Author screen and in a placeholder. Its color will be whatever you set in Preferences, Author, Default Background Color.

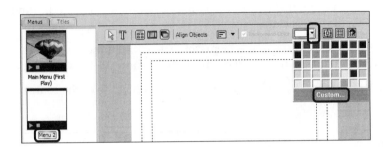

FIGURE 24.14
Selecting DVD Menus, Add Menu adds a menu with a blank, solid-color background.

8. Change the background color by clicking the triangle highlighted in Figure 24.14 and choosing a color from that palette or opening the custom palette to widen your selection.

9. Give your menu some background audio (music, narration, natural sound—any audio file will work). To do that, click the Audio Browse button highlighted in Figure 24.15, select an audio file, and click Open. Note two things:

   ▶ The Menu Type becomes a Timed Still with a duration equal to the length of the audio clip.

   ▶ A Music Note icon appears in the menu's placeholder, indicating it has audio associated with it.

FIGURE 24.15
Add audio to your menu by clicking the highlighted Browse button. Note that your menu becomes a Timed Still and a Music Note icon appears in its placeholder.

10. Create a menu with a video background by clicking the Media tab (not the Title tab—dragging a media asset from there to the menu screen will add a button to the menu) and dragging a video (with audio) to the empty film-strip icon placeholder. After you do that, several things will happen (refer to Figure 24.16):

▶ Two icons appear in the menu placeholder: a triangle indicating this is an animated (video) menu and a Music Note icon indicating that audio is associated with it.

▶ The Menu Type in the Menu tab below the Author screen states this is a Motion Menu with a duration that equals the length of the clip.

▶ The Select Audio line notes the video clip name as the source of the audio.

Watch Out!

Avoid Long Video Menus

Video menus and button animations on static menus can consume large amounts of disc space. The DVD specification allows menus to use up to 1GB of space, which you can fill very quickly if your menu durations are too long (especially if you choose a high video bit rate in the Project Preferences).

I recommend using static menus when they won't take anything away from your DVD's overall look and feel. And when you do use video menus (or animated buttons with static menu backgrounds—both menu types consume the same amount of space) make menu durations no longer than 1 minute. Most viewers select a menu button within 60 seconds anyway.

FIGURE 24.16
Dragging a video from the Media palette to a Menu filmstrip icon place-holder creates a menu with a video background. Note the animation/audio icons in the placeholder and the Motion Menu and Audio files in the Menu window.

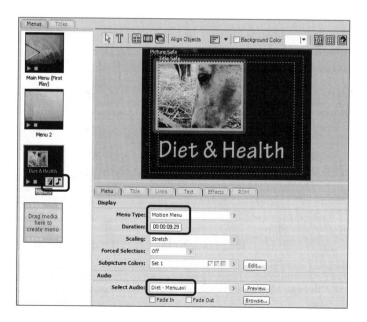

11. You can designate any of these three menus as a Submenu by linking them to other menus. I explain that in more detail in the next chapter. For this task, have DVDit! 5 create a new menu and link it as a submenu to any of the blank menus you've already created. Do that by clicking a menu's placeholder to select it and then select DVD Menus, Add Sub-Menu (keyboard shortcut—Ctrl+Shift+M).

12. As shown in Figure 24.17, adding that submenu places a button (using that submenu's background as the thumbnail image) on the selected menu and adds a menu thumbnail in the Menus palette. Note a couple things:

▶ If you use a non-4:3 background that you had adjusted to fit the background on the selected menu, it will show up as a stretched graphic in the submenu. Stretched is the default action when DVDit! 5 uses a graphic for a menu background.

▶ The new submenu button appears in the center of your selected menu. You can click it and drag it to a new location.

13. To change the submenu's Scaling (if needed), click its placeholder thumbnail to select it and select Zoom, Center, or Letterbox from the Scaling flyout list.

Submenu's Button Does Not Match Changed Scaling

You'd think that changing the scaling on a submenu's background should change the appearance of the button that links to it. But DVDit! 5 does not do this. This is a design oversight and has been prioritized for the next release.

If you want to properly scale this button, it's up to you to do it. I explain that in the next chapter.

Did you Know?

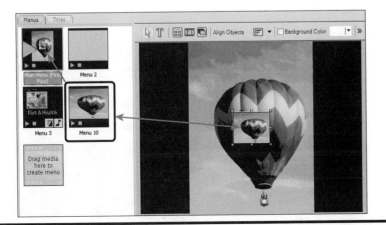

FIGURE 24.17
Adding a submenu to an existing menu adds a new menu placeholder and a button to that submenu in the selected menu.

Summary

Before jumping into menu building, DVDit! 5 lets you adjust a few preferences and project settings. Preferences typically save you a mouse-click or two and automate some processes. Project settings are geared almost exclusively to MPEG transcoding parameters.

After you tweak some options, you begin the DVD project-building process. That starts with some minor video trimming, frame grabs, and chapter placement. You do all those tasks in the Edit interface.

Then in the Author interface, you gather up the rest of your assets, including graphics for buttons and menu backgrounds, and (if you choose) revisit the MyDVD Slideshow interface. With all assets in hand, you create blank menus using static background images (using 4:3 or non-4:3 aspect ratio graphics) or a solid-color background or video backgrounds. From there, it's easy to select a menu and add a submenu button link to it (as well as add that submenu to the Menus palette).

In the next chapter you'll enhance your menus with audio and animations, add buttons and text, and link the media and menus.

As you'll see, it might take more time to plan your project than to create its menus. The menu-building process is straightforward and consists primarily of adding buttons and text to your menu backgrounds. You create links to those buttons and menus at the end of the menu-building process.

CHAPTER 25

Editing Menus with DVDit! 5

What You'll Learn in This Chapter:

- ▶ Adding and building buttons
- ▶ Working with text
- ▶ Scaling buttons, graphics, and text
- ▶ Arranging, aligning, and ordering objects
- ▶ Adding drop shadows and adjusting object opacity
- ▶ Setting First Play and linking media and menus

In this chapter you will complete the menu-building process using DVDit! 5. You'll add buttons to your menu and use DVDit! 5's graphics to build buttons with a customized look. You'll work with DVDit! 5's Text tool to add menu titles and button labels. Then you'll give buttons and text drop shadows.

Finally, you'll connect the dots by setting a **First Play** asset and linking assets—menus, videos, stills, and slideshows—to your newly created buttons.

In the next two chapters you'll tackle some higher-level editing tricks, build buttons in Photoshop, do some manual button navigation work, and burn your project to a recordable DVD.

Adding and Building Buttons

DVDit! 5 offers a full palette of buttons, frames, and text background banners. You can use them separately or layer them to create unique-looking buttons.

You add buttons to menus in two ways:

- ▶ As you did with MyDVD, by adding an asset and having DVDit! 5 automatically add a thumbnail button with a link to that asset.

- ▶ Dragging them from the Buttons palette and later linking them to assets such as submenus and videos.

Try it Yourself   **Place Buttons in Your Menus**

▼

This task shows you how to do both methods. You will try out various button types and combine graphical elements to make a custom button. Here's how:

1. Open a new project by selecting New Project, giving your project a name (I chose `Menu Editing`), selecting a TV standard and file folder location, and then clicking OK.

2. Click the Author button to open that interface, click the Images tab to open that palette, and click the Menus tab to open that palette.

By the Way

> **Graphics Families**
>
> You might have noticed that DVDit! 5 ships with several sets of graphical elements. As shown in Figure 25.1, each background has a name, for example: Cinemontage, Contemporary Green, and Corporation Blue.
>
> If you look in the Buttons and Frames palettes, you'll see graphical objects (button images, objects, navigation buttons) with the same names. DVDit! 5's graphic artists built these to work together.

3. For this task you will work with one family of graphical elements. I suggest Contemporary Blue. Drag the Contemporary Blue background to the Menu placeholder (not to the Title placeholder—that will add a slideshow button). You will add several types of buttons to this menu background, all from the same Contemporary Blue (or whatever background you selected) family of graphics.

4. Open the Buttons palette and select Show Button Images from its drop-down list.

▼

Buttons Equal Images

All the button images should have a twin in the Images palette. Whenever you add a file to the Images palette, DVDit! 5 automatically includes it in the Buttons palette as well. The reason for the two separate palettes is to ensure that DVDit! 5 understands what your intentions are. When you drag an image to an existing menu background, that menu background will change to the new background. When you drag that background's twin button image to a menu, DVDit! 5 displays it as a button with a thumbnail of that image.

By the Way

FIGURE 25.1
DVDit! 5 ships with several families of graphical elements. For every named background, there is a button image, several navigation buttons, a button object, and a frame.

5. Drag a Contemporary Blue (background) button from the Show Button Images palette to the menu screen. Two things happen (refer to Figure 25.2):

  ▶ A button with a thumbnail image of the graphic appears on the menu wherever you released your mouse. It does not have a frame nor a button label, nor is it linked to anything. You take care of all three later in this task and in the "Working with Text" and "Linking Media and Menus" sections that follow.

  ▶ A chime sound effect plays, letting you know "something just happened."

FIGURE 25.2
How your menu
should look after
adding a button
using the same
background image.

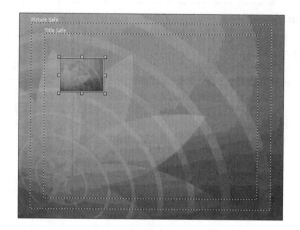

6. Now you'll add an asset and have DVDit! 5 automatically create a **linked** button. Click the Media tab, select the Show Video palette, and add a few video files to that palette by clicking the Import Media button, selecting some clips, and clicking Open.

7. If you drag a video file from the Media palette to the menu screen, you will replace the current static background with that video clip. To make a button, you need to drag a video from the Titles palette. So, put a file in the Titles palette by dragging a video file from the Media palette to the Drag Media Here to Make Title placeholder in the Titles palette.

Did you Know?

You Can Always Reverse a Wrong Move

Remember, you can always undo any action. If you dragged a video clip from the Media palette to the menu screen instead of from the Titles palette (making a new menu background instead of a button), select Edit, Undo or Ctrl+Z.

---

8. Now, drag that video clip from its Titles palette placeholder to your menu background. As shown in Figure 25.3, that action adds a thumbnail of the clip.

9. As currently configured, the button thumbnail will play as a static image in your DVD menu unless you switch on the Animate Button feature. To do so, as shown in Figure 25.3, click the Links tab below the menu screen and click Animate Button.

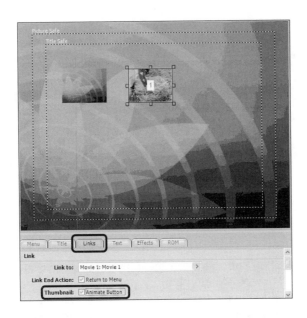

▼

FIGURE 25.3
Create a button automatically by dragging a video clip from the Titles palette to the menu screen.

Button Numbers Appear

DVDit! 5 assigns a number to each linked button. The numbers help you set up button navigation later. If you create a button by dragging a video clip to the menu screen and you don't see any button numbers, select View, View Button Numbers.

By the Way

---

10. Change the thumbnail image for that button by clicking the button to select it and then selecting DVD Menus, Set Button Image; or right-click the button and select Set Button Image—or use the keyboard shortcut Ctrl+\ (backslash). That opens the Set Movie Button Image shown in Figure 25.4. Find a new frame and click Set.

Animated Button Plays from New Thumbnail to End

Normally, an animated (video) thumbnail will play from the beginning of the clip to the end or until the time set for the duration of the motion menu (animating one button automatically changes a Still menu into a Motion menu). If you change the thumbnail of an animated button, the video animation will begin at that thumbnail frame.

By the Way

FIGURE 25.4
Use the Set Movie
Button Image to
change the thumb-
nail image or when
the button's video
animation begins.

11. Add a Navigation button to your menu by clicking the Buttons tab and opening the Show Navigation Buttons palette. Drag the Contemporary Blue (Home) button to the menu. As shown in Figure 25.5, it's fairly small and does not expand to the default button size set in your Preferences. You will change button sizes later in this chapter.

12. Add a Frame by clicking the Frames tab and dragging the Contemporary Blue (Frame) to the Menu screen. After you've placed it, you might need to center it. To do that, hover your cursor over it until it turns into a four-arrow icon, move the cursor, and then drag the frame to a suitable location. Your menu should look like Figure 25.5.

By the Way

Watch Your Button Placement

If your menu doesn't look like Figure 25.5, it might be because you dropped a button or frame onto one of the existing buttons by mistake. This is far too easy to do. If that happens, use the keyboard shortcut Ctrl+Z or the menu commands Edit, Undo to repair that miscue.

13. Add another video from the Media palette to the Titles palette and drag it to the Contemporary Blue Frame. Doing so will cause the entire frame to high-light, indicating you are about to link an asset to this button. Release the mouse button and your clip's thumbnail image will appear in the left side of the frame.

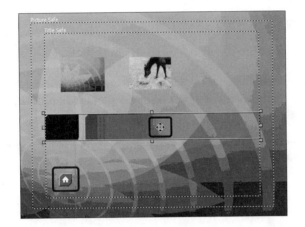

FIGURE 25.5
The navigation buttons do not expand to the default button size. The Contemporary Blue Frame has a built-in text background banner. Use the highlighted Move cursor to change its location.

14. You can use a button graphic in this frame instead of a video thumbnail to give it a different and more consistent look (this step demonstrates how you can build a button using DVDit! 5's graphics). Open the Buttons, Show Button Images palette and drag something other than the Contemporary Blue (Background) button to that frame. That newly selected button will replace the video thumbnail, but that button will still retain its link to the video clip. As shown in Figure 25.6, you can tell the button has a link because the number 2 is in the center of the frame.

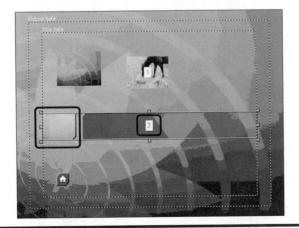

FIGURE 25.6
There is no need to use only video thumbnails in a frame-style button. Add a button image to that frame for a consistent look. Note that the frame button retains its link (number 2) to the video clip.

Working with Text

DVDit! 5 lets you create text using any font on your PC. You can position that text anywhere on the screen; make it bold, italic, or underlined; give it any color or opacity; and add a drop shadow.

In addition, the capability to use text as a button sets DVDit! 5 apart from most other authoring applications in its price category. You can link text to media or menus, which is a handy feature.

Try it Yourself   Enhance Your Menu with Text

In this task, I've limited the work to adding text to a menu or button frame and changing its font characteristics. I cover alignment, drop shadows, and links later in this chapter. Here's how to work with text in DVDit! 5:

1. Create a new menu by clicking the Menus tab, clicking the Images tab, and dragging a background to the Drag Media Here to Create Menu placeholder.

2. Start the process of adding a title to your menu by clicking the Text tab below the menu screen and selecting a font by clicking a font name next to Text Face. As shown in Figure 25.7, DVDit! 5 has the nice feature of previewing every font you have on your PC. Click the triangle (highlighted in Figure 25.7) at the bottom of the list to scroll through more fonts.

FIGURE 25.7
In the Text workspace, clicking in the space next to the highlighted Text Face displays a preview of every font you have on your PC.

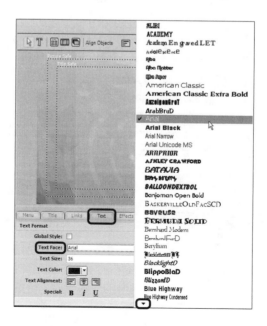

3. Click a font. Then, as shown in Figure 25.8, click the highlighted Text tool (keyboard shortcut—T), and click anywhere in the menu screen. A vertical line appears (it will move ahead of your text as you type). Start typing. Your menu should look something like Figure 25.8.

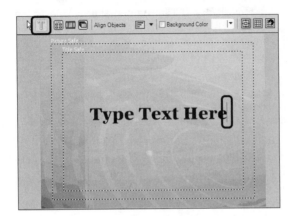

FIGURE 25.8
Select the highlighted Text tool, click inside the menu screen, and start typing.

4. When you're done, click anywhere in the screen and away from the text. That switches on the Select Tool (keyboard shortcut—S) and puts a bounding box around your text. You can hover your cursor inside the bounding box (it'll turn into a four-arrow move cursor) and move the text box anywhere on the menu background.

5. Change the entire text line in one of three ways:

   ▶ Double-click the text to highlight the entire phrase. Whatever you type at this point will replace that entire text string.

   ▶ Click a third time to switch on that vertical text line. You can use the arrow keys to move it left and right or move the cursor to another letter and click to move that line. Wherever it is, when you start typing, you add letters at that point without deleting the rest of the text.

   ▶ With the vertical line displaying, you can drag your cursor to highlight a portion of the text.

6. You can change the Text Face of your already typed text string. Use the Select tool (keyboard shortcut—S) to click it to place a bounding box around it, and then select a new Text Face.

By the Way

All or Nothing

DVDit! 5 does not let you change the font or other text characteristics of a portion of a text string. It's all or nothing. Even if you highlight a few letters, when you click Text Face to open the font display, DVDit! 5 automatically selects the entire text string. To use multiple fonts or font characteristics—size, color, italic, bold, or underlined—within a text string, you need to create separate text elements and then line them up to make them look like a single text string.

7. DVDit! 5 lets you set a Global Style for text. In this way you can have instant access to a consistent style you can use across an entire project or on selected text objects. To set the Global Style, check the Global Style check box, shown in Figure 25.9. Change your Text Face, Size, Color, Alignment, and **Special** characteristics (Bold, Italic, or Underlined). Now, if you add text strings with the Global Style box checked (or highlight existing text strings and click the Global Style check box), they will have the characteristics you set as the Global Style. Unchecking the box and using different text characteristics will not affect the Global Style.

FIGURE 25.9
DVDit! 5 lets you customize a Text Global Style that you can apply to any text strings in a project.

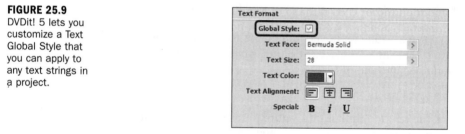

8. You can copy text from one menu and paste it into another (or paste it into the same menu—this is a good way to make a bunch of button labels that all look the same). Select the text string you created back in step 4 by double-clicking it with the Select tool. Copy it by selecting Edit, Copy (keyboard shortcut—Ctrl+C), switch to a different menu by clicking its placeholder in the Menus palette, click inside the menu screen to make it the active menu, and then select Edit, Paste (keyboard shortcut—Ctrl+V).

Scaling Buttons, Graphics, and Text

New to DVDit! 5 are several text and graphics alignment and ordering tools. You can layer elements, such as placing a button object on a frame background and then adding text on top to complete this three-layer object. Or use the menu grid and its Snap to Grid feature to line up buttons.

You also can maintain uniform size and aspect ratios for your graphical objects by resizing them en masse.

Resizing Buttons and Text

Try it Yourself

We'll start with resizing—a fairly simple click-and-drag process. You can resize a single object or a group to maintain uniform size changes. Here's how to do both:

1. Start a new project by clicking the Projects tab, clicking New Project, giving your project a name (I chose **Scaling and Aligning**), selecting a TV standard and a file folder location, and then clicking OK.

2. Go to the Author tab and create a new menu by dragging a background from the Images palette to the placeholder in the Menus palette (I chose the Corporation Blue background).

3. Add some text by clicking the Text tab under the menu screen, clicking the Text tool, clicking anywhere in the menu screen, and typing in anything you want.

4. You can resize text by double-clicking to highlight it (or using the Select tool to put a bounding box around it) and then changing the Text Size. But that's incremental and might not fit your exact needs. Instead, as shown in Figure 25.10, use the text bounding box. Click the Select tool, click the text to create a bounding box, and then drag any corner or edge. Shrink and move a text string to use it as a label with a button.

No Text Distortion

By the Way

The aspect ratio of your text string (and its bounding box) does not change, even if you drag an edge (rather than a corner). You cannot stretch or distort text. However, as I show you in a moment, you can distort a graphical element, such as a button.

Temporary Fuzzy Text

By the Way

You might notice that as you use the bounding box to expand text, the characters get fuzzy. Release the mouse button and the text sharpens. What's happening is that as you expand the text, you are stretching a graphic, which, like blowing up a photo, loses sharpness. But when you release the mouse button, DVDit! 5 recalculates the text face and redisplays it at its new size.

FIGURE 25.10
Use the text bound-
ing box to resize
text. Grab a corner
or an edge and
drag to expand or
contract the text.
After the text is
resized, DVDit! 5
will recalculate the
text display to
sharpen it up.

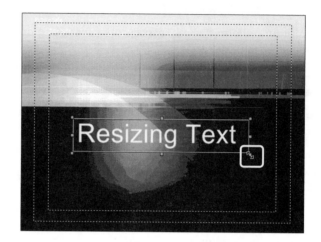

5. Now we'll move on to resizing groups of objects. To see that in action, add three button frames to your menu (no need to line them up) by clicking the Frames tab and dragging the same frame to your menu background three times. I chose the Corporation Blue frame because there are no other graph-ical elements associated with it.

6. Add the menu background button image to each frame by clicking the Buttons tab, selecting the Show Button Images palette, and dragging a background to each frame in the menu screen. Note that, as shown in Figure 25.11, DVDit! 5 lets you know you've properly placed the background by highlighting the entire frame (if you don't see a highlight, press the C key to turn on Selected Highlights).

FIGURE 25.11
Add three frames,
then give them
graphical looks to
match your project
by dragging the
same button image
to them. You can
tell you've placed
the button graphic
properly when
DVDit! 5 displays a
highlight over your
entire button
frame.

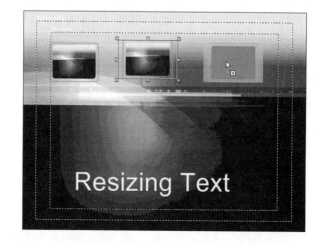

7. To resize them all equally, first select them all. Do that in one of two ways:

  ► Ctrl+click each in turn.

  ► Click and drag a marquee around them. To do that, click above and to the left of all the buttons, and then drag down to the right to encompass all the buttons in a flashing (and barely visible) rectangle—or marquee. Release the button, and bounding boxes should appear around all three buttons.

8. Resize all three selected buttons at once by moving the cursor over a corner of any one of the three buttons, as shown in Figure 25.12, and dragging it. All three buttons will change shape in unison.

9. Save your project, because you will use it in the next task.

Maintaining Aspect Ratio

Dragging a corner handle maintains a button's aspect ratio. Dragging an edge moves only that edge. But, if you hold down Shift while dragging an edge to resize, that, too, maintains the button's current aspect ratio.

Did you
Know?

FIGURE 25.12
You can resize all buttons equally by selecting all of them and resizing only one.

Arranging, Aligning, and Ordering Objects

You completed the previous section with three buttons scattered around your menu. What you'll do in this section is to line them all up—along the left, right, top, or bottom of the menu or centered in a horizontal or vertical line.

You can accomplish this using two routes: menu commands or the menu grid's Snap to Grid feature.

Finally, you'll layer some objects and then use the Order command to make them look the way you imagined them.

Try It Yourself   Aligning and Ordering Objects

▼

This task requires some experimentation to get a real feel for the various alignment options. When you order objects from front to back, sometimes issues occur
when you select an object that's buried under several other graphics.
Nevertheless, after you take a stab at these two operations, you'll get the hang of
them. Here's how they work:

1. Open your just saved project. First try to do some manual button aligning.
   Click a button and drag it to a location that suits you. Do the same for the
   other two buttons, attempting to line them up. To fine-tune your moves,
   select a button and then use the arrow keys to move them in small increments.

2. To line up those three buttons with absolute precision, you'll use the menu
   Align tool. Select DVD Menus, Align (or click the Align Objects button
   above the menu screen) to open the collection of options shown in Figure
   25.13. They are very useful but take some explanation. Here's a rundown:

   ▶ **Relative to Menu**—This is the last option on the list, but the most
     important one. With Relative to Menu deselected, any alignments will
     be relative to the buttons' current positions. So, if you have three but-
     tons going from left to right with overlapping bounding boxes (not a
     good thing with DVD buttons), selecting Align Top will put them in a
     straight line across the top of the menu but will not fix the overlap-
     ping; nor will it space them evenly relative to the menu's edges.
     Selecting Relative to Menu means that any alignment you do will
     place objects (buttons, graphics, and text) in position (left, right, up,
     down, center) symmetrically, relative to the menu. In this case, select-
     ing Align Top will create a straight line of buttons and also separate
     them so there is no overlap (if space permits).

   ▶ **Align Left (Ctrl+L), Align Right (Ctrl+Shift+L), Align Top (Ctrl+T),
     or Align Bottom (Ctrl+Shift+T)**—If you have three buttons in a row
     on top, Align Left or Align Right will pile them on top of one another
     in their respective corners of the menu. Align Top or Align Bottom will
     create a straight, horizontal line of buttons. If you have three random-
     ly placed buttons and have Relative to Menu turned off, selecting
     Align Left, Align Right, Align Top, or Align Bottom will place the but-
     tons in line with the one button that is (respectively) farthest left,
     right, toward the top, or toward the bottom.

   ▶ **Center Horizontally (Alt+Ctrl+H) and Center Vertically
     (Alt+Ctrl+V)**—Depending on the Relative to Menu option, this will
     line up buttons straight up and down or left to right.

▼

▶ **Distribute Horizontally (Shift+Ctrl+H)** and **Distribute Vertically (Shift+Ctrl+V)**—This option evenly spaces the buttons but does not line them up.

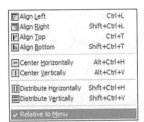

FIGURE 25.13
It takes some experimentation to figure out how to use these alignment options.

3. The best way to learn to use the alignment tool is to experiment with it. Drag your three buttons to scattered locations on the screen. Select all three (use the marquee select or Ctrl+click method). Switch on Relative to Menu and then try each alignment option in turn, using the keyboard shortcuts (which saves opening and reopening the Align menu). Between each instance, use Ctrl+Z to undo any changes so you can see each effect on its own. When you've worked through all six alignments, deselect Relative to Menu and try them again.

4. The other alignment method is to use the menu Grid. As shown in Figure 25.14, click the Show Grid button to switch it on and get rid of the Safe Area lines (to cut down on clutter) by clicking the View Safe Area button (to the left of the Show Grid button).

FIGURE 25.14
The menu grid coupled with its Snap to Grid feature lets you align objects with minimal hassle.

5. You can drag objects (buttons, text, or graphics) around in the menu and eyeball their position relative to the grid lines, or switch on the Snap to Grid feature. The problem is, it's kind of hard to tell when that feature has been turned on. With the grid switched on, you might note that its button is slightly darker and the ToolTip does not show up when you hover your cursor over that button. Use the same visual cues to see if Snap to Grid has been switched on. If it's not on, click that button.

6. Now drag a button around. It should literally snap an edge of its bounding box edge (any edge, depending on proximity to a grid line) to a grid line and hold there for a moment as you drag the button around. In this way you can line up left, right, top, or bottom edges.

Snap to Grid Can Be On When Grid Is Off

Even when the menu grid is off (not displaying) Snap to Grid can be on. This can be disconcerting because as you resize or move an object, both happen in herky-jerky fashion. If you experience that kind of stuttering behavior, switch off Snap to Grid.

7. Now you'll order objects from front to back. In the following steps you will access the Order Command via the Main Menu bar, keyboard shortcuts, and the right-click Menu. To set up this task, create a new menu with a solid color background by selecting DVD Menus, Add Menu (Ctrl+M). The solid color background makes it easier to see what's going on (you can turn off the Show Grid feature).

8. Add Text (type anything you want) and then drag the Filmstrip (Button Object) and Contemporary Blue (or Green) frame to the menu screen (in that order). Your menu screen should look something like Figure 25.15.

FIGURE 25.15
Set up your menu with three objects to try out the Order feature.

BUTTON TEXT LINE

9. Drag all three objects on top of one another. What happens is that the last object added to the menu—the frame—ends up on "top," whereas the first added—the text—is at the "bottom" of the pile. You need to rearrange that.

10. Click the frame (the topmost object). When several objects are piled up on one another, it's easy to select the wrong one, so make sure the bounding box belongs to the frame). Select DVD Menus, Order to open the four-option menu shown in Figure 25.16.

Bring to Front	Shift+Ctrl+]
Send to Back	Shift+Ctrl+[
Bring Forward	Ctrl+]
Send Backward	Ctrl+[

11. Because you selected the topmost object, you will see only two options: Send to Back and Send Backward (it's on top, so you can't bring it to the front). Because you want the frame to be the bottommost object, click Send to Back or use the keyboard shortcut—Shift+Ctrl+[(left square bracket). Clicking Send Backward (Ctrl+[) will move it back only one layer, essentially swapping it with the button object.

12. The text will now be the middle object. You want to bring it to the front. To do that, use the other means to access the Order menu, right-click it, and select Order, Bring to Front (Shift+Ctrl+]).

13. Now, to finish this task, adjust the sizes of the three objects, do some position adjusting (you'll probably need to use the keyboard arrow keys to move the objects around in small increments). When completed, your three-layer graphic should look something like Figure 25.17.

14. To move this, or any multilayered object, as a single unit, drag a marquee around it to select all the graphics, and then drag them to a new location.

FIGURE 25.17
How your text, button, and graphical-layered object might look after using the Order feature to place them in the proper order from back to front.

Adding Drop Shadows and Adjusting Object Opacity

You can apply drop shadows to any object: text, button, or graphic. The Drop Shadow feature has parameters similar to those you encountered in Pinnacle Studio: opacity, angle, color, distance, and size.

You can apply drop shadows to various objects using any combination of those parameters or apply the same set of parameters to any objects using a Global Style.

You use Opacity on an object-by-object basis.

Try it Yourself   Adjust Drop Shadows

▼

Both Opacity and Drop Shadow are in the same menu: Effects. In this task, you'll start with a clean slate, add three kinds of objects, and apply Drop Shadow and Opacity to all of them. Here's how these two features work:

1. Start a new project by clicking the Projects tab, clicking New Project, giving your project a name (I chose `Object Effects`), selecting a TV standard and a file folder location, and then clicking OK.

2. Go to the Author interface, select DVD Menus, New Menu (Ctrl+M) and add four objects (use Figure 25.18 as a reference): text, a button image, a navigation button, and a frame.

FIGURE 25.18
How you can set up your menu to try out the Drop Shadow effect.

▼

Some Navigation Buttons Already Have Drop Shadows

Take a close look at Figure 25.19. Three of the buttons have drop shadows to begin with. This is not a good thing and is probably an oversight on Sonic Solutions's part. Notice that the drop shadows don't all fall in the same direction. So, if you choose to use any navigation buttons with built-in drop shadows in your project, keep in mind that you probably want other objects in the same menu to have drop shadows that match the direction of the navigation buttons' shadows.

One other point—all graphical objects (in contrast to text) that have a resolution less than 768×576 pixels lose sharpness when expanded. The rounded rectangle button in the lower right of Figure 25.19 serves as an example. If the graphic is large to begin with (as are all the button images) they will look sharp at any size.

FIGURE 25.19
Several sets of navigation buttons have drop shadows built in. And all smaller graphical objects lose their sharpness when expanded.

3. Select all four objects using the marquee select technique or the Ctrl+click method.

4. As shown in Figure 25.20, check the Shadow On check box to apply shadows to all four objects.

5. Try out some Drop Shadow parameters. Note a few things:

   ▶ A Size of zero means the shadow is the same size as the original object.

   ▶ As you increase Size, the shadow becomes less distinct.

   ▶ Angle is the direction the virtual light is coming from.

   ▶ The greater the Distance, the farther above the menu background the objects will appear to be.

FIGURE 25.20
Switch on the Drop
Shadow feature in
the Effects window.

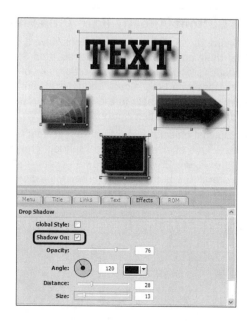

6. As you did with the Text Global Style, you can change the Global Style by clicking that check box and making changes to the Drop Shadow parameters. Then if you add more objects, they will have the same Drop Shadow characteristics. You can use the same Global Style with other menus.

7. Select only one object, switch off Global Style, and adjust its Drop Shadow parameters separately from the others in the menu.

8. Finally, try out the Opacity Effect (below the Drop Shadow window) in the Effects tab. Select any or all objects and move the Opacity slider to a setting less than 100. As shown in Figure 25.21, reducing the opacity not only changes the graphics but reduces their drop shadow opacity as well.

Did you
Know?

Use Opacity on a Layer in a Set

When you build layered objects, as you did earlier in this chapter, you can apply a reduced opacity setting to a single layer as a means to highlight text above that layer, for instance.

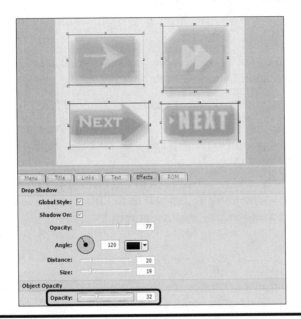

FIGURE 25.21
Reducing the opacity of these objects also reduces the opacity of their drop shadows.

Setting First Play and Linking Media and Menus

In this chapter's final section, I show you how to link assets to the buttons you've created. As I've mentioned a couple times before, this is what sets DVDit! 5 apart from entry-level DVD-authoring products. In DVDit! 5, the basic workflow is to build your menus and buttons and *then* connect them to your assets.

DVDit! 5 shows off another prosumer feature nicely with its First Play tool. As you discovered earlier, Sonic Solutions's entry-level product, MyDVD, has a less-than-ideal version of First Play. It has to be the first video in the project's opening main menu. DVDit! 5 lets you choose any video, menu, slideshow, or still you want. And it does not have to appear in any menu.

Using Studio (or another NLE) you can edit together a sequence of clips, such as an animated logo, brief credits, and a title screen, and have it be the First Play. Upon completion, the DVD then would automatically display to the Main Menu.

Setting First Play Is Easy

Rather than a Try It Yourself task, here's a brief explanation of how to set First Play.

The First Play item can be a Menu or Media Asset. If it's a menu, right-click the Menu's placeholder thumbnail and select Set as First Play.

If it's a media asset, you need to make sure you've added it to the Titles palette.

▶ Remember, in the case of a video, to get it into the Titles palette, first add it to your Media palette and then drag it to the Drag Media Here to Create Title placeholder in the Titles palette.

▶ In the case of a slideshow, you need to first create the slideshow (select File, Add Slideshow), adding a thumbnail in the Titles palette in the process. Or at least start the slideshow creation process by dragging an image from the Images palette to the Drag Media Here to Create Title placeholder in the Titles palette.

After you have your media asset in a Titles placeholder, as shown in Figure 25.22, right-click the placeholder thumbnail and select Set as First Play.

FIGURE 25.22
In the Titles palette, right-click whatever media asset you want to use as First Play and select Set as First Play.

Linking Media and Menus

This is where the rubber meets the road. You've assembled your assets and laid out your menus and submenus with buttons and text; now it's time to link them all. In the previous chapter and at the beginning of this chapter, you noted that when you drag a media asset to a menu, it automatically creates a basic (unframed) thumbnail button with a link to that asset. In this coming task, you use a more proactive method. You select buttons and choose what to link to them.

Higher-Level Linking Tasks in the Next Chapter

By the Way

Basic linking of assets and menus is relatively easy. Things start getting a bit more complicated when you start working with End Actions, Forcing a Menu Selection, or Defining Button Routing. You will work on those three areas in the next chapter.

Adding Links

Try it Yourself

▼

In this task you will work with several menus, including a scene selection submenu, and you will link buttons to menus and media assets. There are three basic methods to add links: drag-and-drop, right-clicking, and the Links menu. I show you all three in this task. Here's how they all work:

1. For this project I set up a full collection of menus and assets. You can do the same or go with some basic assets: a video with chapters, a main menu with some buttons, and a submenu with some button frames for your chapters.

2. The easiest way to link a button to an asset or menu is via drag-and-drop. Figure 25.23 shows how that works. In the Author interface, select your main menu. Click the Menus tab to open the Menus palette. Click and drag a submenu to a button in the menu screen. Doing so adds a red highlight to the button and the cursor changes to a plus (+) sign. Release the mouse button and that audible chime plays and the number 1 appears on the button.

Button Numbers

Did you Know?

Each time you create a button link, DVDit! 5 assigns a button number to the new button. The first link you create on a menu is button number 1, the next is number 2, and so on. If you delete a link, DVDit! 5 reassigns the button numbers to maintain an unbroken sequence.

By default, when a viewer goes to a menu, button 1 is highlighted as the selected button.

If you want a different button to be the default selected button, try to have it be the first link you make to that menu. If not, you can delete links ahead of it to make it first or use DVDit! 5's so-called Forced Selection feature. I cover that in the next chapter.

---

3. You can use the drag-and-drop method to link other menus to the other buttons (or text strings) in any menu. I linked all four buttons in my main menu, and DVDit! 5 added button numbers for each (see Figure 25.24).

▼

FIGURE 25.23
Use the drag-and-drop method to create a link between a menu (or media asset) and a button.

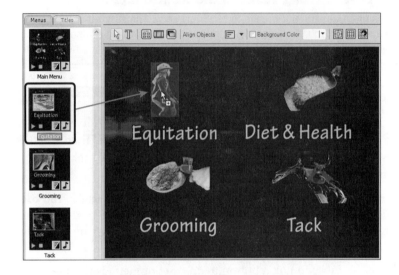

FIGURE 25.24
As you link buttons to other menus or media assets, DVDit! 5 adds button numbers to each linked button.

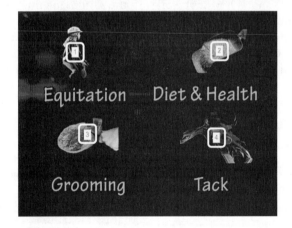

4. Right-clicking a button or a text string to create a link works very well. The caveat is that you have to have added the media asset or menu to the respective palette for it to show up in the right-click linking list. To try this, right-click any button or text string and select Link to open that fly-out listing of possible links (refer to Figure 25.25). Select one to create a link.

Listing of Possible Links Can Become Lengthy

As your project grows, the right-click list of possible links can become unwieldy.

FIGURE 25.25
Use the right-click
menu to add a link
to a button or a
text string.

5. As shown in Figure 25.26, I linked each of the button frames to separate
   videos. As you are adding links to buttons or text, remember to create links
   back to your Main or Previous menus. I dragged the Main Menu placeholder to the Main Menu text in the menu editing screen to add that link (number 4 on this menu, shown in Figure 25.26).

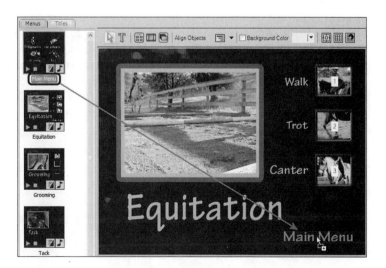

FIGURE 25.26
As you add links,
remember to cre-
ate links back to
your Main Menu or
to the previous
menu.

6. In this step, I link buttons in a scene selection menu to the video clip chapters. You can't use the drag-and-drop method for chapters (in this case—but I explain how you can in another case in the next chapter). You have to use either the right-click method or create a link using the Links menu. As shown in Figure 25.27, click the Links tab to open that menu.

Two Button Points

The DVD specification allows no more than 36 linked buttons per menu. DVDit! 5 will not allow you to add more than that.

Overlapping, linked buttons might not function properly. The best way to check for overlap is to select all buttons (use the Ctrl+click or marquee method) and look at the bounding box handles and see if any touch or overlap. The easiest way to fix that is by using the Align tools.

---

7. Click a button in the menu screen that you want to create a link to and open the Link To listing. As shown in Figure 25.27, the list looks the same as the right-click list. In this case, I clicked the video that I added chapters to (such videos have little triangles indicating the presence of chapters) and selected a chapter.

Create a Link to a Slideshow in the Same Way

If you created a Slideshow, its placeholder will be in the Titles palette. You can create links to it using the same drag-and-drop, right-click, or Links menu methods used for menus and videos.

---

8. Finish linking all your menus and assets. I cover previewing your project in the next chapter, but you can test those waters now. To do that, click the Finish button and click Start from First Play or Start from Current Position. In either case, some unpredictable things might happen, such as instead of going to the Main Menu at the end of the First Play video, DVDit! 5 probably will play some other video. This is not a bug. You need to set the End Action for the First Play video. You'll do that in the next chapter.

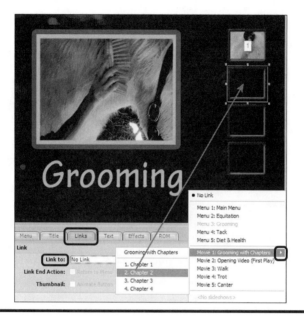

FIGURE 25.27
Use the Links menu Link To listing to add links. In particular, this comes in handy when you're creating links to chapters for a scene selection menu. Note the little triangle next to the video name indicating that this video has chapters.

Summary

DVD authoring involves designing the project's menu structure, creating the menus and buttons, adding media, and linking all the elements. In this chapter, you created and edited buttons; added text; scaled, arranged, aligned, and ordered graphical objects; and added drop shadows and reduced their opacity.

After you completed the menu building process, you assigned First Play status to an asset or menu and then used three methods to create links from your assets and menus to the menu buttons.

CHAPTER 26

Advanced DVDit! 5 Authoring Techniques

What You'll Learn in This Chapter:

- ▶ Creating custom buttons in Photoshop
- ▶ Cool tips and tricks—Easter Eggs, outros, and more
- ▶ Fine-tuning button subpictures and navigation
- ▶ Adjusting menu and media properties
- ▶ Adding ROM Data

In this hour you will try out some advanced authoring techniques. I will show you how to use Photoshop Elements (the lesson applies to the full version of Photoshop as well) to create custom buttons and backgrounds. Perhaps when playing Hollywood movie DVDs, you've encountered "Easter Eggs," invisible buttons that link to special features such as outtakes. I will show you how to create those in your projects.

Some high-end DVDs have videos that lead seamlessly into and out from the menu—**intros** and **outros** in DVD parlance. I explain those techniques in this chapter as well as offer up a few more tips.

Then you will wrap up authoring with DVDit! 5. You'll do some fine-tuning techniques not available in entry-level products such as MyDVD. For example, you will add End Actions, set Forced Button Selections, and define customized Button Routing. Finally, you will add PC files (ROM Data) to your project.

You will do the final testing and burning of your DVD in Chapter 27, "Burning DVDs and Dealing with DVD Duplicators."

Creating Custom Buttons in Photoshop

One of the huge advantages of DVDit! 5 over MyDVD and other entry-level DVD products is how well it works with graphics created in the graphics-industry standard-bearer, Photoshop (I will use Photoshop's much-less-expensive younger sibling, Photoshop Elements, in this section's Try It Yourself task).

If you worked with the MyDVD Style Creator Photoshop plug-in in Chapter 22, "Creating Custom MyDVD Templates with Style Creator," you know it requires some very specific layer names and is geared to creating entire menu templates. DVDit! 5 is much more user friendly. No need to create entire templates—rather, only buttons or single-layer backgrounds. And instead of numerous layer names, DVDit! 5 buttons require only two or three specifically named layers.

By the Way

> ### Creating Menu Backgrounds
>
> You can use graphics created in Photoshop and many other graphics programs as menu backgrounds in DVDit! 5. There are only two basic rules:
>
> ▶ Use one of the seven file formats compatible with DVDit! 5: BMP, JPEG, PICT, PNG, PSD, Targa, and TIFF.
>
> ▶ Stick to a rectangular 4:3 aspect ratio with a resolution equal to (or at least in the vicinity of) the PAL standard: 768×576 pixels.

This customization capability inherent in DVDit! 5 is a *big deal*. And learning how to create your own menu objects is critical to creating professional-looking DVDs.

Try it Yourself   **Creating Menu Graphics in Photoshop Elements**

If you worked with Photoshop or Photoshop Elements in Chapter 22, this will be a piece of cake. DVDit! 5 works with two button types—two-layer basic buttons and three-layer frames. In this task I show you examples of both types and then show you how to make a couple buttons from scratch. Here's how to do all that:

1. Open Photoshop Elements (or Photoshop—their functionality and work-spaces are very similar). Select File, Open and navigate to the DVDit! 5 Navigation Buttons file folder. The default location is C:\Program Files\Sonic\DVDit!\Content\Frames. Select the Travel Passport (Frame).psd file and click Open.

2. That PSD file, shown in Figure 26.1, is a three-layered frame. Note the layer names:

▶ **Overlay**—The button's Subpicture layer. DVDit! 5 allows for only one such layer. That means you cannot have two separate graphics display for the Selected and Activated button states. You can, however, have two different colors. I show you how that feature works later in this chapter.

▶ **Image**—The button itself. You create it on a transparent background so it can have any shape as well as transparency and holes. In this task, I show you how to make a hollow button.

▶ **Thumb**—Use this only for buttons in which you will place a video or still thumbnail animation or image. Nonframe and thumbnail buttons do not have a Thumb layer.

Layer Names Are Critical

DVDit! 5 can use a Photoshop file as a button only if it has these layer names (you need a Thumb layer only for thumbnail frame buttons) and you display them in order from the top layer down: Overlay, Image, and Thumb. You cannot import multilayer files into DVDit! 5 that use other layer names. If you **merge** (or **flatten**) those layers into a single layer, or import any other single-layer graphic as an Image, DVDit! 5 will automatically add a button version of that graphic in the Buttons, Show Button Images palette.

By the Way

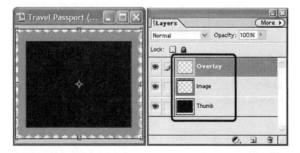

FIGURE 26.1
A basic, three-layered DVDit! 5 frame button Photoshop file. You must adhere to the layer names: Overlay, Image, and Thumb.

3. Before creating a button from scratch, take a look at how the layers work. Unclick the eyeballs for the Overlay and Thumb layers. That leaves the Image, the ragged-edged rectangle shown in Figure 26.2.

Photoshop Effects Need Simplifying

That frame has a 3D look. This is a typical Photoshop effect. You can apply any Photoshop effects you want to a button image, but you have to simplify the layer for that effect to show up when you use the button in DVDit! 5. I show you how to simplify a layer later in this Try It Yourself task.

FIGURE 26.2
How the single-layer Image graphic looks. This is how this frame button will look on a DVD menu.

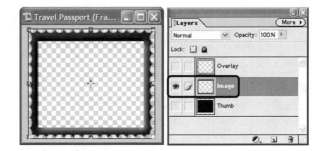

4. Click the Thumb eyeball. You'll see that it's a black rectangle. That rectangle defines where the video or image thumbnail will appear in a button. It can be any shape and color (except white).

Thumbnail Distortion

When you create thumbnail frame buttons, you don't have to use rectangles. I'll give you an example in a moment. The only caveat is that DVDit! 5 will distort the frame Image graphic if necessary to fit the Thumb shape. So, if you create a circular graphic for the Thumb layer, DVDit! 5 will distort the frame (by squashing it horizontally) and then crop the parts that are not within the thumb.

5. Click the Overlay eyeball. In this case, it's a duplicate version of the Image layer in a different color and with no 3D look to it. Overlay graphics can be any shape and any color except white.

Overlay Color Is Irrelevant

One of the confusing things about Overlay colors is that the color you select for the Overlay graphic in Photoshop has no bearing on the color you'll see when the Overlay displays as a Selected or Activated highlight. You choose those Highlight colors within DVDit! 5 and can have any Selected or Activated highlight be any color you want, no matter what color you gave it when you created it in Photoshop.

Keep Subpicture Overlay Graphics Simple

Any effect you apply to an Overlay will not show up in a DVD menu. And it's best to not have any soft edges on Overlay graphics. Subpicture graphics, according to the DVD specification, are very basic. Each pixel is either a solid color or transparent. So, when they display in a DVD menu, soft edges will tend to look jagged and you won't see any effects or multiple colors.

6. Close the Travel Passport (Frame).psd file by clicking the X in the upper-right corner. If Photoshop asks you if you want to save changes, click No.

7. Open a new document by selecting File, New. Using Figure 26.3 as a reference, give your document a name (I chose **DVDit Button-1**), a Width (2"×1.5" is a good minimum size for a button), a resolution of 72 pixels/inch (this resolution works best for TV—a higher resolution is unnecessary), RGB Color, and Transparent Contents. Click OK.

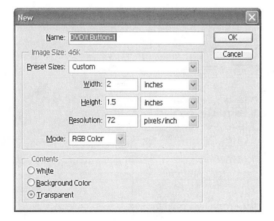

FIGURE 26.3
Use these parameters when building a button from scratch.

8. There are all sorts of ways to create graphics in Photoshop Elements. I have set up one way in Figure 26.4. *Fair warning*: The two buttons I'm going to make in this task will be wacky looking. The purpose here is to show you that it's easy to break out of the rectangle/arrow button mold. Here are the graphic-building steps briefly stated:

   ▶ Click the Drawing tool (keyboard shortcut—U). It'll probably default to a rectangle in the Tools palette).

   ▶ Click the Custom Shape tool in the menu bar. I've highlighted it in Figure 26.4 (when you do that, it'll show up in the Tools palette as well).

▶ Select a Shape from the Shape drop-down list.

▶ Select a Style. I opened the Style palette inside my workspace (instead of having it act as a drop-down list) by dragging its tab from the upper-right corner. I chose a very colorful Nebula Style from the Patterns group.

▶ If you don't select a Style, select a Color.

Did you Know?

Find More Shapes—Find or Create One That's Hollow

You can click the shape's fly-out menu and select All Elements Shapes to see all the cool stuff Photoshop has to offer. I chose a star with a hole in the middle. I suggest you choose the same or some other object with a hollow center.

Even if you choose a solid shape, you can apply a style to it that will make it hollow. In the Layer Styles palette, check out the Wow Neon group. Use these on Arrows and the like to create some very cool buttons.

FIGURE 26.4
How your Photoshop Elements work-space should look if you followed the bulleted points in step 8.

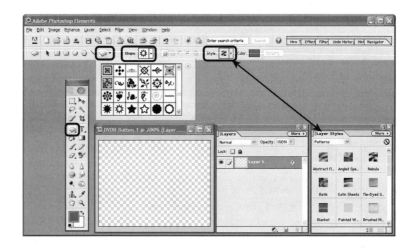

9. Click anywhere in the document and then drag your mouse to somewhere else in the document.

As shown in Figure 26.5, that creates the shape using the style you selected. I went one step further. I switched to a different Style group—Bevels—and dragged the Scalloped Edge bevel onto the star to give it a 3D look as well as the Nebula style.

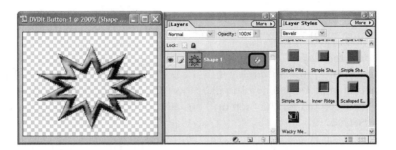

FIGURE 26.5
How my button looks with the Scalloped Edge bevel added. The highlighted little "f" in the Shape 1 layer means effects have been added to this layer. You need to simplify them before saving so they will show up in DVDit! 5.

10. Right-click the Shape 1 layer name and select Simplify Layer so the cool effects will show up in DVDit! 5 (if it is not simplified, DVDit! 5 displays the button in a single color and without the 3D "look").

11. Right-click again, select Rename Layer, and type in **Image**. Failing to give the layer the proper name means DVDit! 5 won't treat it as a button.

12. To create the Subpicture Overlay, you could duplicate the current layer (right-click and select Duplicate Layer) but it's a lot more fun to create something different. To do that, select a new Shape (I chose an eight-point star) and then turn off the Style by clicking its triangle and the fly-out menu button and then selecting Remove Style.

13. Click and drag in the document to create that new shape. As shown in Figure 26.6, Photoshop automatically creates a new layer and places that shape in it.

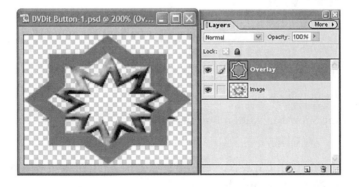

FIGURE 26.6
Adding a new graphic automatically creates a new layer. Name it **Overlay**.

14. Name that layer **Overlay** (right-click, select Rename Layer, and type in **Overlay**). This layer should be above Image in the Layers palette. If not, drag it above Image. Save this file.

15. You create a button frame in the same fashion. You can start from scratch or add a Thumb layer to your current button. To keep things simple, take the latter route. Select a new shape (I chose an oval) and click and drag in your document window to create a shape in a new layer.

16. Rename that layer Thumb (right-click, select Rename Layer, and type in Thumb). Drag the Thumb layer to the bottom of the Layers palette. Your project should look something like Figure 26.7 (I created a new five-point star from scratch for this step and turned off the Overlay display by unclicking its eyeball).

17. Select File, Save As and give this a different name than the previously made button.

FIGURE 26.7
A frame button (I applied a different style to the star and switched off the Overlay eyeball so you could see the Thumb layer better). This demonstrates that frames and thumbnails do not have to be rectangular.

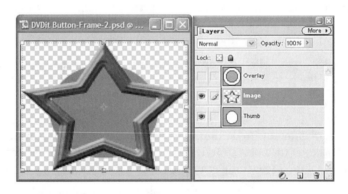

Check Your Work

To see if these buttons work in DVDit! 5, follow these steps:

1. Open DVDit! 5.

2. Open the Author interface.

3. Click the Buttons tab.

4. Open the Show Navigation Buttons palette.

5. Click Import Media.

6. Find your first two-layer button and click Open. It'll appear at the bottom of the Navigation Button palette.

7. Click the Frames tab.

8. Click Import Media.

9. Find your second three-layer frame button and click Open. It'll show up at the bottom of the Frames palette.

10. Drag both buttons to a blank menu.

11. Create a link (so you can see the thumbnail image and subpicture overlay highlights) by dragging a video from the Titles palette to each one.

12. If you don't see the subpicture overlay highlights, turn them on by pressing the keyboard shortcut C to view the Selected highlight or A to view the Activated highlight.

Your menu should look something like Figure 26.8.

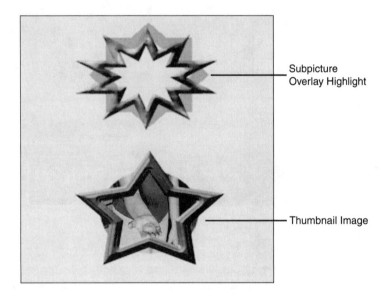

Subpicture
Overlay Highlight

Thumbnail Image

FIGURE 26.8
Test your buttons by adding them to the Buttons and Frames palettes and then dragging them to a menu and creating links.

Cool Tips and Tricks

In this section I give you five nifty tips: Easter Eggs, outros (and intros), creating a chain of videos, adding chapter buttons en masse to a scene selection menu, and how to quickly duplicate buttons, graphics, or text.

Easter Eggs

Many Hollywood movie DVDs have **Easter Eggs**—hidden buttons that link to special bonus content, outtakes, funny bits, or photos of the director's dog. You're on your own in creating or choosing the content, but I will show you how to make an invisible link.

Here's a quick run-through (no need for a full Try It Yourself task):

1. Place a button in a menu and link it to a video clip (you need to link it so you can see its Subpicture highlights). As shown in Figure 26.9, you typically want to put the button in a corner so it won't overlap any visible buttons.

FIGURE 26.9
Place the button you want to convert to an Easter Egg in an out-of-the-way place on your Menu. Set the button's Opacity to zero to make it invisible.

2. Click the Effects tab, click the newly placed Easter Egg button to select it, and drag the Opacity slider to zero. Your button will disappear.

3. Click somewhere in the menu to deselect the button and its handles will disappear.

4. You can tell it's still there by switching on the Selected or Activated Subpictures. Do that using the keyboard shortcuts: A for Activated and C for Selected (alternatively, select DVD Menus, View Selected Subpictures or View Activated Subpictures). Click N to turn off the highlights.

5. You can make this Easter Egg even more difficult to find by reducing its Selected Subpicture color to zero opacity. I show you how to change Subpicture Opacity settings in the next section, "Fine-Tuning Button Subpictures and Navigation." If you do that, the viewer will note that at some point while navigating around a menu, no button will have a Selected highlight. That's the clue that he's found an Easter Egg. If he presses the Enter button on the remote, the Easter Egg button's Activated highlight will display for a moment before taking the viewer to the hidden feature.

6. To make the Easter Egg even more fun, create a button with a wild-looking or fanciful Overlay layer (a *Harry Potter* DVD used an Overlay that scattered stars all over the top of the screen). Or create a text string that says something like, "You found it!" Link an asset to that text and reduce its opacity to zero. So when the viewer moves the remote to that hidden spot and clicks, the Activated Subpicture highlight will pop onscreen, briefly displaying that graphic or message.

7. If you want to be totally diabolical, you can also drop the Easter Egg button's Activated Subpicture highlight color opacity to zero (again, I will explain how to adjust Subpicture Opacity in the next section). So when the viewer notes that no button has a highlight and clicks in the belief that he might have found an Easter Egg, nothing will display, but he will get to see the hidden asset.

DVD Menu Outros and Intros

You've seen DVDs that start with a video that morphs seamlessly into a menu. Some also transition out of a menu. That is, when you click a button, the menu kind of disassembles and then plays the asset linked to that button.

Those DVDs use menu **intros** and **outros**.

Most production work on DVD menu intros and outros takes place outside of DVDit! 5 in your nonlinear video editor. The most basic kind of intro or **outro**— fading up to or dissolving from a video to the menu—takes only a few steps, and you can use Pinnacle Studio or another NLE for that.

But if you want to do other things that require several video tracks and the capability to work with Photoshop graphics with transparent backgrounds (such as flying buttons onscreen), you'll need to step up to Premiere Elements or a higher-level NLE.

After you create the intro and outro videos, it's a simple task to add them to your DVD project. So I'll show you how I created an intro (you can use the same process to create an outro—just reverse some of the steps) and then I'll show you how to use that video as a menu intro (or outro).

Creating an Intro—An Example

Take a look at Figure 26.10. It's a still I grabbed from a video I created in Premiere Pro. There are a few things going on in it:

▶ I used a looping video background. This particular one came from a product called Editor's Tool Kit from Digital Juice (www.digitaljuice.com). It's kind of an expensive collection (starting at $600) of animations. You might consider looking for some freebies. The Main Concept website has a few: www.mainconcept.com/texture_loops.shtml. Main Concept created the MPEG encoder used in Premiere Pro.

▶ I created the horse rider button (highlighted in Figure 26.10) using a couple Photoshop tools.

▶ I added that Photoshop graphic to a Premiere video track and applied the Motion effect to it so it moved from the video (after I froze that video clip) in the frame to the corner of the screen.

FIGURE 26.10
A frame from a video I used as a DVD menu intro. It took several steps to get to this point.

Now take a look at Figure 26.11. This is the final frame of the intro video. All the buttons are in place, as are the submenu titles. Here's how I used this:

▶ I used a frame grab to create an image file of this frame. I used it later to create the DVD menu.

▶ I used the same video background (with its submenu titles but without the button graphics) to create a video background for the DVD menu (I added the button images to that animated menu background later).

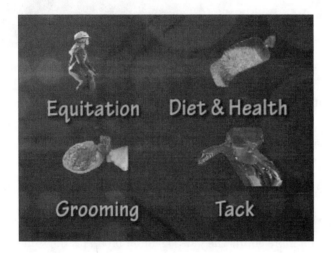

FIGURE 26.11
The final frame of the DVD menu intro video. I used this to create the menu itself.

Now I used the assets I worked on in Premiere and Photoshop to create a menu in DVDit! 5. Figure 26.12 shows some of that process.

▶ I created a menu using the still image I captured of the final frame in the menu intro.

▶ I imported the Photoshop single-layer buttons as Images (DVDit! 5 automatically adds them to the Button Images palette).

▶ I dragged those buttons to the menu template, one at a time, and resized and positioned them to match their duplicates in the template (thereby matching how they looked at the end of the intro video).

▶ Then I replaced the menu template background with the Motion Menu I created without the buttons but with text.

FIGURE 26.12
In DVDit! 5, I used the still frame image, taken from the intro video, as a menu template to which I added, then resized and carefully positioned, the button graphics to match their placement at the end of the intro video.

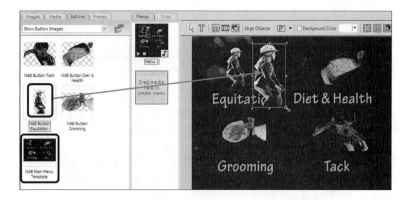

What I have now is a Motion Menu background (with static button images added to it) that matches the final frame of the intro video.

To move seamlessly between the intro video and the main menu, I set the intro video as the DVD's First Play and set its End Action as this Main menu.

I explain End Actions later in this chapter in the "Adjusting Menu and Media Properties" section.

What About Outros?

Outros take a bit more effort. The video-creation process is the same, except you start with the menu video frame and then disassemble it. Typically, the outro video then fades to black and the item the button really linked to starts playing. It could be an intro to another menu (whew—even more work!).

When you've completed editing an outro, you can include it in your DVD project in one of two ways:

▶ Using your video editor, you can add an outro to the beginning of each video asset. The problem with that method is that you can't add an outro to the beginning of a slideshow created within DVDit! 5 (however, you can create a slideshow in your video editor and add an outro to it).

▶ You create a copy of the outro for as many buttons as you'll use to access it, naming each one something like outro-1, outro-2, and so on. Then have each button link to its like-numbered outro and assign an End Action for each outro to go to the asset the button was intended to link to. This will work properly with a slideshow created in DVDit! 5. I explain End Actions later in this chapter.

DVDit! 5 Has No Override Option

With professional-level DVD-authoring products, you don't have to create copies of the outro or attach it to the beginning of each video. Those products typically offer an Override option. Basically, it allows you to put an instruction in a link that tells its linked asset to do something other than its regularly assigned task—its so-called End Action. DVDit! 5 offers a limited version of that Override called Link End Action. I cover it the "Adjusting Menu and Media Properties" section. The reason it won't work for outros is because the only override it offers is to take the viewer back to a menu, not to a media asset.

By the Way

Creating a Chain of Videos

Typically, when adding a First Play video to your project, you want it to be more than a single video. Instead of using your video editor to edit a bunch of videos into one long video, have DVDit! 5 automatically do that for you.

Just drag your assets from the Media palette to the Titles palette. Arrange them into the order you want them to play and set the first one as the First Play. By default, DVDit! 5 will go from the first video clip to the next, and so on, until it comes to a clip with an End Action that tells it to go somewhere else, such as the Main Menu.

Adding Chapter Buttons En Masse Using the Titles Details View

In the previous chapter, I said you could not use the drag-and-drop method to add chapters to buttons you had already placed on a menu. But if you want to add a bunch of simple thumbnail buttons (the type that DVDit! 5 creates automatically when you drag an asset to a menu), a drag-and-drop method will work fine.

You use this method by switching the Title palette view to Details. As shown in Figure 26.13, open the Details view by right-clicking anywhere in the Titles palette (the Menus palette has a Details view, too) and selecting View, Details.

Click the plus (+) sign next to the video that has chapters (videos without chapters don't have plus signs) to view the chapter listing. Use the Ctrl+click or Shift+click method to select some or all of the chapters and drag them to a menu.

Thumbnail images of each chapter's first frame will appear on the menu. Drag them into position and use the Align tool as needed.

FIGURE 26.13
Switch the Titles
view to Details
using the right-click
menu. In Details
view, you can dis-
play a video's chap-
ters and drag them
en masse to a
menu for automatic
scene selection
button creation.

Quickly Duplicate Buttons, Graphics, or Text

Copy and paste is a standard and easy means to add duplicate versions of buttons, graphics, or text to project menus. But DVDit! 5 goes one step further.

It lets you use the Alt key to drag-copy menu objects. Hold down the Alt key and then click and drag any object to instantly create its duplicate.

Hold down Alt+Shift to maintain horizontal or vertical alignment (depending on which way you drag the object). This is a very slick tool.

Fine-Tuning Button Subpictures and Navigation

In MyDVD you have virtually no control over the Subpicture Overlay shapes, colors, and opacities for Selected and Activated highlights. The only way you can adjust them is to create a new menu template in Style Creator. Not an easy task.

In DVDit! 5, selecting from several shapes and setting those colors and opacities is easy. But grasping the Subpicture Highlight color scheme from the get-go is not all that easy. I clear things up in this section.

I also explain how to manually adjust button navigation.

Setting Subpicture Highlight Characteristics and Opacities

Every button has a Subpicture Highlight Overlay layer. DVDit! 5 creates that automatically for each image added to the Button Images palette or uses the Overlay layer you created in a Photoshop graphic.

That Overlay is a single color graphic that displays on top of your button. It shows up when the viewer moves the remote to a button (Selected) or clicks a button (Activated).

What About the Normal Subpicture Overlay?

There also is a Normal Overlay condition, which is how an overlay looks when it is neither Selected nor Activated. But under virtually all situations, you want that to be a transparent layer so that viewers can see your menu buttons clearly through it. DVDit! 5 sets the Normal Subpicture Overlay opacity to zero by default, and there's no reason for you to change that.

By the Way

DVDit! 5 ignores whatever color you applied to the original Photoshop graphic's Overlay layer image. It considers that graphic only to be something like a silhouette to which it applies a color that you choose within DVDit! 5.

Professional-level DVD-authoring software allows you to set any Subpicture color you want for each individual button in a menu (with some limitations). DVDit! 5 does not have that degree of customizability but it has several more possibilities than entry-level authoring products.

DVDit! 5 lets you choose from three combinations of Selected and Activated highlight colors and opacities. It then applies those colors and opacities to every button in a menu. You can select colors and opacities for those three sets on a per-project basis. When you open a new project, all Subpicture color and opacity settings return to their default levels.

Setting Subpicture Characteristics

Try it Yourself

DVDit! 5 also has the very slick feature of letting you choose how that Subpicture highlight will look—its **Style**. We'll start there and then move on to setting Subpicture colors and opacities:

1. As you did in Chapter 25, "Editing Menus with DVDit! 5," create a menu using a solid color background and add several button types to it. If you created buttons using Photoshop, add them along with a DVDit! 5 frame button and an image button.

▼

2. You need to create a link to a button for its Subpicture highlight to show up. So drag a media asset to each button (it can be the same asset). Your menu should look something like Figure 26.14.

FIGURE 26.14
Set up a menu along these lines to examine Subpicture Overlay highlights. Remember, the little numbers are button numbers, created automatically in the order in which you linked the buttons to assets.

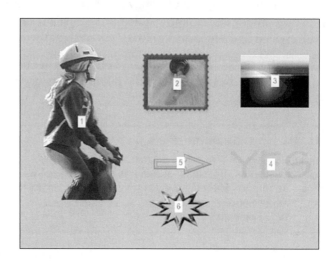

3. Check out how the Selected, Activated, and Normal highlights look by pressing their keyboard shortcuts in turn: C for Selected, A for Activated, and N for Normal. You also can access this highlight display feature via the main menu—DVD Menus, View Selected or Activated or Normal Subpictures—but that is kind of tedious.

By the Way

What the Subpicture Highlights Should Look Like

If you have not changed the default Subpicture color and opacity settings, the Selected Subpicture highlight should give the buttons a transparent (50% opacity) yellow cast. Activated applies a 50% opacity blue color, and Normal is transparent (0% opacity), so its color is irrelevant.

4. To see the five Subpicture Style options, turn on the Selected highlights by pressing C, click a DVDit! 5 frame button, click the Links tab, and open the Subpicture Style list by clicking the chevron highlighted in Figure 26.15.

5. Try each of the five Subpicture Styles for the frame button. Note how each works. A DVDit! 5 frame button has its own Subpicture Overlay layer that typically matches the frame graphic. The other Style options do not use that layer; rather, they apply the Subpicture Color to the graphic or its button bounding box.

▼

6. Try a button that has an irregular shape. Note how you can fill that shape, outline it, or cover the entire bounding box. Try an image button. Note that because it does not have a Subpicture layer, that option is grayed-out in the Subpicture Style list. Figure 26.16 shows each type of Subpicture Style.

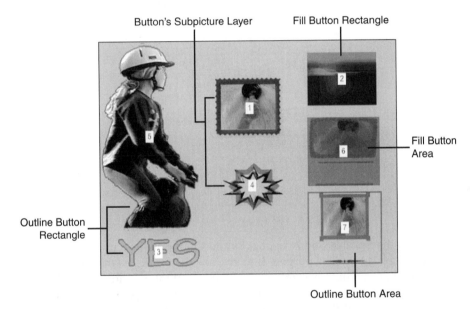

FIGURE 26.16
DVDit! 5 offers five Subpicture Styles—a very nifty extra feature not found in other comparably priced DVD-authoring products.

7. You can change which Subpicture highlight color and opacities you use on a per-menu basis. DVDit! 5 lets you choose from three customizable color sets. To see how they work, as shown in Figure 26.17, click the Menu tab below the menu screen and click the Subpicture Colors chevron to display the three Color Sets. Note that the default setting is for all three to have the same color and opacity settings.

8. Click the Edit button highlighted in Figure 26.17 to open the Edit Subpicture Colors dialog box shown in Figure 26.18.

FIGURE 26.17
You can choose from three customizable Subpicture color/opacity sets.

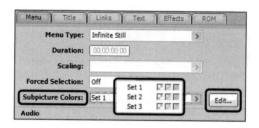

FIGURE 26.18
Change Subpicture colors and opacity settings in this dialog box. You can get immediate feedback in the color swatch. You have to click OK to see the changes show up in the menu screen.

9. Change the Selected and Activated Button Color and Opacity settings for Set 1. Don't be subtle. The purpose is to see how this works, so increase the opacity to something like 75% and pick a color that will stand out (setting the opacity to zero is how you hide an Easter Egg's Subpicture highlight). Your changes will show up in the color swatches. When done, click OK and your changes will show up in the menu screen. Press A and C to see the Activated and Selected colors display.

By the Way

Only 16 Opacity Levels

The DVD specification allows only 16 distinct opacity levels. DVDit! 5's Edit Subpicture Colors dialog boxes let you select any number between zero and 100. In fact, DVDit! 5 ends up selecting the closest opacity level allowed by the DVD spec. Generally, what you see in DVDit! 5 is the same as what you will see when playing the finished disc.

10. Switch your menu back to the default Subpicture color settings by clicking the Subpicture Colors chevron (in the Menu tab) and selecting Set 2 (or Set 3—they have the same settings). Press A and C again to see how that works. Switch back to Set 1.

11. Open another menu, select Set 2, edit its colors to something different than Set 1, and click OK. You can use any of the three color sets on any menu. Note that when you open a new project, all Subpicture Color and Opacity settings return to their default values.

Adjusting Menu and Media Properties

The final authoring step is to make some small but critical adjustments to some of your media and menus. The goal is to define how your media and menus will behave when someone is watching your DVD.

Sometimes you want to adjust Menu Button Routing so buttons display in an order that does not match the default order set by DVDit! 5. When viewers return to a menu, sometimes you want a particular button to be highlighted. You use what's called a Forced Selection for that.

You generally need to assign End Actions to media assets so that when they finish, the DVD jumps to where you want it to go (usually that asset's menu). Finally, you will set Menu Durations and whether they'll loop or play only once.

Menu Button Routing

Menu Button Routing describes the order in which button Selection Subpicture highlights appear as the viewer presses the arrow keys on the remote.

Typically, with buttons arranged in rows, for example, the menu opens with the button in the upper-left corner highlighted. If the viewer presses the right-arrow key, the second button in the top row will highlight. If the viewer then presses the down arrow, the button below it in the second row will highlight.

That button routing is standard, and DVDit! 5 automatically sets that routing for menus laid out like that. Things can get unpredictable when buttons are not laid out in a logical grid pattern. In that case (or others) you might want to do Manual Button Routing.

Generally, it's best to use the button autorouting feature first for all menus. Then fine-tune the routing for individual buttons, if needed, or for menus that do not have an easy-to-follow grid. Here's how to do this:

1. Open a new project, add a menu with a solid color background, add eight buttons, and link a media asset to all of them (to give them a button number—you can use the same asset for each). Your menu should look something like Figure 26.19.

FIGURE 26.19
How to set up your menu to complete this Try It Yourself task.

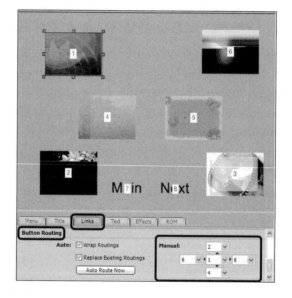

2. Click the Links tab below the menu screen, ensure that you can see its Button Routing section (you might need to scroll down a bit), click the upper-left button in the menu screen to select it, and note how numbers appear in the five slots in the Button Routing section (highlighted in Figure 26.19).

3. Take a look at the routing for the upper-left button (button 1 in my menu—but it could be a different number in yours). That selected button number

will be in the center, and the four other buttons indicate what button will display a Selected highlight when viewers click the respective arrow key on their remote.

4. Uncheck Wrap Routings and click the Auto Route Now button. As shown in Figure 26.20, that turns off **wrapping**. That is, clicking the leftmost button in a row highlights the rightmost button.

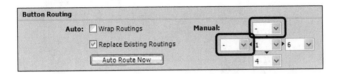

FIGURE 26.20
Turning off Wrap Routings and clicking Auto Route Now means (in this case) that when a viewer clicks the left or up arrows on the remote, nothing changes. The Selected highlight will continue to display over the upper-left button.

5. Usually the manual button routing is only marginally different from the routing selected automatically by DVDit! 5. So recheck Wrap Routings and click the Auto Route Now button.

6. Make some manual fixes. I've demonstrated one in Figure 26.21. In my case, when the upper-left button is highlighted and viewers click the up arrow, I want to highlight the Main (menu) text button. So I select its number (7) in the up-arrow listing (highlighted in Figure 26.21). I previously changed the routing for the down arrow to the button in the lower-left corner (2).

Don't Isolate Buttons

When routing buttons manually, it's easy to isolate buttons—that is, forget to provide any means for a viewer to navigate to them. In the next chapter I explain how to check button routings before burning your DVD. But you can do that now if you like.

To do so, click the Finish button and click Start from Current Position. Use the triangles (arrayed in a circle) below the lower-right corner of the Preview screen (not your mouse—it acts independently of the button navigation) to make sure you can move to and see the Selected highlights for all buttons.

Watch Out!

▼

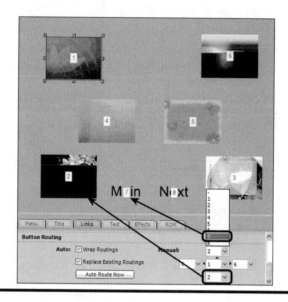

▲

Forcing a Button Selection

Normally, the first time a viewer opens a menu, button 1 (wherever you've located that button) is selected—that is, its Selected highlight displays. When a viewer returns to that menu, the last button clicked (Activated) in that menu will display its Selected highlight.

You can override that feature and have the same button display its Selected highlight each time a viewer returns to that menu—a Forced Button selection.

To do this, use the menu you worked on for Button Routing. As shown in Figure 26.22, click the Menu tab, open the Forced Selection list by clicking its chevron, and select the button number you want to display first, every time the viewer opens this menu.

Watch Out!

Avoid Forced Selection for Looping Menus

You want to avoid using the Forced Selection attribute with looping motion menus (with video backgrounds or static menus with animated buttons) or menus with audio. The reason? Every time the menu loops, the forced selection button becomes highlighted again, creating kind of a spastic jump.

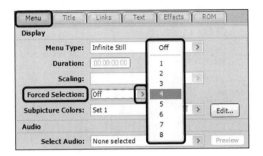

FIGURE 26.22
You can set a
Forced Selection
for each menu.
Select the button
you want to be the
default button to
display its
Selected highlight
whenever a viewer
goes to that menu.

Setting Title End Actions

An End Action is what takes place at the conclusion of a timed menu or media asset—video clip or slideshow. For instance, when a video ends you might go to a new menu or see another video. Menu and Title end actions work differently. You'll work with Title (media asset) End Actions in this section and Menu End Actions in the next.

In entry-level DVD-authoring products, you typically don't have the option to set End Actions. The software selects them automatically. Sometimes they work the way you expect, sometimes they don't. You typically have no recourse but to accept the default behavior. Other times you can rearrange buttons or edit certain clips together to overcome this entry-level authoring shortcoming.

By default, DVDit! 5 sets Title End Actions to the next title (video or slideshow) in the Titles palette. Most likely that won't be what you want, so you need to set End Actions for virtually all media assets.

And, in yet another professional-level feature, DVDit! 5 lets you override End Actions.

Set an End Action

First, here's how to set an End Action:

1. Click any media asset in the Titles palette. It could be a video or a slideshow.

2. As shown in Figure 26.23, click the Title tab below the menu screen and select an End Action from the fly-out list. Simple. But you need to do this for virtually every media asset in your project.

FIGURE 26.23
You will need to set
an End Action for
most media
assets. Access
that feature in the
Title menu.

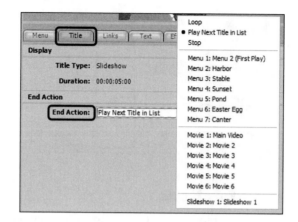

FIGURE 26.23
You will need to set an End Action for most media assets. Access that feature in the Title menu.

Override an End Action with a Link End Action

Sometimes you want your DVD to offer a Play All option that plays all the videos in succession without returning to the menu. *And* you want to let viewers access the videos one at a time. This is a standard feature in DVDs of television series.

If you give this a little thought, you'll note that without some kind of intervention, there's no way to do both. The only way for the Play All feature to work is for the End Action of each video to go to the next video, and the End Action for the last video to return to the Menu.

But that means if you access any one of those videos, when it finishes it will go on to the video linked by its End Action.

DVDit! 5 lets you override that command and bring viewers back to the menu at the end of each video. It does that with what's called a Link End Action. That is, you tell the link to that media asset that the asset is not supposed to perform its End Action. Instead it should return to its menu.

DVDit! 5 gives you only that one Link End Action option—Return to Menu. But it's the most frequent override action DVD authors would use anyway. To set it, do the following:

1. Click a button that links to a media asset.

2. As shown in Figure 26.24, click the Links tab and check the Link End Action check box.

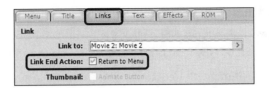

FIGURE 26.24
Override a media asset (video or slideshow) End Action by selecting the button that links to it and checking the Link End Action check box in the Links menu. Now, when the video ends, it returns the viewer to the menu instead of playing another video (in this case).

Adjusting Menu Types, Durations, and End Actions

There are a surprising number of menu types based on combinations of video backgrounds, audio **beds**, and animated buttons. Here's a rundown:

▶ **Infinite Still**—A static menu. It is the simplest to deal with. It has no audio associated with it.

▶ **Timed Still**—Two menu types fit this category:

  ▶ A menu with a still image background and an audio track. Its default duration is the length of the audio clip.

  ▶ A menu with a still image background and no audio track for which you have set a duration (the default time is 30 seconds). If that time runs out before the viewer takes some action, the DVD jumps to some other menu or asset. You set up that link with a Menu End Action. I explain that later in this section.

▶ **Motion Menu**—Two menu types fit this category:

  ▶ A static menu with animated buttons (when you switch on button animation, it becomes a Motion Menu). Its duration is 30 seconds by default.

  ▶ A menu with a video as a background. Its duration is equal to the length of the video clip. If you add animated buttons, its duration remains unchanged. If the button clips are shorter than the menu background video, the button animations will restart.

Replacing a Video Menu with a Still Image? Check the Audio

If you use a video for a menu background and later choose to replace that video with a static image, DVDit! 5 will still consider it a Motion Menu. That's because you replaced only the background. The video's original audio continues to be associated with the menu. You need to take the extra step to remove that audio clip by clicking Select Audio in the Menu window and selecting None Selected.

Watch Out!

Changing the Menu Type and Duration

To see how all these menu types work, click the Menu tab below the menu screen (refer to Figure 26.25). Briefly, here is how you set menu durations:

▶ To change an Infinite Still to a Timed Still *without* audio, click the Menu Type chevron and select Timed Still. A default duration of 30 seconds will display in the Duration window (it will say 29 seconds and 29 frames). You can change the time for this Timed Still or a Motion Menu by clicking in the Duration window and typing in a new duration using Hours:Minutes:Seconds:Frames.

▶ To change an Infinite Still to a Timed Still with audio, click the Select Audio chevron and select from files you've added to the Titles palette or click the Browse button to use an audio file you have not added to the project.

FIGURE 26.25
Click the Menu tab to access the Menu Type window. If you switch to a Timed Still, you can change the default 30-second duration in that window. Adding audio (use the Select Audio window) to an Infinite Still is another way to create a Timed Still menu.

▶ As shown in Figure 26.26, to animate buttons on a menu with a static or video background, click the Links tab, select a frame button that's linked to a video, and click the Animate Button check box.

FIGURE 26.26
To switch on button animation (for frame buttons linked to videos) check the Thumbnail Animate Button check box.

Keep Menu Durations to Less Than 1 Minute

I've mentioned this earlier in the book. It warrants repeating here. There are two reasons to keep animated menus short: They consume a lot of disc space and viewers generally make a button selection within a minute.

Setting Menu End Actions

All Motion Menus and Timed Stills have an End Action. The third menu type, an Infinite Still, has no end action. It simply displays until the viewer takes some action.

There are three types of Menu End Actions: loop, play a static version of the menu, or go to a media asset or another menu.

The default end action is to loop. That is, when Motion Menus or Timed Stills (you used Timed Stills specifically because you can give them an End Action other than to loop) reach the end of their background video clip, audio track, or duration, they start over.

Professional-level DVD-authoring software lets you specify the number of loops. DVDit! 5 gives you only the choice to loop continuously until the viewer clicks a menu button or to go to a still image version of the menu (its first frame) after one play through.

Don't Annoy Your Viewers

Looping menus can become irritating. DVDs players (even the best ones) always pause at the end of a menu loop, so there is always a moment when the audio and video stop.

With professional authoring applications, you can find some middle ground by looping two or three times and then going to a static menu.

Because DVDit! 5 gives you only one choice—perpetual looping versus going to a still frame of the menu—I suggest that you generally eschew looping to avoid annoying your audience.

Menu End Action Link

Your other Menu End Action choice (instead of looping or displaying a static menu) is that at the conclusion of your Timed Still or Motion Menu, you take viewers to either another menu or a media asset like the main video.

As shown in Figure 26.27, to set a Menu End Action to something other than the default Loop, click the Menu tab, click the End Action chevron, and select Still or one of your project's menus or media assets (videos or slideshows).

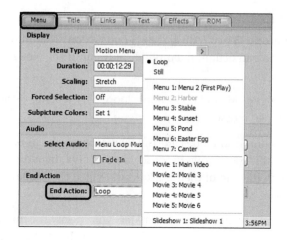

Adding ROM Data

One huge advantage of DVDs versus videotape is that you can play them on a standard TV set or a PC monitor. The other very powerful feature is that DVDs can have PC files on them that are accessible on a PC.

You can store documents, PDF files, images, programs, HTML web pages with links to websites, and even the original video files.

By the Way

> **No Links to Files and No Access via a Set-Top Box**
>
> You cannot create a button link to PC files stored on your DVD. And you cannot access those files via a set-top DVD player. The only way to work with those files is on a DVD–player equipped PC.

Try it Yourself

▼

It's a simple matter to store PC files—called **ROM Data** in DVDit! 5 parlance—on a DVD created in DVDit! 5. Here's how to do that:

1. Gather up all your assets and store them in a single file folder. The DVD specification allows for only a single file folder, but that folder can have subfolders. So you can readily organize your assets into categories.

2. Open the ROM menu by clicking the ROM tab below the menu screen in the Author interface. (It doesn't matter what menu is in that screen—the ROM Data are not connected in any way to a menu or button.)

▼

3. As shown in Figure 26.28, click the Include Data Files in the ROM Folder ▼
   check box to activate the Browse button.

4. Click the Browse button, navigate to and click your file folder, and then
   click OK. ▲

FIGURE 26.28
Add PC files to
your DVD project
via the ROM menu.

Summary

DVDit! 5 is a solid and powerful prosumer/professional DVD-authoring application. One thing that makes it powerful is its numerous options.

As I explained in this chapter you can create custom buttons for it in Photoshop. You can add Easter Eggs, intros and outros, and chain clips into a sequence.

Using its End Actions, you can create Play All links as well as letting viewers play single video clips. Its Subpicture Highlight options give you a wider degree of control over Highlight colors and styles.

You can take control of button navigation, force a Selected Highlight button display, and control the behavior of menus, having them loop, go to a still, or use an End Action to take viewers to a media asset or another menu.

Finally, DVDit! 5 lets you add PC files to a DVD that users can view, work with, and even re-edit on their PCs.

CHAPTER 27

Burning DVDs and Dealing with DVD Duplicators

What You'll Learn in This Chapter:

▶ Checking menu and media links and project flow
▶ Selecting transcoding settings
▶ Using DVDit! 5 to record your DVD project
▶ Printing labels directly on your DVDs
▶ Going the mass-replication route
▶ Using Sonic Solutions's Publishing Showcase
▶ Considering some DVD trends

Now it's time to see the fruits of your labor by recording your project to a DVD and popping it into your TV's set-top player for your viewing pleasure.

In this final chapter, I show you how to use DVDit! 5 to preview your DVD and check for broken links or other unexpected behavior. I explain DVDit! 5's recording options and then have you burn and test your DVD.

I wrap up my book by showing you the steps to take if you want to mass-replicate your DVD and one way to market commercial DVDs.

Checking Menu and Media Links and Project Flow

Before you use DVDit! 5 to burn your DVD, you should test all the links and settings. DVDit! 5 lets you preview the project, mimicking how the finished DVD will play back in the player.

▼

Check Your Links and Test Your Project

In this exercise, you simulate what it's like for a viewer to sit down with a remote control and start clicking through your DVD. Follow these steps:

1. Start DVDit! 5, open a project, click the Author button, and click the Links tab beneath the menu screen.

2. Click the Menus tab to open that palette. Right-click and select View, Details. Click all the little plus (+) signs to display all the button links in each menu. Your screen should look something like Figure 27.1. This is an excellent overview of each menu's links. Click any of the menu names or buttons and note the linking information displayed in the Links menu.

FIGURE 27.1
Open the Menu Details view to get this overview of your menus' button links.

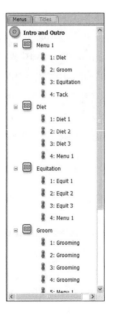

3. Do the same thing in the Titles palette. However, in this case, open the Title menu, click each media asset in turn, and note its End Action in the Title menu.

4. Open the Finish interface by clicking its button at the top center of the screen. This displays the Preview window shown in Figure 27.2.

▼

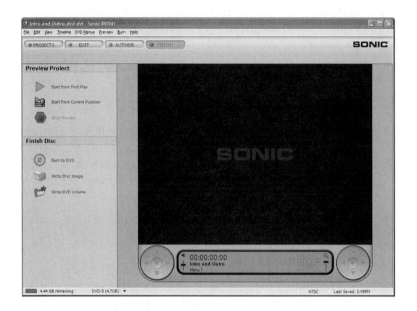

FIGURE 27.2
Click the Finish but-
ton to access this
interface.

5. You have two preview options:

  ▶ **Start from First Play**—This is the best way to get an overall view of
    your DVD's flow. It will play just as it would right after putting your
    finished DVD in a set-top player.

  ▶ **Start from Current Position**—This is very helpful. Instead of slogging
    through several menus and videos, click the Author button, select the
    menu or media asset (video or slideshow) you want to view, click the
    Finish button, and click Start from Current Position.

6. For this exercise, click Start from First Play. That will pop up the Information
box shown in Figure 27.3. It lets you know that DVDit! 5 will display Motion
Menus as Still Menus during Preview. But you can **render** any menu you
choose to see how it'll really look. I explain that in a moment.

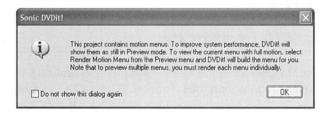

FIGURE 27.3
The first time you
attempt to preview
a project that uses
Motion Menus,
DVDit! 5 lets you
know that the
Preview mode will
show those menus
as still images.

7. Use the Preview controls annotated in Figure 27.4 to navigate through your project. Most are self-explanatory. For instance, the four triangles on the right navigate around the menu buttons. Here are a few that might need some explanation:

> ▶ **Title**—Clicking this takes you to the Main Menu—the one at the top of your menu hierarchy.

> ▶ **Menu**—Takes you back to the previous menu.

> ▶ **Button Numbers**—Use these to Select and Activate a particular button. Most DVD authors choose to not include button numbers on the menu, so unless you remember which button is which, this might not help. But if you include button numbers in the menu, use this keypad to navigate more quickly.

> ▶ **Previous Chapter and Next Chapter**—This jumps back or ahead to the Previous or Next button's menu or movie.

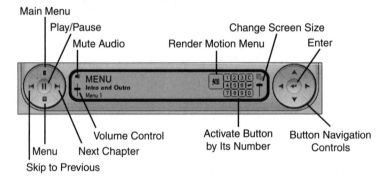

FIGURE 27.4
In general, the Preview controls match those on a typical DVD remote.

8. Try everything, making sure that all the menus do what you expect. View the slideshows, clips, or chapter scenes. After each media asset finishes playing, you should automatically return to its respective menu or to the End Action you assigned to it.

Did you Know?

Full Screen Preview

After Preview has started, press the Escape key (Esc) or double-click in the Preview window to toggle Full-Screen mode on or off.

9. If you want to view a motion menu, navigate to it and click the Render Motion Menu button annotated earlier in Figure 27.4. That will render only that menu. DVDit! 5 permits menu rendering on a menu-by-menu basis only.

10. If any menu buttons take you nowhere or take you to the wrong media or menu, make note of them so you can fix them back in the Author interface. When you complete previewing your project, click Stop Preview and return to the Author interface.

Selecting Transcoding Settings

I went over Transcoding Settings in Chapter 24, "Creating Menus with DVDit! 5." I will do a quick review here and expand on a few items.

There are two places to set Transcoding parameters: Preferences and Project Settings.

Preferences—Setting Finish Parameters

Open Preferences by selecting File, Preferences and then clicking the Finish tab. The only choice is Effort Control. There are three settings—Faster, Medium, and Slower Transcode speeds. The more time spent transcoding, the better the quality of the encoded MPEG video.

DVDit! 5's MPEG encoder analyzes your video to determine the best way to compress it at whatever bit rate you set in Project Settings. The more time it takes to analyze the video frames, the better your compressed video will look.

Project Settings—Transcode Settings

Open Project Settings by pressing Ctrl+E (or select File, Project Settings) and click the Transcode tab. Click the drop-down list shown in Figure 27.5. DVDit! 5 has eight transcode presets—four CBR (constant bit rate) and four VBR (variable bit rate). The highest quality is 8000Kbps (8Mbits per second).

Bit-Rate Rules

The maximum bit rate allowed by the DVD format for the combined video and audio stream is 9.8Mbps. To provide headroom in case there is a spike in the bit rate during compression, DVDit! 5 caps the maximum video bit rate at 8Mbps.

By the Way

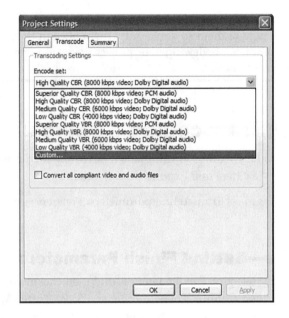

CBR Versus VBR

CBR and VBR are the two types of MPEG encoding:

▶ **CBR** encoding uses the same bit rate for every second of video regardless of the video's complexity, so the quality of the compressed video worsens when the original video becomes more complex (typically action scenes), and bits are wasted when there is not much action.

▶ **VBR** uses higher bit rates for complex sections and lower rates for scenes with less complexity (typically static interviews—"talking heads"), constantly adjusting to keep the overall bit rate at the target value you set.

VBR Is Your Best Bet

I recommend that you use VBR encoding. It can produce the same quality as a CBR encode but at a lower overall bit rate (so you can fit more video on the disc) or better quality than a CBR encode at the same overall bit rate.

CBR generally is useful for applications where you want to avoid bit-rate spikes, typically when streaming video on the Internet.

PCM Versus Dolby Digital Audio

These are the two audio encoding schemes used by DVDit! 5:

▶ **PCM** audio is uncompressed and takes up more room. The PCM audio bit rate is 0.8Mbps for mono and 1.6Mbps for stereo.

▶ **Dolby Digital** takes less room and sounds virtually the same. DVDit! 5's default Dolby Digital bit rate is 0.192Mbps (about one-eighth the PCM's stereo rate), but you can select from five settings between .064Mbps and .384Mbps.

Dolby Digital Audio Is Your Best Bet

This is the industry standard. Using it gives you more room for video (so you can select a higher video bit rate). And the audio quality is on par with PCM.

The only time you should opt for PCM is when the audio quality of your project is more important than the video quality.

Bit-Rate Calculation

At some point in your DVD-authoring experiences, you might need to keep close tabs on the size of your project relative to the space available on a DVD.

The easy way to do that is select a Transcode rate (I always opt for the High Quality VBR (8000Kbps video; Dolby Digital Audio) preset) and watch your project size info in the lower-left corner of the DVDit! 5 interface shown in Figure 27.6.

FIGURE 27.6
Track your project size using this constantly updated Space Remaining indicator. Click the triangle to select from one of the five DVD types supported by DVDit! 5.

As shown in Figure 27.6, you can select from five recordable DVD types supported by DVDit! 5. Generally your choice will be between DVD-5 (single-sided, single-layer DVD recordable disc) and DVD-9 (single-sided, dual-layer DVD recordable disc).

But at some point you might want to fine-tune your Transcode settings to exactly match the size of your project to the space available. You make those customized adjustments in the Compression portion of the Project Settings, Transcode tab shown in Figure 27.7.

A Two-Part Calculation

First you determine the maximum bit rate you can use and still not exceed the space available. Later you will choose the best individual video and audio bit rates that, when added together, approach (but do not exceed) that maximum rate.

To calculate the maximum bit rate, you need to determine the duration of all your videos and motion menus in seconds.

Then you need to know the size of your recordable DVD in megabits (not giga-bytes, the figure you're accustomed to seeing).

▶ A 4.7GB DVD-5 actually has about 4.5GB (4,500MB) of usable space, which equals about 36,000Mbits (multiply 4,500MB by 8 bits per byte).

▶ An 8.5GB DVD-9 has about 8.2GB of usable space, or about 65,000 Mbits.

By the Way

GB Versus Billion Bytes Confusion

This calculation brings us back to the gigabyte versus billion byte confusion I referred to in Chapter 17, "Burning Data DVDs." For this calculation I chose to use the actual number of bytes on the DVD to make these calculations. So even though I used the GB computer-capacity reference based on multiples of 1,024, I really mean billion bytes. The reason is that bit rate is a true number of bits per second and is not based on the listed sizes of your files, which are based on multiples of 1,024.

To calculate the maximum bit rate allowed, divide the DVD's usable disc space by the total video duration in seconds.

For a single-sided DVD-5 (36,000Mbits) and 2 hours of video (7,200 seconds) the maximum bit rate would be

$$36,000 / 7,200 = 5\text{Mbps}$$

Now select a combination of a video bit rate and an audio bit rate that when combined do not exceed 5Mbps.

Typically, you'd select Dolby Digital Audio at .192Mbps (192 Kbps—the unit of measure used in the Project Settings, Transcode tab) so that would mean your video bit rate could not exceed 4.808Mbps (or 4808Kbps).

Having concluded the calculations, make the changes in the Project Settings, Transcode tab, Compression section (shown earlier in Figure 27.7). After you click OK, DVDit! 5 will update the GB remaining display in the lower-left corner of its interface.

Using DVDit! 5 to Record Your DVD Project

This last step of your DVD-authoring process is relatively simple. Primarily, it comes down to selecting from three options:

▶ **Burn to DVD**—This is the primary choice. Use it to create DVDs that will play on set-top players and PCs.

▶ **Write Disc Image**—A Disc Image is a single file that contains all the information in your project. It's a convenient way to save your project and share it with others for additional editing. You can use DVDit! 5 (or optical media recording software like RecordNow) to burn a DVD using a Disc Image.

▶ **Write DVD Volume**—This is a good way to test your project without burning a DVD. A DVD Volume contains all the files that will go on a DVD and stores them in one folder on your hard drive. DVD player software, like Sonic Solutions CinePlayer, can play a DVD Volume. Although DVDit! 5's Preview mode should catch most missing links and the like, testing your project via a DVD Volume takes that preview process a bit further. As with the Disc Image option, you can use DVDit! 5 to create a DVD from a DVD Volume.

Make a DVD Disc   *Try It Yourself*

If all goes smoothly, in a few minutes you'll have a DVD in hand, ready to play on your set-top DVD player or PC. You also can store the Disc Volume or Disc Image on your hard drive. I show you all three options in this task. Follow these steps:

1. Start DVDit! 5 and open your project to the Finish interface.

2. Put a blank recordable disc (DVD-R, DVD-RW, DVD+R, DVD+RW, or DVD-ROM) in your recorder.

Check Project Size

If your project is greater than 4.7GB and you have a dual-layer DVD recorder, make sure you use a double-layer disc. Otherwise, you need to reduce your project size or Transcode bit rate in Project Settings.

3. First, click Write Disc Image (or select Burn, Write Disc Image). As shown in Figure 27.8, if you checked all your links and everything is in order, the Write Disc Image to File window will show up (you might get a Warning message—see Watch Out! "Fix Your Links"). If you want to write a Disc Image, select a file folder, change the project name if needed, and click Save. Otherwise, click Cancel to return to the Finish interface.

FIGURE 27.8
Writing a disc image is a one-step process.

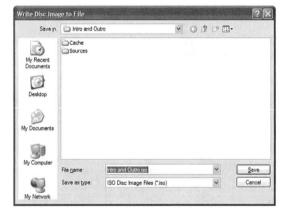

Fix Your Links

If DVDit! 5 displays the warning shown in Figure 27.9, it has discovered that your project has at least one missing link. Professional-level products show you exactly where the problems are. DVDit! 5 merely lets you know something is not in order.

Go back and preview your project yet again. Check everything. You might consider making a DVD Volume and use CinePlayer to completely test your project.

It's possible that something DVDit! 5 considers to be a missing link is actually something you chose not to link to. Or it could mistakenly note that a problem exists when everything is fine.

If you think your project will work fine, click the Yes button to proceed. Otherwise click No and do more testing.

FIGURE 27.9
Before DVDit! 5
burns your disc or
creates a DVD
Volume or Disc
Image, it automati-
cally checks for any
orphaned menus
(menus with no
links) or other
anomalies.

4. Click Write DVD Volume. That opens the Browse for Folder window shown in Figure 27.10. Typically, when you make a DVD Volume, you create a new folder in which to store that volume. So, if you want to proceed, select a file folder in which you want to add the DVD Volume file folder (or go to the root level of your drive—Local Drive C: for example) and click Make New Folder. Give it a name and click OK. Otherwise, click Cancel to return to the Finish interface.

FIGURE 27.10
Usually when you
create a DVD
Volume, you first
create a new file
folder.

5. Now for the real deal. Click Burn to DVD. If you did not just save your project, DVDit! 5 will force that selection. After your project is saved, the Burn to DVD dialog box opens (refer to Figure 27.11). You have a few options:

> **Burn From**—Select the Current Project or DVD Volume or Disc Image you created earlier. If you stick with Current Project (the most likely decision) the Path to that project will display but you will not be able to change it because it correctly identifies the current project. If you select DVD Volume or Disc Image, you'll select a different File Folder or File, respectively.

- ▶ **Device**—If you have more than one DVD recorder, make your selection here.

- ▶ **Copies**—If you want to make more than one copy, note that and DVDit! 5 will prompt you to put in another disc when it finishes burning the currently inserted disc.

- ▶ **Write Speed**—DVDit! 5 selects the fastest speed that will work with your drive and media. If you experience errors (creating a coaster in the process) during recording, switch to a lower speed.

- ▶ **Test Before Writing**—This works only on DVD-Rs in a few older drives. Even if you check this box, it's possible DVDit! 5 will ignore it.

FIGURE 27.11
You have only a few options when burning your project to a DVD.

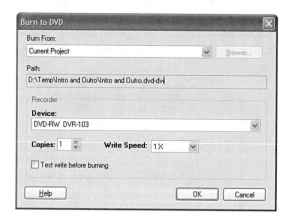

6. Click OK. That will start the burning process, which begins with Transcoding. DVDit! 5 will keep you posted by displaying a Burning progress bar like the one in Figure 27.12 for each item it transcodes in turn. Depending on the Transcode bit rate and Effort Level you selected, this can take considerably longer than the length of your project (that is, longer than real-time).

FIGURE 27.12
DVDit! 5 keeps you informed via a series of Burning progress bars.

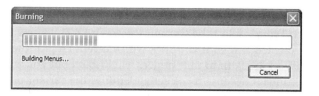

7. When burning is completed, DVDit! 5 ejects your disc and pops up the message, shown in Figure 27.13, asking if you want to create a label. If you click that button, DVDit! 5 will take you to the same labeling software you worked with in the MyDVD chapters. Otherwise, click Done.

FIGURE 27.13
When DVDit! 5 finishes burning a disc, it asks if you want to create labels.

Test Your DVD

Take your DVD to a set-top standalone DVD player and enjoy your DVD project.

If that DVD player is reasonably new and therefore more likely to be fully compatible with all DVD specifications, your DVD should work fine. If not, try it on your PC. Use whatever DVD software player you used in Chapter 16, "Getting Your Gear in Order—DVD Recorders and Media."

If compatibility problems exist with your set-top DVD player, take your DVD to a local consumer electronics store and try it in several of their DVD players.

Printing Labels Directly on Your DVDs

You've seen Hollywood DVDs with artwork printed directly on the DVD. You, too, can give your DVDs that kind of professional look.

The standard ways to label DVDs fall into two camps: marking pens and paper labels. Now, thanks to affordable printers from several companies, you can give your DVDs that Hollywood look by printing directly onto your burned DVDs.

If you are in the DVD-authoring business, this is a great way to impress clients.

I'm aware of three companies that market inexpensive, Direct CD/DVD Printers:

▶ **EZ/CD Print**—(www.ezcdprint.com; see Figure 27.14). They were the first to market. They got their start by converting Epson printers for both paper and direct CD/DVD labeling. Now they offer a consumer-priced printer ($190) and a professional version for $750.

- **Epson**—(www.Epson.com—search on "CD printer"). Offers several direct CD/DVD label printers from $100 to $400.

- **Primera** (www.primera.com)—Offers one low-price printer that works only with optical media (CDs and DVDs—not any kind of paper printing). Its other direct CD/DVD label printers (that work with paper, too) are expensive.

All of these printers ship with label software. Instead of printing to a gummed paper label, you insert a special inkjet-printable, recordable DVD (or CD) into the printer and in about a minute (12 seconds for the EZ/CD Print $750 model), out slides a DVD with a full-color image on it.

Inkjet-printable media are fairly easy to track down. If you run into a dead end, go to EZ/CD's website (www.excdprint.com) and click Data Storage Media.

Going the Mass-Replication Route

Burning multiple DVDs of the same project, one at a time, is tedious. Mass-replication can therefore be an appealing alternative.

These days, working with a replicator is not very difficult. Your finished project recorded to a DVD-R and some liner and DVD disc artwork is about all you need.

To ensure a smooth DVD-replication process, follow these tips:

▶ Start by visiting IRMA—the International Recording Media Association (www.recordingmedia.org). It has a list of member replication firms. Go to http://www.recordingmedia.org/membership/source.cfm (or go to the About page and click the link to search for IRMA member companies).

   You can search specifically for DVD Replicators by State. Many of these companies are **mass** replicators, meaning they deal with film studios and publishers and handle multiple orders annually for millions of copies.

   Few will touch an order of fewer than 1,000 discs. Don't let that discourage you, though. Contact a replicator from the list and ask whom they recommend for smaller orders.

▶ If you want to make a single-sided, single-layer DVD disc, all you need is a DVD-R to serve as a master.

▶ For a double-sided, single-layer so-called DVD-10, you'll need two DVD-R discs.

▶ For DVD-9 (single-sided, double-layer) you generally need to master on Digital Linear Tape (DLT), and that technology is not supported by DVDit! 5.

▶ Be sure you've tested your DVD-R master on a set-top DVD player. Click every menu and press all the remote buttons to ensure that your DVD does what it's supposed to do before you send it off for duplication.

▶ Your most difficult hurdle might be artwork to create your liner and DVD label art. Most DVD replicators provide artwork templates you can use in various graphics programs.

▶ Be sure you proofread everything and check your colors. Your labels can look dramatically different from one replicator to another.

▶ Allow enough time for your project. From delivery of your master along with label artwork, expect to wait two weeks for completion of your order.

Walking Through the Replication Process

Creating DVDs is a multistep process that uses high-pressure injection molds, lasers, and electroplating. Following is a brief overview of the process:

1. Technicians coat a glass master with a very thin layer of light-sensitive material.

2. A sharply focused blue or ultraviolet laser converts digital data into a series of pulses, burning holes into that thin chemical layer along a spiral track (not a series of concentric rings) from the center to the outside.

3. A chemical bath washes away the film at each burnt pulse location leaving tiny pits. A thin layer of metal (usually nickel) is applied as a means to conduct electricity.

FIGURE 27.15
Application of the adhesive to the bottom layer of the DVD prior to the placement of the second layer.

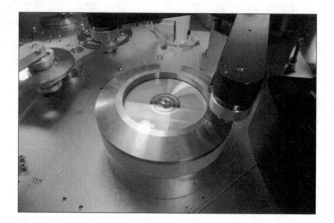

4. This nickel-coated glass master is placed in another bath with an electric current flowing through it. More metal ions fill the tiny pits and then cover them with a thin wafer.

5. That thin layer (now covered with tiny bumps), called the **father**, is a reverse image of the glass master. It becomes the master mold for the actual stampers used to create the DVDs.

6. The stampers are placed in molding machines into which hot, molten polycarbonate is injected under extreme pressure (several tons) to create reverse images of the stampers.

7. Each layer is "metalized," typically with aluminum to create a reflective surface.

FIGURE 27.16
DVDs that have just been through the bonding process.

FIGURE 27.17
Molded DVDs ready for printing.

8. Each metalized surface is bonded to a nonmetalized substrate (see Figures 27.15 and 27.16).

9. So-called single-layer DVDs actually have two such metalized layers (CD-ROMs have only one). Double-layer DVDs have four.

10. Lacquering is applied to protect the reflective upper layer and serve as a surface on which to print labels (see Figure 27.17).

Using Sonic Solutions's Publishing Showcase

 Sonic Solutions, in an alliance with CustomFlix, presents a relatively painless and potentially profitable means to market your DVDs.

For a one-time setup fee (as we went to press it was $30 for Sonic Solutions customers and $50 for everyone else), CustomFlix will help you create an e-store web page, complete with a 30-second video promo, and will fill and ship all your orders (see Figure 27.18 and Figure 27.19).

FIGURE 27.18
CustomFlix offers a relatively simple way to publish your DVDs.

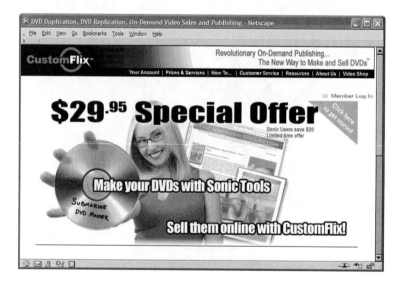

You can have CustomFlix manufacture your DVD in small quantities as orders come in (for which it receives $10 plus 5% of the sales price per item) or have it replicate your DVD in much larger quantities. If you choose the latter option, CustomFlix charges a reduced per-transaction fee but adds a monthly inventory charge.

You set the DVD price and do your own advertising while CustomFlix offers your DVD for sale on at least five websites, including its main store, Amazon zShop, Froogle, its Yahoo! Store, and a store they'll set up for you.

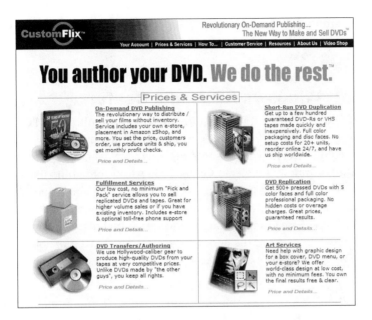

FIGURE 27.19
CustomFlix services include artwork, duplication, e-store setup, and distribution.

If you choose the one-at-a-time approach, you can make a profit with sales of only 10 copies (with a list price of $20). If you try the replication model (1,000 minimum print run), you'll see profits after you sell about 250 copies within a year. But with the greater risk comes greater rewards. After your DVD has annual sales of 500 copies, you start making more per transaction than if you opted for the one-at-a-time scheme.

Visit www.customflix.com/Special/SonicShowcase.html to check out its offerings. When I last looked, it offered a wide assortment of DVDs from a how-to on Cajun fiddle playing to a feature on lighthouses of North Carolina's Outer Banks.

DVD Trends

These are exciting times. DVD technology continues to create opportunities. And I don't see that waning any time soon. So, before bidding you adieu, here are a few final thoughts on where things are going.

DVD Ubiquity

DVDs will be everywhere. Every PC and TV set will have one. Every new nonlinear video editing application will include DVD output as a natural part of the program. Creating slideshows, audio, and home movies on DVD will be as natural as using a VCR. DVDs will become the standard medium for all digital publishing.

Microsoft Windows XP Media Center

Microsoft is taking another stab at creating a standard multimedia PC. Its first foray in the early 1990s failed for lack of a compelling reason to buy. This new standard integrates the PC with the Internet, a DVD player, a TV tuner, and a remote control. Windows XP Media Center 2005 works something like a combination TiVo and online Gemstar programming guide. Watch shows (pausing and rewinding at will), time shift, and operate a CD/DVD player. Media Center shows some real promise. Some major PC manufacturers—including Gateway, H-P, and Alienware—have hopped on the bandwagon. You can learn more about it at www.microsoft.com/windowsxp/mediacenter/default.mspx.

Sonic Solutions, in partnership with Microsoft, created a Media Center application called PrimeTime. It has one simple function: Select a TV program, press a button, and burn that show seamlessly to DVD. Just another example of the coming ubiquity of DVDs.

OpenDVD Format

Sonic Solutions has created what it calls the OpenDVD format. That is, when you create a product using OpenDVD standards, you can open it in any other OpenDVD-compliant product, typically a more expensive authoring tool that lets you fine-tune your original DVD in unique ways. MyDVD is OpenDVD compatible. DVDit! 5.1 is not, but Sonic plans an update to DVDit! that will be OpenDVD compliant.

Will this become an industry standard? I don't know. Sonic Solutions is lining up its many partners, but whether competitors will buy into this remains to be seen. In any event, Open DVD enhances the value of the Sonic Solutions product line and ensures that if you should move up from one Sonic Solutions authoring tool to a higher-level product, you'll be able to use it on existing DVD projects.

Integration with Web

Creating and playing DVDs will take on more immediacy because of Internet connectivity. As you pull in content during the authoring process, you can add links to websites that will enhance your project.

Later when viewers play your DVD on their Web-connected PC or set-top appliance, they can access the latest info using those links. Doing a DVD on your Tahitian vacation? Add some web links to travel sites. Including material about your favorite musician? Add links to that artist's site. During playback, those links will lead to content that will be more current than what you might have included on the DVD.

To accomplish this level of interactivity now takes a high-end video-editing package like Adobe Premiere (and it's fairly limited in scope). In the near future, it will be seamless.

High Definition TV and DVDs

The history of DVD authoring starts with Hollywood studios using high-priced and powerful Computer Aided Design (CAD) workstations and very expensive software to create DVDs.

As PCs became more powerful and DVD recorders dramatically dropped in price, authoring products became consumer-friendly and inexpensive.

That cycle may repeat itself as high definition TV standards begin to coalesce. Putting HDTV on DVD may be a bit of a challenge at the get-go but will quickly take on a consumer-friendly glow as that TV system gains acceptance.

Long Live the DVD Format

DVDs will be around for a long time—as one industry insider told me, a "bunch" of years. What might change is DVD data capacity. Double-sided, double-density discs will become easier to use and author, and blue lasers may finally make a mass market appearance. Because of DVD's near universal acceptance, any new optical format that comes along will need to be backward compatible with DVD video and CD audio.

The future is less about authoring and more about publishing content on DVD. Any kind of software, down to word processors and meeting presentation products, will have DVD output functionality.

Software makers will constantly need to ask: How do we make it easy for consumers to create DVDs?

Upcoming products will take whatever digital content you have and offer easy ways to put it on DVDs.

Summary

Burning DVDs is a three-step process: You check whether your project's links and menus function as you expected; then you tweak the Transcoding options and burn your DVD. After it's burned, you should take the acid test of viewing your DVD in a set-top player.

As you gain experience in DVD production, you might think in terms of marketing your projects. That might start with burning discs one at a time and using a direct-to-DVD label printer for a professional look.

If sales climb, you might use a replicator or turn to the web as a publishing tool. Sonic Solutions and CustomFlix have teamed up to give Sonic Solutions authoring application users a simple and inexpensive means to market and distribute DVDs. Finally, DVDs are here for the long haul. Capacities will increase, as will video quality.

All the while, video-editing software and camcorders will continue to improve in quality. And, as you continue to edit videos and author DVDs, you will discover more creative possibilities.

Index

How can we make this index more useful? Email us at indexes@samspublishing.com

X-Y-Z